ma

Since 1970 Australian cinema has enjoyed a national and international revival
wit'
Ma
Cin   *nal*
red   to

C   se
thre   nd
app   is-
pect   re
gen   of
clas   of
prob   r,
he a

A   es
Aust   n
film

Tom   -
versi   d
is joi

National Cinemas series

General Editor: Susan Hayward

Reflecting growing interest in cinema as a national cultural institution, the new Routledge *National Cinemas* series brings together the most recent developments in cultural studies and film history. Its purpose is to deepen our understanding of film directors and movements by placing them within the context of national cinematic production and global culture and exploring the traditions and cultural values expressed within each. Each book provides students with a thorough and accessible introduction to a different national cinema.

French National Cinema
Susan Hayward

Italian National Cinema
Pierre Sorlin

Australian National Cinema

Tom O'Regan

London and New York

First published 1996
by Routledge
11 New Fetter Lane, London EC4P 4EE

Simultaneously published in the USA and Canada
by Routledge
29 West 35th Street, New York, NY 10001

Typeset in Times by Poole Typesetting (Wessex) Ltd

Printed and bound in Great Britain by
TJ Press (Padstow) Ltd, Padstow, Cornwall

British Library Cataloguing in Publication Data
A catalogue record for this book is available from the British Library

Library of Congress Cataloging in Publication Data
O'Regan, Tom.
   Australian national cinema / Tom O'Regan.
      p.   cm. – (National cinemas series)
   Includes bibliographical references and index.
   1. Motion pictures – Australia. 2. Motion pictures – Social
aspects – Australia. I. Title. II. Series.
PN1993.5.A8073 1996   96–1055
791.43'0994–dc20   CIP

ISBN 0–415–05730–2 (hbk)
         0–415–05731–0 (pbk)

Published with the assistance of the Murdoch University
Board of Research and the School of Humanities

For
Lucy Shanahan O'Regan and Matthew Shanahan O'Regan

Contents

Acknowledgements

The principal readers of my work during the production of this book have been Stuart Cunningham, Carol Laseur, Adrian Martin, Toby Miller, Bill Routt, Catherine Simpson, Rita Shanahan, and an anonymous reader from Routledge. Their assistance has been invaluable. I would like to thank my Routledge editor Rebecca Barden for her forbearance. Thank you too to series editor Susan Hayward for affording me the opportunity to write this book. I have also benefited from the advice and support of Meaghan Morris and Irma Whitford.

Many other people have contributed by reading parts of the book in draft form and providing invaluable feedback. I would particularly like to thank John Hartley, Alec McHoul, Vijay Mishra, Jon Stratton, Julie Cook and students of my 1995 Australian Cinema class who trialled this book. My interest in Australian cinema had its beginnings as a graduate student at Griffith University in the late 1970s and was shaped by my teachers and friends at Griffith and elsewhere at that time, particularly Albert Moran, Sylvia Lawson and Paul Willemen. Without the writings of Thomas Elsaesser, Bruno Latour and Ian Hunter this would have been a very different book.

Long service leave from Murdoch University enabled me to do most of the writing of this book. I am grateful to the University for this support. Throughout this project I have been assisted by some wonderful librarians at Murdoch University and the Film & Television Institute (WA) who helped overcome the tyranny of distance.

List of abbreviations

ABA	Australian Broadcasting Authority
ABC	Australian Broadcasting Corporation
ABC-TV	Australian Broadcasting Corporation Television Network
ABT	Australian Broadcasting Tribunal
AFC	Australian Film Commission
AFDC	Australian Film Development Corporation
AFTRS	Australian Film Television and Radio School
AGPS	Australian Government Publishing Service
ATSIC	Aboriginal and Torres Strait Islander Commission
BBC	British Broadcasting Commission
CDB	Creative Development Branch (Australian Film Commission)
EFF	Experimental Film Fund
ESB	English speaking background
FFC	Australian Film Finance Corporation
GATT	General Agreement on Tariff and Trade
GNP	Gross National Product
MEAA	Media Entertainment and Arts Alliance
NES	Non-English speaking
NESB	Non-English speaking background
SAFC	South Australian Film Corporation
SBS	Special Broadcasting Service
SBS-TV	Special Broadcasting Service Television Network
SPAA	Screen Producers Association of Australia
VCR	Video cassette recorder
WIFT	Women in Film and Television

Chapter 1

Introducing Australian cinema

INTRODUCTION

Australian National Cinema reinterprets André Bazin's original question – 'What is cinema?' in terms of Australian cinema. As the title of this book suggests Australian cinema is a type of cinema – a national cinema. It is one among a number of national cinemas: British, Japanese, Dutch, French and Indian. A national cinema is made of the films and film production industry of particular nations. National cinemas involve relations between, on the one hand, the national film texts and the national and international film industries and, on the other hand, their various social, political and cultural contexts. These supply a means of differentiating cinema product in domestic and international circulation: these are the Australian films, directors, actors and these are the French. National cinemas also partake of a broader 'conversation' with Hollywood and other national cinemas. They carve a space locally and internationally for themselves in the face of the dominant international cinema, Hollywood. National film-makers in-digenize genres, artistic movements and influences. So, for example, *Strictly Ballroom* (Luhrmann 1992), *The Adventures of Priscilla: Queen of the Desert* (Elliott 1994) and *Star Struck* (Armstrong 1982) are not only Australian musicals but each can be seen to Australianize the form. Australian cinema is also a type of national cinema. Like the British and New Zealand cinemas, it is an English language cinema; like the Canadian and Dutch cinemas it is a medium-sized cinema.

Like all national cinemas Australian cinema is a collection of films and production strategies. It is a critical category to be explored. It is an industrial reality and a film production milieu for which governments develop policy. It is a marketing category to be exploited. It is an appreciation and consumption category for domestic and international audiences. Australian cinema is a container into which different film and cultural projects, energies, investments and institutions are assembled. It collects a range of elements – people and things, screen identities, knowledges, strategies, films – that are loosely related to each other; a raft of different institutions and relations, ranging from the complementary to the combative to the completely unrelated. It involves many different agents acting at a local, national and an international level who variously make, consume, produce, discuss, legislate and circulate Australian cinema. Heterogeneous ends, purposes, strategies and varieties of film-making are pursued under its rubric.

Australian cinema is a messy affair. It is a messiness not only in our ways of knowing, reading, consuming and producing films and the larger film-making milieu of which they are a part, but also a messiness among the films themselves with features as far apart as Peter Weir's *Picnic at Hanging Rock* (1975), Bruce Beresford's *Breaker Morant* (1980), Dr George Miller's *Mad Max* films (1979, 1981, 1985 with George Ogilvie),[1] Jocelyn Moorhouse's *Proof* (1991), P. J. Hogan's *Muriel's Wedding* (1994) and Tracey Moffatt's *beDevil* (1993). Australian cinema is fundamentally dispersed. The issue facing those who coordinate Australian film is one of effectively handling this dispersal of films, strategies and ends for personal, financial, cultural, aesthetic, national and political benefit.

The study of Australian cinema asks: 'What are the uses of Australian cinema for those who consume, speak, write about and produce its films?'; 'What is Australian cinema in the situations it creates and finds itself located in?' and 'How do diverse actors make sense of Australian cinema?' In this study, I will address the films, the audience (including the critical audience) for these films, the industry within which they are produced, the local and international markets where they circulate, and the strategic role of government in sustaining domestic production. Undertaking this task involves an interdisciplinarity that draws on film criticism, cultural studies, cultural policy studies and film economics. The discipline which has evolved to undertake this task is national cinema analysis.

National cinema studies examine films and their diverse conditions of production. Such studies routinely survey the connections between text and local and international production, reception and distribution, and between these and the local and international, among society, cultures and peoples. Susan Hayward's *French National Cinema* (1993) and Thomas Elsaesser's *New German Cinema* (1989) are unthinkable without their respective industrial, critical, cultural, social and political milieus. Some studies emphasize the films and/or the discourses of the national cinema; others the hard facts of production, distribution, exhibition and circulation; some the social dimensions of the national cinema. But all national cinema analyses situate the cinema simultaneously as a natural object in the film world (its production and industrial context), as a social object connecting and relating people to each other (its social and political context) and discursively through language, genre and knowledges (its representations).

The issue facing those who study Australian national cinema is akin to that routinely facing film producers and policy makers – one of how to handle and organize this dispersal of films, strategies, viewpoints and ends. The critic's problem is one of writing the national cinema as a hybrid form, the film worker's problem is one of coordinating it as a multifaceted entity. 'National cinemas' present themselves to audiences, film workers and critics alike as so many contingent links among disparate elements, disparate tellings, varied film-making projects. National cinemas are, in this sense, not so much coherent as dispersed.

At one time, this sort of dispersal was considered a problem disqualifying the study of national cinemas from screen theory. Christian Metz contends in his seminal book *Language and Cinema* (1974: 9) that because the cinema was such a 'multi-dimensional phenomenon' it did not lend 'itself to any rigorous and unified study, but only to a heteroclite collection of observations involving multiple and diverse points of view'. For him '"cinema" . . . is not a knowable object'. Under this view – and it is one which has persisted in various ways into the present – the study of a national cinema could be amenable only to observations and not to systematic knowledge.

Although I disagree with Metz, he does have a point. The national cinema writer must take on 'multiple and diverse points of view'. This imposes practical limits on any analysis. If I examine the intersections of text, industry, policy, economics and public reputation, the films necessarily get the more limited attention of synoptic review and not detailed textual exegesis. The reader is confronted with something more, and something less, than journalism, film reviewing, policy analysis, economic analysis and film studies. National cinema analyses poach from these apparently more fully achieved domains, and are dependent on their innovations. They mix and match the concepts and the innovations drawn from each field (thereby running the risk of failing to apprehend each sufficiently).

Metz rightly observes that the insights developed from film criticism's extended discussion of film meaning are not as available to the writer who examines 'the cinema' as a whole. Without the lengthy discursive trajectories and purification of language made possible by concentrating on a particular aspect of the cinema, the national cinema writer cannot match policy studies, economic analysis, and textual analysis on its own terms. National cinemas cannot bracket off all those other components that shape the circulation of films, in order to concentrate on one or two. They need to combine, to give due weight to a heteroclite range of elements in one and the same place and at the same time. National cinema writing is that critical practice which thoroughly establishes and routinely works through the heteroclite nature of cinema.

A national cinema focus forces an analysis of the connections between these elements and insists, however unevenly, on their collocation. The hybrid analytical strategies demanded in examining national cinemas are also its strength. Significantly, national cinema writing is neither the analysis of a film text nor policy discourse; neither film industry journalism and economic analysis nor film reviewing, but a mixture of each. Because a national cinema study needs to deal with texts, technology, language, power and society, it has a chance of holding onto the multiple connections that make the cinema 'possible' and drive it forward. The national cinema writer addresses the multiple personae of the filmmaker: as the one who creates with materials and technologies, who acts politically, who manipulates funding bodies, who lobbies, who needs to know the market, financing and the local and international works of the cinema. Like the national cinema itself, national cinema writing needs to combine the local and the international. The local conditions, the relative speeds of development of domestic infrastructures, the specific and local histories of cinema regulation, politics and governmental subsidies, the discursive fields in which the national cinema is inscribed – these conditions give an inflection to the public's understanding of that cinema.

National cinema analyses are predisposed in some fashion to local history and sociology, to emphasizing the local as well as (and sometimes at the expense of) the international. National cinema writers have no choice: they must deploy hybrid forms of analysis. The special local, critical, cultural, historical and industrial milieu of each cinema needs to be 'translated' into a form available for various kinds of local and international circulation. By showing how these elements are combined, it becomes an arena which can travel along diverse and often public corridors. It can have importance to general readers, to those who programme film retrospectives and film festivals, to film and cultural critics, to policy makers, educators, industry economists, film-makers, politicians, and lawyers in the entertainment industries. It can become essential reading for students of film whether they are film-makers, those involved in the film industry outside the film crew, or screen studies students.

The study of national cinemas is the proof that it is possible to do things with our recognition of the cinema as a multi-dimensional phenomenon. Multiple and diverse points of view can be the subject of our systematizing attention. Whereas Metz used his basic insight to legitimate his turn to the apparently more manageable and pure problems of film language, we use ours to lead cinema criticism back to the impure, admittedly eclectic, but none the less systematizing spaces of the cinema as a social practice. Those of us who do take part in it even think that such messy (John Hartley (1992: 23) calls them 'dirty') spaces are more interesting.

The problem every national cinema analysis faces is one of how to do justice to Australian cinema as a hybrid assemblage of diverse elements, statuses and films. One solution – and this is one adopted in this study – is to demonstrate a film milieu made up of antagonistic, complementary and simply adjacent elements, which are to be made sense of in their own terms. This means keeping the question of 'what is Australian cinema' as firmly and permanently open as it is on the Australian (and international) public record. My task here is not one of deciding which way of seeing Australian cinema is the right one but of showing how each element explains and discloses something about it. When I examine strategies of Australian film production and circulation I do not see my task as one of choosing among them, but rather of elucidating them. The task of national cinema studies, therefore, is not only to make sense of the films produced under its aegis, but also to make sense of those dispersed elements, strategies and purposes that produce, frame and circulate these films.

THE ORGANIZATION OF THIS BOOK

In Chapter 2 – 'Theorizing Australian cinema' – I argue that Australian cinema should be considered as naturalized by a combination of statuses. It is a 'natural' part of the screen world, it is a social bond circulating among people and defining that bond in their circulation, it is an object of knowledge and it is a problem of knowledge. Australian cinema is an assemblage which is simultaneously real, discursive and collective. I draw attention to the diverse knowledges about Australian cinema and how power is exercised through the application of knowledge.

The book then subdivides into three parts. In the first two parts, 'Making a national cinema' and 'Making a distinct cinema', I establish the nature of Australian cinema. In 'Making a national cinema', I consider Australian cinema as a particular kind of national cinema, sharing characteristics with other national cinemas. Here I foreground how certain knowledges, particular discursive figures, cinematic influences, formations of value and routine sense-making procedures normalize Australian national cinema on the horizons of diverse agents. In 'Making a distinct cinema', I consider the character of its diversity, its regularities, its cultural transfers (how it imports and indigenizes genres and film-making norms), and how they contribute to producing a distinct cinema. My emphasis in these first two parts is on those processes of naturalizing which make Australian cinema self-evident. These parts provide a map of the general field of Australian cinema within which the concerns of my third part – about how Australian cinema becomes a problem of knowledge – is established and maintained. In that part I ask: How does Australian cinema function as a vehicle for social problem solving? And how are knowledge, objects and people brought together in Australian cinema?

Making a national cinema

In Chapters 3, 4, 5 and 6 I consider Australian cinema as a national cinema. These chapters compare Australian cinema to other national cinemas and show how the concept of national cinema is made operational in the Australian context. In Chapter 3, 'A national cinema', I survey more generally those characteristics which Australian cinema shares with other national cinemas. I discuss it as a response to Hollywood dominance, as a local and international form, as in part a festival cinema, which has a relation with the nation and the state, and which is messy in its local, national and international involvements. National cinemas are identified as a relational term – a set of processes rather than an essence.

In Chapter 4, 'A medium-sized English-language cinema', I consider Australian cinema as a type of national cinema. Its cinema market, closely resembles that of Canada, the UK and the USA in its English language mainstream, and its 'foreign language' (art house) and ethnic cinemas in the minor stream. Like the Dutch and Swedish cinemas, it is a medium-sized cinema. Like the English-

Canadian cinema, it is a medium-sized English-language cinema. And, like all small to medium-sized national cinemas, it is an antipodal cinema marked by unequal cultural exchange due to the pre-eminent role played by imports.

In Chapter 5, I consider the formations of value of Australian cinema generally. A diverse range of agents – critics, audiences and policy-makers – evaluate Australian national cinema as a whole through a limited number of conceptual means. These include:

1 a relation with a dominant Hollywood cinema in which the national cinema is situated under the sign of culture and Hollywood under the sign of the profane economy;
2 a division of value among national cinemas where some are seen to be prestigious, some 'Other' cinemas, and some simply mundane;
3 a division within the national cinema between its mainstream and its peripheral or independent cinemas; and
4 a positive evaluation of Hollywood and its legacy in local markets, which simultaneously values and devalues the local national cinema.

These four figures interact to produce unstable hierarchies of value. So while some find that Australian cinema lacks sufficient artfulness as a prestige cinema (it is seen to lack innovation at a formal and stylistic level), sufficient cultural difference to be an 'Other' cinema, and sufficient difference from Hollywood as a mundane cinema, others value Australian cinema as a cinema that is sometimes able to speak to the people of Australia and the world, successfully negotiating Hollywood genres, eschewing artiness and committed to entertainment values. Agents also discriminate within the local cinema between the mainstream and the minor stream, alternately favouring one over the other. The Australian national cinema is shown to be traversed by various wills to value.

In Chapter 6, 'Making meaning', I attend to how meaning and value is made from individual Australian titles. I show how particular kinds of Australian cinema and discursive figures are twinned, so as to create a changing public meaning and value for Australian cinema. film-makers, critics, audiences and policy makers routinely make meaning from and assign value to Australian cinema by interpreting it in a number of ways. They relate a film to society and public discourse (its social texts). They compare it to other Australian films, television productions, novels, theatre and poems (its local aesthetic intertexts). They think about its continuities and discontinuities with, on the one hand, British, European and Asian cinemas, and, on the other hand, Hollywood cinema and its production models (its international cinema intertexts). They find it either entertaining or informing; diverting or educational. They berate it for surrendering to commercial values. They castigate it for capitulating to middle-class 'good intentions'. Through such diverse interpretative acts, films – like the larger audiovisual culture they are a part of – have diverse public careers.

Making a distinct cinema

In Chapters 7, 8, 9 and 10, I discuss the characteristics of Australian cinema which contribute to its production as a distinct cinema. I find Australian cinema's specificity to lie, not in any particular set of attributes, so much as in its relational character. This specificity emerges, on the one hand, from its diversifying, unifying, importing and indigenizing, blending and Othering dynamics, and, on the other hand, from its negotiation of its political and cultural weakness and the related importance to it of projecting Australian ugliness and ordinariness.

In Chapter 7, 'Diversity', I discuss the intrinsic diversity of Australian cinema. film-makers typically contribute to this or that pathway of the cinema with varying degrees of intensity over time, with some contributions – to the documentary and the western – being continuous over film history and other contributions – to the science-fiction film and the thriller – being relatively recent. They draw on a range of cultural differentiations from social life, politics and government. They reach out to non-Australian locations for story settings, materials and subjects. Australian cinema is largely of a one-off character and one in which film-makers routinely work across a variety of film forms. In its turn film criticism also bears the marks of this diversity.

In Chapter 8, 'Unity', I consider the paradox of how various agents – film critics, audiences, policy-makers, film-makers – routinely create unities and singularities for this diverse film-making. There are those regularities common to all national cinemas, such as a domestic informational and local symbolic goods archive, representing modal forms of the nation and local speech, which inform the production and circulation of films and provide agents with ways of unifying national film-making. Many of these agents develop a practical map of Australian cinema, in which it appears as a genre or type of dominant film-making or as so many thematic regularities – a masculinist cinema hypercritical of family life and male–female relationships which eschews conventional heterosexual romance structures and Oedipal trajectories. Critics and film-makers also unify Australian cinema around particular stylistic preoccupations – in particular naturalism – and around cultural and stylistic preoccupations with settings and landscape.

In these two chapters, I look at the ways in which agents think and assemble Australian cinema in diversity and at the ways in which they think and produce it in unity. Such processes of creating unity and diversity are not so much opposed as twinned. Sometimes, for example, critics narrow the meaning of Australian cinema to a handful of thematic, plot or other preoccupations, so as to claim that Australian cinema is stylistically and culturally homogeneous. Such narrowing then justifies their arguments for more diversity in the Australian cinema. Unity is specified as a problem in order to permit a greater diversity.

Because of the evident importance of the international cinema in an import culture, cultural transfers are a central issue in and for Australian cinema. Using the work of the Russian semiotician Yuri Lotman, I develop a typology of cultural transfers in Australian cinema in Chapter 9. Lotman's five stages of cultural transfer enable me to theorize the international circulation of concepts, films and styles in the Australian receiving context as multifaceted and multileveled. I use Lotman to reconsider Meaghan Morris's (1988) discussion of the unoriginality of Australian cinema and to position its specificity in the style and character of its negotiation of cultural transfers.

In the last of this section, Chapter 10, I seek more directly the distinctive character of Australian cinema. Here I make a case for its distinctiveness as a *relation* made of the intersection of a number of traits. These are: its manner of dealing with its one-off character and its unoriginality and cultural weakness as a medium-sized cinema, its narrative negotiation of Australian political weakness, its Othering of the Australian, and its blending of melodrama and the art film, and fact and fiction.

Problematizing Australian cinema

Chapters 11, 12 and 13 examine various ways in which Australian film becomes more than 'film in the film world' and attaches itself to social domains and vehicles of social problematization. In Chapter 11, 'Problematizing the Social', I examine Australian cinema as a vehicle for representing and intervening in Australian lifeways, politics and symbolic culture. I consider how film-making organizes social meanings by exploiting social problems – relationship break-down, custody disputes, incest, intolerance, generation gaps, Aboriginal and settler society relations – whether it be to motivate characters and generate tension between them in fiction film-making, or treat them as subjects for documentary and experimental film-making.

In Chapter 12, 'Problematizing gender', I look at one of the most public of problematizations in Australian cinema. The gender cleavage is not only an important structuring difference in front of and behind the camera. While women have always been depicted in the cinema, they still do not drive the narrative or participate in creative, technical and administrative positions to the same extent as men and the opportunities and wages for women actors and performers are nowhere near that for men. The problematizing of gender in social and cultural criticism and elsewhere impacts at the level of representation, politics, work practices and social organization in Australian cinema.

In Chapter 13, 'Problematizing nationhood', I examine how Australian cinema represents the Australian 'people-among-themselves' and defines them in relation to other like peoples. Specifying who the Australian people are, and might become, provides Australian cinema with something to represent, to be, and with materials to exploit. Audiences and critics recognize themselves in films and use them as a source to project their society and nation in a certain kind of way. Policy-makers, film-makers, critics and audiences rely on the existing political, civic and descriptive projects through which Australian society is represented to itself and the larger world. I discern four competing 'projects' for Australian society as a national society – a European derived society, a diasporic society, a New World society and a multicultural society. Here I examine these formulations and their translation into film.

Finally, in Chapter 14, 'Critical dispositions', I turn the point of focus squarely on film criticism and national cinema description. I examine Australian cinema criticism as the intersection of cultural criticism, cinephilic and history discourses and the institutional networks that support them. I discern three different critical styles: 'symptomatic' (or demythologizing criticism), 'explicatory' criticism and remythologizing criticism (remaking its objects). Cinephile institutions are shown to transform through remythologizing film meaning; critical institutions through demythologizing the meaning of films; and historical institutions through narrativizing the relation between past filmic trajectories. I end with a brief self-reflexive examination of my own practice of problematizing Australian cinema. I ask what are the appropriate critical ethics to the diverse problematizations of Australian cinema. I believe that our best ethics are pluralist, as they allow for a diversity of equally valid ends.

This book emphasizes the plurality and diversity of Australian cinema and the open-ended interrelations developed for them. Diversity is taken to be a mundane property of Australian cinema. It is a naturally occurring property of a field and a logical consequence of diverse film-making, of critical and governmental projects. As it is constitutive, diversity is not taken to be an end in itself. My purpose in this study is to demonstrate how Australian cinema is a hybrid assemblage of elements that are continually being improvised, combined and recombined; and to develop a critical ethics appropriate to this situation.

Chapter 2

Theorizing Australian cinema

INTRODUCTION

Australian cinema is a combination of statuses. It is a *naturalized* part of the international cinescape, taking its part alongside other national cinemas and Hollywood cinema. It is a *social bond* uniting (and excluding) diverse people. Australian cinema serves as a vehicle of popular socialization and as a forum for telling uncomfortable truths about its society. Australian films and film institutions negotiate cleavages of ethnicity, gender, race, class and nation. It is an *object of knowledge* which narratively and discursively connects Australia, society, the cinema, genre and various cultural differences. It is a domain of *problem solving* which includes strategies for economic viability, excellence, industry training and equal opportunity for disadvantaged minorities.

Australian cinema is a hybrid form made of objects, people, stories and problem solving. It is a social fact, a figure of discourse, a site for a range of actions and the domain of a range of problematizations. These different statuses simultaneously interact to shape Australian cinema. In his book on science, knowledge and society, *We Have Never Been Modern* (1993), the French intellectual Bruno Latour claims our contemporary world proliferates such hybrids. He calls them 'quasi-objects', since they are simultaneously 'real, like nature', 'collective, like society', and 'narrated, like discourse' (1993: 6). Australian cinema could be understood as one of Latour's quasi-objects. Its assemblage of hetereogenous elements – statuses, elements, ends, strategies and texts – gives it an improvised character. In this chapter I will address each of these statuses.

NATURALIZING AUSTRALIAN CINEMA

For Australian cinema to function, it must be naturalized as an unexceptionable part of the local and international cinema landscape. This naturalizing occurs historically through audiences, distributors, exhibitors, policy makers, politicians and general criticism.

An important element of naturalizing notions of national cinemas and cinema generally occurs through such publications as *Variety's International Film Guide* (Cowie 1995). The 1995 edition has a listing and short essay on each cinema-producing nation's recent films and domestic production contexts. It has essays on profiled international directors: Quentin Tarantino, the Kaurismäki Brothers, Ken Loach, Clint Eastwood and Jane Campion. Campion is self-described here as an 'Aussie directress' and is the director of *The Piano* (1993), *Sweetie* (1989), *An Angel at my Table* (1990, New Zealand) and a host of award winning shorts. The *Guide* profiles the major festivals in which the films of various national cinemas are often first showcased nationally and internationally. We learn that the International Film Festival of La Rochelle in France brought to the cinema world's attention the talent of 'Australia's Fred Schepisi, Germany's Reinhard Hauff and Greece's Theo Angelopoulis' (Jahiel 1995: 382). On page 379 there is a full page photo of the veteran director Peter Weir relaxing at La Rochelle in 1991 (Weir directed 1970s revival titles like *Picnic at Hanging Rock* (1975), *The Last Wave* (1977) and *Gallipoli* (1981), and was most recently the director of the Hollywood feature, *Fearless* (1994).

Festivals also include retrospectives, usually of a director's work. The 1995 Cannes Film Festival honoured twenty years of the Australian Film Television and Radio School (AFTRS) – the first time a film school had been given such a retrospective. The AFTRS counts as its graduates Gillian Armstrong (*My Brilliant Career* 1979, *Little Women* 1994), Phil Noyce (*Dead Calm* 1989, *Patriot Games* 1992), Jocelyn Moorhouse (*Proof* 1985) and Paul J. Hogan (*Muriel's Wedding* 1994) among others. Since the mid-1970s something from Australia has become an unexceptionable part of many international film festivals. However, prior to 1970, there were 'three decades of few local initiatives in feature production' (Pike and Cooper 1980: 305). When it did not have state support, near unanimous public support and investment from inside and outside the cinema trade, the Australian cinema was highly sporadic and dependent. In the 1960s, seventeen features were made without support, 153 were made with support in the 1970s (Jacka 1993: 74). During the 1970s, Australian cinema was naturalized on local and international horizons. Below I will discuss how this naturalization occurred and how it was sustained.

Twenty years earlier, the then prime minister E. G. Whitlam officially opened the AFTRS with these words:

> Film and television are the art forms of the twentieth-century. Every previous art form is to a greater or lesser degree of excellence practiced in Australia. It is quite necessary that Australia should participate in these essentially twentieth-century art forms. ... These twentieth-century art forms are now open to those English speaking people who live in Australia. Australians will be proud of them. The rest of the world will acknowledge Australia.[1]

While Whitlam's remarks about 'English speaking people who live in Australia' strike one today as excluding people of a non-English-speaking (NES) background, he was using the term to indicate inclusive, non-prescriptive, and non-nationalistic ends for film support. Whitlam was stressing Australian-based activity in film art. The 'Australian' was a means to the end of 'art'. For Phillip Adams (1971), the establishment of this Film School was the chance of 'a new industry, making feature films of international standard'. Its first head, Jerzy Toeplitz, was an eminent film scholar and former head of the Polish Film School (when Roman Polanski among others was a student). The AFTRS was not to reproduce the 'high quality mediocrity' of series television drama production then embodied in long running police series like *Homicide* (1964–75) and *Division 4* (1969–75). It would be a vehicle for a more extensive national appreciation of cinema art.

AFTRS was part of a multifaceted policy development that helped naturalize an Australian contribution to the cinema through government subsidy, incentive and investment. The Australian cinema supplemented an internationally defined audiovisual system. This supplement, in the dictionary (not Derridean) sense of 'something added to remedy deficiencies' (*Oxford English Dictionary* 1976: 1160), took a variety of forms. It was a critical supplement, as critics made room on their horizons for a diversely constituted Australian cinema. It was a film-making supplement, as film-makers provided locally produced materials in addition to the international product so readily available. It was a film policy supplement, as policy-makers created favourable production environments in which local exhibitors and international distributors were encouraged to promote Australian product alongside their international, usually Hollywood product. It was a public supplement, as politicians, bureaucracy, and citizens provided for it.

In the same year the Film School was officially opened (it had been running since 1973), Peter Weir's classic *Picnic at Hanging Rock* was released. This film made this supplement a multifaceted reality. It was part financed by one of the largest cinema chains, Greater Union, and by two state film subsidy organizations – the Australian Film Commission (AFC) and the South Australian Film Corporation (SAFC). *National Times* film reviewer P. P. McGuinness (1975, 1985: 188) lauded the fact that with it 'Australian film has truly entered into the field of open and equal international comparisons.' Such national and international *succès d'estime* made Australian cinema more than simply another film industry. It made it a producer of celebrated international films. Previous high profile films of the early 1970s like: *The Adventures of Barry McKenzie* (Beresford 1972), an 'ocker' comedy – an *Animal House*-style film – made entirely with government funding – and *Alvin Purple* (T. Burstall 1973), a sex comedy supported by the Village cinema chain, were commercially successful but achieved neither critical regard nor public endorsement. Others had achieved critical regard but limited success – *Sunday Too Far Away* (Hannam 1975) and before that *Wake in Fright* (Kotcheff 1971) and *Walkabout* (Roeg 1971). *Picnic* centred all these attributes in the one film. It was followed by Schepisi's *The Devil's Playground* (1976), *The Chant of Jimmie Blacksmith* (1978) and *Evil Angels* (1988, aka *Cry in the Dark*), *My Brilliant Career*, *Gallipoli*, Beresford's *Breaker Morant*, Dr George Miller's *Mad Max II* (1981, aka *The Road Warrior*), *Strictly Ballroom* and *The Adventures of Priscilla: Queen of the Desert*. Through these and popular commercial cinema titles like *Crocodile Dundee* (Faiman 1986), and *The Man from Snowy River* (George Miller 1982), Australian cinema gained recognition as an international cinema. In his 'Chronicle of the Cinema 1895–1995', David Robinson (1994: 125) has the 'emergence' of Australian cinema and African cinema as a notable feature of the period 1980–1994.

'Australian cinema' became routinely inserted on the horizon of film institutions, audiences, publishers, investors, politicians, marketers, educators, businesspersons and public servants nationally – and to the extent that it is possible, these same actors internationally. Local films became integral to Australian exhibition and distribution. People financed, produced and worked in the Australian-based film industry and developed policy for it. In Australia it was tagged as the 'Australian film revival' (registering a time in the silent and early sound period where Australia was a film-producing nation); elsewhere it was 'the Australian new wave', 'new Australian cinema' or 'the emerging Australian cinema' (as if no cinema had been produced before).

Crucial to the naturalizing of Australian cinema was 'the supportive and regulatory role of the state' (Dermody and Jacka, 1988a: 48). Australian cinema's re-emergence has been dependent on a 'relatively sweet climate of government support' (Dermody and Jacka 1988a: 48). In 1995, David Stratton (98) claimed the 'support system for film, TV drama and documentaries' was to 'many admirers' internationally 'the best in the world'. It is support which is direct and 'indirect', and is 'mediated by a rhetoric of free-market business and private profit' (Dermody and Jacka 1988a: 48). Through state subsidy, investment and tax concessions (in the 1980s), private (non-film and television industry) and industry capital became involved in Australian film production. The result of this partnership was 524 feature films and 251 telemovies being made between mid-1970 and mid-1993 (Bean and Court 1994: 43). On a feature score alone this is more than were produced in the preceding 70 years! For economists, Simon Molloy and Barry Burgan (1993: 119), this government intervention explains 'Australia's disproportionate share of domestic and world film and television production'.

The Australian government's multifaceted support for Australian film began in 1969. In that year, the proposal of the Film Committee of the Australian Council for the Arts was accepted by the John Gorton led Liberal-Country Party government. Australia would also have a national, state-sponsored cinema in which the state would take over a proportion of the risk involved in feature production by direct investment and taxation incentive. Private cinema trade and television network investment would thus be encouraged. The state would also shoulder some responsibility for industry training (through the AFTRS, Swinburne and the

Technical and Further Education – TAFE – sectors) and for experimentation and script development through direct subsidy and loans.

Most immediately, the state's provision of part of the budget made otherwise marginal commercial propositions viable like feature film, one-off documentary, and high budget limited episode serial television. It enabled the prospect of returns on private and industry investment. State support varied too from providing part of the budget as a means of locking in local and international sources of financing, to underwriting the entire production budget in the case of the recent lower budget feature, *Vacant Possession* (Nash 1995). This support extended from providing direct loan funding through government film agencies in a 'film bank', to providing indirect support by generous tax concessions in the 1980s which encouraged tax minimization investment in features, mini-series and documentaries. These concessions underwrote that decade's tremendous expansion in titles, budgets and aspiration – 335 features in the 1980s (see Jacka 1993: 74, 81–2). Tax concessions made possible high budget Australian themed films like *Mad Max III: Beyond Thunderdome* (Dr Miller and Ogilvie 1985) and *Crocodile Dundee*; in their absence in the 1990s, high budget films became internationally themed, as in Chris Noonan's blockbuster *Babe* (1995).

State sponsorship created favourable environments across a much wider range of film-making practices than would have been delivered through the normal operation of the commercial cinema, video and television industries. It made possible productions, whose commercial prospects were limited but which possessed significant cultural capital, like Tracey Moffatt's *beDevil*. This was the first feature of the acclaimed short-film director and gallery photographer – and the first feature by an Aboriginal and Islander woman. The Australian Documentary Fellowship scheme which operated from 1983 to 1990 was dedicated to excellence and innovation in the documentary. The scheme provided recipients with the resources to make a documentary and a television outlet for its subsequent screening. Generous concessions of this nature have produced a series of experimental and personal documentaries, from Gillian Coote's *Island of Lies* (1990) on the hiding of and resistance to Aboriginal commemoration of genocide in rural Australia, to Susan Lambert and Sarah Gibson's avant-garde experimental documentary *Landslides* (1986) to David Noakes' personal examination of Western Australia – its entrepreneurial history, its boosterism, its Aboriginal dispossession and the sites of reconciliation – in *Bigger than Texas: The Ghosts that Never Die* (1992).

State sponsorship insulated local producers from the full pressures of the market. Ben Cardillo, a Senior Producer at Film Australia, argues that 'unlike the book publishing industry, film and television makers had been somewhat insulated from the rigours of a mass market' in the 1970s and 1980s. Direct state subsidies for production enabled film-makers to deal through 'intermediaries such as broadcasters and international distributors that shared the business risk by offering advances on license fees and distribution revenues' (McIntosh 1994). This insulation consequently gave scope to film-making ambitions.

The central role of the state to film-makers' working lives, particularly in getting a start, makes Australian film-makers not just concerned with establishing their credentials at the box office or securing television ratings points but with mobilizing these state credentials to get a project going. The continuing survival of some forms of film-making can be, at times, due to successful lobbying of state agencies rather than any underlying economic characteristics of the film form or the overall political agenda of the government of the day.

Writing about another national cinema for which state policy has been central – the New German Cinema of the 1970s and early 1980s – Thomas Elsaesser (1989: 3) reckons that the contemporary state wants to 'create and preserve a national film and media ecology' (Elsaesser 1989: 3) rather than simply a national film industry. Like the German Länders, the Australian state – at both a Federal and a states level – sees/saw its role as supporting a commercial industry and a film culture. These national cinemas had from their inception 'apparently incompatible objectives ... to be economically viable but culturally motivated' (Elsaesser 1989: 3).

Australian film policy inherited the principle of dualism from radio and television policy which provided for a national broadcasting (public) sector and a commercial broadcasting (private) sector. In film policy, this was translated into a commercial audiovisual industry dependent on content regulation in television, script development and production investment from state agencies, and a wholly (or almost wholly) publicly supported film culture sector dependent on subsidy and investment. This established a higher budgeted 'mainstream' and a lower budgeted 'minor stream' and all the relations in between. Since 1969 the mainstream and minor streams have been managed by separate institutions. In the early 1970s there was the mainstream Australian Film Development Corporation and the minor stream Experimental Film Fund; from the mid-1970s to the mid-1980s there was the mainstream Industry Branch and the minor stream Creative Development Branch of the AFC; since 1988 the divide has been represented by the Australian Film Finance Corporation (FFC) and the AFC. The various funding bodies in the different states typically functioned as an umbrella for both streams of film-making.

A range of governmental agencies in addition to those mentioned shaped the Australian film-making milieu. The 'national broadcasters' – the ABC (with its large audiovisual infrastructure) and the SBS – influence the area of one-off documentaries, limited-episode drama, telemovies and shorts. To take one example, Jane Campion's telemovie, *2 Friends* (1985) was an ABC production. In its setting and administering of Australian content standards, the Australian Broadcasting Authority (ABA), impacts on the level and character of documentary, feature and dramatic content on television. Various non-film state agencies – like the Aboriginal and Torres Strait Islander Commission and the Office of Multicultural Affairs – have become involved in film production.

Various incarnations of government broadcasting regulatory agencies have administered the broader television industry with consequences for local film production. Their role has been to oversee the viability of an Australian production sector alongside ownership, control and standards. Interpretations of Australian content obligations have not always meshed with those of the film subsidy and investment organizations as in the late 1980s. But through these content provisions, along with state agencies underwriting part of the development and budget costs, commercial television stations and networks have been enlisted to provide funding support for Australian features, documentaries and mini-series. Most crucially, the stations underwrote a viable feature film milieu through their funding of long-running television series and serials which provided continuity of employment for writers, directors, actors and so on.

But the Australian industry is not just a creature of state. State support has always had as its aim private and state partnerships (only where this was not available, could and should the state step in to provide the whole budget). These state institutions interact with a private film and television industry and film culture which the state does not so much create but attempts to interest and enlist on behalf of a diverse Australian film-making. State institutions set themselves up to invite private institutions, investors and so on to influence them.

Most evidently, partnerships are formed through the interaction of the state agencies and the different film industry sectors. (These sectors include feature film-making, mini-series production, long-running television drama, the short film, the one-off documentary, the documentary series, the video-clip, advertising, the avant-garde, experimental, and alternative sectors – such as feminist film-making or electronic arts.)

Cinema exhibition chains and distribution organizations have also provided direct investment in feature production. Village Roadshow became the first with *Alvin Purple* in 1973. Sometimes, as in the 1980s, it has been a priority to attract various non-industry private investors to film production. Since 1988 it has been a policy priority to interest overseas investors in Australian production. David Stratton's (1995: 94–102) article on Australian cinema in the *1995 Guide* noted the continuing importance to Australian cinema in the 1990s of international financing. French money helped bankroll *The Piano* and *Muriel's Wedding*, American financing *The Adventures of Priscilla*. As Kristin Thompson observes, 'a national film industry will tend to take shape following practices in operation within the larger business community in that country and government regulation will encourage certain tendencies which may be peculiar to that country' (1985: 168).

The exhibition and distribution major and minor streams shape Australian film-making ambitions and policy-making. The commercial mainstream is typically the hardest to enlist for Australian cinema. Naturalizing local film on their horizons is an important issue for film-makers – there is, typically, more local product seeking wide release than exhibitors and distributors take up. On the other hand, there are the more specialized commercial and semi-commercial sectors in the repertory art cinema, and the semi-commercial and non-commerical exhibition of the independent sector. These provide a venue for the low budget features and shorts made for film festivals, partly subsidized exhibition venues, minor circuits, galleries, tertiary education, non-commercial screening and more lately SBS-TV particularly in the coveted *Eat Carpet* (1988) slot. The extent of this 'short-film industry' can be gauged by the nearly 200 films produced each year (Clayton, *Australian Financial Review* 17/6/1994: Weekend 15), while its internal diversity is evident in the prizes offered at the annual Dendy Awards – five: for documentary, fiction, general, animation and an ethnic award offered by the Ethnic Affairs Commission (Clayton 1994: Weekend 15).

The Australian film industry is a negotiated outcome of the interaction of these different sectors. Australian cinema is a collection and interaction of different things: local and international economies of production and circulation; investment histories of production and distribution; policy developments; sectors of film-making. Processes of naturalizing Australian film have the effect of making it tangible, unexceptional and multifaceted.

SOCIALIZING AUSTRALIAN CINEMA

For a national cinema to function it must be socialized as implicating, negotiating, expressing, reflecting, bonding society in its most particular and its most general. It is a vehicle for social processes, emerging social movements and identities.

Australian cinema acts as a social bond in a number of ways. Most obviously Australian films, like the media more generally, provide cultural information about the Australian people and their relation to other peoples. Diverse agents take up film stories using them for their own purposes: audiences in their discussions of the films; critics in their reviews, talks and essays on the films and the incidents they depict; film-makers to plunder ideas to make new films; journalists as they attach a prominent film to some social issue of the day; special interest groups to further their own aims and those of their members; and governments in their various capacities. Films are vehicles of social exchange among agents and they define the social (cultural) bond among them by their circulation.[2]

As cinema-going is a social entertainment activity, films intersect with and have an influence on the personal calendars of people (Sacks 1992: 36–9).[3] For me *The Man from Snowy River* recalls the time when I left Brisbane to work on the family farm and my partner went to work in Gladstone in Central Queensland. She shared a house with two women, one of whose boyfriends – a police officer – was obsessed with this film. The local cinema attaches people to each other binding them however loosely together in acts of communal solidarity.

On the drive-in release of this 'kangaroo western' in 1982 patrons tooted their car horns and cinema patrons clapped at the film's end. Patrons in Gladstone booked in advance for the drive-in. The film's extraordinary domestic popularity made it into a public event – more popular than *Star Wars* (Lucas 1977) or *The Godfather* (Coppola 1972) in the Australian market. It became the first local film to become the most commercially successful feature in Australian theatrical box office history. The film collected people from all walks of life. As I wrote at the time 'In the city cinema, [yuppie] Paddington sits next to [working class and migrant] Blacktown; [working class and Aboriginal] Inala next to [middle class] Indooroopilly, the decrepit next to the nubile' (O'Regan 1985a: 250).

When local films circulate before domestic audiences they provide 'a de facto social map for native audiences to situate themselves in culturally and personally' (Lewis 1987: 197). In this way, films routinely involve audiences, film-makers and critics in their various social and cultural identities – as Australians, Queens-landers, Sydneysiders, women, men, Aboriginal and Islanders, young and old, parents and migrants. Sometimes the representation of these identities is in front of the camera: by virtue of being a location based film-making, Australian features are made in many parts of the country and feature many regional and sub-cultural identities. At other times, audiences draw comparisons between the onscreen locations and identities and their own.

Films routinely connect Australian society and other societies. They function to mark the particularities of Australian difference and similarity to the rest of the world. Through them, international audiences find continuities between them-selves and Australians. Australian cinema circulates because of its culture's likeness to and difference from other cultures. Tony Safford, Vice President of Acquisitions at Miramax Films, spoke at the 1994 Screen Producers Association of Australia (SPAA) Conference of the attractiveness of Australian cinema to Americans. He thought it was grounded in 'shared historical origins: each as a British colony, each without the burden of history, each with a "manifest destiny" to conquer its land and indigenous people'. These extended into the present to sharing a 'common language and a broadly similar cultural view'. Governments and private firms alike are concerned with national self-representation. It is also a routine part of national policy to foster international understanding through the work of local cultural industries. For their part, production companies and investors have an interest in having others customize their audiovisual goods and services.

Film-making is implicated in processes of popular socialization and social problem solving (locating social problems, identifying their causes, developing solutions for them). Social activists and film and cultural critics routinely evaluate films for their transmission of cultural values and their stance towards contempo-rary public issues. Governments underwrite, publics support, critics and film-makers assume the capacity of a local film-making to allow Australians to 'dream their own dreams, tell their stories to themselves and to the world' and to 'tell uncomfortable truths about their society'.

From the late 1960s, film industry activists enlisted support from film-makers, governments, the wider public, critics and readerships for a film industry on aesthetic and socio-cultural grounds. These agents yoked film to their purposes. So Australian cinema serves diverse goals: of international publicity and under-standing, of nation-building and citizenship, of cultural protection, of providing education and community information, of situating Australians in their own history, of advancing social understanding and therefore social harmony, of communal integration, of the development of inclusive public and national cultures. The story of cinema after 1969 is one of a media of popular socialization that governments, social and capital élites and the 'knowledge class' – those 'whose existence is grounded in the possession and exercise of knowledge' (Frow 1995: 111) – have yoked to their diverse aesthetic and socio-cultural purposes.

Australian cinema is a vehicle for Australian culture in both a programmatic and a mundane sense. Australian culture is simultaneously a political, social and cultural programme of diverse agents and élites and it has a mundane identity formation and inescapable cultural level in its own right. Australian cinema inevitably shapes this culture in both senses and is in turn shaped by it. It intersects with and articulates various social and national identities.

In a programmatic sense, the cinema is one means of providing a common civic culture for a disparate population. Like other agencies of popular socialization, a national cinema is a vehicle for a 'common culture and a civic ideology, a set of common understandings and aspirations, sentiments and ideas, that binds the population together in their homeland' (A. D. Smith 1991: 11). A domestic film industry – like other cultural industries – helps foster a sense of citizenship and social identities. It creates and represents a common cultural and political core of events and values. It can make 'us' feel good about ourselves. Deborah Jones (1992: xiii) claimed a therapeutic function for *Snowy River*. It situated its audience in Australian history by telling us 'we had a past to be proud of and to be celebrated'. Films chart and nurture a national culture (which can be both given and emergent) and forge an Australian identity (which can be both new and traditional). So Gary Sturgess (1982: 62) can hold Australian cinema mostly responsible for a 'resurgence in national feeling'.

Projects of nationhood are not just confined to government in cultural, educational and civic policies. Commercial enterprises, magazines and national newspapers, parts of television and the cinema all seek the economies of scale of a national reach. Along with legal structures and political parties, these have a vested interest in creating not only national markets but cathartic 'imagined communities' that would sustain these (Anderson 1983, 1991).

As cultural artifacts, films routinely transmit cultural and political values, comportments, histories and identities – and are consumed, praised and criticized for doing so. The national cinema is the 'mobilizer of the nation's myths and of the myth of the nation' (Hayward 1993: 9). Take Peter Weir's *Gallipoli*. It was valued and devalued in Australia as a social document recreating popular memory. It recreated a significant moment of Australia's past – the unsuccessful Gallipoli campaign of the First World War – which is commonly held to have been formative of an Australian identity, marking the moment when Australia 'came of age as a nation'. It is celebrated on the 25th of April every year in grand parades, dawn services and a national holiday. Weir's film transmitted, maintained, extended and repaired this national symbol by giving it a fictional form. It made the Gallipoli campaign real for a generation of school children, adults and cultural commentators ('Until I saw *Gallipoli*, I subconsciously believed that the campaign had been conducted in scratch monochrome by soldiers in their sixties wearing double breasted suits, Akubra hats and rows of medals'; see Phillip Adams 1982: 33).

Its two main characters were recognizable types – Archie (Mark Lee) the idealistic youth sacrificed to a brutal and senseless war, and Frank (Mel Gibson) the survivor. It reconciled classes: the upper middle class Archie with his Aboriginal mate; and most importantly with his rival and subsequent mate, the working class Frank. It reconciled ethnicity – the Anglo Archie with values of Empire and Britishness and the Irish Frank with emergent Australian values and a residual anti-Britishness. It reconciled country (Archie) and city (Frank).

The film was criticized for being neo-traditionalist. For Dermody and Jacka (1998a: 163) *Gallipoli* was 'a simple kind of Baden-Powell "proud" view of the Anzac legend, simplified family entertainment'. It conserved and updated 'myths of the people' and kept them to the narrow range of the Australian Legend (the Aussie battler in Frank, the mateship between the two men, the tension between European gentility and perfidy and rougher emerging Australian values, and the harsh desert landscapes of Western Australia and the Middle East). Here there was a film that produced 'calculated innocence within the ambience of history ... in the playground of the pretty and impressionistic past' (159). For Amanda Lohrey (1981: 29–30) the film recycled militaristic and masculinist myths of young nationhood, leaving out the gross and brutish Australian behaviour in Egypt which was not so much good fun as ill-disciplined soldiers looting and raping ordinary Egyptians. Like so many other Australian features of the centre in this period, it took its 'national identity unproblematically, consenting to the perpetual construction of meaning announced as natural, historical, inevitable, true – and adequate' (Dermody and Jacka 1988a: 25).

Films can also be modernizing vehicles forging emergent national symbols, values and comportments. In 1990s features, there is a trend towards a re-examination of the meaning of the settler culture under the influence of multiculturalism as a new public myth of the people. *Strictly Ballroom* was championed for its multicultural unity-in-diversity: in it 'there is an embracing of all the people who are us' (Jones 1992: xiii). Instead of old world Europe and emerging Australian values, Michael Jenkins' *The Heartbreak Kid* (1993) projects an old (staid) and monocultural society clashing with an emerging, youthful and inclusive multicultural society with the future on its side. Another progressive cultural value is that of reconciliation between the settler and first peoples. This was embodied in the ABC's high-profile mini-series *Heartland* (1994) made in the wake of the 1992 Mabo decision, where the Australian High Court overturned the doctrine of *terra nullius* to recognize prior Aboriginal and Islander ownership. *Heartland* developed a pedagogic romance between a white woman and an Aboriginal man (thereby reversing the customary fiction of white man and

Aboriginal woman). In a symbolic reversal of the black–white relation, the Aboriginal character played by Ernie Dingo teaches, instructs, romances and sometimes patronizes her. This series was part of a process of re-evaluation in which Australian settlement becomes both settlement and invasion. And the non-Aboriginal Australian – no matter how marginal or vulnerable she may be here – is still in some sense a colonist and colonizer.

A larger movement to recognize and value cultural diversity is represented by the mainstreaming of gay lifestyles as in *The Sum of Us* (Burton and Dowling 1994) and *The Adventures of Priscilla*. In these films, the exemplary modern form is of a tolerant national subject and a society able to value difference. In *The Sum of Us*, the female lead retrospectively recognizes the foolishness of her homophobia which had destroyed her promising liason with the father (Jack Thompson) of a gay (Russell Crowe); and despite the father having suffered a debilitating stroke, the film ends on an upbeat note as he takes delight in the prospect of a stable relationship developing for his son. The vox pop television interview has a viewer 'proud to be Australian' after watching this film.

Films then are a means of interrogating the public and civic culture. They inspect, evaluate, describe and project society, its lifeways and its psychic dispositions (neuroses, fears, etc.). Films investigate contemporary public issues, they render social divisions and the incommensurate purposes of people. They register disturbing social and cultural truths, and foster alternative identities within the country.

The film and cultural critic, Meaghan Morris (1980: 135) has persuasively argued that 1970s Australian cinema was fascinated 'with group behaviour, and with relationships seen in the context of social institutions'. She noted the way the films of this era invited critical commentary on dysfunctional aspects and themes in Australian society. Above all, personal relationships, particularly those between men and women in 1970s feature films, like *Petersen* (T. Burstall 1974) and *Don's Party* (Beresford 1976), were shown to be disturbingly dysfunctional:

> Relationships . . . assume the status of a symbolic battleground (comic, grim, or both) for the working out of a variety of conflicts, antagonisms and hostilities; collisions of class, race, culture and environment which become dizzying in their diversity, and which constantly threaten to suggest that beyond the reassuringly familiar outlines of a few national stereotypes of great generality, there might be no guarantees of a binding cultural identity at all.
>
> (Morris 1980: 137)

Local films are expected to disclose awkward truths about Australian society and lifeways. Daniel Scharf, the producer of *Romper Stomper* (Wright 1992) – 'a skinhead racist nightmare erupting somewhere in the western suburbs' (Epstein 1992: 24–5) – connected the film to his Jewish German background and the fact that his mother was a 1936 refugee to Australia. It was

a comment, a mirror, a microcosm of what we see out there. Racism does exist
and should be exposed, we should not bury our heads in the sand. It's a film
about ignorance and intolerance.

(Quoted in Lombard 1993: 18)

Australian cinema is involved in charting existing and emergent social divisions and identities within society. It accommodates, recognizes and promotes the
social divisions constitutive of society. Films provide for alternative – even
counter-identities and histories – as in the Aboriginal and Islander (Moffatt's
beDevil), women's (*Journey Among Women*, Cowan 1977) and migrant identities
and histories (*Silver City*, Turkiewicz 1984). There is a favouring of political
understandings of Australia as a fractured polity over understandings of it as a
people united by shared symbols and myths.

Film-making and criticism focus on society and Australian film's explicit
failures: to be representative and tolerant, its marginalizing, co-option and exclusion of others. There are a variety of unhappy outcomes: suicide for the young
woman in *Only the Brave* (Kokkinos 1994) who is a victim of incest and a victim
of a dysfunctionally heterosexist and homophobic school scene. The gross social
injustices and racism that Jimmie experiences as an Aboriginal in *The Chant of
Jimmie Blacksmith* that drive him to mass murder. Michael Leigh writes of how,
for a century the Australian film industry has used Aborigines and Torres Strait
Islanders for 'its own ends' (Leigh 1988: 88). Documentary film-makers and
cultural critics take mainstream Australian cinema to task, evaluating its record for
presenting categories of people in front of and behind the camera.

In its turn the cinema seems capable of partly remedying, but all too often
contributes to social deficits of, for example, racism, social class, gender inequality and disadvantage. Critics – and a stream of documentary, feature, short-film
and mini-series production – arraign the country, its dominant ethnicity, its
culture, its cinema for their exclusion of whole kinds, classes, ethnicities and races
of people. Dermody and Jacka (1988a: 199) map the masculinism of Australian
cinema of the 1970s and the first half of the 1980s, arguing that the 'Australianization' strategies of this feature film-making characteristically produced a 'particularly inward national drama' in which 'an iconic white "masculinity" generated
'Australianness' (see also Morris 1989: 120).

Franco di Chiera's documentary *Change of Face* (1988) charts the predominance of Anglo-Celtic definitions of Australia's audiovisual culture and how
the dominant ethnicity trivializes people of an NES background in front of the
camera and limits opportunities behind it. A raft of cultural criticism confirms
these findings (see also Dermody and Jacka 1988a *passim*, Mitchell 1993,
Langton 1993, Shaw 1992, S.K. Chua 1993). In Christine Sammers' ABC
documentary *One Australia? The Future Starts Here* (1991) dominant Australian
inventions of national identity and national culture in its cinema and television are
shown to suppress heterogeneity and cultural difference. Activism gives rise to
proposals for a film-making that would engage in 'respectful dialogue'. Stephen

Muecke (1992) calls for a 'respectful appropriation' by White and Black Australians of each other's culture – the evidence for which is to be found in front of and behind the camera.

Cultural criticism whether conducted on screen or in writing is, as Toby Miller (1994a: 21) writes,

> vitally concerned with auditing the denial, italicization, assimilation, and invention that take place each time unitary concepts of nation, community, and society are brought into discourse. This tendency is then connected to a wider move within Australian public life away from essentialist definitions of national identity and towards a more pluralized account of person and polity.

As part of such a pluralized account of the polity, film-making agencies have helped create a considerable body of feminist film-making in experimental, avant-garde, documentary and short and feature film forms. These agencies have also supported a rich history of Aboriginal and non-Aboriginal documentary collaborations, with titles like *Takeover* (MacDougall and MacDougall 1980), *Two Laws* (Cavadini and Strachan 1981), *How the West was Lost* (Noakes 1987) and *Exile and the Kingdom* (Rijavek 1994). Their underwriting of works of 'cultural diversity' created opportunities for Aboriginal and Islander film-maker Anne Pratten (*Terra Nullius* 1993), for the Japanese documentary film-maker Noriko Sekiguchi *When Mrs Hegarty Comes to Japan* (1992) and the Hong Kong film-maker Clara Law (*Floating Life* 1996). It also made possible a domain of documentary film-making focusing on the various diasporic and indigenous communities within Australia. The advent of SBS-TV in 1980 brought an unprecedented acceptance of the principle of the expression of cultural diversity as an accepted subsidy logic.

The 1989 adoption of multiculturalism as a national cultural policy of state 'for all Australians' provided an impetus, albeit in a limited fashion, for cultural diversity to move out of the minor stream institutions and into the mainstream. The ABC mainstreamed documentary film-making, previously the preserve of the SBS, with documentaries like *One Australia?* and Franco di Chiera's *The Joys of the Women* (1993, with its focus on the Australian Italian identities of a choir in Fremantle in Western Australia) and the mini-series *Heartland*. Commercial television produced an ordinary television soap of a multicultural schoolyard in *Heartbreak High* (1994–   ). This mainstreaming of multiculturalism when coupled with the ABC's Aboriginal employment programme and gender inequality as a matter of public concern, ensured that a diversity of offering and viewpoint was maintained, while feature and documentary film-makers became more dependent upon television broadcasters, and film-makers were encouraged to seek greater international integration. The governmental agencies – ABC, SBS-TV, the AFC and the FFC – have also been more inclusive in gender and minorities terms than their counterparts in the commercial industry.

Because state subsidies and schemes are usually developed on cultural grounds, state institutions are open to claims made about the national cinema in terms of a variety of film form, artistic experimentation and innovation, minority viewing, and 'minorities' programming. State logics further compound this cultural orientation through their acceptance of the principle of market failure – the principle that support should go to what is not well supported in the commercial marketplace not to supplement what is well supported.

The state supports mainstream and minor stream film-making. The mainstream may stage social union or division but the minor stream film and television institutions are nearly always the vehicle for the dissident, the marginal and the oppositional, supporting smaller films, feminist films, social problem films, and docu-dramas beside the dominant fare. Minor stream production relies on the purposes behind the state's recognition of it: the disadvantage of particular categories of person, the functional character of a periphery (as a training ground and concept-testing environment), the promise of social amelioration made available through critical voices, dimensions, and the artistic and expressive benefits deriving from maintaining a non-commercial sector. Governmental film agencies routinely support a range of film-making intensely critical of state purposes and mainstream society. Indeed this state support has encouraged independent film-makers and critics to be social issues oriented. Film-makers are critical of the state, society and its practices not only as a matter of principle but also as a means of being noticed and critically regarded. The closer film-makers get to a more commercial orientation the less evident social criticism becomes in film-making. This naturalizes a trajectory from acerbic social criticism to a more gentle acceptance and celebration of Australian lifeways, just as it licences a move from Australia to America.[4] Take Phil Noyce's career, moving from the hard edge of *Backroads* (1977), through to *Newsfront* (1979), *Heatwave* (1982) and *Dead Calm* and then subsequently his American films *Patriot Games*, *Sliver* (1993) and *Clear and Present Danger* (1994).

Liberal democratic nation states like Australia regard the cultural industries they develop policy for not only as so many instruments of popular socialization and unity for a disparate population, but also as calculated and improvised instruments to accommodate, promote and stage social and cultural divisions. Michael Schudson (1994: 42–3) argues just this as a general feature of contemporary cultural policy development in liberal democracies '[i]n their cultural policy nation-states provide less cultural unity than an authoritative statement of the terms in which union and division will be negotiated.'

Governments do not only invest in the cinema because they want to produce well-tempered selves with a fealty to the state (see Miller 1993: ix) – although that is part of their purpose to be sure – they also invest in it for other purposes like its international public relations value, or as part of their wideranging support for the arts, or for the value they place in cultural diversity and difference. These latter purposes say little about managing people and more about creating spaces for the resistant, the marginal and the independently minded. 'Film Art' is useful as a moral and ethical domain for itself, partly insulated from the pressures towards social conformity. It holds at bay the 'social' long enough to permit various minoritarian views and so on to be produced and it enables cultural diversity to mean a diversity of genre, format and approach. As Turner (1993b: 70) notes, various local agendas ranging across a gamut of formats are and have been 'served though national policy initiatives'. Those espousing such agendas have translated themselves into the national cultural policy framework and occupied it strategically.

Australian cinema has a variety of publics. Most obviously there is the cinema-going public which is the target of Australian film-making. But there are also other publics. There is the film-making public made of those involved in producing, circulating and lobbying for Australian cinema; and there is the public for Australian film as a 'public good' which sustains bipartisan political support for film initiatives.

The local film-making milieu is made up of networks of people who form alliances, develop solidarities, organize themselves into professional associations, lobby groups, and develop their own information infrastructures – in short the public. Through these activities, film workers develop a loose sense of a collective identity and commonality of purpose in a broader film and political culture. A united position has been important to organizations like the Screen Producers Association of Australia (SPAA) and the Media Entertainment and Arts Alliance (MEAA). It enabled them to become political players and stakeholders in the audiovisual industries alongside the cinema trade, the television networks and multinational distributors on governmental and media horizons.

By virtue of its reliance on governmental support, the Australian cinema is dependent on the development and rationalization of public support for it. It is also dependent on the mobilization of this support through publicity and ongoing governmental and private sector commitment. The story of Australian cinema since 1969 is in part the story of the creation of a public for it, as a means to enlist government support for film subsidies. Lobbyists needed to argue for a national cinema as a means of enabling their diverse local agendas. This involved attaching the cinema to a variety of social practices (of film consumption, of film and cultural criticism, of cultural policy, of education) and to societal projections of the meaning of citizenship, Australian culture, identity and the nation-state. Before 1969 governments did not see the feature film as a candidate for such attention. The agitation for a film industry in the 1960s was an agitation for the attention of governments to film: for governments precisely to recognize film as a legitimate art form and a vehicle of popular socialization and the registering of social problems. Cultural critics and industry lobbyists had to point out and struggle to have reluctant national and state governments recognize the role of the cultural industries as a vehicle for publicity, popular socialization and dissidence. Lobbyists, directors, actors and cultural critics built a public space in which Australian cinema could become a protected enclave – a public good cushioned to some extent from the commercial pressures of the market.

By virtue of its dependence on the state and, by implication, politics, politicians, critics and their publics, Australian cinema's future relies on its continuing to secure policy and public attention. Film activists have to continue to address and make meaningful the cinema that the 'public' consents to support. The local cinema has to be worthy of public and hence governmental attention. Public interest in Australian cinema must not flag: without it there would be no Australian cinema beyond a trivial level, and no possibility for diverse social purposes including anti-nationalist ones to be entertained. But it has to be put before the public in a particular way. It has to be 'our' film-making to involve us and elicit a response. It has to be made collective on a continuing basis. It is not enough for films to be simply another film; they must be public texts implicating a diverse audience. From the 1970s, Australian cinema became a public text interesting a variety of agents across the social spectrum.

A particular kind of public is important to the maintenance of Australian cinema as a state initiative. It is not the public that individually appreciates particular moments of Australian films – focusing on particular incidents or fetishes of actors, relating and emplotting their private desires and life histories – although informally these help sustain the cinema and our interest in it. Neither is it the Australian cinema that, for example, talks about technologies of incarceration and their efficacy: the terrain of so much Australian cinema from *For the Term of his Natural Life* (Dawn 1927, on the brutality of the convict system), to *Stir!* (Wallace 1980, on prison riots), to *Ghosts ... of the Civil Dead* (Hillcoat 1989, with its electronic zoo jail) to the casual brutalization of inmates in *Every Night ... Every Night* (Tsilimidos 1994). It is a public which has a general citizen's interest in Australian cinema as Australian cinema and therefore in Australian society and culture. Here the public for Australian cinema is a mediating site – one in which Australian cinema is the subject of action and discussion. Australian cinema as a whole is addressed. It is a translation site too, in that Australian film is made sensible to and publicly (rather than simply administratively and privately) implicated in the pronouncements and work of politicians, journalists, public servants, opinion writers, film critics and academics in as much as it is assumed to be of importance to the diverse peoples in Australia.

The achievement of a national cinema is to elevate itself to the sphere of positive value as a public good, so as to have limited protection against the vagaries of entertainment choice and ensure continuity in Australian film production. People addressed as citizens say this type of cinema is a good thing but as consumers they often resist it. Australian-based exhibitors and video shop proprietors routinely talk about the audience's resistance and negativity to local product. Marketing wisdom has it that Australian films and television programmes should de-emphasize and even hide a feature's Australiannness. In 1994, there was no interest on the part of the ABC or the commercial networks in the screening of the annual Australian Film Institute Awards which showcases the best of that year's cinema. Australian films are always having to build their audience, interest the state; they are perpetually emergent.

Australian cinema needs to interest a variety of agents. Part of the task of cinema producers, marketers and critics is to invite these to translate their purposes and ends through Australian film, that is to have them shape it for their own purposes. The national cinema is a commodious social structure. Indeed the history of social attachment to national cinema as a project in Australia, is a history of the association of various local agendas with the national cinema.

Australian cinema socializes us in many ways. As audiences, film-makers, critics and policy makers we routinely sociologize the cinema, organize our personal calendars, differentiate ourselves from other nationals. We are used to Australian cinema connecting, detaching, celebrating and excoriating ourselves. We habitually evaluate Australian cinema as a vehicle for the transmission of cultural values. The national cinema becomes important to government, activists and critics alike for its capacity to intervene in social lifeways whether emergent or with tradition-conserving ends. The exercise of social power sees some contents and agents enabled and others limited. Funding agencies, distributors and exhibitors exercise considerable commercial and public power in deciding which projects proceed. Scriptwriters, directors and producers select story materials from the social materials and forms at their disposal and they use combinations of technology and performance to establish fictional norms and documentary truths. These norms give more screen power to some individuals, some classes of people, one gender (men) and some ethnicities than others. So too are we members of diverse publics and political constituencies for Australian cinema. And without these constituencies, readerships and viewerships bipartisan support for the Australian cinema would lapse. Such projections socialize cinema and television, just as assuredly as exhibitionary, distributive, technical, economic and governmental machinery naturalize it on our quotidian horizons.

DISCURSIVIZING AUSTRALIAN CINEMA

For a national cinema to function it must become an object of knowledge. It must be put into discourse: narrated, discursively represented by tropes, words, phrases, archives, verbal associations, texts.

Our ways of turning Australian cinema into a social bond and a natural entity are also ways of knowing it and of endowing it with meaning and significance. Australian national cinema poses the relation, or otherwise, between the local cinema and nation, between state and society as a category of knowledge. Australian cinema is not only a site where diverse agents – film-makers, critics, policy-makers, investors, distributors, politicians, and publics – organize relations between themselves and things, but it is, at the same time, a site in which these agents produce ways of knowing, reading and appreciating these films, genres, movements, things and histories (O'Regan 1984a, 1984b). Australian cinema is discursively produced. It is shaped by the diverse ways in which the public come to know about it by means of the agents concerned with it. It is a domain in which different knowledges are produced and brought into relation – these are know-ledges about production strategies, distribution and exhibition technologies, markets and taste cultures, policy development and political investment and critical protocols developed by cinephiles, historians and cultural critics.

Many agents make Australian cinema their topic. The texts of Australian cinema are found in the films themselves: in *David Williamson's Emerald City* (Jenkins 1989) there is a reflection on 'nativism' and 'internationalism' in the film industry, in *Newsfront* there is the thematizing of the 'baleful American' influence on Australian popular culture and political culture. The texts are also found 'outside film' in journalism, critical commentary and reviewing, current affairs, publicity, marketing, policy, interpersonal and parliamentary discussion. They appear in different kinds of 'writing'. Obviously a film, a film review, a parliamen-tary speech, policy prescriptions and industry journalism are heterogeneous in character and staged in different sites. They construct different objects and imply different readerships.

Discourse on Australian cinema obeys no general form. It includes the diverse objects of knowledge of film-makers, policy-makers, politicians, a variety of audiences, exhibitors and festival curators. Local and international critics, film-makers and politicans write, speak and speculate about this cinema, endowing it with specific traits, concerns and narrative patterns. Films give textual form to various identities within the nation and represent national characteristics. Politi-cians, film-makers and critics espouse and criticize various kinds of positions on the relation between Australian culture, cinema and society. Bodies of commen-tary – by critics, politicians and audiences – about national cinemas develop over time creating a public reputation for them. The 'fictive' or 'imaginary' (Dermody and Jacka 1988b: 4) reality provided by public reputation is crucial to continuing state and public support for the national cinema. It attracts an interest in it by audiences, distributors and investors inside and outside Australia.

In their turn, films circulate before diverse publics – audiences, critics, policy-makers and other film-makers – who appreciate, interpret and manipulate them. These texts are fashioned from available national and international discursive repertoires: tropes of nation, actual or imagined incidents, stories drawn from the cinema and outside it in literature, theatre, journalism and television. Films fashion textual connections between the output of domestic and international cultural industries. Australian documentarist, feature film-maker and television producer Lee Robinson saw himself as producing in the 1950s and 1960s 'something that was Australian within an international format' (quoted in Shirley and Adams 1983: 201). In describing *Walk into Paradise* (Robinson and Pagliero 1956) and the television series *Skippy* (1968) for example, he was producing an account of his practice, a way of making sense of what he was doing which was also a way of organizing it. Processes of discursivization are central to Australian cinema. Its object of knowledge is a family of ways of knowing produced in a diverse range of settings.

When we distinguish Australian cinema we are already thinking about it in certain ways: charting a loose family of rhetorical relations, posing a loosely connected range of questions to it. 'Australian cinema' marshalls words like 'cinema', 'Australia', 'society', 'nation', 'international', 'genre', 'gender' and 'economics' into productive verbal patterns. Australian cinema is like a tool box. It contains a family of notions, some strongly, others loosely connected. It has different members, identities, relations, trajectories, personalities and ends over time. By associating words and phrases, we build commodious maps of what Australian national cinema is and could be.

In its most minimal sense, 'Australian cinema' is a descriptive device used to bring together the diverse cinema produced in the country. Its rubric allows a wide range of actors – from critics to politicians to lobbyists to film-makers to philatelists – to link a diverse local film-making and film production milieu in order to realize its regularities and dispersal of style, theme and genre. In 1995, the Australian post-office released a set of stamps commemorating the centenary of cinema, which established the story of Australian cinema through a bushranger film (*The Story of the Kelly Gang*, Tait 1906), a hillbilly farce (*On our Selection*, Hall 1932), an outback melodrama centring on Aboriginals and Islanders (*Jedda*, Chauvel 1955), a horror and art film (*Picnic at Hanging Rock*) and a multicultural musical (*Strictly Ballroom*). Australian cinema is equally useful as a rubric to assert the diversity of local output and the lack of any discernible generic, stylistic or narrative connection. What connects Dr George Miller's post apocalyptic *Mad Max* (1979) and Paul J. Hogan's bitter-sweet tragi-comedy *Muriel's Wedding*? David Stratton's book on 1980s Australian cinema *The Avocado Plantation* (1990) indicates the dispersal of that decade's film-making by sorting the productions out generically with chapter titles ('True Stories', 'The Big Country', 'Lovers and Other Strangers', 'A Walk on the Wild Side', 'Author! Author', 'And Justice For All', 'Gun Crazy', 'Them!', 'Come Up Smiling', 'The Kid Stakes' and 'The Children Are Watching Us').

It is also a useful device with which to create a critical image. Pauline Kael's influential criticism of late 1970s and early 1980s cinema, decried its 'simple mindedness' and 'nicely crafted' qualities which made watching Australian films 'like reading an old fashioned novel' (quoted in Hamilton and Matthews 1986: 21):

> 'Made in Australia' is almost like a seal of *Good Housekeeping* on a film. If a young man goes out on a date, it is safe to take a girl to an Australian film, just as it is safe to go to *Cousin, Cousine* or a Claude Lelouch film. It guarantees a certain date appeal, because a film that is terribly exciting can be upsetting to people out on a date.
>
> (Quoted in Hamilton and Matthews 1986: 25)

And this became a tag that Australian films needed to live down, on the horizons of serious critics. The rubric of a national cinema is a powerful means to present the unity and diversity of local film-making.

Among our ways of knowing the Australian cinema are those derived from foregrounding international connections. We want to make sense of the circulation of locally produced product in local and international markets. We connect the local cinema to other national cinemas and construct resemblances and differences alike. We look for and find common policy and producer responses to similar situations (like Hollywood's global dominance). We write of how Australian features should be influenced by the product of other national cinemas. We think about the possibility of the greater enmeshment of national cinemas – like the Australian and New Zealand cinemas – or find reasons for co-productions between Australian and Canadian and British film-makers. We sometimes distinguish between these models: we might favour Australian film-makers looking to Taiwanese models rather than European and Hollywood ones (Berry 1992: 48). We use models drawn from other national cinemas to make sense of our own and derive a sense of what, under optimal conditions, our cinema could be.

We think of how Australian films might extend the cinema. Gillian Armstrong's *Star Struck* takes a quintessential Hollywood format in the musical, and blends an Australian film-making tradition with the American cinema. For Cunningham (1985: 238) it on the one hand reconciles 'in a series of tight parallel cuts, the "contemporary" world of Americanized showbiz and the "traditional" domain of residual Australian culture', and on the other incorporates and transcends the ocker culture of the early 1970s comedies. It can even seem to critics that the 'survival and specificity' of Australian film can be 'ensured by the revision of American codes by Australian texts' (Morris 1988: 247).

We think of ways in which Australian dialogue with the international cinema renovates the local lifeways, political culture and locally produced symbolic culture. In *Film Comment* Harlan Kennedy lauds *Dogs in Space* (Lowenstein 1987), *Celia* (Turner 1989) and *Ghosts of the Civil Dead* for daring 'to introduce Australian cinema – hitherto home of the Golden Narrative – to shifting perspectives, structural experiment, and highly discomforting stories and characters' of the best international cinema (Kennedy 1989: 73). *Celia* becomes 'the identikit Australian coming-of-age movie parodied and disembodied', *Dogs* 'comes on like a post-hippie musical with a cast too zonked out to sing or dance' and is '[c]rusadingly structureless' (Kennedy 1989: 74). Such a way of knowing Australian cinema readily admits and welcomes international influence.

Through these sorts of productive verbal patterns we make connections, link a number of film, social, governmental and international institutions and the agents involved in them. By collecting words we collect things: establishing the relations (or non-relations) among the various components of a film culture, a film-making milieu, a film industry. Agents do not only use discourse on Australian cinema for their own purposes, but they are in turn shaped by this discourse, and the knowledges and meanings they generate are an integral part of these agents' purposes. Discourse imposes its own semiotic limits and possibilities.

Film activists combine this thinking with discourse to create new films, institutions, film policy, to modify existing ones and to transform the relations between them. One of these new 'forms' was the Australian film revival. I discuss below the role a discourse on Australian film played in the development and maintenance of the film revival.

A loose group of small 'l' liberals – Sylvia Lawson, Michael Thornhill, Phillip Adams, Colin Bennett and Joan Long – in newspapers and journals such as *Nation, The Australian, The Age, Quadrant, Nation Review, Current Affairs Bulletin* and the documentary *The Pictures that Moved* (1968),[5] developed a rhetorical strategy in the 1960s and early 1970s to promote the establishment of a government-subsidized 'boutique' film industry, as Adams later called it (1995: ix). Their rhetorical practice was adapted in policy position papers. Their discourse provided critics and subsequently policy-makers with a means of representing an appealing case to government and a variously constituted public for a greatly expanded and government-involved cinema.

These critics attached cultural nationalist tropes to several notions about film and its social uses. Film was the popular art form of the twentieth century. It was the sum of all previous artforms. It had an important role to play in the cultural development of Australia. Australians would be able to respect themselves more if they were to create their own local stories rather than having those stories and locations plundered by foreigners. The cinema could forge progressive identities suited to a changing world. Film was significant in the development of export trade for other commodities. It had an important function in maintaining and refining a progressive sense of national pride.[6]

There was no necessary relation between the components of this discourse. Yet their forceful collocation created a diverse mandate for a film industry. Their several aims and purposes were subsumed as so many more arguments for re-establishing regular feature film production in Australia after a long hiatus. To all intents and purposes, then, they were interchangeable: various notions presenting a coherent, forceful and appealing case for an Australian cinema. There were necessary relations among notions not that were necessarily related. These contingent verbal associations provided a narrative justification for the institutions which are now a natural part of the Australian film landscape: continuing government subvention at a federal and state level, a film school and expanded film training at a tertiary and further education level around Australia, Australian cinema as a subject taught in universities, and so on. Discursivizing was part of naturalizing Australian cinema on public and governmental horizons.

Before the polemical writings of these critics (see Lawson 1965, 1969, 1985a and b) could be published, written and appreciated by audiences, the agitational discourse they contained had to complement, transform and coexist with other discourses. Journal editors and their audiences, for instance, already had to be predisposed to considering publishing and reading articles that urged the re-establishment of the film industry. A major contribution to such a situation was the discourse of an Australian cultural deficiency – a cluster of statements that had become self-evident around the notion that Australia chronically lacked, and desperately needed the leavening effects of culture.

In this discourse, Australians were described as unappreciative of the arts; their environment was inimical to artistic practice, and because of the subsequent lack of any domestic opportunities, Australia's best creative talent was going overseas.[7] These notions, registered as self-evident facts, became material not only for a Senate inquiry in 1982 but for the content of commercial television programmes and newspaper comment. Something had to be done about maintaining and creating a base for cultural activity in Australia. An active policy was needed to produce culture as a presence on Australia's infertile soil. Remedies were sought in coordinated government action and in response, subsidies to the arts became a political issue. The discourse of cultural lack importantly informed the push for increases in the levels of arts subsidies. From it, the feature film agitation gained credence. If Australia lacked a performing arts culture, it also demonstrably lacked a film culture, given the production down-turn which saw 'most of the important features in the twenty years after the war ... made by British and American companies' (Pike and Cooper 1980: 263). If government subsidies were to be given to these art forms, they should be given to the cinema as well. In this, they were helped by the fact that, in the general cultural programme that was emerging, a film production sector had an important role to play. The Vincent Report (1963), a Senate report on Australian television and its lack of local drama programming, asserted that a film production sector was pivotal to any integration and expansion of the Arts.[8] The Vincent Committee reported that between April and June 1962 locally produced television drama made up 2.1 per cent of total drama programming (quoted in the *Overland* version of the *Vincent Report*, 1964: 31). A film production industry for television would provide employment and training for Australian actors, writers, playwrights, drama directors/producers, musicians and dancers. The development of such an industry would enable an Australian base of creative personnel to be built up and it would stabilize other forms of cultural production, particularly the performing arts (see Harris 1964: 25–6). In the feature film agitation of the 1960s and early 1970s these pre-existing priorities were modified. The feature film was the essential cultural prerequisite – not a film production industry for television. It would not only provide employment for creative personnel and maintain other arts forms, but it would also allow for an Australian acknowledgement of the art form of the cinema. But, just as journal editors had to be disposed to publish articles urging a new film industry, John Gorton's government's initial actions to set up an industry similarly had to wait, first recommendations had to be made by an appropriately constituted body (the Film Committee of the Federal Government's statutory arts body the Australian Council for the Arts – the predecessor of today's Australia Council) which reported in 1969.[9] That report began with the following words:

To borrow from another declaration, this Committee holds certain truths to be self-evident. Namely, that it is in the interests of this nation to encourage its local film and television industry so as to increase the quantity and improve the quality of local material in our cinemas and on our television screens.

(Interim Report of the [Film] Committee 1969, 1985)

These recommendations – for a film and television school, a film and television corporation and an experimental film fund industry – then had to fit the policy agenda of the federal government and they needed a good chance of being electorally popular. It was developed for a prime minister, Gorton who not only loved cinema, particularly Westerns, but who cultivated the arts as something politically important and a new direction for his government (Coombs 1981: 245). Gorton was also a cultural nationalist unlike most of his conservative predecessors. The agitational discourse was circulated in cultural policy-making by government, in the submissions and public promotion of industry bodies and in the textual practices of film reviews. It was put on the public agenda and once there, it became self-evident to politicians and a general public. Particular notions about film, and the place of Australian film for its public, served not only as a means to understand film, but also to legislate an industry into existence (Bertrand and Collins 1981: 11–12), to lobby state and federal governments about the necessity for an industry and to formulate oppositional strategies of film-making.

The same characterization of Australian film in the diverse public discussion of reports, parliamentary speeches, reviews and controversies provided a terrain on which disputation could proceed. These institutional sites cohered and contested by saying in part similar things. They used similar language and they associated this 'common' language with their discourses, rationales and projects. Consequently, when repeated, this agitational discourse not only provided evidence of a consensus and sameness of outlook, but also of a more particular contingent repetition in difference across the broad spectrum of community and government.

The components of this agitational discourse became firmly *naturalized* with the establishment of film agencies and the acceptance by both sides of politics of bipartisan support for film subsidies. Federal institutions like The Australian Film Development Corporation (AFDC), the Experimental Film Fund (EFF) and the Australian Film and Television School (hereafter AFTRS) were established between 1970 and 1973, and the AFC in 1975 (which replaced the AFDC and later incorporated the EFF). States-based film initiatives followed these federal initiatives. State organizations were established, starting in 1972 in South Australia then later opening in New South Wales, Victoria, Western Australia, Queensland and Tasmania.

Once naturalized, the components of this agitational discourse became open to *problematization* by government, politicians, critics and the public. This entailed a work of further extension and redirection on their part which could take place without compromising the integrity of the production industry, or state and public support for one. The conceptual (in)coherence and even contradiction within the several parts of the discourse became materials for tactical redeployment by rival agents. By the late 1970s and early 1980s, with a decade of film-making and the institutional division between the Creative Development Branch and the Industry Development Branch of the AFC, it became possible to pose a film industry and a film culture as antagonistic alternatives. These antinomies structured the 1979 Peat, Marwick and Mitchell Services report, *Towards a More Effective Commission: The Australian Film Commission in the 1980s* as well as subsequent criticism (see Phillip Adams 1982 and 'The Meaning of Compliance' 1981). One part favoured a commercial film industry over a film culture, the other a film-making milieu driven by cultural values.

Australian cinema emerged in discourse and discourse was central to it: without the verbal associations and the conditions which sustained them there would have been nothing to produce, nothing to lobby for. Discourse acted as a *mediator* not simply a passive intermediary between facts (nature) and power (society). Latour (1993: 90) describes discourse as 'a population of actants that mix with things as well as with societies, uphold the former and the latter alike, and hold on to them both.' He argues that an '(i)nterest in texts' does not 'distance us from reality' and that texts should not be denied 'the grandeur of forming the social bond that holds us together' (Latour 1993: 90). Discourse requires enunciation, or in Foucault's terms, 'eventalization' (Foucault 1981: 4). It is spoken by agents and carried in a medium. Latour sees discourse as one of those 'actors' which are 'endowed with the capacity to *translate* what they transport, to redefine it, redeploy it, and also to betray it' (Latour 1993: 81). Entrepreneurs and networks of actors treated the agitational discourse on Australian cinema as instruments and materials to be manipulated. They used, betrayed, and played with these repertoires just as much as these repertoires organized and structured them. Processes of discursivizing Australian cinema do not just explain; they function within a strategic, institutional and social field. Discourse may have a relatively independent life of its own because it is 'narrated, historical, passionate, and peopled with actants of autonomous forms' (Latour 1993: 89). But it is not *sui generis*.

PROBLEMATIZING AND PROBLEM SOLVING IN AUSTRALIAN CINEMA

For a national cinema to function it must become a problem of knowledge.
It must unite knowledge and its application, knowledge and power.

The discourses on Australian cinema surveyed immediately above had a strategic dimension. With them we were not only dealing with representations but also with rationalities, strategies of action, discursive techniques fashioned for intervention. These are words with power – who says what to whom, under what conditions, with what force and to what effect. Representations became a basis for diverse actors to intervene. Individuals and institutions applied the discourse of Australian cinema. They used it to create social bonds. A diverse range of actors applied these knowledges to the filmic fact. These verbal patterns created knowledges which were put to work. They linked a number of institutions and established relations among them and they sustained existing rhetorical configurations and produced new ones.

Attending to discourse led us to things, to agents, to networks, to institutions, to governance in the general sense of processes of controlling and managing. We are dealing with a question of knowledge and the relations among actors: verbal associations and actor networks (Latour calls these 'chains of association', 1987: 202). These words, these knowledges were ways of organizing relations among the several actors. They were words 'used' for pragmatic purposes and ends. The knowledge(s) about Australian cinema produced a range of applications in the hands of actors.

The 'we' of the last paragraph covers not only those who write on national cinemas like myself,[10] but also the multitude of actors within the national cinema itself – film-makers, government officials, film festival coordinators, multinational distributors, private investors, cultural critics and audiences, publishers and the National Film and Sound Archive. Each agent conceptualizes, analyses, recognizes and, indeed calls 'Australian cinema' into question in particular ways, for its own practical purposes. Like the film critic, these agents also connect (and disconnect) films, policies, institutions, and different national cinemas. Each has definite ideas about what Australian cinema currently is, what it is likely to become and what they would like it to be. As film activists they use such knowledges to explore these relations whether to lobby, to justify, or as tools to think out strategies or undergird polemical positions.

When film lobbyists Barry Jones and Phillip Adams made a case to prime minister John Gorton in 1969 that federal support should revive the Australian industry they argued the classic case for a national cinema. Such a cinema would represent Australia to themselves; Australians should participate in this popular and culturally prestigious art form; and they argued for an educational mechanism – a film school – to secure this excellence. They spoke of Australia's lack of ongoing production, its lack of representation on the international festival circuit, and the impact of a steady and dominant diet of American film and television on Australians. These notions are still at the heart of the Australian government's twenty-five year commitment to an Australian national cinema and were most recently reaffirmed in the Creative Nation statement. Diverse agents used these notions to act, to envisage the possibility of a feature film revival, to capture the imagination of politicians and a diverse public including critics. They used knowledge to enlist powerful allies.

Knowledge and its application can be seen in the ongoing problematizing of gender inequality in the Australian film industry since the early 1970s. Feminist activists and their organizations like Women in Film and Television (WIFT) identified the problem as under-representation in front of and behind the camera.

They lobbied for programmes to improve the employment situation and education campaigns to combat sexism. They called for more 'women centred' stories and ear-marked production funding. These actions cut across other ways of rendering Australian cinema. And these activists were partially successful. Some of Australia's highest profile directors are women. Some of its most popular and famous films have been women centred: *Picnic at Hanging Rock*, *Caddie* (Crombie 1976), *My Brilliant Career*, *The Piano*, *Muriel's Wedding*. Women have worked at the highest levels in the film industry: heading the AFTRS, Film Australia, the AFC, Film Victoria, SBS-TV and ABC Drama. This feeds back into 'knowing Australia' as a more female-friendly industry, providing opportunities which are not as available elsewhere. But it equally provides a cool appraisal of just how far there is to go for there to be genuine equality.

The ends of cultural national and feminist objectives are sometimes commensurable, sometimes not. Sue Milliken, current Chair of the AFC entertains a remit for the industry as a whole. She is also an activist for Australian culture and equal opportunity, particularly for women in the industry. At other times, feminist critics of Australian cinema oppose themselves to cultural national ideals as a matter of principle, registering these as a nationalism that is never beneficial to women and asserting the primacy of women's interests over 'national' and other general interests.

But both are at loggerheads with the market orientation of distributors and exhibitors towards a commercially viable Australian film-making or even just making money. Exhibitors and distributors 'know' and 'expect' that Hollywood 'blockbusters' – often male-centred stories like *The Lion King* (Allers and Minkoff 1994) or *Forrest Gump* (Zemeckis 1994), or *Speed* (De Bont 1994) – will tend to be the typical high grossers in the Australian market and not Australian films, let alone Australian films with women-centred storylines.

Australian cinema is explicitly considered by these agents as so many *problems of knowledge*. It follows that one of the ways we come to understand Australian cinema is through the various wills to produce knowledge about it. 'Problematizing' has acquired two distinct senses. It is a technique in the armoury of criticism and it is a technique of policy and governmental processes. The first version makes problematizing synonymous with 'criticizing' or 'rendering questionable'. Film and cultural critics perform this problematizing when they debunk Australian cinema. They register it as constructed, fictive, imaginary and therefore chimerical. For Dermody and Jacka (1988b: 4), this cinema is an 'imaginary construct in the minds of the public and its own members and proponents'; it is a 'construct . . . frequently in excess of its own reality'. Problematizing becomes the critic's resource to make sense of the field examined. It enables the critic to establish a critical distance from the field in question. The second version of problematizing – and the one which informs this analysis – sees calling into question as a means of bringing objects, things and outcomes into being. Locating the problem is tied here to solving it practically. Michel Foucault drew attention to such problematizing as a routine part of modern governmentality. Ian Hunter describes it as the productive processes by which things are made 'an object of ethical care and attention'. So to make something into a problem, to call something into question is, in Hunter's words (1994: 46), 'to hold it up for inspection in the light of what it might be' and 'to picture its reconstruction around certain norms'. Problematization is synonymous with the 'application of knowledge' more generally (47). It is a critical comportment and a general operation of those in the field. It not only represents and so defines the problem(s) facing say Australian cinema, but it develops solutions for it (them). Latour (1993: 79–82) calls this process mediation – emphasizing the active and coordinating work of probematization.

Problem solving is, of course, the promise of policy and the domain of government in its most general sense – to control and manage through strategies and plans of action adequate to the circumstance. Problem solving is, then, a crucial component in the practice and interaction of the different experts in a film milieu – film-makers, censors, film policy advisers, various industry and professional organizations. These players – like those Rose and Miller (1992: 177) generally describe – unite 'systems of thought' and 'systems of action'. The sphere of government is given over extensively to 'a continuous problematizing of the domains in which it operates'. Government is not only a property of the state but of private industry: distributors and exhibitors also govern the film market by managing it through their plans of action. Adopting such a wide definition of government allows for the problematizing of Australian cinema, not just by state instrumentalities but by all those involved in policy-making. We go from the specialist video shop proprietor who has a policy of deliberately downplaying a film's Australian origin so as to maintain its rental value (or displaying Australian cinema in a separate small site down the back of the shop thereby confirming this same estimation), to the governmental agencies forging film policy and the distributors and exhibitors handling Australian features in certain ways.

Following Foucault's lead, Hunter is keen to identify how the 'application of knowledge and the exercise of power – problematization and intervention – allows it [government] to bring new levels or departments of social existence into being'. The action of problematizing projects the Australian national cinema just as it provides instruments for its debunking and reconstructing. This also means that the 'deployment of an expert knowledge of the domain to be governed' (by it) is critical to the exercise of power (46).

Government, Hunter argues, 'engages with social reality by representing it with intellectual instruments that show this reality only in the light of what it could be, under an optimal administration of its natural and human resources'. It entails inbuilt failure as '[d]emonstrating its own failure ... is the means by which government opens up new tracts of social life to bureaucratic knowledge and intervention' (Hunter 1994: 134).

Problematization is one of the means of holding the critic's and government's interest in the national cinema. It supplies film-making with vision, potential, possibilities and unfinished business. Just as a national cinema requires both its blockbuster, financial successes like *Crocodile Dundee* and *succès d'estime* like *Picnic at Hanging Rock* and *The Piano*, it also requires a plan and vision for (national) cultural futures. (Perhaps national cinemas, by virtue of their reliance on government funding, partly require the language of failure, in that failure is paradoxically, part of its success on governmental and critical horizons.)

Australian cinema is not so much a field governed by a coherent or unified power but rather it is one of those dispersed governmental fields traversed by 'a will to govern' (Rose and Miller 1992: 190–1). In this sense, problematizing is integral to the very shape and contours of Australian cinema. It provides knowledge(s) and truth(s) about it.[11] It brings objects and departments of social existence to things and is a means to a variety of governmental ends.

AUSTRALIAN CINEMA IS A QUASI-OBJECT

> For a national cinema to function it must be a quasi-object: simultaneously natural, social, discursive and governmental – an entity, a domain of practical action, a field of practical knowledge and their application.

As one of Latour's hybrids of 'reality, language, society and being all at once' (Latour 1993: 89), the story of Australian cinema is more than mere discourse, more than the mere things of cinema, the genres of international cinema, more than a story of a social bond between a people, their society and their cinema. Latour claims 'quasi-objects' always come to us in each of these three guises '[a]s soon as we are on the trail of some quasi-object, it appears to us sometimes as a thing, sometimes as a narrative, sometimes as a social bond' (1993: 89). None of these repertoires of naturalization, socialization and discursivization should be privileged above the others. People lead to discourse, power leads to things, things to narratives and fictive dimensions. Australian cinema is a hybrid entity embracing each. It is always a mixture that is not established in a stable hierarchy.

It is therefore futile to use the discursive character of Australian cinema as a critique of its naturalness; to use its collectiveness to denigrate its discursive character; to use its naturalness to denigrate the collectivities that produce it. Given the hybrid character of Australian cinema, it makes no sense to ask whether it is more a natural entity, or a social entity or a fictive discursive entity. For there is no decision on status to make regarding an object that is always already real, social and discursive.

We can, of course, purify the cinema into one of nature, society and discourse. We then make it only a matter of discourse, or only a matter of economics, or only a matter of the power of certain classes of agents. Alternatively we may isolate each into barely overlapping compartments (volume one of Dermody and Jacka's study of Australian cinema is about its industry/political economy; while volume two is about the films – their relation to other Australian films, Australian peoples and some international cinema). We can connect these repertoires of naturalization, discursivization, socialization by making one determining factor with respect to the others. We habitually give ascendancy to discourse (semiotics); or to nature in the economy; or to society and political power. But by doing so we miss something important: the constitutive work of *mediation* and *problematization* in objects that are simultaneously 'real, social and discursive'. Our quasi-objects Latour observes are:

> much more social, much more fabricated, much more collective than the 'hard' parts of nature, but they are in no way arbitrary receptacles of a full-fledged society. On the other hand they are much more real, non-human and objective than those shapeless screens on which society – for unknown reasons needed to be projected.
>
> (1993: 55)

Latour argues that quasi-objects 'mix up different periods, ontologies and genres' (1993: 73). Surveying the feature film output of any year it is supremely difficult to categorize the films as a single group belonging to the same temporal order. Take the 1994 films: *Country Life* (Blakemore) drew on the well-crafted style of the revival classics like *My Brilliant Career*. *Body Melt* (Brophy) embedded its contemporary splatter stylistics in a retro televisual frame of the 1960s television police series, *Homicide*. *Muriel's Wedding* updated a tradition of Australian storytelling centring on the antics of a 'daggy' family featuring strong father/strong daughter relations and mentally defective siblings – the archetypal Rudd family story retold this time in a coastal city and contemporary context. Finally, *The Adventures of Priscilla* drew on the 1950s backstage musical with the 'putting on a show' involving drag queens mainstreaming gay lifestyles on the road to Alice Springs. All these films occupy the same space; none is animated by the same concerns. We can only produce coherence by sorting through them, finding thematic or stylistic continuities, declaring some to be outmoded and others quintessentially modern. For Monica Zetlin (1994: 64) *Country Life* was outmoded as it harked back to 'an Australian cinema long thought over, and perhaps wisely so, to ... "middle brow film-making"'; 'it was out of kilter with the modern 1994 releases like *Muriel's Wedding, The Sum of Us, Priscilla*, and *Bad Boy Bubby*' (de Heer 1994).

Quasi-objects require hybrid analysis capable of moving among facts, social power and discourse. We need to find ways of holding these several elements together. Latour calls for a 'new constitution' which would allow us to address more than only a part of the hybrid. It is one which would allow us to focus on the mediation and problematizing aspects of Australian cinema. It means recognizing how the cinema is made of commodious textual, conceptual, social, structural and technological assemblages.

As a quasi-object Australian cinema is an unprincipled assemblage of diverse elements. I borrow the concept of unprincipled assemblage from Ian Hunter's *Rethinking the School* (1994), where he uses it as a way of considering the school system. He argues that 'assemblage' is a useful way to characterize the school not only because of its impure character, diverse purposes and comportments but because the school is not derived from the application of first principles. Rather the school system is continually and pragmatically 'improvised' (Hunter 1994: xxii). The quasi-objects Latour describes and which I take national cinemas to be are also highly impure, they are also assemblages of materials that are tactically improvised, and they are also put together from different spheres of life and serve 'a mixture of spiritual and worldly ends' (Hunter xxii).

Australian cinema is an *unprincipled assemblage*, in that there is no general principle that coheres its component parts or allows for a unitary explanatory principle productively to combine its many facets. It is an imperfectly integrated assemblage because it is a hybrid of people, texts, elements, social practices, discourses and technologies with all manner of relations between them. It is the accumulation and juxtaposition of its various (stylistic, critical, political) tendencies, the elaboration of its incommensurate (aesthetic, political, intellectual) values, its competing (filmic and social) identities and the contradictions, disjunctions and complementarities of these.

There is no ideal or complete development of a national cinema to which Australian cinema might strive. There is no fundamental identity or expressive (in)capacity underlying Australian cinema. Contrary to those principled critical analyses which presume to embody such an ideal for Australian cinema or import another to substitute for it, it has an open-ended and highly contingent character. Hunter enjoins us to put to one side the temptations to ethical absolutes and the opportunities to use such analysis to develop a personal or collective ethos.

Australian cinema is not a unified field with a unitary principle of organization governing it. National cinema criticism, in its turn, cannot provide anything more than a contingent grasp of its object. This means we should foreground the intrinsic noisiness and mixed character of a national cinema with its different production traditions, critical orthodoxies, exhibition, distribution, policy apparatuses and publishing structures. We should approach this messiness not to reduce and purify it to some unifying principles or tendencies or general themes but to exemplify it, to sort it, to emphasize its incommensurate values and ends. This is to envisage Australian cinema as a patchwork of mediations, of problematizations.

To do this we face a practical difficulty. Ian Hunter (1994: 90–1) observes that the problem we face in describing this kind of institutional network is that it is '"wiser" than any of its constituent personae, who, after all, represent comportments of the person assembled and trained under its aegis'. There can be no privileged point in the cinema where all the diverse elements could be summarized into a generalized principle. It is the network – made of a collection of hybrid entities – that governs the cinema's form and character. The various ways in which agents know Australian cinema depends on their place in this web (and this includes me). It also depends on the manner in which they negotiate its pathways, intersections and divergences. This situation imposes on the national cinema critic a modicum of modesty. How can her or his position be other than the view from one or other vantage point? And what is the function in this network of this critical vantage point? If our object is itself an improvised web, so too are our national cinema analyses similarly improvised. Such a situation requires a plural approach to the matters before Australian cinema.

Part I

Making a national cinema

Chapter 3

A national cinema

INTRODUCTION

'What does Australian cinema *have in common with other national cinemas* – no matter how diverse?' This chapter answers this question by establishing the characteristics of national cinemas generally through a survey of different aspects of Australian cinema. In inspecting Australian and other cinemas, I aim to generalize the shape and outlook of national cinema as a category. Like all national cinemas, the Australian cinema contends with Hollywood dominance, it is simultaneously a local and international form, it is a producer of festival cinema, it has a significant relation with the nation and the state, and it is constitutionally fuzzy. National cinemas are simultaneously an aesthetic and production movement, a critical technology, a civic project of state, an industrial strategy and an international project formed in response to the dominant international cinemas (particularly but not exclusively Hollywood cinema). Australian cinema is formed as a relation to Hollywood and other national cinemas.

NATIONAL CINEMAS AND LE DÉFI AMÉRICAIN

Alternative cinemas gain their significance and force partly because they seek to undermine the common equation of 'the movies' with 'Hollywood'.

(Kristin Thompson 1985: 170)

If you can't stand the heat, get out of the kitchen, living in the twentieth century means learning to be American.

(Dusan Makavejev quoted in Elsaesser 1994: 24)

The American cinema looms large as a term of reference for every national cinema in the West and many beyond. Curiously, the US cinema is in many respects like other national cinemas. It relies in the first instance on the certainties of its domestic market, it is embedded in a particular industrial, policy and aesthetic milieu, it has dynamics that are simultaneously local and international, and it negotiates particular social, cultural and ethnic differences within the USA. But Hollywood is not usually thought to be a 'national cinema'.

The term is reserved by critics, film-makers, policy makers, audiences and marketers for national cinemas other than the US one. For them, national cinemas provide a rubric within which cinema and television product can be differentiated from each other and from the dominant international Hollywood cinema. There is Hollywood, and there are national cinemas. Hollywood is an avowedly commercial enterprise. National cinemas are mixed-commercial and public enterprises. While the US government assists Hollywood's commercial ends, in other national cinemas there is a higher degree of formative government assistance involved in creating and sustaining them. Australian cinema, for example, is what it is today because of the ongoing governmental assistance to it since 1969. From the end of the Second World War to 1969 Australian feature production was sporadic and marginal because it lacked such assistance.

The American national cinema is in its reach the most international of national cinemas. It is the pre-eminent supplier of international products in various national markets. It is the closest thing we have to an audiovisual lingua franca in the world. It also has had an historical stranglehold over many of the world's cinema and more lately video markets – and this market presence is most evident in Europe, the Americas and Australasia. These countries are culturally closer to the USA than those in Africa and large parts of Asia. This makes Hollywood a particularly important term of reference.

Along with India, Hollywood is one of the few cinemas that consistently dominate their domestic box offices. In the USA and India the national cinema *is* the cinema. Differences are disclosed mostly *within* the local cinema. There is, to be sure, a minor US market for the product of other national cinemas in its ethnic cinemas and its 'art cinema' circuits, indeed Elsaesser argues it was the 'US distribution practice of the art-house circuit which gave the term "art cinema" its currently accepted meaning' (Elsaesser 1994: 24). Within the US, other national cinemas occupy minor niche markets and do not threaten Hollywood's American hegemony. It makes little sense to think of these cinemas in the same 'national/ international' terms that we do for national cinemas. Differentiations between the American cinema and imported product is not something US producers need to negotiate, marketers to market as 'their advantage', and American politicians to concern themselves with (unless it is to try and remove barriers to its international circulation in other national markets). Yet these are the things of central concern to film workers in other national cinemas. Rather US producers, politicians, etc., are primarily concerned with differences within the American cinema.

In most countries which have their own national cinema, cinema-going, cinema distribution, cinema viewing and cinema criticism are not primarily oriented to the local national cinema, but to the cinema more generally, and more particularly the dominant international cinema. Most national cinemas do not dominate their domestic market. American and to a lesser extent British and European cinema is central to the Australian audience's experience of the cinema, television and video. So too the local production component of the cinema, television and video industries in Australia makes up only a fraction of their total turnover. So, for example, Australian features made up between 5 per cent and 21 per cent of the local cinema box-office in the 1980s (AFC 1991: 71) which means that Australian cinema-goers saw an Australian film 'between 5 and 20% of the time depending on the films available in any particular year' (AFC 1991: 71). This situation is repeated in television drama where in 1990 local television drama comprised 16 per cent of total drama programming on the commercial television networks, 7 per cent on the foremost public service broadcaster, the ABC and a negligible proportion on the SBS (ABT 1991: 32).

The international cinemas are more naturalized parts of the cinema landscape than are the various local cinemas. Within most countries people experience the cinema more as another cinema than as their own national cinema. Andrew Higson notes that this international cinema, particularly Hollywood cinema and television, has become 'an integral and naturalized part of the national culture . . . of most countries in which cinema is an established entertainment form' (Higson 1989: 39). One of the consequences here is that, as Geoffrey Nowell-Smith writes of Britain, the American cinema is 'by now far more deeply rooted in British cultural life than is the native product' (1985: 152). Diane Collins puts this case in its strongest form for Australia (1987: 2):

> For most of this century Australians have watched little else but American movies and America's domination of Australia's film culture extended far beyond the screen. Australians saw (and see) these films in American-style picture shows; news of the latest releases came (and comes) via the American industry's publicity methods. It was not long before locally made films were modelled on Hollywood production styles and America's movie world meant more to many Australians than homegrown celebrities.

At best, Australian films supplement the audience's and the exhibition and distribution industry's mostly Hollywood diet.

National cinemas are structurally marginal, fragile and dependent on outside help. In their own domestic market and internationally, they are often structurally dispensable in that exhibitors, distributors and audiences can make do without their product, though they cannot do without international product. The 1991 figures for Australian theatrical releases well illustrate this point: of the 238 theatrical releases, 60 per cent were sourced from the USA, 10 per cent from the UK, 14 per cent from Europe (7 per cent France), 9 per cent from Australia; of the remainder 3 per cent were from the Far East, 2 per cent other, 1 per cent Canada and less than 1 per cent from New Zealand (calculated from Curtis and Spriggs 1992: 75). The lack of distributor and exhibitor interest in Australian cinema is a continuing leitmotif of Australian film history. The exhibition and distribution combine, Union Pictures, chose to consolidate itself and expand during the First World War and immediately after at the expense of local production. Film activists of the 1960s regarded with justification the Australian film trade as simply an extension of the American film industry. They saw themselves as representing Australian interests, while the dominant exhibitors – Hoyts and Greater Union – represented American interests.

While most national cinema producers face difficulties in their home market, this same domestic box-office is generally crucial to all national cinemas (even Hollywood has historically relied on 45 per cent–75 per cent of its revenues from its domestic market). National cinemas generally need as good an access to their domestic box-office and to the international market as they can get to be viable. But only part of their local box-office is available – in the Australian case between 3 and 21 per cent of the box-office from 1977 to 1993 (Reid 1994: 82). Clearly they need help – and this is where government is important, as is other non-cinema backing and international involvement, whether by way of direct investment, co-productions, or simply revenues from having had a major international success.

Every national cinema activist negotiates to win ground for its national cinema in this market context. The aim of a national cinema is one of producing a local presence alongside the dominant imported presence in both the local and international markets. The task of a national cinema is to graft itself as a minor component on to the existing communication circuits and networks of cinema and television. The aim of a national cinema in this market and cultural environment is not to replace Hollywood films with say Australian films so much as to provide a viable and healthy local supplement to Hollywood cinema. National cinema producers hope, at best, for some limited import substitution and some limited overseas presence. And this is the case for all bar the largest of national cinemas – in the 1992/93 financial year, the value of Australia's audiovisual exports were $65 million, while its import bill was a massive $437 million (Given 1994: 19). Policy-makers recognize the limits of import substitution given the cultural and economic characteristics of the Australian market; and generally the limits in export.[1] Naturalizing a local contribution to the cinema and local and international audiences to a national cinema is an unending and fraught process. A sense of the minor and subordinate role of domestic production is never far away from debates or writings on any national cinema. The local cinema needs to be worked for anew and presented to every new generation of critics, viewers, exhibitors, distributors and politicians. National cinema activists and film-makers have to think out, work at, legitimate, lobby for, self-consciously articulate and market their difference from the dominant international cinema and each other.

'[T]he cinema', Geoffrey Nowell-Smith writes, 'has always been international, both culturally and economically' (1985: 154). In this context, national cinemas routinely negotiate the extraordinary internationalism of the cinema. They do so from an unequal basis. National cinemas can expect to be no more than a junior partner to the dominant international cinemas. As Elsaesser observes '"national cinema" makes sense only as a relation, not as an essence, being dependent on other kinds of film-making, to which it supplies the other side of the coin' (1994: 25–6). A national cinema necessarily 'functions as a subordinate term' (26).

A national cinema, as it is understood on everything from festival schedules to publishers lists, is a production industry operating in the context of a more significant international, usually Hollywood, market presence. For Australian and European cinema alike the 'shape' of the national cinema was partly defined by the impact of and competition provided by the North American film production and distribution industry (K. Thompson 1985: 168) and a subsidiary component of 'runaway' and 'off-shore' productions of that industry – like Stanley Kramer's *On the Beach* in 1959 or Steve Gordon's 1993 *Fortress*.

National cinemas like Australia's evolve strategies to respond to Hollywood's pre-eminent place on the cinema horizons of the Western world and beyond (I make the 'Western' qualification here to allow for the significant circulation of Indian and Hong Kong cinema in African and Asian contexts). They are thus, local film production, film policy and critical strategies designed to effectively *compete with, imitate, oppose, complement* and *supplement* the (dominant) international cinema. The relation between the local and the international cinema provides many 'national cinemas' with their identity and force.

Because Hollywood looms large for those cinemas culturally closest to Hollywood cinema such as the English-speaking cinemas of Canada, Australia, the UK and New Zealand, the need to imitate and oppose Hollywood is felt especially keenly. British, Australian and Canadian film producers often tackle the competition head-on at home and abroad: with titles like *Crocodile Dundee, Four Weddings and a Funeral* (Newell 1994) and *The Fly* (Cronenberg 1986). These sorts of films circulated as Hollywood major product: Warner Brothers, for example, handled the international distribution of the *Mad Max* films. At times various British studios, distributors and exhibitors have sought to try to become a British Hollywood major. Being directly competitive, internationally, is an option mostly available to the English language cinemas.

This means producing films that are, if not imitative, then consonant or interchangeable with the international product. Australian film-makers are often held to 'imitate' American films, whether it be Carl Schultz's Sirkian melodrama, *Careful He Might Hear You* (1983) or Dr Miller's 'revenge/road movie' cycle *Mad Max* (1979, 1981, 1985) cycle. As local cinema and television drama markets are dominated by imports, the local product is shaped by these imports. The prevailing international styles, techniques, technologies, programme concepts and sensibilities are used, adjusted, and transformed in their local enactment in national productions and criticism. In such circumstances of 'internationalization' and 'hybridization', it is often difficult to ascertain where the local ends and the other national or international begins (Dermody and Jacka, 1988a: 20).

Another strategy to 'counter' Hollywood competition is to compete indirectly by seeking complementarities. This market niche option can take a number of directions. It can seek local specificities in domestic social events, issues, stories and myths foregrounding the coherence of the national cultural system such as the shearers in *Sunday Too Far Away* and the famous racehorse *Phar Lap* (Wincer 1983). Elsaesser notes the 'importance of the texture of speech and voice for our idea of a national cinema' (Elsaesser, 1994: 26); there are the Australian accents in the work of script-writer and playwright, David Williamson in the 1970s with

Don's Party, Stork (Burstall 1971), *The Removalists* (Jeffrey 1975) and *The Club* (Beresford 1976) which foregrounded the Australian vernacular. These may draw on what Alison Butler (1992: 419) has called 'more localized approaches to cultural codification'. Alternatively it can seek an aesthetic distinction by promoting cinema product as 'Art'. Sometimes a national cinema takes on an 'avant-gardist opposition to Hollywood style' (Butler 1992: 419). Or it can do both. Doing both is central to the 'art cinema' as a strategy for a national cinema. As Elsaesser (1994: 26) notes 'one function of auteur cinema, before the advent of television, was to transcribe features of a nation's cultural tradition as figured in other art forms (the novel, theatre, opera) and to represent them in the cinema.' This can be seen in the coincidence of Australian auteurs and the literary *oeuvre*: Armstrong and Miles Franklin's *My Brilliant Career*; Weir and Joan Lindsay's *Picnic at Hanging Rock* and Weir and Christopher Koch's *The Year of Living Dangerously* (1982); Schepisi and Thomas Kenneally's *The Chant of Jimmie Blacksmith*; Beresford and Henry Handel Richardson's *The Getting of Wisdom* (1977) and Beresford and David Williamson's *Don's Party*. It can also be witnessed in the focus on the Norman Lindsay legend in John Duigan's *Sirens* (1994). Lindsay was not only a painter, novelist, poet, children's story writer and publisher but a cultural phenomenon in his own right, who scandalized Sydney society for three decades. Steve Neale (1981) argues that Art and national identity are fused for the Germans in the 1920s, essentially for market niche reasons. Australia did not have this fusion until 1970 or thereabouts.[2] This doubling was first an explicit project of Australian film policy and later embodied in Peter Weir's *Picnic at Hanging Rock*. Here, for the first time, a nation's character seemed embodied in a personally idiosyncratic and poetic cinema as opposed to slick Hollywood commercial entertainment (and its Australian predecessors that sought to be only entertainment).

Critics and film-makers oppose Hollywood screen dominance, seeing in the local product alternatives to Hollywood norms and values. They invoke Australian film's humanist values, its black humour, its quirkiness. For Australia's festival cinema – *Breaker Morant, Sweetie* – the aim is not to directly compete so much as to complement Hollywood product. It has what Butler (1992: 418) would call its 'nationally specific styles', its 'misreadings' of Hollywood norms.

National cinemas provide a means to identify, assist, legitimate, polemicize, project, and otherwise create a space nationally and internationally for non-Hollywood film-making activity. Just as 'the international' makes no sense without nations, so, in cinema terms 'national' makes no sense without 'le défi américain'.

NATIONAL CINEMA AS A LOCAL AND INTERNATIONAL FORUM

So, national cinemas can be seen as a response to the internationalization of the cinema. They are not alternatives to internationalization, they are one of its manifestations. National cinemas, whether in the guise of a local film industry producing a variety of films or of a purveyor of the national culture or whatever, are from inception vehicles for international integration.

In Australia's case, the project of a national cinema in the multifaceted sense advanced so far, did not emerge until 1969, well after Hollywood had consolidated its international reach and control over the Australian market. At that point, formative government assistance was put into place and an Australian national cinema became a project capable of enlisting a large array of local and inter-national actors – politicians, arts bureaucrats, voters, critics, audiences, film-makers. Before that, it was simply a struggling commercial industry, producing, or striving to produce, popular entertainment capable of intermittently enlisting government support, or it was a producer of unaffiliated product showing great promise but achieving no theatrical release like Cecil Holmes' films *Captain Thunderbolt* (1953) and *Three in One* (1957).

As one of the forms the internationalization of the cinema takes, national cinemas *localize* the cinema and explicitly *contribute* to the international cinema at one and the same time. As Kristin Thompson (1985: 168) observes:

> few national cinema industries operate in isolation; through foreign invest-ment, competition and other types of influence, outside factors will almost invariably affect any given national cinema. Such effects have implications for most types of historical study – whether of film style, industry working, government policy, technological change or social implications.

National cinemas work to be local while streamlining themselves to be of interest to audiences outside Australia. Bruce Beresford's *The Adventures of Barry McKenzie* – a classic comedy of an 'ocker' in England – came out of a period where film policy and criticism emphasized securing a local following and gave near exclusive priority to representing Australia to itself. But the film was also from its inception international: self-consciously made for the British and Australian market it was successful in both (the Barry Humphries comic strip on which the film was based was more popular in the UK than in Australia). *Barry McKenzie* has as its erstwhile hero the monstrous Barry McKenzie who in order to acquire his inheritance must visit the 'old country', England. Apart from the opening sequence in Sydney and a brief sequence in Hong Kong immediately following, the rest of the film is concerned with Bazza's assorted English adventures. If, with his double breasted suit, airways bag, and his braggadocio, McKenzie is a camp parody of a by then outdated Australian masculinity (his clothes belong in the 1940s and early 1950s not the the 1960s or 1970s) he is also the Australian abroad, the colonial Candide. Episodically structured, improbably connected, the film has a farcical structure in which narrative is clearly at the service of set piece performances by Barry Crocker (Bazza), Barry Humphreys (Edna Everage and other roles), Spike Milligan and Peter Cook. In many ways the film can be regarded as a 'rewriting' of *They're a Weird Mob* (Powell 1966). It encourages not so much the 'identification' with its Australianness, but a suspending of illusionist belief, thereby producing its fantasy of the 'hyper-Australian' intersecting with an equally 'hyper-Britishness'. The film could be simultaneously, depending on where you stood: 'us sticking it up the Poms' and 'us dealing with those frightful Australians'.

This process of streamlining has a bearing on what is selected from the cultural archive – British/Australian implications in the colonial or post-colonial eras are foregrounded in many Australian films, including notable successes like *Gallipoli* and *Breaker Morant*. Michael Blakemore set his film, *Country Life* (1994) in turn-of-the-century Australia. The metropole/province relation was configured as a British/Australian relation within an Australian family. Sometimes it can be updated, as in Mark Joffe's *Spotswood* (1992) where the English efficiency expert comes to an Australian moccasin factory. The workers here are more interested in racing slot cars than working and he is eventually 'bent' towards his eccentric workers. Here again the British connection not only lies with Anthony Hopkins' presence in the lead role but in the many ways the film evokes the Ealing comedies of the 1940s and 1950s. In *Film Review 1993–4* James Cameron-Wilson described it as 'an exquisitely judged social comedy, which is written, directed and played at just the right pitch, evoking fond memories of Ealing' (in Cameron-Wilson and Speed 1993: 99).

Similarly the 'American in Australia' and, to a lesser extent, the 'Australian in America' are constant figures in the local cinema. Sometimes American 'innocents' are done down but eventually triumph over the disturbed, psychotic, murderous or rampaging monsters who happen to be Australian. Stacy Keech and Jamie Lee Curtis are the only 'normal characters' in *Roadgames* (Franklin 1981). They do battle across the Nullabor plains with an odd assortment of weird Australians including a sex murderer, unfriendly police officers, and cranky drivers. Jimmy Smits is the charismatic American University Professor in Melbourne falsely accused and imprisoned for rape in *Gross Misconduct* (George Miller 1993). He is the victim of the overheated sexual gaze of a beautiful female student who turns out to be a victim too – of incest – which retrospectively explains and justifies her actions. In *Razorback* (Mulcahy 1984), Carl (Gregory Harrison) comes to Australia to avenge the death of his wife at the hands of the eponymous wild pig, and in the process he also sorts out the malevolent local kangaroo shooters who have a symbiotic relationship with the pig.

American men provide love interests for Australian women in Chris Thomson's 1989 film *The Delinquents* – Charlie Schlatter is Kylie Minogue's love interest in this film of love on the wrong side of the tracks, and in the Second World War story *Rebel* (Jenkins 1985) – Matt Dillon plays a GI deserter in Sydney hidden by a night club singer, Debbie Byrne.

Americans are often 'problematic' figures and presences which Australians need to negotiate and come to terms with – often making the Australians feel inferior. In Mora's *Death of a Soldier* (1986), James Coburg plays a senior American commander in Australia during the Second World War dealing with the lines of demarcation between the American military police and the Australian civil police force over an American soldier wanted by both for a series of murders of local women. Eric Roberts in Dusan Makavejev's *The Coca-Cola Kid* (1985) is a Coca-Cola executive sent to Australia to bring Coke into the back-blocks – like the Anthony Hopkins character in *Spotswood* he achieves his goal but in the process is changed. *Dallas Doll* (Turner 1993) has Sarah Bernhardt as a morally questionable character who is simultaneously desired by and repelled by nearly every character (all Australians) in this film. She seduces nearly everyone in the family – the father, the son and the mother. Eventually the Australians turn the tables on her, or, in the case of the mother, simply assert themselves.

Finally American actors sometimes play Australian characters. Notably Meryl Streep in *Evil Angels*, Robert Mitchum and Deborah Kerr in *The Sundowners* (Zinnemann 1960), and Richard Chamberlain in *The Last Wave* (where the Chamberlain character is given as having a South American heritage).

Equally, there can at times seem to be an almost seamless web between working to be local and being internationally successful. Indeed just about every national cinema at some stage goes local in order to go international. It was an article of faith in the 1970s for the national cinema to be local in front of and behind the camera and even to be substantially locally financed. Film critics like the influential critic of *The Age* (Melbourne), Colin Bennett, in the 1970s found evidence of the wisdom of this position in Schepisi's 1970s classics – *The Devil's Playground* and *The Chant of Jimmie Blacksmith*, Armstrong's *My Brilliant Career*, Miller's *Mad Max*, and Noyce's *Newsfront*. The presence of international actors in Australian films of the decade became another, and sometimes unwanted and distracting 'noise'.

If this local orientation is now explicitly repudiated as *the* only model for a national cinema, it persists because it is a structural necessity in the Australian cinema – which like the New Zealand and German cinemas – relies so critically on the work of first and second time directors for success. Their best directors, cinematographers and actors become expatriates after a decade or less in film-making. Some of the most successful and high profile Australian films of the 1990s were either their director's first feature: Jocelyn Moorhouse with *Proof*, Geoffrey Wright with *Romper Stomper*, Baz Luhrmann with *Strictly Ballroom*, Paul J. Hogan with *Muriel's Wedding*, Ray Argall with *Return Home* (1990), John Ruane with *Death in Brunswick* (1991), Geoff Burton and Kevin Dowling with *The Sum of Us*, or their second feature: Stephan Elliott with *The Adventures of Priscilla: Queen of the Desert*. Additionally, many highly regarded – although not always commercially successful 1990s releases – were also the work of first-time or second-time feature directors: Jackie McKimmie (*Waiting* 1991), Tracey Moffatt (*beDevil*) and Pauline Chan (*Traps* 1994) and Alexis Vellis (*Nirvana Street Murder* 1991). By definition, first time directors are not that internationally integrated, as they are yet to prove themselves. Their locally set, locally produced and locally acted productions are their international calling cards. Australian cinema of the 1990s was – with the exception of international blockbusters set outside Australia – increasingly dependent on 'sleepers': low budget films that exceeded all expectation for success. But these were not 'sleepers' of the *Mad Max* variety. They were films from directors whose national and international careers were often established in advance through international film festival screenings of their shorts and features.

The 1990s cinema looked a lot like that of the mid- to late 1970s when there was a similar turn towards Europe and attention was being paid to gaining recognition in the international European and North American festivals. As in the earlier period, there was a shortage of Australian investors, the industry needed to rely on 'first time' directors to give the Australian industry a palpable form, and the state funding institutions played a much larger role than they did in the 1980s. It is worth noting that these 'local productions' were sometimes underwritten by state investment and subsidy in partnership with international financing, for example *Muriel's Wedding* was underwritten by French finance through CIBY Sales, with a principle involvement of Film Victoria and subsidiary involvement of the Queensland Pacific Film and Television, the NSW Film and Television Office, the AFC and the FFC.

'Going local' does not only hold out the prospect of a culturally authentic, low budget cinema just possibly able to recoup its money from the domestic market and attractive to international audiences in its Australianness (using the local to go to the universal). It also opens on to two other possibilities:

1 the prospect of a commercially oriented exploitative cinema – a crassly commercial cinema, recycling possibly regressive notions and ideas (the 1970s 'sex comedy' classically embodied by *Alvin Purple* is often taken to be an instance here, as was the first *Mad Max* at its time of release); and
2 the prospect of a quirky, eccentric cinema to one side of the international norm as a means of establishing international attractiveness. In *Sweetie* and *Strictly Ballroom*, *Muriel's Wedding* and *The Adventures of Priscilla Queen of the Desert* a space is created for what has become an international expectation of Australian 'quirkiness', 'eccentricity' and 'individuality'.

In these features, the banality and richness of contemporary, usually urban settings and culture, are foregrounded and turned away from their usual moorings in realist social problem film-making. So Peter Castaldi praises *Strictly Ballroom* for its combination of the conventional romance fairy tale and Australian sub-urbia, its back streets and its dreams. This combination 'liberates the suburban from the grip of the realists and lets fantasy run free' (Castaldi 1994) as the film-makers 'took the back streets of any town and dressed them up in the most colourful, outrageous and wickedly witty way'. In making *Sweetie*, Campion took the 'short films' for which she had become internationally famous and made them longer without sacrificing their signature 'look'. As Campion reported

When I made them [my short films], I never thought in the future I'd have the opportunity to make such personal, off-the-wall films. But then I saw how people enjoyed them, and I thought I'd like to make a feature which went even further than they did. I decided I didn't want to ape the kind of films made by other people: I wanted to invent my own.

(Quoted in Stratton 1990: 373)

In so doing, she legitimated the AFC's policy of developing talent and stylistic and plot innovation through the short film. Campion provided an example for subsequent film-makers: film-makers would be encouraged as much as possible to keep and extend the concerns and signatures of their short films into their features. In critical and marketing terms, her short films' prestigious international circulation created expectations for the director's long awaited first feature. *Sweetie's* enumeration of what Anne-Marie Crawford and Adrian Martin called 'a world defined, at a fundamentally banal and everyday level, by alienation, irresolution and incohesion' (Crawford and Martin 1989: 56–7) provided a larger statement of the work in her short films. These same characteristics are also the domain of the many everyday stories of *No Worries* (Elfick 1993), *Return Home* and *A Woman's Tale* (Cox 1991).

So to be 'wholly local' in a pure form in front of and behind the camera is not the natural condition of a national cinema – even when it looks to be doing precisely that. Most national cinemas seek to involve international players (actors, directors, distributors, festival organizers, composers, television buyers) in the creation, financing and circulation of national cinema and television texts. A feature film-maker's domestic career often hinges on getting their film into and comporting themselves appropriately at the Cannes, New York, Venice, Montreal, Toronto and London film festivals. In their choice of actors, locations, production personnel, story and dialogue, local producers routinely take into account the requirements of international circulation. Such considerations are crucial to getting films to circulate internationally, to bringing in international distributors, to securing pre-sales and co-production partners. National cinema film-makers keep abreast of contemporaneous international technical, stylistic, storytelling and organizational instruments for film-makers indigenizing them to local circumstance.

Particularly when we move to its higher budgeted form, every Western national cinema strives to be explicitly international in its textual form. No national cinema can survive on 'sleepers'. Those who make sleepers want to operate with higher budgets and a bigger scale. At some stage each national cinema has to produce expensive films and this means becoming more explicitly international. This is riskier though because more money is at stake. It also entails enlisting a lot of international allies in advance. But it is the only way of escaping the low yields and lower production values typical of the purely local product. Compared to *Crocodile Dundee* and *The Piano*, *Strictly Ballroom* and *Romper Stomper* were minor successes internationally. Half of *Strictly*'s global revenues were generated in Australia; compared to 10 per cent of *The Piano*'s $(US)112 million (Given 1994: 13). The sleeper *Mad Max* could never hope to compete with its high budget successor *Mad Max II* (aka *The Road Warrior*) – it was the latter, not the former, that changed international film-making, sparking many imitations, the latest of which is Kevin Costner's *Waterworld* (Reynolds 1995). Higher budget productions also benefit the local and international image of the Australian cinema. They raise the industry's infrastructure, update its domestic technological base, employ and train a large number of professionals to industry standard and drag the smaller Australian films in their wake both locally and internationally. They help create the international currency of the local cinema. (Securing an attachment on Jane Campion's *The Piano* was important to Margot Nash making the transition from documentaries to low-budget features with *Vacant Possession*.) As one Australian-based director, Werner Meyer, put it to me in 1992: what the Australian industry needed was another *Crocodile Dundee* – not because this was the sort of film he made or liked but because 'it made everything easier for everyone else in the industry'. But, of course, this is harder to achieve successfully. Sometimes the international requirements in the make up of international films change: liberal tax concessions made it possible in the 1980s to make a 'quality' blockbuster with a predominantly Australian cast, finance and explicitly foregrounded Australian connections with titles like *The Man from Snowy River*, *Mad Max II*, *Gallipoli* and *Dead Calm* being the result. But, in the 1990s, it required a project with an international setting and connection – often co-productions with Australian involvement more behind than in front of the camera, in titles like *The Piano*, *The Black Robe* (Beresford 1992) and *Green Card* (Weir 1991) which I will discuss later.

If all national cinemas are implicated internationally, Australian cinema has been remarkably implicated. This can be measured in a variety of ways, like the international financing of Australian features and televison dramas (between 1988/89 and 1992/93 financial years foreign investors accounted for 39 per cent of production funding, government agencies 33 per cent and Australian private and commercial investment 28 per cent (Bean and Court 1994: 37)), or the international actors appearing in Australian cinema (some American actors not already mentioned include Tina Turner, Lee Remick, Kirk Douglas, Linda Hunt, Tom Selleck!), or, indeed the international directors working behind the camera in Australian productions. British, American, Canadian, German, Polish and Yugoslav directors have made films in Australia from Australian stories and sometimes with Australian financing. Sometimes the films of major international directors have had a lasting impact on the subsequent shape of the national cinemas they worked in, however briefly.

There can, at times, be a happy mutuality between Australia as the location for other imaginings and these imaginings as 'ours'. Some of these films became owned by Australians as theirs. The most obvious examples here are: Harry Watt's *The Overlanders* (1946), Jack Lee's *A Town Like Alice* (1956), Fred Zinnemann's *The Sundowners*, Robert Powell's *They're a Weird Mob*, Nicolas Roeg's *Walkabout* and Ted Kotcheff's *Wake in Fright*. These directors took Australian cultural artifacts – literature for Powell, Zinnemann, Kotcheff and previous 'images' of Australia for Roeg – and transformed them into films.

Some 'location' film-making projects have been crucial to Australian cinema providing models and opening out new territory for local film-makers to follow. *The Overlanders* may have been an Australian/British western but it was also a 'docu-drama' and possibly the first Australian art film. It opened the 'outback' to a different fictional emplotment and eschewed the melodramatic norms which had been essential to the 1920s and 1930s Australian cinema. Romance was downplayed. There was an absence of close-ups. The 'vast open spaces' were shot as spectacle (a repertoire still in evidence). More important was the space it created for a mutually advantageous British–Australian partnership. Through it Australia became an on-screen presence in Britain – something that was, at best, unevenly achieved in the preceding decades.

The post-1970 Australian cinema revival is particularly indebted to the Australian work of the British directors Powell (for *Weird Mob*) and Roeg (*Walkabout*); and to the Canadian, Ted Kotcheff. They prepared local and international audiences and critics for the Australian films that followed in the 1970s and beyond. Powell's *They're a Weird Mob* was a forerunner to the 'ocker' films of the 1970s and the multicultural cinema of the 1990s with its repertoires of ethnicity, ethnic mixing and cultural non-comprehension – still in evidence in *The Heartbreak Kid* and *Romper Stomper*.

Wake in Fright's prototypical middle-class male school teacher experiencing a vernacular working-class male regional culture fashioned the male ensemble film. With its dystopian view of mateship and misogyny, *Wake* introduced the idea of endemic and structural evil to Australian cinema. These rhetorical figures have persisted through to the present and have helped organize the terrain of much subsequent Australian storytelling from *Don's Party* to *Romper Stomper*. The preparedness to accept, exploit, entertain and at times exaggerate this possibility provided an important maturity to Australian film-making and undoubtedly aided its circulation in the international festival market. It helped create – after the figure of New German Cinema's 'unmastered past' – an unsavoury Australian past and present centred largely on the deeds, misogyny, limited horizons, and xenophobia of white (Anglo) males. Kotcheff's film prepared the way for that mix of hyperrealism, excessive masculinity, ambiguous sexuality, and misogyny so insistently present in subsequent Australian cinema.

In Roeg's *Walkabout* landscape was worked into the film as a 'character'. As the British critic Dilys Powell wrote on its release:

> it is to the eyes that *Walkabout* speaks. Mr Roeg has painted an Australian landscape, blazing, enormous; and his desert really is a red desert; the sand burns brick red.
>
> (1989: 261)

Such an emphasis on landscape as character is evident in many later films, but notably Peter Weir's *Picnic at Hanging Rock*, Paul Cox's *Exile* (1993) and Robert Scholes' *The Tale of Ruby Rose* (1988). Roeg's emphasis on the uncanny and the other-worldly, the mundane and the spiritual, and the tragic clash of Aboriginal

and non-Aboriginal peoples in the Australian continent opened directly on to
Weir's *The Last Wave*, Schepisi's *The Chant of Jimmie Blacksmith*, Moffatt's
Night Cries – A Rural Tragedy (1989), the children's films *Storm Boy* (Safran
1976) and *Manganinnie* (Honey 1980), and even Barron film's remake of *Bush
Christmas* (Safran 1983).[3] Roeg's observations about the film are pertinent to this
discussion:

> It couldn't have been made anywhere else and it was an utterly Australian
> film. ... But it did something, I think, and I like to hope that it touched
> emotional chords that were international. I think that helped in some way to
> open doors for Australian movies.
>
> (Quoted in White 1984: 25)

Walkabout and *Wake in Fright* were seminal films for the Australian film
revival to critics, audiences and film-makers alike. Actor Jack Thompson claims
both films to be 'searching looks at the Australian ethos' and credits them with
demonstrating 'not only to the rest of the world of film-makers but to ourselves
that we were capable of making feature films' (quoted in White 1984: 27). While
neither was particularly successful in Australia, Thompson notes that they were
'transitional films' signalling the transition between a feature industry marked by
the 'almost totally foreign-made films being made in Australia' and an 'Australian
cinema'. These two films became particularly important to the 1970s film revival,
in that they created Australian cinema as an international territory in the cinema
and provided directly for an Australian place. They were noticed by critics and
industry figures.

National cinemas are one of the means by which the local and the international
reconfigure each other. Our above example foregrounds British, American and
Canadian film-makers refashioning the audiovisual representation of Australia
and Australians and more than this, reconceptualizing the form, approach and
stylistic means of the Australian cinema that followed – which was largely
Australian produced, directed and scripted. But such refashioning is only part of
the general circulation of any national cinema as it 'travels' outside its domestic
context and enters new contexts. Thomas Elsaesser (1994: 25) writes of how

> European films intended for one kind of (national) audience or made within a
> particular kind of aesthetic framework or ideology, for instance, undergo a sea
> change as they cross the Atlantic and on coming back find themselves bearing
> the stamp of yet another cultural currency.

The international appreciation of national cinemas in, for example, festivals
'assign different kinds of value' to the product and in the process the films acquire
a 'new cultural capital beyond the prospect of economic circulation (art cinema
distribution, a television sale)'. Quite provocatively Elsaesser claims that 'the
New German Cinema was discovered and even invented abroad, and had to be
reimported to be recognized as such' (1989: 300). Australian cinema from the
1970s fashioned this international process as an intrinsic part of marketing

Australian cinema to local audiences. Selection at Cannes provided an imprimateur for local audiences. It also rehabilitated local directors.

When Fred Schepisi's *The Chant of Jimmie Blacksmith* came out it died at the box-office after eleven weeks. Schepisi lost a lot of his personal savings accumulated over a decade of working as a television commercials director. He was attacked from all sides. film-maker Terry Bourke claimed this film and Weir's *Last Wave* had led Australian film-making away from commercial values and genre film-making. Veteran director and former Channel 9 boss Ken G. Hall weighed in by claiming that Schepisi should have known that films about Aborigines are box-office poison. From the other direction, James Ricketson weighed in claiming *Jimmie Blacksmith* was a 'dinosaur', an 'ersatz Hollywood monster' and that the industry would be better funding 'four potential [low budget] *Mouth to Mouth* (Duigan 1978) than in funding one *Jimmie Blacksmith*' (Ricketson 1979, 1985: 226–7). The film's humanist values were attacked by an academic screen criticism inimical to humanism. Mudrooroo (then known as Johnson – 1987: 50) questioned the novel and the film's politics. He later wrote that the film's lingering image was that of 'a beserk boong hacking to death white ladies'. He noted the consternation among the Aboriginal family of Jimmy Governor and how they, on seeing the film, sought legal advice to try and stop its screening. It was left to Pauline Kael to salvage the film's Australian reputation somewhat. Albert Moran and I incorporated Kael's 1980 *New Yorker* review of the film into our 1985 collection *An Australian Film Reader*, partly because it provided a different view on the film as well as providing an instance of the importance to Australian cinema's international circulation of the New York critical establishment. Susan Dermody and Elizabeth Jacka (1987a: 148) noted how the republication of this review suggested that *Jimmie Blacksmith* 'may be one of the underestimated and overlooked films of the 1970s'. Through this and similar critical rethinkings, Schepisi was brought home, even though his subsequent career was now mostly in the USA.

The local as much as international terrain informs perceptions and the success of the dominant, imported cinema and national cinema product in international circulation. Historically, cinema and television is international in its outlook and sensibility, while local in its national configurations. Borders – especially national borders – are significant to explaining the circulation of Hollywood and national cinemas alike. These influence the viewing of international cinema as surely as they do the local product. In answer to the question of 'what happens when a text crosses national or other borders' Alison Butler (1992: 419) answers

> There is mounting evidence that the refunctionalization of texts is not just a manifestation of occasional resistances, but the very condition of possibility of such border crossings. Productive – and indeed unproductive – misreading is perhaps the paradigmatic operation which governs the reception of films outside – and sometimes inside – their original national contexts.

If this is the terrain of an imagined 'America' bearing sometimes a limited relation to the actual USA, it is also the terrain of the 'imagined' Australia or 'Britain'. Both *Crocodile Dundee* and *Four Weddings and a Funeral* were criticized at home for providing a 'tourist's-eye view' of Australia and Britain. They both exported a view of Australian and British life 'which is more like the rest of the world wants it to be than it actually is' (Roddick 1995: 15). Here, the worry is that the 'imagined Australia' (an outback 'ocker' doing battle with crocodiles and New York escalators) or 'imagined Britain' (upper middle class twits 'off to a smart wedding in a battered Land Rover' (15)) directly impinges and shapes domestic film production. But if Butler is right, such repositionings are an unexceptionable part of the cinema landscape – and a part that film-makers are acutely aware of. Take Stephan Elliott's account of the different audience responses in France, Australia and the USA to his film, *The Adventures of Priscilla, Queen of the Desert*:

> At a screening we had for an Australian audience, they laughed at all the Australianisms. The Americans laughed too, but at different jokes. There is a line where Tick says, 'Bernadette has left her cake out in the rain … ' Last night, they [the French audience] didn't get it, whereas the Americans laughed for ten minutes.
>
> (Quoted in Epstein 1994: 6)

Elliott went on to observe that his film – like *Strictly Ballroom* (Luhrmann 1992) before it – was changing from 'territory to territory' to become 'a different film in different territories' (Elliott, in Epstein 1994: 6). This difference Elliott observed extended to its public meaning: it could be seen in the US gay response which saw it 'as the big one that will bring gay lifestyles into a mainstream' while Australian audiences 'embrace it as just another successful Australian film' – 'a musical with actors who are really recognizable' (7). And so it was for *Crocodile Dundee* too (see Crofts 1992).

Such a situation leads Elsaesser (1994: 26) to declare that

> national cinemas and Hollywood are not only communicating vessels, but (to change the metaphor) exist in a space set up like a hall of mirrors, in which recognition, imaginary identity and miscognition enjoy equal status.

The local dimension of a national cinema does not only reside in the specifically local cultural codifications or domestic production traditions, but also lies in the movement of localization, the movement of indigenizing other nation's cinema product and their production models. National cinemas are one of the means by which cultural transfers are routinely accomplished in the international cinema. More than this, these cultural transfers embodied in the locally produced cinema are themselves a form of localizing and indigenizing processes. Localizing becomes the means of internationalizing; internationalizing the means of localizing. The local and the international are ineradicably mixed in the constitution of the national cinema project.

NATIONAL CINEMAS AS FESTIVAL CINEMAS

We [Americans] want Australian films to seem real and convincing (as if there are real films of real Australia), certainly more real and convincing that most people imagine Hollywood films to be. I suppose this is the defining characteristic – a prejudice to your advantage, really – we have towards Australian cinema, perhaps Australia as a whole. . . . Your cinema is to us a 'specialized cinema', an art house cinema supported by festivals, critics and filmgoers who want something different . . . but not too different, who want a more real and convincing cinematic experience, who want to experience this sense of 'Australianicity', an Otherness that is, in fact, not all that Other.

(29)

Tony Safford (1995) was here speaking to the Screen Producers Association of Australia conference in 1994. He was not only defining the particularity of Australian cinema to Americans but defining as well the space of a festival cinema more generally. Like part of the output of any national cinema, Australian cinema circulates in that principally non-Hollywood ('festival') space of the 'foreign film' in world cinema markets. Since the 1970s film revival, there have been a handful of internationally recognized Australian cinema auteurs (notably Peter Weir, Bruce Beresford, Fred Schepisi from the 1970s generation; Gillian Armstrong, Phil Noyce, George Miller of the 1980s generation; more lately, the Australian-trained Jane Campion) and avant-garde cinema stylists (Albie Thoms in the 1960s, Tracey Moffatt in the 1990s), internationally renowned documentarists and ethnographic film-makers (David Bradbury, Denis O'Rourke, David and Judith MacDougall, Bob Connolly and Robin Anderson), feminist experimental film-makers (Helen Grace, Laleen Jayamenne), indigenous film-makers (Moffatt and Prattan) and a band of recognizable, adaptable actors used by accomplished mainstream and art cinema directors (Judy Davis, Jack Thompson, Sam Neil, Russell Crowe). Their works mark out the routine Australian membership and presence at the Cannes, Berlin, Toronto and even Singapore film festivals as something from Australia now becomes an unexceptional though minor norm at international festivals and subsequently in repertory film and 'quality' television markets.

Bill Nichols has made a number of points about the function of this film festival cinema:

The festival circuit allows the local to circulate globally, within a specific system of institutional assumptions, priorities and constraints. Never only or purely local, festival films nonetheless circulate, in large part, with a cachet of locally inscribed difference and globally ascribed commonality. They both attest to the uniqueness of different cultures and specific film-makers and affirm the underlying qualities of an 'international cinema'.

(1994: 68)

This festival context adds 'a global overlay to more local meaning' (1994: 68) providing 'a continuous, international pattern of circulation and exchange of image-culture'. Here Australian cinema can be seen to observe John Orr's (1993: 6) dictum that 'cinema is often at its more powerful in film-makers who emerge from distinctive *national* traditions' and that what he calls 'the neo-modern moment has its origin in the national cinemas of Western Europe and the United States where it engages with Western capitalist modernity'.

The different European national cinemas of the 1950s to the present and the Asian, African and Latin American cinemas of the present provide the Australian cinema audience and local film-makers with an important social and cultural experience of modernity, and not just in the cinema. That Australian film-makers should want to contribute to it should come as no surprise. Furthermore Nichols suggests that within this festival optic Hollywood occupies an 'oppositional rather than an inspirational position' (1994: 74). The film festival circuit displaces this centre rather than 'bolstering' it (74). It provides a way of valuing its own product at the expense of Hollywood. And therein lies its attraction for Australian film-makers and audiences alike. It naturalizes the local as internationally acceptable, just as it provides a space to one side of the mainstream Hollywood competition. In doing so, it does not so much compete, as circulate and organize an alternative space to the common vernacular of Hollywood. As noted, an important component of this festival circuit is the art cinema, whether in its major and still dominant form of the European art cinema, or in its emergent form as films from outside the 'Western, Eurocentric centre' (Nichols 1994: 74).

Director Paul Schrader once described the difference between the European and the Hollywood film as one of attitude:

> American movies are based on the assumption that life presents you with problems, while European films are based on the conviction that life confronts you with dilemmas – and while problems are something you solve, dilemmas cannot be solved, they're merely probed or investigated.
>
> (Quoted in Elsaesser 1994: 24)

Elsaesser (1994: 24) contends that this 'might explain why a happy ending in a European art film is felt to be a cop-out, a fundamentally unserious mode of closure'. He asks: 'isn't one of the characteristics of "modern" cinema (until recently synonymous with the art film) its metaphysical doubt about master narratives of progress, preferring to be sceptical of linear time and the efficacy of action?'

Consequently the largely European derived 'art film' model and its televisual equivalent in 'quality television' has had an impact on Australian production schedules and television priorities. This poses its own obligations upon Australian cinema: a cinema created for the representation of modernist cultural themes (existentialism, the absurd, alienation, 'boundary situations') and modern political issues (class, gender, race) providing the doubling of aesthetics and politics. The best representatives of this tendency in Australian cinema usually combine fragments of all of these: from Peter Weir's *Picnic at Hanging Rock*, to Paul Cox's *Man of Flowers* (1983) to Gillian Armstrong's *The Last Days of Chez Nous* (1992), to *Sunday Too Far Away* to *Don's Party*; from *The Piano* to *The Chant of Jimmie Blacksmith*.

Not surprisingly many of Australian cinema's narrative resolutions and thematic preoccupations (though not necessarily their means of realization) are classically those of the international art cinema. As Debi Enker observes about Australian cinema's thematic preoccupations:

> Characters are repeatedly alienated and driven apart, condemned to loneliness, or at the very least to being alone. In this context, the dearth of happily resolved love stories is entirely appropriate ... Australia's film-makers have concentrated more on the spaces that separate people, on communities that stifle the spirit and circumstances that drive lovers apart. It is a much darker and despairing vision than that of a frontier paradise promising freedom and unlimited scope for fulfilment.
>
> (224–5)

Enker goes on to note that this includes films as diverse as *Mad Max* and *Picnic at Hanging Rock*, *Caddie* and *Nirvana Street Murder*, *Breaker Morant* and *Monkey Grip* (K. Cameron 1982).

More than any other film-making project before Campion's *Sweetie* Cox's *My First Wife* (1984) fits in with European art cinema protocols. Perhaps this is why his films easily fit within local and international art film circuits. The chief interest in the film is in the break up of a relationship seen from the man's (played by John Hargreaves) perspective. The viewer is invited continually to identify with his sense of grief, remorse, betrayal. In consequence, the wife remains both a cipher and an enigma for him and for us as viewers. To realize this narrative structure, *My First Wife* entails the strategies (the feelings, intensities, excesses, and neuroses) of art cinema. There is a trading in of narrative development for a vivid tableaux. It relies on an interiorizing of conflict, upon states of mind, feelings, sentiments which find their expression in repeated scenes. One such scene is the flashback to the wedding scene which provides the film's narrative image. The image here is of the Wendy Hughes character, the first wife, in her wedding dress (it's also the image used on the video dustjacket). It promises literally what is not in the present time of the film. The image of the wife at her wedding is recalled as his memory. It is insistently returned to: a counterpoint to the present of a conjugal relationship in crisis.

My First Wife invites interpretation. It is, as Bill Routt and Rick Thompson (1987: 32) would put it, a text which despite its attractive surface is not 'for everyone', as it contains, and has wrapped itself around enigmas and secrets. The enigma to be explored by viewer and film-maker alike is the meaning for the John Hargreaves character (and we viewers) of his previously unquestioned relationship with his wife. This enigma distilled in the film's narrative image – the Wendy

Hughes character at her wedding happy in love with the John Hargreaves character – is the pretext and subtext of the film.

The film is built around what Horst Ruthrof (1980: 102) calls a 'boundary situation' in which 'a presented persona, a narrator, or the implied reader in a flash of insight becomes aware of meaningful as against meaningless existence'. David Bordwell (1985: 208) sees this situation as a defining characteristic of much art cinema. Certainly *My First Wife*'s impetus wholly derives from the main character's recognition that he faces a crisis of existential significance. Cox's film insists upon a degree of psychologizing as the protagonist's state of mind is visualized. This messes up the dividing line between reality and fantasy, past and present, suggesting an uneasiness with the literal present. In this Cox's bears comparison to some of Peter Weir's films – *The Last Wave* particularly – where liminal states of mind are externalized into a heightening of reality, into a literal present gone awry.

In nearly all of Cox's films there are clear moments of excess which suggest the relation of the film-maker to the apparatus. In *My First Wife* there are the sequences which are distorted, which refuse to show clearly, which de-representationalize, and thus diminish the scope for us to see anything clearly. Because they go on just a shade too long, they carry more than the existential weight of the husband's state of mind. They draw attention to themselves as play with film stock, with the form of film. They pose another disrupting enigma, that of film play. The viewer is encouraged to read different meanings into the film – not only in the end there is only the family, but also in the end there is only film and its experience.

With its invitations to psychological depth, its dislocations, its willingness to fragment, its use of the 'boundary situation' – Paul Cox's cinema is one for which readings of personal vision are appropriate, fit easily and are encouraged by the films themselves. The figure of John Hargreaves in *My First Wife* is irresistibly a stand-in for the author. If like so many 1980s films the central journey is 'His' journey, it's a journey which we are advised to speak of in personal terms.

But it's not only the kernel of interpretation at the heart of Cox's films that is refracted in their critical circulation. There is also the drive to make cinema meaningful, to reinvent it, to place oneself, one's whole being at its service. If this involves the cinematizing of the personal it also carries the megalomaniac's dream of total control and total risk. This licences his films to come stuffed with chaotic excess, prejudices, intellectual and physical obsessions, unreasonableness – thereby encouraging the reader in his or her turn to engage with them. There are few directors in Australian cinema who so insistently invite the labour of the auteurist as Paul Cox.

The festival circulation of director as auteur and the close proximity of self-expression and personal vision to national and intersubjective vision, ensures that the kind of attention the festival and related circuits confer upon a film generates a certain kind of public reputation. It gives Australian cinema generally more value, just as it permits the construction (as with all auteur-based projects) of a singular career and a star persona. As Nichols goes on to note, a transformation is involved in this passage from the local to the international:

> The entry of national cinemas and the work of individual film-makers into the international film festival circuit itself constructs new meanings, and it is these new meanings that we, as festival-goers, are most likely to discover.
>
> (71)

While this international standing and circulation may have little to tell us about what, if anything, connects any of these Australian directors, film-makers and actors it does signpost cultural estime (however liminally as birthplace or site of training) and public relations value. Both are critical to sustaining the domestic reputation of the industry on governmental and other horizons within Australia.

NATIONAL CINEMAS AND THE NATIONAL

> Only by being aware of its national identity can a film industry be international.
>
> (Volker Schlondorff 1977, quoted in Elsaesser 1989: 306)

If national cinemas are an intrinsically international form, they are also national forms. As Schlondorff's comment suggests, national cinemas do not only persist as a means to counter or accommodate Hollywood, they are sustained and shaped by local purposes of a social, economic, cultural and national nature. Moreover they need to be conscious of these. Recently Phillip Adams reflected on his and Barry Jones' insider involvement in bringing about federal government support for a film industry in 1968–9. Here Adams explicitly brings together 'national identity' and film export – associating the former with a 'boutique industry':

> We [Phillip Adams and Barry Jones] weren't arguing for a major film industry. Just a modest effort that would allow us to explore our national identity (whatever that was) and to export it to the world's film festivals. At no stage did Jones or I believe it was either possible or useful to make more than ten or fifteen features a year, but our travels had convinced us that there was an opportunity for a boutique industry, that would make culturally specific films for up-market audiences everywhere.
>
> (Adams 1995: ix)

Every national cinema attempts at some point to turn its national distinction into an asset, not a liability. It strives at some point to be locally attached. National cinemas have to do so because the national cinema's place on the horizons of local (and international) cinema and television drama viewers is more marginal than is its international counterpart. Consequently the local connection to government, to non-cinema kinds of backing, and to international involvement whether by way of direct investment or co-productions are going to be all the more important. For this reason there is no clearer instance of this localizing moment than in the ways national cinema producers, promoters and activists call on and mobilize local resources to naturalize their films on the local industry, on local governmental, private enterprise and community horizons. These agents routinely move outside the 'film world' and call on whatever vehicles are at their disposal to bind audiences to the local product and naturalize the local cinema. They characterize the national cinema product as a story of the local people-among-themselves framing their histories, their stories, their lifeways, their locations. Going local at some point is a way of securing the resources with which to compete at home and abroad.

The vehicles drawn on are often 'outside' the typical film communicative circuits. The educational apparatus was enlisted for Peter Weir's *Gallipoli* (1981), as schools around the country organized matinée visits to the cinema during school time for its screening. This had been done before with John Heyer's *Back of Beyond* (1954) – a documentary film commissioned by the Shell Film Unit to capture the 'essence of Australia'. Schepisi drew on a dramatic local incident: the Lindy/Michael/Azaria Chamberlain story of a dingo, Uluru (Ayers Rock) and the ensuing court case which made world news in *Evil Angels/Cry in the Dark* (with Meryl Streep and Sam Neill in the lead roles). David Elfick drew on the late 1980s and early 1990s story of rural crisis, with a generation of workers on the land walking off, for his film *No Worries*. National cinemas often work to produce social purposes as a means of enlisting local audiences. Again *Gallipoli* is an instance where the film's launch and the public discussion surrounding it provided a national lesson in civics. It also provided a marketable Australian image abroad in the historical film. Elsaesser argues that countries like Australia and the UK 'without a strong and continuous tradition of film-making may have to depend on an ability to "market" the national history as spectacle for international success'. National history like the dramatic contemporary public event provides film-makers with a 'common currency' which they might otherwise lack. It 'establishes a signifying system of motifs, oppositions, antinomies and structural binarisms: the very stuff of narratives' (Elsaesser 1989: 293). Elsaesser was thinking here of historical titles like the British *Chariots of Fire* (Hudson 1981) and the Australian *We of the Never Never* (Auzins 1982). This history need not be glorious either. It can be ignominious as in *The Chant of Jimmie Blacksmith*'s insistence on white Australia's racist history (the Aboriginal survival becomes Australia's 'un-mastered past' like the Holocaust for Germans); it can be about national defeat in the First World War at *Gallipoli*; and it can be about the sacrifice of principles of justice for the sake of a post-war order, as Japanese war criminals are set free and an innocent Japanese man is convicted as a scapegoat in *Blood Oath* (Wallace 1990).

These different survival options are connected to the strategies and agencies of nation-building of the state and private sector. The two dominant film-makers of 1930s and 1940s Australian cinema – Charles Chauvel and Ken G. Hall – operated in a period where there was just not the same degree of formative state support as there was after 1969. Yet these commercially minded directors were explicitly nationalist. Chauvel proclaimed his mission to be one of 'featuring Australia' as a character in his films. Later national cinema producers had outside help to survive in what Elsaesser (1989: 3) calls 'the politics of culture [support]' of the state. As Tim Rowse (1985: 67) observed, '[n]ation states promote a sense of nation-hood. That is one of the functions of cultural policy.' Curiously this enabled them to be less explicitly nationalist.

A. D. Smith (1986: 129–39) distinguishes two features of the common national culture that are important to any discussion of a national cinema. There is the *national political* – the common political and civic culture involving citizenship and equality before the law; and there is the *national cultural* – the cultural core of memories, values, customs, myths, symbols, solidarities and significant land-scapes shaping 'Australian' identity. For Smith no state can be workable without both a national political and national cultural sense of itself. The cinema and television matter to public policy makers, interest groups, lobbyists, film-makers and audiences as targets for their national cultural and national political projects and ambitions.

Film-making and film industry policy sustains both kinds of national defini-tions. The agitators for Australian cinema in the 1960s and early 1970s sought national political support for Australian cinema as a national cultural institution concerned with identity and self-expression – 'dreaming our own dreams, telling our own stories'. A measure of a self-respecting mature nation was the possession of a national cinema. Their emphasis on an open-ended national cultural ambition for the cinema helped legitimate the creation of film-making infrastructures which sustained mainstream, oppositional and peripheral cinemas. It also created a space for alternative Australian identities. If this last had been dressed up as an explicit national political project, rather than as part of a national cultural project, it might well have not got off the ground.

Film-making and film and television policy can sometimes emphasize each at the same time. In 1980 the beginnings of a fifth television network – the SBS-TV – started in Sydney and Melbourne. It was legitimated by a policy of multi-culturalism that was initially conceived as a national political project, highlighting those ethnically and culturally diverse NES background peoples in Australia. At the same time, the establishment of a generous tax concession régime encouraging private investment in film and television production (called 10BA) largely underwrote a film and mini-series boom in which the 'national cultural' was consistently foregrounded and with it the established settler culture and its Australian history. It should be noted that the 1980s was that decade in which the Australian state played the least important role in the selection of film properties and funding (reduced to 16 per cent compared to the 1990s' 39 per cent) – but it still had an indirect role through its certifying of film and mini-series as Australian to qualify for tax concession purposes. This role limited the degree of inter-nationalization of production through the decade and inhibited the development of story properties set outside Australia. Some of the most popular Australian cinema and mini-series television of the 1980s revisited formative national moments in the national symbols-myths complex, such as the Boer War in Bruce Beresford's international 'breakthrough' film, *Breaker Morant*, the First World War in

Gallipoli; the legend of the eponymous race-horse of the 1930s in *Phar Lap*; the bodyline cricket controversy of the 1930s between Australia and Britain in *Bodyline* (Schultz, Ogilvie, Marinos and Lawrence 1984). These productions restated and updated old myths 'dedominionizing' Australia by accentuating its 'non-English' characteristics (see Kapferer 1988: 167 and Davidson 1979 *passim*). The most popular features of the decade – *Crocodile Dundee* and *The Man from Snowy River* – revisited Australian 'bushman' archetypes and in the *Snowy River*'s case the famous poem once taught universally in Australian schools.

While this was happening some policy-makers, critics and film-makers subscribed to a different national political object. This was a reconstructed objective of a 'multicultural' Australia which was to become an increasingly important definition of Australian nationhood from the mid-1980s, culminating in the 1989 National Agenda for a Multicultural Australia. As Rowse observed in 1985 (75) it 'yields an Australianism defined by inner diversity, rather than by a homogeneous sense of being different from Britain'. It envisages an 'Australia linked in a relaxed diversity of inheritances to all the nations of Europe and Asia by the encouragement given to ethnic plurality among migrants' (75). Cathy Robinson, current Chief Executive of the AFC, observed in November 1991 that multiculturalism ensured that 'cultural policy and cultural nationalism could no longer be so easily equated' (Robinson and Given 1994: 20).

The two movements for locating a national cultural identity and a multicultural reality found some congruence in a handful of the mini-series of the late 1980s foregrounding the NES experience of the Australian mainstream, in programmes like *The Dunera Boys* (1985, Jewish refugee experience of Australian internment), *Cowra Breakout* (1985, Japanese prisoner-of-war internment in the Second World War), *Fields of Fire* (1987, 1988, 1989, Italian-Australian experience in the cane fields of north Queensland) and *Always Afternoon* (1988, a German national's experience of discrimination during the First World War).

Sometimes the two can be in conflict. With the increasing importance of multiculturalism as an official policy of state over the 1980s and a sense of the inevitability of industry internationalization by the late 1980s, film policy makers and bureaucrats certifying films as Australian for investment purposes gave policy a more national political hue. They became concerned with industrial markers – how many were involved in the making of it and in which positions. At the same time, broadcasting regulators at the then Australian Broadcasting Tribunal were concerned to evolve national cultural terminology and notions, seeking textual markers for something to be Australian (see Cunningham 1992: 56–60). For the first the issue was an employment and deployment one involving principles of equity and access. For the second it was a national cultural issue. The conflict between these two arms of government confronted a national political assessment with a national cultural one.

Both critical commentary and film industry thinking had, by the late 1980s, moved towards the notion that, in Rowse's words, 'Australianness should mean nothing more than that a number of residents of Australia were employed in the making of it' (75). This had the advantage of 'not beg[ging] the question of what people who live in Australia are concerned with' (79) and therefore living up to the promise of multiculturalism. It also had the advantage of opening the industry to what Ross Gibson (1992: 81) has called 'international contamination', in which Australian cinema could be envisaged as a large family of projects made with some Australian involvement. This entailed a significantly more commodious notion of what could be 'Australian' in order to permit some exploitation of the opportunities afforded Australia as a cultural producer in the English language, like the French–Australian co-production *Green Card* – the vehicle for Gerard Depardieu to reach a wide English-speaking audience – or Vincent Ward's remarkable *Map of the Human Heart* (1993), with its tale of an Inuit's unrequited love and Pauline Chan's *Traps* – a story of a marriage falling apart set in Vietnam of the 1950s. The preferred Australian was now what Ghassan Hage has usefully called a 'cosmopolite' – a '"mega-urban" figure, detached from strong affiliations with roots and consequently open to all forms of otherness' (Hage 1995: 76). As Deborah Jones (1992: xiv) writes in the context of *Strictly Ballroom* 'to be Australian now is to be much more like other people, anywhere, than we may have admitted in the past'. And it produces a film-making whose 'identity' is uncertain, like *The Piano* and *Sirens*.

When Elsaesser writes that 'no other European country, it seems, is as unsure of the meaning of its culture as Germany, or as obsessed with its national identity' (1989: 49) – he could just as well be writing of Australia. As with the New German Cinema, the Australian cinema since the 1970s has resolutely set about problematizing its national identity, taking on, or perhaps 'trying on' successive identities, holding together apparently incompatible national cultural and political objectives and using the nation as a means of questioning and interrogating its very national possibility and merit as such. Because of the importance of 'nations' to a national cinema, national cinemas inevitably involve questions of relative national merit.

In their own ways, Germany and Australia have problematic international identities and these influence what their cinemas can be and how they can be taken up. Both have as part of their very cinematic identity this movement of problematizing the nation, the culture, and even the society itself. Germany's Nazi history is sometimes compared to Australia's Aboriginal and Islander genocide. But mostly Australia's problem is not Germany's one of the specific kind of cultural value it musters, but rather the absence of (any) value and therefore any distinguishing culture in international circulation.

Like the German cinema, the Australian cinema has also been 'innovative and coherent' (Elsaesser 1989: 61) in its margins: its women's cinema, its films about marginal groups (the skin-heads of *Romper Stomper*, the bikers of *Stone* – Harbutt 1974), the sub-cultural lifestyles (*Monkey Grip*'s Carlton milieu, the transvestites of *The Adventures of Priscilla: Queen of the Desert*), and minority interests (the displaced persons of *Silver City*, the Greeks of *The Heartbreak Kid*, the Japanese war brides in *Aya* (Hoaas 1991), the disabled in *Struck by Lightning* (Domaradzki 1990), the Murri Aborigines of *Fringe Dwellers* (Beresford 1986) – and perhaps,

most significantly, in its documentary tradition. Films produced under this logic
are often seen as the true heart of Australian cinema: not only where it is at its most
experimental, innovative and coherent but where it deals with the toughest issues
and where it is 'most Australian'.

Yet, as with the New German cinema, films produced under this logic also
suffer a legitimation gap in that they are marginal to a significant part of the
audience. At times their audiences are more virtual than actual – films to mark
time, to develop talent, to get noticed to make a high budget film. But equally, as
with the New German Cinema, Australian cinema in its minor streams has highly
specific audiences in mind making films appealing to a small part of the audience
'from a sense of shared values and assumptions' (Elsaesser 1989: 154) but running
'the risk of being either parochial (the in-group film) or esoteric'. The cinema here
'served an audience for confirming or validating individual experience and
feelings' opening on to a 'desire . . . directed at the film-maker, to represent only
a "correct" political or ideologically unambiguous standpoint'. There was a
constant 'need for self-confirmation and self-validation in the guise of criticism
and ad hoc political theory on the part of the spectators' (159). If this is
particularly true for the independent cinema in Australia with *Filmnews* until
1995, *Cantrill's Filmnotes* and *Metro* serving as vehicles to make it so; it is also
true of a critical milieu seeking as a matter of some urgency to work out whether
the mainstream *The Sum of Us* or *Bad Boy Bubby* or *The Piano* have got their
respective sexual politics right – establishing in short whether these films can
legitimately speak to 'us' in the way Campion's short films, and Ana Kokkinos'
Only the Brave apparently do/did.

Like the New German Cinema, the search for an audience is continually
foregrounded as a problem in Australian cinema. Even the villains were the same:
the exhibition and distribution sector concerned with exhibiting American pictures, the local audience trained to accommodate the wrong product, the Americans who have colonized our subconscious in a thoroughly mediatized landscape
– *Kings of the Road* (Wenders 1975) meets *Newsfront*! To some degree the
responses are also similar: Kluge's experimentation with form in his 1970s films
echoes the experimentation in distantiation found in Australian feature 'documentaries' like Cavadini and Strachen's ethnographic experimentation in the service
of a political cinema in *Two Laws* (1981) or in John Hughes' Walter Benjamin
inspired film *One Way Street* (1993). As in New German Cinema, there is
considerable attention to getting the film processes right – ethically and politically
– to obtaining the right forms of consultation particularly with respect to marginal
groups. Herzog's propensity to 'test borderlines, limits and extremes' finds its
Australian equivalent in Denis O'Rourke's dramatic gestures on the Pacific rim –
in his documentary features *Cannibal Tours* (1988) and most extraordinarily in
The Good Woman of Bangkok (1992). Schepisi's treatment of the media and the
courts in *Evil Angels* (aka *Cry in the Dark*) as instruments of systemic harassment
replicates Margarethe von Trotta's *The Lost Honour of Katharina Blum* (1975).

Elsaesser (1989: 309) notes that 'Australia . . . has seen a revival as a national cinema similar to that in West Germany'. He also notes the parallel with the new Australian cinema. Elsaesser and Dermody and Jacka make the state central to their account. For their part, Dermody and Jacka see Australian film-makers as having three different responses as handmaidens to the state, its reputation and its ethos. One has been to subscribe to state purposes, to the dominant national cultural purposes in a bland mainstream feature film-making, which they call the AFC-Genre; another has been to subscribe to and stress the industry and therefore commercial purposes espousing genre film-making; and yet another – and this is by far the most dependent one on the state – is to resist both. This estimation very much consigns the mainstream product to the sidelines as either nakedly commercial or as a bland product. It certainly has been incoherent and less evidently 'innovative' in a formal and minoritarian sense. Yet this 'absent centre' at the heart of mainstream Australian features – this seeming dependence on 'other cinemas' and their norms, genres and so on – is actually one of the most fascinating aspects of Australian cinema, enabling it to speak so powerfully to local and international audiences alike in *Strictly Ballroom*, *Mad Max II* (*The Road Warrior*), *My Brilliant Career* and *Crocodile Dundee*.

THE MESSINESS OF NATIONAL CINEMAS

If there is a considerable 'local' aspect to national cinemas, there is considerable fuzziness surrounding them. At some time or other most national cinemas are not coterminous with their nation states. As we have seen, production funding is international. Formal co-production treaties between countries provide frameworks to produce films which may have little to do with either country. Peter Weir's romantic comedy, *Green Card*, is typical of the high budget strand of Australian film-making in the 1990s: it has an Australian director, it is funded by French and Australian investors and its post-production was carried out in Australia. This is a French/Australian co-production set and filmed in New York and is the story of a 'marriage of convenience' between a French man played by Gerard Depardieu and an American played by Andie MacDowell. He marries in order to gain permanent residency in the USA and she to secure an apartment only available to a married woman. The comedy and the developing romance between the two evolves once they are subject to an official investigation over the status of their 'marriage'. Yet unlike the rapid-fire comedy dialogue of similar Hollywood romantic comedies casting opposites – physically, emotionally, intellectually – *Green Card* has a slower delivery of dialogue, and is consequently more muted, slow and observed. It remains true to the green card experience of the Depardieu character speaking and mastering English as a second language. This and the film's ending, where the Depardieu character is deported at the precise moment the couple realize they love each other, signifies the intrusion of the European-Australian 'reality principle' which refuses to solve the problem in a happy ending but instead substitutes a new dilemma for the old. There are no Australians in front of the camera, yet. It is, with its FFC backing, Peter Weir's 'Australian film' of the 1990s.

Many smaller national cinemas are also in product, orientation, industry and language at some stage a part of each other. Deciding where the national leaves off and another national begins is difficult in these cases because the 'national' involves both. This is particularly so for Australia and New Zealand. Close cultural, language and historical links forge an Australasian film-making and identity. Vincent Ward, Jane Campion and Cecil Holmes (regarded by some as film-makers, whose promise made evident in *Three in One* and *Captain Thunderbolt* – was tragically not able to be fulfilled) are all New Zealanders. Franklyn Barrett – with Longford and McDonagh – the finest of Australian silent film-makers, came to Australia after a film-making career in New Zealand. There is a long history of Australian directors making New Zealand films which includes Longford's *A Maori Maid's Love* 1916). Some silent films – like Beaumont Smith's *The Betrayer* (1921) – managed Australian and New Zealand locations. And New Zealand actors have always had a strong presence in Australian films from 'the clever New Zealander' Vera James (whose father secured the New Zealand distribution rights for her film *A Girl of the Bush* (Barrett 1921),[4] to Sam Neill in *My Brilliant Career*, *Dead Calm* and *Death in Brunswick*.

Campion's explicitly Australian-based work is sometimes claimed for New Zealand cinema. *Sweetie* was screened in Sydney as part of a festival of New Zealand cinema. Is Campion a New Zealander or an Australian? Sometimes she describes herself as an Australian; just as often she associates her work – particularly her New Zealand based stories – with her Kiwi identity. This gives rise to debates over whether *The Piano* is an Australian or a New Zealand film. Does her work spanning the Tasman Sea and that of Vincent Ward (*The Navigator: A Medieval Odyssey* 1988 – the AFC and the New Zealand Film Commission's first co-production) presage the development of a more integrated 'Australasian' film market to undergird an Australasian identity?

The Piano was set in New Zealand and made by a New Zealand director and of its three principals two were American and one a New Zealander. The Australian connection is solely that the AFC provided Campion with script development money and that Campion is Sydney-based, has lived in Australia for seventeen years, was trained at the AFTRS, and has used Australian film subsidy and production régimes to develop her talent and film properties. Yet *The Piano* is not simply another international production with some Australian involvement, it also represents Australasian film-making and a growing convergence and integration of the Australian and New Zealand film-making, exhibition and distribution sectors in the 1990s. This emerging situation is reminiscent of the integrated market that existed before television fractured what was a highly integrated Australasian audio-visual market.

Sweetie, *The Piano*, *Map of the Human Heart* and *An Angel at My Table* are just some of the high profile 'mixed productions' involving Australian and New Zealand collaborations of creative personnel which became an unexceptionable part of the cinema landscape in the 1990s. The 1990s also saw the return of New Zealand to the Australian imagination after so long being the 'poor relation'. Films set and shot in New Zealand gained significant audiences and acclaim from the Australian market, as *An Angel at My Table* and *The Piano* were followed up with Lee Tamahori's *Once were Warriors* (1994) and Peter Jackson's *Heavenly Creatures* (1995). Campion's films project in these terms an Australasian identity reflecting the close economic, cultural political, social and historical links between Australia and New Zealand and the significant New Zealand migrant presence in Australia. It is worth remembering in this regard that every Western national cinema is, at some stage, as a matter of national cultural policy interested in fostering international values, cooperation, mutual understanding and economic integration. The rethinking of the Australian–New Zealand relation on both sides of the Tasman at virtually every level in the late 1980s and through into the 1990s is a case in point. *The Piano* is one consequence of this rethinking. For David Robinson (1994: 125) the film becomes 'in its combination of Australasian and Hollywood practices . . . a paradigm of new international art cinema'.

Many smaller national cinemas are also at some stage part of larger national cinemas. Think of Austrian cinema with respect to German cinema; or Australian and New Zealand cinema with respect to English and American cinema. The Australian cinema of the 1930s consciously foregrounded its diasporic links to Britain – both as a means to create product suitable for sale in the UK and as a way of giving expression to a dominant (but by no means uncontested) cultural ideal of the day projecting Australia as a British-derived society. In 1930, W. K. Hancock wrote in his authoritative work on Australians (1961: 28) 'if such a creature as the average Briton exists anywhere upon this earth, he will be found in Australia'. Ken G. Hall's *The Squatter's Daughter* (1933) set up a seamless movement from Australia to Britain and then back again. The talented musician denied opportunity within Australia in *Broken Melody* (Hall 1938) goes to England to claim his destiny as a composer of merit, to return later to Australia and reclaim his romantic love and retrieve his place in his father's affections and bail out the family farm.

The post-war Australian feature cinema up until the decisive explosion of the 1970s was significantly – and mostly – a consequence of the outreaching of other national cinemas – British, American and even French and Japanese cinemas. The 1966 film *They're a Weird Mob* is a pivotal transition film between the 'outreaching of others' and the 'on local terms' of the 1970s. It looks back to the British and American location films of the 1950s and 1960s; and it looks forward to an 'Anglo-Australian film industry' characterized by creative partnerships like that between J. C. Williamson and Powell and Pressburger. Post-1970 Australian cinema used subsidy and television industry consolidation to forge on its own terms international partnerships in place of the off-shore productions of the 1950s and 1960s.

So too, nation states are only one among a number of organizers of films, their circulation, production and meaning. Large regional international organizations such as the European Community are taking over some of the functions of nation states and evolving film policies fostering international cooperation. So too it is a policy priority of the Australian, Canadian, English and New Zealand film organizations to pursue greater production, policy and industry links between themselves to better coordinate and integrate their markets to mutual benefit. This parallels and updates the relatively integrated 'Commonwealth' film market of the 1950s involving these same countries. *Black Robe* is an example of this increasingly formalized association between the government funding agencies of these Commonwealth countries. This film is veteran director Bruce Beresford's 'Australian film' of the 1990s. There are a host of Australians in the crew and one in the cast, in Aden Young (who grew up in Canada). It is a Canadian/Australian co-production. It is also a Canadian film set in Canada telling the story of colonization and most particularly the religious colonization of the Indian peoples of Quebec. At my local video library *Black Robe* is located on the 'festival' shelves and marketed on the dustjacket as being in continuity with the director's 1980 classic, *Breaker Morant*.

Other organizers of film production and circulation are multinational distributors, satellite television networks, international festivals, television networks and co-production arrangements. Most of this is not new. The transnational European film ideal of today had its predecessor in the Film Europe movement of the 1920s and early 1930s (K. Thompson 1987). Co-productions emerged in the 1960s to facilitate continental European film-making.

Sometimes this fuzziness in the national cinema is structural to the nation. Take for instance the language and regionally based 'national' cinemas within India and Canada. The Canadian state, for example, supports two national cinemas: an English-speaking one based in Toronto and Vancouver and a French-speaking one based in Montreal. And there are the various diasporic cinemas which in some guises have the stature of a cohesive 'national' cinema – like the 'overseas Chinese', 'Indian' and Jewish cinema which gains Australian audiences. Jewish film festivals have become a phenomenon in Australia and the USA, whose product is drawn from across the world including Australia. Australian cinema's contributions to a Jewish cinema have been limited: they include Henri Safran's comedy *Norman Loves Rose* (1982) and Jackie Farkas' searing short film *The Illustrated Auschwitz* (1992) which recounts a survivor's experience of the Holocaust and how her memory of that is connected to her first post-Holocaust cultural experience of watching *The Wizard of Oz* 1939). Are the growing body of short films shot in Italian, Spanish and Greek a contribution to the Italian, Spanish and Greek 'national cinemas' or are they 'Australian cinema'? Although not part of any larger diaspora, diaspora-like structures have emerged surrounding 'first peoples' or 'Aboriginal' film-making and screening events, which bring together culturally diverse first peoples who have been marginalized in different parts of the world by processes of colonization. Is there an Aboriginal and Torres Strait Islander cinema we can call an indigenous national cinema emerging from the spaces of non-Aboriginal and Aboriginal partnerships? The AFC sponsored a touring season of films in 1995 called *Hidden Pictures*, promoting an indigenous cinema whose beginnings are located in collaborations between non-Aboriginal film-makers and Aboriginal actors and individuals – in Ned Lander's tale of an Aboriginal band on the road in *Wrong Side of the Road* (1981) and Phil Noyce's low-budget road movie *Backroads*. The openness of these film-makers to Aboriginal input and their preparedness to allow that input shape the final product prepared the way for Aboriginal film-makers like Tracey Moffatt and Anne Pratten and a greater role for Aboriginal voices.

Like many national cinemas, Australian cinema operates within the multi-ethnic context. Fourteen per cent of Australian households spoke a language other than English at home and these homes sustained 'ethnic video' and cinema outlets for screening imported, culturally appropriate product and for the screening of locally produced materials. With 22 per cent of its population born outside the country courtesy of a large post-Second World War migration programme and a generous refugee programme (on a per capita basis Australia accepted more Indo-Chinese refugees than did any other country, see Lombard 1993: 18), Australian cinema may not be the natural non-Hollywood cinema of a minor but not insignificant proportion of the population. With such a multi-ethnic society the 'typical Australian' is now a product of several ancestries to the extent that Australia's cinema audience is shaped by a variety of cultural influences – which are increasingly seen in its cinema – as in the Spanish family in *Strictly Ballroom* and the Greek family in *Death in Brunswick* and *The Heartbreak Kid*.

National cinemas function within internally divided provincial contexts sustained by provincial governance and regional identities. Because many nations are, like Australia, Canada, the USA and Germany federations, state or provincial authorities are also organizers of film production and circulation through, for example, various state film authorities and the local basis for censorship provisions. Elsaesser (1989: 49) notes Germany's 'long established reflex of regionalism, and centuries of decentralization' commenting on its impact on German cinema and the politics of culture support. Australia is like Germany in this respect: regionalism is a standard reflex – the Australian states existed before 'Australia' did as a governing entity and decentralization is not only intrinsic to the European settlement of Australia but to Aboriginal and Islander society before it. Some Australian states, notably the populous New South Wales (Sydney its capital was the major centre for film production and still is) imposed film quotas in the 1930s. One of the important features of the Australian film revival was that production funding has been provided by the different states since 1972. Some Australian exhibition chains have been locality- and state-specific. And various kinds of sub-national identities provide alternative cultural materials and spaces to exploit.

A good example of this regionalism is Argall's *Return Home*. Its Adelaide setting stresses the cultural particularity of regional Australia. It foregrounds the significant migration to the metropolitan city from provincial Adelaide. It is also about diminishing living standards and downward mobility that is a marked feature of the lower middle class and working class experience over the 1980s and 1990s. One of the characters, Noel is rehabilitated by his journey home from Melbourne. The film is structured as a dialogue between two brothers, Steve (Adelaide) and Noel (metropolitan Melbourne). Each has what the other lacks. Steve owns a failing small garage business but he has family. Noel has no family but is successful and has big city Melbourne values. We are invited to read their different values in relation to the changing geographic 'landscape' of Australia. The narrative is resolved in favour of provincial Adelaide and family, as Noel returns to lend his skills to rejuvenate his brother's business. This affirmation of home has a utopian dimension, as Adelaide and South Australia have bleaker prospects compared to the booming economies of Queensland and Western Australia and the industrial heartlands of Sydney and Melbourne. Here Adelaide can be remade by the return of sons and daughters it has lost to the metropolis. Watching *Return Home* I was struck by the many parallels between it and Edgar Reitz's mini-series *Heimat* (1984). Both Australian and German cities have a deeply provincial character, with competing regional centres having different outlooks. There is the same 'rootlessness', as a post-war order was made and fashioned as a significant 'break with the past'. Both have seen significant internal migration – in Australia's case north to Queensland and west to Western Australia, and to Australia's two metropoles of Sydney and Melbourne. *Return Home*'s regionalism is achieved through its suburban characters, language, and the minute, often nostalgic descriptions of everyday life in the spacious single-storey suburbs of Adelaide. The film interweaves ideas of provincialism and homeland – giving voice to that other side of Australian life – its provincial character. Here the suburban heartland is centred on the nuclear family, its local horizons, the immediate and locality-bound networks which are gently opposed to the modern city, Melbourne and its alienated vision of glass. Like *Heimat*, *Return Home* consistently exploits the tension which Kaes (1989: 168) identifies there between 'staying and leaving, between longing for distant places and homesickness'. Argall's film is a troubling objection to the changes wrought on traditional Australian communities struggling to keep their provincial lives, hopes and lifeways intact in the face of declining economic circumstance and profound structural change.

In this chapter Australian cinema has been shown to possess the typical characteristics of a national cinema. National cinemas are marked by their *relational* character and by the co-presence of, on the one hand, the local and national and, on the other hand, the international. In the next chapter, I will further identify it as a type of national cinema.

Chapter 4

A medium-sized English-language cinema

INTRODUCTION

What kind of national cinema is the Australian cinema? How is it like some national cinemas and unlike others? I begin by emphasizing the broader English language cultural milieu of Australia, stressing how much the cinema market in Australia is like that of other English-speaking countries. Hollywood, as the dominant English language cinema, places insistent pressure upon non-American Anglophone producers. Producing in English presents Australian, British, New Zealand and English-Canadian cinema with advantages and disadvantages alike. I then emphasize the consequences for Australian cinema of being a medium-sized cinema. Like all medium and small countries, Australia has a minor place in the international trade in national symbolic images. Australian and English-Canadian cinemas face particular problems by virtue of sharing a similar exhibition market, market size, producing in English, and being a minor place in the international trade in national images. The chapter concludes by considering Australian cinema's antipodal identity – its implication in and negotiation of unequal cultural exchanges.

THE AUSTRALIAN CINEMA MARKET

The theatrical market in Australia, the USA, the UK and English Canada consists of a mainstream exhibition market exclusively oriented to English-language product, a minor stream geared to the sub-titled 'foreign film', and a semi-commercial and informal ethnic market geared to providing culturally appropriate product to many ethnic minorities.

Hollywood cinema dominates mainstream exhibition in these countries, consistently taking since the First World War between 75 and 99 per cent (in the case of the USA) of the box-office. The Hollywod share of the Australian market was 95 per cent in 1917 and 1925, 75 per cent in 1952 and 76 per cent in 1992 (K. Thompson 1985: 81; PEP 1952: 242; *Screen Digest* Dec. 1993: 279–80). The Hollywood cinema is often identified with the cinema in Anglophone countries. In Anglophone markets, Hollywood titles attract significantly more audiences than do their English language competitors. In their study of the economics of Australian film and television in the early 1990s, Simon Molloy and Barry Burgan (1993: 25) note that British films in Britain, and Australian films in Australia attracted fewer admissions per film than did imported – principally Hollywood – films. In Australia in 1990 46,000 people attended the average local title while 161,000 attended the average imported (Hollywood) film; in the UK the figures were 272,000 compared to 440,000 (*Screen Digest* April 1992: 86).[1]

Historically, the next most important influence in popular exhibition is the British cinema – the British share of the Australian and Canadian markets in 1950 was 20 per cent and 5 per cent respectively (PEP 1952: 246–7). British features were 7 per cent of Australian film imports at the end of the Second World War, 25 per cent by 1959, 9 per cent in the 1970s, 10 per cent in 1986 and 4 per cent in 1992/93 (Bell and Bell, 1993: 189; di Chiera 1980: 8; Office of Film and Literature Classification 1993: 27).

After these two cinemas comes the minor market presence of other English-language cinemas: Australian, English-Canadian or New Zealand. There are exceptions: with the decline of British cinema over the 1980s and with tax concessions creating a local feature boom, the Australian share of its local market moved beyond the British share for possibly the first time.

This mainstream commercial cinema accounts for nearly all of the box-office in these countries. It includes a range of product from popular, to exploitation, to 'quality', to festival film-making. Consequently the main competitors to Australian films are the English-speaking films of the USA, the UK, Canada and, to a lesser extent, New Zealand.

In Australia, Hollywood and the other English-language cinemas achieve their box office dominance despite Anglophone features making up only a proportion of the 35mm features and videos coming into the country for theatrical release. In 1991 79 per cent of these were English language – but between 1973 and 1978 only 41 per cent were. More Italian (13 per cent) and Hong Kong (9 per cent) films were shown for commercial screening between 1973 and 1978, than Australian (2 per cent) and British (9 per cent) films, but their combined box office was completely dwarfed by that of the Australian and British films (see PMM 1979: appendix 1).

Hollywood product also dominates the theatrical markets of non-English speaking (NES) countries of continental Europe and beyond. The major difference between the continental and Anglophone markets turns on what product occupies the minor competitive position in mainstream exhibition. In the English-speaking markets this position is occupied exclusively by other Anglophone cinemas, in the NES markets this competitor position, after Hollywood, is taken up by NES product and the English-language product from outside of Hollywood. It is also significant that in Japan and in some continental European markets – particularly France and Italy – the domestic product competes more effectively at home with the Hollywood product than does the British, Australian and English-Canadian. Outside the English language, language does not present as high a barrier to popularity. Audiences are either used to dubbing into their own language in the larger markets or sub-titling in the smaller language markets. In Canada, Australia and the UK, dubbing is rare. Sometimes dubbed titles have worked in these markets – as with Bruce Lee's Kung Fu titles of the early 1970s – but they rarely do. This is because an absence of lip-synch is seen to be a flaw in imported films, and not as it is outside the English-speaking market, where it is the accepted norm. Consequently NES films tend to be presented in sub-titles in Anglophone markets.

The sub-titled 'foreign films' make up a minor commercial form in art houses, as part of the 'festival' or 'repertory' cinema market. 'Foreign' here means foreign-language. The repertory circuits, film societies and the film festivals brought 'foreign films' into Australia in a sustained way from the 1950s – and earlier in the UK, the USA, Canada and New Zealand. These are the next most important markets in terms of public visibility and commercial development. Foreign language festival films made up 18 per cent of 35mm features imported in the 1970s (di Chiera 1980: 8), indicating a market where profits are generated by smaller audiences per title and high product turnover. In the 1990s, this repertory cinema often screened independent American and other English-language product alongside continental European and Asian features from Hong Kong, Taiwan, China and Japan.

With the advent of the film society movement in the 1940s and the development of international festivals in Australia in the 1950s and beyond, the 'foreign film' broadened considerably the cinema-going experience. It gave rise to a new phenomenon: the film intellectual. This subtitled film bore the imprimatur and authority of culture. These valued cinemas – in the 1960s French, Italian, Japanese and Swedish – provided local critics, film-makers and policy-makers with the means to rethink what Australian cinema could be. Critics and lobbyists – Thornhill, Lawson, Adams, Jones – imagined a different destiny for Australian film-making as a festival cinema and not just commercial entertainment (see Thornhill 1967). If the box-office take of repertory cinema is miniscule compared to the mainstream entertainment cinema, this cinema none the less provided a regular and important part of cinema-going for an influential section of filmgoers.

The festival cinema is sometimes a half-way point between the mainstream and the ethnic cinemas. Some festival cinemas – like the Italian and German cinemas in the 1960s and 1970s and the Chinese cinemas from the 1970s – functioned also as ethnic cinemas. The Italian cinema was an 'art house' cinema of note in the 1950s and 1960s with directors like Fellini, Antonioni, Visconti, Rossellini and de Sica, and Italians were the largest NES community in the 1950s and 1960s. The Chinese cinemas regularly appear on repertory schedules in the 1990s alongside French and other European cinemas and attract ethnic audiences from the Chinese diaspora in Australia. The Melbourne *Herald-Sun* carries a regular review column entitled 'Chinese Cinemas'. Such cinemas attract crossover audiences – the 'foreign film' audience and the ethnic audience(s) creating a hybrid identity and commercial viability as 'art cinema' and 'ethnic cinema'. What was valued about the post-war Italian, French and the German cinema by the art-house audience was its modernist articulations; just as the Japanese and now the Hong Kong and two China cinemas provide an image of Asian modernity.[2]

Despite the fact the ethnic cinemas are the least evidently commercial form, 40 per cent of all 35mm feature films imported between 1973 and 1978 were registered as for ethnic consumption. Furthermore this underestimated the NES films coming into the country for ethnic community screenings (di Chiera 1979: 2, 74). With the advent of video in the 1980s and its widespread ethnic community uptake, many more films on video now circulate among ethnic communities without reference to official channels, thus making it exceedingly difficult to determine relative figures.[3] The ethnic 'market' provides for an astonishing array of product. The ethnic cinema and video market is characterized by high volume, small but intensely committed audiences, and limited commercial development.

There have been and still are minor ethnic commercial cinemas (variously based on the larger ethnic groups – Italian, Greek and Chinese) and in the case of two of the larger groups from 1994, Italian- and Chinese-language pay-TV services. In the 1950s and 1960s Greek cinema was exhibited in Sydney and Melbourne – and on a shared basis in Brisbane. Greeks made up the second largest NES community and cinema operators relied on this large, relatively self-sustaining, and concentrated ethnic community to make their marginal operations viable.

Alongside these is a myriad of usually non-commercial exhibition venues, including ethnic home video devoted to screening NES films to the 100 or more ethnic migrant groups in Australia. Because none of these groups individually makes up as large a cohort as say the Francophones of Canada, only a handful of communities can develop a commercially recognizable form of cinema and video exhibition and distribution. Consequently, the ethnic sector is substantially catered for by non-commercial and semi-commercial exhibition and ethnic video sustained through community networks. Ethnic clubs and churches hired out halls and cinemas and used the clubs themselves for the screening of product. Alternatively, delis (mixed grocery stores), butchers and travel agencies serviced community video needs.

These three markets loosely match the three television sectors in free-to-air television. The mainstream which dominates television ratings is represented by the commercial networks and the main national broadcaster, the ABC. The repertory market is mostly served by SBS-TV which screens foreign-language product (festival cinema, high budget NES mini-series) and sometimes the ABC which occasionally screens an NES movie. The ethnic market is also served by SBS-TV in its ordinary NES TV-series and movies. The establishment of SBS-TV in 1980 brought television into the alignment long present in the cinema. It provided a venue for the circulation of NES product on free-to-air Australian television – just as the ABC provides such a venue for British television product.

Government funding through the two national broadcasters provides for a greater diversity in imports than would otherwise be the case. Again this replicates a situation in continental Europe where public broadcasters underwrote a diversity of film and TV product. The precarious character of the ethnic market helps explain why 'ethnic television', as SBS was called in the early 1980s, was underwritten by government and why in the 1990s it looked to advertising sponsorhip. SBS-TV works on low purchase prices for its NES imports – and this fits into its import logic of a market developed to accommodate a large volume of NES product attracting low ratings (typically 1–3 per cent of sets in use). To make its foreign-language product work, SBS-TV has typically sought a hybrid programming logic taking on board repertory cinema and quality television titles from France, Italy, Germany, Japan and more recently Hong Kong and the two Chinas. The state through SBS-TV has actively sponsored and developed Australia as a cultural import market with half of SBS programming hours in NES languages. Through SBS-TV, a television export market was developed for the homeland of one of the largest NESB ethnic groups in Australia – the Greeks.

The influence and significance of the ethnic cinema, video and television can sometimes be obscured. It is often invisible to the censor, audiences for individual titles are small and ratings consistently low. But this cinema cumulatively provides a distinct repertoire of film-making and television experience for NES people. It helps model several 'taste cultures' and different experiences of the cinema within Australia, shaping different kinds of relations with that cinema product for a significant few. Its legacy is apparent in the work of emerging film-makers of an NES background who are encouraged to draw on it to shape their contribution to Australian cinema. Italian cinema looms large for Italo-Australian director, Monica Pellizari with her short films evoking Australian Italy (*Velo Nero* 1987, *Rabbit on the Moon* 1987, *Just Desserts* 1993) and owing a clear debt to Italian features, comedies and Fellini.

With the advent of SBS-TV in 1980, this diversity of imported product has become more visible and publicly available. Under a multicultural remit, film policy has supported the production of short films and parts of feature films and mini-series in NES languages. Short films are sometimes all in a foreign language. These are 'independent' productions – productions not connected with the trade but dependent on state support. Feature films and mini-series productions have evolved to feature a component – usually the minor component – in NES languages with the other component being mostly in English. Examples here are the mini-series *Cowra Breakout*, and the features *The Heartbreak Kid* and *Gino* (McKimmie 1994). Because of multicultural policy and the close proximity of the state to film-making, this model is being drawn on stylistically and content wise in limited ways in production slates. Indeed SBS used the injection of government funding to help produce what was claimed (Harari 1995: 20–3) as the first Australian-produced feature that was mostly not in English – *Floating Life* (Law 1996) – centring on a Hong Kong couple planning to migrate to Australia who have one daughter in Germany and another in Australia. It is filmed mostly in Cantonese and German.

Australia, the USA, English Canada and the UK all have significant ethnic markets with a great many similarities, but some differences. Australia, for example, has not got the economy of scale to sustain 'ethnic' production as have the US Hispanic and Iranian communities. The Australian market is most like that of smaller communities in the USA and English Canada, in that there is a commercially developed form for only the largest language communities. But, unlike these, the Australian market builds bridges between the minor stream and the English-language mainstream, cultivating different kinds of public transparency and encouraging a general public space of interaction.

Due weight needs to be given to each of these markets. Each has had consequences for local production and consumption. The make-up, dimensions and character of the cinema and television markets shape the terms in which local audiences respond and film-makers produce the local cinema. Forms of cinema, video and TV provide the structures and templates through which the national cinema – including the very idea of a national cinema in its contemporary form – was created and subsequently viewed. Each of these sectors instruct local film-making, institute campaigns for it and orient its consumption and criticism. The impact of the repertory and ethnic 'import' markets is felt in the hybridization of English-language production traditions. And, yes, the Hollywood cinema remains the single most important influence. It is the *lingua franca* in cinema, video and television in Australia and beyond. British product continues to be the next most evident and continuing influence by virtue of its minor but nodal position in the English language.

AN ENGLISH-LANGUAGE CINEMA

As natural languages are the basis for cultural systems, communications corridors, markets, international trading systems and political alliances, they form cultural areas above the level of the nation. Australia and its national cinema is part of the larger family of English-language cinemas and cultures including the USA, English-speaking Canada, New Zealand, the UK and Ireland and to a lesser extent South Africa, Anglophone India and Singapore. Its cinema is a fragment of the larger Anglophone cinema, its culture a bit of the larger English-language cultural area. Membership of this larger, Anglophone cultural area shapes Australian culture and its cinema.

Despite the international promise of the festival and national cinema ideal of international cultural exchange, most national cinemas are mostly language cinemas. They rely more on fellow language speakers for profit than on anyone else. Hollywood is, despite its global reach, primarily an English-language cinema. The same tends to be true for the Australian cinema. Between 1985 and 1991 53 Australian features were released in the UK and 64 in the USA compared to 27 in France, 26 in Germany, and 10 in Spain; in that same period 113 features were screened on free-to-air in the UK compared to 17 in France, 70 in Germany and 12 in Spain – US cable took 85 movies and 11 telemovies in that same period (Sue Murray 1992: 65). As an English-language cinema, Australian cinema is oriented in the first instance towards English-language audiences.[4]

With its large market and considerable wealth, the English language is the dominant audiovisual language. The problem facing competitor language markets is that they either have the numbers of speakers but not the wealth, or the wealth but not the number of speakers. Hindu/Urdu has 86 per cent of the number of English speakers but only 5 per cent of English-speakers' GNP; Spanish has 64 per cent of the English-speakers' population but only 15 per cent of its GNP (Wildman and Siwek 1988: 86); whilst Japanese, German and French have a greater proportion of English speakers' GNP but do not have as many speakers. As Wildman and Siwek note:

> Japan, which has over 98% of the Japanese-speaking population, has a GNP only slightly greater than one quarter of the GNP of countries claiming English as an official language, and the Japanese-speaking population totals less than one third of the English-speaking population. The number of French speakers is 27% of the number of English speakers, and the combined GNP of French-speaking countries is less than 20% of the total for English-speaking countries. German totals are slightly less than 25% of the English totals on both counts.
>
> (86)

Wildman and Siwek suggest this gives English-speaking producers significant advantages in the international marketplace. They are able to invest more in image and sound than their counterparts and this investment ensures their product achieves greater international circulation. Consequently English is the international language from which to dub. Furthermore, as easily the largest market in the English language, US producers dominate that language and because they do they dominate global film markets.

Without language barriers, British, Australian, New Zealand and Canadian films have a better chance of breaching the huge North American market and so producing major international films than any other nations. Some Australian films – *Crocodile Dundee*, *The Man from Snowy River* and the *Mad Max* trilogy – can, as Sue Murray (1992: 65) head of Marketing at the AFC notes, 'claim their place as dominant entertainment forces'. *Crocodile Dundee* was the most successful film internationally in its year of release and the most successful foreign film ever in the US market – it made $174.6 million dollars in its US theatrical release. Only British, Canadian and New Zealand film-makers have this kind of possible North American circulation *occasionally* available to them.[5]

These non-US English markets have a greater capacity for integration and off-shore production with Hollywood majors than do non-Anglophone markets. One of the consequences of British film quotas in the 1950s and 1960s was to encourage extensive American investment in British film production with the unintended consequence, as Thomas Guback (1969: 35) observes, that quotas guaranteed 'American companies producing in Britain a reserved place on British screens'.

In the 1990s, Australia has become a significant off-shore production and facilities centre for international companies attracted by favourable exchange rates, competitive production and crewing costs (claimed to be 25–30 per cent less than Los Angeles costs), a state of the art studio at the Gold Coast subsidized by the Queensland government, one under construction in Sydney in conjunction with News Corporation, and the capacity of Australian locations to double as American, European, Asian locations and 'geographically unspecific' locations for action features like *Fortress* (1993), *Sniper* (Llosa 1992), *Escape from Absolon* (1994) and *Street Fighter* (De Souza 1995). With Queensland's success in attracting offshore production through the Village Roadshow studios on the Gold Coast and its associated Warner Brothers Movie World theme park, a number of state film agencies now pursue 'foreign production' and the competition among states is fierce. Toby Miller (1994b) has argued that the Gold Coast Studio 'sets up a third tier in Australian-based screen production in addition to notions of culturally valuable film culture and commercially driven film industrialism'.

By virtue of the common Anglophone culture presented on screen by Hollywood, all other things being equal, the cinema tends to be more important to social and cultural life in the English language countries. (Continental European cinema admissions were double those of North America in the 1960s but this was owing to the delay in Europe in the development of the audiovisual industries, particularly multichannel commercial television; so the comparison should be with North America in the 1960s and continental Europe in the late 1970s and early 1980s.)

The greater commercial standing of the English-language cinema confers additional benefits. Cinema attendance has tended to be historically higher in Anglophone markets than in comparable continental European markets. In the early 1950s, British audiences averaged twenty-seven cinema visits annually whereas French audiences averaged only eight visits (Political and Economic Planning 1952: 170). In 1994, Australian cinema attendances per head were 3.57, New Zealand 3.88 and Spain 2.21. Despite the considerable difference in population between Spain (39 million) and Australasia (Australia and New Zealand) (21 million),[6] the 1994 gross box-office in Australia and New Zealand was higher at $(US)376.8 million (Australia $330.3 million, New Zealand 46.5 million), than Spain's $336.1 million (*Screen Digest* Sept. 1995: 206–7). This and the possibility of international export enables the Australian cinema to work from a larger industry base than its population size suggests.

By virtue of its size, wealth and international dominance, English-language cinema is the most internally differentiated and diverse of all language cinemas. While much energy has gone into describing the classical Hollywood style, the US cinema in conjunction with the British, Canadian and Australasian cinemas has always produced a large variety of product from its commodious space. Take many prominent European auteurs like Jean Renoir, Luis Buñuel, Billy Wilder, Douglas Sirk – not to mention the minor Australian, New Zealand and Canadian contributions – and you have a large and impressive variety, significantly contributing to and often dominating the formats and various taste cultures in the cinema. This makes it notoriously difficult to describe these cinemas, as their significant internal diversity and fragmentation is explicable only in terms of the enormous diversity of the Hollywood cinema.

In general, these English-language countries are quicker to take up innovations.[7] Canada is, for example, a major innovator in theatrical exhibition, distribution and new audiovisual media which are subsequently taken up elsewhere – the multiplex is a Canadian invention and, arguably so too is cable television. In English-speaking countries cinema infrastructures were renovated in the 1980s and 1990s, earlier and more thoroughly than in NES countries. Apart from the Gulf states and Japan, the take-up of VCRs in the home was consistently higher and occurred earlier in the English-speaking markets. Australian VCR penetration was amongst the highest in the world in 1991 – 72 per cent of television households, with the UK at 71.5 per cent, the USA at 71 per cent, and Japan at 70 per cent – only Kuwait was higher that year at 85.5 per cent! These figures are considerably higher than the estimated world VCR penetration of television households of 33.8 per cent (Molloy and Burgan 1993: 60). Because English-language cinemas are exposed directly to Hollywood, because they are exposed so quickly to change, because they are at the technological and distributive cutting edge, they need to be innovative, to continue to have constantly shifting centres and mobile identities.

English-language cinemas invest more money in individual feature production than do their NES counterparts. *Screen Digest* (April 1992: 85) estimated that in 1990 the average production budget for US features was $7.6 million, UK features was $(US) 5.32 million, and Australian $(US) 3.3 million compared to the European community average of $(US) 2.8 million. Directly competing against the high budget Hollywood cinema, non-US Anglophone cinemas cannot afford to have the same scale of production values as can NES cinemas. Australian and British feature film budgets tend to be higher than film budgets in continental Europe and there is less reliance on easy options for conveying story information like dialogue. The proximity to Hollywood requires higher investments in the image to be competitive, so non-US English-language cinema has to access more production capital per film than do NES national cinemas – despite the fact that they have proportionately less access to their own box-office.

Each of the advantages of operating in English also turn out to be a disadvantage. The higher standards of imaging required to be competitive make it harder to get productions up. They also make non-US English producers more self-conscious about their international potential and international considerations insistently impinge in production and pre-production. With higher budgets they need the prospect of North American circulation.

The ability to attract American and other international productions creates problems for the local industry. Film critic, Peter Thompson (1994), suggests that with greater offshore production in Australia 'a two-tier industry could develop with the top rank eventually pricing itself out of the international marketplace and the indigenous industry strangled by lack of capital investment'. He observes that '[a]lmost no locally produced films can afford to use the new studio facilities because Australian budgets are pegged by various factors at about the $3 million mark'.

Because innovations are taken up earlier, the English language countries are more directly and quickly exposed. If the local cinema can be a worthy substitute and rival for Hollywood for popular audiences locally and internationally in, for example, *The Piano*, *Crocodile Dundee* and the *Mad Max* trilogy, it does not have the protection and advantage afforded by the barrier of language.

The French and Italian cinemas can seem to persist autonomously – in the sense of being spaces of separate development and marked difference from Hollywood and other national cinemas. But such autonomy is not as available to non-US English-language film-makers, critics, audiences, or policy makers. The connections between the local and the Hollywood cinemas are encountered more often, materially and insistently. For French cinema these connections are encountered less often, making for a space of positive appropriation and incorporation that does not appear to compromise French cultural autonomy. Non-US English-language cinemas are not as structurally or as textually independent.

The familiar lament in Anglophone countries outside the USA is that 'our film industry would have been able to develop more fully and separately, if it were not for the fact of the English language'. Local film-makers do not have the 'wall' of language for protection. Hollywood provides greater domestic competition for the local product in English-speaking rather than in NES countries. The almost non-existent cultural barriers to Hollywood cinema's circulation and audience uptake in the English-speaking countries is indicated by the US market share in 1992 – Australia 76 per cent, the UK 93 per cent, Ireland 92 per cent – compared to France 58 per cent and Italy 68 per cent (*Screen Digest*, Dec. 1993: 279–80)![8] As Hollywood cinema crowds out local product, these countries cannot maintain a local presence approaching France's 1993 figure of 40 per cent (Ciment 1995: 165). The upper end of Australia's share of the domestic box-office is the 1982 level of 21 per cent and the 1988 level of 18 per cent (that year saw *Crocodile Dundee II*, *The Man from Snowy River II*, *Young Einstein* (Serious 1988), and *Evil Angels* earning 'significant box office returns' (AFC 1991: 10)) – but it has usually been below 10 per cent since production subsidies stabilized in 1975 (in twelve of the seventeen years from 1977 to 1993 Australian box-office share was below 10 per cent (calculated from Reid 1994: 82).

Local product feels Hollywood competition intensely because of its culture's social and cultural proximity to the USA. There is not as large a gap between the locally produced cinema and the dominant Hollywood cinema – both share a common language and a raft of common cultural infrastructures. Like the USA,

Australia is a new world society, a former British colony, and both are societies formed by polyethnic migration. Hollywood's 'minority' cinema, such as its Jewish (*Hester Street* (Silver 1974), *Crossing Delancey* (Silver 1988), *Avalon* (Levinson 1990)) and gay cinema (*Longtime Companion* (Rene 1990), *Making Love* (Hiller 1982)) serve equally well for Australian Jews (see Freiberg 1994: 199) and gays and lesbians. The Australasian, British and Canadian ambivalence to the USA lies in the fact that the Americans are 'us' in ways they cannot be for other NES countries.

Producing in English provides audiences, critics and film-makers with more ready points of comparison between their output and that of the Hollywood cinema. By virtue of Australian cinema's participation in the Anglophone cultural area, this will be so whether or not imitation was intended by film-makers or thought to be an issue for viewers. So Australian, British and Canadian film-makers can be readily seen as lesser versions of US film-makers locally and abroad. Producing in the English language also encourages a sense amongst audiences, distributors and exhibitors that the local cinema is interchangeable with US and to a lesser extent British films. Sometimes Australian films are confused by international audiences with British and American films. The very possibility of making distinctions among the various cultures in English is undercut by the coherence of the English-language cinema and cultural system and the dominance of it by the US and to a lesser extent the British.

Hollywood impacts at all levels. Australians – like their British and Canadian counterparts – routinely get more information on US films than on Australian titles. They learn in their popular media about the performance of films released first in the USA. Burgan and Molloy contend that 'the US market (and, in general, any highly visible foreign market: e.g. UK, France) is an uncertainty filter for the Australian market' for audiences, distributors, exhibitors and critics alike. They continue:

> The box office performance of new films, notwithstanding the flow of usual gossip, is the essence of film news that appears in the entertainment sections of the print media and on television entertainment shows. The reduced uncertainty that is attached to US film thus confers on it an inherent desirability in the eyes of distributors, exhibitors and consumers.
>
> (30)

They see this as 'a rational response by risk averse agents to the lower uncertainty associated with "road-tested" US film' (30). So Australian film distribution and exhibition is 'naturally' oriented to Hollywood and to a lesser extent British product. And it has been so since the first decade of this century.

Local exhibition and distribution practices including ownership patterns have evolved to facilitate this relation. There are few commercial barriers to limit Hollywood's Australian circulation, or US company expansion into Australian exhibition, distribution and video rental markets.

The most seminal economic analysis of the consequences of this relation for local production was the 1973 Tariff Board Report on the Australian film and television industry. (The Tariff Board was a Federal government industry advisory body now called the Industry's Commission.) The Tariff Board found Australian exhibition and distribution to be marketing mechanisms for foreign, not Australian films (7). The cinema trade was an extension of the American and British production industries and fundamentally skewed away from local production. Distributors were really forwarding agencies, remitting practically all their returns to their overseas principals to be divided there (41). They had no competence to create campaigns, make trailers, assess projects or launch films (42). Exhibitors, on the other hand, were efficient mechanisms for the Australian screening of groups of foreign films with proven track records overseas. Some of these films were from their own stables (47); Fox, the American major then in American hands had a majority shareholding in Hoyts, and Rank, then a British major, had a 50 per cent equity in Greater Union. Similarly, their affiliation with particular distributors dictated an exhibition policy favouring their source of supply. They just were not geared to the needs of Australian film production and had not been for most of the century. As the Board reported:

> To say that the Australian distribution/exhibition network is to a great extent an integrated part of the marketing activities of foreign film producers is to emphasize that there is no substantial distribution exhibition system operating specifically with the purpose of marketing Australian produced films.
>
> (43)

Australian films were independently produced, they were not 'their' films and they were an unknown entertainment commodity without promotional campaigns. Australian film, the Board concluded, was crucially independent of mainstream exhibition and distribution and consequently commercial local films did not have 'exhibition opportunities commensurate with their box office potential'. Their 'country of origin and the distribution company to which they belonged' influenced their screening opportunities too much. The cinema market was structurally prejudiced in its practices, its orientations and in its patterns of ownership and control against Australian features. Practices of block and blind booking further locked exhibitors into taking a proportion of Hollywood, and to a lesser extent British product, irrespective of a film's earning potential, so as to get that handful of hits that exhibition revenues are dependent on. There simply was not room for Australian product in mainstream exhibition and distribution.

The Board recommended government intervention in the market along US anti-trust lines to secure 'genuine and effective competition between the major elements of production, distribution and exhibition' (7). This consisted of intervention in the patterns of ownership and control: divestiture of cinemas by the major chains, genuine bidding for film, and an end to practices of block booking and blind bidding. Such a structural intervention was not pursued. Under pressure from the major chains: the Motion Picture Export Association of America

(MPEAA), and a business sector hostile to trade practices legislation, these recommendations were not followed.[9] Another of its recommendations – the continuation and expansion of government production subsidies was followed.

Australia's import orientation licenced government intervention into the audio-visual sector which was and still is designed to secure Australian cinema production levels beyond a trivial level (see Molloy and Burgan 1993: 92–101). Government funding provided for a more extensive – albeit limited – Australian presence. It created opportunities within Australia for writers, directors and actors. Without that funding, and the infrastructures that went with it, such as the AFTRS, it is doubtful that the world would have known of Mel Gibson, Peter Weir, Jane Campion or Judy Davis. The figure of 2–3 per cent Australian titles for theatrical screening in the 1970s is the achievement of a government funding régime that does not counter this import orientation but does leaven it somewhat.

After two decades of generous government support, Molloy and Burgan's analysis of the contemporary Australian cinema and television industries confirms many of the Tariff Board's diagnoses. It demonstrates a continuing situation of exhibition dominance as three exhibitors dominate the market: in 1990 Hoyts (34 per cent market share), Village (22 per cent) and Greater Union (20 per cent) dominated the domestic box-office (Molloy and Burgan 1993: 54). Distribution, in its turn, was dominated by three major firms with US links. Both exhibition and distribution were oriented primarily to Hollywood. However, a minor market for local films and the infrastructures for handling them evolved, to the extent that Australian films made up on average 9 per cent of the domestic box-office over the 1980s. Between 1980 and 1991 Hoyts and Roadshow distributed 20 per cent of the Australian films released, while the Greater Union organization handled 11 per cent (Molloy and Burgan 1993: 53). A series of minor distributors such as Ronin Films and Beyond International emerged to handle Australian product alongside these distributors.

So I have argued that natural languages play a part in making some national cinemas more marginal than others. If a national cinema is a part of a smaller and/ or poorer language community it will be dwarfed by the films of larger and wealthier language communities. By the same token, if a national cinema is part of a coherent and significant language community dominated by a larger inter-national cinema – then it will be marginalized by the primary node of that language community. The smaller Australian and larger UK markets are domi-nated by the USA. Australian, English-Canadian and British producers are condemned to unequal English-language competition with the USA, while simul-taneously taking advantage of the cultural and economic benefits of being English producers.

A MEDIUM-SIZED CINEMA

Australian cinema's minor status as a national cinema is not only a consequence of its operating in English but of its market size. Australia's is a medium-sized cinema, the Australian market a medium-sized cinema market. Like its Dutch and Swedish counterparts, Australia does not have a huge cinema and cinema market as does the USA, it does not have a large cinema market as does the UK, France, Italy and Germany, but by the same token none of these are small countries.

National cinemas are, as a rule, more solidly commercially grounded in larger than in smaller countries and in wealthier than in poorer countries. French cinema producers never faced the prospect of an industry 'blackout' that Australian film-makers faced in the 1940s, 1950s and 1960s. Medium- to smaller-sized national cinemas like Australia's have a more difficult time of it because they are simply not big enough to sustain Britain's or France's annual production. In 1993 France produced 152 features and released 133 titles (Ciment 1995: 165) – in that same year Australia released eighteen features (Reid 1994: 83) while feature production in the 1992/93 financial year was twenty-three titles (Court and Bean 1994: 43). Australian cinema does not have as captive export markets in former colonies and European states as does France.[10] Elsaesser describes French cinema (1994: 26) as 'a national cinema with such a diversity of strands that it makes its auteurs (Godard, Resnais, Truffaut, Rivette) almost marginal figures in the overall constellation'.

Like the Swedish cinema of the 1960s, the Australian cinema of the late 1970s and 1980s was known through a limited number of auteurs and actors. Like Ingmar Bergman and Liv Ullman in the Swedish cinema of the 1960s, Australia was known in the late 1970s for directors, Armstrong and Dr Miller, and their actors Judy Davis and Mel Gibson. As David Robinson (1994: 125) notes 'stylistically the literary drama [*My Brilliant Career*] and the dystopian road movie [*Mad Max*] could not have been more different, but both expressed a distinctive (and internationally marketable) Australian voice'.

Servicing 18 million people, Australian cinema is not large enough to support an extensive film production industry, nor the scale of local production in higher budgeted movie and limited episode serial television. As a medium-sized producer, it cannot as easily differentiate itself through either, producing a sufficient volume of suitable product or readily occupying a market niche as can the larger French, Italian or British cinemas (these are readily known in their own right). In part because of the difficulties of delivering a 'brand name', diverse Australian product circulates locally and internationally.

Medium-sized cinemas do not have as extensive or valuable export markets as do larger cinemas. They have difficulty holding their best and brightest in front of and behind the camera because of the limited professional options available. Their local product is not as critically valued in itself but is evaluated – often pejoratively – with respect to imports. When exported, their features are rarely as popular or as critically respected internationally as are those of the USA and the major European cinemas (also available in those markets).

Courtesy of its medium-size status, cinema in Australia is primarily import-oriented. Unequal exchanges characterize the general Australian cultural marketplace in publishing, video, television, CD sales as well, and are a factor, irrespective of size, scale or product exhibited and distributed. Imports provide audiences, film-makers and critics with their most significant experience of the cinema. As already indicated Australian distributors and exhibitors are more concerned with imported feature films. Their French and Italian counterparts are that much more interested in their own local product because it makes up a more significant portion of the box office. Local films are more incidental for Australian audiences and critics. Australian-produced cinema is a more marginal cinema in its home market than are the cinemas of major film-producing countries in their home markets.

Australian cinema producers, their audiences and policy-makers work in an environment in which their local cinema is a minor part of the local experience of the cinema. If this is a characteristic – to some extent – of *all* national cinemas, it is a particularly acute characteristic of minor national cinemas such as the Australian, English-Canadian, Dutch, Austrian, Belgian, Singaporean and Malaysian ones. Australian cinema faces intense international competition on two counts: it is an Anglophone cinema and a medium-sized national cinema. By contrast British cinema is Anglophone but large; French cinema Francophone and large; the Dutch cinema Dutch-speaking but medium-sized.

Yet Australia is larger than Belgium, Holland, Austria, New Zealand, Singapore and the Scandinavian countries. It can produce more films than these countries and it has developed more extensive export markets. With the benefit of generous state support since 1969 it has been able to figure disproportionately for its size as a national cinema in world film and television markets.

Recognition of Australia as a medium-sized cinema was important in getting film production subsidies up. Scandinavian and Canadian examples legitimized an Australian subsidized cinema on governmental horizons in the late 1960s and 1970s. Looking outside of the normal points of comparison – Britain, the USA and the larger European countries – was strategically necessary in order to think a different destiny. Australian 'best practice' was as a small- to medium-sized country whose achievements were to be measured against Sweden, The Netherlands and Canada. It also involved tempering a vision of what Australian cinema could be to a minor supplement: a 3–15 per cent market share! If imports are necessary to sustain cinema and television schedules in all 'national cinemas', medium-sized and small markets are natural import markets. They are not large enough to have the scale economies to control their local market above a minor level. There is a closer association of exhibitor and distributor interest with the imported product and a more distant relation with the local product. Small to medium-sized countries often see political and cultural purposes in diversifying imports and can even, as we have seen, use public funding to do so, as with the SBS-TV experiment!

Because they are not at the centre of definitions of cinema, medium-sized cinemas tend to be known in more particular ways. Like The Netherlands and Canada, Australia is on the margins of the international trade in national images. It is not France, and Sydney is not Paris as a location. Their minor place in an international symbolic geography constrains what a medium-sized cinema can be and how its output is internationally consumed. Moreover this place is not just secured through Australian or Canadian or Dutch actions, it is also – and more powerfully – secured through international actions which circumscribe local film-making options and meanings.

International audiences and critics customize the Australian cinema for their own purposes. International film-makers use Australian locations and stories as materials for their storytelling. Australian film-makers and producers negotiate the constraints of this minor place in their selection of story materials and in their negotiations with international investors. In this way Australia is a shared symbolic resource for international film-makers and audiences – a resource, an archive, a set of human and non-human materials. Australia becomes a site for the international projections of audiences and film-makers from other cinemas to find some purchase on and connection with Australian culture, its people, its history, its locations and its stories. Both these international actions connect with a long tradition of Australia as 'a projective screen for European aspiration and anxiety' (Gibson 1992: x).

By virtue of its medium size, Australia and Australians become known internationally for a narrow range of things: peoples, stereotypes, myths and settings. They are known as 'outback' types, freaks, Aboriginal peoples and convicts. At the height of the hillbilly classic, *Crocodile Dundee*'s extraordinary worldwide success in 1986/87 many Australian tourists were reportedly sick of the responses they encountered overseas. They came to resent the film's 'outback' yokel version of the Australian type – rejecting it in favour of their sophisticated urban sensibility. David White wrote in 1984 (23) of how Australia emerged on the horizon of 'overseas scriptwriters' as precisely this particular type:

> Scotland might be the home of mean men in kilts, France a place of racy women of easy morals, Mexico of a race of Speedy Gonzales and the East a hotbed of scheming venality. Australia was simply a huge land, characterized by its remoteness and a sparse population of amiable yokels.

Australia's place in the *National Geographic* imaginary is a freakish one of exotic landscapes, vegetation, Aboriginal peoples and weird animals (even Peter Weir felt it necessary to include shots of koalas in *Picnic at Hanging Rock*). There is no doubt that the ways of knowing Australia by its flora, fauna and landscape courtesy of nature documentaries and genres of landscape photography privilege the countryside and wilderness. They do not foreground the culture of urban or regional Australia – particularly in the European imagination.

Such estimations have a wider relevance in structuring the interpretation of Australian cinema generally. Amanda MacDonald (1995: 57) shows how Serge Grunberg's major 1994 essay on Australian cinema for *Les Cahiers du Cinéma* (September 1994) entitled 'Longue Distance' 'participates in a long-standing French discursive habit of mythologizing Australia as the desert island of the South Pacific'. The first serious attention paid by *Cahiers* to the Australian cinema turns on confirming rather than interrogating this 'desertification'. The tendency for '"Ah, L'Australie – ces grands espaces!" ("Ah, Australia, those wide open spaces!") . . . makes of Australia a collection of emptinesses' (57–8) – filled by nomads obsessed with political correctness, sharing the Anglo-Saxon obsession with homosexuality (*The Adventures of Priscilla: Queen of the Desert, The Sum of Us, Only the Brave*), and lacking real history and a sense of place.

Australian cinema's penchant for producing 'freaks' (like Mick Dundee, Barry McKenzie, Sweetie and Muriel) and 'monsters' (*Razorback*, the men in *Wake in Fright* and *Don's Party*) intersects with Australian 'freakishness' as a news item on international screens. This is also an historical freakishness. First there are Australia's indigenous peoples – probably the world's most anthropologized people – who have exercised the European imagination for the past 200 years and are central to the Western sociological archive in the work of Durkheim, Freud, Fraser and Mauss (Miller 1995). Second there is a settler society created in the late eighteenth century by convicts – ambiguously a nation founded by criminals and gaolers and by a form of (white) slavery.

Indigenous people amidst an ancient landscape attracted Roeg and the two German auteurs – Werner Herzog and Wim Wenders – to make *Where the Green Ants Dream* (1984, centred on the clash between traditional Aboriginal lifeways and a mining venture by European Australians in the central desert) and *Until the End of the World* (1992, where the last third is centred in the central Australian desert amidst an Aboriginal community). International documentary film-makers like John Pilger have used the genocide, dispossession and mistreatment of the Aborigines and Torres Strait Islanders to provide potent international images of a corrupt, invading criminal people dealing harshly with Aboriginal and Islander peoples.

In its turn, the convict settlement period in Australian history attracted Alfred Hitchcock and Hans Detlef Sierck (Douglas Sirk) to make *Under Capricorn* (1949) and *To the Distant Shore* (*Zu Neuen Ufern* 1937) respectively. The convict period in Sydney worked well with Hitchcock's thematics. Here was a society where former murderers could be prominent, legitimate businessmen. It is one of the few places in the nineteenth century where the Ingrid Bergman character (the daughter of Irish aristocracy) and the Joseph Cotten character (the family strapper) could publicly consummate their relationship and seem to prosper and get away with it. But it is also a dystopian space where questions of recidivism, secrets, and dark and unspoken pasts were never far away, intruding into the present and constituting an inner family stain. Nowhere is this clearer than in the troubled marriage between the ex-convict businessman and husband, played by a classically troubled and brooding Joseph Cotten and his drunken, neurotic and hysterical wife played by Bergman. The Mandalay of *Rebecca* (Hitchcock 1940) became the Sydney mansion on the edge of the city, Mrs Danvers became the malevolent housekeeper, who out of her twisted love for the Joseph Cotten character, feeds the Bergman character's alcohol habit and neuroses and fuels the Cotten character's jealousy of his rival. It is the housekeeper who precipitates the shooting of the rival which almost repeats the earlier shooting. We ultimately learn that it was the Ingrid Bergman character who killed her brother and not the Joseph Cotten character.

For his part, Sierck's *To the Distant Shore* narrativized the female convict system. Again there is an innocent convict victim – except this time it is a prominent singer (Zarah Leander) taking the punishment for the counterfeiting crime of her lover. She escapes convict status by agreeing to marry a free settler who genuinely loves her (the Rock Hudson function in some of Sirk's later Hollywood films). She uses him to rejoin her fluctuating lover who has since come to Australia. The lover rejects her and plans instead an advantageous and socially acceptable match. But he cannot bear to be without the Zarah Leander character and commits suicide on the eve of his wedding. The woman, freed now of her passion and able to see her lover for what he really is, freely 'selects' her settler in marriage.[11]

Many films – local and international – have narrativized Australian criminality of the late eighteenth and nineteenth centuries. Alongside the many convict feature films and mini-series, are the staple of bushranger films. Like many of the convicts, these bushrangers are often also victims of circumstance. The Ned Kelly story, for example, which has been retold in at least six features and one mini-series, typically thematizes Ned's declaration of war on the police as a natural response to cruelty and discrimination, accidental circumstance, and as a form of working-class resistance to arbitrary authority. And Rolf Boldrewood's classic bushranging novel *Robbery Under Arms* – with its gentleman bushranger, Captain Starlight, as its centre (most recently played by Peter Finch in the 1957 version and Sam Neill in the 1985 version) – has been made into five features and one mini-series.

The international – British and American – interest in telling Australian stories was more significant after the Second World War, becoming almost semi-permanent. This was at a time when the Australian trade moved decisively away from local production and when Commonwealth film policy was non-existent outside of support for its Documentary Film Unit. With the Hollywood consent decrees breaking up vertical integration within the US industry – i.e. the control of exhibition, distribution and production by the same companies – greater opportunities were created for English language producers in the American market. The British sought to shore up their Commonwealth markets through offshore productions and involvement in exhibition in Australia, Canada and South Africa, while gearing themselves to the American market and attracting Hollywood offshore involvement to the UK. Prior to this, British and American producers were largely uninterested in exploiting Australian locations and stories (Routt 1994b).

In the late 1940s and 1950s, Australia was a place to make 'British' westerns and 'location' films. A division of symbolic labour emerged within the larger British film industry which included sections of the Australian industry. The British would produce studio productions and urban-based storytelling, while their Australian and South African films would foreground rural and outback scenarios in male-centred stories. With westerns dominating film schedules in this period, Australia's exotic locations made it possible for British and Australian producers to make, in the 1950s and 1960s, both nineteenth-century westerns *Eureka Stockade* (Watt 1949), *Bitter Springs* (Smart 1950), *Robbery Under Arms* (J. Lee 1957) – and contemporary westerns (*The Overlanders*, *The Phantom Stockman* (Robinson 1953) and *Walk into Paradise*). In comparison, pre-Second World War features gave a more important place to urban stories and Australian women, as melodrama-accentuated productions dominated. Bush-centred films typically gave a central place for women in titles like *The Squatter's Daughter* (Hall 1933) and *A Girl of the Bush* (Barrett 1921).

By the 1970s, the British/Australian connection had become more sophisticated as a result of the continuing and organized structural exchanges put into place for television. Co-productions could still feature the colonial period and the early years of this century but they could also venture into mini-series set in the post-Second World War period like *The Leaving of Liverpool* (Jenkins 1992), *Brides of Christ* (K. Cameron 1991) and *The Act of Betrayal* (Clark 1988, centring on an IRA informer living a new life in Australia while being hunted for his past).

Minor national cinemas like Australia's constantly worry that an international cinema will reproduce 'ossified' stereotypes rather than present emergent senses of a culture and people. Australia becomes here not an urban multicultural society but a place peopled by Mick Dundees, the Bryan Brown of *Breaker Morant*, the Tom Burlinson and Sigrid Thornton of *The Man from Snowy River* and the nomadic Mel Gibson traversing a desert-like landscape in the *Mad Max* trilogy. If, as David Rowe suggests, 'all forms of international symbol exchange are in some ways touristic' (Rowe 1994: 17), the insistent presence of internationalization in a medium-sized market can entail the entropic projection of touristic images back into Australia, rejuvenating images, types and stereotypes that may not have been otherwise sustained. Hence a certain quaint and retro quality accrues to medium-sized national cinemas.

The government funding of an Australian national cinema from the late 1960s had as one of its purposes a greater Australian role in shaping Australia as a place in the cinema. For the 1969 Australian Council of the Arts report, cinema would assist in 'Australia's efforts to interpret itself to the rest of the world'. There was a 'public relations potential of an indigenous film and television industry'. Australians would no longer leave it to 'British and American companies to visit us and make features and series revolving round such *exotica* as Cobb and Co. and Ned Kelly' (my emphasis). This was an explicit strategy of normalization – a strategy which can only ever be partially successful by virtue of the minor place in the international trade in symbolic national images available to Australia and the fact that only a handful of Australian films become dominant entertainment product.

A MEDIUM-SIZED ENGLISH-LANGUAGE CINEMA

Like English-Canadian cinema, Australian cinema is a medium-sized English language producer which has required state intervention to sustain production beyond trivial levels. While Australian films can claim their place as dominant entertainment forces, they only occasionally do so. For Sue Murray (1992: 65) local film-making is 'best viewed in the context of European and American independent production'.

Australian film-makers face the same problems as American independents. Their features are to one side of the dominant major Hollywood product. Their budgets are much lower than the product the US majors sponsor. There is a lot of unaffiliated product looking for theatrical exhibition. But they can produce 'sleepers' which can count in North America and beyond as 'dominant entertainment' fare and their product is able to circulate viably as 'minor' commercial product in North America and beyond, as did *Breaker Morant*, *Muriel's Wedding* and *The Adventures of Priscilla: Queen of the Desert*. As with the American independents, the influence of the Hollywood majors on Australian film-making is clear. It needs to be similar to, yet different from the high budget Hollywood product. Too similar, and the competition from the major Hollywood product is too evident, with the local product being compared negatively. Too different, and the local and international audience can be alienated and trained into accepting Hollywood protocols as they are. As Stephan Elliott put it:

> the only way it [making films] is going to work is if Australians start taking gambles and do the unusual pictures that the Americans won't. We don't have the money, we don't have the manpower, we don't have the movie stars to compete with expensive American films head on. All we are left with at the end of the day is lower budgets, ingenuity, freedom and imagination.
>
> (Epstein, 1994: 86)

In the early 1990s this 'Australian difference' had become in Paul Malone's words 'the prevalence of parody, especially of urban/suburban mundane pretentiousness and portentousness ... a contribution to ocker grunge' (Malone 1994: 69). And this is, after all, not far from the strategies of US independents to produce 'off-beat', 'quirky' films that are 'right on the edge'.

But there are limits to this comparison. Australian producers are not as closely related to the Hollywood major product. Their product does not have the same standing within the USA and beyond. Sometimes being Australian gives local film-makers a market edge over American independents but, for the most part, being non-American counts against Australian producers.

Australian film-makers are like the continental European producers. Their films largely occupy the place of the 'foreign film' in European and North American markets alike. They compete with non-Anglophone films at Cannes. By virtue of the 'festival' cinema option, they draw on European production models to inform their productions. Their sales tend to be made on a territory-by-territory basis after completion. They tend to be structurally marginal to the mainstream market. They create a product without the international commercial standing of the Hollywood product. While being shot in English is an advantage in terms of sales to NES markets, this is counterbalanced by the fact that both make up a minor place in the cinema – if you want non-Hollywood English-language product, you will normally go to the more familiar British cinema.

Australian producers are also like the British cinema producer (as a European producer) in that they operate in similar exhibition and distribution markets: they have the same problem negotiating a US sale, they too have difficulty producing an adequate film-making response to Hollywood, they draw significantly on British production models and responses to the Hollywood cinema and they often forge partnerships with the British industry for co-productions and financing. Because the British cinema has been the only continuous and credible English-language response to Hollywood over the century, Canadian and Australian producers are going to be that much more interested and shaped by it. In the long list of 'faults' of Australian film-making – a reliance upon social realism, docu-drama, social problem film-making, too much dialogue, emotional underachievement of actors, colourless 'ordinary' leading men and women – these are just as surely problems with British cinema! But the Australians and Canadians are unlike the British producer in that they are working from a smaller domestic market base.

The problems facing Australia in its unequal competition with Hollywood have made a relation with the British film industry, film-making and its production models that much more historically important. Other incentives are provided by the cultural proximity to the UK and the possibility of British export, given that the UK is the only large country market and the only country outside of Ireland and New Zealand routinely interested in Australia.

The British relation is a constant refrain: whether it involves the populist 1930s director Ken G. Hall, the Ealing Studios director Harry Watt, or a Stephan Elliott of *Priscilla* fame (who looks forward to a career '[u]sing British money and shooting wherever I want, I'll be able to retain creative controls as long as I stay nimble. The second you land into the big Hollywood pot, you lose control and have 40 people cutting your film' (Epstein 1994: 10)). The two dominant directors in the 1930s – Charles Chauvel and Ken Hall – foregrounded the British connection yet were also proud of their knowledge of and capacity to work within and adapt Hollywood production protocols (see Cunningham 1987a: 81–9; Hall 1980 *passim*). Although this might be 'the last hurrah for empire' in the face of the dominance of Hollywood (Cunningham 1989a: 55); its means of realization was typically more American than British. By contrast, the more internationalist cinema of the 1940s and 1950s adopted British production models while producing a film-making that confirmed the nativist 'Australian' statements of Chauvel's *Forty Thousand Horsemen* (1940) in films like *The Overlanders* and *Eureka Stockade*. British directors in the 1960s and early 1970s confirmed this in *They're a Weird Mob*, *The Age of Consent* with its British artist played by James Mason going native in the Australian tropics, Tony Richardson's *Ned Kelly* (1970) with

Mick Jagger as the eponymous Irish Australian bushranger/freedom fighter against British rule), right down to Nicholas Roeg's updating of *Back of Beyond* with its story of children lost in the desert, in *Walkabout*. Australia's implied connection with the UK necessarily produces such outcomes. In some ways, the Australian film revival had its basic 'national' repertoires set by British and North American directors and studios (re)imagining Australian difference as an internationally marketable commodity from the 1940s. This mutual interpenetration of British and Australian cinemas led Pauline Kael (1986: 247) to quip that *Chariots of Fire* was 'probably the best Australian film ever made in England'.

The 1970s and 1980s saw local film-makers and critics modelling their films and criticism through a complex amalgam of these US and British influences. Critics wrote of 'Hollywood Genres, Australian Movies' (Cunningham 1985) and of 'Australian Movies and the American dream' (Glen Lewis 1987). film-makers move between each. Peter Weir made his landmark revival film, *Gallipoli*, which US-based critic Marcia Landy, claims is a remake of the British 'art cinema' classic, *Tell England* (Asquith and Barkas 1931, see Routt 1994b: 68–9). And the resemblance between the two films is uncanny – the Gallipoli campaign, the futility of war, the friendship between two men. Weir's next film was very different. He again used David Williamson as one of the scriptwriters, but the film, *The Year of Living Dangerously*, was a political thriller set in Indonesia.

The British and American connection is explicable in that Australian culture is as Bell and Bell (1993: 202) observe a culture melded of 'various British and US heritages' – 'a distinctive subset of American-accented culture, not its colonized or disempowered victim'. These heritages can, at times, seem to dominate Australian cinema and culture. In 1958 Tom Weir (1985: 144) wrote in *The Nation* that the Australian film industry was 'bastardized' 'undeveloped' 'weakly articulated' and 'torn between two dominant cultures'. John Tulloch characterized the Australian industry of the 1920s and 1930s and 'Hollywood's ultimate control of Australian cinema' as being 'the result of competing imperialisms within Australia' (1982: 40) – British colonialism *and* American cultural imperialism. Stuart Cunningham (1991) used the terms 'second cinema' to characterize Australian and Canadian cinema's place in the 1930s through to the 1950s. He found (1991: 13) a 'semi-peripheral' or '"dominion capitalist" relationship in a global audio-visual political economy'. He insists on Australian cinema's complicity in that '[i]t is the effective alignment of Australian interests with British and American interests, even as those latter interests shift and enter into competition, that characterize the Australian cinema's "Second World" status'. Dermody and Jacka (1988a: 20), for their part, argue of the 1970s revival that Australians are 'fixed in a series of radically unequal economic and cultural exchange with Britain and the US'. They continue:

> The 'second world' we inhabit is bound to reproduce the first world [UK and the USA], but needs to assert a measure of independence, of product differentiation, to market or circulate our reproductions. ... Second-world countries

like Canada and Australia are riddled with post-colonial ambiguity and anxieties. . . . our identity becomes both clamorous and permanently obscure. . . . For where do 'we' end and the 'other' begin? Who is the other by which we define our difference, ensuring 'us'? Britain? America? How are 'they' to be satisfactorily disentangled from what we have internalized and hybridized from them? Our film industry proclaims its central role in revealing an identity we don't know we have until we recognize it.

These are not only different interpretations of the Australian dilemma with respect to the dominant nodes of the English language, they are also descriptions of different situations. Dermody and Jacka are writing about the well-funded, post-1970 Australian cinema and not the straitened circumstances of production in previous decades where British and American agency played such a crucial role. Consequently the relation between, on the one hand, the Australian film industry and, on the other hand, the English and American industries seems to be less about structural conditions that about 'local mindsets'.

Dermody and Jacka's quotation also opens on to the powerful sense in both Australian and Canadian film-making projects that there is a need to work at trying to produce national differences rather than these being self-evidently apparent. Such a culture has to be self-consciously made, fashioned, created and found by them. Their cinemas are perpetually emergent. This can be a project firing the imagination of critics, film-makers and policy-makers turning on a sense of 'auto-creation' (creating oneself out of a relation to oneself). Here it seems one can and should be creating a culture from scratch – and with this experiencing the 'violence' of an identity achieved through a separation, sometimes painful, sometimes difficult, sometimes impossible – from that with which one is familiar in the USA and Britain. Alternatively it can be the struggle to reclaim a past hidden from view, crowded out by the contemporary force of American imaginings.

Any projection of Australian difference seems always threatened, overwhelmed, compromised by the equally threatening projections of Australian likeness and indistinguishability. film-making becomes a protective mechanism, an umbrella for a weakly developed Australian culture which is, itself, always under threat. At the same time, what that culture – the dominant American and, to a lesser extent, British one – is like and how it is structurally integrated into the cultural industries or the larger English language cultural area, provides an alternative collection of identities and projects. These are based on an identity as part of this larger cultural area. Here the project is one of participation, not separation; interchangeability, not a longed-for incommensurability; shared culture, not cultural specificities. film-making becomes a facilitatory mechanism for participating in a common English-language culture, a common new world society, a shared entertainment culture, a transnational film industry. The Australian cinema becomes an 'accent' – critics and film-makers can think, with Graeme Turner (1986: 8), that Australian cinema has 'a kind of Australian accent

which is audible and distinctive when placed in relation to that of other English
speakers' – or they can simply think that the Australian and Canadian are
indistinguishable from this larger cultural area. But Australian and Canadian
participation in an English-language culture dominated by American and British
culture can seem equally attenuated from inside and outside. It is available more
as an Australian and Canadian recognition than others looking in on them.
Canadians refer to a shared North American culture, Americans to a US culture;
Eric Michaels speaking as an American observer of the Australian scene reckons
Australians imagine themselves as becoming 'Yanks' while in reality they are
becoming something different (1990: 62).

   In both countries, two seemingly opposed industrial and critical strategies have
evolved. One crafts a film-making from a focus on the specifically Canadian or
Australian themes and national specificities: producing an international art cinema
vehicle, taking local 'events' like the Azaria Chamberlain story, or popular
national narratives – *Anne of Green Gables* (Sullivan 1985) in Canada and *They're
a Weird Mob* in Australia to craft a popular product. The cinema is associated with
cultural values – aesthetically in an art or quality cinema and culturally in the
sense of the all too mundane national culture and its archive of myths and symbols.
The other crafts the Canadian and Australian as close as possible to the American,
becoming to an extent interchangeable with it producing, or rather trying to
produce, dominant international cinema.

   These two models – Dermody and Jacka (1988a: 12–13) describe them as
'industry 1' and 'industry 2' respectively – seem to pose a great alternative facing
Australian and Canadian production and policy-makers. Graeme Turner (1993b:
70) maintains that this produces the structural tension of Australian cultural
policy as

> a small and economically weak nation is torn between adjusting what it does in
> order to compete internationally (and these adjustments often seem to mean the
> denial of specificity, the thorough internationalization of its activities), or
> alternatively maintaining a close relation between its actitivies and a sense of
> national identity – even where this incurs economic penalties.

In film this boils down to whether or not film-making should emphasize Australian
or Canadian singularity (and use this as either the route to a universality of appeal
or a pact with its local audience)? Or should it emphasize what is universal (the
American), utilizing the generic norms and aspects common to film-making and
social experience (and use this as the road to universality and local and international success)? Through operating these antinomies we pose 'quality' Australian productions with a literary precurser like *My Brilliant Career* against a
low-brow action genre, or a 'quality' cinema (the English speaking version of the
European 'art film') against a 'commercial' cinema.[12]

The product of both attempts in Australia and Canada also suffers from their dismissal locally and in the USA (and beyond) as either well-intentioned and boring in the case of 'quality' film-making, or as a lesser version of the American and therefore not particularly interesting to Americans, the British, continental Europeans or Asians.[13] As Safford put it: Australian and Canadian cinema are 'an independent and, thus marginal cinema, forever to be dominated by our own. The British make better films anyway' (Safford 1995: 28).

For the Australians and the Canadians, the cultural proximity with the USA ensures that the 'Australian' and the 'Canadian' can easily become stand-in substitutes for the American or British with only small shifts of emphasis. If film-making is always a matter of selection and combination then it is comparatively easy to select and combine in such a way that the Australian or Canadian location could be American (*Fortress*, the second *Mission Impossible* series (Bole and Manners 1989) or British (Hall's *The Silence of Dean Maitland* for example in 1934; and Franklin's *Patrick* in 1978). Downplaying the obvious Canadian or Australian markers is an important market reality, given the significance of the Hollywood majors and minors to international distribution and the successful taking up of Canadian and Australian films. 'De-Canadianization' and 'de-Australianization' are typical strategies to get product past these institutional gatekeepers – and not only into the USA but also into Europe, Japan, Latin America and even the home market. Thus for film-makers whose 'market' includes the USA (and this can be either US distributors for international circulation and/or actual US audiences) it is quite typical for them to feel compelled to efface signs of national difference in their work (see Parker 1993: 220).

The close identification of the American cinema as a programme for Canadian and Australian cinema is not just a move made for the purposes of transmission, or profit, or reputation, it is culturally appropriate. Richard Franklin, one of the most underrated of 1970s directors, made this argument in 1980 (411). He argued that Australia was close to America culturally and that our films should acknowledge this, as too often they failed to. Instead, they focused on the differences. For Franklin, the Australian audiences' relation to the cinema was defined through Hollywood and its genres and that 'next to the pub there is a Colonel Sanders'. He used this to argue that it was 'downright culturally inaccurate' to focus just on the residual Australian and to screen out all the other influences and therefore to speak of there being a film-making that was specifically Australian. In this sense, a horror film like *Halloween* (Little 1978) and Franklin's own 'horror' contribution *Patrick* was more 'Australian' than films like Bruce Beresford's *Don's Party* which made much of Australian speech, literally accenting the differences. Franklin implied that if one was to make cinema in Australia, to make a cinema that engaged its audience emotionally and psychically, then it would be through Hollywood genres. For Franklin, recognizing this entailed a strategy of internationalization. In his *Roadgames* he had Stacy Keach and Jamie Lee Curtis on the Nullabor as an American truck driver and hitchhiker respectively.

Canadian and Australian producers experience these two film-making options as dilemmas more acutely and routinely than do continental Europeans who, it should be noted, also have their 'mid-Atlantic production' and 'Euro-puddings' (even the USA has its avowedly 'international' films). At the root of both of these seeming alternatives is the extent to which we can define and espouse Australian cinema and Australian culture as a separate and relatively autonomous entity in the cinema (a national cinema) and with it a sovereign nation among nations (national culture among national cultures), and Australian cinema and society as a collection of film-making projects and social modalities that are part of the larger English-language, European and Western – and increasingly Asian – cinema and culture.

The close proximity of both terms can be seen in the following remarks from Dr George Miller:

> we are Australians, we are Australian film-makers. I think, without even trying, the Australianness comes through in the film, so you can't suddenly export yourself, as it were, and make films without that Australian point of view. Even though our culture reproduces to some degree the American, British, European and, in a little way, Asian culture, I think that makes us even in a very subtle way peculiarly Australian and you can never get around that.
>
> (Quoted in David White 1984: 96)

Australian cultures seem to be an accentuation of these cultures and Australian cinema a pathway within their film-making. For Dr George Miller, this is not a problem; there is no choice to be made between them. The coming together of these diverse cultural accents constitutes the inescapably Australian and relational character of these films. The Australian voice in the cinema is a way of being hybrid. If Miller is right, there must be a natural inability to decide between these international/national terms in the Australian context. This suggests the artificial nature of the opposition between the specifically Australian and the international Australian. This situation is not a good thing nor is it a bad thing; it is simply an aspect of who Australians are and what their film-making project is. The tension between Australian singularity and American (and other) universality is overt, organizing the differences between and within film-making projects alike. The Australian cinematic identity, its culture, its projects for the cinema are shaped by these binaries – neither of which tell the whole or the true story. The careers of individual directors, scriptwriters, producers and funding agencies back up Miller's assessment.

Australian film-makers find it easy to work within American film-making and cultural norms. Fred Schepisi maintains that it is 'easier for Australians to go and work in that area [Hollywood, universal film]' than it is for many other nationals. He goes further:

and I don't mean to sell out and make commercial films and bland, mass appeal things. It's the way we grew up: we didn't necessarily grow up with a great culture of our own only; as much, if not more, we grew up with English culture and American culture. . . . While we're not American or English it's part of us, it's just as much a part of us as being Australian. So it's not like we're going over and working in some strange area entirely.

(Schepisi to Koval 1992: 42)

If Schepisi is talking about Australian directors in Hollywood he could also be talking about tensions in the work of Australian-based directors. Phil Noyce directed the 'very Australian' *Newsfront* with its residual anti-Americanist, anti-cold war rhetoric in the late 1970s and later directed the (pro-American) Tom Clancy Hollywood thriller *Patriot Games* – yesterday's anti-American becomes today's Australian American director. This schizophrenic quality which makes distinguishing between American, British and Australian components of the culture so difficult, always shifting intergenerationally and historically, leads to an unsettling quality in local and Canadian product, in part because their product can look like American and British film without quite being that. As one of the American fans of Canadian film-maker, David Cronenberg put it to him:

the fact that you make your films in Canada makes them even more eerie and dreamlike, because it's like America, but it's not. The streets look American, but they're not, and the accents are American, but not quite. Everything's a little off-kilter; it's sort of like a dream image of America.

(Quoted in Parker 1993: 221)

Contrast this with Miramax's Tony Safford's account of what 'Americans want from Australian cinema':

Over in America, we have a profound sense that you have some kind of distinct history, culture and identity to express. We're just not entirely sure what. This vagueness is actually a great advantage when seeking the attention of American distributors who will occasionally present something different . . . but not too different; and when competing for the hearts and minds of American filmgoers who will occasionally seek out something different . . . but not too different.

(Safford 1995: 27)

Take those most cinephile of films the *Mad Max* cycle. The films translate and transform international styles, themes, and stories. Ross Gibson identifies the character of the *Mad Max* cycle as one of a dialogue between two orders of knowledge: the national culture and the international popular culture:

The [*Mad Max*] stories take into account the undeniably complex inter-relationships now existing in Australia between an orthodox, officially sanc-tioned National Culture and the constantly mutating complex of images and ideas that comprises the international popular culture that gets imported and consumed here with such enthusiasm.

(Gibson 1988: 29)

Mad Max's significant images lingered well beyond the time and place of their screening, the images – despite (or perhaps because of) the film's generic origins – articulating collective neuroses and fears. The film's violence was implied rather than on-screen. A measure of its cinematic achievement was that audiences remember a violence in excess of what was literally there. From its opening: the parallel cutting between the mayhem of the chase and Max's excessively slow driving preparations (which recalls moments from Sergio Leone's *Once Upon a Time in the West* 1968); the film announced itself as display, as having a relation to the cinema generally. This relationship was enhanced by its singular feel for *mise-en-scène*, and its delight in traversing the surfaces of space, bodies and equipment.

Mad Max was one of those films which, despite the fact that in terms of its story line it narratively resolves itself, audiences are still invited to keep returning and adding to it. From the beginning it was a film which could carry a sequel. Hence the pleasurable surprise and palpable disappointment of audiences for *Mad Max 2: The Road Warrior* and *Mad Max 3: Beyond Thunderdome*. What was on screen was not how they had projected the story forward, nor could anything on the screen succeed in closing the story off. The cycle's quality of excess made it capable of being considered both as an international film *par excellence* and as a reworking of Australian historiographical understandings (Gibson, 1992: 158–77). In *Mad Max* Dr Miller and Byron Kennedy created the single most powerful male lead in Australian cinema – Mel Gibson. From the first time we see him – a fragment of his body – the film insists as only Charles Chauvel before him had, with Robert Tudawali as Marbuk in *Jedda*, that here was a screen presence that could stop a story. Max, once he has duly buttoned up, put on his sun glasses and turned the ignition does indeed stop the chase, stop that part of the story. But the film had predicted this through its cross-cutting and the deliberately different and slow responses of Max. The film had, by marking the absence of action on Max's part, created Max as a figure of powerful action.

If *Mad Max* conjured up an everyday murderousness this was probably due to its carnival of flesh and body. At its heart, *Mad Max* was a story of mutilation, disempowerment and re-empowerment. Its maiming was carefully choreo-graphed: a hand missing here, a limb there, a leg in plaster, a body beneath a tent in too appalling a shape to be seen. Thus the film inscribed upon the male bodies on screen an almost hysterical anxiety – a fear of literal and symbolic castration. Max's body bears the marks of his journey. But unlike Charlton Heston in Anthony Mann's *El Cid* (1961) there is, at the end, no woman to deny in favour of the greater good. This is because the death of Max's wife and child has been the making of Max. Their death was what convinced him to take on the role of avenger and not the earlier 'vegetable' fate of his mate.

Mad Max invites collusion, not distance from its audience. In this he is unlike a Bond or a Rambo. Max is emotionally and physically vulnerable. The social power of the film lies in this engendering of a sense of collusion. Its vehicular violence makes sense in relation to the testing of masculinity at traffic lights or on country roads. The kinds of scenes played out in *Mad Max* are the kind of waking nightmare that makes karate schools popular.

The staging for *Mad Max*'s striking, disturbing, and surreal images is country roads. This makes good sense financially, as country roads are cheaper for staging action scenes. Less needs to be controlled and there's less mess to clean up. But it does not end there. *Mad Max* is Australian gothic. Its country road location can be understood in relation to everyday talk of roads and horror stretches. Thus economic necessity meshes with a social landscape in which it is quite logical to depict the spectacular murderousness of the high speed head-on collisions on country roads, rather than the more routine violence of the city traffic accident. To put the contrast crudely, Americans dream of freeway pile-ups and their exploitation films have 'crazies' driving spectacularly through crowded city streets; Australians dream of cars coming over hills on the wrong side of the road.

In *Mad Max*'s climax Max kills the leader of the motorcycle gang who has been responsible for the death of his wife, child and friends. The generic convention leads us to infer that Max will extract ultimate retribution by his own hands. But he does so not by his own hands, gun or car. Instead he forces the bikie into a head-on collision with a truck. The film goes from a giant close-up of the bikie's eyes to a long shot (subsequently shown to be Max's perspective) of a semi-trailer (prime mover) gradually and inexorably grinding the bikie and his bike into the bitumen. The truck appears out of nowhere. There is hardly a truck in the rest of the film. Is it too outlandish to suggest that this disruption of the film's carefully contrived diegetic world works for its Australian audiences because it captures all too well the motorists' routine nightmare of their own death? It is a death which comes from not paying enough attention to the road and is delivered by that most impersonal of agencies, a semi-trailer.

Dr George Miller, when asked by an interviewer whether his reworking of a quintessentially American genre was 'Australian' or not replied that he thought it was. He based his reply not just on the fact that American films were the ones that he grew up with and knew best, but because in Australia road accidents were 'a socially acceptable form of violence' with Australia having the 'highest incidence of road trauma in the world', and because:

> The Americans have a gun culture – we have a car culture. ... Out in the suburbs it's [cars] a socially acceptable form of violence. That's the wellspring a film like this has.
>
> (Miller, quoted in Kaufman and Page 1979: 8)

In the Australian film-making milieu, we are dealing at every move – if my analysis of *Mad Max* is correct – with a space that constitutively includes both the options of Australianization and de-Australianization – separately and singly and sometimes in the same film. These two options are simply extreme forms of political, marketing and sense making options, which belie the space of a hybrid film production industry and film-making which typically incorporates both aspects. Even the Australian film-making most concerned to accentuate the difference, and dominated by a concern for the nationally-specific (historical and contemporary) – the 1970s and 1980s classics such as *My Brilliant Career*, *Breaker Morant* and *Gallipoli* – are readily assimilable into the American 'quality film'. These are the kind of films which will be awarded an Oscar, as Peter Weir's and Bruce Beresford's subsequent Hollywood careers and Jane Campion's *The Piano* demonstrate.

AN ANTIPODAL CINEMA

The balance of cultural and economic exchange between 'us' and 'the other', whether Britain or the United States, remains drastically unequal. We are post-colonial, without being post-revolutionary. We cannot in any way afford too much difference. But without some, we shrivel in self-esteem and are obliged to live in an uninterpretable void, a place-less, story-less limbo.

(Dermody and Jacka 1987b: 11)

Such is one assessment of the consequences to Australia of unequal cultural exchange: a hopelessly compromised antipodal identity and culture. But such antipodal relations can have a positive face in the work of McKenzie Wark, Morris, Routt, Gibson, Cunningham, Tulloch and Turner. Unequal cultural exchanges are the normal condition of most nations in the world (given that most are small- to medium-sized). While a measure of unequal cultural exchanges holds for large countries such as France, the UK and Germany, and can be seen in the disproportionate presence of Hollywood on their screens, this inequality is that much more marked in small- to medium-sized countries.

Australian cinema relies on innovation, through producers and audiences alike adjusting local cinema and cultural traditions to common international formats most evident in contemporaneous US and to a lesser extent British imports. Australian cinema can simultaneously appear too 'American' by the fact of evident and imagined imitation and not 'American' enough in the textual and on-screen results.

Australian cinema routinely faces the problem of differentiation. If it strives to be too like Hollywood major product, or the British cinema or the European art film then comparisons will inevitably be made which disadvantage it. With the original already at hand, Australian cinema must not imitate so much as negotiate. Given the importance of Hollywood in the Australian market, Australian cinema's difference from it has to work somewhat differently than it would if there was a language barrier.

The Australian film-maker inevitably comes to be different from her or his audience. The audience can happily wonder or unhappily lament the non-coincidence of Australian and Hollywood film-making norms or the lack of Australian experiment of the kind associated with French and Brazilian cinema. The audience can imagine Australian versions principally because they do not have to do any more than have that fleeting image of what it could look like. The film-maker, by contrast, learns the hard way that copying is actually difficult; unlike variety and infotainment television there is no remaking of the copy; there is, rather, the burden of originality, the reality of differentiation. Trying to be the same leads to a confrontation with difference, to questions of accent, domestic social texts, scale, budgets – questions of what can or cannot be staged, in other words the need to differentiate, to occupy the spaces that Hollywood does not. To be like 'Hollywood' is to aspire to the conditions of the majors but to pursue in reality the strategies of the undercapitalized North American independents (and none of this need be entertained by the audience who only need to work through so far).

For Wark what is important about these 'unequal flows' (of cultural product and cultural power) is that they give rise to 'problematic uses of displaced cultural matter' (1992: 437) in the receiving country. He claims that the 'almost over-whelming flow of dominant culture' makes it difficult in the antipodes to draw 'a line between self and other' (437). To be antipodean then is 'to write from the perspective of the *minor* term in any and every vectoral equation' (443, my italics).

One consequence of such unequal flows is that 'the national always hinges on a problematic relation to the international, and the cultural to a crisis-prone antipathy to the economic' (442). In antipodean contexts it is not possible to separate the economic from the cultural or the national from the international in ways that it is possible 'in a metropolitan country' (441). Furthermore, the uses to which this 'displaced matter' of the 'dominant culture' are put seem 'perverse' and 'paradoxical' cross-cultural readings (435); they also lead to equally perverse and paradoxical writings and film-making. That is to say the situation is neither a one-off anti-imperialist retort, a hegemonic surrender, a co-option or an equal negotiation.

Something of this is evident in Tony Safford's appraisal of *Mad Max 2: The Road Warrior* and *Camera Natura* (R. Gibson 1984) – two films which drew him 'to this strangely familiar far-off place':

> *The Road Warrior* strikingly recasts a familiar American genre – a cowboys and Indians shoot-em-up – on to a post-punk, post-holocaust Australian landscape. Ross Gibson's *Camera Natura* is a bizarre and hallucinogenic compilation on Australian identity using maps, paintings, writings, myths, photography and cinema. For me . . . these two films are the true expressions of what I would call Australian cinema or, better, an 'antipodal cinema' – fractured, chaotic, oddly informed by cinematic and cultural history by virtue of being so close yet so far away from me.
>
> (Safford 1995: 29)

In the antipodean context there is an 'experience of a lack of common narrative, central authority, unity of place and time'. And this underwrites the experience of its cinematic diversity. Further:

> All authority in antipodean experience is either too close and too shallow or too distant and too obscure to have any real effects. One either worships imperial power or resents it – both relations at a distance.
>
> (Wark 1992: 443)

This antipodal character takes on a characteristically Australian form. These dynamics occurred in Australia through 'the combination of shared language with the 'tyranny of distance' which 'made us neuroticly fixated on the antipodean relation' (Wark, 1992: 437). In a similar vein, Ross Gibson (1992: xi) finds that Australia 'is both a long way from the world ... *and* it is nowhere in particular, in the swirl of electronic information and entertainment'. This makes Australia something of 'a depot and a clearing house' for 'ideas, raw materials and artifacts'. These are however transformed, they become 'feral ... both wild and captive' (Gibson 1992: xi). The term is increasingly used as a metaphor for (white) Australian society with, for example, its convict roots. In some circumstances it has become a kind of celebration of the bending, the transformation and the indigenizing alongside a necessary recognition of its possible inappropriateness and flawed character.

No account of the similarities and differences of Australian cinema to others can ignore its relative geographic and cultural isolation. In one of David Perry's films from the mid-1970s a voiceover for an image of a Nescafé coffee container says words to the effect that everywhere else seemed exotic because Australia was so isolated, but then air travel came and we imagined that everywhere was the same. A similar argument has been most forcefully put by Bertrand and Routt (1989: 4) in terms that fit Wark's antipodal model:

> Australia is an island at the end of the world, necessarily insular and isolated. Its people identify themselves accordingly: constantly seeking to be the same as everyone else – denying the insularity and isolation – and at the same time different, in aggressive celebration of those same conditions.

It is surrounded on all sides by sea; and three sides by vast oceans; and on the fourth by a Melanesian and South-East Asian states – all of which are at large distances from the principal Australian population centres. Bertrand and Routt go on to argue that these terms are also the historic terms of film-making and debates about it. This dynamic helps explain some of its ambiguous and oscillating characteristics: wanting to produce the same films, denying the consequences and reality of insularity and isolation, yet aggressively celebrating these differences.

This also produces interpretative uncertainties: when are we looking at something the same, when are we looking at something different? Gibson would argue that this is typical of Australian artifacts 'recognizable yet chimerical, present yet exotic' (xi). For Bertrand and Routt (1989: 4):

> Simultaneous similarity and difference, and the tensions created thereby, have affected both the organization of the Australian film industry as a socio/ political/industrial institution and the ideology of the films which are made

here. Similarity and difference structure the debates that have raged for so many years around the issue of whether the production industry should be aimed primarily at an international or a national market, whether Australian films should speak of whatever may be specific to Australia or only what might have 'universal appeal'.

What is different for some about Australian cinema is what is the same for others; what is culturally similar is also that very film which is dissimilar; one person's original Australian film or television programme is another's imitation (see O'Regan 1993: 14–17). This axis also structures Australian understandings of what is produced and imported. It produces anxiety about lack of originality and the effect on Australians of what is imported; just as it promotes vigorous assertions of originality, identity and Australian competence to produce cinema to an international standard.

Something of this sense of Australian particularity in its relationship with the international film industry and global film economy can be seen in Cunningham's (1991: 14) argument that '[u]nlike Third World countries, dependence and political-economic development in Australia were not mutually exclusive.' He suggests that cinema 'at every level' in Australia has been informed by 'complex relations of dependency'; *but* these 'cannot simply be posited as relations of domination and inhibition'. Bell and Bell suggest that a better term for dependency might be 'implication'. This still recognizes the junior partner status and marginal characteristics of these relations from the Australian perspective, but it stresses local agency more. These unequal but interdependent relations facilitate as much as inhibit the Australian cinema.

Antipodality moves in two directions. Australia shares the same industrial and modernizing cultural connections that The Netherlands, Belgium or the Scandinavian states experience *vis-à-vis* the UK and the USA. And it shares specific social and cultural similarities in Australia's cultural identity as an English-language 'new world' society founded like the USA on British imperial expansion. Perhaps it is not surprising that so much Australian cinema narrativizes its antipodality – simultaneously acknowledging interdependence (which is all too prone to abject dependence) and avowing personal integrity. This is the cinema of the 1970s which Max Harris (1979) lionized for thematizing 'how people can live with themselves when they have chosen to work in an insistently corrupting and disruptive world'. The drama of national subordination (and a necessary division between national identity and state that accompanies it (see Kapferer), is one played out often in Australian film. In *Newsfront* it is the Bill Hunter character refusing to hand over to his Americanized brother his film of the notorious water polo game between Hungary and Russia in the 1956 Melbourne Olympics.

Australian cinema is structured by the options available to it in the international system, given its exhibition and distribution market, its English-language character, its size and place in the cinema and its close connection with, and difference from, American and British culture. Acutely posed are the problems of both its own distinctiveness and its own capacity to pass for being American and British. These structural characteristics see Australian cinema operating in conditions of permanent and unequal cultural exchange with respect to the international cinema(s). The antipodal condition is central to the Australian negotiation of its possibilities. Australian film-makers need to provide inventive solutions to being on the margins of the more dominant film cultures of the USA, UK and continental Europe.

Chapter 5

Formations of value

PROMOTING AND DEVALUING AUSTRALIAN CINEMA

Value is an inescapable feature of all cultural objects. Disputes over value are likewise inescapable (see Frow 1995, B. Smith 1988). Value is especially significant for Australian cinema. It needs to be positively regarded by audiences, distributors, exhibitors, investors and critics. The 'public' needs to feel well disposed towards Australian cinema to sustain ongoing governmental commitment. Governments need to see their film support as both a public good and electorally valuable in order to justify their outlays in the face of competing demands. Australian cinema needs not only a cinematic identity but a positive one. It needs not only an international presence but international standing.

Only Hollywood and parts of Indian and Hong Kong cinema can get by without acquiring too much cultural authority. They can be simply commercial and/or exploitation cinema. But not so the Australian national cinema. Its precarious commercial position makes activists seek cultural authority inside and outside film networks. They publicize the social and aesthetic value of Australian cinema, enlisting the help of two distinct vocabularies of value.

The first of these vocabularies espouses cultural values, dialogic cultural exchange and the ecology of a film culture. Cultural values are opposed to a solely commercial calculus, dialogue to exploitative unequal exchanges (imperialism) and a film culture to the economy of a film industries. In this vocabulary national cinemas are seen to be intrinsically more significant than Hollywood. Prestigious and Other or Third national cinemas are more worthy than 'run of the mill' national cinema. Films of a local minor stream are more credible than those of the commercial mainstream. These more valuable aspects of the cinema accrue the symbolic benefits of higher cultural authority by being associated with notions of heterogeneity, innovation and diversity at social, aesthetic and political levels.

The second of these vocabularies connects culture and commerce rather than unilaterally opposing them. Cultural value is connected with a commercial calculus, necessarily unequal exchanges and film industries more generally. Varieties of popular art in a popular film-making are preferred to the élite art of 'quality' and Prestigious film-making. In this way Hollywood is valued as a vernacular popular cinema uniquely able to speak to the people of the world. This vocabulary reverses the direction of the first: national cinemas are seen to be intrinsically *less valuable* than Hollywood. Prestigious and 'Other' or Third national cinemas are *less worthy* than 'run of the mill' national cinemas. Films of a local minor stream are *less credible* than those of the commercial mainstream. Hollywood accrues the symbolic benefits of higher cultural authority by being likewise associated with notions of heterogeneity, innovation and diversity at social, aesthetic and political levels (with similar concepts of the first vocabulary only marshalled to different ends). Hollywood functions as a free-floating signifier of value able to be attached to a variety of local projects. Here an evident relation to the dominant cinema is valuable, while that to national cinemas is devalued.

Agents use both of these vocabularies to promote Australian cinema. They use the first to generate meanings of Australian cinema's significance, advantage and intrinsic worth as a cultural phenomenon both to the side of – and sometimes altogether outside of – the commercial operations of the Hollywood cinema. The category of a national cinema generates cultural capital by pushing aside commercial value sufficiently to allow for culturally valued films with some commercial potential. The very idea of a national cinema envisages a partnership of private capital and public funding to serve culture (in both the aesthetic and socio-cultural sense). The claim of cultural value is foundational to the establishment of the space of a festival cinema, the foreign film, the British and Australasian quality film, and alternative cinema alike. The national cinema idea provides a rhetorical means to think the necessity of public support, interest, help and marketing edge, without which Australian cinema could not survive. Activists especially use this vocabulary of value to argue for and legitimate those directions in the local cinema which most need the ballast of cultural value – a prestige, festival film-making and varieties of independent film-making (alternative, avant-garde and experimental, political, feminist, multicultural and Aboriginal film-making).

Agents use the second vocabulary to generate meanings of the significance and value of a local popular vernacular cinema able to speak to and connect with local and international audiences. They draw on Hollywood as the dominant model to legitimate an Australian film industry (see O'Regan 1984a). This vocabulary promotes a local film industry and attracts to the Australian cinema some of Hollywood's glory. Funding organizations, politicians, critics and film-makers value a popular cinema in its relation to Hollywood. *Mad Max II: The Road Warrior* is praised as 'an honest-to-goodness movie-movie of such breathtaking velocity' (Andrew Sarris quoted in Peary 1989: 207). Given the significant American presence in popular cinema, festival, quality and the various alternative cinemas, American film-making provides a privileged relation for agents in the Australian film milieu (including critics, audiences, film-makers, policy-makers and the cinema trade). Allusions to Hollywood provide a positive legitimation for independent films. Adrian Martin (1988a: 98) praises it as the true local heir to Hollywood's cinephilia, vitality, energy and innovation.

The combination of cultural value, separate to some extent from the market, and of commercial value connected to the market and Hollywood, is integral to the promotion of Australian cinema. It helped fashion a broadly based bi-partisan political programme for an Australian national cinema, by justifying that which could be simultaneously an alternative to and a supplement of the dominant Hollywood cinema, a film industry and a film culture. Agents in the film milieu want features to be profitable domestically *and* internationally, to be popular *and* well regarded by a large section of the home populace, to be innovative and excellent *and* conform to contemporary film-making norms, to be critically regarded *and* to be politically and socially acceptable. For every argument that it is the 'proper function of a national cinema to consciously and overtly strive to redefine and present those distinctions that make a difference culturally – if only to make them for a place in the popular memory' there is a corresponding argument that Australian cinema 'can afford, like Hollywood, to confuse itself with the world at large, and to be the commonplace stuff that the world's dreams are made on' (Routt quoted in AFC 1991: 66). film-makers want to create films across a variety of formats and genres, to make a popular film after a prestigious one, an industry documentary after a personal one. These two vocabularies of value shape how the local cinema is marketed. Publicists and critics take the spontaneous dancing in the aisles for *Strictly Ballroom*, the Cannes and Academy Award for *The Piano*, Nancy Reagan liking Bryan Brown in the mini-series *A Town Like Alice* (Stevens 1981) as evidence of discernment and use these to sell Australian quality to local audiences.

Both these formations of cultural value also *devalue* Australian cinema. Every national cinema attracts opprobrium from agents in the film milieu inside and outside the country. Australian cinema is an 'imitative' not an 'oppositional' national cinema. It is not a prestige cinema, unlike the French and Italian cinemas. It is not an Other cinema, unlike the Japanese and Taiwanese cinemas. In lacking artfulness and cultural difference, it is a mundane national cinema. In only its independent cinema can it aspire to innovation and cultural diversity. Critics, film-makers, lobbyists and audiences routinely single out the festival and independent parts of the national cinema as better, more progressive, 'eccentric' or artful than the bulk of mainstream Australian cinema (see Martin 1988a, 1994c, 1994d).

In any positive assessment of Hollywood, the Australian cinema also suffers. It is patently not Hollywood. It is a less popular, lesser version of it. It lacks Hollywood's vitality and energy, its powerful characterizations and production values (McFarlane and Mayer 1992). Audiences also routinely cite Australian cinema's inferior production values and lack of star appeal – reporting the consequence of its undercapitalized imaging compared to the highly capitalized Hollywood image (see, for example, Spectrum 1978). In video release, Holly-wood's popularity eclipses that of a shabby local cinema whose rental value to a video shop is increased by downplaying its local origin.[1] Hollywood even has the progressive social and aesthetic value which an Australian cinema lacks. In both cases, most Australian efforts are routinely compared with international films and are found wanting. The value of Australian cinema and its mainstream and minor stream alike are routinely contested by audiences, the cinema trade, critics, and film-makers by recourse to the same vocabularies of cultural value.

As we have seen, these two value formations are not sealed off from each other, but are typically pressed into service to promote and criticize Australian cinema, often marshalling elements of both formations of value. These formations rarely come to us in a pure form. They are nearly always mixed together. The national cinema ideal, the mundane, prestigious and Other cinemas, and the mainstream and minor stream film-making all emerged historically as a response to unequal cultural exchange and nonsymmetrical power relations in the cinema. The national cinema and independent ideal are not sensible without what they seek, in a very limited practical way, to overturn, delegitimize, reverse or even to graft themselves on to. Agents are therefore simultaneously against Hollywood and for it; against the mainstream and for it; simultaneously calling for a prestigious and culturally Other national cinema and wanting a popular mundane cinema. Both the support for the different types of national cinema and their denigration are foundational parts of any film milieu.

These formations of value provide the constitutional politics of any national cinema. They provide a commodious space for processes of valuation to be mundanely accomplished by a variety of agents who enlist them for their diverse ends. They provide tools, perspectives and contents to be drawn on in film-making, policy development and criticism. They legitimate and keep alive a variety of film-making and critical options. They provide multifaceted ways of valuing, knowing, acting and believing in an Australian cinema. They enable powerful distinctions to be made between national cinemas and the Hollywood cinema, between different national cinemas. and within national cinemas. They interact to provide for an economy of cultural value, a distribution of value, which at any moment defines the public standing of Australian cinema through an unstable hierarchy.

Since agents use both vocabularies of value to promote and demote Australian cinema alike on public and critical horizons,[2] neither should be regarded as having any especial standing *vis-à-vis* Australian cinema. Rather our attention needs to be on the *processes* of cultural evaluation that *operationalize* these vocabularies. Consequently this chapter is not concerned with determining the value or otherwise of Australian cinema but with attending to those vocabularies used by agents to ascribe positive and negative attributes. As establishing, maintaining and repairing cultural value is the customary practice of agents in the film milieu my concern is therefore with the governance of value in Australian cinema.

Creating and contesting hierarchies of value is integral to the very nature of film as symbolic good. Films ask audiences, critics and film-makers alike to value them, to measure their significance, not only in dollars at the box-office but in talk – word of mouth, publicity and critical estimation. The direction of the resulting hierarchies of value is neither stable nor without contestation. The field of

Australian cinema is one of an assemblage of competing, contesting and complementary value formations. It is driven by the will to value. Consequently our attention must be on the organization of evaluation in a field characterized by a dispersal of cultural value and authority (see B. Smith 1988: 148–81, Frow 1995: 22).

In the rest of this chapter, I chart the general form and distribution of these evaluations. I examine how Australian cinema is advantaged as a national cinema, how it is disadvantaged as a type of national cinema, how its minor stream is advantaged over its mainstream and finally how all of these three are contested through a re-evaluation of the dominant Hollywood and mainstream Australian cinemas.

VALUING THE NATIONAL CINEMA, DEVALUING HOLLYWOOD CINEMA

The national cinema ideal takes as the natural order a world where national cultures are sovereign cultures entering into mutually beneficial international dialogue. These cinemas each produce for their own markets and then exchange films or, alternatively, enter into co-production arrangements as equals.[3] National cinemas have conversations with other national and international cinemas,[4] where the local space of adaptation and revision is respected as a sovereign space. Films respect their local particularities and use these as a means to reach the universals of the cinema and humankind. For prominent playwright and scriptwriter, David Williamson (quoted in 'Writer's Offensive', 1980: 1), films work 'both at home and internationally' because of 'their uniqueness and integrity'. Local film-making should, ideally, project itself without outside interference and enter into international dialogue on its own terms and timetable.

These notions undergird the creation of a 'market' for 'foreign films' – a festival and alternative cinema – and they endow such features with interest and cultural value. They also provide a positive ideology for co-production arrangements. 'Evidence' is marshalled to support this national cinema ideal. Under the 'quality film' mandate of governmental policy-making over the latter half of the 1970s, a productive dialogue with British and European cinema developed. These influences modernized Australian cinema's aesthetic norms taking them beyond the melodrama, location westerns, and hillbilly films of the first half of the century. Ramona Barry (1994:9) recalls *Picnic at Hanging Rock*'s 'complete rejection of the classic Hollywood narrative in favour of a more esoteric European style'. Here was a film which demonstrated that 'success was attainable without having to imitate or compete against the far more established populist Hollywood style'. *Black Robe* is a co-production which secures the best of both worlds – an Australian and a Canadian film – that 'we can all enjoy' (Marshall and Turner 1992: 93).

We can, I think recognize in the national cinema ideal a dream of escape from the transnational fully blown and profane capitalist economy of Hollywood towards a more respectful cultural terrain characterized by barter, cooperation, human values, and the mercantile economy of the 'festival' film, co-productions and international festivals like Cannes. There is even the possibility of a site beyond economic accounting altogether, in the projection of a dependent national cinema transcending capitalism and preparing an exit to socialism (Willemen 1994: 204). Barbara Herrnstein Smith (1988: 112) sees such ideals as a 'recurrent impulse', given the centrality and 'inexorability of economic accounting in and throughout every aspect of human . . . existence'.

To endorse the national cinema is to endorse human and cinematic potential to the side of economic calculation. Such a cultural calculus is held out whenever agents pose an indigenous cinema with a direct and natural relation with its domestic audience. It also provides a way of establishing hierarchies of value between national cinemas and between parts of a national cinema. There are, it seems those film-making projects – particular national cinemas and particular tendencies within a national cinema – which are cultural, and those which are compromised by economic accounting. Those which are commercially driven are in Willemen's (1994: 204) terms a 'second cinema . . . seeking to find a lucrative niche' within the international cinema. In a series of broadcasts in 1981, John Hinde claimed that with the 'ocker cycle' of films of the 1970s there was the possibility of an indigenous cinema which Australians would need culturally, but this possibility was 'suppressed by the snobberies of a minority who didn't need them' (Hinde 1981: 123) like himself. After this, for Hinde, Australian cinema became just another struggling film industry interchangeable with the imported product.

The national cinema ideal needs these terms and the 'evidence' naturalizing them. These notions envisage Hollywood as usurping national sovereignty, recklessly distorting cinema markets globally, and contaminating local audiences, film-makers and exhibitors. Hollywood dominance of domestic screens and of box-office receipts breaches the sovereign national culture and turns the cinema away from its natural inclination. Action is therefore necessary to counter Hollywood's 'imperializing' presence so as to ensure the survival of local traditions, the transmission of social and aesthetic values, even culture itself. In this way, the existing international order of the cinema – which like any market is unequal since it is made of agents who do not conduct their transactions on the same footing – is reconfigured as an unnatural perversion of the cinema.

As the sovereign national space is invaded and bypassed, it becomes possible to call for local action and international negotiation at GATT or the new World Trade Organization (1995), in EC media policy or in national cinema policy addressing the aggrieved circumstance of a local national cinema. In this way governmental funding for an Australian film industry in 1975 was legitimated on the grounds that:

Australia, as a nation, cannot accept, in this powerful and persuasive medium, the current flood of other nations' productions on our screens without it constituting a very serious threat to our national identity.

(Interim Board Australian Film Commission)

The Hollywood competition is a cultural imperialism, precluding the local and engaging in unequal and unfair competition. Critics and film-makers working within a national cinema lament with Susan Dermody and Liz Jacka (1988a: 12) the interference caused by locally produced films having 'had to compete both at home and abroad within a set of viewing expectations that is American, or formed by American culture abroad'. Australian cinema is for them a 'perpetually displaced national cinema' (1987b:10). The national cinema fails to dominate the domestic box-office and win local audience loyalty because Hollywood has precluded it from developing an organic or 'seminal' (Hinde 1981: 24–5)) relation with its domestic audience. Australia's problem for John Hinde was that 'a local audience [was] debauched on other people's pictures' (1981: 148). Hinde and other critics, lobbyists and film-makers make American 'predators' responsible for precluding a natural and direct relation between the Australian product on screen and the local audience.

With the Americans there can be no principled equivalence, no conversation, no real communication. In the opinion of The Interim Board of the Australian Film Commission (1975: 36) '[l]ocations should not be given away to make decorations for overseas [i.e. Hollywood] films, but kept as a vital part of those films to be made by Australians'. Its justification: 'The Australian scene is as much a national resource as Australian minerals'[!] It follows that our identity, locations, stories need to be protected against overseas, i.e. Hollywood theft. Like all cultural imperialisms, Hollywood's effects are experienced not only in the perverted complexion of markets and investment but in the perversion of the national subject itself – the value and identity of a nation's citizens. America's offence is psychical: they are the privileged group, globally enforcing their world view. Australians respond by becoming identified with this American point of view and in the process their identity, history and culture are devalued.

Critics locate an abjection among audiences and film-makers alike to explain why a positive relation between the Australian audience and the Australian-produced cinema is so difficult to achieve. Dermody and Jacka (1988a: 20) argue that Australians and Canadians 'feel second best . . . forced to second guess what their authentic indigenous culture should be'. Some countries like France are able to see Hollywood infringing a glorious national cultural tradition which existed before this American century; 'Asia' can imagine a glorious future in which its present circumstances will be changed in an Asian twenty-first century, but 'new' nations like Australia have no glory to be subsequently corrupted, nor any future apart from more of the same. Their national cinema is a child, or an adolescent, trying to grow up and become something, but whose development is permanently arrested in a second cinema (Dermody and Jacka 1988a: 20).

The 'Australian' film, the Australian style and sensibility can seem yet to be adequately represented, yet to emerge, yet to find (adequate) expression, yet to be made. Sometimes it seemed to be there but then it was lost. Activists in the 1960s and critics in the 1980s find the beginnings of a genuine Australian cinema in Raymond Longford and Lottie Lyell's silent cinema – most particularly *The Sentimental Bloke* (Longford 1919) – judged by Ina Bertrand and William Routt (1989: 20) as 'among the very best films made anywhere before 1920 . . . one most certain entry this country has in the world's gallery of great films'. But Lyell died in 1925. Longford was treated shabbily by an American oriented trade that reviled him, unhappy with his antipodal innovations, so much so that Longford was lost to films, spending his later career working as a clerk on the Sydney wharves, dying, his work unrecognized in 1959.

The Australian industry too is full of 'sell-outs': films, film-makers, exhibitors, distributors and sometimes even audiences who make Australian cinema into, what Dermody and Jacka (1988a: 23) call, a 'neocolonial 'second cinema' that consciously and unconsciously strives to reproduce the Hollywood models of production and circulation, counterfeiting the local sense of historical reality'. Ramona Barry (1994: 9) laments *The Man from Snowy River* – it is:

> a deceptively un-Australian film. It fell neatly into the Hollywood western genre where boys become men and women fell at their feet no matter how feisty they started out. Even Hollywood legend Kirk Douglas was wheeled in for authenticity. It was a case of Australians looking overseas for their national identity and finding one they could be happy with. . . . Audiences lapped up this contrived national identity, leaving many of the more realistic cinematic ventures in the box-office dust.

Richard Franklin, became, for a time, the embodiment of these same problems in 1980. He was even asked to leave the country in an editorial in the *Sydney Morning Herald* (see S. Murray 1995: 57) and Actors Equity ran a strident campaign against his film *Roadgames* for its use of two American actors in the lead parts. Franklin, Simon Wincer (*Harlequin* 1980) and Tony Ginnane (producer of *Race for the Yankee Zephyr* – Hemmings 1981) were targeted by playwright and scriptwriter David Williamson,[5] in his capacity as spokesperson for the Australian Writers Guild, as producing 'concocted and contrived products made to crack the American market' (quoted in 'Writer's Offensive', 1980: 1). Their problem was that they were making an 'international product' (seen interchangeably as exploitive, commodified and American) which at worst ignored the local, and at best exploited it for profit in international circulation.

While the international cinema with which Australian cinema has respectful relations changes, what does not is the need to distinguish between respectful and disrespectful relations. With this comes a desire to expel some foreign elements in a bid to recover the national.[6] And this is an important theme in some films themselves, often arising when an American is included. Consider *Newsfront*'s attempt to sort out the ambiguous American legacy and the local. The American/

Australian relation becomes a family and political matter in the context of the Cold War. These relations are embodied in the juxtaposition between the Australian 'everyman' Len Maguire (Bill Hunter) and his grasping brother, Frank (Gerard Kennedy) and the circulation between them of the independent woman, Amy McKenzie (Wendy Hughes). Frank abandons her for his commercial career in the USA and returns to Australia thoroughly Americanized, while Len is abandoned by his wife, Fay (Angela Punch-McGregor) and an intolerant Catholicism that is prepared, like Frank, to do the handiwork of the US-inspired Cold War.

Just this sort of anti-Americanism permitted a generation of critics and film-makers to be attached to the national cinema as a progressive good, enabling them to be simultaneously anti-capitalist, anti-American and pro-internationalist (Routt 1994a: 218). Our righteousness – I include myself here – was sustained by a certainty that we apprehended culture and with it the need for non-exploitative dialogue. We envisaged the national cinema as a non-productive expenditure beyond, and antagonistic to, Hollywood's tawdry market values. The national cinema ideal thus licensed – albeit in a highly qualified way – a form of nationalism.

The national cinema ideal problematizes the international exhibition/distribution/production order. As this order is characterized by unequal national and language contributions, transnational operational and capital intensive investment and technological innovation, the national cinema ideal clears a place for a lower budgeted national cinema grafting itself on to this order without disturbing its fundamental relations too much. Lobbyists, politicians, critics and film-makers find it strategically useful in legitimating a variety of structural remedies. Intervening in the marketplace of distribution and exhibition habitually becomes the political economy solution to righting the perceived wrong of a national cinema which is disconnected and marginal to its domestic exhibition and distribution instruments (Tariff Board 1973: 20–1). This option is more talked about than enacted. Mostly the national cinema ideal provides inflated *publicity* for the local cinema which is then used by agents to naturalize the local cinema on diverse horizons.

Quotas limiting Hollywood screen presence so as to secure a minor local presence have been a feature of cinema markets since 1920 and are now integral to television. Profits from the screening of Hollywood programming are siphoned off to assist in the development of a local production capacity in cinema, television and VCR markets. The means to do so varies from country to country: in France it is monopoly importing agencies, in the UK box-office seat levies or in Australia proposed quotas on pay-TV operators. National governments have created subsidy schemes, tax concessions and grants to encourage the production of local programmes in cinema and television. Such measures have assisted domestic production but they do not substantially alter the organization of the international cinema market.

Sometimes the national cinema ideal has an even more basic purpose: to ensure that politicians, policy-makers and audiences recognize a film production sector. Part of forging a well-grounded Australian cinema supplement in the late 1950s and throughout the 1960s involved training politicians, government, critics and the general public to differentiate between an Australian film production industry and the American extension of Hollywood cinema in the Australian exhibition and distribution industry. The differentiation was neither that meaningful, nor pertinent to government as recently as the early 1960s. Once adopted though, it permitted existing relations within the cinema and television industries to be *problematized.*

The national cinema ideal permitted two industries, two interests, to be recognized: a production industry and an exhibition/distribution industry, in what had been previously a single Australian film industry dominated by the exhibition and distribution sector.[7] When this division became meaningful, equality, disadvantage and fair dealing between the two 'industries' could be mounted as an issue by the production industry agitation. In an era where there was concern to 'buy back the farm', this became an issue of American versus Australian interests.

Through these rhetorical means, a nearly non-existent feature film production industry and a marginal television drama production industry effectively campaigned to have themselves recognized by government and the media alike as the collective voice of the Australian film industry. The idea of special aid to this sector depended on constructing, then having the public recognize, film production as a needy, disadvantaged sector conferring pro-social and tangible national benefits while having the exhibition/distribution sector seen as largely foreign-owned and dedicated to the imported product. The idea of separate industries with opposing interests and priorities was circulated before diverse publics: to government by lobbying, to cultural readers through journals, film reviews and quality newspaper articles, to popular audiences through the mass circulation tabloids and television. A polemical cultural criticism was aligned with commercial industry bodies like the then Producers and Directors Guild of Australia in the umbrella organizations of the Australian Film Council.[8] The legitimate needs and grievances of the film production sector (indeed its very existence) all had to be naturalized on the governmental agenda. A measure of government recognition of production was the brief given to the federal industry advisory agency, the Tariff Board to investigate ways of assisting Australian film production and the subsequent establishment of the Australian Film Commission and various complementary state film bodies.[9]

The resulting naturalization of Australian cinema grafted the local industry on to the existing (local and international) cinema circuits. It did so without altering the rough division of international labour in the cinema and television industries: where distribution is dominated by the Hollywood majors and their associated companies and partnerships; while the exhibition side in the cinema and video chains and television stations leaves greater space for local control (though always with strong international links increasingly expressed in joint ventures).[10] The vilification of the major cinema chains – Hoyts (which was then controlled by 20th Century Fox and afterwards in American hands), Greater Union, Village, and the American major distributors – was meant to redress this situation by embarrassing these companies into working for local product. In the event, production subsidies and industry partnerships evolved, and producers benefited from the national and international facilities of the major chains and distributors.

What the national cinema ideal is necessarily blind to is that the Hollywood cinema has created cinema in the West, sustained its infrastructures, provided the incentive to invest in building and renovating exhibition infrastructures. It has created the multiplex rebuilding in Europe and Australasia of the 1990s and produced the incentive to invest in cinema technology, special effects, and the image sufficient to routinely attract a paying public to the cinema spectacle. For these reasons, the national cinema ideal in any practical implementation leaves substantially intact the exhibition, distribution and production nexus of the dominant international cinema – at best fiddling at its edges with a national cinema supplement or Australian content rules on television. It cannot challenge this nexus too much without compromising its own very possibility. It can establish, if not a directly competitive market reality for the national cinema, than a subsidized festival cinema market to one side. The national cinema ideal enables this cinema to acquire cultural capital that symbolically reverses the commercial order of the cinema, where unequal exchanges, dominance, hierarchies, the size and length of the multinational and national exhibition and distribution networks rule. It sounds strong minded and principled but it is constitutively weak in the alternative market realities it produces and sustains. At most it can only tinker, engaging in various supplementing activities justified by rhetorics of national sovereignty and sustained by formulas of abjection.

MAKING DISTINCTIONS AMONG NATIONAL CINEMAS

Some national cinemas are identified more in international and domestic circulation as prestigious or festival cinemas, some as Third cinemas and others as mundane cinemas. Historically the French cinema has been valued as a prestige cinema. African and Latin American cinema are valued as Other or 'Third cinemas' and are appreciated for their difference. The Australian and British cinemas are mostly mundane cinemas, seen to lack distinction and great value. Prestige and the Other cinemas maintain the national cinema ideal while mundane cinemas are compromised and complicit with Hollywood.

These 'types' provide a rough map of international standing in the cinema. The landmarks of film art when they are not in Hollywood are in the larger continental European national cinemas (of France, Germany, Italy and Russia) and Japanese cinema. These cinemas are the producers of distinctive auteurs and stylistic movements. British and Australian film-making contributes little to film art – indeed their prominent film-makers are often subsumed within Hollywood. For their part, the Bombay and Hong Kong cinema – both popular vernacular cinemas – appear in Western film markets and scholarship as Other cinemas (although Hong Kong cinema product is increasingly producing titles which, like Kurosawa's Japanese cinema of the 1950s and 1960s, is art and Other). Of course, there are exceptions. Bruce Lee's film cycle in the early 1970s crossed over and became a popular international cinema.

Some national cinemas have their feet in a number of camps. While a mundane cinema in Japan itself (as is every national cinema at some point), the Japanese cinema that circulates in the major film festivals, film history discourses, and art cinema houses outside Japan is a prestige and Other cinema – its prestige complements and drives interest in its Japaneseness. This gives rise to speculation about what is borrowed and what is authentic – where does John Ford's influence end and Akira Kurosawa's Japaneseness begin? What is a negotiation of European modernism and what a native cultural tradition? Taiwanese and mainland Chinese festival film-making is following this same path. Sometimes the film-making that represents the national cinema internationally in festivals and art cinema circuits is a stream specifically created for international consumption. Japanese, Brazilian, contemporary Taiwanese and mainland Chinese festival directors have built careers creating such product.

These distinctions affect how national cinemas are written. Prestige cinemas are usually written about in a different language from the cinema in question; they are often written by a national of a different country and they are destined for an audience other than the national audience of that cinema. The cinemas dealt with tend to be the famous large, 'art' cinemas, and those cinemas which have contributed significant cinema movements (Italian neo-realism, the French New Wave, New German Cinema). In the English language, these writings include English and American books, for example, Susan Hayward (1993) and Alan Williams (1992) on French cinema; Elsaesser (1989) and Timothy Corrigan (1983) on New German Cinema; and Donald Richie (1991) and Noel Burch (1979) on Japanese cinema. Writers and their readerships/viewers produce this cinema as something to be critically valued and pondered. They explicate films as the work of auteur directors; plot them as expressions of the various cultural movements – avant-garde, modernism or post-modernism; they 'read' films as symptoms of larger cultural, aesthetic, social and political unities such as fascism in Italy (Hay 1987), or post-war German cinema's 'unmastered past' (Kaes 1989). Such critics concern themselves with the conditions of production to better support their valuations of the films. Consequently production conditions occupy a subsidiary role to the 'being' or identity of the cinema.[11] This cinema seems to be attached to larger aesthetic and political 'movements' – modernity, postmodernity, and various avant-gardes. Not surprisingly such cinemas find their greatest assertions of value in the festival circuit, film retrospectives, and critical discourse on the cinema. Susan Hayward observes that this biases the film history, of say French cinema, to 'the province of high art rather than popular culture'

(1993: xi) such that its 'moments of exception and not the "global" picture' are typically addressed (ibid.).

Relatedly, there are the writings on the Other cinemas which are at some cultural, political and aesthetic distance from the dominant currents of Western and Hollywood film-making. Traditionally this has been the domain of the popular Indian (Rajadhyaksha 1986) and Chinese cinemas (Dissanayake 1988), but Japanese cinema is sometimes included here, as too are the Third World cinemas (Armes 1987) including the various Latin American and African cinemas (Diawara 1992). These cinemas make up an alternative space in the cinema whether as a foil to the first cinema, as an alternative aesthetic and political praxis, as a political counterpoint to the West, as a challenge to the norms of the major Western cinemas, or as a local negotiation of the larger themes of tradition and modernity. On this last point Robert Stam (1993: 239) appreciates modernity in Brazilian cinema as one of 'devouring imported cultural products as the raw material for a new synthesis, one which attempted to turn the imposed culture back, transformed, *against* the colonizer' [my emphasis]. He contends that this Third cinema develops as a 'cinema of research and experimentation, equidistant from both mainstream and auteurist cinema' (Stam 1993: 242). Critics find this cinema politically and aesthetically important because it projects alternatives to 'the festival cinema', 'the "first cinema" of Hollywood' and the second cinema of the Australian film revival. What connects both the prestigious and the Other national cinemas is that – in the English language – these provide one major basis for appreciating difference in the cinema. Taken together both project valued alternative cultural and aesthetic spaces.

Because their object is marked not by exoticism but by mundanity and therefore banality, writings on mundane cinemas are written in the same language and do not inspire as much external interest. They are often authored in the same country as the national cinema in question and are destined for an audience that is significantly made up – like the films themselves – both of people from that place and a smaller international readership. Such cinema is marginal to criticism. It combines none of the artistic dominance of continental European modernity nor the cultural and aesthetic difference of the Third cinemas. It can even lack cinematic merit. Truffaut once commented that Britain and cinema were contradictory terms. Writing in 1970, John Baxter (109) likewise claimed that the Australian is

> not a cinema minded person. He does not think in images, nor in the electric arcs of film. His existence, fragmentary and spare, feeds on passing things, not the deep continuing convictions that sustain great art.

This linking of national characteristics with a capacity to contribute to the cinema is inane – after all Truffaut acknowledged his debt to Britain's greatest director, Hitchcock, just as Kieslowski does to Loach. Such silliness contributes to habits of thinking, and ways of valuing British and Australian cinema, in which they become simply ordinary. As Andy Medhurst recently declared:

> British cinema is a cardigan. Cardigans are familiar, dependable and warm, with a leaning towards shabbiness, which is how many of us see much of our national cinema. That's a blinkered view, but again, like a reliable old cardigan it's very hard to give up.
>
> (1995: 16)

Writing for a local and a French audience keen to see a showcasing of Australian cinema at the Georges Pompidou Centre, Scott Murray (1994b: 143) writes that

> the vast majority of Australian cinema is mediocre. Far too many directors approach their work with little passion or innovation, without any sense of a personal vision or cinematic style. Rarely do they take hold of the material and breathe life into it; rather, they cautiously and routinely transfer the written page to the screen, often oblivious to the merits or otherwise of the original script.

The critic diagnoses the national cinema's failure – its dullness and its badness – and only sometimes explicates its successes and achievements. The British, English-Canadian and Australian cinemas suffer the reverse of French cinema: the local picture is ignored for the sake of the global picture.

Film-makers, policy-makers and cultural critics alike incessantly worry over the quality, depth and value of what is produced. Their major strategy is synoptic and symptomatic. They are frequently insistent about providing their international readers with the larger and therefore unflattering picture of cinematic history in the country: Australian film-makers 'have not consistently reached the high levels of the best European cinema' even though 'the best is certainly of world standard, and some of the directors (particularly Dr George Miller) are among the world's finest' (Scott Murray 1994b: 143). Such critics rigorously eschew turning the moments of exception into the rule.

Because of their emphases on the mundane, critics are sometimes just as much concerned with the conditions of production as they are with the films produced (on Australian cinema see Dermody and Jacka 1987b; on Canadian cinema see Pendakur 1990). Sometimes these conditions are even thought to be more interesting than the films themselves. Dermody (1981: 12), for example, makes the case that, in 1930s Australian cinema, 'the energy that went into ... producing the very means of production ... reached the films only in' an 'indirect form', leading her to write not about the Australian sound film but rather about the Australian who invented a rival sound system, thereby resisting Hollywood control.

Such cinemas also become interesting in their margins, where a mundane cinema meets the 'Others in its midst' and in their auteur directors. Contemporary British cinema becomes innovative, interesting and exemplary in its Asian and West Indian themed films like *Young Soul Rebels* (Julien 1991), *Sammy and Rosie Get Laid* (Frears 1987) and *My Beautiful Laundrette* (Frears 1985). Australian cinema becomes something more substantial in its margins: its Aboriginal and Islander peoples collaborating with white film-makers in *Two Laws* and *Exile and the Kingdom*; its Aboriginal film-maker Tracey Moffatt in *Nice Coloured Girls* (1987), *Night Cries* and *beDevil*; its 'multicultural' cinema of *Death in Brunswick* and *The Heartbreak Kid*; its 'camp sensibility' of *The Adventures of Priscilla: Queen of the Desert*; and in its structures to accommodate and nurture the work of women directors notably, Jane Campion (*Sweetie*), Jocelyn Moorhouse (*Proof*) and Gillian Armstrong (*The Last Days of Chez Nous*).

Australian and British cinema's auteur directors are seen as exceptions. Often this estimation is confirmed by their subsequent career in North America. An exception here is Powell and Pressburger whose subsequent *Australian* career is treated as an exile and punishment for *Peeping Tom* (1959). Going to Australia, like Jean Renoir going to America, can only be evidence of a creative pair in decline. The British Alfred Hitchcock is like the Australian Peter Weir. Australians and Britishers have their gifted film-makers for only so long. They often do their best work in Hollywood. British, Australian, Canadian and New Zealand cinema become vehicles for developing potential, for leading to bigger things elsewhere – and this is at all levels including the demotic, exploitation end of production. The little known thriller, *Dangerous Game* (1988, released 1991) was the Hollywood 'calling card' for director Stephen Hopkins and cinematographer Peter Levy – who went on to make *A Nightmare on Elm Street 5* (1989) and *Predator 2* (1990, see Gul 1993: 311).

Unlike the Third cinema, the mundane cinema does not attempt a viable socialist exit. It is criticized for capitulation. Sam Rohdie sees Australian feature film-making as a film-making created on the terms of the national bourgeoisie, implicated in and restrained by multinational corporations, and beholden to Hollywood aesthetic norms and packaging. Like Australia itself, Australian films serve US foreign (including cinema) policy, projecting a conservative cinema in its politics and textual practice. Australian film-making provides 'mediated reproductions of the social relations and imagery of the colonial - capitalism that has helped form it and has caused it to conform' (Rohdie 1985: 273).

Unless they foreground the Others in their midst or claim their offshore auteurs as their own, gloomy prognostications like Rohdie's are part of the mindset of festival audiences, critics and film-makers discussing Australian cinema. Its identity, value and critical worth seem always in question. Critics can imagine only a limited role for themselves. They are reconciled to their limited capacity to effect changes and seek smaller, less manifesto-like results than the political and aesthetic ambition of a 'Third cinema'. They find some virtue in doing 'after-the-fact explanatory exercises' which frequently 'come not to praise but to bury'. Critics write in resigned lamentation for that which cannot be but is still desired.

They typically experience 'aching gaps' in Australian cinema, 'absences' that are 'sorely felt':

> Where in Australian film is the appetite and readiness for the marvellous, the appeal to exaltation, impatience with the sham of official public culture, insistence on emotions and ideas experienced to the hilt?
>
> (Dermody and Jacka 1988a: 241)

Australian cinema becomes a cinema of the centre. For Adrian Martin (1988a: 97), an eminent Australian film critic, writing in 1988 'Australian cinema has too often been, since its mid-1970s renaissance, the home of good intentions, liberal ideology and comfortable worthiness.' This is an ordinariness which film-maker and director Tim Burstall once described as 'town councillor art' (quoted in Bromby 1979: 87). Every time commercial television in Australia repeats *Crocodile Dundee*, its critical value diminishes with declining economic value; no such logic attends the rarer revival on SBS-TV of *Les Diaboliques* (Clouzot 1954) and *Les Enfants du Paradis* (Carne 1943) whose value appreciates with time – these are films one looks forward to again and again. They are not antipodean Hillbilly films (J. W. Williamson 1995).

If this mirrors the larger medium-based distinction between cinema (as a culturally prestigious form) and television (as a mundane and demotic mass form), it also opens out on to the ways a mundane cinema is implicated in, and is partly an annex of, the local *television* industry. Not only are industrial and economic relations involved here, but so too are aesthetic ones. In a significant reconsideration of his past position on Australian cinema, Adrian Martin (1994a: 15) now argues that Australian and British cinema is aesthetically a 'televisual cinema' geared as it is to

> a different intensity, a different mesh of style, content and 'social text' than either a pumped-up Hollywood spectacle or a lush, visionary, European art film.

He no longer sees this televisual relation as a problem. Contemporary Australian cinema is a post-television national cinema in several ways: it operates in an audiovisual context in which television is the dominant player; a multifaceted Australian national cinema occurred *after* television had reached multichannel maturity in the major capitals (by 1966 the then four major cities – Sydney, Melbourne, Brisbane and Adelaide – had three commercial stations and a well-funded public broadcaster). Television production, including advertising production, sustained technological and employment infrastructures for actors, writers, directors, producers, camera operators and technicians. That the subsidized cinema which developed after 1970 should bear the traces of television should come as no surprise.

In subsidy arrangements and in public positioning, the cinema's relation to television has been central. In the 1970s the Australian feature film was an alternative to television. During this establishment period feature film-making needed to separate itself from television to claim its alternative and separate public identity. After a decade of film support and the 1980s tax concessions under-writing private investment in Australian film-making through division 10BA of the Australian Taxation Act, the feature film and television sectors came together in the documentary, mini-series and feature areas (see O'Regan 1986). Then, in the 1990s, the subsidy structure made a relation with television just one among a number of relations with local and international players. If a relation with television is a defining characteristic of Australia's mundane cinema, it is a defining relationship in all contemporary national cinemas. What is, perhaps, surprising is that we don't see so readily how televisual all national cinemas actually are – the mundane British and Australasian cinemas only more clearly demonstrate this general condition.

MAKING DISTINCTIONS WITHIN THE NATIONAL CINEMA

The same distinctions made among national cinemas are made within national cinemas to value local output. Australian cinema has its 'festival' films *(Sweetie* and *Picnic at Hanging Rock* – the only Australian titles to make the 1995 list of the BBC 100 films), its Third or counter cinema *(Night Cries* and *Serious Under-takings* (Grace 1983) and its mundane cinema *(Muriel's Wedding)*. But the mapping of prestige, Other and mundane on to Australian cinema effects a limited transformation, as these classifications take a specific form organized around the structuring binary of the mundane mainstream and the independent minor stream. The local film milieu has, in Susan Hayward's formulation (1993: 14), developed for French cinema, a 'cinema of the centre' and a 'cinema of the periphery'. Against the reality of a mundane Australian audiovisual industry is held out the nascent possibilities of its local periphery. What is replicated in this binary notation is the *very* same division as that holding for Hollywood versus the national cinema, for the mundane versus the prestigious and Other. The periphery represents an escape from economy into dialogue; the mainstream an overly close association with commercial values and the market.

In this opposition, the festival option hovers somewhere in between – some-times more on one side, sometimes more on the other side. From the mid-1970s to the early 1980s, a 'quality film' policy, critical rhetoric and film-maker inclination connected the festival cinema to a marginal cultural economy distinct from a mainstream television industry. From the late 1970s through to the early 1990s, the 'festival' option was more closely associated with a minor stream of Aus-tralian film-making. In the 1990s, there is once again a return of festival titles marking Australian cinema as a special domain to the side of the televisual mainstream in *Muriel's Wedding, The Piano* and *Proof.* These are popular films which are also prestige films circulating in film festivals.

From the late 1970s there have been various attempts to make the festival cinema and the Other cinema converge in an alternative or oppositional cinema. James Ricketson advocated a 'poor cinema' in 1979. Both Jacka (1988a) and Dermody (1988) proposed a 'local' and 'eccentric' cinema in 1988. Various cinema activists advocate a multicultural and Aboriginal and Islander cinema from 1988 (see di Chiera's documentary *A Change of Face* 1988). James Ricketson, who went on to direct an episode of the mini-series *Women of the Sun* (1982, which provided a view of Australian history since the white invasion from Aboriginal women's perspective) and *Blackfellas* (1993), argued for a 'poor' cinema in the place of 'rich movies'. For him, John Duigan's *Mouth to Mouth*, a story of 'four outcast teenagers', featuring unemployment and homelessness in contemporary Melbourne, had all the attributes of a poor cinema:

> It is contemporary, socially relevant, intelligent without being elitist, enter-taining without compromising its content, challenging but not didactic, aware of its audience but not pandering to its expectations.
>
> (Ricketson 1979: 5)

The aesthetic and the social interpenetrate in the selection of subject, the political orientation to it, and the aesthetic means of its realization. Raffaele Caputo (1993: 19) notes how Duigan in this film was able to

> achieve a sense of social and ideological critique, and maintain dramatic tension with subject matter that is well served by an *art brut* style: gritty surface, disconcerting compositions, episodic development, rapid cutting of sequences ... atonal use of natural sound, and juicing baroque sensibilities out of minimalist acting.

Liz Jacka's (1988a: 126) specification of the *local* gave emphasis to 'a particular and specific set of circumstances and forces that operate at any given time and place'. It did not 'entail any particular exclusion of what is not Australian ... the local is a huge accretion of influences from many sources, from traditional through technological to what is sometimes called 'junk' culture'. For Susan Dermody (1988: 132) the local was attached to a cinema that is 'a little like a recessive gene, perhaps a mutant one ... eccentric to the [prevailing] field of aesthetic choice'. These 'local' films make Australian cinema worthwhile, sus-taining their interest in it. Some of the films Dermody cites are: Nadia Tass's *Malcolm* (1986), a comedy built around a simple-minded loner inventor, Mal-colm, who forges an unlikely friendship with a criminal fellow-lodger which leads them to robbing banks with the aid of his inventions; Lowenstein's *Dogs in Space*, a 'lifestyles' film structured around experiences and incidents of a share-household active in the new music scene in Melbourne in the mid-1980s; and Ian Pringle's *Wrong World* (1986), a drama which has its drug addict, going cold turkey lead (Richard Moir) develop a transitory though meaningful relationship with another addict (Jo Kennedy). These all suggest alternatives and provide pointers to future directions in the Australian cinema.

In the 1990s, cultural value clustered around a revived 'Third' and 'multi-cultural cinema' option. This was based on two developments: a strategic convergence of festival and Other cinemas in the 1990s which opened out the festival cinema to move beyond the first world prestige cinemas of Europe and selected Japanese (Kurosawa, Ozu, Mizoguchi) and Indian (Ray) auteurs to embrace more of the world; and the need to articulate and legitimate alternative forms to that of the feature films – in the short film, the experimental film and so on. The associating of non-European and marginal European with festival and prestige cinema ends, opened out a space for diasporic and oppositional cinemas within the first world to be included in the Third cinema. Jim Pines and Paul Willemen in 1989 updated the influential formulation created out of earlier Latin American manifestos of the 1960s, to attach the Third cinema to the film-making of marginal Other film-makers from the 'Third World in the First World' like African-American and Latino-Latin cinema in the USA, Black and Asian film-making in the UK, or Aboriginal and ethnic film-making in Australia. There is an equation made between hybrid people and hybrid art forms: Pauline Chan, Monica Pellizari and Tracey Moffatt become exemplary here (see Chapter 13).

The periphery also has a longstanding history as the alternative Australian cinema. From the 1960s, this alternative was embodied in the short film, the experimental, the avant-garde, the personal film and the handmade film. These constitute their own régimes of value and purpose which connect in various ways to the mainstream feature. One of the reasons for the uptake of Helen Grace's *Serious Undertakings* and Ross Gibson's *Camera Natura* is not only their accessibility but their function as a mediation site connecting formal experimentation and political progressivism. This cinema is valued for its oppositional and non-conformist moments: when it critically interrogates national cultural, political, social and filmic ways. Sylvia Lawson (1985c: 330) finds Helen Grace's short film *Serious Undertakings* to be one such text:[12]

> the film's chief task is demolition: it assails the prescribed boundaries of feminism, the terms of authentic nationality, the proper concerns of male and female, notions of what can be included in the past, and the proper place of history.

The film mixes the retelling of Henry Lawson's classic short story 'The Drover's Wife' over images of the city and a woman and her child in a stroller negotiating it. It draws on classic images from Australian art. Various men and women discuss this art. Male actors discuss their relation to feminism and are 'silenced' by a woman doing the vacuuming. Their image is distorted and their voices decayed. There is dramatic rendering of an act of political terrorism. The Odessa Steps sequence from Eisenstein's *Battleship Potemkin* (1925) is replayed.

While acknowledging national specificity, such films manage to be resolutely internationalist in politics and outlooks. The rubric of a progressive national cinema becomes a vehicle for recognizing the disadvantaged in the USA and Australia alike (Jacka 1988a: 126), permitting and encouraging networks of international solidarity, whether these are configured as logics of first peoples, diasporas, the environment, socialism, or gay and lesbian film-making. The national cinema can be in these moments a Third cinema of the first and second world: anti-imperialist, anti-racist, anti-homophobic, anti-sexist, socialist and multiculturalist. Critics can call for the 'de-colonization' of Australian cinema and culture (Lawson 1982: 19–32). They can attach the Australian cinema to an agenda of reconciliation between indigenous and settler Australia (Langton 1993). They can hold out the prospect of an Australian cinema which could forge *new* cultural spaces in the film world as neither festival nor mainstream, neither Hollywood nor art-film. The prospect of a peripheral cinema enables film-makers, critics and policy-makers to have a 'progressive' engagement with the national cinema. It is a value formation tailored to public subsidy instruments in a liberal-democratic state. Through it, the national cinema can be envisaged as a domain of aesthetic and political intervention.

The Other cinema is an asset in that it makes the national cinema more fulsome and diverse. It functions as its conscience. Yesterday's radical politics and peripheral film-making becomes today's taken for granted norm. It works as a testing ground for later take-up, as the 'cinema of the centre' relies on the peripheral cinema for some of its stylistic, narrative, technological and representational innovations. The logic of industry training helps underwrite avant-garde, oppositional, experimental productions including experimentation with new technologies (see Penny 1994: 328–37). Obviously the 200 short films made in Australia are more numerous than the twenty odd features and the handful of television dramas whose format can be settled for a number of years. For all of those like John Ruane and Geoffrey Wright who use their short films (*Queensland* 1976 and *Lover Boy* 1988 respectively) to launch their subsequent careers making features (*Death in Brunswick* and *Romper Stomper*), there are those for whom peripheral film-making is their 'self-professed 'marginal' activity' (Martin 1994c: 203) such as the work of Arthur and Corrinne Cantrill (*Waterfall* 1984). The periphery grafts on to the national cinema reality a variety of purposes and projects alternative to, and sometimes oppositional to, those of 'the centre'.

The divide between the periphery and the mainstream is fluid. Sometimes the differences between them are a matter of perception. Sometimes they are structurally embodied in the various industry sectors; sometimes they are a matter of ideological contents, sometimes of form and style. film-maker Richard Lowenstein straddles short political films, video-clip production (with it avant-garde stylistics) and theatrical feature production in *Strikebound* (1984, adopting a political thematic sympathetic to the Australian Communist Party of the 1930s), and in his later *Dogs in Space* and *Say a Little Prayer* (1993) – both set in the subcultural milieu of drugs and inner-city youth – by marrying narrative film-making and video-clip derived stylistics. Albie Thoms' experimental cinema of the 1960s was partly underwritten by his work on *Skippy*, filming rock bands and the ABC's *GTK* programme. Indeed, as Willemen argues, this dependence is necessarily part of any oppositional cinema:

> a cinema which seeks to engage with the questions of national specificity from a critical, non- or counter-hegemonic position is by definition a minority and a

poor cinema, dependent on the existence of a larger multinational or nation-alized industrial sector (most national cinemas operate a mixed economic system, but that does not alter the argument: it merely creates a little more breathing space for film-makers).

(1994: 212)

Willemen is identifying here the relational character of any independent cinema, as its proponents push the boundaries of the contours of a minor market form – the festival cinema – and utilize semi-commercial and non-commercial subsidized screening spaces for political and avant-garde cinema. The independent cinema is meaningful through the will to value and the desire to coordinate the assigning of value.

If we want to understand the relation governing the peripheral cinema's separation from the mainstream, its selection of and need to project antinomies of national specificity versus nationalism, experimentation versus conventionality, political progressivism versus conservatism, culture versus the economic, its own self-understanding won't tell us much. Rather, we need to see the peripheral cinema as embedded in a fluid industrial and critical situation which it does not so much apprehend as intervene in so as to provide a protected space for a variety of more marginal film-makings and for rising film-makers to gather resources.

Agents occupy a principled position through valuing national cinemas against Hollywood, prestige and Other against the mundane, the cinema of the periphery against the centre. The claim they make for attention is that of 'moral notables' (Hunter 1994: 176). They do so because this is often the only authority they have available to them in the film industry/popular entertainment system. After all, their claim is for 'what we might become' and 'what ought to be', not 'what we are', 'what is' or even necessarily 'what realistically can be'.

THE INTERNATIONAL CINEMA AND NATIONAL CINEMAS

Let us now turn to that formation of value which privileges Hollywood, US influences and commercial dynamics and consequently devalues national cinemas, and prestigious, Other and peripheral local cinemas. Audiences, policy makers and film-makers attach to Hollywood and commercial cinema progressive aesthetic, cultural and political values that show up the national cinema's negative, regressive and conservative values. Because the national cinema ideal gained legitimacy from the presumption of its preferable moral, ethical and aesthetic values to those of Hollywood (Jacka 1988a: 125), any re-evaluation of the standing and legacy of the American (US) cinema downgrades the standing of the national cinema.

The demonization of Hollywood is replaced by suspicions about the self-serving make-up of the project of national cinema. Because national cinemas garner resources for themselves through a close association with cultural, educational, industrial and political élites, they are criticised for this cosy association. The need for national cinemas to both dispose local materials and also be popular drives a close association with some national traditions and public institutions which leaves them open to criticism. Iconic masculinity has been a privileged marker of a public and collective identity in *Gallipoli* and *Breaker Morant*, while an iconic femininity has been a marker of a private and individual identity in *Sweetie*, *My Brilliant Career*, *Caddie* and *Picnic at Hanging Rock*. Australian cinema is closely associated with an homogenous, monocultural, masculinist, xenophobic and exclusionary national identity. At the same time, policy has privileged notions of quality associating the cinema with respectable, not popular culture – and this is seen as one source for its unpopularity – its élitism and unpreparedness to engage with where audiences are 'at'.

The national cinema has a tenuous relation with its domestic audience, creating 'a pervasive legitimation gap' for it (Elsaesser 1989: 42). Australian cinema is continually criticized for failing to accomplish Hollywood's complicity with local audiences. It fails to live up to its promise to be seminal. It displays the divergent relation between the national cinema and local cultural consumption. No amount of cultural capital ever sufficiently closes this gap. By definition a minority product, national cinemas emerge from cultural policy needing at some level to enact a high/low culture divide while, at the same time, registering the contingency of what is art and what is not.

Charges of the irrelevance and failure of a national cinema are made even during highpoints of a national cinema's local and international standing. Those local production traditions thought to be independent of Hollywood are described as chauvinist, élitist (and pro-British), normative, backward-looking, hopelessly out of touch with a popular audience and not a little condescending. Such devaluations can question the very existence of the protected audiovisual enclave. When John Docker (1991) criticized the notion of quality in film and television policy and the related emphasis on drama in the Australian television content provisions, his intervention was widely seen as playing into the hands of those television stations and Hollywood multinationals for whom the 'national cultural infrastructure' for drama production was either an onerous burden or competition to be squeezed (Cunningham 1992: 61–5).

National cinemas are seen to be irrelevant to contemporary circumstance. They are 'an anachronism' (Jacka 1988a). Phillip Adams (1995: x) reckons that '[t]hese days the notions of national identity' that a national cinema depended on, seem 'doomed' in the wake of 'global culture (still a euphemism for American culture)'. This is a longstanding recognition. The 'ever-expanding international film, media and information economy' (Elsaesser 1989: 3) of today, threatening the fragile 'ecology' of the national cinema, was as evident in the 1920s, 1960s, 1970s as it is in the 1990s. The standing and importance of sovereign states and national identities always seem to be eclipsed by a burgeoning internationalization. Today the national is being made less central in Europe with a new reach for global culture and regional trading blocs above the level of the nation. But there is not a lot new for the Australian cinema here. Trading blocks were the building blocks of Empire, the English language has functioned as a coherent language and trading market for most of this century.

It is true, however, that more extensive regional and global instruments have emerged to facilitate international economic, political and cultural integration. When coupled with multichannel television and pay-television services, such conditions are reconfiguring the position of the national product. The need to fill channel schedules and to spread the cost of the international financing of film and television increasingly brings with it the need for hybrid productions, including co-productions. Herb Schiller, for example, explains the present situation of the international cultural political economy as the triumph of 'transnational economic interests' over the mechanisms of accountability, which derive from sovereign states and their international organizations (Schiller 1993: 47–58, T. Miller 1994a: 31).

Perhaps the most important new ingredient is the partial shift of cultural policy in nation states away from cultural nationalist positions concerned with managing the external relations of a sovereign national culture towards facilitating and problematizing internal relations of what are now seen to be fractured and divided national communities. Cultural policy problematizes a national cinema, the nation, national identity and national culture with reference to internal cultural diversity. It responds to communities within the nation – other local national identities, various unassimilated ethnic identities, assertions of diasporas stretching across nation states, and indigenous peoples. The development of such non-national instruments below and above the level of the nation-state are not eroding the nation state so much as inaugurating another turn in the national coordination of a nation's internal and external relations.

The valorization of the local and Other national cinema influences are replaced by endorsements of Hollywood's positivities. The national cinema ideal neglects what Richard Collins (1990: 157) has called the 'productivity of US cultural influences ... on the Nouvelle Vague, the New German Cinema, or on Italian film-makers like Sergio Leone or ... Gianni Amelio'. Dr George Miller, as the director of the *Mad Max* films and later *The Witches of Eastwick* (1987) and *Lorenzo's Oil* (1992), has indicated the influence of Hollywood genre films on his film-making. Finding Hollywood so positively in the constitution of the national cinema product questions the idea of contamination. There is an Australian dialogue with Hollywood. To be sure this is an asymmetrical dialogue, but a dialogue none the less. To make films for North American circulation is as legitimate a form of international exchange as any other. Valuing Hollywood reverses the traditional hierarchies of influence. It is positive to be Hollywood-influenced and negative not to be. Brian McFarlane and Geoff Mayer's recent study (1992) finds that Australian cinema lacks the protocols of Hollywood melodrama and needs them to become effective film-making.

Devaluing the national cinema and admitting to the value of Hollywood is part of how film-makers – like Baz Luhrmann (*Strictly Ballroom*) and Geoffrey Wright

(*Romper Stomper*) – declare the 'newness', 'relevance' and 'importance' of their work. They want to contribute to some other part of that broad repertoire of international film-making, usually but not always another part of the Hollywood cinema. Devaluing the local cinema provides a new generation of critics, film-makers, bureaucrats, politicians and audiences with a means to step in the face of the previous generation. Revaluing Hollywood also pluralizes what can count as progressive image making. If, as Martin (1988a: 98) would have it, the American cinema is the home of cinephilia, any rethinking of Hollywood's progressive legacy legitimizes the cinephilic terrain where films

> do not presume to show real life: rather, they head straight for the mediations of this life experience, its privileged metaphors, that are contained in the popular cultural well of cinematic images and fictions.

For Martin, cinephilia is a more legitimate terrain to inform Australian cinema than its preoccupations with the naturalistic – 'neutral, steady gaze on the events it portrays' – and the ornamental – its tendency to 'seize on a device for its good looks (or sounds) and then wed it to the first ... available cheap poetic effect' (100). He finds Australian cinephilia not only in the obvious places of Australian genre cinema – *Roadgames* and *Patrick*, Mora's *Howling III: The Marsupials* (1987) and most importantly the *Mad Max* cycle, but also in the experimental and avant-garde itself, the work of Moffatt, Brophy and Marie Craven.

Hollywood is seen to enact what the national cinema ideal held out as its preserve – namely a natural and direct relation with the local audience. It is the vernacular and seminal cinema in the West. Kim Schroder and Michael Skovmond (1992: 7) argue that American cultural products – particularly cinema and television – 'by breaking away from traditional, class-based notions of good taste, could be absorbed by the actual tastes and desires of large numbers of working-class people'. Hollywood film and television provided working-class consumers with 'a symbolic resistance to the paternalism of the national cultural establishment'. They did so by providing working class people with, in Tony Bennett's words, 'a repertoire of cultural styles and resources ... which ... have undercut and been consciously mobilized against the cultural hegemony of ... traditional elites' (quoted in Higson 1989: 40). For Adrian Martin, Hollywood provided a point of resistance at school to Australia's British-oriented cultural establishment (1994b: 12). Soren Schou (1992: 143) writes of how Hollywood cinema and American culture more generally revitalized the cultural life of the receiving country and prepared it for modern living:

> American films ... told us about a life many of us were going to live, an urban or suburban life. In Denmark, daily existence was changing for many people as we left our agrarian past and approached a new status as an industrial nation. A new self-awareness was sought in order to come to terms with the changing world, new and more sophisticated ways of looking at life, new ways to communicate. The inspiration had to come from the most advanced industrial

nation in the world. American popular culture became a guide during this mental transformation ... One could say that it was instrumental in bringing about the 'mental' modernization of Denmark. But it should be emphasized that the modernization occurred in a specific, American form not strictly inherent in the process of modernization itself.

(1992: 157)

Bell and Bell (1993: 201) similarly argue that Australia experienced 'a strongly American form of modernization'. They do not see this as a cause for lament or celebration. It is, rather, an inescapable social fact.

Such revaluations of Hollywood which aim to defuse primary pro- and anti-Americanism raise serious questions about the desirability of wanting goodness and worthiness from a national cinema.[13] What Australians want from their national cinema, Bill Routt contends 'is a quality cinema, a cinema of all good films, a cinema of good intentions.'[14] They don't want all the other things which go with it: lack of quality, bad films, bad motives. Routt (1994a: 219) finds fault with this notion of 'value':

Surely the point about 'national identity', like 'national cinema' – to those who think such things important – is never whether any specific one exists or not, but whether a *worthy* one exists or not. Value is not spoken about directly these days, especially in film studies, but value is what bulks up behind 'Australia' and 'Australian cinema'. No one wants to know more than they can learn in the least possible time about the dull films made here, the bad ones, and no one wants just a country or just an Australian film industry. Everybody wants something 'good'. They want to make 'Australia' and 'good' the same thing. *Which is stupid. And lends itself to evil.* [my emphasis]

Our desire for an aesthetically and morally worthy cinema is a problem. It suggests that wanting an Australian film to have aesthetic and/or moral value is inevitably a desire for *a* kind of cinema: a cinema of worth, a cinema of quality, an edifying cinema, a 'politically correct' and an aesthetically satisfying cinema. In principle this excludes too much: a dull and bad cinema, a naive cinema, a demotic cinema, an exhibitionist cinema, an exploitationist cinema, an imitative cinema, a retro cinema, a cinema of bad intentions – in short, a popular cinema with its dubious moral values and undecideable viewpoints.

This desire places unnecessary strictures on film-making and criticism. It imposes upon film-makers and critics alike an exemplary moral and spiritual demeanour and a continuing capacity for self-reflection and problematization. But there is no ideal or complete development of a national culture or identity underlying Australian cinema and neither should there be. The national cinema, the national culture, the national identity are always impure and hybrid assemblages of the good, the bad and the dull. Consequently this kind of principled position on a national cinema is open to Ian Hunter's criticism that in presuming 'to embody this ideal as a moral absolute and as a personal ethos' this position 'begins to look self-righteous as a spiritual comportment and fanatical as a civic one' (Hunter 1994: xxii).

For Routt, there is a flaw in the whole project of a national cinema, and this is with wanting 'Australian' and 'good' to mean the same thing. This criticism is not that the films that get made in Australia show both good and bad, it is that we want to impose the good side as well. We want a good national identity not a flawed, second best or blinkered one. For Routt this desire is a problem. Flaws, misconceptions, blinkers, derivativness, banality, evil are part of any cinema, of any art, of any identity. Our solutions even – and perhaps especially when we are righteous – are themselves also flawed, blinkered and misconceived. This suggests an ideal of a less principled criticism and film-making demeanours as a goal in Australian film-making and criticism, to allow for diverse film-making ends (not just the standard alternative, oppositional and avant-garde variety but varieties of popular cinema including exploitation cinema. The national cinema-based demand that art – and a popular art like the cinema – be aesthetically and/or morally good, places normative strictures on that art. These are strictures that do not apply to much Hollywood cinema and Hong Kong cinema and these cinemas are, as Routt would claim, better for its absence.[15]

The move to question the established value of a national cinema has several consequences. It suggests that the dull and bad films may have as much to tell us as the worthy ones. And this would liberate Australian film criticism to investigate its impressive archive. It *is* productive, contrary to what John Hinde says, to want just a film industry. We do not have to berate or discover some hitherto undisclosed goodness in the comic strip cinema of Brian Trenchard-Smith (*BMX Bandits* (1983), *The Man from Hong Kong* (1975)) and Lee Robinson (*Walk into Paradise*, *King of the Coral Sea*, *The Phantom Stockman*, *Skippy*). We can simply attend to it. There is nothing wrong with the achievement of the English language national cinemas when they create a popular vernacular product. The teen movies (*Love in Limbo* (Elfick 1993), the splatter movies (*Body Melt*) the exploitation films (*Howling III*) – these facets of commercial film-making 'beyond the pale' can make their return amidst the 'quality', 'local' and 'eccentric' films.

All national cinemas can be legitimately inspected as mundane cinemas. At some point they always are. In *New German Cinema*, Thomas Elsaesser explicitly refuses to see this cinema as mostly a prestige cinema and instead insists on normalizing it to its mundane contours. Elsaesser (1989: 153) distinguishes 'between a concept of the New German Cinema as it constituted itself within the European art cinema, backed by the star directors and functioning largely outside Germany, and a New German Cinema as the direct consequence of the subsidy system and with a distinct existence inside Germany'. In short, inside the country New German Cinema is a mundane cinema, while outside it is a prestige and, to some extent, Other cinema. This distinction is important. Because the films that count internationally and are selected to represent Australia are not Australian cinema but specific Australian films.

Conceiving a national cinema as a mundane cinema is important to any national cinema. It refuses to see only its exceptionalism. It talks to the heteroclite character of a national cinema in ways the self-defensive ethos of the oppositional and the self-congratulatory ethos of the prestigious cannot.

Sometimes there is an attempt to value the mundane cinema as such and to celebrate a diverse film industry by using those moments of spectacular local success to open out on to cultural and aesthetic discussion. In 1982 I wrote an article for *Filmnews* on *The Man from Snowy River* which was subsequently republished (1985a) in reaction to the then prevailing and subsequent reflexive denunciation of this film as in Rose Lucas' (1993: 103) words, 'a shamelessly opportunist pandering to the box office and to American film markets in particular'. This was a film with no redeeming features: aesthetically, politically and culturally. By using an 'American colonizer' the 'heat' was taken off our 'fine Australian pioneers' who were 'involved in an identical process of encoding the landscape within their own territorial and ideological parameters'. The film was also particularly 'objectionable' because of its 'stereotypical equation of women with a passive landscape to be cultivated or a horse to be ridden'. 'The love interest, Jessica ... is virtually indistinguishable from the missing horse'.

Snowy River was ideologically bad, technically bad, masculinist, poorly scripted and shamelessly commercial. We needed, I thought, better tools than these to explain a film which supplanted all previous successful Hollywood films to become the most successful box-office film in Australian theatrical exhibition (it was later eclipsed by *E.T.* (Spielberg 1982) and *Crocodile Dundee*). We also needed a better way of respecting the audience that had made it so successful than a declamatory critique that turned the audience into dupes of exploitative Americanized film-makers.

In my essay, I argued that film and cultural intellectuals had much to learn from *Snowy River* and its firm situation in Australian popular culture. *Snowy River* is a story loosely based on the famous Banjo Patterson poem. It has the main lead Jim leave his mountain home after the death of his father 'at the hands' of brumbies. He is forced out by the older mountain men who tell him he must earn the right to return to the high country. He works as a horse wrangler on the plains for a wealthy and hard American squatter, Harrison (Kirk Douglas). There he meets and falls in love with Harrison's daughter (Sigrid Thornton) and is subsequently forced to leave. He is able to return to the mountains when he catches Harrison's prize colt which has escaped to the brumbies. He succeeds, where everyone else has failed, in the film's central spectacular chase sequence. He and his surrogate father – Harrison's despised half-brother Spur (also played by Kirk Douglas) – win back their self-respect and community respect.

Film criticism needed to set aside its notions as to what constituted a 'well made' film in order to work out how this film connected with audiences. How was it that, for example, those very scenes that were, for critics, evidence of poor scripting, staginess and touching animal clichés, were also those appreciated and identified by audiences as what they liked about the film (O'Regan 1985a: 244)?

Identifying the film as a commercial film – a film made for money not critics – as a final shaper and clue to its meaning did not help either, because all that encouraged us to do was 'see it as imitative in a bad sense, dismiss it as if it had no significant structures, regard its commercial success as a "con"', (245). The tools we needed to explain its phenomenal success involved recognizing what this sort of film was – 'a kangaroo western', a popular melodrama mixing actors from Australian television soaps with Hollywood (Kirk Douglas). It also involved a strategy of address on the part of the film-makers which envisaged its audience as the 'whole of Australia' where Australia was seen to be not so much as a 'unified national character' but 'diverse publics'. The film-makers saw themselves as providing something for each – 'parents, kids, those who never go to the cinema, cineastes, adolescents of both sexes'. I argued that the film displayed the marks of this selection when 'what appeared plausibly and appreciatively as kitsch and quotation appeared to other audiences as something real, new, genuine' (250). We also needed to recognize aspects of Australian popular culture for what they were. I wrote:

> The terrain *The Man* inhabits is that of the cigarette commercial, clothes, fashions, real estate, tourism, soap opera (melodrama), bush dancing, John Ford and John Wayne. In other words, the film is firmly situated within Australian popular culture. The 'fictive space' of Australia and the locale that the film calls upon is one formed in and informed by television, the press and radio; rather than the state, existing Australian feature films, or . . . literature.
>
> (245)

The film was also situated in contemporary values and debates. So Harrison (the bad guy) rails against feminism. Jim (the Man) talks in the language of animal liberation when he breaks in the colt from Old Regret. Clancy admonishes the predatory Harrison in terms that make sense 'only within an ecological frame of reference'.

I thought cultural critics could learn from this film. It could help them understand just how localized and specific to them were some of the ideas they imputed as a general Australian condition. I was specifically thinking about the 'bush as alien, foreign, mysterious, uncolonisable, predatory or revengeful'. In the stead of these, the film posed a much more ordinary, banal and pragmatic relation with the bush: 'it is a commercial, ecological, desirable, pleasurable, traversable, and indeed acquirable space' (246). White Australians were not 'Europeans', they were not 'intruders in the bush'; nature was not a 'hermeneutic' (as in *Picnic at Hanging Rock*) and Aboriginality and Aboriginal culture did not 'provide the keys to an experience of . . . the Australian landscape' – as in *Walkabout*, *The Last Wave* and *Manganinnie* (247). The bush is not separate from the film-maker and the audience. It is simply available. 'It is not alien although it is unfamiliar' (247). The outback folk in turn were not 'the vicious, nasty, racist, ugly, predatory people of *Wake in Fright*, nor the European peasantry of *My Brilliant Career*', rather they were 'variously simple, naive, dignified, affectionate, likeable and resilient'. What

I felt could be taken from this film, was just how misguided and unconnected to life experiences and contemporary popular culture were ideas 'about an in-authentic Australian culture', 'an alienating threatening landscape', the opposition between 'European gentility and Australian vulgarity' and urban fantasies about country people that deny them their humanity and culture.

Like the trenchant criticism of *The Man from Snowy River*, I was overstating my case (country people are just as racist, predatory and awful as anyone else); there is no reason why people can't feel 'alienated from the landscape' – it was only that I and most people I grew up with didn't. I'd ignored the gender dynamics; and my reference to Aboriginal people not providing the keys to 'coming to terms with the landscape' for white audiences can't simply be left there. My criticism was born of a reaction to what I saw as a hegemonic film and cultural criticism unprepared to find anything in this film. From another angle, just such a sense of grievance animated Rose Lucas's criticism. She was objecting to what was for her a hegemonic film and cultural practice – evidenced by the film's phenomenal success – which marginalized her critical sensibilities and sense of identity.

Hollywood's role in making, inventing and repairing cinema and making, shaping and repairing our sense of ourselves reconfigures the Hollywood legacy. We are not outside Hollywood, we are implicated in ongoing negotiations with it. Bell and Bell (1993: 201) write that 'the history of the US in Australia is one of negotiation, albeit negotiation that has frequently been conducted within the language and culture of the greater power, and within a global economic structure in which Australia has experienced very little power'. Their revision stresses the asymmetry of the negotia-tions mostly favouring the dominant Hollywood and not the subordinate national cinema. But they also insist on the multifaceted productivity of American and Hollywood cinema for diverse audiences in nation states:

> the degree and quality of 'Americanization', through even the most clearly American media presence in Australia, depend on local accommodations, including resistances or reinterpretations of the meaning of 'America' in the local and receiving culture.
>
> (1993: 93)

John Caughie (1990: 45) argues that this situation encourages a curious game of identification and non-identification, such that the non-American 'plays at being American' with all the 'tactics of empowerment' and 'games of subordination' that this implies. This imaginary Hollywood and America can project on to the American a figure of immense potence, leading to the kind of audience identi-fications with stars charted by Edgar Morin (1961: 71–96); to Aboriginal identifications of Americans as saviors rescuing Aborigines from white Aus-tralians collected by Debbie Rose in Central Australia (1990: 163–70); to letters to the editor in times of recession, which urge Australia to apply to become the USA's 51st state; to Sylvia Lawson's (1982: 21) poignant recognition of an imaginary landscape in which Americans and Europeans were film-makers and Australians something else. Equally, in its mode of reversal, this play at being

American can project the American as a curiosity, a monstrosity, or an inferior. Hollywood 'may be marketing dreams which are dreamed in quite diverse ways, a fantasy of the Other as quaint, perhaps, rather than as compelling object of desire' (Caughie 1990: 46). Irony here promotes distance, engaged disengagement, and 'affected' superiority.

The reality of complicity, implication and qualified (rather than intrinsic) resistance to Hollywood and the social and aesthetic productivity of Hollywood makes the anti-Americanism so foundational to the grievance of a national cinema chauvinist and nationalist. As Routt (1994a: 218) cannily observes:

> In the writing on film which has gone on since May 1968 there has been a great deal of anti-American sentiment masquerading as reasoned politics. ... The ideas that 'classic narrative' is somehow linked in some fundamental fashion to Hollywood and thus to capitalism (and that the bourgeois art cinema of Europe and Japan offers a politically palatable alternative) seem specious on the face of it, but they are what everyone knows these days.

If the local audience's viewing preference for American cinema is not a duping, then in an important way the American cinema must be admitted as the Australian cinema. Hollywood and Australian cinema are simply two options for the viewing audience. Responsibility for image-making nationally is shared between imported and local production. There are moments of direct competition between Hollywood and the national cinema, but there are also complementarities and synergies, as both configure and contribute to forms of cultural reproduction. That the local cinema is the minority cinema experience of the Australian majority is not something to be made good, nor is it a sign of its failure.

Both Australian and Hollywood cinemas ordinarily produce negative and positive outcomes. Domestic film-making traditions are internationally informed in their content and style. The co-presence of various imported product and local product, suggests that local film production strategies are negotiated responses to the competition and complementary dynamics created by the presence in the home market of the Hollywood and minority imported product. They are conversations with the dominant local cinema, the Hollywood cinema, and with the other minor cinemas. If Australian cinema has relied more on theatrically and naturalistically derived protocols, this may be to do with the differentiation strategies available to it, given the imaginative spaces that Hollywood cinema occupies.

Devaluing the national cinema ideal through a revaluation of Hollywood attacks some of the foundation legitimations for a national cinema. Emphasizing the productivity of Hollywood's influences and constitutive character queries the very idea of sovereign national cultures in their strong form as autonomous, auto-creating and auto-identifying entities. New hierarchies of influence and dialogue challenge the pre-eminence of non-American relations. Hollywood's social and cultural positivity challenges the national cinema's mortgage on social and cultural progressivism. Hollywood becomes just as (or even more) important an instrument for generating cultural capital. Finally, refusing to be anti-American removes possibilities for nationalist righteousness.

Yet these devaluations are productive for the national cinema project. They renovate national cinema practice and criticism. Various local film-making projects have different priorities – they often enlist these repertories as their allies. film-makers look to Hollywood. They prioritize meeting the audience as a way of distinguishing their work. Devaluation does not simply debunk. Sustained attacks on national cinemas and notions of a (singular) national culture in Australian policy-making from the mid-1980s did not result in the jettisoning of the often criticized notions of 'distinctively Australian' nor the abandonment of 'cultural nationalist' rhetoric. Policy-makers redefined these notions. They co-associated cultural nationalism with the difference and diversity arguments, connecting the former to the latter in multicultural policy technologies. They also projected national identities sufficiently attenuated to allow for co-productions and strategies to attract offshore productions. The project of a national cinema became associated with multiplicities at two levels: many types of film-making consonant with prevailing international film-making, and the representation and involvement of minorities in front of and behind the camera. If, as Ross Gibson (1992: 81) reckons, 'the audience for Australian cinema . . . is now perhaps more interested in the world rather than the boundaries that could theoretically separate the nation from the remainder of the international community', what seemed needed was another definition of Australia. It would be one which 'welcomes a sense of international "contamination"' – and we see it in films such as *Green Card*, *Black Robe*, *The Piano* and just as equally *Strictly Ballroom*, *Muriel's Wedding* and *The Adventures of Priscilla: Queen of the Desert*.

THE FUNCTIONAL CHARACTER OF REGIMES OF VALUE

All national cinemas need to be prestigious, Other and simply mundane. All seem to need to reject and embrace Hollywood. Australian cinema needs its prestigious films – like *Sweetie* – which although not a 'big hit' provide it with internationally sanctioned cultural legitimation. Australian cinema has its 'Others within' and 'without' that it defines itself in relation to and seeks to incorporate. Pauline Chan's *Traps* becomes of central interest to the Asian cinema journal *Cinemaya*, principally because she is Vietnamese as well as Australian (Teo 1995, Berry 1995). It needs its mundane element: it is popular, aesthetically unexciting, even banal films, which although popular with domestic and international audiences do not seem especially meritorious and are often a critical embarrassment – like *Crocodile Dundee* – which maintain a broadly based public profile for the local cinema. These are all needed for a national cinema to function and enlist widespread public and exhibitor, distributor, investor and film critic support.

Film policy in most countries with national cinemas reflects this mixed scenario. Some policy-makers may want to create an 'art' cinema – but film-makers use this policy desire to create something more and less than a prestige cinema, as in the New German Cinema of the 1960s and 1970s (Elsaesser 1989 *passim*). For their part, Australian film policy-makers and producers want to have their foot in two camps. They usually want prestige with popularity and not necessarily in the same film. As we have already noted, the policy document that set in train the post-1970 Australian film revival – the report of the Film Committee of the Australian Council for the Arts – suggested in 1969 (1985: 171) that 'frankly commercial films' (a mundane cinema) were one of the major initial aims for Australian film policy, alongside the production of a 'percentage of serious interpretive feature films, or art films, which may or may not have box-office potential – the sort of films that will gain acceptance at international festivals' – a (prestige cinema); a 'constant flow of short experimental films' patterned on British precedent (an Other cinema); and lastly the nurturing environment of a film school. The committee saw this mix of initiatives as securing the objective of a 'quality' cinema (174). The very idea of 'quality' is a typically British and Australian policy notion which suggests as an ideal a cinema situated somewhere between a prestige art-house and mundane cinema and a minor stream of experimentation and Other cinema in short films or lower budget film-making generally.[16]

For over a quarter of a century film policy and film subsidy institutions have consistently and necessarily favoured firstly a mundane cinema, secondly a prestigious cinema and thirdly a counter cinema. Government funding institutions have favoured popularity and prestige in feature productions. The economic calculus produced by the 10BA tax concessions in the 1980s encouraged a popular mundane cinema at the expense of a prestige or Other cinema. The Other cinema has in its turn functioned as a moral barometer for the Australian cinema. The differences among these are frequently blurred. The principle supporter of the mundane cinema in the 1990s – the FFC – underwrote Tracey Moffatt's first feature *beDevil*. Many Australian titles have routinely crossed the boundaries between the (international) art cinema and a mundane cinema, the Other and the mainstream. This is particularly so in an Australian cinema where the entry level is often as it was for Jane Campion through the independent cinema (*A Girl's Own Story* (1983) *Peel* (1982)), into a prestige cinema (*Sweetie*) and thence to a mundane popular cinema (*The Piano*).

Film and cultural criticism has largely favoured a prestige and Other cinema more than the mundane cinema. Cultural criticism values the self-evidently marginal, which is resistant and different, more than the dominant values of the mainstream cinema. Cultural critics and political activists celebrate an emergent hybrid form in Tracey Moffatt's *Night Cries* and a powerful Aboriginal and Islander identify, just as before they preferred Duigan's *Mouth to Mouth* and Wallace's *Love Letters from Teralba Road* (1977) to *The Last Wave* and *The Chant of Jimmie Blacksmith*. Sometimes populist critics celebrate the mundane cinema of, for example, *The Man from Snowy River* for its easy establishment of complicity between its audience and the screen. The result is an equilibrium of sorts in public space. The mundane cinema is economically strong and popularly valued but critically devalued; against this, the prestige, Other and oppositional cinemas are rhetorically strong but draw on a more limited patronage for their critical and political value.

What is problematized – as an application of knowledge for governance – is the two value systems at work in these examples. The one which promises a film-making ecology separate from or to the side of the market, and the one which promises the utility of the market itself as the conferrer of value. What is exciting about Australian film-making since 1970 is an overall picture marked by this double problematization and an Australian cinema which functions in the space between these problematizations. Australian national cinema needs the subsidized 'ecology' to sustain even its most evidently populist – let alone art house or avant-gardist – ambitions. Policy-making explicitly has to recognize and accommodate the different values in place. It can't denigrate Hollywood too much because if it does so, it distorts Australian culture and overly proscribes film-makers' options. At the same time, it can't diminish too much the national cinema ideal. Proponents of a prestigious cinema cannot wish away its mundane components. Proponents of an oppositional cinema cannot wish away its mainstream. Proponents of a mainstream need its prestigious and Other components. Each leads inexorably to the other.

When the Australian film magazine *Cinema Papers* invited leading film and cultural critics to write on the neglected Australian films they loved, their work divided between mainstream features and the independent cinema. Four took up the invitation and wrote on mainstream features – on David Stevens' *The Clinic* (1983), Lee Robinson's *King of the Coral Sea* (1954) and Paulette McDonagh's *The Cheaters* (1931) – or international features made in Australia – Luigi Zampa's *Bello Onesto Emigrato Australia Sposerebbe Compaesana Illibata* (1971). The rest focused on low budget features born out of an oppositional impulse: Bert Deling's *Pure S* (1976), Jim Sharman's *Shirley Thompson versus the Aliens* (1972), Haydn Keenan's *Going Down* (1983), or experimental and avant-garde films as in Stephen Harrop's nine–minute *Square Bashing* (1982) and Arthur and Corinne Cantrill's *Waterfall*. I think we are now seeing in the field of Australian cinema a recognition by critics of the plurality of values.

The dominant international is no worse than the local. The British, European and Asian influences are no better than the American influence. Neither national cinemas nor Hollywood, neither the mainstream nor the minor stream, have a mortgage on modernity, aesthetic innovation, progressive politics and the like. American dominance is a matter of fact not an opportunity for moral posturing and anti-Americanism. The marginal position of Australia and its national cinema is also a matter of fact not value. There are many opportunities for film-makers in the many ways that Hollywood is the vernacular English-language cinema and Australian cinema can be a participation in that cinema and an extension of it. Australian cinema's place is as just another struggling national cinema attempting to forge spaces within, alongside and even outside those provided by the dominant cinema. Hierarchies of national cinemas (like prestige, Other and mundane) are at best relative and contingent – they are not possessions or essential attributes of particular national cinemas or parts of a national cinema. Every national cinema is at some time prestigious, Other and mundane. Every national cinema product is under some conditions progressive or regressive, innovative or conventional. And every hierarchy of value is reversible. Film policy for some time now has explicitly recognized this diversity of ends, film projects and purposes. It is time film criticism and film analysis did likewise. The first step towards this is to recognize just how limited are the descriptions we generate from our habitual vocabularies of value in the cinema. These formations were designed to favour some kinds of internationalism over others, to carry with them their own positivities and negativities in imagining the local. They were constructed in such a way as to bear enlistment by diverse agents in the film milieu. This makes them adequate political instruments and perfect for campaigning. But they are clearly inadequate as a means of understanding the film milieu.

Chapter 6

Making meaning

INTRODUCTION

In the previous chapter, I was concerned with the standing of Australian cinema as a generalizable entity; in this chapter I am concerned with the routine accomplishment of meaning with respect to Australian films. How do film-makers, critics, audiences and policy-makers make meaning from Australian films? They interpret it and value it in a number of ways. They relate a film or television series to society and public discourse. They compare it to other Australian films, television productions, novels, theatre and poems. They think about its continuities and discontinuities with British, European and Hollywood productions. They find it either entertaining or informing, or diverting and educational. They berate it for surrendering to commercial values. They castigate it for capitulating to middle-class 'good intentions'. Through such diverse interpretative acts, films and television programmes – like the larger audiovisual culture they are a part of – have diverse public careers.

Picnic at Hanging Rock had such a career. On its release, film critic, P. P. McGuinness reviewed it for the 'quality' weekly, *The National Times*, comparing it to the work of Swedish director Bo Widerberg (not inappropriately given its art-house release in Europe). He found an advantage in Weir's film's 'extra dimension of horror' (1975; 1985: 189). Stephen King (1981: 387) described it as one of his personal favourite horror films (the other reference points were all American horror movies). Adrian Martin (1980) celebrated it as a welcome example of 'fantasy' in Australian cinema. Film and cultural critics discussed the film and the novel it was based on. Some reckoned it suffered in comparison with the novel. As an exemplar for subsequent Australian films, *Picnic* was variously interpreted as a 'period' or 'nostalgia' film. Dermody and Jacka (1988a: 97–8) see it as the beginning of an indigenous genre, the AFC-genre. The film invoked social inter-texts of feminism, lesbianism, social class and as a 'spin' on the local 'child lost in the bush' news and fiction stories. For Ian Hunter '[l]esbianism is in the film in the same way as the disappearance is, not to be thought about as a human reality, but as an emblem of the girls' otherworldliness' (1976; 1985: 192); while

> The upper class characters and the director know intuitively that causation is too crudely rational and proletarian for the refined realms of the spirit and art. Accepting intrinsic class differences is one of the conditions for accepting the film. Being upper class is one of the conditions for entry to the other world.
>
> (1985: 191)

Later readings voiced landscape and environmentalist concerns. John Carroll (1982: 223) found the film 'visually dull' compared to the 'uncanny and mysterious, wild beauty of the rock itself'. At the time of its production Hal McElroy found in it a production strategy of the 'middle course ... making films that are intrinsically Australian, but thematically have international subjects'. And '[w]hat England and America can't do is a *Caddie*, a *Devil's Playground* or a *Picnic at Hanging Rock*' (Walsh 1976: 41).

These repertoires position the local cinema with reference to the international cinema, television and international concerns and local symbolic culture, local lifeways and public culture. They construct diverse purposes for cinema. They hybridize and problematize the cinema. These diverse cultural repertoires provide machinery to make films mean.

They turn on a will to:

1 emplot local film-making across local and international coordinates alike, so as to indigenize and internationalize the cinema;
2 distribute film-making purposes across coordinates of industry and culture. entertainment and cultural values, so as to emplot the cinema along the contours of the dualist repertoires which sustain government involvement and make the cinema and television more than just another industry;
3 embed the Australian cinema into the world of social life – particularly but not exclusively Australian life – via attention to social texts, in order to anchor the cinema in available social texts.

None of these repertoires count more than others. Different parts of the film complex have an interest in furthering one or other of these terms. A film's relation to other Australian film and aesthetic texts is part of film viewing and the professional interests of those who market, appreciate, study and write about the Australian produced arts. Australian film-making informs and is informed by local cultural production in a variety of media forms. Films do make adjustments to Australian cultural history with its canons, high points and low points. Australian films have an aesthetic history in which their aesthetic-cultural inter-texts are foregrounded. The relation to the various Australian – and to a lesser extent – international social texts is also part of viewing. Films concern Australians as a people-among-themselves (and people in the international community). This relation is important in constructing plausible film stories. It is also in the professional interests of those who deal with the public and engage politically, to attach their social programmes, analyses and interest to a film or television programme. The relationship to the international cinema, whether in its popular mainstream variety or in its minority, 'quality', 'art-house' or 'political film-making' varieties, is one all film-makers need to negotiate. Their audiences routinely negotiate these in their cinema-going and television viewing. As Sylvia Lawson once asked: for an Australian audience which has 'just seen *Close Encounters*, *Saturday Night Fever*, *1900*, or *Seven Beauties*; what do they want, or need, to be told by a movie made in their own community?' (1982: 27).

These critical repertoires provide critics, marketers, film-makers and audiences with ways of making sense of existing Australian cinema in a retrospective apprehension of it. But these critical repertoires are not simply ways of apprehending film-making for criticism and consumption. They provide these agents with ways of creating this cinema, prospectively producing it: they are forcefully used. The film-maker needs to be aware of contemporaneous international cinema in its Hollywood and British/European dimensions: Hollywood films because they are the main fare for his or her domestic and international audience; British and European cinema because these provide points of reference, as they are to some extent a response produced in the context of Hollywood dominance. Producing Australian film entails some knowledge of local films, both to define the difference of this project, to keep abreast of what is locally working at the box-office, and in a subsidy-driven industry to identify what projects are getting up, and to identify personnel – actors and crews for future reference. In addition, because local film-makers come out of a particular cultural social milieu they will produce films with reference to the prevailing social problematizations circulating in that milieu.

Film-makers, in the process of enlisting diverse investors and later audience constituencies, typically mobilize diverse interpretative protocols and constituencies to get films off the ground. Their film is like this or that Australian film. It follows on from the international success of some usually American or European/British film. It takes up such and such a public issue and event. It has this well-known theatre piece successful in New York in *The Sum of Us*. Here is an opportunity to connect the American director of the stage play with the Australian cinematographer as co-directors. Or here is a notable literary property in the teen novel/autobiography section, *Puberty Blues* (Beresford 1981), investment in which would make a good bet.

A film project has different meanings for different people at different moments of the production and consumption process. This is not dissembling on the part of the producers and directors – to be successful, a film requires multiple coordination and diverse uptake. The film itself also has to be 'rhetorically strong' enough to bear this diverse uptake. As a 'mass medium', mainstream and minority cinema alike have to travel far in social and cultural space in order to be successful. As extremely expensive symbolic commodities, films have to travel far in economic space in terms of the extent of money and people that need to be enlisted to get the production off the ground. It should not be surprising that films are 'laden' with diverse, disconnected and sometimes contradictory meanings as they travel through social space. Films which are not able to marshall a number of these repertoires face difficulty justifying their presence on production schedules and on audience horizons.

STRICTLY BALLROOM AND THE COMPLEMENTATION OF REPERTOIRES

Films that become major 'events' like *Strictly Ballroom* persist on a number of horizons and provide audiences with richly diverse points of engagement. Even the most evidently generic 'event' cinema can be made malleable. The box-office hit of 1992, *Strictly Ballroom* was described by R. Horton (1993: 6) in *Film Comment* as 'simultaneously a camp vehicle and a straight-sappy Garland-Rooney musical'. Its director, Baz Luhrmann, was keen to accentuate this connection with the classical Hollywood musical, emphasizing the continuity between Gene Kelly in *Singin' in the Rain* (Kelly and Donen 1952) and *An American in Paris* (Minnelli 1951) and Paul Mercurio. And these connections are dazzling. Like Kelly, Mercurio as the Scott Hastings character dances through almost the entire film – all his movements are evidently choreographed rather than blocked out; and in the best musical tradition the prototypically utopian finale makes dance a universal condition.

Luhrmann also suggested that the ballroom world was 'a metaphor, or a microcosm, of the world at large' in which 'people's desires are so passionately expressed' (Luhrmann quoted in Taylor 1992: 8). Writing in 1994 to coincide with the film's television screening, Peter Castaldi acknowledged its claim for a place in the international cinema as having 'reinvented the dance film'. It was, he said, a forerunner to the 1994 Australian 'hits' *Muriel's Wedding* and *The Adventures of Priscilla: Queen of the Desert*. It cleared the way for these films because of the way it combined the conventional fairy tale romance with Australian suburbia, its back streets and its dreams:

> They [the film-makers] took the back streets of any town and dressed them up in the most colourful, outrageous and wickedly witty way. What is essentially the story of ugly duckling Fran [played by Tara Morice] getting her wish to dance with handsome prince Mercurio and (without kissing the frog) becoming a princess herself, is in fact a celebration like no other of everything Australian. *Strictly Ballroom* underneath its lavish frocks, its wonderful performances and crackerjack pace liberates the suburban from the grip of the realists and lets fantasy run free.
>
> (Castaldi 1994)

For Castaldi, Luhrmann Australianizes the fairy tale. In article after article the film's standing ovation, the dancing in the aisles and repeat screening at Cannes are mentioned, providing the European seal of approval on the film's quality. Film festivals and award ceremonies followed. It was awarded the Prix de la Jeunesse (Youth Prize) at Cannes, and judged the Most Popular Film in the Vancouver,

Toronto and Palm Springs International Festivals. For its part the British Academy of Film and Television Arts gave it awards for Best Costume, Best Production, and Best Original Music Score. Its Cannes reception enabled it to gain entry into the important international markets. There were also trenchant criticisms. Not surprisingly given its 'fairy tale' qualities, Pat Gillespie (1993: 52) lambasted the film for 'toying superficially with people's bitchiness, obsessions with image, winning and peer groups' and its 'one dimensional' characters. But such criticisms were minor voices. Here was a film in which these interpretative templates largely complemented each other: it was simultaneously 'so Australian', a trailblazer for subsequent Australian and international cinema, a retro homage to the Hollywood musical, a camp and a quality film recognized by discerning audiences at the world's most prestigious festivals.

The same complementarity of repertoires is in evidence in lobbyist and policy-making rhetorics. They often assemble their arguments for an Australian cinema as a patchwork of these repertoires. The initial arguments for Australian cinema were, as we have seen, explicitly organized in ways that brought each together. Australians had a cultural right to cinema which would explicitly organize the Australian social text. Australians had a right to participate in the 'universal film language'. There should be Australian stars, studios and commercial film-making as well as serious, quality films. Here both sides of the dualist opposition, the social and the aesthetic intertexts, were mobilized to form a doctrine of cultural rights – creativity rights and viewing rights for the Australian social text to be represented and for Australians to participate in the range of national cinema.

ROMPER STOMPER AND THE COLLISION OF REPERTOIRES

Romper Stomper, by contrast with *Strictly Ballroom*, was a controversial film. It was made to be so. Its deliberate textual ambiguities eschewed any simple moral equation. It was a rollercoaster ride from start to finish. Viewing it was a draining experience (and deliberately so, the director wanted people to be exhausted by it). It had powerful, engaging performances by Russell Crowe, Jacqueline McKenzie and Daniel Pollock (Crowe and McKenzie's careers took off after these performances; Pollock died soon after). Its marketing strategies centring on a film about skinheads and racist violence were bound to generate controversy. The film was taken to task – and defended – for its 'moral' credentials. Was it glamourizing the skinheads? Was it endorsing racist violence through its magnetic performances (remember 'one in six Vietnamese adolescents have suffered, or has been threatened with physical violence based on racism' (Lombard 1993:18))? Was its depiction of Vietnamese defending themselves racist? Was it an adequate portrayal of the suburb in which it was set? Why was the Mayor of Fitzroy so intent on lambasting the film? And above all, was it right for Australians to make this kind of film?

Its director added to the controversy. He aggressively defended his skinheads as an integral part of Australian public culture – they were not 'other' than our (good righteous) 'selves':

> Skinheads are not aliens. They are a part of this culture and they represent something about it – exaggerated, not pleasant, but nonetheless real.
>
> (Quoted in Quinn 1993a: 4–7)

We follow their lives. Hando's gang moves from racist thugs to victims of large-scale retribution by an Asian gang that destroys their home. They subsequently acquire 'new digs' through violently evicting and verbally abusing a gay couple from their squat. Gabe, by then Hando's epileptic 'girlfriend', orchestrates an 'excessive' retribution of her own on her rich father and his house for his incestual relationship with her. The emerging love triangle between Hando, Gabe and Davey triggers the breakup of the gang (Dave moves out of Hando's orbit into Gabe's). Acting in revenge for Hando's treatment of her, Gabe betrays the whereabouts of the remains of the group to the police. The police arrest the group, killing the child member of the gang in the process. Hando, who escapes, subsequently hounds Gabe who is now with Davey. He penetrates what Nicole Mitchell has called 'the mock Bavarian cottage in which Gabe and Davey are ensconced',[1] with the 'reference to the big bad wolf' being underscored by the caged dogs he passes to get to the house. He makes them commit an armed robbery and kills a shopkeeper in the process. In a climactic finale, Hando tries to kill Gabe for setting fire to their car. Dave and Gabe together kill Hando while Japanese tourists look on. There is no simple moral equation (bearing out Wright's statement 'what I hate most is to be given a simple moral equation'). Such a position on social problems undoubtedly encouraged accusations of racism. In defence, Wright claimed the audience was too exhausted after these gruelling sequences to be motivated to commit copycat acts of violence.

Wright also gained further notoriety for his trenchant criticism of film funding bodies and of other Australian films for their characterizations and their moralism. The funding bodies were not 'as brave as they could be'. The problem with Australian films according to Wright was that:

> Most Australian films lack motivated characters. The characters don't seem to want anything very much. There doesn't seem to be any dramatic mainspring. There's not much at stake. I think most Australian films are dull.
>
> (Quoted in Friedman 1992: 6–11)

Wright's skinheads wanted something. Their lives, their 'turf', their community and identity was at stake in a gross inversion of 'identity politics'. They had energy. They were engaging. They might all be ugly and be prepared to betray one another but they had 'conviction and drive'. Perhaps most contentious of all, the social problems documented – violence, incest, gangs, misogyny, racism – are not treated as the issue. They are simply there to motivate the narrative. They function as maguffins – story elements that mislead the protagonists and audience alike as to the nature of what is going on – as in so many American thrillers/investigation stories.

The film turns out to be a love story. But even here a love triangle with a difference emerges. Rejected and mistreated by Hando, Gabe takes revenge. She is rewarded with his mate Davey who walks out when she does. With Davey, she has more control over the situation: she is filmed on top in their love making and her own pleasure is insisted on. Contrast this with the earlier sequence where her face is pressed against the shower screen as Hando screws her from behind. When she later overhears Hando trying to convince Davey to choose between him (male bonding) and her (heterosexual) love, she exacts vengeance by burning the car – Hando's means of escape. With it goes the last vestige of their community and Hando's hopes. Each time Gabe refuses to be marginalized, refuses to be denied her own say. In so doing, she provokes Hando into attempted murder. Davey is forced to side with Gabe and tries to save her and himself from Hando. The film exacts a cunning reversal; Davey, not Gabe, is the object of exchange, the object in circulation, in this love triangle. He circulates between the two strong characters. Hando's assertion to Davey that he was going to give him Gabe anyway, is meant to ring hollow. In the film's logic she is not to be 'given away', or 'fought over'. Davey has that position. Terrible things have been done to her, but she is not a victim nor is she to be treated as an object by her father or Hando.

People were outraged that the 'social problems' in this film were not treated in their own right and with full integrity. Some reckoned it was bad film-making to have the Vietnamese so quickly disappear (they thought the film was about race relations). But for some this also represented the maturity of this film: it represented a preparedness to hinge these 'problems' as 'family matters', not externally out there, but by implicating us not as pretext but as subtext. We, the audience, are made to sympathize with Hando (an extreme position) all the better to turn on him and reject him later as an evil monster that we want dead (an equally extreme position). It excited the cinephile imagination for its cinematic achievement: 'nowhere to be found [was] the patchiness in acting and directing that has blighted several Australian films' (Epstein 1992: 24–5). 'At last', another critic told me, 'we've found another Australian director who knows how to make a film.' In these terms, it arguably opened up a new terrain for Australian cinema: '[t]here is less Australianization and the arguably civilizing capacity of Australian ironic humour is completely missing. For this reason the film is frightening' (Epstein 1992: 24–5). This was an Australian storytelling that aspired to the 'big picture' look and acting. The moral hesitation with which we regard Hando and Gabe's actions is the hallmark of the gangster film (see Routt 1989b). Adopting Routt's discussion of the Hollywood gangster film, Hando/Gabe also

> displays himself to me ... but his thrusting himself forward is also a demand, a challenge to deal with the Other or close my eyes. I am being asked 'What do you see?' – I am being asked for interpretation. But to display something is at once to impart information and to attempt to persuade – that is to assert. The

gangster film catches me up in a rudimentary condition of the cinema: that it may only make assertions, that even at its most literal it is also demanding judgement, soliciting value . . . What draws an audience to it is not an image of the Self reflected from the screen, but the Other incarnate: spectacular, evanescent, intransigent . . . The experience of popular cinema . . . arises out of the tension between what is properly of the Self and of the Other. In it, as in all exhibitionist display, the gaze is flung back at the gazer.

(Routt 1989b: 125)

As Karl Quinn (1993a: 1) asserts, *Romper Stomper* is a 'spit in the face of expectations of what an Australian film should be'. Not because it makes us deal with the Other (as we will note in a later chapter 'othering the Australian' is part of the tradition of Australian fiction), but because of the way it makes us deal with the Other, the kinds of complicity, the kinds of implication and the kinds of hesitation. This is the 'Other' we abhor not applaud!

The controversy surrounding the film created its audience. It also turned people away. *Stomper* was decidedly less popular than *Strictly Ballroom*. As we have seen, the textual logic of the film intersected with the different cultural repertoires which controversy counterposed. The Australian multicultural intertext (social text) was at odds with its cinephile ambitions. Its project was to change existing storytelling coordinates, break with cultural traditions, and assimilate a quintes-sentially American storytelling at the heart of Australian storytelling. Its public critical divisions demonstrated just how brutally confronting it was: David Stratton on the high profile SBS-TV programme, *The Movie Show*, could not bring himself to talk about it, saying that it should not have been made. By contrast, his co-host, Margaret Pomerantz extolled the film's virtues. film-maker Teck Tan and critic Chris Berry were adamant it was anti-Asian. Tan said 'I was put in the position of Asian victim again, and it didn't do much for my psychology' (Berry 1993: 44). *Filmnews* declared it to be narrativizing a dystopian multiculturalism, as opposed to the benign multiculturalism of *Strictly Ballroom*. In one the ethnic is to be expelled and competing groups fight for control over suburban space, in the other the 'gift of culture' enables Scott and Fran to transform ballroom dancing and bring the two communities, (Anglo) Australian and Spanish together. The most shocking aspect of *Romper Stomper* was not its exposure of Australian racism, but its discomforting reversals of these positions. For Adrian Martin what sticks in his mind is

when the neo-nazi Hando . . . takes time out from dodging the death-blows delivered by Australian-Vietnamese to philosophize – and compares his historical plight as a member of a vanishing species to that of 'the fucking Abo'.

(Martin 1994a: 15)

These skinheads are the white trash who not only perpetrate violence and hatred but also see their community invaded and destroyed. Their pub is taken over. Their 'home' is destroyed. There is no sentimentalizing of ethnicity. The Vietnamese invade, outnumber and effectively dispatch the neo-Nazi threat. At the same time, these neo-Nazis do their own 'invading' and dispossession – gratuitously bashing children on skateboards, violating shops and shopkeepers, dispossessing the marginal gay men from their squat, invading Gabe's father's house and chaining him to the toilet and destroying his car.

Our cultural repertoires do not simply provide a means of representing a phenomenon, they also intervene in producing the phenomenon. Both movements are crucial here. Critics, film-makers, marketers and politicians variously view Australian cinema in relation to social texts, aesthetic intertexts and the continuum of international cinema practice. They also construct Australian cinema through these relations. The competition among these agents for public authority is partly conducted by operationalizing these different critical templates. They make different objects and create so many divergent purposes for the cinema. Contrariwise, the complementarities and cooperation between these agents produce an eclectic, multifaceted and pleasurably differentiated and controversial Australian film-making.

DISSENSION OVER THE REPERTOIRE

Much dissension over a film's meaning in Australian public contexts comes down to which repertoires should be deployed. Sometimes this dissension takes place within the making of a film. Take Steve Jodrell's *Shame* (1988; for critical comment see Crofts 1993, Partridge 1988: 38). This film has been described as a 'genre-twister', an interesting mutant of the 'road movie', a feminist *Mad Max* and a dyke film. On its Perth release local television presenters wondered about the extent of the rape of adolescent girls being 'covered up' in 'our' country towns. All these understandings turn on the film's structural conflict between its naturalistic acting and camera presentational qualities sitting oddly within a script that selfconsciously produced the film as a 'genre' piece. Jodrell is a naturalist drama director. While the script-writers (Beverly Blankenship and Michael Brindley) saw it as a genre reworking, the director was more inclined to regard it as a 'social problem' film! The film oscillates between these poles, ending finally with a 'social problem' rather than 'genre' ending. It was initially written with a 'genre' ending in mind but was changed during production to a social problem ending, where the death of the girl who dared to stand up to rape is treated as an opportunity for moralizing and the communal recognition of the social problem.

Arguments that film-makers and critics have as to the appropriate focus and ends of film production turn on which of these repertoires should predominate: cultural critics emphasize the social problematizations on offer, film critics the extent of the relation with the established cinema and its social dimensions. Sometimes the dissension is a struggle for the meaning of the film and the future of the film industry. The alternative to film culture or film industry debate of the 1980s was classically a debate between the two sides of the dualism policy:

education and entertainment, culture and industry, British/European art cinema models and Hollywood genres, mapped over an inwardly oriented relation between local social texts and the Australian literary and cultural tradition, and emphasizing those matters that concerned the world.

These different cultural repertoires not only provide materials for struggle over public meaning of Australian film generally, they offer alternative 'moralities' for film-making and its consumption. Something of the stakes involved here can be glimpsed in the struggle that developed over the attempt to expand the repertoire of Australian stereotypes of freakishness to include the Filipina in *The Adventures of Priscilla: Queen of the Desert*.

The film opened with a largely benign press. Together with *The Sum of Us*, *Priscilla* was mainstreaming gay lifestyles. The margins – transvestism – were being celebrated and normal 'heterosexuality' derided. Like *Strictly Ballroom*, this was a feel-good movie, but properly 'camp' in the tradition of *The Rocky Horror Picture Show* (Sharman 1975). It was shocking then to hear Melba Margison of the Centre for Filipino Concerns saying:

> That film, the way we have been treated there is actually killing us. For us, it is the murder of the dignity of Filipino women. It will encourage more violence against us.
>
> (Cafarella, in *The Age*, 7 October 1994)

She added that the Filipino character in the film, Cynthia, was:

> a gold-digger, a prostitute, an entertertainer whose expertise is popping out ping-pong balls from her sex-organ, a manic depressive, loud and vulgar. The worst stereotype of the Filipina.
>
> While all the main and secondary characters in the film were treated with respect, humanized and dignified, the Filipina was treated with condemnation, dehumanized and stripped of any form of dignity. Her dignity was killed. That is the word. Violently killed.

One of the film's producers, Al Clark, rejoined:

> The film is a gentle satire with enormous affection for its characters. Cynthia, the Filipina character in the film is a misfit like the three protagonists are, and just about everybody else in the film is, and her presence is no more a statement about Filipino women than having three drag queens is a statement about Australian men.

Clark's was a 'cinephile' appreciation. He stressed the Cynthia character as a stereotype among stereotypes. She was also a misfit in a film of misfits who were portrayed more sympathetically than the 'ocker men'. In response to the argument that the film-makers had a responsibility to present minority groups 'realistically and sympathetically', Clark said:

If that were the primary consideration in films, there would be no vulnerable characters, no folly, no absurdity. People would be policing their attitudes all the time. They would be policing their portrayal of everybody. The whole point of a big noisy musical set on the road is that people of all kinds should collide with each other.

(Quoted in Cafarella 1994)

The Melbourne *Age* (10 October 1994) editorialized a position that could reconcile these competing 'moralities': film-making's need for stereotypes and a minority's concern as a marginal and vulnerable group for fair and reasonable coverage:

It is, perhaps a pity that a film with a message of tolerance and acceptance for homosexuals should feel the need of what looks very much to us like a racist and sexist scapegoat.

The vehemence of this response and the subsequent attempted editorializing 'resolution' of it which has continued in critical writing since (see Quinn 1994/5: 23–6) meant that the film became partially problematic. It injected a note of wariness into what had been up to that point a celebration about the convergence in this film of a social text mainstreaming gay lifestyles and 'acceptable gay culture' and an Australian film-making tradition which had been extended to include the transvestites Mitzi and Felicia alongside the freakish Nino, Barry McKenzie, Stork, and Alvin Purple.

Critical multiculturalist repertoires were mobilized. The film acquired an ambiguous reputation for the way that, in attempting to 'rehabilitate' a marginalized group, it denigrated other 'marginalized' groups like Asians and women. As a colleague, Mark Berger reported to me in discussion that:

There seemed to be a sort of white male mateship thing going on in which the rules are altered slightly to allow gay men and transexuals in (as long as they are white), who are after all still 'male'.

The dissension over the meaning of the film is not reconcileable. Popular film-makers work with hesitations, moral ambiguities, and not the moral equations that sustain so much identity politics and critical intellectual debate. These form, if you like, the basis of their morality and their ethics. Without risking being bad, such films, it is felt, simply will not work. The director of another 'problematic film' *Death in Brunswick*, John Ruane, insists that stereotypes are 'a bit in the eye of the beholder' (Koval 1992: 36). Elliott and Ruane seem to be saying that the answer to 'minority' concerns may not be found in limiting or overcoming stereotypes, but in proliferating them, working with them, inverting them, shaking them around.

Elliott and Clark would insist that the similarities between Cynthia and the other transvestites were palpable. Like them, she was 'in control'. She manipulated the situation. She escaped from being chained by the Bill Hunter character to perform (and without him doing that his character would have been altogether too benign for the hard edges of this film). Subsequent to that, she left him for the city and one presumes more performances (just as the transvestites come from the city). Curious confirmation of this cinephile position comes from San Francisco where patrons of the movie were reported (*Weekend Australian* 22 October 1994) to be going to the movie prepared 'with plenty of ping-pong balls which they throw at the screen at an appropriate moment'. They were not making a protest. They were celebrating Cynthia's performance (which was also the only 'straight' heterosexual moment in the film but also its most camp parody). The report continued 'It reminds one of that other interactive movie with strong Aussie ties, *The Rocky Horror Picture Show*' (that film's director is an Australian).

In Elliott's favour it must be noted that the 'ugly, daggy, monstrous Australian' is a part of the culture (which has proved fertile ground for multiculturalism's sustaining of a mild ethnic supremacist position *vis-à-vis* the broader Australian culture). In a culture which has so routinely delivered dystopian visions of Australian life and concentrated on its materialism, its shallowness and its stupor, not to accommodate the various ethnicities in these terms is to 'other' them once more (it leaves them as the perpetual Other, always good and always the victim, virtuous but dull, boring and uninteresting). In such circumstances there should be room for the 'ugly, daggy, monstrous (ethnically different) Australian'.

For an identity and critical multiculturalism politics, this set of 'ethics' does not see the difference between the accented and unaccented sign. Oppression, victimization and bastardry – these are crude, immediate and present. Such film-making is experienced as outrageous and hurtful. Worse, it perpetuates stereotypes which lead to excessive violence against the Filipina. The Filipina should be treated with the same respect as the transvestites:

> She [Margeson] said prejudice in the media about Filipino women had contributed to an increasing level of violence that now accounted for the deaths of four children and seventeen women (fourteen of these murdered) between 1980 and May this year . . . A Filipino woman is 5.6 times as likely to be killed by her spouse or former spouse than an Australian woman.
>
> (Cafarella 1994)

The facts of racist violence are used to counter unwanted representations. Undoubtedly, the producers might have expected that only the cinephile and gay pride parts of the repertoire would be mobilized, which would have benefitted the film's career as a 'feel-good' movie – and not social texts portraying the film as misogynist and anti-Asian.

MOBILIZING PART OF THE REPERTOIRE

Outside the benign 'event' film like *Picnic at Hanging Rock* and *Strictly Ballroom*, the controversial 'event' film like *Romper Stomper*, the dissension over the different moralities contained in each repertoire, there is almost a division of labour in operation as these different repertoires are distributed across film forms and critical institutions. While it is possible to put a film or television programme in any of these different positions, they are ordinarily positioned by their producers, critics and audiences more in one position than another. Historically Australian cinema criticism, like the cinema itself, has tended to emphasize certain things about particular films.

Some features and television programmes are made to be read and marketed as 'true to the actual'. Documentaries are obviously going to be more concerned with social problematization than with explicitly foregrounding the relation to the film world or to its generic features (the 'docu-experiments' of John Hughes, Helen Grace and Gillian Leahy are exceptions here).

Social problem films like *Fran* (Hambly 1985) and *Annie's Coming Out* (Brealey 1984) tend to be developed in relation to their social intertext and downplay their melodramatic aspects. The more successfully these films mobilize their social intertext – in *Fran* a 'problem' single mother who eventually loses custody of her children, in *Annie's Coming Out* a physically disabled person struggling to communicate and show her mental and expressive capacity – the less they get discussed in terms of their representational techniques and generic conventions, since that would compromise and even seem to callously deny the social problem surveyed.

The television mini-series of the 1980s often foregrounded their social texts and with this their citizenship (education and informing) purposes. Such was the case with *The Dismissal* (Dr Miller, Schultz, Ogilvie, Paver 1983), given its focus on Australia's major constitutional crisis this century when an elected federal government was sacked by the Queen's representative. Even here other inter-pretative protocols were present, such that the mini-series, particularly after the controversy surrounding its political interpretation had subsided. Television criticism discussed it generically in relation to contemporaneous American films and mini-series about American politics. Its production protocols were considered in relation to British models of docu-drama, whilst some compared it to other Australian mini-series and assessed the extent to which it innovated or conformed to them.

The international art film can be seen as a means of delivering, in a relatively coherent package, a film-making which could be readily and easily recognized as simultaneously social text driven, cultural intertext driven and as a participant in international cinema. Sometimes these links are at the production more than the reception level. *Bad Boy Bubby* is close to some Eastern European, particularly Polish cinema. *Last Days of Chez Nous* demonstrates a firm grasp of the French and German art film right down to Bruno Ganz's presence.

Self-consciously, genre films ask to be judged in relation to their Hollywood intertext and only secondarily in relation to Australian cinema and social inter-texts. Exploitation and action films are going to be rather more defined by the generic templates of the film world and popular cinema and television.

Yet social intertexts, cultural intertexts and international filmic intertexts range over the entire continuum of 'commercial' and 'quality' production. The independent film-making espoused in the now defunct *Filmnews* often defined itself variously in relation to the Australian social text, contemporaneous international developments, and other like texts both nationally and internationally. It is also rash to assume that a film is automatically dealing with one or other intertext at the expense of the others. It often depends on critical and viewing habits, promotional purposes and the inflection given to social issues. Carol Laseur (1992) has shown how Australian exploitation and cult films like *Howling III: the Marsupials* and *Hostage* (Shields 1983) often carry strong social intertexts but rarely if ever get described or lauded for their sensitive handling of social problems. Perhaps this is one consequence of a film milieu that structurally co-associates the publicly funded with quality and independence and the privately funded with commercial and genre-dependence. Consequently it is difficult to promote a place for 'badness as goodness' in Australian exploitation cinema. Anna Maria dell'Oso cannot recognize *Roly Poly Man*'s (Goldsworthy 1994) 'bad goodness', but she can laud as worthy Australian films lensed in Spanish like *El Angelito* (Sepulveda 1993). Unlike the US situation, where exploitation cinema is lauded for its often progressive elements and experimentation, Australian exploitation cinema is generally regarded as conformist – it is on the 'commercial' side of the dualist repertoires in circumstances where liberal state funding keeps open a non-commercial space.

This division of labour within film-making is repeated in the different forms and institutions of film criticism. In a quality daily review, the critic situates an Australian cinema in relation to the mainstream Hollywood cinema and, less regularly, art cinema and independent release. Australian films will consequently tend to be situated on the horizons of this international cinema and well-known Australian films. *Cinema Papers* critics will emphasize filmic intertexts – Australian and international more than social texts. They are also going to be more concerned with matters of style and their realization. Those who write for *Metro* are more interested in some way of combining these pro-filmic concerns with social and political problems and progressive concerns. In its turn, film studies tends to be similarly interpenetrated, mixing references to international cinema and localizing the prevailing critical models and concerns, owing to its shared international protocols.

Brian McFarlane's *Australian Cinema, 1970–1985* (1987) and his later effort with Geoff Mayer *New Australian Cinema* (1992) surveys Australian cinema with reference to itself and international, particularly British, cinema in the case of the latter. Graeme Turner's *National Fictions* (1986, 1993c) surveys Australian cinema in terms of a specifically Australian set of concerns which are present also in the literary tradition. Adrian Martin's film criticism typically positions Australian cinema in relation to international cinema – particularly Hollywood cinema, experimental and avant-garde cinema – see his essay on Australian

'Fantasy cinema' in Scott Murray's edited collection *The New Australian Cinema* (1980) and his practice in *Phantasms* (1994b).

Critical intellectuals are more interested in foregrounding the adequacy of a film's social problematizations and investigating its ideological values. Their emphasis upon the social text opens out on to films as social history, as social record, as political statements. They find cultural relations between films and social context, film-makers and the social imaginary, cultural stereotypes and cultural exactitude. Works on Australian nationalism and culture such as Stephen Alomes *A Nation at Last* (1988) embed Australian cinema within ideological and cultural concerns at the level of the social text, in this case nationalist discourses. Feature articles on social problem film-making like the ABC mini-series *The Leaving of Liverpool* will emphasize the social text of the migrant experience of child orphans in brutal and repressive Catholic schools in the 1950s and its legacy for survivors.

These repertoires are selectively used to conduct industry politics. Where industry actors justify film production in cultural terms, they mobilize arguments related to Australian social texts, aesthetic texts, and international forms of cinema assumed to be the most appropriate vehicles for such texts. Whereas, justifying a film production in entertainment values tends to mobilize arguments related to the existing international – principally Hollywood – cinema, in circumstances where similarities rather than social differences are stressed. During the 1990s these alternatives became mixed up, as co-productions became more important, the multicultural concerns of independents became those of the centre and the social texts of films could be international and not exclusively Australian (see Jacka and Cunningham 1993).

Each of these repertoires has a changing priority on the public record. The general positioning of Australian cinema on public horizons changes as one or other of these repertoires are emphasized. During the 1970s, Australian cinema tended to be situated more in terms of the Australian cultural and social text axis, with other reference points being subordinated to this axis. This led to exasperation on the part of critics like Adrian Martin (1980) and Stuart Cunningham (1978) who worried about the naïve aesthetics of a film-making whose only sense of aesthetic and moral mission seemed to be true to the actual, as if film-making did not have to pass though a panoply of techniques, genres and norms to make its meaning.

During the latter part of the 1980s Australian cinema tended to be situated rather more in terms of the international cinema axis, downplaying its relation to the social text and Australian symbolic texts. This trend could be seen in how Meaghan Morris's (1980, 1988, 1989) work moves from establishing the 'auto-creating' aspects of Australian cinema in the 1970s to the 'hetero-identifications' of the late 1980s.

Each of these repertoires is dynamic and changing. While the general outline of the repertoires does not change, the 'contents' do. Nowhere is this more evident than with the social text. The cinema's social texts turn on diverse axes of cultural differentiation that enable distinctions to be made at a policy-making, critical and film-making level.

Take the Australian social text. When notions of Australian society and Australian nation change, there is a disturbance at the level of the public culture. Australia went from being seen as a class-based, gender divided society with a strong urban rural dichotomy (differences within the form of the same; for example, the same accent), to a society made up of a mixture of diasporas, ethnicities, languages, variety of Australian English, sexual orientations. Cultural diversity was privileged and with it figures of unity in diversity, hybridity, multi-ancestry, linguistic diversity (sameness through difference). In this process, priorities were reorganized. Women, gays and ethnics become 'the battlers' – Muriel, Mitzi and Nick (of *The Heartbreak Kid*). These different senses of relevance and identity conferred through social text give Australian cinema, in a sense, a particular 'right to exist'.

REPERTOIRES AS A NATURAL SCAPE

Australian cinema simply exists on a continuum of Australian (and international) social texts, cultural and international cinema intertexts, purposes of enlightenment and exploitation. These repertoires are part of the landscape of Australian cinema. They have long become self-evident, and are un-selfreflexive, interpretative and creative norms. That some critics will be more interested in situating films in relation to Australian films and locally produced performing arts, some in relation to international films and others in relation to social issues, is as natural a phenomenon as is the film criticism of Meaghan Morris, which draws upon all these different coordinates to review and shape discussion of film meaning. These templates do not simply enable critics to see different films and then use the templates to organize their perceptions of difference and sameness and assert the viability of their filmic interpretation over others; they also enable audiences viewing the films and film-makers organizing a film project to utilize a range of socially meaningful interpretative protocols.

Each of these terms is integral to the naturalization, socialization and discursivization of Australian cinema. They are a 'naturally occurring', but socially constructed and discursively represented, set of combative points, points of agreement and points of non-contact which are the means by which Australian cinema is positioned and thought.

These tendencies give various directions to the film milieu. They collide, interact, complement and co-shape each other. They deliver a range of interconnected though disparate activities organizing consensus, stabilizing and generating conflict about film meaning.

Although 'taking sides' over which repertoire is the most important is intrinsic to the natural combativeness of the film milieu and institutions within it, we should not here privilege social texts, local Australian cinema, international trajectories, or one side of the dualist divide. To disclose the full repertoires of film meaning we must attend to how they work. This means acknowledging the co-presence in Australian film-making and critical formations concerned with handling film of quite different though contiguous interpretative templates for organizing film meaning.

Our task is to sort them out – not to purify them and put each into neat compartments but to find how their interaction creates Australian cinema as a hybrid public entity which is capable of diverse production, of critical and emotional investments. This sorting activity does not approach Australian cinema as a 'dirty' object to be 'cleaned up' through rigorous critical insight (locating their contradictions, paraphrasing their contents, writing principled criticism of them) or through privileging one of these repertoires over the others by, for example, arguing for Australian cinema's relationship to its Australian and/or international filmic intertexts at the expense of its social intertexts, and various non-filmic and cultural interests. Instead this sorting finds ways in which this messiness can be opened out on to a patchwork coherence facilitating the creation of new entities capable of extension through time and space. Throughout this book, I am concerned with this patchwork rather than breaking it down into component parts.

Future chapters will provide some explanation for the persistence of these cultural repertoires and their relative stability in the cinema's diversity and unity, logics of cultural transfers and its distinctiveness. The concern for the cinema to engage with social texts is close to the national cinema trope of a cinema of the people-among-themselves participating in the great social themes of our time. *Sylvania Waters* (Hill and Woods 1992) is both a story of the Australian people (Rowe 1994) and, the contemporary family in Western capitalist nations (Stratton and Ang 1994a). The attention to Australian aesthetic traditions turns on 'Australian distinctiveness' and making a distinct contribution to the cinema. The logic of cultural transfers and a diverse cinema output map Australia's participation in the various pathways of international cinema.

All of these interpretative and interventionary acts can, in one way or another, be reduced to two intersecting variations:

1 the dualist repertoires of education and entertainment, film culture and film industry, public service broadcasting and commercial broadcasting, quality and demotic cinema, art cinema and popular cinema, with its international entailments British and European cinema and Hollywood cinema as reference points; and
2 Australian intertexts – at one extreme Australian aesthetic culture and at the other extreme social texts (this includes to a lesser extent international social texts).

These can be represented on the following grid.

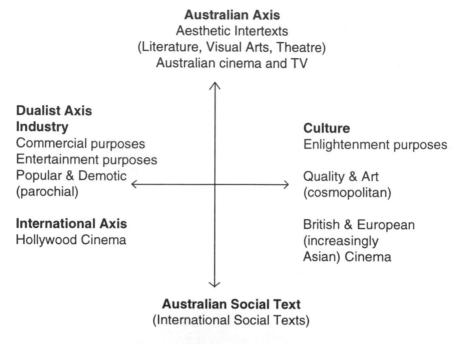

Australian Axis
Aesthetic Intertexts
(Literature, Visual Arts, Theatre)
Australian cinema and TV

Dualist Axis
Industry
Commercial purposes
Entertainment purposes
Popular & Demotic
(parochial)

Culture
Enlightenment purposes

Quality & Art
(cosmopolitan)

International Axis
Hollywood Cinema

British & European
(increasingly
Asian) Cinema

Australian Social Text
(International Social Texts)

Figure 1. The Australian cinema matrix

Making an Australian film mean is a point around which naturalizing, socializing and discursivizing movements intersect. What is disclosed at this point is the hybrid dimension of the cinema as simultaneously international, local, social and discursive (generic). These repertoires provide a store that is drawn on by members of the film milieu for a variety of purposes. film-makers, critics, policy-makers can pursue one to the exclusion of others, they can mix them up, they can create heirarchies of value, pitting one against another. These repertoires can be 'purified', made to be 'interpenetrated' and 'opposed' alike. Some repertoires and some aspects of particular repertoires are emphasized more at different times. These emphases are a consequence of politics, dispositions of forces and the entrepreneurial purposes of those institutional actors who attach them to particular industry programmes and film-making projects. The discursive career of films and television programmes are not only a habit of consumption and criticism, it is part of the activity of the producers themselves in creating, constructing and marketing films.

Because my purpose is to understand the fields in which Australian cinema circulates and comes to mean, I have imposed a somewhat agnostic position upon my practice. I do not want to say that, as critics, we should focus on one or other of these repertoires (that the references to other Australian cinema texts should organize our film appreciation – this would be difficult, given the absence of a large and ongoing canon of Australian film that large numbers of people are familiar with) or that Australian cinema should be positioned exclusively in relation to the international cinema. I do not want to demand that film-makers should be more concerned with local social texts and less with genres and international production orientations or vice versa. All of these are important and useful issues to address. Such partisan positions are the naturally occurring rhetorical and institutional features of a film landscape that I have set out to describe.

My strategy is one of making sense of Australian film. I have provided a generous model with which to approach film meaning, insisting upon the place of each of these assembled elements, rather than attempting to drive one or other out. If we want to directly and immediately participate in the making of Australian film meaning, then we are inevitably involved in more direct tasks than these contemplative ones. But if our purpose is to understand a film-making milieu, if we are trying to understand the dynamics of Australian cinema and grasp its dimensions and rhetorical dynamics over time – then we need to consider the ways in which Australian film meaning is structurally, institutionally and discursively organized in order to be self-evident. Without a grasp of the repertoires of film meaning and their different objects and purposes, we can still be effective partisan critics, but that is all we will be. We will be unaware of the structuring matrices through which the cinema is understand and positioned. And to be unaware is to lose the possibility of envisaging something different.

I have shown how Australian film-making is sustained by a number of repertoires. Inasmuch as each are sustained by institutions, ideas and means of deployment each repertoire produces film as a cultural matter. Sometimes we distinguish the anthropological culture of the social world from the aesthetic milieu of production, genre, performance and narrative; we distinguish social criticism from textual criticism; we distinguish public politics from textual politics. But each are thoroughly cultural matters and none is more cultural than the other.

In this chapter I have shown Australian cinema to be necessarily an 'in-between' phenomenon. Australian films are not necessarily 'transnational culture', nor are they 'local culture'; they negotiate local and international production traditions. Such 'in-betweenness' fits a milieu in which Australian cinema and television producers, as well as critics and audiences negotiate a large dose of Hollywood movies and locally-produced infotainment, series and serials.

Part II

Making a distinct cinema

Chapter 7

Diversity

A DIVERSE CINEMA

> Like so many others, I had assumed that a cinema that had been in the international spotlight for almost 15 years, and gained such recognition with its New Wave, was a known quantity. It wasn't until the UCLA Film and Television Archive sent me to Australia to take a first-hand look at the full range of production that I realized how much we [Americans] had been missing. I was thrilled to discover a film culture of such exceptional diversity, richness and significance. I found a wealth of outstanding film and television unseen in the US, along with many talented directors, writers, actors and directors of photography unknown overseas. I was impressed by Australia's innovative schemes for nurturing new talent and supporting a wide range of film and television productions.
>
> (Broderick 1988: vi–vii)

Broderick's promotional remarks were made in the context of introducing the *Back of Beyond* festival of Australian cinema which he curated in Los Angeles in 1988. Australian cinema is a diverse cinema and television made of projects with little in common. It is a family of rivalrous, complementary and disconnected film-making projects. Feature film-making, television drama, documentary, short film and experimental projects compete with each other for the public's attention, a slice of government funds and critical scrutiny. These several film forms also provide for a well-rounded film-making milieu and film appreciation culture.

Additionally, within each of these forms there are noteworthy differences of emphasis, genre and style such that there are large variations in each category of film-making. Take some theatrical releases for 1991: what, if anything, connects John Ruane's black comedy of ethnic interrelation, *Death in Brunswick*, Peter Weir's romantic comedy *Green Card*, Jocelyn Moorhouse's 'art film' *Proof* with its conceit of a blind man taking photographs, and John Duigan's coming of age boarding school film about two outsiders, *Flirting*?

There is no one Australian feature cinema, documentary cinema, independent cinema, television drama or avant-garde. There is little in the way of a common form among these several projects. Instead Australian cinema contributes to the various pathways of the cinema and television dramas.

CONTRIBUTING TO THE CINEMA'S PATHWAYS

We can talk of the relative strength of the Australian contribution in the various formats and genres of cinema and television. These vary over time. Two of the strongest Australian contributions stretch over the entire history of the cinema: the 'western' genre and the documentary.

The Australian contribution to the western goes back to the beginnings of Australian film in its multi-reel bushranger film *The Story of The Kelly Gang* in 1906. The exploits of the Kelly gang, who conducted a sustained campaign against the police and held up towns donning armour fashioned from plough shears, proved a consistent reference point for Australian cinema (features made in 1906, 1920, 1923, 1934, 1951, and 1970). Mick Jagger played the hero in the 1970 version of *Ned Kelly* directed by Tony Richardson. Ian Jones and Bronwyn Binns' mini-series *The Last Outlaw* (Dobson and Dr Miller 1980) drew on Jones' own historical research to fashion a revisionist account of the story as the 'Kelly outbreak' – a minor political rebellion. This mini-series was first broadcast 100 years to the day on which Kelly was hanged (Moran 1993: 261). Yahoo Serious later updated the Kelly myth to a contemporary setting in *Reckless Kelly* (1993). Here Ned sits astride a motorbike, has an Aboriginal side of the family, holds up banks and thwarts the plans of his arch enemy to sell the Kelly island to Japanese investors for towing to Japan. He saves the day through his own bravery and the money he has earned from his Hollywood career.

The power, reach and strength of the 'bushranger film' for local audiences proved so popular in the early years of the century that it was banned in the most populous state of New South Wales. Yet there have been a number of bushranger films. Rolf Boldrewood's novel, *Robbery Under Arms* has been remade no less than five times (1907, 1911, 1920, 1957, 1985/6). In 1985 the then South Australian Film Corporation released a feature and a year later a mini-series version of the film.

The bushranger as 'working class' hero was given an added inflection in Cecil Holmes' *Captain Thunderbolt*. Holmes took the unusual step of having as the voiceover narrator an entirely unsympathetic 'trooper', whose cruelty to Thunderbolt and others drove the hero to escape custody and pursue a subsequent career as a Robin Hood of the New England tablelands. This figure's continuing obsession with capturing Thunderbolt drives the narrative. Cunningham (1987b: 95) recalls it as 'a particularly confident, stylistically and politically radical short fiction' claiming it as 'the best treatment of the ... bushranger theme in the Australian cinema'. He also notes its 'outrageous piece of cinephilic interpolation in homage to Eisenstein ... the black suited, brandy swilling, cigar chomping, bloated capitalists are framed vertically from floor level underneath a glass-topped table'. A bushranger film animated by similar cinephile concerns was Phillippe Mora's *Mad Dog Morgan* (1976) – again based on a true story – about the eponymous bushranger of the 1860s who 'had a public reputation as a maniacal killer, but the film attempted to break through the legend to present Morgan as a poor Irish victim of a violent society and a repressive colonial administration' (Pike and Cooper 1980: 379). Mora makes the colonial administration criminal and psychotic in its demonizing of Morgan and subsequent barbaric handling of his remains (his sympathetic treatment of Morgan is in marked contrast to the 1911 version of the story). It also explicitly connects what happens to Morgan to the criminal and random violence of the white gold diggers against their Chinese counterparts. It is also the first of the 'schizo' roles which Dennis Hopper later made his own. With typical Australian 'difference' Hopper's Mad Dog is the hero not the villain. Mora said that Dennis Hopper 'brought an insanity to the role, and an intensity that most actors would have found impossible to create' (quoted in Pike and Cooper 1980: 379).

Fred Schepisi's *The Chant of Jimmie Blacksmith* also centres on an historical outlaw – Jimmy Governor – an Aboriginal driven to mass murder by prejudice. (Schepisi's screenplay was based on the 'documentary fiction' of the same name by Thomas Kenneally – most famous for his later documentary novel which Spielberg made into *Schindler's List* 1993.)

There are also Snowy Baker's athletic westerns of the 1920s such as *The Shadow of Lightning Ridge* (W. Lucas 1920) in which

> Baker was put through a series of amazing stunts: these included leaping from a galloping horse on to a moving train; fighting with a guard in the horse box, underneath the frightened animals' hooves; riding his own horse Boomerang along a narrow fifty-foot log above an abyss while his police companions crawl across on hands and knees; and, in a final piece of daring, jumping Boomerang from thirty feet up a mountain through a roof of a remote hut to save Brownie Vernon as heroine from the real villain.
>
> (Tulloch 1981: 93)

The 1946 cattle drive western has its Australian equivalent in the 'drover' films which in Australia often had a contemporary setting: *The Overlanders* told the story of an epic cattle drive from the West to the East coast in the 1940s, *The Sundowners* that of a droving family (with its Hollywood actors Robert Mitchum and Deborah Kerr and director Fred Zinnemann adapted from the Australian novel by Jon Cleary).[1] There has also been a supernatural western *The Phantom Stockman* where Chips Rafferty is invested with Phantom-like powers not unlike those Paul Hogan calls upon to defeat the Latin American drug cartel in *Crocodile Dundee II* (Cornell 1988).

Another interesting variation of the contemporary western was provided by the mini-series *Alice to Nowhere* (Power 1986) in which two thieves and killers hijack the Birdsville Mail and hold the mailman and three others hostage (the mini-series followed the journey of the mailman in John Heyer's mytho-poetic 1954 documentary *The Back of Beyond*). For Moran (1993: 49) this series 'belongs to a familiar cycle ... of 1950s westerns such as *Rawhide, The Fastest Gun Alive* and *The Fiend who Walked the West*'. This mini-series is a contemporary version of the stage coach western which has, as its predecessor, *Whiplash* (J. Lucas and Maxwell 1961) which centred on the Australian version of Wells Fargo, the Cobb and Co stage-coach line. (It featured Peter Graves who came back 30 years later for the remake on the Gold Coast of the Hollywood series he starred in, *Mission Impossible*.) There have been goldrush mini-series in *Rush* (Arnold, Taylor and Jenkins 1974) and *Eureka Stockade* (Hardy 1984), and a riverboat mini-series in *All the Rivers Run* (G. Miller, Power, Amenta 1983). *The Man from Snowy River* is a western melodrama, as too is its family television mini-series successor, *Banjo Patterson's The Man from Snowy River* (T. Burstall, Lawrence, D. Burstall 1994) – set twenty years on from the famous ride. Like the earlier *Whiplash*, this mini-series had American production backing – this time from the Family Channel (in 1994 it was screened on New York cable-TV at 6 pm on Saturdays).

For its part, documentary is the oldest continuous tradition of film-making in Australia and one of the most important. Newsreels survived in the cinema, when feature film-making declined in the 1940s, 1950s and 1960s and during this period the documentary provided opportunities for intellectuals to be involved in the cinema. There is hardly any aspect of Australian film-making – fictional or experimental – which has not been touched in some way by the documentary. The documentary lays most claim to being Australia's major, even singular, contribution to world cinema and television programming. In virtually every major documentary genre there are outstanding Australian examples. The classical documentary has a high point in Heyer's *The Back of Beyond*; the political documentary in Joris Ivens *Indonesia Calling* (1946) and in David Bradbury's career, stretching from *Front Line* (1980) through *State of Shock* (1989) to *Nazi Supergrass* (1993). The docu-drama *The Overlanders* successfully straddled two genres, being both a careful documentary reconstruction of a notable cattle drive during the Second World War and an oddball western. Ethnographic film-making began in Australia at the same time as elsewhere and today a number of its foremost contemporary practitioners are Australian-based film-makers – David and Judith MacDougall, Bob Connolly and Robin Anderson with productions such as *Takeover* and *Black Harvest* (1992). Collaborative documentaries involving political activist white film-makers and indigenous people are well represented: Cavadini and Strachan's *Two Laws*, David Noakes' *How the West was Lost*, and most recently Frank Rijavek's *Exile and the Kingdom*.

There are also the 'fly on the wall' documentaries – most famously the 1992 'reality fiction'/'reality soap' of *Sylvania Waters* following a Sydney family with the rhythms of a soap opera. That most recent realm of the 'personal' documentary

– in which the film-maker becomes a personality in the film, interposing himself or herself in the story – is well represented in the work of Barbara Chobocky (*Maria* 1991), Graeme Chase (*Modern Times* 1992), Noakes (*Bigger than Texas*) Gillian Coote (*Island of Lies*) and O'Rourke – the result of which is his self-proclaimed 'fiction documentary' *The Good Woman of Bangkok*. Then there are the experimental documentaries: the feminist experimentation of Mitzi Goldman and Trish FitzSimons' *Snakes and Ladders* (1987) and *Serious Undertakings* and John Hughes' Walter Benjamin project *One Way Street*, described by Adrian Martin (1994d: 300) as 'tele-doco/essay film/new image research hybrid'.[2] There are the social diversity documentary series like *Chequerboard* (1969–75) and *The Big Country* which began its 20 year career in 1968; the raft of nature/wildlife documentaries; and the artist documentaries like Christina Wilcox's *The Nights Belong to the Novelist* (1987).

Unlike the documentary and the western, other genres of film-making are relatively recent. The 'art cinema' is a post-Second World War phenomena in Australia, beginning perhaps with *Clay* (Mangiamele 1965). The science fiction film more or less begins with Sharman's *Shirley Thompson versus the Aliens* in 1972. That film was described by its director, Jim Sharman, as 'a psychological thriller cum 50s rock musical/science fiction/fantasy movie ... the only A-grade B-movie loathed by underground, art-house and commercial management alike' (Pike and Cooper 1980: 338). In it the eponymous heroine is visited by aliens and is committed to an insane asylum when she tries unsuccessfully to convince people of the aliens' existence.[3] The science fiction film moves assuredly on to the post-Apocalypse film-making of the *Mad Max* trilogy in the late 1970s and early 1980s. Two interesting later variants are the 'tall story' science fiction comedy of *As Times Goes By* (Peak 1988) about 'the encounter between a young surfie and an alien in outback Australia' (Epstein 1993: 241) and the 'psychological' science fiction of de Heer's *Incident at Raven's Gate* (1989) where the impact of the strange force on the different characters and their relationship with each other drives the narrative rather than any pyrotechnics or special effects.

Some genres move in and out of centrality. While there was a steady though minor stream of thrillers from the late 1950s beginning with *The Stowaway* (Robinson and Habib 1958) and *The Seige of Pinchgut* (Watt 1959), the thriller did not become central to feature film-making definitions until the 1980s when Scott Murray (1994b: 97) described it as 'a main staple of the 10BA era'. That decade's political thrillers included the high budget ($7 million) thriller *Ground Zero* (Pattinson 1987) centring on the cover-up of fall out from atomic bomb testing in South Australia. This film's paranoia recalls the British mini-series *Edge of Darkness* (1985). *Heatwave* (Noyce 1982) and *The Killing of Angel Street* (Crombie 1981) centre on ordinary people dealing with corrupt property developers who are prepared to eliminate or compromise people who get in their way. John Duigan's *Far East* (1982), was set against an unstable South-East Asian political situation. For its part, *Dead Calm* provided Phil Noyce with his directorial ticket to Hollywood, while providing Nicole Kidman with the platform for her Hollywood career.

The Woman-centred narrative is one feature genre that has maintained an ongoing though minor presence on production schedules, particularly from 1970. Its success sometimes sees it touted by public and critics alike as representative of Australian cinema. The woman-centred film has been a regular feature on production slates, whether it be the Raymond Longford, Lottie Lyall and Arthur Higgins collaboration *The Woman Suffers ... While the Man Goes Free* (1918) or 1970s titles like *Caddie, My Brilliant Career, The Getting of Wisdom*, 1980s titles like *Fran, Hightide* (Armstrong 1987), and in the 1990s *The Last Days of Chez Nous* and *The Piano*. This film-making has survived owing to the predilection for social problem film-making on Australian cinema schedules in the 1910s, the 1920s and since 1970, and the unusually significant though still minor presence of women directors and producers in Australian film. Public campaigns of the domestic feminist movement have been strong, and a prioritizing of relationships as a central point of focus in Australian cinema has been necessary because it has had to rely less on action and more on relationships.

Another genre with a consistent though minor presence on film-making lists is the Australian melodrama. The Australian industry is routinely an expert producer and now a concept exporter for its television soaps and mini-series. No one could safely suggest that Australian features lack emotion, intensities, excessive feelings and altered states if they put together the following films, beginning with *The Woman Suffers ... While the Man Goes Free* and moving through Barrett's *The Breaking of the Drought* (1920), with its dual plot lines of the onset of drought and the squandering of the family fortune in the city. Ken Hall's *Broken Melody* – possibly his finest feature – has as its conceit an Australian Chopin, living penniless under the Harbour bridge, made accidentally famous through a benefactor and returning from England to conduct his own operetta about his lost love 'Raggedy Ann' (who is the substitute singer in the role unbeknownst to the conductor/composer). There is also Chauvel's great family melodrama *The Sons of Matthew* (1949) and his Aboriginal melodrama *Jedda*. In the mid-1980s, titles like *Jenny Kissed Me* (Trenchard-Smith 1986) explored the hysterical 'father' seeking to maintain a fatherly relationship with his non-biological 'daughter' after the break up of his live-in relationship with the child's mother. The film *Silver City* manages its love triangle of marriage, mistress and duty, whilst Lex Marinos' *Indecent Obsession* (1985) brings the male lead's heterosexuality into public question. In *Careful he Might Hear You*, two sisters (played by Wendy Hughes and Robyn Nevin) battle each other for the custody of the child PS – a film which pushes Australian melodrama towards high melodrama. Finally, there are the 'burnt' misanthropic lovers of Bill Bennett's *Jilted* (1987).

In the mini-series, melodrama is a staple. One of the most sucessful of mini-series both domestically and internationally, *Return to Eden* (Arthur *et al.* 1983), has Rebecca Gilling playing a wife who survives her husband and his lover's attempt to murder her for her money by feeding her to crocodiles. She returns complete with a new identity and a new face created by a master surgeon (who promptly falls in love with his own creation) to wreak vengeance upon her husband and his lover. For its part, Kennedy-Miller's *Dirtwater Dynasty* (1988) makes the convolutions and coincidences of the early twentieth-century film classic, *The Breaking of the Drought*, look restrained in comparison. People are struck by lightning, father and son are torpedoed at sea not long after being reunited, a mother contracts terminal illness and is unable to care for her children, and the existence of daughters is kept from fathers by grandparents. In one excruciating scene a father asks directions from his real daughter – he is looking for her and she needs him (their true relationship is unknown to both of them at the time). Families are not on speaking terms and neighbours are implacable foes over a lifetime.

There is the action cinema of *Forty Thousand Horsemen*; the romantic comedy in *The Sentimental Bloke*, the mad-cap comedy in *Around the World in 80 Ways* (MacLean 1988) and *Young Einstein*; while *Star Struck* and *Strictly Ballroom* pay their homage to the musical and teen movie simultaneously. The horror film is rendered in *Patrick*. *Shame* draws on elements of the road movie, as its feminist bikie lawyer rides into town.

For the obvious reason of budgets and special effects infrastructures, there have not been many Australian epics – the two that particularly stand out are Norman Dawn's 1927 version of *For the Term of His Natural Life* and Dr George Miller and George Ogilvie's Cecil B. de Mille homage *Mad Max III: Beyond Thunderdome*, with Mel Gibson as Max and Tina Turner as the queen of barter town.

There is a rich and important tradition of Australian 'location' films from Frank Hurley's strange *Jungle Woman* (1926) to Robinson's *Walk into Paradise* – both set in Nui (New) Guinea – to Chauvel's *In the Wake of the Bounty* (1933, Pitcairn island), to Weir's *The Year of Living Dangerously* (Indonesia), to Faiman's *Crocodile Dundee* and Cornell's *Crocodile Dundee II*. This aspect will be discussed further below.

The depth of Australia's contribution to cinema can also be seen in more marginal feature and experimental areas. The cinephile imagination has produced a minor strand of Australian exploitation film-making in the 1980s and 1990s (Laseur 1993, Martin 1988a). These have included those which do violence to well-known Australian television identities in *Turkey Shoot* (Trenchard-Smith 1982) and the later *Body Melt*. In the first film, these identities were hunted down to be raped and brutally murdered, while, in the later film, the identities literally decompose into a colourful sludge before our eyes after taking vitamin pills. There have been parodies of the horror film in the Australian *Howling* film, *Howling III: the Marsupials* and in *Razorback* (although this film takes itself a little more seriously than the former). In *Howling III*, the central conceit is marsupial werewolves – produced from the mating of kangaroos and humans – which are an endangered species with pouches. Then there are Sandy Harbutt's *Stone* (1974) with its bikie cop struggling to solve a spate of murders amongst a motorcycle gang; and Frank Shields's *Hostage* where the story of Christine Maresch is retold as a graphic tale of blackmail, German neo-Nazis, robbery and domestic violence.

The Australian surf movie of the 1960s and 1970s was popular enough to justify Albie Thoms making a film about it for German television (*Surf Movies* 1981). Writing in 1975, Thoms noted how between 1960 and 1975 no fewer than twenty-four features had been made, its practitioners being among the most experienced in the country, and that this phenomenon had led to the creation of 'an independent, vertically integrated film economy to control production, distribution and exhibition' (1978: 85). He claimed that surf movies like *Crystal Voyager* (Falzon 1973), *Rolling Home* (Witzig 1974), *Morning of the Earth* (Falzon 1972) had 'greatly extended the range of pictorial imagery in Australian film, and closely observed Australian lifestyles ignored by other film-makers' (89). In conversation with the author, Thoms claimed not unreasonably that this cinema provided many Australians with their only *filmic* image of Australia in the 1960s.

Rolf de Heer directed, in *Dingo* (1992), a 'jazz film'. Miles Davis's 'cool jazz' sound becomes here the authentic outback sound of the eponymous hero who risks all for his music. De Heer cuts and frames his shots as much as possible to the music, attempting not just a film about jazz but a jazz film. Lowenstein's *Dogs in Space* is similarly structured and driven by the music. Adrian Martin (1994d: 300) insists on the 'rich tradition our experimental cinema is', citing Corinne Cantrill's *In this Life's Body* (1984), Arf Arf's *Thread of Voice* (1994) and Michael Lee's *Mystical Rose* (1976) as exemplars.

Indigenous film-making is represented in the films of Tracey Moffatt (*Nice Coloured Girls, beDevil*), Essie Coffey (*My Survival as an Aborigine* 1979), and Anne Pratten's *Terra Nullius*. Peter Loizos (1993: 167–87) devotes a whole chapter of his book on ethnographic film to Australian ethnographic films made between 1972 and 1980 'which are distinctive by virtue of the strong voices of their Aboriginal subjects, reaching us through their collaborations with white film-makers' (*Coniston Muster: Scenes from a Stockman's Life* (Sandall 1972); *Mourning for Mangatopi: A Tiwi Bereavement Ceremony* (Levy 1975); *The House Opening* (J. MacDougall 1980); *Waiting for Harry* (McKenzie 1980)).

From the mid-1970s, there has been a steady stream of feminist film-making. It stretches from Jeni Thornley's quasi-autobiographical *Maidens* (1978), through women and politics documentaries like *Red Matildas* (Connolly and Graham 1985), to the experimental fiction of Susan Dermody's *Breathing Under Water* (1992) and Gillian Leahy's excoriating account of a relationship breakup in *My Life without Steve* (1986). This last is sometimes regarded as an 'essay film' – after the tradition of mixed comment and narration of Godard, Marker and Ruiz (Leahy and King 1994: 246). Two other 'essay films' are Ross Gibson's essay films on Australian film and landscape – *Camera Natura* – and his later discussion of a forest and its peoples in *Wild* (1993). Animation is well represented by *Grendel Grendel Grendel* (Stitt 1981) and Yoram Gross's impressive work, from the contemporary *Blinky Bill* (1994) to *Dot and the Kangaroo* (1977).

CHARACTERISTICS OF CINEMATIC DIVERSITY

The history of Australian film is largely a history of the combinations of possible projects and an indication of which of these are ascendant. A range of conditions sustains these combinations: the nature of state support offered, the policy framework for delivering it, the extent to which talented film workers concentrate in an area, the international opportunities available in commercial and critical terms through working in a film form, and the critical celebration of this or that film-making.

This range and depth is part of a routine dialogue with the cinema and television in its international diversity. Adrian Martin's (1994b) critical practice in his book *Phantasms* makes this evident by placing Australian cinema within the general cinema topics under discussion – like the teen movie; in this way Australian cinema provides one more, and not an especially privileged, example. Mostly, Australian cinema is a dialogue with English-language cinema and television – which is mercifully the most internally differentiated of all cinema and television enterprises. Sometimes it is also a dialogue with the non-English-language international cinemas: Jane Campion's films like *The Piano* and *Sweetie* relate to the French cinema. This diversity within a format (the feature film, the television mini-series and the documentary) and among formats, is fundamental to its identity as a cinema.

The range of these contributions means that Australian cinema is a cinema without a strong identity and market presence. It does not have a market and aesthetic niche in some evident cinematic domain, like say the French cinema or Hong Kong's action cinema. Instead, it grafts itself on to other cinemas – including other national cinemas – producing an Australian version of them. Pauline Chan's *Traps* presents itself as a French location film but its dialogue is in English and Vietnamese. *Country Life* is a 'theatrical film' at home in the British and US filmed stage tradition which clearly betrays its Chekov adaptation. Brophy's *Body Melt* is a low-budget schlock movie glorying in its bad taste, visual excess and sick spectacle.

Such diversity is sometimes a problem and sometimes an advantage. Either way it is unavoidable. Production fragmentation has created a cinema and cinema personnel notably flexible and able to work across different types of film-making. In the 1960s and 1970s, Albie Thoms not only, as noted earlier, directed episodes of *Skippy*, mounted *GTK* – a short rock music show which was a forerunner to the contemporary video-clip – made a low-budget feature *Palm Beach* (1979) with a complex soundtrack and multiple perspectives, but also created 'personal films', whether by scratching the negative Brakhage-style or by basing his *Bolero* (1967) almost entirely around a tracking shot (in order to observe, in Thoms's (1978: 80) own words, 'the effect of movement on perception within the framework of Ravel's music').

Such flexibility also suggests weakness. There is, it seems, never enough follow-through. There just is not the critical mass to enable sufficient specialization in a format, style or genre. There cannot be the same degree of honing of skills from film to film in a screen format (such honing is available to larger film industries or those whose film output has a more stable identity). Dr George Miller diagnoses a problem of cohesion in Australian film and television acting which he attributes to a lack of critical mass and rehearsal time:

> In Australia ... we don't have a big enough acting population to have developed cohesive acting ensembles. Look at any Australian film and it has been cast from mainstream theatre, classically-trained people out of NIDA [National Institute for Dramatic Art], people from soap operas and commercials, and some who have never acted before. And they are all up there on the screen together, with very little rehearsal. It is not surprising there is a lack of cohesion.
>
> (Quoted in Scott Murray 1988b: 36)

The differences within Australian cinema are as significant as any unities it might possess. Moreover these differences are closely related to the differences within the imported Hollywood, British, European art-house, avant-garde and ethnic cinemas themselves. While there are differences between the imported and local projects, the local product must be understood as being in continuity with these international cinemas. In a screen and publishing culture like Australia's, in which imports figure so largely, there is a natural inclination to counterpose the local to the imported and to seek rivalry, incommensurability and adjacency there. While it can be useful to do this, it should not distract from giving due weight to the continuities between Australian and the international cinema that are so fundamental to Australian cinema's identity and structural make-up.

DIVERSITY AS CULTURAL DISPERSAL

Diversity in Australian cinema is also found in its representations: its negotiation of Australian cultural diversity. film-makers routinely mobilize – and critics draw on – the many axes of cultural differentiation made available from Australian social life, politics and government. A national cinema is obliged to enact, express and represent the national lifeways and aspirations of people in Australia – through projecting these specificities it finds its identity and its market niche in the international cinema. Cinematic diversity can be found both in front of the camera and behind the camera.

In front of the camera, Australian cinema includes films and mini-series centred on the Japanese-Australian experience: the prisoners of war in Kennedy-Miller's *Cowra Breakout* or the Japanese war-bride struggling to survive in a crumbling marriage in Hoaas's feature *Aya*; features centred on social class in *Sunday Too Far Away*; on gender in *My Brilliant Career*; on sexual-orientation in *The Sum of*

Us; and region of Australia in the Adelaide of *Return Home*. Issues of age are centred in *Spider and Rose* (Bennett 1994); religious and non-religious affiliation in *Nostradamus Kid* (Ellis 1993); NES migrants in *Silver City*; the interaction of English-speaking-background and NESB people in a Melbourne suburb in *Death in Brunswick*; Aboriginal and settler in *The Chant of Jimmie Blacksmith, The Last Wave* and *Night Cries*; disability in *Annie's Coming Out* and *Struck by Lightning*; occupation in the film workers of David Williamson's *Emerald City*, the pearlers of *King of the Coral Sea* and the drovers of *The Overlanders*. Social values and subcultures find representation in the urban-band-drug subculture of *Monkey Grip*, the 'back of the beach' culture of *Muriel's Wedding*, the fishing town in Gillian Armstrong's *Hightide*, or the inner city street culture of *Going Down*. Existing social differentiations provide cultural coordinates which are not simply contents to be disposed by diverse film-making practices, but are also ways of making sense and making meaning in their own right and thus contributing powerfully to film meaning.

To this representational diversity can be added the cultural diversity behind the camera of Australian film-makers and producers – Aboriginal (Tracey Moffatt), Vietnamese (Pauline Chan), New Zealander (Marie Maclean, Vincent Ward, Jane Campion), Dutch (Paul Cox, Rolf de Heer), Hungarian (Carl Schultz), Greek (Aleksi Vellis, Nadia Tass), Polish (Yoram Gross, Sophie Turkiewicz), French (Henri Safran, Phillippe Mora), Jewish (Ben Lewin, Bob Weis). There are also gay directors and scriptwriters (David Stevens and Stephen McLean) and film-makers from the different parts of Australia: Melbourne (Geoffrey Wright), Adelaide (Ray Argall), Brisbane (Denis O'Rourke). Feminist, Aboriginal and Islander and NESB film-makers variously emphasize how important to film meaning and film-making their creative involvement and direction is, to 'getting it right' and bringing a minority perspective to bear on film.

Many of these cultural differentiations have a structural place in social policy making and in commercial dynamics. For example, special training, access and equity provisions and sometimes funding programmes are available to women, people of an NES background, Aborigines, the disadvantaged, and people in regional areas. These programmes provide one of the reasons why Australia produces many more women directors and producers than do other comparable countries. Institutions like the Australian Film Commission problematize gender and Aboriginal representation in front of and behind the camera. The Australian Film Commission employs an Aboriginal officer, Wal Saunders, and commissioned Marcia Langton (1993) to produce a landmark report on film-makers' relations with indigenous peoples – '*Well I heard it on the radio and I saw it on the television*'.

Similarly, film-makers of the 1990s from an NES background emphasize ethnic backgrounds in storytelling more than did their predecessors – as in Barbara Chobocky's films *Maria* and *Witch Hunt* (1986), *Aussie Rules* (1993) and *Learning the Ropes* (1993). That they do so is partly owing to public redefinitions in the wake of the bringing of multiculturalism into centrality and the ear-marked funding available to NES film-makers and film topics through the SBS and some governmental film programmes. Because of SBS-TV's minority mandate and the fact that it is an important route into television for low-budget productions, independent film-makers and one-off programme makers, a generation of film-makers are entering film-making and achieving public visibility through SBS's minoritarian, multicultural logic. These circumstances affect the selection of story materials and lead to an accentuation of, and a visibility afforded to, ethnic cultural differentiations. SBS-TV has purposely created drama in its *Under the Skin* (1994) and *Six Pack* (Pavlou *et al.* 1991) projects which have been developed with outside producers or it has taken up with projects already developed, such as the shorts for its *Eat Carpet* slot. As the second national broadcaster gaining audience shares of between 1 and 4 per cent on average and with an average audience share one-fifth that of the ABC, SBS-TV operates on lower budgets. It does, however, attract favourable critical attention and governmental recognition on the basis of its multicultural, cultural diversity remit.

Criticism, film-making and policy making will always promote some axes of cultural differentiation and endow some contending voices with more power. How these cultural materials intersect gives a changing set of priorities to the 'cinema of the centre' and the 'peripheral cinemas' alike. Indeed there is something of a division of labour between the two cinemas as regards which cultural differentiations are dealt with. (The ABC and the commercials focused on demography, class, region, age and values-based on-screen indicators; the SBS-TV on ethnic diversity, race and minority communities. This can be mapped over the division between high-budget and low-budget film-making.) If national cinema and television drama will always centre on the dominant ethnicity and its social values, minorities will not be simply excluded. Australian cinema has evolved its particular instruments – including structural and critical instruments – to think and produce its margins.

LOOKING OUTWARDS AS AN AGENT FOR DIVERSITY

Another production factor encouraging diversity in Australian film and television production is its longstanding practice of reaching out to other locations for story settings, story materials and subject. From its inception, Australian cinema has participated in a wider international storytelling – whether it be Chauvel's docu-fictional account of the mutiny on the *Bounty*, *In The Wake of the Bounty* or Vincent Ward's *The Navigator: A Medieval Odyssey* with its 'brilliant conceit of having five men and a boy tunnel from a Middle Ages ravaged by Black Death to a present day of industrial horror and reflecting glass' in 1980s Auckland (Scott Murray 1993b: 254); whether it be Eric Porter's *Marco Polo Junior and the Red Dragon* (1972) – Australia's first animated feature, or Ian Pringle's negotiation of a Dostoyevskian legacy in *Prisoner of St Petersberg* (1990). As it is in the nature of culture and the cinema to be international and to cross borders, Australian film-

makers have taken up and redisposed internationally shared repertoires of locations, images, nationalities, styles of performance, stories and orientations
towards story materials. This interest on the part of film-makers and
audiences alike stems from being part of the international audience for films
and stories and the free-floating character of repertoires of national images and
situations in global image markets.

When an 'inward looking' national drama seemed a characteristic of feature
film-making in the 1980s, Meaghan Morris (1989: 119–20) observed that documentary and television production were operating with 'a complex and current
sense of 'Australia' as a culturally and racially mixed society in the Asia-Pacific
region'. She continued:

> When compared to the nostalgic insularity of the mainstream commercial
> cinema, ordinary mini-series like *A Town like Alice*, *Vietnam*, *Cowra Break-
> out*, and *A Dangerous Life*, documentaries like Gary Kildea's *Celso and Cora:
> A Manila Story* [1983], Dennis O'Rourke's *Yumi Yet* [1976], *Ileksen* (1978),
> and *Cannibal Tours*, *First Contact* [1982] by Robin Anderson and Bob
> Connelly, *Bali Triptych* [Darling 1987], even the routine TV current affairs
> shows screening every week, all appear to emerge, if not from a different
> country, then from another time in that country, with a different sense of
> place.
>
> (119–20)

Sometimes a film-making fascinated with the outside world has been more
important than locally centred productions. In the 1950s, the major feature film-
making partnership of the era of Lee Robinson and Chips Rafferty made feature
films and documentaries in Nui Guinea and the Pacific with and without French
co-production partners. One of their films, *Walk into Paradise*, was Australia's
most internationally circulated film of the 1950s and 1960s. It featured Chips
Rafferty as a District Patrol Officer keeping the peace in the Nui Guinea
highlands. It represents Australia's version of Rudyard Kipling's 'white man's
burden'. In Andrew Pike and Ross Cooper's words, it uses the 'formula of a
comic-strip yarn in an exotic location' (1980: 290). Such reaching out is also
significant in the less strained production circumstances of film-making of later
periods. Take the example of the independent documentaries which the ABC pre-
purchased between 1989 and 1992. Of these 140 documentary programmes from
independent film-makers, 29 per cent were 'about international non-Anglo subjects' (Sammers 1993: 164).

For the several sectors of film-making, the significance of making films outside
Australia varies over time. Sometimes it is more important to feature film-making,
sometimes to mini-series production, sometimes to documentary, and sometimes
to television drama. When domestic financing – both public and private – cannot

meet the costs of production alone, outreaching often becomes central to Australian high-budget production strategies in the one-off and high-budget documentary series areas, in feature film-making and mini-series production. In these circumstances, international pre-sales, financing, and co-production pressures are keenly felt, and looking outside Australia for story materials and settings becomes a way to bring on board a variety of partners.

We can see this in mini-series like *A Town Like Alice*, with its Malaysian and outback Australian locations in 1980, before the sweet funding environment of the tax incentives permitted mini-series experimentation focusing on Australian relations to itself; and we see it again in the 1990s when the local underwriting of high-budget mini-series came under increasing pressure, so that productions emerged like *Bangkok Hilton* (K. Cameron 1989, involving the rescue of an innocent Australian national abroad – Nicole Kidman – from a Bangkok jail) and *Children of the Dragon* (P. Smith 1992, plotting an equally naïve middle-aged Sydney medical specialist caught up in the events of Tiananmen Square).

Looking outward has sustained a variety of orientations from the 'us over there' of *Breaker Morant* (South Africa), *The Adventures of Barry McKenzie* (the UK) and *Echoes of Paradise* (Noyce 1988, Thailand) to the 'us and them' of *Blood Oath* (Indonesia), the mini-series *Cowra Breakout* and the series *Embassy* (1990–2, Ragaan); from the 'them for themselves' of, for example, John Darling's ethnographic documentaries *Lempad of Bali* (1980) and *Bali Triptych*, to the 'them and us together' of O'Rourke's documentary *The Good Woman of Bangkok* and Darling's *Bali Hash* (1989, which juxtaposed Balinese rituals with those of the Hash House Harriers). Because Australia is an immigrant society, notions of 'them amongst us' are important, whether in *Cowra Breakout*, *Silver City*, *Aya*, *They're a Weird Mob* or the host of documentaries on ethnic communities in Australia and their sometimes fraught relation with the mainstream, like *Witch Hunt* (on the notorious social security conspiracy case 1978–83 which saw hundreds of people of a Greek background arrested in dawn raids – all charges were later dismissed).[4]

Sometimes outreaching work gets overlooked because Australian film and, by implication, its identity and culture, is understood solely in terms of itself and its national borders. Documentarist John Darling has made his film-making career mapping Indonesian subjects – usually minorities in Indonesia, with the documentaries *Lempad of Bali*, *Bali Triptych*, *Bali Hash* and *Below the Wind* (1994). But he considers that critics, policy-makers and other film-makers sometimes see his work as marginal to the Australian documentary, film-making and culture more generally, given his Indonesian settings and his determination to address the Balinese on their terms. These orientations can threaten the sense of the unity and integrity of an Australian industry, as Australian cinema becomes interchangeable with American, British or European cinema. *Bali Triptych* could just as well have been a BBC or Granada documentary. Nicole Kidman in *Bangkok Hilton* is the 'European' in trouble in the Far East like the boy-man in *Midnight Express* (Parker 1978). These projects acutely pose the Australian cinema not so much as 'for itself' but give it an alternative identity as an extension of the British, American or European film industries.

The secure place such reaching out has on Australian cinema schedules has ensured an extra diversity of content, setting, storytelling, and social and political orientation. It comes in a variety of film genres and styles and takes in a diverse cultural geography from Nui Guinea to Japan to the UK to Latin America. It provides film-makers and audiences alike with diverse kinds of engagement, confusions and opportunities. Sometimes this orientation fits an Australianist project. At other times, Australian cinema is simply participating in an international storytelling or ethnographic documentary tradition for which its Australian production base is incidental. Sometimes it can seem colonialist. At other times – as Chris Berry (1994: 46) provocatively suggests for O'Rourke's *The Good Woman of Bangkok* – it takes a 'step into a difficult postcolonial space called "Australia in Asia"'. The 'outward' face of Australian cinema has expanded the ways Australians have of knowing their region and the world. It has introduced more complex pictures of the nation and society and provided a variety of vantage points on Australia, its international relations and its international spheres of cultural interest. Australian cinema's outward orientation is simultaneously central to Australian self-definition and to processes of public accommodation of its ethnic and cultural diversity. This is apart from any economic logic, entailing the 'inevitable, unstoppable increase in international co-production' (Martin 1994a: 15).

A DIVERSE FILM CRITICISM

Film criticism simultaneously negotiates, singles out, celebrates and denies this diversity. Adrian Martin (1994a: 97) notes that critical responses to Australian cinema 'are almost always polarized'. He cites as an example Baz Luhrmann's *Strictly Ballroom*. Helen Garner can describe it as a 'profound piece of popular entertainment', while John Flaus can lambast it as 'trifle served as main course ... brazenly derivative, redundant and sentimental'. Martin suggests that one of the downsides of this polarization is that it 'is very difficult, and maybe even impossible, for an Australian critic to get any real perspective on this national cinema as it takes shape from one new film to the next'. Indeed Australian cinema writers (and I am included here) sometimes deal with this diversity of criticism by ignoring it.[5] Dermody and Jacka in their two volume study of Australian cinema ignore most reviews of the films they discuss. If they had not, their discussion of the films would have become more complicated and the manuscript more unmanageable. Scott Murray's (1993a) edited collection of reviews of Australian film from 1978 to 1992 often leaves out in its single entries some of the more important reviews and critical discussions of the films in question.

The feature cinema's diverse generic and stylistic engagements can produce problems of identification for critics. Just what type of movie is Sharman's *The*

Night of the Prowler (1979)? Just what should this or that film be compared to; how should it be situated? David Stratton makes the point again and again in his study of 1970s feature film-making, *The Last New Wave* (1980), that Australian film critics have often wrongly recognized what is before them. If we add to this a critical reflex demanding Australian cinema be something definable and worthy, Australian films can be pressed into a shape and a service not necessarily their own.

Critics are only too well aware that the popular and funding success of one kind of project means, in a small industry, the *denigration* of another. In these circumstances film criticism becomes unavoidably tactical. Supporting the diversity of Australian cinema (or wishing to add to this diversity) often means denigrating one (usually the currently popular) stream of Australian film and television drama production. That stream then stands for an homogenous Australian film and television industry.

Successful Australian films carry a socially representative weight, such that a lot is invested in the one or two Australian films per year that constitute the public reference points for what makes an Australian film. This situation in turn encourages a sense of reaction to it, as the public and critical success of this or that film seems to get in the way of other projects and other representations. This ensures that critics, film-makers, social lobbyists, minority groups and even policy makers can routinely criticize films for what kind of film they are not, and for what they do not contain. Critical attention is skewed away from thinking about exactly what the film is, as a film, and negotiating what contents it actually works with. Underwriting this tendency further are the various voices of 'minority politics' – feminist, ethnic, indigenous, gay and lesbian – which legitimate these exclusion arguments by associating representational absences with systematic exclusion.

Australian film criticism also has its centre and peripheries – its status quo and oppositional elements – in the communicative circuits of Australian film criticism. There is the general public film criticism in the dailies and major journals including the one specialist Australian film publication available on newsstands – *Cinema Papers*. This film criticism and industry reporting are largely concerned with the mainstream industry, and with defining its shape and trajectories, such that director Stephen Wallace could claim that Australians 'seem to have always granted the critics in the popular press an unfettered right to define what our cinema is, who is important and what line it is taking' to the detriment of the 'much wider group of people who have engaged with screen culture in this country' (*Age* 25 August 1994).

Yet there is also a minority, specialized and oppositional film criticism and commentary in small circulation art and culture journals which is less concerned with the mainstream and more concerned with covering and supplying criticism for the 'missing beat'. The public for this criticism is specialized and sometimes associated with professional pedagogy such as the Australian Teachers of Media's *Metro* magazine or *Continuum: the Australian Journal of Media and Culture*. There is a sense among those who curate and promote this sector that it has 'a marginal status, withheld from a general public trained only to be impatient or dismissive towards it' (Martin 1994c: 202). Yet writing on it is comparatively well supported, often in major publications.[6]

The two spheres are separate. It is possible to be well known in the latter but get little or no mention in the former. Sometimes there is more Australian film criticism of the 'independent' product than of the 'mainstream'. Not only is this criticism due to the oft-quoted 'quality' of independents work compared to the 'middle of the road' product of the centre, but also it is due to the development of a critical space which manufactures this as a taken for granted myth of Australian cinema, underwriting the existence of a vibrant short film sector. The difficulties of critically crossing from one to the other are structural. Consequently a whole domain of film-making can fall into the critical cracks – especially that film-making on the edge of minority and general public circulation – and film-makers can rightly lament with Stephen Wallace, who often directs this kind of cinema, the dearth of film criticism.

To some extent, there is always going to be a gap between those who simply go to the cinema for entertainment and those who professionally write about it. Their purposes, training, self-understandings and the markets they read and write for occur in different institutional and cultural spaces. Only a small proportion of the popular audience reads cinema reviews. An even smaller proportion buy specialist magazines such as *Cinema Papers*. And an even smaller proportion read the professional screen/media/cultural studies journals. The readers and writers for these publications look for something different. Whether they see their role as 'more discerning', or as more politically aware, or as simply critical, their commentary on contemporaneous Australian cinema is already driven by supplying something different and something more than is provided for in the public spaces of the promotion and public circulatory contexts of review and enthusiasm. At the same time, in a democratic polity, critics retain some reference points to the 'common touch'. *Cinema Papers* sees itself as the Australian magazine of record for the Australian feature film industry, prioritizing coverage of the 'mainstream' product of domestic cinema exhibition and distribution. However, its interest in the cinema and its possibilities ensures it is going to be more concerned with *Sweetie* than *Crocodile Dundee*. But the Australian-based reticence for *Crocodile Dundee* was not expressed in *Cinema Papers*.

Film criticism is also driven by the kinds of cultural differences on the public agenda and in the films at the time. Criticism typically selects some differences to emphasize, rather than others. Moreover these change over time. In 1980 Meaghan Morris described the cultural diversity of the 1970s cinema as persisting in 'collisions of class, race, culture and environment' and the 'relations involving men with women' (1980: 137). In the 1990s, cultural diversity is typically critically expressed in many of the same terms, but class is now less important, sexual orientation and ethnicity more important. Morris (1993: 155) notes one of the consequences of this shift: she sees 'whiteness almost before ... maleness' when surveying 'our national icons', so important has 'race and ethnicity' become. With this came an explicit foregrounding of the concepts of dominant ethnicity (the Anglo-Celtic), masculinism and heterosexism in Australian cultural criticism in order to organize criticism and found a progressive politics.

Through the changing application of such cultural coordinates, film criticism retrospectively transforms the terms of appreciation of the cinema, adding to the unstable meanings accruing to diverse film practices. Morris' 'dizzying' cultural diversity of 1970s cinema became in its 1980s reinterpretation a masculinist cinema (Dermody and Jacka 1988a) and from the late 1980s a monocultural and inward-oriented cinema (Morris 1989, Turner 1989: 104). Moreover, these structured absences are seen to persist into present film-making (Shaw 1992; S. K. Chua 1993). For Tony Mitchell (1993: 133) there is a 'regulated diversity' to mainstream film and television offerings which sets limits to the representation of minorities as the 'wog the Anglo wants to see'. Within this context, Mitchell writes of how the portrayal of ethnicity in Australian television situation comedies is one which requires 'Aboriginal and migrant performers ... to caricature or stigmatize their ethnicity'.

Critical polarization is systemic. Take the Australian television drama series *Embassy* which could be appreciated (see Hooks 1990, Mike Harris 1990) as ABC-TV taking account of criticism that it had not developed 'any sense of Australia as part of the Asian region' in its drama output (Jacka 1991: 52). Frost (1994a: 192) reports how Singaporean and Malaysian undergraduate students studying in Australia watched the series because it was 'situated in Asia and dealt with issues relevant to the region' (they also had a generally positive response to it). Alongside this came a competing and gradually ascendant view of *Embassy* in the wake of Malaysian government complaints about it in the writing of Evans, Perera (1993) and S. K. Chua, in which it became a particularly potent example of Australian racism, orientalism and insensitivity to the region.

Critical estimation of Australian cinema's various orientations is bound to attract criticism. Take the products of Australia's outward international orientation in features such as *The Year of Living Dangerously* which stresses 'us and them' and 'us over there'. It has been criticized for the way it looks, from one cultural perspective to another without space for the subjectivities and textualities of the 'Other'. Sylvie Shaw (1992), Chris Berry (1994), S. K. Chua (1993) and Pereira (1993) see Australian features like *The Year of Living Dangerously* and *Far East* as occupying a colonial and orientalist position. Asia and Asians, Berry (1994: 35) argues, function in Australian cinema and television 'as a fetishized other against which Australia constructs that identity [as an imagined community]'. This suggests to S. K. Chua (1993: 29) that Australian cinema recognizes the Asian as 'out there', rather than allowing 'Australianness to be inscribed with any kind of Asian ... subjectivity'.

Also coming under critical scrutiny is that orientation which implicates Australia and the Australian audiences as observers rather than participants, telling stories about others rather than about us. Berry takes the impressive ethnographic film-making of Bob Connolly and Robin Anderson to task. In a trilogy, these film-makers charted the colonial legacy to a highland community of the Australian involvement in Nui Guinea: *First Contact*, *Joe Leahy's Neighbours* and *Black Harvest*. Berry (1994: 42–3) criticizes this trilogy for its 'safe distance on its subject matter' which is achieved by its 'assuming the uninvolved, objective stance of classic documentary form in which the film-maker (and the audience) is in a position of epistemological sovereignty as the one that knows, and those on camera are objects to be known about'.

So too, the very outward orientation itself can be criticized for forestalling more local agendas. Sammers, for example, has argued that this international orientation in the early 1990s came at the expense of surveying Australia's own ethnic and cultural diversity. In calling for more attention to the processes of Australian auto-identification, as in her documentary *One Australia?*, she was not being parochial. She was noting that one facet of Australian cinema's cultural diversity – its internationalism – was getting in the way of the expression of another facet – its social diversity.

For our purposes, critical polarization simply exists and needs to be attended to for its consequences on Australian film-making and our understanding of it. Doing so suggests, on the one hand, the importance in Australian film and television production of the kind of structured polysemic ambiguity which simultaneously permits diverse critical and audience uptake and, on the other hand, a critical system dispersed and varied enough to encourage and sustain divergent readings of the same film and television programmes.

CONCLUSION

Australian cinema is significantly internally differentiated. It comprises so many different strategies of production and circulation, genres of film-making, performances secured, rhetoric of camera work, and relations posed between films and historical audiences, and critical outlooks. Obviously all national cinemas are to a greater or lesser extent like this. An important difference among them is the way this fragmentation is organized, facilitated and encouraged, including which kinds of film-making may become dominant. Australian cinema and television proliferates axes of differentiation and its diversity of production and criticism which must, in part, be a consequence of the film-making available in Australia – both imported and local. At the same time, some kinds of film-making and some axes of cultural differentiation become ascendant at particular times, organizing debate and criticism.

If we think of Australian cinema as being made of incommensurate and adjacent projects we can conceive of this cinema's productive differentiations within and between particular categories of film-making. We need to recognize the routine dispersal of Australian film-making projects, because only by doing so can we deal ordinarily with the cinema before us. In this chapter, I have insisted on the Australian cinema's dispersal in competing, antagonistic and adjacent critical and film-making projects.

This diversity of production and outlook confronts critics, film-makers and lobbyists with a number of options. First, they can celebrate this diversity as making up a multifaceted film culture. This book is animated by just such a pluralist perspective – a perspective shared in the work of policy-makers and politicians concerned with a whole film culture, or by curators like Peter Broderick commissioned to signal the diversity of Australian film work to a Los Angeles audience. We like to point to the spread of Australian activity, seeing in it something for everyone, however small.

But equally the limits of this pluralism are readily apparent. Some schools of film-making are more dominant than others. Some film-makers believe their careers have been stymied because they do not fit prevailing moulds: the cult success of Sandy Harbutt's bikie exploitation film, *Stone*, did not result in anything like a continuous career for Harbutt despite this film's promise – a fact he later put down to his being an inappropriate person and his exploitation projects not fitting the prevailing culturalist agenda of the AFC. Geoff Gardner (1993a: 65) laments the interrupted career of Albie Thoms, seeing his experimental feature, *Palm Beach*, as a

> terrible reminder that there are people of great ability who have never been able to pursue their craft in the Australian industry, while dozens of mediocrities have had the chance to squander countless dollars and a multitude of opportunities.

The interrupted career of Scott Murray, the current editor of *Cinema Papers*, and director of *Devil in the Flesh* (1989, aka *Beyond Innocence*) is often put down to the 'problematic' standing of such cinephile films and sensibilities on Australian production schedules. Despite its awards and critical acclaim Helen Grace's political/experimental/feminist film *Serious Undertakings* was not followed up – although not for want of her trying to initiate other projects.

Second, film-makers and critics can be more partial about their cinema. Audiences often talk about Australian film as if it was one kind of film: usually in the form of a popular Australian film from their past that journalists may have promoted as representative of Australian cinema. film-makers are confronted with the pressing demand of selecting from the repertoire of film-making and promoting some and not other parts of it. Funding agencies need to make choices between projects. It matters to them that there is a funding differential between formats, genres and individuals, particularly if one's area is weakly funded. Critics likewise unashamedly promote their preferences for a film, a sector of film-making, a genre within that, a production orientation, and a production budget. As Martin (1994c: 201) recently observed for advocates of the short film:

> One staked out one's ground with a claim to the strategic primacy and exotic specificity of Super 8, or video art, or experimental, or whatever, and then one

railed against those other territories unfairly favoured through the cultural networks of subsidy, promotion and criticism.

Some of the criticism of Australian cinema's uniformity has as much to do with the need for film-makers and critics to sponsor *more* of one kind of film work, than it has to do with describing an existing production reality. Because we want Australian cinema to be one thing more than another we want it to be homogenous; because we see it as too much of one and not enough of another we criticize the Australian cinema for its homogeneity.

The dissonance and conflict in the cultural politics of Australian film stem from the rivalries which come out of the preferences of critics, film-makers, policy-makers and bureaucrats. Each want different combinations of film-making and axes of cultural differentiation. Cultural politics is necessarily made up of so many single-minded individuals whose passions for genre cinema, short films, cinephile films, documentaries, festival cinema individually and collectively, provide the commitment necessary to sustain film-making careers in these forms and styles and a film criticism capable of matching and supplementing these commitments. Getting, keeping and stripping power and legitimacy from someone else is fundamental to the entrepreneurial milieu of film-making, policy development, film criticism and governmental subsidy regimes in their striving for accountability. Cultural politics will always be made up of those seeking to universalize their position. The sum of such rivalries over the shape, location and trajectories of national film production helps, paradoxically, to underwrite the diversity of Australian cinema.

But equally fundamental to sustaining this diversity are the processes of consensus creation, of coalition building, of power sharing and working at securing complementarities of production and criticism between sectors, personnel and production orientations. Without it, there is no industry lobbying, no capacity to enjoy a wide range of films and move between the variety of formats. There needs to be a space for the *noblesse oblige* which can recognize the value of a diverse film-making milieu for film-makers and audiences. film-making is inescapably a collective enterprise, with loose collectivities and solidarities between the different parts of the film-making milieu being critical to its everyday functioning.

Australian cinema is made up of various identities and exhibits many tendencies. Juri Lotman notes that a culture – in his terms a semiosphere – is made of rivalrous, incommensurable and adjacent elements (Lotman 1990: 135). The film-making that fills the Australian audiovisual space has these characteristics too. These films (as the 'languages' that fill the semiotic space in Lotman's terms) also 'relate to each other along the spectrum which runs from complete mutual translatability to just as complete mutual untranslatability' (125). I am labouring this point because at policy, critical and audience level it is important that Australian cinema be seen for its heterogeneity. It is fundamentally driven by tendencies towards diversity. This diversity is an unexceptionable characteristic of the local cinema. Like the Hollywood cinema, Australian cinema contains many competing and complementary elements. These make it difficult to define an overarching framework for Australian cinema. It, follows, however that any definition of this cinema's 'character' must give due weight to: a diverse cinema made up of rivalrous and complementary film projects; a cinema which makes contributions to several pathways of the cinema, and a cinema with an unstable identity and market niche.

Chapter 8

Unity

INTRODUCTION

Constructing a sense of unity is one response to the diversity of Australian film-making. Here I survey the ways Australian cinema becomes generalizable as a unity for critics, marketers, audiences, producers and film-makers. Talking of Australian cinema's national specificities, considering Australian cinema as a genre, elucidating its narrative, thematic and stylistic preoccupations and generalizing about its uses of setting, light and landscape produce a sense of its regularity, unity and convergence. These moves are driven by a will to see Australian cinema as a connected family of film-making projects and a coherent film industry. Such unities produce the definiteness of Australian cinema as *something*. These positivities of unity are functional. Under conditions where variety is typically valued, Australian cinema's unity can be an unfortunate characteristic needing to be made good, through alternative policy and film-making dedicated to securing difference. For marketing, product recognition, industry and lobbying – and some criticism, unity can be a positive, contributing a sense of Australian cinema as a progressive social institution. Notions of unity provide a way of negotiating, organizing coherence, and foregrounding aspects of Australian cinema and society. Unities of different sorts are a natural accomplishment of any film-making milieu no matter how diverse.

NATIONAL SPECIFICITIES COMMON TO ALL NATIONAL CINEMAS

National specificities – socio-cultural and structural features – give a certain commonality to cinema. Some of these consist of those things that occur in every national cinema but are specifically realized in each. As we have already noted, each national cinema stresses its social texts, drawing as it does on its public record and the cultural archives particular to it. These common archives of information, story and archetype are shared by film-maker and local audience alike and are mobilized by film-makers and film-marketers seeking to exploit their 'local' advantage. These social texts, national stories and myths still obey the *general* form of stories existing elsewhere. What is different in each national cinema is the contents and inflections given to these general forms.

The intertextuality of film-making is not only an accomplishment turning on relations with other films but also on relations with other social, performance, and textual entities outside film. film-making in Australia always has had an important relation to *local* orders of information, literature, theatre, poetry and the visual arts, news and journalism. Australian film-making's relation to the Australian stage was important in the first fifty years of this century (see O'Regan 1987),[1] and persists enough into post-1970 film-making for critics to mull over the prevalence of 'the model three-act script' and the scriptwriter auteur (Martin 1988a: 97).

With half the commercial television schedule being Australian-produced, television provides a sizeable archive to inform feature film and experimental production such as *Body Melt*'s and *Nirvana Street Murder*'s clear references to the Crawford police series of the late 1960s and early 1970s. The former connects these police series' look and plot with the splatter movie; and John Conomos claims that the latter film blends successfully 'the familiar codes, icons and stylistic visuals' of these police series with 'the basic thematic and visual interests of the action-comedy' (Conomos 1993: 321). Even though many shows are concept remakes these concepts still have to be indigenized. Now that the old relation of inferior television versus superior film is becoming eclipsed, critics can see and value the important consequences to Australian cinema of its relation with television (see Martin 1994a; O'Regan 1986).

Non-fiction is disproportionately represented in Australian publishing and film. Documentary film and non-fiction writing favours Australiana and matters of Australian, not universal, significance (L. Murray 1984: 150). There is a clearly discernible influence of the documentary on narrative film-making, most obviously in the many 'docu-fictions' like Chauvel's *In the Wake of the Bounty*, Watt's *The Overlanders* and Brealey's *Annie's Coming Out*, but also, and less obviously in 'naturalistic' acting and film-making once a more observational style became ascendant in the documentary (which sometimes leads to a sense of underacting in films). film-makers often closely follow the 'public record', whether in the 1980s mini-series *Bodyline* or Mora's feature film *Death of a Soldier*.[2]

National cinemas also have specific institutional infrastructures – governmental and private.[3] While film policies are internationally shared, such policies need to be worked out on the ground in each country and adjusted to local circumstance. Film business conditions do vary in terms of the laws, the access to capital, equipment and taxation and so on. And film training conditions likewise. The circumstances of a film and television industry which needs to directly compete in its domestic market with the most expensively produced film and television drama in the world ensures that the industry and film training organizations like the AFTRS are almost excessively concerned with developing appropriate standards of imaging and securing a sufficient funding platform to produce a competitive product. Also the kinds of film-making opportunities available for the local product both domestically and internationally varies among national cinemas and biases output in some directions. These combinations of conditions form the basis of traditions of local film-making which are not original as such but are based on local inflections of larger film-making traditions.

While socio-culturally Australia shares much with a variety of other new world societies (see Chapter 13), these common processes are realized differently in Australian cinema. Take the example of the indigenous peoples in Australia, Canada, the USA and New Zealand. The relation between the indigenous population and the state, the degree of their relationship with, incorporation into and exclusion from settler lifeways and national myths and symbols, their filmic representation and their involvement in film production varies in each country. Unlike New Zealand, Canada and the USA there is no long history of conceiving an Aboriginal nation within the Australian nation in the way the Maori nation and the first nations of Canada and the USA are configured. New Zealanders are always astonished at the formal lack of Aboriginal recognition on public occasions and in national representations. The 'available discourses' on Aborigines (see Muecke 1992: 19–35) in Australian film turn on the 'Aboriginal problem' and the traditional Aboriginal lifeways – emphasizing, on the one hand, the documentary and social problem film-making and, on the other hand, Aboriginal Otherness in narrative and ethnographic treatment. This tends to leave little space on film for Aboriginal modernity – but see the work of Moffatt and the music videos of Yothu Yindi (see Muecke 1992: 179–85).

When Hollywood was using Native Americans to construct its mythical West – becoming that force which needed to be overcome in order to establish American civilization – Australian government officials were worrying about the threat to White authority in remote Aboriginal communities posed by showing westerns in which natives killed whites. Peter Malone notes 'a complete absence of Aborigines or themes in Australian features' after 1913, with only a couple of exceptions, until the late 1940s. Malone states '[t]hey were either ignored or stories not considered interesting or relevant' (1987: 137). In 1955 Chauvel remedied this situation for Australian film-making somewhat with his first colour film and last feature film *Jedda* (see Cunningham 1992: 156–64). This first Aboriginal-centred story is a western melodrama reminiscent of King Vidor's *Duel in the Sun* (1946). Like that film *Jedda* has a triangle, as the Aboriginal girl brought up white (the Jennifer Jones function played by Ngarla Kunoth) circulates between the half-caste head stockman (and respectability) with whom she has grown up and who is more like a brother than a lover to her (the Joseph Cotten function played by Paul Reynall), and the traditional man Marbuk who strides into the narrative with a brooding, criminal erotic masculinity (the Gregory Peck function played by Robert Tudawali). Marbuk lures Jedda to him through the power of his 'singing' (ritual chanting) and then he steals her away. The fugitive couple are pursued by both white and Aboriginal law. White law wants him for abduction and murder; Aboriginal law wants to punish them both because Jedda is the 'wrong skin' for Marbuk. Eventually both plunge off a cliff to their death. Contemporary Aboriginal opinion is divided on this film. Marcia Langton (1993: 45) derides it as a colonialist fantasy which 'rewrites Australian history so that the black rebel against white colonial rule is a rebel against the laws of his own society'. Chauvel inverts the 'truth on the black/white frontier, as if none of the brutality, murder and land clearances occurred'. Mudrooroo (Johnson 1987: 48), however, provides a different judgement. He writes that 'it is to Chauvel's credit, or perhaps in spite of Chauvel, that the only dignified Aboriginal male lead that has been allowed to exist in films made by white directors in Australia, is in *Jedda*, and though Marbuk does die in the end, it is because he has offended tribal law rather than because of anything the whiteman has shot at him.' Of Jedda herself, he observes (53) how her 'very passivity reflects the passivity of adolescent black girls locked up in mission compounds, thick with stories of savage myalls prowling the fence of the compound ready to steal them away'.

In the contemporary period, Aborigines are being written back into the picture under pressure from Aboriginal and other activists. Some films – like Weir's *The Last Wave* – undertake major revisions of the national identity in order to acknowledge the realities of dispossession and second class citizenship and question the moral legitimacy of the 'white settler culture'. *The Last Wave* is structured around the journey of a white lawyer, David (Richard Chamberlain) as he interacts with two Aboriginal people Chris (David Gulpilil) and Charlie (Nandjiwarra Amagula). What starts out as the story of a liberal and well-meaning industrial lawyer lending his expertise to an innocent and dispossessed Aboriginal defendant to get him off a charge of which he is innocent, becomes instead the lawyer's journey away from his family towards a recognition of his psychic affinity with these Aboriginal men, and an awareness of the meaning of his own dreaming and his society's destiny to be destroyed by a giant tidal wave. As Routt (1994a: 225) observes: this 'Australian finds identity with or through Aboriginal people' and the film seems to be saying 'we can only get to the real Australia through the experience of Aboriginal people.' Here there is an intertwining of fates and destinies with dystopian consequences. David, at first unwittingly, and then later deliberately transgresses Aboriginal law – making public the secret survival in an urban setting of the Aboriginal dreamtime and his own destiny to re-enact the primal encounter between the indigenous Aborigines and non-Aboriginal invaders, in a fight in the sewers after which he kneels on the beach as the tidal wave approaches. The tidal wave is ambiguously linked to the white treatment of Aboriginals and Islanders in Australia. For Routt (1994a: 225), the film says that 'the destruction of Aboriginal culture is a self-serving lie, that the culture is more powerful than the white man's history and the white man's photographs'.

Unlike New Zealand which had mechanisms for structural accommodation, Australia is seeking to add on and accommodate indigenous initiatives to structures that evolved without Aboriginals being parties to the negotiation of their form and content. From the late 1980s ABC and SBS-TV have evolved Aboriginal employment programmes and during the 1990s the AFC has worked on Aboriginal and Islander issues culminating in the employment of an Aboriginal officer.

Sensitive accommodations of an Aboriginal presence have, more often than not, taken part in the domain of documentary film-makers, where there has been a degree of collaboration between white film-makers and Aboriginal peoples.

Local variations on a theme extend to other cultural specificities. There are those cultural and social features – sometimes called the 'anthropological culture' or the Australian 'way of life' – which provide particularities for films to draw on and use as an archive. The anthropological culture not only provides contents but also the ways of doing (performance) and making sense, that film-making takes up and makes its own. Think of the styles of self-presentation of the 'back of the beach' family in *Muriel's Wedding*, the monstrous middle-class professionals of Beresford's *Don's Party* or the interplay John Conomos (1993: 321) notes in Aleksi Vellis' *Nirvana Street Murder* between Greek Australian men and their Anglo-Celtic counterparts 'in terms of *machismo* posturings, street-wise bravado, sub-cultural rituals and anti-Anglo-Celtic obsessions'. Audiences and critics often find an Australian 'sense of humour' evident in films like the laconic and economical humour of *Sunday Too Far Away* and *The Sum of Us*. Cinema works with local vernaculars of suburban architecture and fragments of social life contained in it, like those observed in Paul Cox's feature *Lonely Hearts* (1982).

There is the Australian English 'language' which not only includes the stage and screen 'Australian accent' but also its regional, class and ethnically differentiated speech like Aboriginal English, Asian-Australian English, Southern European-Australian English which is slowly finding audiovisual representation outside of non-fiction. Australian English is a family of English accents like, yet unlike, other English accents. Australian English entails sufficient particularities of usage to warrant the development of Australian English dictionaries based on Australian usage, despite the tremendous amount shared with the UK and North America. Tim Rowse (1985: 70–72) suggests that this Australian English has become a privileged site for defining and celebrating the Australian and Australianness in cultural production of the 1970s and 1980s. Screen and stage performances, he suggests, have taken two directions with this accent. In one, the accent is 'relatively incidental to the performance', in the other, it draws 'attention to itself as vernacular' (79). For one, the Australian language is simply used transparently, for the other it is a topic in its own right. For 'human drama' film-making, the accent is largely incidental, for comedy and tragi-comedy the language is part of the act, part of the persona (70), as in *They're a Weird Mob*, *The Adventures of Barry McKenzie* and *Crocodile Dundee*. These latter kinds of performance encourage the audience to watch as an 'outsider to the Australianness being invoked' (70).

The Australian language has functioned as an ideological standard bearer for an Australian identity in that it presents itself as the site of irreducible (Australian) difference. Rowse is scathing about what he sees as the result – a 'provincial narcissism' (71).

Each national space also organizes its own varieties of nationalism, and myth and symbols complex (see Chapter 13). The invention of tradition in each country can look remarkably similar in intent but the content varies from country to country. Themes of communal solidarity can mean duty in Germany and mateship in Australia, as represented in *Gallipoli* and debunked in Hannam's *Break of Day* (1976). If military involvements are part of the cultural repertoire of many nations, differences occur within the same general form such as which kind of military campaign, whether it was a defeat or victory, or conducted on home or foreign shores. Gallipoli was an offshore defeat, the American Civil War a domestic drama.

The general outline of nationalism and its symbols is modal and is common to all national cinemas, but the working out of these symbols in themes, accents, adaptations, and concept indigenizing, negotiates specific national contents with social, cultural and aesthetic entailments. If these commonalities mean that national specificities and differences are produced within the form of the same, they also powerfully sustain and give credibility to the notion of a distinctive Australian cinema.

AUSTRALIAN CINEMA AS A GENRE

One of the powerful ways we have of organizing continuities and similarities among diverse cinema and television practices is to treat Australian cinema and television drama as its own 'genre' of film-making. To do so is not as silly as it first looks. Genre is, after all, a commodious category capable of holding together divergent performances, contents and settings, stylistic features and so on. Sometimes, as in the mid-1980s, Australian videos were even generically marketed, just as 'Australiana' is a marketing category for Australian booksellers and publishers.

Generic understandings of Australian cinema are probably inevitable because of the circumstances of their viewing. For the general audience Australian titles might optimistically make up one in ten cinema titles viewed, one in twenty or so video titles viewed (a more speculative figure), and between one in five and one in eight drama titles viewed on television. In the cinema and on video these viewings can be some time apart. The audience notes the Australian setting, *mise-en-scène*, actors (known and marked as Australian) and publicity (if a success). Together with the period of forgetting between one film viewing and the next, this noting of Australianness provides sufficient materials to create a generic sense of Australian cinema, no matter what the differences are among films.

In marked contrast to this typical experience of Australian films, critics and producers often watch Australian features and short films *en masse* through the Australian Film Institute's annual award screenings. These screening conditions also assist generic understandings for significant critical taste brokers, as films are juxtaposed, connected and made interchangeable through the force of film festival viewing conditions. Either way, the comparing and contrasting work we sometimes do during and after watching a film necessarily involve us in making comparisons with other Australian films: this exercise is fundamental to establishing the intertextual character of genre and to creating a sense of the character of Australian cinema. Our doing so is aided by the public discourse on Australian film which provides social and reception context repertoires for making sense of this or that film, whether to ourselves, to people we talk with about these films, or in their critical discussion before diverse publics.

The generic understanding of Australian film poses it as a form of cinema. Here the axis is turned around a little. What is emphasized here is not the *continuities* a film has with genres of film-making established in the UK, Hollywood or Europe but Australian film *as a genus*, as a type. This interpretative move has the advantage at least of recognizing the *interpenetration* of Australian film-making practices despite their diversity. Whether this process produces unexpected and new connections and meanings, or limits the range and possibility of these meanings will depend on the circumstance, the critic and the films. Perhaps the setting, Australian language, familiar faces and modest on-screen look – courtesy of a small- to middle-range budget (internationally), helps create an artificial sense of the boundedness of Australian cinema. More than anything else this Australian boundedness makes it difficult to count as 'Australian cinema' those films made by Australian residents but produced outside Australia and not ostensibly about this country.

These perceptions of the generic unity of Australian cinema are partly a consequence of some film-making projects being more popular than others. There are only one or two, at most five, Australian feature films in any one year that a wide-cross section of the public sees and that get taken up in subsidiary general public circulation – on radio, on television and in newspaper features. In 1992, it was *Strictly Ballroom* and *Romper Stomper*; in 1994, it was *The Adventures of Priscilla: Queen of the Desert*, *The Sum of Us*, *Muriel's Wedding*, *Sirens* and *Bad Boy Bubby*. Consequently these come to represent the Australian cinema output and trends in it. This may be notwithstanding the fact that they may be untypical of the films released. For example, other 1992 releases were: Rolf de Heer's 'jazz film' *Dingo*, Esben Storm's 'Aboriginal deaths in custody' thriller *Deadly*, Armstrong's art cinema tale of a marriage breakup, *The Last Days of Chez Nous*, none of which bear much, if any, resemblance to *Ballroom* or *Stomper*.

But the successes inevitably present themselves as 'touchstone successes' and so find the horizon line of public explanation. The 'trends' found become the basis for sweeping cultural and critical statements, not to mention industry and critical attention. This also happens in Australian television drama. Domestic audiences for Australian television soaps could be expected, in practice, to watch two to three of the six or so on offer. These soaps, like those couple of successful films each year, come to bear a culturally and critically representative weight as representing the practice of Australian television drama generally.

There is also a structural reason. Although diversified, the Australian production industry is small in comparison to the US, Japanese, British or French film and television production industries. This means that not only do producers within the different genres and formats of film production jostle with one another for financing and public attention, but so do producers of the different genres and formats. The limited popularity sample provided by the two to four titles that garner public attention converges with the limited funding base and state subvention to register and make particular kinds of film-making ascendant at particular times.

For these reasons, Australian cinema tends to be periodized, as changing projects become dominant. The early 1970s is the 'ocker' film era of a 'frankly commercial' film policy in *Alvin Purple* and *The Adventures of Barry McKenzie* (O'Regan 1989a). The mid-1970s to the early 1980s is the 'nostalgia' film era of a 'quality and worth' film policy in *Picnic at Hanging Rock* and *My Brilliant Career* (Turner 1989). The 1980s is the 'industry' era where genre cinema and blockbusters dominated with 10BA tax concession finance in *Mad Max II* and *Crocodile Dundee* (O'Regan 1989b), whilst the 1990s is a film era marked by the 'international film' (*The Piano*), and cultural diversity and quirky films like *Strictly Ballroom*, *Proof* and *Romper Stomper* going from being 'long shots to favourites' (Reid 1993).

Within the film milieu of each period, those popular titles or spectacular flops which can be grouped into a cycle, become the object of scorn for rival film-making projects and provide critics with scope for disputatious generalizations about them. So just as the denigration of 'the coarse vulgar rubbish' of *Alvin Purple* and *The Adventures of Barry McKenzie* made way for a quality film-making of *Picnic et al.* in the mid-1970s, so in its turn this 'quality film' came under scrutiny in the late 1970s. Critic after critic, film-maker after film-maker maintained that what Australian culture needed was contemporary representations, not nostalgia films set in a mythic past. Australians needed to be resituated within their own culture and history with new and more relevant symbols than that of the Australian legend, mateship and the Aussie battler. film-makers needed to engage with genre cinema replacing Australian battler victimhood with 'heroes' – initiators and perpetrators of action. Critics enjoined the Australian industry to make films 'that deal now with what it means or feels like to be alive in Australia' (Bennett, 1979). film-makers needed to deal with 'the structure and fabric of Australian society and stimulate us by exploring contemporary individuals, institutions, issues'. Films needed to be tougher-minded so that they could respond 'to the threat of the Australian landscape rather than lyricising it, or the potential excitement of its cities, instead of ignoring it' (McFarlane, 1980: 61).

And today we have come to know the 'quality film-making' of this period through this accepted wisdom. We know that the period films did little to reflect the 'contemporary realities of an urban, middle class, postcolonial multicultural society' (Turner 1989: 115). We know that, for the most part, these were 'beautiful, untroubling films', that 'they were politically conservative', and that they 'said virtually nothing about contemporary Australia' (Turner 1989: 104). Susan Dermody and Liz Jacka in their study of 1970s and 1980s film-making describe this film-making as a genre in its own right – the AFC genre (named after the funding agency, the AFC). Films of this genre include: *The Devil's Play-*

ground, Picnic at Hanging Rock, Caddie, My Brilliant Career, The Chant of Jimmie Blacksmith and *Breaker Morant*. They were character not action-based narratives with a past setting. Stories were 'relatively unshaped' and more 'interested in "sensibility" in the tradition of the novel rather than the moral and action of the more plotted melodrama' (1988a: 32). Characters were 'morally inoffensive' and 'bland' (1988a: 33). Acting was genteel and naturalistic, with Australia having 'a large number of actors expert in this kind of performance style' (Jacka 1988b: 82). Dermody and Jacka (1988a: 33) also distinguish a gender dynamic, as films 'centre on strong, assertive women verging, as in *My Brilliant Career* on the larrikin ... the male characters are recessive, sensitive in temperament and doomed to failure (including failure at the box office)'. Specifically the AFC genre and period drama consisted of films

> foregrounding their Australianness through the re-creation of history and representations of the landscape; lyrically and beautifully shot; and employing aesthetic mannerisms such as a fondness for long, atmospheric shots, an avoidance of action or sustained conflict, and the use of slow motion to infer significance.
>
> (Turner 1989: 100)

Like all such generic estimations these notions illuminated and obscured the films. Because these estimations are so much a part of the film culture's work of retrospectively accounting for what it has done in order to move on, these notions necessarily involve forgettings. We have to forget the horror dimension to *Picnic at Hanging Rock* and downplay its lesbian thematics. *The Chant of Jimmie Blacksmith* is about how mainstream Australian society created a serial killer who successfully evaded the police for a time. Mora's *Mad Dog Morgan* makes the colonial administration criminal and psychotic. Cowan's *Journey among Women* rewrites the colonial story through the then emerging feminist metaphor of the colonization of women. *Newsfront* mobilizes a host of textual resources, newsreels, both black and white and colour, fragmented narrative and a blending of fiction and documentary, all of which still astonish. The supposed incapacity of the 'nostalgia film' to speak to contemporary reality makes it forget the critiques of cultural, intellectual conformity, parochialism and a society inimical to new ideas that are central to Thornhill's *Between Wars* (1974). The lack of 'contemporary relevance' in *The Irishman* (Crombie 1978) has to downplay the explicit and social intertext of advances in technology which deskill and render redundant previous trades and connect this 'nostalgia' film to the new wave of industrial displacement happening in the 1970s. How do Weir's three films *The Cars that Ate Paris* (1974 – a gothic tale of a town living off cars and human remains), *Picnic* and *The Last Wave* connect with the lack of an Australian appetite for the marvellous and the uncanny in its cinema? What are we to make of the close proximity of the teen-pic to many 'period films'? After all, Gillian Armstrong did not need to move very far to go from *My Brilliant Career* to her teen musical *Star Struck*. And what are we to make of Schepisi's *The Devil's Playground* (1976), a film regarded at the time of its release as a disturbing and unsettling film, which is surely a precurser to Ann Turner's later use of children on the edge of fantasy, reality and murder in *Celia*?

NARRATIVE AND THEMATIC PREOCCUPATIONS

A related way of disclosing the unity of Australian cinema acknowledges differences among films but looks to larger regularities of theme, plot and representation for a sense of unity. This process enables critics and film-makers alike to create connections between projects that would otherwise be kept separate. They give a fragmented industry and production context a semblance of coherence. So it is possible to assemble the thematic concerns of Australian cinema in its emphasis upon ordinariness, its male predominance, its eschewing of heterosexual romance; its highlighting of father/daughter, mother/daughter relations with their unusual Oedipal concerns.

Australian cinema is often celebrated and denigrated for its ordinariness. Max Harris (1979) eulogized the way actors in the Australian cinema were in proportion to their surroundings being 'real, not overblown'. Actors like Helen Morse, Angela Punch-McGregor, Jack Thompson and John Mellion were 'in the business of being ordinary; and they are there to demonstrate that sensibility can be more astoundingly present in the ordinary than the extraordinary'. For Tom Ryan these characteristics mark the individual as a 'consumer of history rather than a participant in its course' (1980: 125); Australian films place the protagonist as victim not agent of history, whereas American film makes the protagonist drive the narrative and so become an agent of history. Graeme Turner (1989: 116) notes how this feature is also common to literary narratives where the 'individual is subordinate to the structures of society and they are skeptical about the possibility of the individual ever effecting social change'. We should, however, be careful with such generalizations, as a lot of Hollywood cinema – social problem film-making for instance and the suspense thriller – also relies on making its characters 'victims of narration'.

Another often-noted characteristic of Australian cinema is a masculinist bias which sees a 'peripheral part' played by women in 'most Australian cinema' (Morris 1989: 117). Meaghan Morris (1989: 119) notes that the cinema's view of women is diametrically opposed to that circulating in Australian television drama which

> creates a quite different impression of family life ... [the] most popular local shows have created a glowing Australia of loving couples, happy families, and friendly communities ... Furthermore, a substantial documentary cinema offers much more nuanced and varied representation of family life than either film or TV drama. Few fictional Australian women have been created with the detail of Gillian Armstrong's documentary trilogy *Smokes and Lollies* [1976], *14's Good, 18's Better* [1981], and *Bingo, Bridesmaids and Braces* [1988].

For Dermody and Jacka the preponderance of the 'male ensemble' film in the mid-1980s repeated the historical exclusion of women in Australian history, providing a way to unify films as diverse as *Mad Max* and the experimental docu-drama *The Dismissal* (based on the events leading up to the dismissal of the Whitlam Labor government in 1975), and Paul Hogan's vehicle to 'serious acting', *ANZACS* (Dixon, G. Miller, Amenta 1985). The reality of this thematic preoccupation in the most popular films and mini-series of this era was well brought out by Jane Campion when she declared on graduating from AFTRS that she wanted to work for Kennedy-Miller when they stopped making boy's films.

A related thematic regularity is the 'bleak' and 'hypercritical' view Australian cinema has about both (nuclear) 'family life and male–female' relationships especially in a contemporary setting. Morris (1989: 117) suggests that the prevailing themes of the relations between the sexes have been 'violence, hostility, alienation, misery and a difference of values and desires ... that verges on incommensurability'. Consequently there are 'few romantic comedies; few fully developed adult love stories, fewer still happy endings'. These constitute something like a 'segregationist' norm.[4]

Enker suggests that it is almost subversive in Australian cinema to have the couple remain united: Paul Cox's *Lonely Hearts*, Peter Faiman's *Crocodile Dundee* and Baz Luhrmann's *Strictly Ballroom* stand out in this regard. filmmakers, she argues, have a 'collective discomfort with heterosexual love stories and skepticism about the possibility for enduring passion'. She further notes that '[t]here is a striking absence of the grand passions that are intrinsic to, and characteristic of, French and American cinema' (218). These predilections and absences are not based on any especial demography – the Australian divorce rate is, after all, the lowest of those countries with high divorce rates such as the USA, Canada, the UK and the Scandinavian countries (McDonald 1993: 162). Rather than reflecting any supposed passionless characteristic of Australian people and their lives, these tendencies in the Australian cinema have more to do with the need to differentiate between product in the international market.

As Creed observes:

> Australian films also frequently – and perversely – tend to construct the 'normal' heterosexual couple as in excess. Marginalization of the couple is accompanied by the general failure of Australian films to deal convincingly with encounters between the heterosexual couple which are sexually charged and erotically powerful.
>
> (Creed 1992: 22)

Creed's analysis of Moorhouse's *Proof* suggests that while it

> is not about a homosexual relationship its exploration of male bonding, based as it is on the exclusion of woman, suggests that all relationships between men involve a degree of homoeroticism. Woman is represented as an abject figure who must be located outside the territory of the male couple.
>
> (1992: 16)

These characteristics enable Karl Quinn (1993b: 322) to criticize the film for its 'nasty touch of misogyny', because the Genevieve Picot character 'loses out' in the triangular relationship between herself, her blind lodger she is in love with and his male friend whom she sleeps with. (For her part, Picot was reportedly delighted with this female role of complexity, substance and agency.)

These thematic characteristics are importantly underwritten by popular socio-logical and national descriptions of Australian society that start to emerge in the late 1950s and are summed up in the aggressive song from *They're a Weird Mob* 'It's a man's country sweetheart'. These putative descriptions of Australian social life and mores created specific imaginative spaces for creative and critical work. Three texts represent this masculinist assertion in its first 'positivity': J. D. Pringle's *Australian Accent* (1958, 1978), Russell Ward's *Australian Legend* (1958, 1980) and John O'Grady's *They're a Weird Mob* (1957). Ward turned the relationship among men to a foundation of the establishment of national values. That this turn was not 'natural' is evident from previous films. Chauvel's 1935 film *Heritage* has competition for women and not homosocial bonding as the wellspring for Australian democracy. Chauvel, Hall and Longford all typically put women at the centre of their narratives just as Australian serial television has, from *Bellbird* (1967–77) to the present.

In *They're a Weird Mob* the vocabulary for the next thirty years of a strand of 'big picture' Australian film-making was mapped. Australian language, parti-cularly men's work place and pub-culture language, was foregrounded as a public comportment. The alternative, in terms of familial values, to the excessively masculinized Australian public culture is the softer and more attractive ethnic culture and the culture of Australian women. Consequently, the public and self-conscious reputation of the Australian is marked by these binaries of a public masculine and a private feminine, as well as a sharp segregation between these.

Then there are Australian cinema's unusual Oedipal concerns stemming from these narrative preoccupations. Barbara Creed notes that:

> Regardless of the mode in which Oedipal issues are addressed, Australian texts generally do not endorse the fulfillment of the subject's proper Oedipal destiny; rather they use this classic narrative form in order to provide their protagonists with a means of escaping from the social and familial demands of society. This is particularly marked in mother/son and mother/daughter narratives.
>
> (Creed 1992: 15)

Creed observes that the protagonists of both mother/son and mother/daughter narratives 'do not direct their desires towards the proper goal, a number of prohibited fantasies dominate', such as 'a desire to love only the mother and a desire to bond only with one's gender counterpart' (Creed 1992: 22). So we have in films like *Proof*, *Strictly Ballroom* and *Death in Brunswick* the son – not the daughter – hating the mother, with this 'antagonism' being 'posited as a necessary step, not just in relation to his desire for a woman, but also in relation to his desire to bond with a man/mate.' (22). By contrast, in mother/daughter films like

Hightide, Shame and *A Woman's Tale* 'the bond with the mother is not replaced or undone, nor is there a male figure who comes between mother and daughter.' Male lovers 'are virtually absent' (22). Creed continues:

> By refusing to represent the mother as a figure of abjection and the daughter's rejection of the mother as necessary for the initiation of her desire for the father/ husband, these texts present an unconventional representation of mother/ daughter relations.
>
> (22)

It is something of a continuing but necessary critical challenge to find ways of bringing together and making coherent the range of Australian film-making. Such bringing together, whether in the commentary of critics or film-makers, is also crucial to establishing a sense not only of what is there (and what its preoccupations are) but also establishing what is not, in order to instead define new presences. The male bias legitimates affirmative action in the cinema both behind and in front of the camera. The Anglo-Celtic bias suggests the need for a cinema reflecting Australian cultural diversity.

This move to produce coherence and to give to Australian cinema a certain representativity is crucial to how critics, policy-makers, film-makers and bureaucrats problematize Australian cinema. This mobilizing, encouraging and identifying of progressive and regressive tendencies in the cinema has direct consequences. Locating ethnic, female, gay and lesbian and regional under-representation and Anglo-Celtic, masculine, heterosexual and metropolitan (or top end of town) over-representation is crucial to encouraging and facilitating an increased presence and the organization of structural programmes to bring about representation and the material means to achieve it. Similarly, suggestions as to an endemic aesthetic and political timidity as the norm of Australian cinema by Sam Rohdie, Scott Murray, Sue Dermody and Liz Jacka promote a film-making and film criticism which would deliver a more whole and complete Australian cinema.

The hyperbolic locating of the sameness of Australian cinema is therefore crucial to differentiating projects. It assists a range of film-making projects to survive and cultivates the necessity for a differently constructed 'crop' of films. Negative views of Australian cinema's homogeneity are central to maintaining its internal diversity. They also have the advantage of exerting a form of pressure on film funding institutions to move in certain directions.

STYLISTIC PREOCCUPATIONS

Critics and film-makers alike see Australian cinema as driven by a band of *stylistic* choices. As noted earlier Adrian Martin (1988a) identifies 'naturalism', 'ornamentalism' and a minor stream of 'cinephile cinema' as making up the stylistic domain of Australian cinema. Naturalism 'plays down form altogether for the sake of a seamless fictional illusion', ornamentalism 'throws around a few novel, flashy formal effects in the name of local colour, or "style" in the empty sense' (97), while cinephile cinema allows 'form or style' to 'truly animate a subject' (98).

For his part, Ross Gibson claims that there are two 'dominant modes' of Australian cinema: 'the lower-budget end of the Hollywood storytelling tradition – "the classic realist text" ... and ... a functional, documentary realism' (1992: 74). For Gibson

> All the other traditions of world cinema (for example, European avant-garde experimentation and quality narrative, surrealism, and the more magical genres of industrial cinema, such as the musical and the science fiction fantasy) have played only minor roles in the history of cinema in Australia.
>
> (1992: 74)

Martin and Gibson produce reasonably congruent estimations of a cinema locked into a narrow expressive bandwidth. Both see Australian cinema as having a limited negotiation with the repertoires of world cinema. And Gibson's emphasis on 'realism' and its relation with 'pictorialism' in Australian visual representation loosely matches Martin's 'naturalist' and 'ornamentalist' categories respectively. Dermody and Jacka also argue that naturalism dominates Australian feature film-making and television drama production, with minor streams of film-making in other performance styles.

There is no doubt that the most important single style in Australian film-making is *naturalism*, understood as an ideological strategy *and* as a family of production and performance strategies. These two features of naturalism often get confused.

1 Naturalism as an ideological strategy

'Naturalism' is here another term for realism. Adrian Martin has provided the most sustained criticism of such a strategy in Australian film-making. In his 1988 essay, 'Nurturing the Next Wave', he defines naturalism through the realist injunction for film-making to be 'true to the actual' – to give '"a slice of life" or window on the world' (1988a: 97). Here 'content is *a priori* naturally more important than form' such that '*how* these films speak and shape themselves – the politics of their invisible or calculatedly transparent form – is usually dismissed ... as an exotic irrelevance'. Instead of form, what is important is the force of the content: film as social action. For Martin this results in a film-making which asks 'what do I want to say with film' and not 'what do I want to *hear* and *say* on film?' (92). The 1994 chairperson of the Australian Film Commission, Sue Milliken, neatly encapsulated this view in her comment on the prevalence of '[Hollywood] action films' at the cinema box-office:

> As a film-maker, I'm only interested in making films that have something to say. It's depressing that the films which reach the widest audience are the ones that have littlest to say, because film is always a medium for change.
> Still, there are many people in the world who, on the whole, are much better

educated than 30 or 40 years ago. That does mean a bigger audience for arthouse films.

(Milliken, quoted in S. Williams 1994)

Naturalism as an ideological strategy attaches film-making to social, political and cultural orders. To be successful, Australian film-making needs to inhere in these orders to some extent. Critics, reviewers, film-makers, marketers, audiences, policy-makers and so on routinely use the film to talk about these social orders. It is therefore natural to invoke a 'realist' register for film-making that is, by no stretch of the imagination, naturalist. ALP Federal President in the early 1990s and quiz show contestant celebrity, Barry Jones, once praised *Mad Max* for having the characteristics of his outer Melbourne electorate. As noted in Chapter 2, the idea of a national cinema relies on just such a realist/naturalist projection. Given this, it is not surprising that a cinema whose *raison d'être* is national cultural expression (or the registering of national specificities in its oppositional guise) should be approached as a domain of naturalism *as an ideological figure* of realism. As the self-professed realist ambition is for the film to be judged in its connection to social orders, ideological naturalism is the normal recourse for social critics to make sense of Australian cinema, for lobbyists to promote it, for audiences to appreciate the 'Australian supplement'; film-makers to take advantage of the local situation (what is available to them and not as available to the imported product), and for cultural critics to explore a specifically Australian experience of film-making. Whether the film-making style supports or undermines such reasoning, this will be the case.

When a predominance of naturalism in Australian cinema is suggested by critics and film-makers, it usually turns on naturalism as an ideological figure. Most criticism of Australian cinema turns on its realist biases. 'Pretending to let 'life itself' speak, naturalism denies the fact that all films are fantasy-machines, filling and prompting our imagination of the possible' (Martin 1988a: 99). For more explicitly political positions, ideological naturalism maintains the status quo. It accepts what is constructed in dominance – the nation, masculinity, heterosexism, the dominant ethnicity – without either permitting the expression of *difference* or allowing form and experiment to develop appropriate means for marginalized voices to find expression.

Martin also suggests that the dominance of naturalism in Australian cinema is what marks the yawning stylistic gap between Australian and Hollywood cinema. This owes itself to the marginalizing of cinephile traditions in Australian film-making – whereas such cinephilia is integral to the Hollywood cinema:

> Cinephile films do not presume to show real life; rather, they head straight for the mediations of this life experience, its privileged metaphors, that are contained in the popular cultural well of cinematic images and fictions. A naturalistic film, on the other hand, asserts that it is a unique object, a glimpse into 'life itself' unfolding.

(Martin 1988a: 98)

Naturalism encourages an Australian cinema which revolves around a pre-modernist relationship with and disposition of materials (in which cinematic form is a neutral conveyor of predetermined information). It is apparently a cinema yet to grasp its mission as cinema; while the Hollywood cinema with its self-referentiality, its emphasis on myth and its negotiation of the imaginary is seen as modernist and even post-modernist. Martin connects Australian cinema's 'orna-mentalist' inclination to this naturalist bias, claiming that film-makers graft this ornamentalism on to pre-existing materials to spice them up.

Naturalism as an ideological figure shapes these tellings of Australian cinema's unity. Whether this unity is produced by relations to the local environment for Gibson (1992) or by an endemic failure to grasp the cinema as cinema for Martin (1988a), what is created is an *ideologically defined stylistic unity* to Australian cinema.

What makes this unity more plausible is its close association with film-making practices in which naturalist performances and styles are dominant. The relation between naturalism as an ideological strategy and naturalist film performance strategies in Australian film is a complex one, given that these two do not always match. The rhetorics supporting and criticizing a national cinema bind the two closely together, but film practice is dominated by naturalism though scarcely by a realist ideology. Naturalism as social problematization is not the same as naturalism as a performative or stylistic enterprise. By 1994, Adrian Martin had admitted as much. Naturalism had become another film performance style some-times obscured by an 'anti-realist bias'. He now saw Australian film-making traditions as 'somewhere between varieties of naturalism and the tall tale'. Naturalism becomes a commodious term for a collection of production strategies.

2 Naturalism as a performance strategy

Naturalism is possibly the single largest and most internally differentiated set of performance styles in film and television. Film, like photography, is a naturalist medium (see Bazin (1971), Balázs (1970)). Naturalism is the dominant style of film acting across nearly all genres and styles of film-making – Richard Blum (1984), suggests that American film acting in the sound era is in 'the Stanislavski heritage'. Television drama, from the sit-com to the mini-series to 'the soap', is the home of naturalism. It deploys naturalistic rhetorics by virtue of constraints of resolution and image size, dictating reliance on smaller gesture suited to the intimate requirements of close-ups and medium close-ups, shot-reverse shots, serial formats, and lower investment per unit of screen time. It almost dictates productions 'on a human scale', centring relationships, and the effects of action on character.

Additionally, naturalism's close relationship with documentary informs the changing of naturalist styles in the docu-drama and its close relation, the social problem film. As changes to documentary occur, changes in other areas of film-making follow. This naturalist rhetoric inherited from the documentary is usually going to be different from the soap naturalism animating *Neighbours* (1985–) (although the 'reality fiction' *Sylvania Waters* following a Sydney family did show just how close these two could be). Documentary and other 'reality' productions in television and the newsreel have long fed into Australian film-making. Sometimes this occurs in unexpected ways. Lee Robinson's action adventure cinema of the 1950s in *King of the Coral Sea* and *The Phantom Stockman* worked off locations he had already 'created' in his documentaries. In these films the narrative sometimes takes time out to render, in a classical documentary expositary mode, in the case of the former, the quotidian spectacle of the pearling industry and, in the case of the latter, painter Albert Namatjira at work creating one of his internationally famous canvasses. Robinson here was returning to settings and situations on which he had earlier made documentaries.

Naturalist observational documentary rhetorics are in evidence in the oddly distanced and observational camera in Glenda Hambly's *Fran* – which made the audience complicit with and at the same time distanced from Fran. The result is a certain sympathy but ambivalence towards Fran despite the stuff of full-blown melodrama that is the film's plot. While Fran loves her children she puts her sexual and romantic interests above them and is subsequently oblivious to her lover's implied sexual abuse of her daughter. Eventually her relatives and friends spurn her and the welfare agencies step in to break up the family. What is produced is more a space of 'interrogation' of the character and our relation as viewers to the action – the position taken in observational documentaries.

Naturalism is also the domain of the 'drama' category on video shelves and in cinema schedules (and Australian films are often found here beside Hollywood's Oscar winning films). Naturalism as 'drama' betrays its stage roots as the predominant form of nineteenth- and twentieth-century theatre in the West, in 'well-made' plays and stage melodramas alike. This path leads to a film-making with obvious debts to playwrights like Ibsen and Chekhov and the performance styles developed by Konstantin Stanislavsky and the film-making experiments and theorizing of a D. W. Griffith and V. I. Pudovkin. Sometimes the debt is acknowledged, as when Michael Blakemore adapted Chekhov's *Uncle Vanya* to his *Country Life* (1994).[5] Mostly though, the influence is less acknowledged, as for some of the most popular Australian titles of the 1970s and early 1980s from *Caddie* to *Picnic at Hanging Rock*, from *Breaker Morant* to *My Brilliant Career*. These so-called 'nostalgia films' owe a clear debt to a cinematic tradition that draws on naturalist 'drama': the 'quality' British and Hollywood films and 1950s and 1960s television experiments with the one-off play.

Naturalism is the primary vehicle for that important stream of Hollywood film-making which has always persisted side by side with the high budget special effects and action cinema – the smaller 'issues oriented' film where actors portray 'realistic people in recognizable situations' (Blum 1984: 70). Fred Schepisi's *Evil Angels* is, after all, close to many of Streep's Hollywood vehicles and confirmed her reputation as an actor's actor and this as an 'actor's picture'. The extent to which Australian cinema produces and nurtures directors for this kind of cinema is evident in the Hollywood careers of some of Australia's most famous established directors – Beresford (*Driving Miss Daisy* 1989), Weir (*Green Card*), and even that most 'cinematic' of Australian directors, Dr George Miller (*Lorenzo's Oil*). One of the side points about this 'drama' orientation is that it more often appeals to an older audience. Mid-to-late 1970s Australian feature film-making – the nostalgia film – attracted just such an audience. In stage-of-life terms, the historical audience 'matured' from the 'ocker' films of their youth into the 'serious quality films' of their twenties and thirties. Dr George Miller talks of *Lorenzo's Oil* as his 'adult film', made after marriage and children, and I do not think I would have appreciated this film as much without having had sick children of my own.

Sometimes this cinema is disparaged as 'theatrical film-making', in which the scriptwriter and the actor dominate. For Martin Australian scriptwriters are encouraged to 'craftily and preciously cultivate what they want to say' and not what 'they might want to see and hear' (Martin 1988a: 97). Martin later claimed that Franklin's *Hotel Sorrento* (1995) was flawed in this regard – keeping too close to the stage play on which it was based. If this can sometimes be a problem, Dilys Powell's 1980 assessment of *Breaker Morant* suggests the cinematic effectiveness of such film-making at its best:

> there are no visual refinements ... The trial proceeds bleakly: an almost military directness, faces in severe close-up; nonetheless, *Breaker Morant* engages one's emotions more powerfully than many a film with closer attention to cinematic style.
>
> (Powell, 1989: 294)

A minimalist naturalism is entirely appropriate and effective *cinema*. Beresford's subsequent and distinguished Hollywood career (e.g. *Tender Mercies* 1982) shows just how close Australian naturalist cinema is to much of Hollywood cinema.

The 'drama' legacy is undoubtedly more complex than as simply a theatrical tradition transposed to film. The theatre's naturalist tradition provided workable, plausible and successful models which met film-making and television's production requirements. Just as with documentary naturalism, this legacy is often found in unexpected directions. Australian television drama's great journeyman scriptwriter, Ron McLean, once reported to Albert Moran that he had rewritten Edward Albee's *Who's Afraid of Virginia Wolf* (immortalized in the Richard Burton, Elizabeth Taylor screen version) no less than sixteen times for Australian serial television. Equally I have spoken to scriptwriters who claim to have modelled episodes of children's drama series on Shakspeare's *The Tempest*.

The second path leading from video's drama category is the naturalist melodrama – the dominant form of cinematic melodrama on film and in the television 'soap'. As noted in Chapter 5, Australian cinema has produced many full-blown melodramas, and television is routinely an expert producer and concept exporter for television soaps and mini-series. Moreover, melodrama's shifts of feeling and intensities are never far away in Australian cinema. The tragi-comedy and dramatic, almost uncontrolled, mood swings of Paul J. Hogan's *Muriel's Wedding* are fuelled by just such intensities. In *The Adventures of Priscilla: Queen of the Desert*, the Terence Stamp character provides the film's emotional centre for a certain section of the audience. The uncontrollable mirth of fellow cinema patrons sits oddly with one's own tears. Perhaps this proximity to melodrama and sentimentality is naturally there, given that relationships are going to be that much more important in Australian cinema and the main line of action. Such is even the case in sci-fi films, as in Rolf de Heer's *Incident at Raven's Gate* where the extra-terrestrial force remains inexplicable while insinuating itself in a love triangle involving the two brothers and the wife of one of them. One brother maims his married brother; the wife in turn maims her lover then kills her husband, and finally brother and sister-in-law can go off together to be restored to their house as if nothing had happened. All this emotional mayhem is secured through a matter-of-fact naturalistic performance!

Australian feature film-making is often a hybrid of these two facets of the drama category – the well-made screenplay and melodrama with its popular resonances. Unlike the larger film industries, the Australian industry cannot separately support each format. On their own they cannot attract the necessary Australian patronage and later video and commercial television sales. The logic is for a bit of this and a bit of that – enough to keep both constituencies happy. The naturalist logic of much Australian cinema is to be in the domain of melodrama on the one hand and attempt to be firmly situated in the quality (drama) film on the other. Hence the charge of sentimentality without passion (*The Irishman*) and passion without sense (*Jenny Kissed Me*). P. P. McGuinness's criticism of *The Irishman* in the *National Times* (24–30 March 1979) was that it had no redeeming drama – its 'values' were those 'of the three minute cigarette commercial', its connection to 'the realities of modern Australia' was through an 'appeal to escapism'. The same reviewer (*National Times*, 20–26 March 1978) earlier damned Ken Hannam's *Dawn!* (1979) with its imputed bisexual swimming star as being 'like a *Women's Weekly* feature translated directly to the screen without any intervening human intelligence or sensitivity ... clearly made for the mass magazine market'.

Australian popular cinema does have a close connection with the commercial popular culture. After all, in style, training, and continuity of employment advertising has been crucial to sustaining the feature film-making infrastructure in Australia. The acceptable 'pictorial' look (usually delivered on a small budget) has been developed over many years in advertising as the highest budgeted-per-second of screen time production in Australia. In recognition of this, the ACS (the Australian Cinematographers Society) regards advertising cinematographers more highly as experts than those who might cut their teeth on low budget shorts and features. Martin's sense of an 'ornamentalist' logic at work in Australian cinema is partly shaped by this proximity. A peripheral industry in the English language has to compete directly with Hollywood in terms of its standards of imaging and its need to present well. This encourages, in its turn, criticism of 'ornamentalism' and 'surrender to ... slick commercial values' (McGuinness *National Times*, 20–26 March 1978).

UNITIES OF SETTING AND LANDSCAPE

Another site for convergence in film-making lies in landscape and lighting. Much has been made of this by film-makers and critics. They argue that Australian cinema has developed a distinctive cinema by virtue of having to shoot in a different light and in a different topography than the Anglo-European. Visitors to Australia often comment, as Gideon Bachmann did in 1978, that:

> There is a sense of space in this landscape that I have never felt anywhere else, and a quality of light which seems unique in its brittle horizontality and transparence. A life rhythm results from these facts and from the great distance to elsewhere. ... Nothing in Australia can be shortened or abstracted.
>
> (Quoted in Baxter 1986: 112)

Cinematographer Russell Boyd also speaks of his accommodation to Australian light:

> It's something one becomes conscious of as a kid, to the extent where I guess the light's something you can't easily escape in Australia. And I guess when you transfer that to using that quality on film, one has to be prepared to suffer the rigours of the hard Australian light, and also to try and not only communicate those on film but also to control the contrast of it, by either lighting or placement of subject against the sun or using early morning light or late afternoon light. ... it's certainly far different from the European, which is obviously much softer and more diffused, and much more in fact controllable.
>
> (Boyd in Baxter 1986: 113–14)

The evidence of this visual sensibility lies in those Hollywood films and television programmes shot with an Australian sensibility. Dean Semler's Academy Award-winning cinematography on *Dances with Wolves* (Costner 1991) made the featureless US landscapes so often avoided in US films resemble the Australian landscapes featured in Australian 'nostalgia films'. Simon Wincer's direction of the Hollywood mini-series *Lonesome Dove* (1989) brought a similar landscape emphasis along with the many other stylistic similarities of the Australian mini-series of the early 1980s.[6]

It is a commonplace that landscape is central to Australian culture. Ross Gibson has connected this cultural concern with film-making trajectories. He argues for 'a recurrent, almost mesmerized, preoccupation with topography on the part of Europeans who have attempted, over several centuries, to define a non-Aboriginal culture' (Gibson 1992: 1). In Australian cinema, '[i]t is a leitmotif and a ubiquitous character' (1992: 63) and '[i]ts presence throughout the history of Australian film-making is such that the country has come to represent something much more than an environmental setting for local narratives' (1992: 63). Indeed, for Gibson 'the majority of Australian features have been about landscape' (63). The landscape and this sensibility both become an important international differentiation: '[t]he landscape cinema has asserted both Australia's difference from the rest of the world and also the nation's singularity of constitution within its own boundaries' (69). The landscape appears to provide a key to Australia's identity, a preoccupation further underlined by the fact that these are the imaginings of one of the most urbanized of societies.

I don't want to assert too much particularity here. In the USA, Canada and New Zealand wilderness, bush and significant landscapes – like Uluru (Ayers Rock) in the Australian context – take on an emblematic identity. Agents from all these countries construct the same deep pasts in the landscape and the sea. The landscapes of each also provide an apparently open and continuous point of identification. So, Australia is a new nation in an old, old land. A sense of youth and beginning anew is paradoxically associated with an ancient landscape, a unique flora and fauna and, more lately, Aboriginal people and their heritage (as the world's oldest peoples).

So central was a rural and frontier setting to Australian film-making in the 1920s that John Tulloch (1981) in his study of films of the 1920s uses the term 'films of the bush' to record it. I take him to be suggesting a nativist narrative and thematic preoccupation running through diverse titles. He quotes the American director Wallace Worsley's 1932 comment in order to get at the special inflection of the 'Australian Legend' running through this and later Australian cinema:

> The drama of Australia is not as it is so frequently represented overseas – a drama of an Australian falling victim to the wiles of a native girl . . . or of a white woman living amongst Aborigines, but the drama of man's struggle against nature in the face of great physical and mental hardship, his eventual triumph, and his magnificent reward.
>
> (Tulloch 1981: 345)

But the legend in this form continues in part because it still addresses contemporary realities – of drought-ravaged farming and grazing communities, and its usefulness as a metaphor for life's struggles, as in Elfick's *No Worries*. It is also a legend that has often given women an important role. Women were at the heart of the bush narrative right up until *Wake in Fright* – with famous titles like *The Squatter's Daughter*, *A Girl of the Bush*, the Rudd cycle, and all of Chauvel's titles. Women are also present in Chauvel's documentaries and their filming (Cunningham 1991: 3–4). In Chauvel's great *The Sons of Matthew* (1949) the opening of the rainforest lands in the Gold Coast hinterland is rendered as a tale involving the struggle of (white) men and women against the natural world including their natural inclinations. A woman, Cathy, is the earth that the male lead, Shane, says he wants.

We now draw attention to the *exclusion* of the Aboriginal presence from this legend or the *undesirable* place of this presence within it; in *The Overlanders* the

Aboriginal men are either part of the landscape or an exploited part of the droving workforce without a voice. Of late the Aboriginal presence is getting written back into the bush and pioneer legends. As Lattas observes (1990: 66), in public mythology there is a tendency today to mix the bush with the first Australians – the Aborigines:

> the primordial and primitive otherness of Aborigines is seen as capable of providing a form of spiritual unity for the nation, it can provide the necessary mythology capable of overcoming that fragmentation of the nation which immigration and multiculturalism have produced.

The Australian legend is being Aboriginalized to provide accounts of Aboriginal accomplishment. Like the white settlers of the legend, Aboriginal agents struggled with and accommodated their culture to an environment – indeed theirs is the superior accommodation. The bush legend also offers a space of solidarity between non-Aboriginal and Aboriginal people offered, for example, in Ross Gibson's essay film *Wild*. Aboriginal people can become privileged markers of the legend, in that there is not only the Aboriginal achievement of living so success-fully and for so long in such a difficult environment, but there is also an Aboriginal ethic of care for the environment in which 'triumph' is replaced by adaptive accommodation. In *Where the Green Ants Dream*, the Aboriginal 'care' ethic of the land is contrasted with the commercially oriented and exploitative relationship of 'the European' in mining and agriculture.

As in Canada and New Zealand – but not the USA, the Australian presentation of 'landscape' now feels impelled to negotiate the indigenous viewpoint and presence. It cannot be so evidently empty, primeval, Other. The model of such an adaptive accommodation is still John Heyer's landmark documentary, *The Back of Beyond* (1954). Here the 'bush type' (Ward 1978) and Aborigines accommodate the landscape and negotiate a cosmopolitan Australian heritage later exploited by Roeg, Herzog and Wenders.

There are, of course, good economic reasons for the Australian focus on the landscape, topography, and bush. Car chases and car crashes are easier and less costly to stage on country roads. There is an 'ease' to a location that can make up for a lack of investment and budget for art direction, or precise studio control. As noted already, international images of Australia are predominantly topographical images which constitute exploitable features for domestic and international consumption.

But making the landscape so central also falsifies the film-making record. Australian cinema is not dominated by rural and outback stories. There are more city and town stories. And there are stories which combine the two. It has to be remembered that these city and town landscapes are not especially Australian in look. Furthermore 'Melbourne' light is not Alice Springs or Perth light. The visual look of many of Cox's films like *My First Wife* and *Lonely Hearts*, and Ruane's *Death in Brunswick* testify to a different sensibility for which we do not have as easy a rhetoric to apply to. Here the urban landscapes could be easily and readily

European (English, German, Dutch). For the argument to hold in the urban context, film-makers require high summer and not the southern winter rains or Melbourne's four seasons in a day.

CONCLUSION

The last two chapters have shown us that the character and direction of Australian cinema and television is simultaneously made of dispersing and converging tendencies. The handling of dispersal and convergence, diversity and unity in film-making projects and the relationship between both provides Australian cinema with its characteristic shape. Yet each have entailments which cloud as much as illuminate.

Because critics, film-makers and policy-makers want a generalizable picture of the Australian cinema, they give priority to one or other: to either diversity or unity. In 1990s policy-making and criticism, diversity is foregrounded; in the 1970s, unity was foregrounded – and both provided ample scope for a diverse and multifaceted film-making milieu. Australia's film culture can always be deconstructed to reveal either its *differences* of scope and emphasis or its redundancies and *typicalities*.

Particular values have been associated with each of these tendencies. Typically, an ideological emphasis promoting the dispersal of Australian cinema emphasizes the intertextual relationship with international cinema and the affiliations this cinema has with that larger international cinema. An emphasis promoting convergence emphasizes a film's relation to the Australian cinema and Australian socio-cultural formations and national specificities. Dispersal leads us to Australian universalism, participation in the international cinema and a sense of how unnecessary it might be to draw borders around Australian film, or to imagine Australian identities. Convergence leads to Australian particularism, the singularity of Australia's film culture, the integrity of a film-making and cultural milieu which inevitably produces, reflects and creates Australian identities. Yet there is nothing 'natural' about these associations. Sometimes an unfortunate unity can lie in Australian cinema's relation to the international cinema. Thus the closeness of the relation with international cinema was often criticized in the 1960s and early 1970s: 'location films' and 'kangaroo westerns' brooked the nativist difference in Australian cinema and so disabled an original Australian contribution to world cinema. Christine Sammers was criticizing Australian universalism in the internationalization of the Australian documentary in the early 1990s, when she argued that this came at the expense of the representation and address to Australia's internal diversity – its urban neighbourhood stories and therefore multicultural Australia (Sammers 1993: 164).

The movements to dispersal and unity are part of the contending pressures and speaking (and knowing) positions on and in Australian cinema. To emphasize one at the expense of the other is to do Australian cinema a disservice. The competing orientations, critical appropriations, audience expectations, and institutional, political and film-making trajectories, each moving along on its own timetable, are central to the makeup of the Australian film and television landscape. Lotman (1990: 135) suggests we should not be surprised about the existence of such competing systems: 'the attentive historian of culture will find in each synchronic section [of culture] not one system of canonized norms, but a paradigm of competing systems.' Australia's national cinema – and the culture of cinema in Australia – is assuredly one such paradigm of competing systems shaped by the various wills to unify and diversify this cinema.

Chapter 9

Negotiating cultural transfers

INTRODUCTION

The international cinema has always been important to Australian film-making. The Australian contribution to the several pathways of the cinema turns on local film-making as a negotiation and dialogue with the international cinema. But this is not, as we have seen in Chapter 4, an equal dialogue or a symmetrical negotiation. Australian agents negotiate with the international cinema on a permanently unequal basis making *cultural transfers* much more important to Australian film production, circulation, appreciation and criticism. It is a film and television milieu configured by flows and transfers (of concepts, genres, styles, texts, fashions, etc.) which shape film-making, criticism and consumption in a variety of antipodal ways. In this chapter I will theorize on this variety by drawing on the work of Yuri Lotman (1990) and Meaghan Morris (1988), who have made cultural transfers central to their understanding of national cultural formations and Australian film respectively.

Both Lotman and Morris considerably advance our understanding of the integral role cultural transfers play in the formation of cultures. They take us beyond the simple import/export, unoriginal/original dichotomies and related notions of cultural imperialism which are usually used to distinguish receiving and sending cultures. They take into account the mutuality of a situation in which cultural imports are connected to local cultural production and its export, while unoriginality and derivation is connected to the very possibility of originality. For Lotman this relation holds for receiving and sending cultures alike. Both Lotman and Morris lead us to see that the alternatives of an Australian culture, either always captured by international components or always remaking and repositioning the imported culture on native terms, are not so much contradictory interpretations but part of larger and unavoidable semiotic processes.

Lotman is particularly useful, as he has elaborated his model of cultural transfers in the context of his general theory of culture as the 'semiosphere'. For Lotman cultural transfers are central to culture and cultural development generally. A culture cannot turn itself into a sending culture without being at some point a receiving culture. More importantly for this study, he distinguishes *processes* of cultural transfer and he gives us a way of linking these as the successive stages involved in the unfolding story of any culture's development. These are: a first stage where imported texts 'keep their strangeness' and are valued more than those of the home culture; a second stage where 'the imported text and the home culture ... restructure each other' (so, for example, *Bad Boy Bubby* indigenizes the Eastern European art film); a third stage where 'a higher content is found in the imported world-view which can be separated from the national culture of the imported texts' and is attached to the local product (thus Australian films – like *Mad Max* and *Newsfront* become better films than their original Hollywood and quality film exemplars); a fourth stage where 'imported texts are entirely dissolved in the receiving culture' (*The Chant of Jimmie Blacksmith, Proof*); and a fifth stage where 'the receiving culture ... changes into a transmitting culture directing its product to other, peripheral areas of the semiosphere' (Lotman 1990: 146) in *The Piano, Crocodile Dundee* and the television series *Police Rescue* (1992–   ) and *Bananas in Pyjamas* (1991–   ).

For Lotman, national cultures need to pass through these five stages (Lotman 1990: 146). Cultures cannot become transmitting cultures – without passing through stages one to three. For Lotman, as a professional historian and semiotician of culture, it makes no sense to oppose these stages to one another, as they are part of a general process. Both the abject home culture of stage one with its cultural cringe, and the confident producing culture of stage four with its thorough indiginization of imported models are not only part of a continuum of cultural exchange but are organically interconnected. Such *natural* semiotic processes are to be identified for what they are – part of the general condition of any culture.

Lotman's model came out of his historical study of Russian cultural history in the eighteenth and nineteenth centuries. While I do not want to push too far the analogy between eighteenth- and nineteenth-century Russian culture and late twentieth-century Australian culture, it is significant that both countries – Russia then and Australia since European settlement – were 'frontier areas', Russia to Europe, Australia to the UK and the USA. For both, cultural imports and the language of those imports were valued over a vernacular. And in both competing pull factors were generated, in the Russian case, by its various ethnic cultures and, in the Australian case, by Aboriginal and Islander and NES peoples.

After expanding on Lotman's model and applying it to the Australian film milieu, I will then consider how Australian cinema history can be written as a succession of these stages; and how these stages are often co-present at any one time. I will connect Lotman's model to Morris's model of Australian un-originality, concluding with a brief discussion of the composite international identity of Australian cinema.

LOTMAN'S MODEL OF CULTURAL TRANSFER

First stage

The first stage identified by Lotman (1990: 146) sees '[t]he texts coming in from the outside keep their "strangeness"', such that they are 'read in the foreign language (both in the sense of natural language and in the semiotic sense).' Also, '[t]hey hold a high position in the scale of values, and are considered to be true, beautiful, of divine origin'. Australians routinely hold Hollywood film-making, British cinema and television and the European and now Asian cinema in higher esteem than the local product. Industry people – distributors, film-makers and exhibitors – regularly report that audiences, from their perspective, are un-warrantedly resistant to quality local product.

Critics and film-makers are often just as resistant, preferring other imaginings. For the cinephile, American not Australian cinema is 'the cinephile's heaven' (Martin 1988a: 92) – the cinephile believes he or she is appreciating this imported product on its own terms. Theirs is a loving regard for modes of film-making often not their own. Australian cinephiles praised Richard Franklin in the 1960s and 1970s because he was successful at doing films the American way. As Adrian Martin (1988b: 130–1) describes his standing then:

> Few [film] journals at the time are complete without the latest bulletin concerning his training at the University of Southern California film school and particularly his apprenticeship on the set of Hitchcock's 1968 *Topaz*. Franklin ... stands for know-how, technical mastery, cleverness within convention ... a species of home-grown Hitchcocko-Hawksianism ... Eventually, Franklin climbs enough steps of the industry ladder to make what is for some cinephiles a breakthrough Australian film, *Patrick* (1978), a unique instance of American cinema lessons well absorbed and put to work. Hostile commentators ... dub Franklin's work 'trans-Pacific', but the cinephiles stay with him as he starts to make the ritual move back to Hollywood – first with the co-production *Roadgames* ... and then the real thing a bona fide American movie, *Psycho II* [1983]: the Hitchcockian circle is closed, and other films follow. ... Franklin's 'Americanism', whichever country he practices it in, is declared by his loyal cinephile cohorts to be brave and under-appreciated by Australian film culture at large.

Franklin's own film-making and pronouncements (Franklin 1980: 411) dovetail with this estimation. He insisted upon the cultural appropriateness in Australia of the Hollywood imaginary, berating those who would accentuate what is different about Australian speech and lifeways and ignoring what was imaginatively held in common. For Lotman (1990: 146):

> Knowledge of the foreign language is a sign of belonging to 'culture', to the elite, to the best. Already existing texts in 'one's own' language, and that language itself, are correspondingly valued lowly, being classed as untrue, 'coarse', 'uncultured'.

As the cinephile example shows, criticism does not have to be animated by what a cultural élite finds 'the best'. Variously the Hollywood cinema, American independents, European and Asian art films, the avant-garde, exploitation, political, multicultural, or feminist cinema show up the limits and inadequacies of local efforts. The film critic calls on this international repertoire to introduce to Australian cinema some film performance style, genre, or social problematization.

Audiences are often animated by similar concerns. For John Baxter (Baxter 1986: 22) there was something disturbing about the idea of Australian feature film-making:

> Both *Bush Christmas* and *The Overlanders* had left me disturbed rather than glowing with national pride – rather like a Catholic hearing mass said for the first time in English rather than Latin. There was only one proper place for making films and that was America: I didn't care to see fantasies enacted right on my doorstep. It was a common reaction.

I find that students express similar sentiments. Australian cinema is the 1990s equivalent of the lowly, coarse and uncultured – unhip, boring and not with the times. And this includes those who want a career in film-making. They see their task as renovating Australian film-making through participating in the life worlds of contemporary cinema and embracing whatever topics and issues appear internationally prevalent.

During this stage, Lotman (146) suggests there is a 'dominant psychological impulse . . . to break with the past, to idealize the 'new', i.e. the imported worldview, and to break with tradition, while the 'new' is experienced as something salvific'. Instances of this stage abound in criticism, film-making and film policy development. The need for a new start is undergirded by a recognition of the worthless character of Australian film history and production traditions. Film policy-makers, critics and film-makers go through this first stage to create the threshold for the second stage of concept indigenization. Without the standing of Hollywood, the British quality film and the European art film there could have been no basis from which to legitimate an Australian film industry.

Australian film criticism is full of routine comparisons between the qualities of the international cinema and the 'lowly' qualities of the Australian cinema. People feel this difference. The devaluation of Australian-produced culture and elevation of Hollywood and international art cinema is a natural part of the Australian experience of the cinema and culture more generally. The standing of British culture in the 1960s devalued the Australian accent to such an extent that the playwrights and stage actors the feature revival drew on often had to be retrained in the vernacular and the Australian accent. The voice coach became an important component on the set of Crawford television series and serials from the mid-1960s to the 1980s, by which time actor training institutions had delivered an Australian accent.

The consequences for local film-making are not always benign. It can seem to

Andrew Pike, distributor of Jackie McKimmie's *Waiting*, that 'if *Waiting* had been in French with subtitles it would have done a lot better and cost a lot less to launch' (quoted in House of Representatives Standing Committee on Environment, Recreation and the Arts 1992: 10). The problem for film-makers is that they may be a cultural stage ahead of their audience. For Pike, *Waiting* is an Australian version of the French relationship film. McKimmie 'indigenizes' the French model and comes out at the end with a film recognizable as such, but true to the Brisbane bohemian milieu her film describes. Was the audience that generally makes French films Australian art-house successes simply not ready for the Australian supplement?

Sometimes this first stage is referred to retrospectively and disparagingly as the 'cultural cringe', whereby anything imported is valued come what may. The standpoint of later stages promotes this stage as a false consciousness to rail against as a means of moving on to and legitimating later stages of cultural transfer. A retrospective description of this first stage lies in Philip Noyce's *Newsfront*, where the 'Road to Gundagai' is sung by an American performer – a poignant moment where the Bill Hunter character notes the loss of local values and indigenous cultural materials to Americanization. Such a lament calls forth Noyce's own film, which restores these values, legitimating it as the bearer of true values and investing its lead – the Bill Hunter persona – as the bearer of the best and worst of such residual Australian values in this and later roles.

Lotman's first stage is essential to the introduction of new formats, critical paradigms, and combinations of film-making. Without it there can be no system regeneration, no second stage of indigenizing the imported culture from which to begin. It also encourages a healthy disrespect for the local product and it enables people to dream of an outside from which to reposition the local.

Second stage

The second stage where the 'imported texts and the home culture restructure each other' is evident when Scott Murray took Raymond Radiguet's 1923 novel *Le Diable au Corps* and set it in Australia during the Second World War as *Devil in the Flesh* (1989 – a remake which in its turn influenced the subsequent French remake). John Duigan updated *Casablanca* in his *Far East*. Such cinema adaptations are a feature of film-making.

This second stage is present in a more rudimentary form in the huge number of concept remakes on television worldwide – when the rights for a television quiz, variety or sports show are acquired and the format is applied with small changes to accommodate local circumstance.[1] It is present in criticism when critics take the different theories developed for other cultural formations and sometimes apply them with only minor changes to accommodate the Australian context. And, it is a component of the documentary, given the substantially local character of much documentary circulation which enables more rudimentary concept re-makes because the original is not as publicly available.

Typically, feature film-makers and television drama producers operate in the more advanced stage of a full-blown adaptation – as the Hollywood, British and European originals already have a market presence. In this second stage, Lotman insists, 'translations, imitations and adaptations multiply' and 'the codes imported along with the texts become part of the metalingual structure.' This second stage gives rise to a relatively strict division of labour: the Australian is the content, the flavour, the accent and the social text, while the international provides the underlying form, values, narrative resolutions, etc.

If Australian cultural product is so often at this second stage, this might explain why so many national and international film critics find it, on the surface, unadventurous and derivative even when at its most independent. The idea that Australians are an unoriginal lot – one of the first things visiting Americans seem to note about Australian culture – might stem from the prevalence of productions and criticism at this stage. The critic's claim that Australian cinema is mostly locked into the classical Hollywood paradigm and is a pale imitation of the Hollywood original is often an implied argument that Australians incompetently clone Hollywood cinema. Some want Australian cinema to be 'a good clone', a cinema more like Hollywood which could eliminate Australian difference; others want it to be something altogether different from Hollywood and more like that of another national cinema – continental European, British and more recently Taiwan and Hong Kong cinemas. What is being argued over here is *what* should be indigenized. Of course it might be only that those critics and audiences who see Australian product at this stage may not have worked through the consequences of negotiation, which the producers have, in which case they 'mistake' what they see.

Despite the prevalence of this second stage in the self-understanding of Australian cinema by those who produce it, there are few directors who have made 'Hollywood in Australia': Richard Franklin in the 1970s and in his later Hollywood films like *Psycho II*, perhaps the Simon Wincer vehicles, *Harlequin* and *Quigley Down Under* (1992) and his American efforts *Lonesome Dove* and *Free Willy* (1993). The other prime candidates, George Miller of *Snowy River* and Dr George Miller of the *Mad Max* trilogy and Ken Hall in the 1930s (Tulloch 1982: 30), were more American influenced with their stories rooted in longer standing local cultural materials.

Furthermore, as 1970s criticism of Australian cinema shows, much of the talk about the surrender to Hollywood values in film-making was a complaint that revival films were often not Hollywood oriented enough, given that they lacked the strong characters, narrative drive, and energy of Hollywood cinema. To praise or criticize Australian cinema entails projecting its failures or possible successes as lying in its adopting and modelling Hollywood and European, and now Asian precedent, or as the rejection of all these. We don't seem to have much of a language to talk about a cinema which only adopts so far and only rejects up to a point. We do not see it as Lotman does as a natural thing fundamental to the ecology of any culture. It is alternately seen as bad, or improperly realized.

But there is more to this stage. It includes 'a predominant tendency to restore the links with the past, to look for 'roots' (Lotman 1990: 147). The 'new' is now interpreted as 'an organic continuation of the old, which is thus rehabilitated'. Peter Weir's *Picnic at Hanging Rock* makes sense not just as a lush and quirky European art film or a classy horror film, but in its connections with longstanding local traditions of storytelling, based as it is upon a screen adaptation of Joan Lindsay's novel. It was connected with nativist ideas about the threatening bush and tall stories and ghost stories about child disappearance and horror met with in the bush.

Lotman notes that ideas of organic development come to the fore at this stage. Cultural criticism, publicity and policy discourses held that the films of the 1970s revival connected Australians with the past. The films became part of a larger narrative of a culture undergoing development and flowering maturity. Producer Joan Long told the Moving Pictures Enquiry in 1991 that this was a time when 'after years of drought for Australian films there was a hunger, almost a craving, to see our past on the screen' (House of Representatives Standing Committee on Environment, Recreation and the Arts 1992: 8).

The prevalence of 'revision' and 'extension' suggests an Australian cinema as less an imitation (as in television quiz shows) than as a *transformation* and a *negotiation*. Australian cinema is consequently less derivative than we might like it to be or criticize it for being. Differences get forged in likeness. Roger and Philip Bell (1993: 80) note that in conditions where local films compete against a dominant American product, 'the cultural effects of the competition between local films and American genres' are 'complex'. They argue that it is neither a matter of 'simple imitation or ... the direct imposition of American values on Australian settings'. Instead, Australian films disclose 'very complex negotiations'. Drawing on John Tulloch's (1981) study of 1920s cinema *Legends on the Screen*, they argue that these negotiations are observable in 'the way local films represented conflicts that had parallels in the films of Hollywood' and in the way the audience restructures the imported product:

> The 'vamp' – the exotic 'world-weary sexual creature' – who was an emblem of city degradation was accompanied by another Hollywood type – the 'Girl-Woman' – who might either be 'a pure and helpless victim or else pure and capable of spirited activity'. Tulloch points out that the cultural resonance of these types was strong in a local industry where the vamp had also customarily been contrasted to the bush heroine. The cultural meanings that Australian audiences read from the Hollywood genre films may have been peculiar to their own background – both social and cinematic.

The norms, thematics and styles of the dominant cinema are central to Australian cinema, structuring it in similarity, differentiation and interpenetration.

Third stage

Lotman's third stage stresses

> a tendency ... to find within the imported world-view a higher content which
> can be separated from the actual national culture of the imported texts. The idea
> takes hold that 'over there' these ideas were realized in an 'untrue', confused or
> distorted form and that 'here', in the heart of the receiving culture they will find
> their true, 'natural' heartland. The culture which first relayed these texts falls
> out of favour and the national characteristics of the texts will be stressed.
>
> (146)

Lotman's third stage crucially involves perceptions. It re-evaluates the home
culture's product in a situation of assumed international comparison. Australian
films can be appreciated at Cannes and the other major international film festivals,
because they are true to the film-making ideals derived from over there but
renovated and innovated here. So Jane Campion becomes the auteur director who
is the first woman to win the Palme d'Or for a feature film. The AFTRS proudly
notes (1993: 1) that 'Jane is the first Australasian to have five films accepted into
the Cannes Festival, three of which were produced whilst she was an AFTRS
student'. The establishment of a film's international credentials establishes its
domestic credentials as an exemplary local product of international standard.
Lotman's third stage opens out onto the heartfelt pride of many producers and
filmworkers about the quality and innovation of their product in an international
frame.

The third stage is evident in the appreciation of the *Mad Max* cycle. Stuart
Cunningham (1985: 237) has commented on how the *Mad Max* cycle in its
'complete mastery of the genre [of road movies], sheer technical virtuosity and
aggressively decadent vitalism – outdoes Hollywood on the grounds it knows
best'. So too there is the idea that Australian cinema holds on trust what is
forgotten in the American source culture – perhaps the humanism of a Frank Capra
or the relations on a human scale lost to an American cinema more concerned with
machines, special effects and dazzle than people. This can even extend to a
retrospective celebration of the Australian sex film. Scott Murray (1993c: 14)
defends John Lamond's *The ABC of Love and Sex Australian Style* (1978) in these
terms:

> given the American cinema's obsession in the 1980s with naked bodies as
> objects to be abused and mutilated, to be pierced violently by knives and cut
> apart by chainsaws, there is much to applaud in the 1970s' [Australian
> cinema's] almost mystical adoration of nude bodies and sex.

Fourth stage

The fourth stage assimilates the imported matrices making them entirely its own.
'[T]he imported texts are entirely dissolved in the receiving culture'. For Lotman
(1990: 146):

During this stage ... the culture itself changes to a state of activity and begins rapidly to produce new texts; these new texts are based on cultural codes which in the distant past were stimulated by invasions from outside, but which now have been wholly transformed through the many asymmetrical transformations into a new and original structural model.

Mad Max does not only 'outdo' Hollywood but with *Shame, Neighbours* (1985–   ) and *The Dismissal* also perhaps provides original structural models for their respective genres. It is no longer a copy. Each has its international consequences, the Australian soap and the 'Australian model' of television become seen as objects in their own right just as the *Mad Max* trilogy led to the Hollywood *Lethal Weapon* (Donner 1987, 1989, 1992) series and *Waterworld*.

Sue Milliken, chairperson of the Australian Film Commission reports:

> We've got over the cringe and the strut, when Australians didn't know whether to try to be totally American or totally Australian, to be successful. Now they're just being good.
>
> Most of our films today are neither protesting their Australianness, or defending it, or embarrassed by it – they just are. They're celebrating quirky idiosyncratic aspects of our society, but are not just 'feel good' movies. There's an edge. . . . We're producing a totally different genre from the Big American commercial blockbuster with a high budget and fifteen writers.
>
> (Hawley, 1994)

As noted earlier, this stage spills over from the second stage of concept extensions, where the model is not so much copied as revised and extended, to such an extent that differences are as important as any similarities. Sometimes it is a toss up whether the concept extensions that start to develop in the second phase are in this fourth stage. Undoubtedly many Australian television drama concepts, documentaries and features belong in this 'in between' stage – perhaps necessarily so, as domestic cinema and drama production tradition need to constantly take account of contemporaneous stylistic, performance and technical developments. As a result, productions will be in part at this fourth stage and in another part at the second stage. As Dermody and Jacka (1988a: 181, 187) observe *The Man from Snowy River* combines 'pyrotechnic television-advertising for action', 'serviceable television drama for dialogue' (signalled by the presence of actors Lorraine Bayley and Tom Burlinson in pivotal roles) and an epic Western form in its plot devices, spectacular landscapes and mythic iconic characters (Kirk Douglas alongside an 'iconic' Jack Thompson).

There are limits to Australian participation at this fourth stage. There is not the level of production activity to sustain it, nor is there the dominance of local 'symbolic' culture at the box-office and on the television schedule. Yet these facts should not downplay the achievements of this phase. A phase curiously undeveloped in Lotman's account, in part, I suspect because it looks least like a cultural transfer!

Fifth stage

The fifth stage sees

> The receiving culture, which now becomes the general centre of the semio-
> sphere, changes into a transmitting culture and issues forth a flood of texts
> directed to other, peripheral areas of the semiosphere. . . . As with any dialogue,
> a situation of mutual attraction must precede the actual contact.
>
> (Lotman 1990: 146)

Of course the idea of Australia as at the centre of the international audiovisual
semiosphere is largely chimerical for reasons outlined in earlier chapters. Although individual films and television series regularly become 'dominant entertainment forces', these tend to be exceptions not the rule – a result available to
only a small handful of films and series at any one time. None the less there is an
Australian ambition within just about every reach of cinema and criticism not only
to be particular and local – to speak to the women and men of Australia – but also
to be universal and to speak to the world. The trajectory of many actors,
cinematographers and directors to Hollywood and to dividing their work between
Australia and North America makes sense in this context.

Historically there have been worries about the consequences to Australian
culture of its confusing itself with the world. To do so seems to sell out Australian
particularity – to make something for someone else is often taken to mean having
the *world define just who you are*. Just about every film I can think of as being at
this stage has been criticized as selling out Australian specificity – *Mad Max*,
Crocodile Dundee, *The Man from Snowy River*, *The Piano*, *Babe*. The fifth stage
is routinely criticized for looking suspiciously like the first stage.

Australian cinema as a succession of stages

Journalistic, film institution and public relations histories of the industry favour
tellings roughly consonant with these five stages. The successful film of the day
marks the 'arrival' of Australian film-making and the maturity of the culture. This
arrival follows from an earlier period – now in the past – marked by either 'cultural
cringe' or 'cultural strut'; such announcements have been regularly, though
intermittently, made over the past twenty years. It is succeeded by regular
announcements as to 'what's wrong' with Australian cinema, that film-makers
need a better appreciation of Hollywood or European and Asian models.

Such tellings do have their truth. Some decades of Australian film-making are
more about one or other of these stages. In the 1950s up to the mid-1960s the
imported culture – whether American or British – was more highly valued in
feature film-making and television drama. There was hardly any Australian
feature film production. The Americans knew how to make films, the British
quality television. This is a self-abased culture thoroughly imperialized by
Hollywood in the 1950s and early 1960s, such that Australians were abjectly

'flattered, not to say grateful, for their own country on screen' in *The Sundowners* (see Lawson 1965, 1985a: 155).

From the mid-1960s another movement slowly developed, as imported formats such as the American and British police series in television drama were indigenized with *Homicide*, *Lassie* – which was indigenized to become *Skippy* (perhaps Australia's most successful television export) – and avant-garde and art cinema were experimented with. The latter began with Giorgio Mangiamele's *Clay* which is a story of a sculptor who shelters a fugitive and subsequently kills herself when he is apprehended. It is told through the subjective responses of the sculptor. This was followed by T. Burstall's *Two Thousand Weeks* (1969) which Pike and Cooper (1980: 316) describe as 'about the isolation and frustration of an artist in ... the wasteland of Australian culture'. Government support and an established television infrastructure consolidated these developments over the 1970s. These factors gradually transformed a receiving culture into a producing culture with the 'ocker' cycle of *Stork* and *Alvin Purple* (T. Burstall 1973) in the early 1970s.

By the second half of that decade, the third stage could be evidenced in 1970s film-making like *Picnic at Hanging Rock* and *Sunday Too Far Away*, as the receiving culture became a sending culture and Australian films became known locally as the 'last new wave' (antipodean vigour in the image of the celebrated French *nouvelle vague*).[2] Australian successes at Cannes permit an Australian recognition of its film-makers' superior film-making capacities.

The fourth stage of assimilation probably begins in long-running television drama in the 1970s and feature film-making and mini-series production in the 1980s. Television drama has been put on a highly industrialized footing since at least the landmark television soap, *Number 96* (1972), and in feature film and mini-series in the 1980s with the liberal funding regime of 10BA. Here the American and British originals are so thoroughly dissolved that the fourth stage has arrived. Australian television drama had assimilated the British and American lessons and turned them into something else: a particular kind of soap opera exportable in its original form and through the tailoring of its concepts. The *Mad Max* cycle, *Gallipoli*, *Phar Lap*, *The Man from Snowy River* become evidence of a fourth stage in 1980s cinema. Then in some sites, Australia arrives at a fifth stage of being the centre of the semiosphere. *Crocodile Dundee* becomes in 1986 the most successful non-Hollywood international film, the Grundy organization pushes the sale of Australian television and concepts in Europe and beyond, pursuing a strategy of parochial internationalism (indigenizing Australian concepts in, for example, the Dutch and North American markets). Rupert Murdoch introduces Australian style television to Britain through his satellite operations and later, in his STAR TV operations, in Asia. This leads to a fifth stage where an Australian originated film-making confuses itself with its region and the world in *The Piano*.

But in each of these stages there are countervailing indications. While the 1980s did see greatly expanded film and television exports, these exports still amounted to only a fraction of the dollar value of imports. The production industry was also going into decline by the late 1980s with the diminishing value of tax incentives, the hiatus created before the FFC emerged, and a dramatic turn around in the debt the Australian television system was carrying. Receivership for two of the three commercial networks ensued, as did a forced sale of the third, which reduced the monies available to local production (see O'Regan 1993: 48–53). Additionally a prolonged recession in the early 1990s diminished private investment coming into the industry necessitating a more outward orientation to local production.

The co-presence of stages

While different periods do seem to foreground one or other of these stages, in general these stages are co-present at any one time: starting again, devaluing the Australian-made and valuing the imports, concept remakes, valuing the local for its international competitiveness, assimilation into emerging production traditions, and international export. Since the advent of a mature television industry and state support in the 1970s, the co-presence of these different stages is the unexceptionable norm in the cinema and television. The Australian film-making milieu almost naturally consists of each of these stages at any one time.

Australia is simultaneously always at the first stage as imports innovate, become the harbingers of new social trends and youth styles, and are generally held in high esteem; at the second stage as everything from drama to critical concepts are indigenized; at the third stage as Australian product is seen to be 'better than the original' and Australians see themselves to have customized the imported concept to its advantage; and at the fourth stage as Australian texts and criticism seamlessly assimilate what was once imported leading to domestic production and the emergence of critical traditions. Finally, at the fifth stage Australian product 'colonizes' parts of the world with, for example, *The Piano* or *Breaker Morant* or *Crocodile Dundee* and television series like *Skippy, Neighbours, The Flying Doctors* (1985) and *A Town Like Alice*.

Some productions are made in the language of the original, barely assimilating new film-making forms. Others involve remakes with varying degrees of indigenization. Some take these concepts some distance from their original, becoming something identifiable in their own right, such as *The Piano* and *Mad Max II*. And this movement enables film-makers and critics alike to discover the higher standing, more human values of the Australian product of *Breaker Morant* and *My Brilliant Career*. Still others – *Dead Calm* and *The Year of Living Dangerously* – have been able to confuse the Australian with the world, being exported around the globe. When this happens, an American career usually follows and the talent is often lost to the Australian industry.

Each of these five stages is represented in the interpretative work of Australian film and cultural critics. Take *Crocodile Dundee*. The critical manoeuvres are various. J. W. Williamson (1995) saw the film as respectful to the original concept: *Dundee* is the quintessential hillbilly film. Meaghan Morris saw it as disrespectful to the Hollywood original of Jungle Jim, Tarzan and *I Love Lucy* (1951–7) (1988: 248–9). Morris regarded its concept extensions and transformations as something new – a form of 'positive unoriginality'; Veronica Brady damned it as a bad copy of a bad kind of film when she claimed on ABC-TV that Dundee was an Australian Rambo. Ruth Abbey and Jo Crawford (1987) questioned its authenticity and cultural integrity, entitling their *Meanjin* article 'Crocodile Dundee or Davey Crockett?'. For Ramona Barry (1994: 9) it was creating 'what the world thinks we do best – cracking jokes, eating bush tucker and being basically naive to technology and the culture of the civilized world'. It was an un-Australian film. By contrast in my 1988 article I saw a resourceful textual fabric built on a 'canny play of "intermedia" sources', a 'complex interplay of textual elements such as parody', and a 'necessarily multilayered audience response' (O'Regan 1988: 158). This was a concept extension and transformation which provided a seamless continuation of Hogan's television and advertising persona. Ex-politician and judge Jim McLelland (1987) saw in Dundee neither Rambo nor Davey Crockett but 'a special sort of ocker' who 'lives out his own values'. The dispute over the meaning of this film turned on *which stage* it was assigned to. A decision as to the status of its cultural transfers was integral to the film's denigration and appreciation. Obviously the third, fourth and fifth stages are more culturally prestigious. Given this, a typical *critical manoeuvre* is to claim that internationally successful work like *Dundee* is something other than a stage four and five production. Consequently, one person's original is another's fake.

Australia as a frontier area

Lotman talks of 'frontier areas' of the semiosphere. We can usefully adopt his terminology and combine it with McKenzie Wark's 'antipodal relation' in order to see Australia as a frontier area of the English language. For Lotman (1990: 141) frontier areas are those where 'semiotic processes are intensified because here there are constant invasions from outside'. Such boundary areas are characterized by 'bilingualism, which as a rule finds literal expression in the language practice of the inhabitants of borderlands between two cultural areas' (142). This Australian 'bilingualism' (accommodation of different cultures within the one language) lies in the capacity of film workers and audiences to work in terms of the 'sending culture' and in their own receiving culture. The frontier area is further underwritten by a high level of cultural imports. Such 'bilingualism' leads to largely interchangeable senses of identity and culture. Australia becomes in Lotman's terms a 'disorganized space'.

With the five stages being mostly co-present in the Australian 'frontier' there is an inevitably mixed scenario. Lotman (126) continues:

> across any synchronic section of the semiosphere different languages at different stage of development are in conflict, and some texts are immersed in languages not their own, while the codes to decipher them with may be entirely absent.

The conflict between stages of development is evident in the polarization of critical interpretation and uptake which has sometimes little to do with the 'languages' of the film's producers. film-makers like Jackie McKimmie with *Waiting* are literally waiting for their audience to believe that an Australian contribution to the urbane French drama comedy of relationships is possible. Or Ken Cameron, whose film *Peter Kenna's Umbrella Woman* (1987) had to wait six years after its release for a means for it to be read by Adrian Martin:

> *The Umbrella Woman* does not deserve its composite reputation as a con-servative, conventional, bland 'costume drama' in the style of some Australian films of the 1970s; it is a corrosive, despairing, highly 'materialist' portrayal of certain values underlying Australian life.
>
> (Martin 1993: 225)

A culture creates for Lotman (1990: 142) 'not only its own type of internal organization but also its own type of external "disorganization"'.

The Australian space is further disorganized courtesy of migration and ethnic dynamics. Australia is not only a 'boundary area' in the English language, but is also a 'boundary area' for the Greek, Vietnamese and Italian speakers in Australia. These communities operate in the spaces within and between language, maintain-ing a diasporic relation to their home cultures and an orientation to the broader Australian English-language culture. Another form of disorganization is produced by Aboriginal and Torres Strait Islanders' orientation to the dominant settler culture and to their own indigenous traditions. For these and other minority groups the processes of semiotic transformation impose themselves in the opposite direction to which US and British models and norms solicit reaction in the broader Australian symbolic goods context. While this Australian centre is obviously going to be more weakly developed, given its own status as a boundary area, it none the less constitutes a centre.

MORRIS'S POSITIVE UNORIGINALITY

Lotman's position is supported in Meaghan Morris's landmark essay on *Croco-dile Dundee*. Morris theorizes the domestic reality of cultural transfers indirectly by attending to its byproduct: the nexus of originality and unoriginality. She notes 'that the one distinctive feature of Australian culture is its positive unoriginality' (1988: 245). She then assays three constructions of 'unoriginality and national cinema' (246).

The first of these is *unoriginality as an endemic Australian problem* and an undesirable end for Australian cinema. It is 'a byproduct of "cultural im-perialism"' which sees Hollywood norms dominate the 'programming of pleas-ures', American majors the Australian film market and a history of 'disastrous meddling by American studio interests in Australian film production . . . and . . . the use of Australia as exotic backdrop to rising American stars'. The mission for an Australian cinema would be to create an 'originality' and 'authenticity' (247) which would counter these circumstances. Morris continues:

> an argument with these reference-points often combines a call for collective originality with a realist aesthetic ('cultural exactitude'), an essentialist model of audience (the eye of the beholder as site of national perception) and a politics of primary anti-Americanism.
>
> (246)

The path to originality involves sorting out which are the acceptable 'Australian' production orientations and foreign influences. Critics and film-makers distinguish between film-making practices, declaring some tributaries of an authentic Australian cinema and others not. (So we get the preference for Raymond Longford over Ken Hall; in the early 1980s the preference was for the films of Phil Noyce – *Newsfront* – and Bruce Beresford – *Breaker Morant* – over those of Simon Wincer and Richard Franklin.) It also entails a search for a specifically Australian voice where the Australian is an ideal to which to aspire – the possibility of the Australian yet to be made. This notion of Australian originality turns on the classic tropes of a national cinema in its first sense as an 'inward identification', whilst in its negotiation of a terrain in which 'the international question' is never far away it is concerned to expel the imperializing foreign element.

The second construction of unoriginality is *positive unoriginality*. It turns on originality as a 'natural and necessary thing in modern times' (247). Here unoriginality is celebrated and pluralized in a 'cheerful acceptance that it is a natural and necessary thing in modern times'. The prognosis for Australian cinema is 'imitation' and 'unspecificity':

> Film is an industry in a Western mega-culture, and Australia is simply part of it; ideals of originality independence and authenticity are sentimental anachronisms, inappropriate to the *combinatoire* of industrial cinema ...

Australian film-making can provide an exemplary instance of a style or type of film-making – 'an ideal of positive unspecificity' represented by Franklin's *Roadgames* and in a more contemporary setting Chris Noonan's *Babe* (1995) with its deliberate British-looking farmyard and not-quite-American accents (spoken of by Noonan as a way of retaining a certain Australianness). Here the model and the Australian instance are coterminous. In both cases, the Australian text is valued through comparison.

Morris's third construction of unoriginality sees the '*survival and specificity of Australian film ensured by the revision of American codes by Australian texts*' (247 my emphasis). By extension these could also be British, European and Hong Kong cinematic codes. This position 'salvages some of the cultural assertiveness of one, and all the economic pragmatism of the other' – rejecting as it does 'hostility to Hollywood' and 'base denials of Australian contexts'. So the *Mad Max* films successfully 'appropriate' the 'road-movie genre'.

Morris's three models provide us with several orientations. Take the domestic context. In the first, the Australian context is protected through a screening out of foreign influences – and this distorts by denying the local productivity of, for example, American influences; in the second, the internationally shared elements of the Australian context are emphasized – and this distorts too because it denies local contexts and traditions; in the third the international and local are brought into alignment – this simultaneously admits the local and the international and forges a productive relation between them. Take questions of genre: in the first, there is a sense of the possibility of native genres developing – as Australian cinema becomes a sovereign space in the cinema. In the second, Australian cinema is part of that international cinema without discernible or necessary independent existence. So David Bordwell and Kristin Thompson (1986: 96–8) cite *Mad Max 2/The Road Warrior* as 'constructed along classical Hollywood lines' and compare its narrational strategies to those of *The Big Sleep* (Hawks 1946). In the third, independence and participation are stressed: Australian film-makers negotiate genres making small changes to a formal system, subtly transforming it in the process. For Ross Gibson (1992: 158–77) the *Mad Max* trilogy is a new structural model for the apocalyptic narrative and Australian historiography.

Morris's 'positive unoriginality' thesis neatly maps over our three prevailing models for understanding the relation between the national cinema and the international cinema: localism, internationalism and parochial internationalism. Under localism, the Australian culture is or could be a sovereign space. It has or could have its own production traditions, contents and symbols mobilized in film. If cultural transfers occur, these do so in a 'dialogic' fashion where the Australian instance becomes a superior example of the general type or a new structural model is created rather than an insipid imitation. The culture in this third and fourth stage has clearly defined borders, contents, and characteristics. But only some parts of the symbolic culture – audiences, film-makers and critics – have arrived at this stage. Moreover, those local production traditions and stories that are at a further stage are assimilated versions of previous cultural transfers. Morris is reluctant to recognize this fourth stage in its 'high' mode as producing new structural models. Instead she emphasizes the jingoist and anti-internationalist entailment of localism.

For an internationalist position, Australian-produced is simply international cinema – no more, no less. film-making is an intrinsically international medium. National cultural consumption and production produce forms of continuity and sharing – various transnational commonalities. Australian films are made inter-changeable and universal with those of other countries. There is no distinction worthy of the name here. Sometimes this internationalism, this interchangeability can provide the basis for international understanding. Sometimes it amounts to a form of imperialism creating a desultory and inauthentic culture. Whether projected negatively by élites as Americanization, or positively as shared international cultural repertoires or styles, this internationalism emphasizes international likeness and communicability. Such internationalism is generally true, in the sense that even at its most autonomous, cultural transfers are involved. But it is limited too. In an environment where Australian audiences and critics are as likely to compare Australian films with the adjacent American, British or art cinema output as they are with other Australian films (and so doing be at Lotman's first and second stages), they are prone to misunderstand their fourth and fifth stage production traditions and assume that local work has no distinguishing (and certainly no distinguished) features. Sometimes overseas critics recognize the textual and aesthetic difference in the Australian product more than an Australian critic trained into a kind of seamlessness, in which the Australian form of production is so naturalized as to not be anything in particular and thus seems more or less interchangeable with the US product. Local critic Neil McDonald suggests, for example, that Fred Schepisi's Hollywood films have adapted so well to American conditions that they are 'indistinguishable from the overseas product' (quoted in AFC 1991: 62). Yet Schepisi's Hollywood films have maintained a consistency of approach in which moral and ethical problematization is of the same kind as found in his earlier Australian film-making and in the rich humanist stream of Australian film-making in general. Lotman provides some support for this internationalist position in his first, second, third and fifth stages. But Lotman also deflates this position seeing the same 'international' culture as having local effects. There has to be 'mutual attraction' for any such cultural transfers to be realized.

And this is precisely what is accomplished in our third model of parochial internationalism. All national consumption and production is internationally derived but simultaneously localized. If it is always international in some form, this internationalism is inevitably produced locally as a parochial entailment. Parochial internationalism stresses simultaneously how Australian cinema is shaped by, blended with, and transformed by the various elements of the international and national cinema. Every one of Lotman's five stages of cultural transfer can be seen as forms of parochial internationalism. But it too is misleading. As a concept it more readily refers to Lotman's second and third stages where the restructuring of the international text or concept is most evident. It would need to be reworked to fully describe Lotman's fourth stage, in which the imported models are so thoroughly indigenized as to make emphasizing their by now distant relation to the local product of little value.

CONCLUSION: SOME IDENTITIES FOR AUSTRALIAN CINEMA

These arguments open out onto the different international identities for the Australian cinema. Firstly, Australian cinema is a part of that international cinema. Australian film-makers participate in an international cinema where place and point of origin scarcely matter. *Red Matildas* and *For Love or Money* (McMurchy, Nash, Oliver and Thornley 1983) are continuations of the 'international women in progressive politics' and 'women in work' films like *Union Maids* (Reichert and Klein 1976) and *The Life and Times of Rosie the Riveter*

(Field 1980). Australian cinema is an integral part of the English language cinema and part of the larger Hollywood and British industries.

Second, Australian cinema is implicated in this international cinema. It has an 'in-between' identity as both 'for itself' and 'as part of the dominant cinema'. This view of Australian cinema stresses its negotiation of its implicated and junior position. Here the 'dominant cinema' structures the Australian cinema. Australian film-makers and critics copy and adapt formats, they parody and mimic international norms. It is the Australian cinema of Lotman's second, third and to an extent fourth phase.

Third, Australian cinema enters into dialogue with the international cinema. Its enmeshment provides for a mechanism of cultural exchange of various degrees of reciprocity. Here every film-making culture appropriates, raids and reconstructs cultural elements from outside itself thereby indigenizing the concept, the style and so on. This figure allows for 'hybridity', for new syntheses to emerge in the Australian productions of the local and the imported, and for a sense of rejoinder and reply. The extreme of this position might find its justification in Bakhtin's remark that 'the dialogic encounter of two cultures does not result in merging or mixing'; 'Each retains its own unity and open totality, but they are mutually enriched' (quoted in Stam 1993: 242). Here the two cultures of the cinema – indigenous Australian and the exogenous American and British, to take the English speaking coordinates – remain separate and retain their integrity through this process. This fits the concept extension part of the second stage and Lotman's fourth stage. Here cultural exchange alters the 'host' culture. Australian cinema adjusts its local terms and conditions and is reinvigorated and diminished alike through that contact. In Australian film criticism, both the local and the international bleed one into the other. In the film criticism of Meaghan Morris, Ross Gibson, Bill Routt, Stuart Cunningham and Graeme Turner the imported product provides raw materials for an Australian reinterpretation.

Fourth, Australian cinema is responding to much the same collection of elements and forces as those of other national cinemas and cultures. These include the same forces of industrialization and modernization, global economic restructuring and international economic interdependency, and common technological, scientific and urban innovations. These are social facts that form the raw materials for the camera to record and scripts to emplot. At the same time, these forces and developments entail international aesthetic movements and systems of cultural exchange – modernism, post-modernism, genres, Hollywood – which provide a shared international cultural repertoire that film-makers exploit. These reduce the cultural distance between nations and places, constructing international social, cultural and economic resemblances and allowing for the development of cultural units such as Hollywood and the international festival cinema capable of circulating between them. Australian cinema is a variation on a common international theme and has a 'family resemblance' to other national cinemas. Australians 'hit upon' some of the same strategies and structures as do other cinemas precisely because they are in similar stages of development. It also suggests that the 'mutual attraction' which permitted US imports in the first place must have something to do with the way Australia is itself configured as a society – the political and cultural characteristics it shares with the USA. It should not be surprising that Australia borrows directly; nor that it should independently invent much the same things.

There is – as in all these other terms – an undecidable relation involved. The co-presence of Lotman's five stages suggests as much. Some cinema will be more directly within the international cinema; some more exogenous to it. Sometimes viewers, producers and critics will experience the same film as indigenous and exogenous. The various social, technological and cultural commonalities mean that Australian cinema is simultaneously part of and an expression of these commonalities. Morris's generally agnostic position on Australian unoriginality and Lotman's own emphasis upon the general nature of cultural transfers make them sanguine about cultural transfers. The historian of culture should probably not take sides too quickly or take up the teleological invitation of seeing five sequential stages in which the latter stages are superior. She or he should afford each stage its due. There are no right kinds of cultural transfer. I am quite happy to call *Babe*, *The Piano* and *Fearless* 'Australian films', to support Australian imitations like *Roadgames* and *Harlequin*, to find the indigenization of 'drama' in *Country Life* or the 'adaptations' of *Back of Beyond*, *Mad Max*, or *Neighbours*.

Lotman and Morris emphasize the agency of the receiving culture in any cultural transfer relationship. They draw attention to a culture's necessary orientation toward 'imports' and how imports and local texts restructure each other. Both direct our attention to the international participation inherent in all national cinemas and to the different sorts of participation on offer. National audiences, critics and film-makers appropriate, negotiate and transform the international cinema in various ways. The centrality of cultural transfers in the Australian context suggests that the distinctiveness of Australian cinema may be found in its *negotiation* of cultural transfers. Any claims we may make about the space of – and distinctiveness of – Australian cinema must turn on the participation, negotiation, adaptation and hybridization following on from unequal cultural transfers.

Chapter 10

A distinct place in the cinema

Better still, sometimes, as in *The Overlanders*, a western theme is borrowed – in this case the traditional cattle drive – and set in a landscape [that is] central Australian, reasonably like the American west. The result, as we know, was excellent. But unfortunately no attempt was made to follow up this paradoxical achievement, whose success was due to an unusual combination of circumstances.

(André Bazin 1971: 141–2)

Bazin's insight can be usefully reworked. It suggests that Australian cinema's distinctiveness can be found in how it borrows, its one-off nature and the resulting paradox of its achievements. *The Overlanders* 'borrows' a quintessentially American 'western' theme. Australian film history is rife with texts that could have been followed up: think of John Heyer's extraordinary *The Back of Beyond* with its extending of the language of the classical documentary, *Newsfront*'s blending of its diverse inscriptive materials, the permutations on the *Mad Max* cycle that ended with *Mad Max 3*. Australia's contribution to this or that pathway of the cinema is what it becomes known for and is what critics and film-makers then map.

This sense of borrowing is conveyed by the words critics use to place Australian cinema. The title of a 1985 essay by Stuart Cunningham was 'Hollywood genres, Australian Movies' (significantly written during the 1980s 'turn to genre'). Graeme Turner (1986, 1993c) writes of an Australian 'accent' to familiar stories, themes and genres. Cunningham sees *The Back of Beyond* as 'an adaptation of, while remaining in accordance with, its master stylistic ensemble' (Cunningham 1988/89: 160). Meaghan Morris writing in the context of *Crocodile Dundee* sees Australian films 'disadvantaging the original' (Morris 1988: 248).

Countless critics – Australian and otherwise – have registered this cinema's unoriginality (Morris 1988: 246–7). Sometimes they convey it positively as an addition, supplement, renovation or subversion; sometimes negatively as a derivative, a poor copy, a slavish imitation or as being formally conformist. Australian difference is something smaller, more modest, a small irruption, an unexpected point of departure, a subtle transformation, a 'tentative defiance of the codes' to open a new space in the cinema, a point of resistance, or a regional dialect of the American or British cinema. Critics register Australian cinema's similarity to the international exemplar, so that difference is registered within the larger context of this similarity – rather than similarity being registered within the larger context of differences, which is how the Western 'festival audience' measures, for example, mainland Chinese features.

In this chapter, I will assay some of these points of Australian distinctiveness: its unoriginality and cultural weakness, its ways of negotiating political weakness, its relational character which blends the art film and melodrama, fact and fiction, and the important roles played by ugliness, ordinariness and othering the Australian.

UNORIGINALITY AND CULTURAL WEAKNESS

Perhaps the idea of Australian 'positive unoriginality' has its apotheosis in Stephen McLean's 'high camp' parody of tourism, *Around the World in 80 Ways*. In this story Mum (Diana Davidson), decides to go on an 'around the world' package holiday to get away from her bleak life looking after her senile near-blind husband (Alan Penney) and her younger no-hoper son Eddy (Kelly Dingwall). Before she leaves she commits Dad to a nursing home. Dad, on learning of Mum's departure on the same package holiday as his next door neighbour Alex Moffatt (Rob Steele), enlists the help of his two sons Wally (Philip Quast) and Eddy to follow her. Together with a nurse from the nursing home (Gosia Dobrowolska) the two sons led by Wally pretend to take Dad off around the world, by reconstructing the world in their suburban backyard, Moffatt's house, swimming pool and his used car yard. Each has their own motives for this deception: Wally needs Dad's money to pay his debts so he can get his 'Big Banana' and tourist business back, Eddy wants the money for a new sound system and the nurse wants to try out a new stimulation therapy for the aged.

The world constructed in the Sydney backyard by the sons and the nurse is much more interesting than the outside world Mum explores from the confines of her packaged holiday. Australia emerges in this film as a post-modern simulacrum. It copies poorly and the badness of the copy is wonderful. The backyard pool doubles up as Hawaii as the son provides the right sounds. Supermarket checkouts become airport customs; drycleaners ticket counters; Wally's tour bus with its banana emblem is an aeroplane – taking off is going up hills, landing is going fast over bumps. The garage becomes the Vatican. Las Vegas is created from the used-car yard and bits of Holden cars. King's Cross prostitutes become 'geisha girls' and are much more interesting for that (by contrast Mum's flight cannot even land in Tokyo because of a hurricane). An (in)competent Australian invention of the world is attempted.

Inadvertently, Wally – the trickster homosexual son – sets in train the restoration of the family. Dad with his 'galloping senility' is, through his therapeutic journey, restored to sensuality, virility and Mum. He even turns the tables on his sworn enemy and rival for Mum's affections, Moffatt, destroying his obscenely ostentatious triple-fronted brick veneer and publicly revealing his toupée. The unloved baby brother more interested in sound than life, develops a 'normal' relationship with the glamorous nurse who is seduced by his train set. For her part nurse Ophelia proves that her cure works and acquires the right lover (her fiancé is given as being like Moffatt). Mum's trip around the real world is a series of disappointments and disasters including her love life. She returns home to Dad to start a dancing studio – and they 'grow younger'.

The strategy in *Around the World in 80 Ways* – and *Crocodile Dundee* – is to transform what is the culturally weak Australian position into a comic vehicle that turns the tables on the culturally strong. Using Meaghan Morris's (1988: 249) formulation, the film clearly disadvantages the original. film-makers of other medium-sized and smaller cinemas adopt just such a strategy. Olle Sjögren (1992: 157) observes that, as a 'small country', Sweden

> is forced to transform its culturally weak position into a comedic national virtue. Comedy becomes a funny mirror for reflecting upon one's cultural weakness. It allows one to admit that one longs for a more exciting life without threatening the life one is leading. Through parodies one can indulge one's fascination with another, more exciting culture, while simultaneously dismissing the indulgence as a joke.

Likewise the Australian cinema of *Around the World in 80 Ways* is variously seen, appreciated and situated on a continuum of similarity moving from outright mimicry, to ironic imitation, adjustment, negotiation, transformation, resistance and subversion. All these movements entail relations of implication, not violent resistance. Australia is a 'little' nation. Parody, irony, self-deprecation and an incapacity to take oneself or others seriously are part of an antipodal strand of Australian comic cinema stretching from *On our Selection* (Longford 1920, Hall 1932, Whaley 1995) to *The Adventures of Barry McKenzie* through to *Muriel's Wedding*. With such self-deprecation comes an equally strong tendency to 'debunk' the nation and its national 'heroes'. 'Taking the mickey' out of the New Yorkers in *Crocodile Dundee* is not that far apart from rendering Australian history in *Eliza Fraser* (T. Burstall 1976) as, in Tim Burstall's words, so much 'bullshit' (cited in Bromby 1979: 87).

Revising and debunking a nation is a natural repertoire for an import culture. Because of its size, its minor symbolic and political place, the extent of cultural transfers including immigration, Australia can have little of the grandeur, sense of destiny, global importance, and so Nietzschean pretensions of a large country. Moreover its attempts at mythmaking are going to be lower-budgeted and not up to the same standard of spectacle and performance of the American imports. Take *Burke and Wills* (Clifford 1985) – a serious drama – in which great emphasis is placed on the absurdity of Burke and Wills's journey. These men die of thirst and starvation amidst a prospering Aboriginal community. They are too ignorant to know how to communicate with the Aboriginal people who offer help. For their part the Aboriginal people gaze on, wondering at such foolishness. What a powerful rewriting of the Burke and Wills myth this is: these explorers who do not die alone, their heroism simply ethnocentric incompetence, but who are none the less ours! The audience is left in an uneasy place: simultaneously recognizing stubbornness, useless heroism and incompetence.

But equally, the culturally weak position goes to the heart of self-representation and the attributes and capacities ascribed as Australian in 'drama' productions. Tom Ryan's description of the 'battler' logic of much 1970s historical cinema is apposite here:

> Perhaps the most significant recurring narrative pattern is that which locates the characters in a position of powerlessness in relation to the movement of the historical periods in which they are placed. In contrast, say, to American narratives which are 'typically stories of strength and energy expended in the pursuit and acquisition of or extension of control over geographic areas or political enterprises', these Australian narratives decline the option of stories tracing characters' rise to power. It is not that the Australian films should place their characters in positions of power, in the interest of the assertion of 'national identity' and similar nonsense, it is simply that they do not.
>
> (Ryan 1980: 120)

From a culturally and politically weak position, characters are not 'overblown'. Australian cinema produces 'narratives peopled by characters who are governed by forces beyond their control, and who are shown in a position of defeat at the close of the film' (Ryan 1980: 120). Ryan mentions in this regard films as different as *Between Wars* (Thornhill 1974), *Mad Dog Morgan, Caddie, Break of Day, The Irishman, Newsfront, Dawn!, The Odd Angry Shot* (Jeffery 1979) and *My Brilliant Career*. Such a fatalist storytelling is a close relation to the 'Australian Legend' which, as we have seen, pitted 'humans against nature' – bushfires, droughts, floods, creatures (rabbits, kangaroos, dingos). Nature – the natural environment, society, international events – often defeats or at least bends the human to its will. History itself becomes a natural event. For a medium-sized country this fatalism is understandable, as its general course cannot be much altered and its capacity to act internationally on its own is limited.

Local film-makers, critics and audiences are often critical of such a cinema. They want it to overcome cultural weakness. They take on the American-speaking position and project a less defeatist, more independent, less 'sheltered' country.

NEGOTIATING POLITICAL WEAKNESS

Australia's politically weaker position is sometimes *narrativized* in films. Perhaps the most famous film in this regard is *Breaker Morant*. The battler is variously the men on trial for war crimes – Breaker Morant (Edward Woodward), Hancock

(Bryan Brown) and Witton (Lewis Fitz-Gerald) – and the men's small town solicitor played consummately by Jack Thompson. The film chooses to focus on them and their actions rather than on the agreement between the Australian and British governments that these men should be convicted and expeditiously executed to secure peace and placate the German and Dutch governments.

Bruce Kepferer has identified an anti-state sentiment as a characteristic of Australian nationalism. Perhaps this is because the state, unlike the people, can have only limited autonomy; it sees itself as having to fall into line behind powerful friends – the UK, the USA, Japan and more lately Indonesia – because of its weak position. The state, unlike the people and the nation, is constitutionally, morally and ethically compromised. If this drives a nationalism in which the Australian is constituted in partial defiance of these norms – Australian anti-authoritarianism – it also permits the development of a common international brotherhood against the state.[1]

Stephen Wallace's *Blood Oath*, which had a successful minority cinema release in Japan, provides a contemporary update of the Morant story. It is a film based on a Second World War crimes trial in which an innocent Japanese soldier was executed to cover up for the war crimes of his superiors. It begins with a distance between the Australian prosecutor (Bryan Brown) and his Japanese prisoner. The film works to close that distance while simultaneously opening an increasingly yawning gap between the Australian and his American allies – his superior officers, and between the Japanese soldier and the collaborating high command who make this soldier a scapegoat for their crimes. The Australian lawyer, as in *Breaker Morant*, again 'loses his case', gradually coming to recognize that he had no chance of winning from the start. He and the Japanese soldier he represents are the victims this time of another Empire in the making – the American and the future Japanese one. The logic of the film at this point is clear. The ordinary Japanese soldier is brought into the 'Australian family' which is then aligned against the power élite that controls both their destinies.

Over the course of the film, both rediscover their mutual marginality. The Japanese prisoner is abandoned by his commanders and made to carry the can for war atrocities just as ordinary Japanese suffered at the hands of their fascist rulers; he is an ideal scapegoat as he is of lowly rank and non-conformist (he is a Christian). For his part, the Australian finds the limits of 'Australian action' and fails his duty of care to uphold the principles of justice and a fair trial. His principled actions meet with fierce resistance and his own marginalization by the American and Japanese high commands. And this historical record of friendship is the more remarkable precisely because of the brutal nature of the Pacific theatre of war in the Second World War. The film's hopeful projection of a space of Japanese–Australian dialogue and mutual understanding out of the ashes of an horrific war is one utopian projection of Australia's special relationship with Japan.[2]

AUSTRALIAN CINEMA'S IN-BETWEENNESS

Melodrama and art film

Australian cinema proliferates generic hybrids. There is a chronic indeterminacy in Australian cinema's generic workings. Most importantly, it brings together the art cinema and the melodrama. Often this characteristic is seen as a problem but sometimes it is seen as an advantage of Australian cinema (for my part, I think we should simply attend to it not denigrate or celebrate it).

In *New Australian Cinema*, Brian McFarlane and Geoff Mayer argue that Australian films characteristically fall between the classical cinema and the art cinema:

> Many Australian films fail, or refuse, to develop the possibilities of either the classical cinema or the art cinema, and appear to slide into an aesthetic 'hole' that represents neither narrative paradigm. The characteristically recessive characters, subdued or virtually nonexistent climaxes, and tentative closures indicate, as other film commentators have also noted, a cinema that is not sure of its projected audience and/or its ability to develop fully the conventions of either melodrama or any other dramatic form.
>
> (239)

McFarlane and Mayer would be happy if Australian cinema was not so 'in between'. Instead of acknowledging its blending of, for example, the art film and melodrama, as a distinctive characteristic of Australian cinema to be investigated and teased out, they criticize it. For them Australian cinema 'in betweeness' is the major problem; Australian cinema hybridity needs to be sorted out into distinct, purified and hermetically sealed enclaves of film-making: the art film and that of Hollywood melodrama. Australian cinema should, they think, choose between these two modes. Because it fails to conform sufficiently to either of these prevailing models, it is seen to fail aesthetically and at the box-office. They assume that if film-makers adopted one or the other then they would make films which would better connect with local and international audiences.

But what if this hybridity which they disparagingly label 'falling between' is not a problem? What if, as Sam Rohdie, once suggested its mixing of these characteristics marks its 'formula' for success. Here is Rohdie (1982b: 39) talking about *Picnic at Hanging Rock* and *Gallipoli*:

> The films get doubly sold: within an art market (world bourgeois film festivals, Berlin, Cannes, New York), and as conventional mass entertainment. One has the alibi of art while enjoying more common pleasure (in touch with the 'others') with the secret enjoyment of a self-congratulatory, more sophisticated taste. Consequently, we see the discriminating New Yorker queuing to watch *Gallipoli*, and *Picnic at Hanging Rock* screened in the art-house cinema-d'essai circuit in Italy – a film seriously considered by 'serious' critics not a film for the bin of film 'spazzatura'.

Like McFarlane and Mayer, though for different reasons, Rohdie is critical of such an adaptive and successful accommodation of art-house and Hollywood protocols. But cultural critics can sometimes endorse this position as when in 1980 Max Harris eulogized Australians and their film-makers:

> We simple, sun-bronzed vulgar yobs are producing films characterized by a delicate portraiture of human sensibilities. We have taken over and developed the idiom of Losey without falling into the trap of being arty-crafty after the fashion of French film-making.

The materials of Australian cinema suggest not so much the exercise of obvious binaries as the emergence of hybrids. Moreover these hybrids formed from the dialogue with the international cinema are equally informed by the other strands and projects of the Australian film milieu – the adjacent film-making, televisual, documentary and infotainment culture. If there is an Australian production tradition here, it might be found in Fred Schepisi's discussion of his problems working in Hollywood:

> It always disturbs me that they talk about film scripts as though they're plays. They talk about a first, second and third act, a thesis, antithesis and synthesis . . . This is not a way to make original films.

> (Koval 1992: 43)

Schepisi's eschewal of the evident and predictable dramatic structure of the classical cinema makes his cinema eccentric to the classical norm. And such Australian eccentricity is always going to be made good by more attention to 'the script'! Yet Schepisi is also an Australian director with an American Hollywood career. *The Russia House* (1990) is dressed up as a thriller, but it wants to explore the ethics and circumstances under which one should betray one's own country. The same criticism that McFarlane and Mayer level at Australian cinema for falling into a hole between the art film and the Hollywood melodrama can be levelled at most Schepisi films, from his Australian titles like *The Devil's Playground, The Chant of Jimmie Blacksmith, Evil Angels / Cry in the Dark*) to his Hollywood vehicles – *Barbarosa* (1982), *The Russia House* and *Six Degrees of Separation* (1993). Schepisi's inability to fit into *either* and yet, in a sense, do *both* should not be regarded as a failure.

Blending of fact and fiction

Another component of Australian cinema's hybridity lies in its blend of fact and fiction. Given that the documentary is never far away in Australian cinema, it is not surprising that it should impinge on fiction and fiction on it. Writing in 1988 Graeme Turner notes that, since the 1970s revival, it has become increasingly characteristic of Australian documentary cinema that any investigation of history is interrogated and shaped, often through fictionalization; it also has become increasingly characteristic of Australian feature films and television drama that Australian fictions are rooted and situated in material contexts, historicized and politicized through the deployment of documentary styles.

(1988: 75)

Turner cites the mixed modes of the mini-series *The Dismissal* – in which actors impersonate rather than play the politicians involved in the Whitlam dismissal, and *Scales of Justice* (Jenkins 1983) with its documentary style 'low-lit, grainy, lots of hand-held cameras, a script that does not sound like one' (74) which turns the events portrayed into 'allegations – if not of specific occurrences, at least of customary practices within the judicial and legislative system'. For its part, *Newsfront* 'derives much of its force and its appeal from the acute and intelligent blending of newsreel footage with live action' (74).

Turner also singles out documentaries – like *Cane Toads* (Lewis 1987), *God Knows Why But it Works* (Noyce 1975) and *The Nights Belong to the Novelist* – which draw heavily on narrative devices. Mark Lewis's cult documentary, *Cane Toads*, dealing with the biological, ecological and social history of the cane toad in Queensland is shot through a raft of styles from a playful classic expository documentary parodying itself, to a 'range of fictionalizing methods, with references in the framing, the soundtrack and the editing to such classic *auteurs* as Hitchcock and to such classic monster films as *Jaws*' (Turner 1988: 70). Christina Wilcox's *The Nights Belong to the Novelist* – a study of novelist Elizabeth Jolley – makes the 'line between fact and fiction ... even less distinct' (70) alternating sequences of the author and dramatized sequences from her novels.

Such blending was a staple before the 1970s revival. Chauvel's *In the Wake of the Bounty* moves in and out of narrative film about the mutiny on the *Bounty*, history documentary, travelogue, musical and high melodrama (Errol Flynn played Fletcher Christian). Just after the Second World War, Harry Watt created *The Overlanders* as docu-drama – the film served as a western, an informative classical documentary about the rigours and jobs involved in cattle driving, and a fictional recreation of a real event. The same blend is present in Ron Maslyn Williams's documentary fiction *Mike and Stefani* (1952). Here the real-life couple recreate their pre-war lives for the camera and this is then blended with images of the couple in refugee camps and their interview by an uncommunicative and unfriendly immigration official. Critics sometimes regard this as Australia's first 'neorealist' film – appropriately Italian neo-realism comes into Australian filmmaking via the documentary! As Albert Moran (1991: 47) notes:

> Like the neorealist films of Rossellini, de Sica, Visconti and the other Italian film-makers, the causes of character actions in *Mike and Stefani* are concretely economic, political and historical, most especially to do with World War Two and its aftermath.

For its part, *Back of Beyond* moves in and out of being a travelogue documentary following mail person Tom Kruise, a film of mytho-poetic montage sequences, a full-blown fictional retelling of a story that is introduced as a myth of the track (and this story of two girls getting lost is what most people remember about this film; after watching it so many times, I still find it almost unbearable), and a voiceover commentary which is more a prose poem than an information voiceover.

While occupying the space of the documentary, *From the Tropics to the Snow* (Mason and Lee 1964) looks like an early 1960s Jean-Luc Godard film applied to government documentary film-making. The film begins by proudly announcing 'this is a film about a film', as its central protagonists – Unit film-makers – have a heated debate about what should go into a commissioned documentary to present Australia. The film fictionally renders tensions over alternative 'contents' for documentary film-making: alternative formal, expressive and ideological positions on Australian documentary production at the time. The fictional side is further underwritten by the gratuitous use of a 'sex interest' – all these male film-makers are distracted by the pretty woman taking the dictation. She subsequently turns up in odd ways in their projections of alternative scenarios for a documentary presenting Australia's tourist potential. In the process, the institutional documentary is revealed as a construction and the repertoire of stock documentary images and voice-overs begin to look entirely fictive.

From the Tropics to the Snow not only indicates how rhetorical 'truth telling' can be but also how the 'world' described by documentary film-making is itself a rich and self-sufficient system of symbols – genre, discourses, stereotypes and archetypes. And might not this precisely explain why Australian cinema takes on board documentary styles even when film-makers do not have to? (John Hughes' experimental docu-fiction, *Traps* (1986) – not to be confused with Chan's (1994) feature of the same title – provided such a disconcerting blend of fact and fiction that it confused people about exactly what was its status.)

A minor variant of this blending is the 1970s Australian sex film which self-consciously used the device of the documentary. John B. Murray's *The Naked Bunyip* (1970) incorporates the fictionalizing of the 'real' that had been a feature of tendencies in the French 'new wave' and the American avant-garde narrative cinema. The fictional framework has a shy young man (played by Graeme Blundell) chosen by an ad agency to conduct a survey on sex in Australia. As Pike and Cooper (1980: 325) note, the young man is

> soon adrift in a sea of sexual experience as he investigates homosexuality, transvestites, prostitution, strip clubs, pack-rape, permissive morality, pornography – everything in fact except 'normal' heterosexuality. Within its fictional framework, the film consisted mainly of interviews, unrehearsed and unscripted, and recorded with direct sound.

This film-making targeted the documentary interest in sexual lifeways, mixing fiction and documentary in unexpected ways, creating in the figure of the fictional market researcher a stand-in figure for the equally bemused and titillated audience.[3]

Even film-makers known for their 'straight' documentaries deploy in the same film a range of documentary and fictional styles. For a political film, this range is a difficult balancing act because it has to be clear and unambiguous about 'the truth', if political purposes are to be foregrounded and not the politics of film-making. Phillip Noyce's *God Knows Why But it Works*, about the work of an outback doctor who has devoted his life to Aboriginal health problems, mobilizes two lines of action. As Graeme Turner (1988: 71) relates it:

> The first is a realist, traditional documentary style, following the doctor around as he talks about his work; the second is a highly theatrical dramatization of key events in his life, often performed without sets or any realist paraphernalia at all.

David Bradbury's *State of Shock* begins in a similar fashion. Static close-up shots of Alwyn Peters take us through his recollection of the events which led up to him killing his partner after a drunken binge. These are intercut with the workshopping of a play dramatizing the same event, with Ernie Dingo as the fictional Peters. A third, though minor, strand is provided by the shots of Peters hunting with a rifle in 'his country' of which he and his family were dispossessed, and by shots of his mother still living in the house that is the scene of the crime.

Bradbury brings his three strands together in an extraordinary sequence. It begins with the climax of the play – the murder of the woman, having completed the stage murder, Ernie Dingo then steps out of character to comment on his character's next actions. We then cut to inside the house where the crime was committed. The camera tracks through the house as if it was Peters himself, finds the mother on a bed who asks 'is it you', and proceeds past her into another room. The gaps between the obviously fictional world of the play, the documentary world of the present and the documentary recollections of the real life characters spoken to camera are collapsed at this point. The film-maker delegates his editorial voice to the stage play actor, Ernie Dingo. The mother recreates herself reliving those events. Alwyn Peters breaks down recollecting these events. This also marks a turning point in the film: thereafter a naturalist observation documentary alternates with talking head interviews. (In the next chapter, I will discuss the political sensitivity surrounding Bradbury's subject matter and Aboriginal criticism of particular sequences from this film.)

There are several ways in which the documentary in the fiction and the fiction in the documentary in Australian film-making can be accounted for. Firstly, non-fiction is a central source for the recreation, retelling and remythologizing of Australian history, contemporary lifeways and politics. It easily dwarfs the fictional symbolic culture in importance as a common public reference point. Besides, 'docu-drama' or 'faction' has been a central plank of Australian storytelling from the popular literature of the 1940s and 1950s, like Ion L. Idriess and Frank Clune's 'true stories' to the later feature cinema and mini-series attention to fictionalizing the public record. Additionally, this relation to the documentary makes cultural sense. In Australia, the information and political culture is a major carrier of identity. It is also the most Australianized domain of image making. The symbolic rhetoric of Australia and Australian lifeways is largely defined by the factual genres. In these circumstances, fiction film-makers naturally work from this already advanced generic, stereotypical, archetypal *audiovisual* rhetoric to fashion stories. Without much international circulation, the documentary develops in a more self-sustaining fashion. Australian documentarists are likely to use the 'imported models', but like their American feature and television counterparts, their audience may not know that they have. Documentary, news, and before television the cinema newsreel, also provided a storehouse of types, stereotypes, shorthands of intonation, gesture, performance styles, *mise-en-scène* and explorations to be drawn upon for fiction film-making. The 'public record' and the 'documentary style' are predominant repertoires for binding an Australian audience into a film or television programme whether it is the re-enactment of *Joh's Jury* (K. Cameron 1993) or the bicentennial mega-production *Australia Live* (Faiman 1988).[4]

Second, for part of Australia's film history, film-makers could only make documentaries. The desire to participate in a wider repertoire saw documentary filmmmakers pushing the limits of the documentary. Think of those polished film-makers of the 1950s John Heyer and Ron Maslyn Williams. Many 1970s generation film-makers emerged from documentary. The Commonwealth Film Unit (a documentary production unit) produced the feature film *Three to Go* (Weir, Hannant, Howes 1971) with one of its three stories, 'Michael', was directed by Peter Weir. Feature directors in the 1970s and 1980s continued to return to documentary, such as Gillian Armstrong' with her trilogy following the lives of three females from early adolescence, to teenagers to twenty-something women in *Smokes and Lollies, 14's Good, 18's Better, Bingo Bridesmaids and Braces.* Third, documentary styles and emphases on ordinary people in complex situations – such as the Doctor's work in *God Knows Why But it Works* – fit a fictional tradition which combines the tall story and 'the battler'.

Fourth, the selection of documentary forms of lighting, shooting and 'look' in feature film-making is an attempt to turn a minus into a plus. Through it Australian film-making can find a place for itself in the cinema – not through directly competing in look and style but by doing so indirectly. Australian film-making cannot hope to match mainstream American cinema's standards of imaging: it cannot put up the same investment per second of screen time. The number and complexity of camera set-ups are going to be limited. There will be less generous shooting ratios, less time spent in rehearsal. The lower level of on-screen investment will normally show. In these circumstances, attempting to turn this disadvantage into an advantage makes sense. The documentary look legitimates limited set-ups, documentary lighting, the '*art brut*' look Caputo (1993: 19) finds in *Mouth to Mouth*, and a documentary naturalism in actor performance. If this sometimes entails 'observation' more than 'characterization', it also fits an

Australian emphasis on socially recognizable types. An added advantage is that the USA does not dominate the documentary in the way it does fictional genres. Many of Australia's finest feature film cinematographers – like Dean Semler – began in documentary. Documentary cinematographers are especially able to create a 'big picture' look on low budgets using the existing urban and country landscapes.

Fifth, documentary and fiction blends are appropriate to broadcasting and film policy's dualist emphases. The mixed broadcasting situation of the ABC, SBS and the commercial stations is underwritten by a philosophy that broadcasting should divert and educate, entertain and inform. This gives documentarist and documentarist-inflected repertoires a continuing place in the television system. Film policy in its turn gives a structural place to educating and informing which ensure a place on funding horizons for the documentary, docu-drama, a fiction film-making close to the public record, and a fiction film-making deploying documentarist rhetorics. In such an environment, it is natural that documentary should foreground fictionalizing the documentary and documentarizing the fiction. The dualist inheritance also helps explain the remarkable number of titles about teachers and teaching: *Picnic at Hanging Rock*, *The Devil's Playground*, *The Mango Tree* (Dobson 1977), *The Getting of Wisdom*, *Fighting Back* (Caulfield 1983), *Flirting*, *The Year My Voice Broke* (Duigan 1987), *Fast Talking* (K. Cameron 1984), *Moving Out* (Pattinson 1983), *Street Hero* (Pattinson 1984) and *The Heartbreak Kid*.

THE IMPORTANCE OF UGLINESS AND ORDINARINESS IN AUSTRALIAN CINEMA

At its Cannes screening, a *Variety* critic found of *Muriel's Wedding* that '[t]he director seems to take a perverse pleasure in drawing attention to the ugliest aspects of (Australian) life'. At the centre of this ugliness is Muriel/Mariel. She is overweight. Her taste in clothes is appalling. She is the dowdy best friend typically put at the edge of a film. She does not slim down by the film's end (to reveal the physical swan in the ugly duckling). We have to see double. This ugly duckling is a swan; the problem is with *our vision*. Paul J. Hogan, the director and scriptwriter for *Muriel's Wedding*, argued that:

> Usually in Australian films, definitely in Australian television, definitely in American films, the central character is usually the Sophie Lee character. You're invited to enjoy the wondrous personality of Tania, to put an emotional investment in her. For me the question is: 'Is the Sophie Lee character in *Muriel's Wedding* any less self-centred and deeply stupid than the Demi Moore character in *Indecent Proposal* [Bergman 1993]?' I think not! However, we accept stories about Tanias every day and Muriel in these stories is left out or consigned to a position of best friend, one to feel sorry for. . . . I wanted to put

that kind of character centre stage and the beautiful best friend in the position of living horror.

(Quoted in Wignall 1994: 33)

For all Hogan's protestations to the contrary, such an inflection is common in Australian cinema and television. Such ugliness is a recurring feature of Australian cinema. Members of the screen trade saw the principal leads of Longford's *The Sentimental Bloke* – Lottie Lyell and Arthur Tauchert – as 'barren of beauty' representing a 'national ugliness' (Tulloch 1981: 44). *Newsfront* focuses on the Bill Hunter figure who has a body and a look that would put him at the margins of much cinema. Lee Robinson and Chips Rafferty put Charles (Bud) Tingwell and not Rod Taylor at the centre of *King of the Coral Sea* (the same Taylor that Hitchcock was so cunningly able to later exploit as male bimbo in *The Birds* (1963)). David Elfick made his coming of age film, *Love in Limbo*, focus on the nerd who fails to lose his virginity at a Kalgoorlie brothel and not on the conventional outlaw figure played by Aden Young. *Roly Poly Man*'s private dick is the unlikely Paul Chubb: in its own way an inspirational choice – for here is an actor who admires the work of silent comedian Buster Keaton and models his own performances where possible on his. Relatedly, fashionable Australian soaps turn on the conceit of an ordinary neighbourhood with characters on a human scale, from *Bellbird* to *Neighbours*, from *A Country Practice* (1981) to *Home and Away* (1988). Their claim to ordinariness is central to the operating strategies of these soaps, just as the extraordinary is central to *Models Inc* (1994), *Dynasty* (1981–9) and *Dallas* (1978–91).

Some of Australia's most acclaimed actors, like Judy Davis, are not conventionally beautiful. In 1980 Max Harris reported that actors like Helen Morse, Jack Thompson and the late John Mellion were as 'ordinary as Omo commercials' (for him at least their lack of Nietzschean pretensions and overblowness were an asset, not a liability). In much of *Hightide*, Davis's expressions and looks are a consistent pasty white which, if it were not for the storyline of a mother becoming maternal and interested in the daughter she abandoned many years before, would look almost vampirish and positively sexually voyeuristic. Armstrong makes Davis look worse than she can be made to, and makes her cinematographer, Russell Boyd, turn some of the most beautiful coastline in Australia into landscapes without promise – miming the bleak prospects of its central characters.

For its part, Heyer's classic, *The Back of Beyond* is full of its quota of ordinary people doing everyday things under extraordinary conditions. Men sit in lounge chairs smoking, with a desert stretching to infinity for a living room. For relaxation jazz records are played on a wind-up gramophone and used for dancing to amid sandhills. In surroundings empty of any sign of life on the Birdsville Track, a woman and her child wait in Sunday best for the mail truck to take them to town. The film is a classic 'tall story' – a tradition of storytelling premised on the ordinary, the mundane, the tawdry and the banal – but it gradually opens out on to the unexpected and extraordinary which is, at the same time, rendered as an extension of the ordinary and the mundane.

Far from being eccentric, Paul J. Hogan's casting and storytelling sits within a well-represented strand of Australian storytelling. Many Australian stories focus on people who would be in the periphery, and cast physical types into central roles who would normally be cast into supporting roles. Evidence of Australian cinema's apparent casting against the obvious is provided by Hollywood's casting of Australia's lead actors – apart from Mel Gibson and to a lesser extent Bryan Brown in the *F/X* (Mandel 1985, Franklin 1991) cycle of films – as the 'baddy' or as the bit player to the main lead. Think of the way Judy Davis is used by Cronenberg in *The Naked Lunch* (1991) and by the Coen brothers in *Barton Fink* (1991).

Sometimes this centring of the ordinary, the daggy (unstylish), the ugly and the mundane is seen as a mistake. Films should have attractive people who are pleasing to the eye, 'stars' who are larger than life, and a degree of spectacle, if they are to be successful. Beautiful landscapes should not be made to look so bleak. From this point of view, such storytelling is wrong-headed and Australian casting practices are miscasting practices. To attempt to 'cure' the national ugliness of actors like Lyell and Tauchert, the trade ran competitions judged by Hollywood personnel. Their ugliness provided evidence of Australian cinema's 'inferior production values' (Tulloch 1981: 49). But is there something wrong with basing a story around Lyell and Tauchert and Muriel/Mariel (Toni Collette)?

'Australian ugliness' is not just reserved for the 'look' of actors. In many Australian films, artless characters are centrally represented. Barry McKenzie is a simpleton (his 'dagginess' is signposted by his doublebreasted suit and his airways bag – a camp parody of an outdated masculinity in keeping with Muriel's excessive 'love' for ABBA). Bubby (in *Bad Boy Bubby*) is the child-man who retains his childlike qualities right to the end – despite getting married and having children. Crocodile Dundee, and Nino in *They're a Weird Mob*, are possibly the only ones who become socially competent. But even here there is a rub; cultured Nino learns the 'lingo' and embraces the lifeways of uncultured yobboes, and Mick Dundee remains the yokel in the Big Apple. Hollywood cinema also uses the 'everyman' simpleton to good effect; except that Forrest Gump – like Frank Capra's naïve men played by James Stewart and Gary Cooper – became somebody. These are heroes and agents of history: men of destiny whose simpleness disorders public institutions. By contrast, Bubby becomes a small time rock performer and father of twins and raises a family in the shadow of an industrial area. And Barry McKenzie is put on the first flight home after disgracing himself on British national television.

Sometimes this attention to ordinariness fits ideological and performance naturalism's requirements for a storytelling in which actors are in proportion to their surroundings, actions take place on a 'human scale' and there is a concern for 'truth to the actual'. That was one of the reasons Max Harris found for liking

Australian cinema. But *Muriel's Wedding* is a tragi-comedy, *The Sentimental Bloke* a romantic comedy: neither genre is notably driven by concerns for 'realism'.

Perhaps Morris is right when she suggests that something else happens in Australian cinema, as the demands of drama undergo permutation and some of the strategies associated with comedy and the action film – such as the unashamed use of stereotypes and undeveloped characters – find their way into the most serious drama. Unlike the Hollywood 'drama', its Australian counterpart is often less interested in 'psychological characterization' (1980: 138) or the 'moral dimension' (141) than with *stereotyping* and organizing the resulting 'types into relationships which highlight opposition' (145). Such a cinema is naturally less interested in beauty than in social types, character types. The result is a cinema of *character actors*. For Morris:

> Stereotyping is a highly formalized way of defining a figure by a few essential characteristics sanctified as typical by convention; it is not a debased or inferior form of art beside the greater refinement of something else. It depends on a cultivation of the precise things which characterize a person, a place or an object in an immediately convincing way. Stereotyping in fact, is an art of identification and recognition; in a sense, it makes it possible to control difference by making it easily interpretable.
>
> (146)

Morris associates stereotyping with a tendency to 'social observation' which relies on socially recognizable types, cultural stereotypes which play on recognition (shades of the blending of fiction and documentary here). Not surprisingly then, Graham Shirley finds the silent cinema festival audience in Poderone in Italy slower on the uptake than its Australian counterparts. The response to *The Sentimental Bloke* was not 'unanimous' and 'it took a while for the audience to realize that this was indeed comedy' (Shirley 1994: 43).

Rapport and recognition are partly dependent on an Australian cultural training in recognizable types and situations. Such recognitions are central to *Muriel's Wedding*'s Australian uptake by, for example, social commentator, Frank Devine (1994) who sees the film as finding drama, dignity and audiences among 'the back-of-the-beach Australians'. In a film-making called by Australian Film Institute head, Vicki Molloy a 'comic strip style' cinema, considerable media attention focused on its 'types'. Its lead, Toni Collette, reported that she was brought up in Blacktown, in Sydney's western suburbs, was the daughter of a truckie and a telephonist and that people like her were looked down on by beachside suburbanites: 'I was surrounded by Tanias. I fell right into that Muriel category.' (*Sunday Mail*, Brisbane, 9 October 1994).

Sometimes this ordinariness takes us into decidedly unconventional directions. Bubby's (of *Bad Boy Bubby*) notions of the sexually attractive body are unconventional: the threatening cornucopia of flesh of his aging mum, who keeps him simultaneously as her baby and her sexual partner (in its classic 20 minutes 'theatre of cruelty' opening) enables his positive desire for the younger but equally well-endowed (Ruebens-like) Angel to make sense for him and for the viewer. The film works – in part because of the lasting impression created by that first twenty minutes – to put us in his position, positively dismissing the conventionally beautiful women as ugly in sequences worthy of Fellini. Bubby even murders Angel's parents by clingwrapping them, in revenge for their treatment of her which includes their insistence on how 'fat' and unattractive she is.

While Paul J. Hogan and his producers Jocelyn Moorhouse and Linda House would probably not see *Muriel's Wedding* as an update of the Rudd tradition, there are surprising continuities between this film and the popular Rudd cycle which dominated Australian cultural production from the 1920s to the 1940s. The Rudd family is a lot like Muriel's. Consider Routt's (1989a: 29) assessment of them:

> There is some reason for regarding the Rudd family as especially significant in Australian popular culture. Books, plays, a radio series, a comic strip and six films were devoted to it, not to mention such unabashed plagiarisms as Beaumont Smith's 'Hayseeds' series of films. Yet the Rudd family, at least as it is depicted on film, is a peculiar one. ... the Rudds do not seem very 'wholesome' and the particular circumstance of their unwholesomeness is the mental degeneration of many of the Rudd children. Dave, the eldest son, is perhaps the clearest example of this. In both the 1920s and 1930s versions of the family, Dave is portrayed as a stereotyped rural idiot. The same might be said for one of the daughters, Sarah, whose attempts at clandestine meetings with Billy Bearup provide comic relief in some of the films of the series.

Routt notes that the exceptions here are the father, Dad Rudd, and the 'strong woman' – the eldest daughter, variously Kate (in both versions of *On Our Selection*), Nell (*Rudd's New Selection!*, Longford 1921), Jill (*Dad and Dave Come to Town*, Hall 1938) and Ann (*Dad Rudd, M.P.*, Hall 1940). In *Muriel's Wedding*, the rural, struggling, small plot selector and his family is replaced by the 'back of the beach' people. Dad played consummately by Bill Hunter is a small town councillor on the take, prepared to bribe police and sales people to protect the family name. The benign and patriarchal Dad Rudd, whose children are another of his burdens together with bushfires, drought and kangaroos eating his crops in *On our Selection*, has become the awful patriachal father of *Muriel's Wedding* responsible for his wife's ruined life and his children's lack of emotional and mental maturity. In both cases, the eldest daughter is the *only* member of the family most like her respective father. And both are the ones to 'escape' the family: Kate and her various other personae into marriage to an eligible and more wealthy neighbour who is suitably colourless in comparison to her and her father, and Muriel into and out of marriage. It is significant that Muriel ends her marriage at the point where she realizes her potential to become like her father and so takes steps to break the cycle.

Routt sees the patriarchal family and the father–daughter relation in the Rudd cycle as a displaced metaphor of settler colonialism: Dad as 'Prospero'; Kate/Nell/

Jill/Ann as 'Miranda'; and Australia as the fairest child of the (British) motherland. *Muriel's Wedding* converts this into a wholly Australian affair. It is
Australian patriarchy that is unproblematically under investigation and that is the
problem; the film is anti-marriage in so far as marriage means the continuation of
the dysfunctional patriarchal marriage. Muriel crucially leaves her family to her
Dad who is now stripped of power, authority, wealth and his lover. Muriel refuses
to play Mum, leaving Dad to become the mother function and pick up the pieces
of what he has wrought – graphically represented by the burnt backyard and the
singed clothes on the Hill's clothes-line (Mum's last defiant act before committing
suicide).

Muriel's Wedding and the Rudd family provide, if you like, a positive take on
Australian ugliness. Sometimes Australians want to disown such ugliness. The
fact that Australia told itself stories like those in the Rudd cycle, confirmed for
some the unflattering image of Australia as an uncultured, untutored and unsophis-
ticated place full of bumpkin and possibly inbred halfwits. The 'ocker' cycle of the
early 1970s oscillated between implication and denunciation. Its 'freaks' and
'monsters' were praised for capturing the energy and materialism of urban life and
a film-making marked by 'excess rather than a tasteful balance' (Rohdie 1982b:
39), and were panned for demonstrating an ugliness and collective immaturity the
nation could well do without. Perhaps the greatest asset David Williamson had as
a playwright and scriptwriter for titles like *Don's Party* and *Stork* was his
'ambivalence' about Australian 'ugliness'. Tim Burstall noted that his work of this
period eschewed the easy avenue of denunciation without implication:

> Does Williamson approve or disapprove of what he describes? If what he is
> doing can be seen as an indictment of modern Australia – its vulgarity, its
> crassness, its shallow social goals – then he can be praised. But if it is sensed
> he is either the impartial recorder – or what is worse – a man who rather
> relished the vigour, energy and 'tastelessness' of the life around him, then he is
> described as . . . hollow, a man without vision.
>
> (Burstall 1977: 50)

There is a stream of Australian film-making that does not bother with ambivalence and ambiguity. It wants to denounce. Showing 'the ugliness that you do not
want to own' is a regular part of Australian film culture. Such is the terrain of
Jackie McKimmie's *Australian Dream* (1987), whose monstrous characters are
cruelly mocked. It turns on excoriating Australian lifeways and culture in a mode
of hypercriticism. Les Murray has disparagingly called this the 'host of routine
excoriations of Australian life and culture, the Godzones and the Australian
Stupors' (Les Murray 1984: 150) as found in the literature of Ronald Conway,
Robin Boyd, Anne Summers, Marylyn Lake, Donald Horne and Elaine Thompson. Such work often projects itself as an antidote to the unthinking celebration of
Australian life and lifeways and its parochial, sexist, racist and ethnocentric
outlooks. Adrian Martin (1988a: 101) notes that excoriation is often the domain of
'Australian gothic' film-making. He criticizes Greg Woodland's *Tripe* (1985) not

just for the banality of its excoriations but for the superiority of the film-maker to what is described:

> There is something relentless and unforgiveable in the way current gothic time and time again zooms in on Australian suburbia as the natural home of all backward, pathological grotesques. In this world, fathers are tyrannically patriarchal at the dinner table, repressed daughters are droolingly tarty once given freedom, and dutiful sons are stiff-necked conformists seething with lascivious desires. The film chalks up the obligatory point for itself as being insightfully critical about the way the 'masses' must live ... whilst ultimately high-handedly condemning the characters to remain fixed in the hell of their perpetual conservativism. Life in action? This is more like a game in which all the moves are rigged in advance, with all the spoils going straight to the film-maker-as-superior-being.
>
> (101

Undoubtedly 'the Ugly Australian' is often a middle-class fantasy which projects a relation of alterity to the viewer and film-maker who is, above all, not like that, thank God. The candidates for ugliness are, however, surprisingly limited: the non-deserving working class of *The Last of the Knucklemen* (T. Burstall 1979), Australian men in *Wake in Fright*, *The Umbrella Woman*, suburban culture in *Tripe*, the *nouveau riche* in *Sylvania Waters* and the middle-class 'ockers' of *Don's Party*.

Parts of Australian culture are monstrous – but no more monstrous than parts of other cultures. The difference is that Australian self-denigration is an important component of the culture alongside its celebratory self-promotion. It is a disarming feature of Australian film-making and culture generally that it should be so prepared to emphasize and dramatize the worst parts of the culture; and to present these as representative of it.

But only projecting the ugliness can get in the way of projecting other perspectives. Marcia Langton criticizes a tendency of Australian film-makers to go only for the excoriating stories that paint 'the whites' as complete oppressors:

> [film-makers] edit in the 'gub' and 'kadiya' stories [centring violence and horror] and leave Aboriginal stories of good times with white people – the flotsam and jetsam of the working models – on the cutting room floor. These film-makers want to see 'Europeans' portrayed only as oppressors and all the complexities eliminated.
>
> (1993: 37)

The problem here is that excoriating repertoires do not project any Aboriginal agency (as they are *only* the victims of this ugliness). They often deny Aboriginal survival and integrity. Take the late Tom Haydon's remarkable documentary, *The Last Tasmanian* (1978). The documentary told the story of the 'swiftest and most complete genocide in history' – that of the Tasmanian Aboriginal people in the nineteenth century. It takes the moral high ground. White supremacism, the complicity of an emerging social science of anthropology, grave robbing, colonialists poisoning and removing the Aboriginal people are all foregrounded. The Aboriginal people are victims and they are all wiped out. Haydon 'talks strong' and likens Australia's colonial history to that of the Jewish Holocaust. Aboriginal people were outraged. Tasmanian Aboriginal people like Michael Mansell were particularly outraged. It denied them again their very existence.[5] Genocide, yes, but not complete genocide – exaggeration in the name of anti-racism can be another form of Australian racism.[6]

The tendency to accentuate the mundane which projects an Australia that is alternatively more daggy and downmarket than it is, or more racist, sexist and homophobic than it is, is sustained by several conditions. Traditions of storytelling accentuating the tall story and social types demand Australian 'monsters' and 'freaks' who are none the less 'ordinary'. The need to differentiate the local product sees Australian ugliness staked out as Australia's territory in the cinema – an antidote to the pretty, well-dressed and well-coiffured people on offer in some genres of the cinema. It fits the cultural logic of a medium-sized producer to take the culturally weak position in which Australia is in the supporting cast on the world stage, and turn it into a strength: Australia as a cast of colourful 'freakish' characters whether it is Muriel, Bazza McKenzie, or Mitzi in *The Adventures of Priscilla*. At the same time, traditions of the documentary necessarily focus on 'bad news', and the human drama focuses on social problems: both, in their turn, reproduce the figure of 'the Ugly Australian' (intolerant, racist, sexist and boorish).

OTHERING THE AUSTRALIAN

Another feature of Australian storytelling is to invite its audience to, in Rowse's words, 'stand in an external and observing relationship' to definitions 'of things essentially and ethnically Australian' (1985: 70). Rowse describes this as an 'important ambivalence in the wider [Australian] culture'. Every feature of Australian storytelling discussed so far 'fits' to some degree this othering of the Australian: its situation between the melodrama and the art film, its centring types and social observation, its freaks and monsters, and its subsidiary stream of excoriations of Australian lifeways. All these turn on establishing relations of alterity between the audience and what is on-screen.

Othering the Australian is present in the way films ask their audience to play anthropologist to their culture, as in *Puberty Blues* and *Petersen*, or to laugh at the Australian stereotypes in *They're a Weird Mob*, *Strictly Ballroom* or *Muriel's Wedding*. It extends to the manipulation of the art film's 'boundary situation', as when the socially dysfunctional relationships in *Don's Party* place the viewer apart from the action; or through a young migrant boy's experience of the broader Australian culture in *Moving Out*, which promises alienation on all sides; or in the way the audience is asked to judge the lifeways of other Australians (not us) in the horrific *Wake in Fright*. In even the most mainstream productions, this process of othering is in evidence. Take the momentous beginning of the mini-series *The Dismissal*, where the internationalizing of the Whitlam dismissal in 1975 functions to take its audience away from its own 'take' on this event, placing them as outsiders to the familiar events that unfold in a new way. Through this strategy the events are powerfully mythologized by their being internationalized alongside events of global significance.

Another version of this othering process lies in the importance to the Australian uptake of many films, of their acclaim and popularity outside Australia; this not only retrospectively values and signals the importance of Australian productions but also provides an extra richness to viewing: viewers can imagine themselves as the British and Americans watching *Strictly Ballroom* – a film which surprised 'us' as much as 'them'. The Australian audience is imagining itself as the foreign audience for this or that Australian film. The audience wants to try to read the 'imported' text in the language of the original, holding on to the Australian and the overseas reading simultaneously.[7]

I want to consider in detail perhaps the most classic statement of Australian alterity, *They're a Weird Mob*. It forges a path for later comedy films and humourists to follow. Barry Humphries, Paul Hogan, Austen Tayshus, Wendy Harmer, Max Gillies and Vince Sorrenti have all made careers as comics of Australian alterity. *They're a Weird Mob* is in a long line of comic strip cinema which includes *The Adventures of Barry McKenzie*, *Strictly Ballroom*, *Muriel's Wedding* and *The Adventures of Priscilla*. It brought into the foreground sociocultural differentiations – particularly ethnic differences – which had hitherto been in the background of Australian storytelling. *They're a Weird Mob* was also the most popular Australian film of the 1960s. It was a screen adaptation of the most popular Australian novel of the late 1950s and early 1960s, written by John O'Grady under the pseudonym of Nino Culotta.

While later commentators have focused on the significance and cultural inappropriateness of an Australian of Celtic extraction adopting an Italian name, few note the function of this pseudonym in the book and the film's reading strategies. The book is written by Nino who is its central character: we 'make believe' that we are reading autobiography. (Again an Australian fiction passes itself off as 'faction'. The book's claim of 'documentarist' observation enables it to focus on small incidents and everyday behaviours; Nino's 'education' shifts the Australian dualism of education and entertainment to an ironic sense – not the education of young Donald but of 'Nino the wog'.)

They're a Weird Mob is to late 1950s and early 1960s Australian culture what C. J. Dennis' *The Sentimental Bloke* was to Australian culture in the first twenty years of this century. Made as a co production between prominent local theatrical company J. C. Williamson's and the then-disgraced English pair, of director Michael Powell and scriptwriter Emeric Pressburger (after the scandal of *Peeping Tom*), the film was a raging success in Australia but the makers' hopes of international success in the UK and Italy were not met.

Pike and Cooper, in keeping with critical response to this film, put its popularity down to 'the novelty of seeing a homegrown entertainment' after 'a long drought' (1980: 309); later they disparage the film for failing to say as much about 'the life of migrants in Australia' (1980: 337) as Zampa's *Girl in Australia (Bello Onesto Emigrato Australia Sposerebbe Compaesana Illibata*, 1971).[8] Displaying none of the genius of their *Red Shoes* (1948), it is a lesser Powell and Pressburger film. Powell did not think much of the film either. In his long autobiography, he has little to say about it.[9] Since the advent of multiculturalism in the late 1970s, *They're a Weird Mob* has acquired a reputation as the apotheosis of the repressive assimilationist policy, with its exhortation that Italian wogs should strive to become 'Dinkidi' Aussies like Nino.

But the film is barely about the assimilation of recalcitrant Italian communities: it is more about Nino as a cipher for directing attention onto 'them', i.e. Australians, in order to better project 'their particularities'. He does not try to change the Italians or the Australians he meets. He simply tries to understand them. Only with Kay's father does he argue his Italianness and then only to point out that the Pope is Italian. For her part, Kay appears at home in the Italian party she arrives at in search of Nino and finds it attractive and welcoming (this ethnic party, liked by an Anglo woman for qualities unavailable in Australian lifeways, is repeated in *Caddie* and *Kostas* (Cox 1979) and becomes the viewpoint of an Anglo man in *Strictly Ballroom*.)[10]

They're a Weird Mob's strategy of othering has the Australian disclosed through an outsider. His gaze on 'them' discloses who 'they', and therefore 'we' the audience are. He is the naïve one abroad in a strange land. He is the audience's stand-in. We see Australia and Australians through his eyes. We see his fellow Italian migrants through his eyes. We experience the discrimination the Italian family suffers on the ferry through his eyes. Unlike *The Adventures of Barry McKenzie*, the strange land is Australia. The film's conceit is that audiences should see themselves through the eyes of the Other, the 'New Australian'. Nino is like Bazza McKenzie in London and Crocodile Dundee in New York. In Dundee fashion Nino has become Sue (like him she is a journalist; but unlike him she continues her career in journalism; for Nino, builder's labouring is what is available to him at least until he writes the book about his Australian adventures).

Nino Culotta is in a long line of 'overseas' subjects who render the Australian comprehensible to locals and others. Some of the earliest literature on Australia is a travel literature produced for 'home country' – usually British – consumption, but becoming popular, with Australians disclosing who they were and what they were like then. Ex-convicts, William Makepeace Thackeray and Charles Darwin all wrote works covering Australia in the nineteenth century. In the twentieth century at least two of the most popular sociologies of Australians, their govern-ance and lifeways, W. K. Hancock's *Australia* (1930, 1961) and J. D. Pringle's *Australian Accent* (1958, 1978) were written for a UK audience but found their major market in Australia. J. D. Pringle, an Englishman brought out to edit *The*

Sydney Morning Herald, wrote *Australian Accent* for prospective English migrants. *Australian Accent* and *They're a Weird Mob* more or less parallel each
other.

O'Grady Australianizes the genre, taking over the rhetoric of the 'outsider' in
order to explain and render Australians to themselves in two directions. First, the
book/film is created from inception for Australian consumption – it ironizes the
speaking position of the authoritative outsider. Second, it innovates through
having, as the outsider, someone culturally devalued in the Australian context: the
'Itie', 'the wog', Nino Culotta. Nino is not one of the more culturally valued
English, French and Americans surveying a lesser society – like Sue Charlton in
Dundee. Rather the Italian and the Australian are equalized: both function in the
broader English language cultures as bit players and provide comic light relief in
the international cinema.

In the film, the 'Australian' becomes something akin to a sub-culture, and
Australian English a sub-cultural argot. The film makes much of its announcement
of Australians as a strange lot. The notion of Australia as 'down under', and
therefore an 'upside down place' *Alice in Wonderland*-style, is visualized by the
opening sequences of streetscapes etc. being upside down. As in *The Sentimental
Bloke*, where much of its mirth is still generated by its wonderful intertitles,
They're a Weird Mob foregrounds 'comic-poetic' Australian speech. Pike and
Cooper concede that '[m]ost of the humour dwelt on the incomprehensibility of
Australian slang to the newcomer' (309).[11]

Nino's first mistake is to believe Australians speak English. Since he speaks
(correct) English, he presumes he will not have any problems. But Australians
speak Australian English. The film charts his mastery of another language. Nino
undergoes a series of incongruous pedagogic lessons on building sites, pubs and in
lounge rooms about Australian language and therefore lifeways. And this mastery
changes him to 'one of them' – such that, by the end of the film, the gap between
his vision and that of the other characters in the fiction has been abolished. He has
now become one of 'them', whom the audience gaze at *from outside*; but here is
the rub, 'they' are 'us'.

Nino's trajectory, from middle-class Italian to working-class but upwardly
mobile Australian, has him trade in a tennis racket for the pickaxe and a career in
journalism in for that of a 'brickie's labourer' and eventually a builder. The film
insists that he is *repeating* the trajectory of his prospective father-in-law – the
working-class Australian builder of Irish descent (he is purposely called Kelly)
made good. Nino's journey downwards in order to go upwards is paralleled by
sophisticated, successful 'rich woman' Kay's agreement at the end of the film to
live with him in a tent while they build a house (she also *repeats* a trajectory, this
time that of her mother).

The Australians Nino encounters have limited horizons and even more limited
interests. They barely communicate with their female partners; their drinking
rituals verge on alcoholism. Their weekend activities like hunting rabbits are
boyish in the extreme and not a little dangerous. They are scarcely cosmopolitan

– little more than peasants who happen to live in the city (the connection between these working-class Australians and the bulk of Southern European migrants – who unlike their Northern European counterparts were often unskilled and semi-skilled – slotting into the working-class is not one often made but clearly evident here). There are also sufficient scenes of public drunkenness, casual racism and misogyny to suggest that Nino has got himself into a culture and lifestyle he may be better off without.

They're a Weird Mob also makes for an interesting comparison with two later films. The first is Michael Pattinson's *Moving Out* in which a young Italian boy, Gino is 'the family's go-between with "Australian" society' (Gardner 1993b: 134). Here the cross-cultural encounter has become confrontational:

> In its presentation of the cultural confrontation between Italian peasant stock, dominated by insular and rigorous family values, and the panzer battalions of Australia desperate to impose their ignorance on any new arrival, we can discover a battle between cultures that ends with both sides alienated and confused.

Another variation is provided by Jackie McKimmie in *Gino* (1994) from a Vince Sorrenti script about a would-be stand-up comic, Gino (Nicolas Bufalo). For stand-up comedy, othering by telling tall stories about one's own usually monstrous family is a central comic technique. In this film, the butt of its humour and Gino's stand-up comedy routine is Italo-Australian culture. The community is outrageously caricatured. Gino is the audience's guide through the intricacies of Italian-Australian lifeways – eating habits, family interactions and sexual niceties – as he explains that, over the last few weeks, life had became altogether too complicated. Gino's relation of alterity to his community sets up an on-screen 'us' and 'them' audience relation. The audience which this community is to be explained to is the 'wider Australian community' and in a comedic finale 'themselves'. Gino becomes the community's bard; he reconciles the tension between himself and his hopelessly inarticulate and uncommunicative father about the worthiness of his chosen career (stand-up comedy) over architecture; he makes his father laugh at himself and puts his future father-in-law's nose out of joint and establishes for himself and his partner, Lucia (Zoe Carides) an independent space, while simultaneously remaining in the family.

The film reverses *They're a Weird Mob*'s comic strategy, in that the community to be explained is the Italian-Australian community, not the 'Aussies' who are confined to bit parts just as were the 'Italians' set apart from Nino in *Weird Mob*. This time the audience is invited to laugh at 'them' as 'they' ultimately laugh at 'themselves'. The drama is not built out of cultural incomprehension between the Italian Nino and the Australians he encounters, lives with and eventually comes to understand and appreciate; it is one of a clash of cultural values between generations in the Italo-Australian community: an older generation which wants their children to grow up in their image, and the younger generation which wants to strike out into other areas, like be a stand-up comedian and in Lucia's case not be the traditional Italian wife. *Gino* does not project this as a tension between an older generation and their Australian children but as a generation gap in a socially stratified Italo-Australian community. Whereas Nino was one of the few normal people in *They're a Weird Mob*, the normal people here are the 'would be' stand-up comedian Gino and his partner Lucia. The rest, like Gino's working-class mother and father and Lucia's father – who inhabits an unbelievably gaudy Italo-Australian palazzo – are all larger-than-life caricatures. But the film gets away with its caricatures because the tensions are all staged in the Italo-Australian community, which is posed as simultaneously stifling, claustrophobic and delightful, generous, familial and convivial: in short the qualities of *They're a Weird Mob*'s 'Aussies'.

Like Nino's incompetence in 'Australian' lifeways, the Australians who are not marked as ethnic in *Gino* are shown to be comically incompetent in Italian lifeways and protocols. Gino's manager, played by John Polson, keeps putting his foot in his mouth while attempting to be gracious; his sister's lover, Trev, who walked out on her on their wedding day is utterly overwhelmed by the prospect of this family (Trev also really belongs in this family – his car, with its number plate 'TREV', splutters and starts throughout the film).

The film is simultaneously about the Italian diaspora and about a well-known part of the Australian community that many people of a non-Italian background are related to or encounter. 'They' are not a 'they', 'they' are also 'us'. Sorrenti and McKimmie take the quintessentially Australian repertoire of 'caricature' and 'types' and embed it in a storytelling turning on alterity to create a caricatured community as in *Weird Mob*. They show that at least for this tradition of Australian storytelling, the way forward is not to overcome the stereotype (as well-intentioned criticism would have it) but to proliferate them and create rich and multifaceted ethnic stereotypes. In a culture which so disarmingly and powerfully creates images of its own monstrosity and evil, the various minorities will have 'arrived' when they can claim some share of the quirky, the monstrous and the evil, as is available to the broader community in *Muriel's Wedding*, *Don's Party* and *Wake in Fright*. *Gino*, *The Heartbreak Kid* and *Nirvana Street Murder* are all important films in this respect.

If inviting the domestic audience to 'other the Australian' is an Australian production tradition, it also makes sense as a strategy for cultural export. It is not that far a distance to travel from constructing the Australian as Other for a local audience, to constructing it for the overseas gaze. Peter Faiman/Paul Hogan manage their American and Australian audiences in *Crocodile Dundee*; likewise Ken Hall and Bruce Beresford (in *It isn't Done* (1937) and *The Adventures of Barry McKenzie* respectively) manage their British and Australian audiences through a repertoire of stereotypes. All are effective examples of a seamless wedding of a local film-making idiom and cultural style and an international projection of what might be interesting in Australia.

The management of both a local and an overseas site through 'othering the Australian' extends to documentary. The BBC–ABC co-production (with British creative control), *Sylvania Waters*, fitted both production traditions. In Australian film-making it fitted the excoriation and 'social types' film-making; to the British it was the 'fly on the wall' documentary unveiling the quotidian Australian 'reality' behind the public face presented by *Neighbours*. Noeline is from a long line of Australian 'monsters'. Here the legend of Australian awfulness is a marketable commodity abroad – fitting British estimations (exploited by Barry Humphries's personae Dame Edna Everage and Sir Les Patterson) of Australians as a boorish, uncultured and brash lot (Rowe 1994), and an information culture in which news from 'down under' will inevitably be some unusual freakish story. Even a mainstream event like the election of a new prime minister can fit this 'freakishness': Bob Hawke's election as prime minister in 1983 was presented on UK television as the Aussies electing a former world champion beer drinker.

Part of the appreciation of *Sylvania Waters* in Australia turned on imagining British responses to its screening there. This provided an added frisson to its viewing. For some, viewing it could be a 'national humiliation' as 'our image [was] muddied again' (Rowe 1994: 98). Talk-back radio was sometimes obsessed with sorting out whose alterity was at stake: was this a British view of Australia, or was this an Australian view of itself? How Australians constitute themselves for the other's gaze was central to textual, critical and audience uptake strategies. Once again a local storytelling – despite its *verité* practices – created 'types' and 'stereotypes' not psychological characterizations. It became 'reality soap'.

CONCLUSION

Such a film-making has helped construct Australia as a minor place in the cultural geography of world cinema. The image of Australia that emerges is benign and unflattering. It is a nation of bit characters peopled by harmless though quirky people, by physically unappealing people with limited mental attributes, and by mongrel bastards who murder and dispossess their Aboriginal population, mistreat women, migrants and others. Australia itself becomes a place where weird things happen – both naturally and socially, something to be expected of a society derived from a nation of white crooks/slaves and jailers.

Equally, Australian cinema becomes a cinema peculiarly able to air its society's dirty linen, prepared to look seriously and unflinchingly at its own history, able to dramatize and give dignity to the ordinary, the handicapped and people on its margins, telling stories of people not normally centred in fiction. The Australian film-making that shows Australian racism, sexism and homophobia provides evidence of a tradition of anti-racism, anti-homophobia and anti-sexism sufficiently entrenched to sustain a film-making which excoriates Australian lifeways. Like the New German cinema, the image of Australia as a racist and sexist country is one largely sponsored by Australians and their public institutions.

Australians sometimes see the composite image this cinema creates as a problem. Muriel and Noeline, like Bazza, Mick Dundee and the cast of *Neighbours, embarrasses* them. *Sylvania Waters* encapsulates Australian 'bad taste and lack of distinction' (Rowe 1994: 16). Such film-making also helps underwrite opinion polls which claim Australians lack national self-esteem. But medium-sized countries, liable as they are to buffeting by external forces, cannot afford too much self-esteem. Besides national self-esteem – given its close relation to chauvinism and exclusion – is the last thing any self-respecting nation wants or needs.

Part III

Problematizing Australian cinema

Chapter 11

Problematizing the social

INTRODUCTION

More than a 'film in the film world', Australian film attaches itself to social domains and becomes a vehicle for social problematization. Such problematization is further underwritten by Australian cinema's close relationship to information orders, weaker participation in international genres brought about by its one-off nature, and its reliance upon social intertexts and national specificities in film-making, marketing and audience uptake. Film-making is a prime domain in which changing socio-cultural problematizations occur, both in front of and behind the camera.

If aesthetic structures such as genre, entertainment norms, and industrial and economic practices structure the social texts film and television programmes deploy (such that they form the *cultural requirements* of nearly all film-making), these social texts powerfully enter Australian film-making. film-making requires social texts even when at its most generic. *The Adventures of Priscilla, Queen of the Desert* draws upon national-cultural-social specificities to tell its story. Social texts *are the already discursivized materials of public record*. They provide a ready resource for film-makers supplying a new angle, a new setting, a novel inflection to an old tale. *Priscilla* 'dresses up in drag' the road movie. These specificities provide materials for a film-making described by Harlan Kennedy (1994: 11) in *Film Comment* as combining 'Frederico's [Fellini] kitsch, Robert's [Altman] open plan serendipidy, and Jean's [Renoir] compassion'. The social texts, like the filmic intertexts, formed intertextual points of reference for film reviewers, the film-makers and the film's diverse audiences.

With their smaller budgets, their greater reliance on dialogue – telling as much as showing – their limited capacity to stage spectacle, the one-off character of production and their difficulties in working on the technological cutting edge of special effects, national cinemas like Australia's are more 'sociologically' and 'people' reliant. They rely more on social texts, on human proportions, on modest backdrops and upon the techniques and strategies of what the video shops call 'drama'. Even when working within action, horror and science fiction genres, Australian film-making creatively solves its production budget limitations by focusing less on the public spectacle of machines, objects, and spectacular viruses than on the impact of these sometimes unseen monsters on an *interpersonal* rather than *public* scale. In Rolf de Heer's *Incident at Raven's Gate*, the alien force that kills and transforms people into zombies affects a handful of characters whose relationships with each other are important. The events in turn cannot be made public, as the authorities apparently well used to such happenings ruthlessly want to keep the public from knowing. The *paranoid* qualities of Australian cinema owe as much to the limited production horizons as to any Australian propensity to paranoia.

National-cultural-social specificities are not only represented in film but are *enacted* there as part of the *political* business of film-making. Bureaucracy, politicians, critical institutions and commercial interests have long been in the business of being concerned for the socio-cultural aspects of film-making. As a means of representing society in general and social institutions in particular, film-making is an ideal vehicle for representing socio-cultural problematizations – public concerns, public 'morality' and political messages. film-making processes and film-making institutions are subject to the same general governmental problematization as are other domains of social life – like anti-discrimination, access and equity, and multicultural programmes. In the film-making domain, the selection process for students of the AFTRS is carefully monitored in terms of gender and ethnic outcomes. film-making programmes are explicitly directed toward showing cultural diversity. Statistics are collected on women's participation in the film and television industries. The Federal government's 1994 'Creative Nation Cultural Policy Statement' committed an extra $13 million to the SBS-TV for production dedicated to exploring Australia's cultural diversity. Social problematization does not simply hold the industry publicly accountable, it creates new domains – sustaining film-making spaces and issues.

Cultural critics, governments and commercial interests each provide film-makers with incentives to problematize *in certain directions*. film-makers transform, translate and occasionally lampoon contemporary problematizations. In the ABC's mini-series *The Damnation of Harvey McHugh* (Sarell *et al.* 1994), just such a gentle lampooning of 'political correctness' and 'access and equity' programmes takes place. The eponymous Harvey gets a promotion and the chance of permanency by pretending to be gay. He is acquitted of a charge of attempted political assassination (of which he is innocent), because his friend (also innocent) confesses to the crime to gain public literary recognition from potential readers and Arts bureaucracies sympathetic to prisoners.

The general direction of contemporary social problematizations becomes part of the social tapestry of film production and consumption. *The Adventures of Priscilla, Queen of the Desert* and *The Sum of Us* are sensible against the background of the Sydney Gay and Lesbian Mardi Gras as a nationally televized event in 1994, the acceptance of gays in the military, the treating of gay couples as families in the 1994 census, and an anti-discrimination campaign combating homophobia. Like cultural criticism, film-making often acts as the conscience of government. Christine Sammers's documentary on Australian multiculturalism and national identity *One Australia?* made the case that governmental programmes and community attitudes have not gone far enough.

Socio-cultural problematizations are most directly experienced in the subject and orientation of documentaries where the tenor, phrases and language of socio-cultural problematizations are readily adaptable. Within fiction formats social problematization is relatively direct, as in a 'social problem' film like *Annie's Coming Out* – where the insensitivity of parents and carers to the physically disabled, but not mentally handicapped, is explicitly narrativized. In the thriller, social problematizations are embedded either to mislead the viewer or as a backdrop for the principal story. The Aboriginal deaths-in-custody issue in *Deadly* misleads us as to the true nature of the crime, while the Italo-Australian community and the Italian-based 'mafia' function as a backrop in the mini-series *The Magistrate* (Mueller 1989).

Governmental influence on the direction of social problematization in films can sometimes be direct, as government monies are central to generating part of the production budget for commercial projects and sometimes all the budget for more marginal product. For their part, the investors, distributors and television networks are influenced by governmental problematizations. They also problematize for their own purposes. Television station management's concern with ratings and demographics, their public relations concern to demonstrate themselves as good corporate citizens in touch with changing community attitudes, dictates a certain complicity with and a capacity, at times, to be ahead of the audience. Similarly, a film industry's concern to maximize the paying audience in a market dominated by a late teen/early twenties demography entails adopting and transforming attitudes, values and an emergent social situation consonant with emerging social problematizations, as in *The Heartbreak Kid*. The very need for a storytelling suitable to as many young consumers as possible drove the creation of the television series spin-off of the film, *Heartbreak High*. film-makers, advertisers and television networks have a commercial interest in the extent to which demographic cleavages are cultural cleavages, where generational styles, tastes and cultures might be emerging. Without governmental underwriting, the cinema would still become a vehicle for social problematization, as the social record provides a commercial incentive to follow from and tap public issues. The cinema routinely produces representations that are as much interventions into as they are reflections of social formations.

Social problematizations are drawn from the many axes of differentiation in Australian society like those between ethnicity and ancestry, race, birthplace, class, gender, sexual orientation, region within Australia, age, religious or non-religious affiliation, migrant and Australian-born, Aboriginal and settler, social values and subcultures. *Sunday Too Far Away* is a film about class struggle and class-based identities and values: the vernacular working-class shearer against the employer grazier supported by the state and 'scabs' (strike breaking, non-union labour). For a film criticism within which gender and location are foregrounded, the film becomes another example of Australian cinema's masculinism, the predominance of the male ensemble film on film-making schedules and of the model of industrial citizenship based on working-class men and a cultural preference for the (masculine) bush over the (feminine) city.

Partiality is intrinsic to problematizing social domains and to configuring social life for intervention and illumination. Socio-cultural problematizations necessarily select *some* elements from the dizzying array provided by available axes of cultural and social differentiation. By providing materials to think with, problematizations *shape* film meaning and market film product by *accentuating* an aspect of the film. Such problematizations also *regulate* film meaning, directing film-making and film criticism along certain corridors. Some elements of the cultural mix get foregrounded and represented, some themes and stories get favoured, some axes of cultural differentiation are promoted and some differentiations achieve political and institutional form. Seen from this perspective, Australian society and its cinema is created from a series of axes of cultural differentiation of varying strength and durability, depending on the elements of the cultural mix activated in the film-making, policy making and the political and social record of the day.

Take Stephen Crofts's and Dilys Powell's reviews of *Breaker Morant* in 1980. Crofts does not go along with the social texts, content and thematics of the film, rather he locates its exclusion of women: '*Breaker Morant*'s exclusion of women in any terms other than the sexist, helps consolidate the film's 'Australian' values of mateship and maleness' (420). For Crofts the film promotes a jingoist nationalism. Powell, a British critic, saw a different film. *Breaker Morant* was about 'a new kind of conflict ... modern war'. Citing the climactic speech of the eponymous hero at his trial, she continues:

> In modern war soldiers are changed; you can't understand the changes unless you are involved. The quality of *Breaker Morant* is just that. It involves you in the basics of war. And war changes not the soldier only, it changes all of us. After all, one comes out of Mr Beresford's film sympathizing with a man who shoots his prisoners.
>
> (Powell 1989: 295)

The very provisionality of problematization is partly responsible for the dynamism of film meaning and film culture. The terms of social analysis, value and representation can change quickly becoming in the process a vehicle for a generational changing of the guard in criticism, film-making and film policy domains.

DURABLE CULTURAL DIFFERENTIATIONS

Only some cultural differentiations become the basis for durable projects. These have institutional and structural support in politics, policy-making, government and commerce. Because these institutions shape film-making the cleavages they support are perpetuated as socially and culturally significant. The more important of these are: federal/state/interstate, city/country, locality, social class, generational and subcultural, sexual preference, religious, national and international, Aboriginal and non-Aboriginal, ethnic and gender cleavages. This chapter deals with most of these cleavages – the last two (gender and ethnicity) are dealt with in the next two chapters. Each of these cultural differentiations provides a means of problematizing a social domain, making it available for filmic expression and critical exploration. These cleavages provide continuity and stability *in the foreground and background* of storytelling. One cultural cleavage may be foregrounded in a film and televison programme – like the Greek-Australian ethnicity in *The Heartbreak Kid* – but other cultural cleavages will inevitably criss-cross these like gender, generations, locality and social class (these cleavages provide diverse ways into a film and television programme for a culturally diverse and differentiated audience). Arch Nicholson's *Buddies* (1983) is a 'male buddies film' featuring Anglo men and women (more men than women). It is also a regional film in address and in its exaggeration of its local gem-field culture. It was enthusiastically taken up by audiences in Central and North Queensland but not elsewhere.

As a Western Australian-based documentary film-maker, David Noakes pursued at various times a states-Federal political argument about film-making in the West. In his *How the West was Lost*, Aboriginal/white relations are foregrounded, as the story of colonialism and a pastoral strike in the Pilbara region is told from an Aboriginal perspective. It was not a purely 'regional' story of interest only to Western Australians, it was made to travel nationally and internationally. Its story of the Aboriginal resistance through a pastoral walkout of Aboriginal station hands was told by juxtaposing the community's designated negotiater (white) Don McLeod with the Aboriginal men. With such a predominantly male point of view, Noakes balanced the film by having a female voiceover.

Federal/state/interstate cleavages

These cleavages are not only politically and constitutionally important, but also socio-culturally important. Each of the six states and two territories – and, indeed, their different state capital and major regional centres – have their socio-cultural specificities, their own social and demographic mix, histories, local, national and international orientations, and sense of identity for film-makers to draw on. Melbourne, Sydney and Perth are much more 'multi-ethnic' cities than is Australia's third city, Brisbane, whose phenomenal growth over the last twenty years has been fuelled by internal migration (Brisbane also makes up less than half the total Queensland population, whereas Melbourne, Sydney and Perth dominate their respective states, thereby further ensuring Brisbane's less than achieved hegemony over the state). Perth, for its part, is the most English of Australian capital cities – with the highest proportion of its population, in any capital city, born in the UK. From a Sydney and Melbourne vantage point some of the work coming out of Perth and Brisbane can look old-fashioned and even 'monochrome' (white and Anglo), with out-of-date concerns.

The federal/state/interstate axes are most important at a policy and institutional level – they impose a federal logic upon governmental agencies. These axes are representationally important to the semiotics of Australian politics, sport and informational orders but not so much to fiction.

The importance of geographic/cultural divisions and identities based on state cleavages is indirectly signposted by the careful crafting of Australian television series and serial production toward what Toby Miller (1994b) has usefully called 'the homogenising urban non-specificity of many Australian programmes'. This 'nowhere' space was developed out of the need in the mid-1960s to create a general *Australian television space*. Existing drama series with a local sense of place like *Consider Your Verdict* (1961) were 'too Melbourne' to travel well into the Sydney market and beyond. The solution was a television drama that downplayed *specific geography* and instead emphasized the *commonalities* of its urban (including country city) communities across Australia. In this way, producers sidetracked the deeply felt provincialisms of Australian life generated by the state boosterisms of NSW, Victoria, Queensland, South Australia, Tasmania and the Northern Territory.

City/country (metropolitan/regional) cleavages

The geographical cleavage between city and country cuts across state boundaries. Although less important than in 1947, when the rural population numbered 31 per cent of the total population, in 1986 14.5 per cent of the Australian population were still in rural areas (Ian Castles 1992: 149). These country communities maintain a keen sense of their difference from their urban counterparts. Regional Australia is given some policy recognition, for example, in SBS-TV and ABC-TV's charter. When SBS-TV went national, 'regional diversity' was added to its 'special' mandate. In ABC-TV a regional coverage retains a more structural presence (although it is of less importance than earlier, as there has been a progressive winding back in regional television production infrastructure and a loss of interest in rural storytelling, with the ascendance of the predominantly urban-based multicultural myth).

Additionally, these communities in feature film-making – particularly the 'white' country communities – have come to represent all that is bad in the Australian settler culture and which a metropolitan sensitivity can take its distance from: racism, xenophobia, misogyny, violence, intolerance of difference, homophobia and aggressive masculinism in a film-making stretching from *Wake in Fright* through *Weekend of Shadows* (Jeffrey, 1978) to *The Adventures of Priscilla: Queen of the Desert*. Even the so-called 'nostalgia films' with their rural settings constructed the bush as something you needed to overcome in order to be who you could be (writing rescues Sybylla from rural idiocy in *My Brilliant Career*); it is what you grow out of and leave, as in *The Year My Voice Broke*.

The contemporary reputation of these communities is the inverse to that of the first half of the century, where the 'good' bush was contrasted with the corrupting and wicked city in films like Franklyn Barrett's *The Breaking of the Drought*. The representational significance of the 'bush' and the rural community as a symbol of Australia is under pressure, now that the 'Australian legend' – variously 'man' [*sic*] against 'nature' and a national identity forged by itinerant workers – is criticized for male exclusivism, ethnocentrism and its closeness to the dispossession and continuing marginalization of Aboriginal communities (as a majority of Aboriginal and Islanders live in rural and regional Australia).

Yet these communities – particularly the country town – continue to be a setting for television series, particularly popular television soaps from *Bellbird* through *A Country Practice* and *The Flying Doctors* in the 1980s to *Law of the Land* (1993). Unlike the feature film and mini-series driven by 'big ideas', the ordinary television series exploits the opportunities for interrelatedness, closeness and caring in the country town settings. It permits people of diverse backgrounds, occupations, ages and values to routinely interconnect and collide. Friendships and relationships can be formed across social and cultural cleavages without stretching the bounds of story motivation. The country town functions simultaneously in this storytelling as the (utopian) village community whose friendliness, interrelatedness and closeness also borders on the (dystopian) prospect of a provincial, claustrophobic community intolerant of difference and meddling in each other's affairs. It is simultaneously desired and pushed away in equal measure.

Country town settings in television soaps also function as metaphors for the suburban experience. The distance between *A Country Practice* and the Ramsey Street of *Neighbours* is slight in this regard. This is not what suburbia is, but what it could be. The Australian 'garden' suburb is often modelled on and sold as a kind of *country* living. Like the abstract idea of the suburb, such country town settings often lack geographical specificity: Wandon Valley and Bellbird are nowhere in particular.

David Elfick's work is one of the most interesting treatments of country town/ rural communities. He has attempted to wed a sense of country lifeways to contemporary multiethnic formations. His mini-series *Fields of Fire* connected the established country settler culture, the 'new chum' English migrant, and the marginalized Italian community in the North Queensland cane fields. Here the rural community is a *multicultural community*. *Fields of Fire* spawned two sequels. (Finding multi-ethnic cosmopolitanism in the countryside has its precedent in John Heyer's 1954 classic, *The Back of Beyond*, see Gibson 1992: 80.) Elfick's *No Worries* explicitly connects the (Anglo) rural girl, Matilda, and her parents' loss of their farm and place in the world, with the experience of exile of a Vietnamese child in a multicultural neighbourhood in Sydney. *No Worries* achieved some critical applause but earnt most of its commercial business in screenings in regional Australia where, one suspects, the journey to the city and the hardships and cultural confrontations experienced there became an allegory for urban Australia's marginalization and lack of understanding of the culture of regional Australia.

Another interesting turn in 'rural' representation is provided in Ross Gibson's essay film, *Wild*, which brings Eric Rolls's nativist ecological understanding of the Piliga Forest generated by his farming career and his interest in ecology as described in his book *A Million Wild Acres* (Rolls is also a voice in the film), to Eric Michaels' work on Aboriginal audiovisual tellings. Gibson takes from Rolls his displacement of the predominantly urban-Australian 'myth of the alien bush'.[1] As poet Les Murray would have it:

> A received sensibility almost had me subscribing to its agenda, in spite of my awareness that the bush wasn't alien to me at all, but a deeply loved vastness containing danger and heavy work, but also possessing a blessedly interminable quality which was and is almost my mind's model of contemplation. It was years, though, before I had a character in a verse novel discover that 'the bush is sensible' it'll kill you, but it's – 'decent'.
>
> (L. Murray 1984: 153)

Wild makes central just such a country person's sensibility and aligns it to Aboriginal sensibilities of bush and landscape as cultural materials.[2]

Locality cultural cleavages

The locality-based cultural cleavages are a close relation to federal/state and urban/rural cleavages. Perhaps the most public one is that between Sydney and Melbourne (which also stands as a NSW/Victorian divide). Novelist and scriptwriter, Helen Garner, notes that both Gillian Armstrong's *The Last Days of Chez Nous* and Jane Campion's *Two Friends* (1985) 'were imagined in Melbourne [by her] and shot in Sydney [by them]'. She 'didn't think this would matter', but

> the two big cities of Australia are tonally as distinct from each other as Boston is from LA, or Lyon from Marseilles. The very image of a *house*, on which both films heavily depend, bears one sort of psychological emphasis in warm, open Sydney, and a completely different one in Melbourne, where dwellings are enclosing, curtained, cold-weather resisting: more like burrows.
>
> (Garner 1992: xii)

Given the Sydney and Melbourne base for the Australian film industry and feature film-making and mini-series production's use of locations and historical incident – compared to the studio and controlled environments of long-running television series and serial productions – these 'specificities' have strongly emerged since the 1970s.

Feature film-making and documentary productions emphasize the 'internally exotic' peoples and built and natural landscapes. Such an emphasis is sustained by a repertoire of regionally inflected 'types' – as in the outback type, the country redneck or the traditional Aborigine, and 'regions' – as in the tropics, the desert, the high plains and the rainforests.

A few film-making projects capitalize on 'myths' of regional specificity circulating in the wider society. Carl Schultz's caricature of Queensland's Gold Coast, *Goodbye Paradise* (1983), is unthinkable set anywhere else in Australia. Like the tele-movie, *Joh's Jury*, about the goings on in the jury room for the trial of former Queensland premier (equivalent of a state governor), Johannes Bjelke-Petersen for perjury, this feature attracted its principal audience in Sydney and Melbourne. A programme more akin to the Gold Coast's own (promotional) self-understanding of beach babes and male bimbos, the series *Paradise Beach* (1993), was, by contrast, unable to attract sustainable ratings elsewhere in Australia or on its US release. Its antecedent was possibly Igor Auzins' *High Rolling* (1977) with its escapades of a trio – an American carnival hand (played by Timothy Bottoms), an Australian tent boxer and a 16-year-old young woman hitchhiker – the film had a modest commercial release. (Probably the most successful 'Gold Coast' film is Paul J. Hogan's *Muriel's Wedding* but the fictional town of Porpoise Spit could also be Caloundra, Coffs Harbour (NSW) or Mandurah (WA)).

Social class cleavages

For a society that sometimes presents itself as free of the class divisions found in Britain, social class has been an enduring feature of Australian political institutions, audiovisual representation, and national self-understandings. Social class has been an important marker of *social inequality* because of the importance in the Australian polity of *industrial citizenship* through the different trade unions, the arbitration system, the Australian Labor Party, the once powerful industrial base of the Australian Communists and the labour-based myths associated with Australian nationalism and its icons.

The importance of class-based cleavages and their utopian association with socialism can be seen in the shearers versus the wool growers in *Sunday Too Far Away*, the mine workers versus management in *Strikebound* (Lowenstein 1984), the wharfies in the mini-series *Waterfront* (Thomson 1984), the rural poor in the mini-series *A Fortunate Life* (Cole and Safran 1986), the itinerant workers and their families in *The Battlers* (Ogilvie 1994). The partial decline in the 1980s and 1990s of class-based emphases is not related to the gap between rich and poor diminishing (in fact it has widened). It is a consequence of alternative problematizations of social life and national lifeways – particularly gender, ethnic and indigenous issues – becoming more central. These work off differently constituted notions of disadvantage and history (for these the 'traditional' Anglo male working-class culture is just as likely to be oppressive, misogynist and prejudiced). Yet the institutions representing class divisions are still with us. Since the collapse of communism, class no longer provides a utopian vision of nation. As a consequence, the mini-series *The Battlers*, with its foregrounding of fractured families, structural unemployment and exploitative labour conditions was widely regarded as an 'unmodern' mini-series – a throwback rather than an imaginative retelling of the present.

Generational and subcultural cleavages

Generational cleavages are important social facts. Governments evolve youth and aged policies. Social researchers talk of life cycles and generation gaps. Advertisers capture the youth market. Television ratings supply *demographic* information. Psychological profiles of consumer types are critical to marketing and to launching television series and feature films aimed at 'youth'. Generations become 'knowable' and 'distinct' – the 'baby-boomers' and 'Generation X' become the basis for situation comedy, jokes, documentaries and feature film-making.

Generational cleavages are cultural matters, in that each generation is exposed in their formative youth to a largely *different* archive of musical style, television series and features. The cycles of passionate engagement with music, performers, television drama and films in youth become the basis for the subsequent commercial value of these in the narrowcast environments of video and pay-TV. Generations 'grow up' with different histories of information and style.

These generational cleavages are simultaneously transnational – Madonna in the early 1990s rather than the Beatles of the late 1960s; the video-clip versus the radio star – and locally inflected through 'national' performers and programming. The 1990s is the domain of ABC-TV's *Rage* (1988–   ) rather than the variety format of *Countdown* of the 1970s and early 1980s. The generation that encountered in its formative period the Australian police series – *Homicide, Division 4* and *Matlock Police* (1971) – appreciated different styles than that growing up with *The Heartbreak Kid* and *Home and Away* in the mid-1990s.

Bill Bennett's *Spider and Rose* stages this generational clash of values, musical archive, language use and performance and living styles, by throwing together two 'representative' people of each generation. Spider, the young ambulance driver on his last day of work, is confronted by the equally implacable force of the elderly Rose played by the redoubtable Ruth Cracknell. In its turn, the fact that the film got made is driven by several factors – the intertext of the television sit-com *Mother and Son* in which Cracknell plays the truly monstrous and devious mother, the emerging older demographic in the cinema audience, and the political development of 'grey power' as an identity politics alongside other identity politics.

Then there are the different subcultures, like the surfing subculture of the 1960s that sustained the surf movie, launched David Elfick's career, and formed the basis of *Puberty Blues*'s excoriating critique of the sexism endured by surfie chicks. There is the 'wog' subculture of *Acropolis Now* (1989) and the skinhead culture of *Romper Stomper*.

The most important group interested in subculture and the different generations are the cultural industries – particularly the commercially-based cultural industries. These cleavages can be given a commodity form in part *because they do not impinge so closely on the community idealism* that producers run across by foregrounding, for example, religion, ethnicity or locality. Here it matters that the 'archive' of the second generation youth of a non-English speaking background is significantly shared with that of her or his English-language culture counterparts for whom culture is mostly in English.

Sexual preference cleavages

The mainstreaming of gay and lesbian issues made varieties of sexual preference into cultural cleavages – the majority heterosexual and the minority homosexual one with bisexual preferences in between these. In the social formations of the 1980s and 1990s, gays and lesbians form identifiable communities – which, like diasporic ethnic communities, have their geographical concentrations, bars, bookshops, newspapers, videos and 'public' self-presentations to themselves and the wider community – such as the Sydney Gay and Lesbian Mardi Gras. Gays and lesbians talk of their communities and the 'straight' community. We have already noted some obvious examples of the mainstreaming of gay culture in popular Australian cinema and television – usually involving gay men – such as the transvestites of *The Adventures of Priscilla*, the gay son in *The Sum of Us* and the gay nurse in ABC-TV's soap *G.P.* (1989).

Stephen Dunne, editor of the *Sydney Star Observer* (gay and lesbian community newspaper), when asked to speculate on 'gay culture crossing into the mainstream culture' said:

> Straights seem to like that *frisson* of difference, that slight air of decadence and naughtiness. . . . The way to walk on the wild side in the '90s is to feel that frisson of fun, to blur your sexuality. . . . What's happening with gay culture now is the process all minority groups experience when they stop being reviled and start becoming visible. First you are marginalized, then you are fetishized and considered sexy and dangerous, then you gradually reach the centre and become mainstream.
>
> (Dunne, quoted in Hawley 1994)

With the emergence of heterosexuality and homosexuality as two poles, a middle term has developed consciously to exploit sexual ambiguities in mainstream storytelling. Such a reworking is evident in John Duigan's *Sirens*. The sirens of the title are the sexually liberated women who pose for the controversial artist, Norman Lindsay, in the 1920s and 1930s. The fulcrum of the story is shifted from Lindsay and the clergyman conducting an intellectual argument about Lindsay's work, pornography, and sexuality, to the relationship between the models and the clergyman's wife. Over the course of the film she is sexually liberated. This is achieved through her bonding with the women, with the supposedly 'blind' male artist model, and her coming to terms with the bush. Duigan reworks the Lindsay story so that Lindsay becomes a chronicler of these women's autonomous sexuality and power. His fantastic mythological Amazonian women are made into 'realistic' depictions. The woman has two 'orgasmic experiences' on one night with the male model – she goes to him, and the next night in a dream – as the other female models stroke and caress her naked body as she floats in the water in a rock pool. Lindsay, played by Sam Neill, paints this last stage of the chronicle by inserting the woman as another of the sirens on his recently completed large canvas. These parallel lines of action make the bush into a place of sexual myth.[3]

The prevalence of such ambiguous sexual moments in 1990s film encouraged columnist Mike Gibson to see *Muriel's Wedding* as 'different' and a welcome return to normality(!) in his regular column for the *Daily Telegraph-Mirror* (7 October 1994)

> What makes *Muriel's Wedding* even more remarkable in the current Australian movie making climate is that it's a film about heterosexuals. The romantic scenes actually feature men making love to women ... There are a lot of good things happening in this country.

Apart from the film's insistence that it is women making love to men, the film is not so clearly straightforward. Ultimately, it is a film about the friendship and bond between two women. This friendship – not bonding with a man – is the best thing in Muriel's life. The heterosexual scenes are opportunities for broad comedy, with the single exception being that between Muriel and her husband after Muriel's mother's funeral. And the one really erotic scene, is that between Muriel and her friend on the tropical island – where they lie head to head and talk. At this moment we, the audience, are looking at them erotically, yet they do not do so to each other. This encouraged William Routt to comment in correspondence with the author:

> *Muriel's Wedding* and *Talk* [Lambert 1994] are both about women who are just good friends, and both have these narrow-escape heterosex sex scenes, in some kind of hysterical proof that these women are just good friends, just good friends. Neither film needs the heterosex. Neither film even allows the women to construct or to see each other erotically, although we see them erotically. What's going on? Why can't they just fall into each other's arms – just once? The love that dares not speak its name, dares not speak its name again.

Religious cleavages

Religion continues to be an important cultural differentiation. In the 1986 census, 26 per cent of the population registered as Catholic, 24 per cent Anglican, and 23 per cent other Christian, 25 per cent of the population did not state a religious affiliation, while non-Christian religions made up 2 per cent (of this 2 per cent, 35 per cent were Muslims, 25 per cent Buddhists and 20 per cent Jews). Religion is another cultural cleavage connecting and dividing Australians. It opens on to so many communities of association, education, marriage and social training. For some of these denominations church and ethnicity are coterminous – Greeks and the Greek Orthodox faith, for instance, provide one of the reasons for Greeks not marrying as much outside their community and creates a seamless connection between the Greek community clubs and the church. The same thing happens with the British and Anglicanism. For others the church is a *multi-ethnic* institution. Australian Catholicism takes in people of an Irish, Italian, Polish, Dutch, Portuguese, Croatian and Vietnamese background, not to mention converts from a variety of backgrounds. Likewise Australian Jewry takes in, for example, people of a Russian, Polish, German, English, Middle Eastern and North American background. Australian Islam combines peoples from the Middle East, Turkey, Bosnia, the Indian sub-continent and South-East Asia. Within these multicultural church frameworks cross-cultural marriages are facilitated (remember how Nino convinces Kay's father of the rightness of her choice of man in *They're a Weird Mob*, by pointing out the Italian given pride of place on her father's wall: the Pope). Denominational schools and church associations become the basis of intermarriage patterns and life-long friendships.

One of the important transformations of Australian society wrought by its post-Second World War mass immigration programme was the emergence of Catholicism as the largest single religious denomination to displace Anglicanism. This demographic fact is marked by the foregrounding of Catholicism in three high-profile and hugely successful 1990s mini-series. From the brutal Catholic orphanages in the bush of the 1950s in *The Leaving of Liverpool* to the 1960s setting of *Brides of Christ* (about a group of nuns experiences of the Church's modernization after the Second Vatican Council of 1962–5) to the contemporary *The Damnation of Harvey McHugh*, in which the hero is a devout Catholic boy negotiating a determinedly 'worldly' public service. *Brides of Christ*, the most uncompromisingly Catholic in its attentions, achieved extraordinary ratings for the ABC in both its screenings – even its third screening on a commercial network achieved impressive ratings. While Australian Catholicism has been represented before – most notably in Fred Schepisi's 1975 feature *The Devil's Playground* – it has never had this kind of centrality in popular storytelling.[4] When, on rare occasions, it turned to religion, popular film-making before the 1960s explicitly centred on Protestant clergy in a storytelling which did its best to de-Australianize itself, like Ken Hall's *The Silence of Dean Maitland*. There, the story of a clergyman's temptation and subsequent cover-up of a murder takes place in a setting which, while never announcing itself as British, none the less looked that way.

Australian storytelling, like its Anglo-American and British counterpart, has focused a determinedly secular story-space.[5] Sometimes the explanation for a lack of religious storytelling is sought in Australians' lack of religiosity. Although the proportion of atheists and agnostics – like myself – is probably highest among cultural producers and critics, the fact religion does not enter so powerfully into myths of nation and society projected in the cinema may lie, paradoxically, in its continuing importance. The bitter sectarian cleavages – between varieties of

Protestantism and Protestants and Catholics – that marked Australian social life until the 1960s, pitted a largely Irish-derived Catholic minority against an English-derived Anglican (the largest church denomination until the 1980s) and non-conformist Scottish churches (Presbyterian, Methodist). If Australia was overwhelmingly Christian, signposting this necessarily led to sectarian questions and with it religious and political rivalries and fractious ethnically-derived community idealisms. A consensus politics kept a lid on sectarianism and a 'new world' production strategy looked to less schismatic cleavages. Not surprisingly, Australian storytelling tends to downplay such religio-cultural cleavages – moving either on to the safer ground of 'ethnic colour' provided by the stage Irish, the Scot, the Cockney or Jew (Mo – Roy Rene) – and the later and similar ethnic stereotypes – or alternatively addressing a general and not specifically Australian religious experience with, it must be said, the inflections of Protestantism. (This is, after all, the country which sometimes claims as its first feature film the retelling of the story of Christ and early Christian martyrs in *Soldiers of the Cross* (Perry and Booth 1900) and for whom Hollywood religious spectaculars and books pulled significant audiences.)

Charles Chauvel's foundation 'myth' story, *Sons of Matthew*, is one of the few important Australian features in which religion is mixed with nation and ethnicity. (The biblical overtones to this creation story were emphasized when, during the screening of the film to a class, a janitor in his fifties stepped into the theatre – and remembered the music and the name of the film 'Sons of Adam'!). The film is important for what it does not say as much as for what it does. As the historical audience would be only too well aware – the English Protestant Jane has married the Irish Catholic Matthew. Their progeny the 'first Australian O'Riordan', Shane, is most like his mother while the second born Barney (significantly the Celtic redhead) is most like his father. Both men are rivals for Cathy McAllister (the 'Australian' McAllister of a Scottish father). Cathy in her turn is most like – and even looks like – Jane. Her move from Barney to Shane is explicitly signposted as her growth to maturity (the mother tells Barney: 'as a woman she chose Shane') and destiny – in Shane's words: 'You are the Earth, Cathy. That's all I want'. Shane's conflation of woman and earth leads back to his Irish ancestry. Like his father he is marked by his love for the soil – the only character who shares this passion is the Scottish-descended Cathy (a Celtic 'brotherhood'/'sisterhood' perhaps?). Australia becomes the 'promised land'; the Tambourine mountains a 'new Israel'. And the sons' and Cathy's period in the rainforests become their 'testing' and 'purgation', like Christ's in the desert. (Significantly, in this the driest continent on Earth, their testing involves coming to terms with the wet.)

The film wisely says nothing of the contemporary politics of the mixed marriage (not long after this film was made in 1948, my Catholic father asked my Protestant mother to marry him with the words 'will you marry me in my church').[6] Rather the film focuses on the shared Christian religious observances – prayers and grace. It self-consciously emplots this Australian creation story within religious coordinates: its opening frame quotes from the New Testament. And the mother, Jane, is consistently posed as the Madonna figure. The film works a double union – an overt staging of a unity of faith in Christianity – out of sectarian differences presumed by the historical audience – and a 'national union' of different nationals (English, Irish and Scots) creating a new unity: their Australian children. The film's utopian spell sacrifices sectarian and ethnic idealisms to the higher unities of Christianity and the Australian, as a holy, secular family.

Sons of Matthew also provides the first explicit representation of the Australian as a member of a new ethnic division and a distinct persona – the Anglo-Celt. It incorporates the previously marginalized Irish Catholic component, placing the Irish in the ambiguous position of the father (who becomes in the creation story harmless, impotent Joseph) to the stronger English Protestant Mother (Mother Mary, Jane). In its turn the film marginalizes both in favour of their progeny, the mix of both – the (Anglo-Celtic) Australian. *Sons of Matthew* provides one of the first expressions of a truce in the sectarian/ethnic conflicts between Irish (a working-class minority) and English (the middle-class majority) with the Scots, as ever, somewhere in between the two. Australia becomes the new Israel in another sense: the bitter ethnic and nationalist conflicts of the British Isles are 'resolved' in Australia by being made matters of family and blood. The culturally Christian Anglo-Celt succeeds a diasporic sense of Britishness. If Britishness only half-heartedly incorporated the more independently inclined Celtic component – the Irish and Scots – the Anglo-Celt inscribed them at the centre. (It is worth remembering that when Australia was 'British to the bootstraps' in the 1950s, surveys showed some 20 per cent of the population – predominantly of Irish descent – favoured the abolition of the Queen as head of state.)

While Australia is still predominantly a Christian country, the marked and marginalized religious cleavages are not based around the major but the minority churches, cults and non-Christian churches – usually but not necessarily built on ethnicity (the extraordinary rise in importance of Christian fundamentalist and evangelical churches in the 1980s and 1990s is determinedly 'new world' in its strategies). These Muslim, Christian fundamentalist and other minority religions occupy the position of repressive tolerance that the Catholic church did for the first half of a century of film-making. The Seventh Day Adventist family, Lindy and Michael Chamberlain, in Schepisi's *Evil Angels* is condemned by a bigoted society for their 'difference', which includes their religious difference. The same evangelical church in Bob Ellis's semi-autobiographical film, *The Nostradamus Kid* (1993), is mocked for its fundamentalism, its sexual repressions and its intolerances by its determinedly athiest storyteller.

The Aboriginal and Islander/non-Aboriginal (settler) cleavage

The cleavage between the indigenous and settler culture(s) has become increasingly central since 1970, when the logic and claim of Aboriginal and Islanders as first peoples began to be made in its contemporary form. This is not only an equal rights claim for 'an equitable share in the distribution of goods in society' (although Aboriginal activists' were successful in the 1950s and 1960s through appeals to equal rights, equal opportunities and an end to discriminatory treatment) but, like the Amerindians, 'they feel that their historic ownership of their respective lands should entitle them to something more' (Sykes 1989: 215). The second part of the Aboriginal claim has taken longer to be publicly recognized, but has been central from the 1970s in, for example, Michael Mansell's activism. Citizenship rights, land rights, self-determination, Aboriginal deaths in custody, native title and an agenda of reconciliation all mark a quarter of a century of the Aboriginal presence being raised as a central political and moral issue for Aboriginal and non-Aboriginal Australia.

In this period Aboriginal and Islanders have achieved a degree of symbolic centrality in projects and discourses not entirely of their making. Their 'care for the country' is a routine part of the environmental argument against ecological destruction and development. As the first Australians, they have pride of place in a decolonizing Australian nationalism, marking the first peoples that belonged here and made this their home (unlike the 'problem' identity for other Australians, Aboriginal and Islanders are seen as having a secure identity and sense of belongingness).[7] Aboriginal and Islanders constitute the settler culture's 'original sin' – they are the peoples whose country 'we' invaded, who 'we' dispossessed. Their dispossession is becoming – like slavery and the US state – the settler culture's 'original sin', its genocide, its holocaust, its guilty history, as in Tom Haydon's documentary *The Last Tasmanian*. Political documentaries often made with the collaboration of Aboriginal communities chart this usurpation over the twentieth century, as in Frank Rijavek and Noelene Harrison's *Exile and the Kingdom* which shows the consequences first of the pastoral and pearling invasions and then by mining in the Pilbara region of Western Australia. The Mabo High Court decision recognizing the persistence of native title gave symbolic, public and legal recognition to settlement as a process of usurpation. This decision is also the biggest and most long-running news event in Australian newspaper, radio and television history.

Aboriginal survival and activism ensures that the settler culture has to re-imagine itself not as victim of imperial predation and colonial or neo-colonial servitude, but as a perpetrator and oppressor of indigenous peoples. Foregrounding the logic of first peoples necessarily re-invisages colonial history. It problematizes the 'pioneer legend', it disturbs the comfortable legitimacy of settler institutions and lifeways, and it necessitates reconciliation as a public project. Feature films of the 1970s as diverse as John Honey's *Manganinnie*, Schepisi's *The Chant of Jimmie Blacksmith* and Igor Auzins' *We of the Never Never* (1982) are part of this re-envisaging.

Aboriginal and Islanders are also a 'problem' community for government, bureaucracy, citizenship, health authorities and policing. Aboriginal male violence and drunkenness is a social problem in *State of Shock*. They are second class citizens forced into the bottom of the labour market in *Lousy Little Sixpence* (Alec Morgan 1983). They are the most disadvantaged minority in *One Australia?*. They are a problem for policing as an unruly and homeless people in *Genocide* (Oxenburgh 1990). They are often welfare-dependent (significantly the collaboration documentary, *Two Laws*, defines one of its breakdowns of their history as 'welfare times'). No other group in Australia has been subjected to what Brian Winston once called 'the tradition of the victim' in the documentary and social problem film-making. The issue is not that Aboriginal social problems are focused, but rather the *ways* in which they are focused. As John Hartley put it to the Aboriginal Royal Commission into Black Deaths in Custody hearing, 'in stories about them Aborigines are not included as part of the audience for these stories.' As a marginal group, their rights to consent to be filmed were often abrogated by documentary and current affairs programmes; as 'social problems' their spokespersons were – and to an extent still are – ignored in favour of the more 'authoritative' (and white) experts. Current affairs and documentaries on the 'Aboriginal problem' whether about health, drunkenness, or housing have been with us from the start of television and still structure films like *Fringe Dwellers* and *Blackfellas*.

Anthropological ways of knowing Aboriginal and Islanders have been sustained by traditions of ethnographic and observational film-making. From the 1970s the ethnographic interest increasingly gave Aboriginal subjects some control over the process of filming (Loizos 1993: 185). The involvement of political activists like Martha Ansara and Essie Coffey in *My Survival as an Aborigine*, and Cavadini and Strachan in *Two Laws*, opened out additional opportunities for Aboriginal/non-Aboriginal collaboration and forged new audiences. *Survival* linked Aboriginal and feminist concerns, *Two Laws* brought together the ethnographic and the political film. Both provided new ways of imparting cultural information – colonizing, if you like, these forms for Aboriginal purposes.

The massive and diversified interest in, and presence of, Aboriginal and Islanders on the public record is not always wanted by Aboriginal and Islanders. They object to stories that they do not create, or at least, co-create because such stories impact on them. These stories provide the wider community with ways of 'knowing Aborigines' which Aborigines then need to negotiate. The imbalances involved in this 'authoring', see the Aboriginal emerge as a 'figure of discourse' in the absence of continuing interchange such that, as Marcia Langton has trenchantly put it:

> Australians do not know and relate to Aboriginal people. They relate to stories told by former colonists.
>
> (1993: 33)

Part of the Aboriginal and Islander criticism is that such tellings focus the way Aboriginal and Islanders are meaningful to non-Aboriginals, rather than how Aboriginal and Islanders are meaningful to themselves. They foreground an unequal hetero-identification at the expense of an auto-identification. These circumstances provide the background for Aboriginal demands for complete 'control' over their representation. But as Marcia Langton (1993) points out, this is not always realistic or desirable:

> To demand complete control of all representation, as some Aboriginal people naively do, is to demand censorship, to deny the communication which none of us can prevent.
>
> (10)

Instead of imposed identities and the utopian demand for complete control Langton proposes how Aboriginal and non-Aboriginal might together forge 'intersubjective' spaces. Wal Saunders, an Aboriginal working for the Australian Film Commission's Indigenous Branch, suggests that in these matters

> There are only two ways to go: either stop non-indigenous film-makers from using government money to make films about Indigenous people, or to allow only collaborative projects which ensure that Indigenous people have the right to creative and artistic control. In light of the fine works that have come from such collaboration, I personally opt for the latter.
>
> (1994: 7)

Saunders' agenda for a more codified 'collaboration' is part of an Aboriginal and Islander strategy of reappropriating and renegotiating the terms of representation in each of these larger 'fields of interest'. Collaboration means here a more central bargaining position for Aboriginal and Islanders in the shaping of film meaning. It is the middle position between complete control and no controls. In a sense it is also necessary, because structurally an indigenous cinema is limited by its relatively small population base of 1.5 per cent of the Australian population and a chronically disadvantaged and dependent condition.

As in feminism, the logic develops for both mainstreaming and a separate film-making space. A host of different strategies emerge: videotape exchanges, Aboriginal programme windows on ABC-TV, indigenous 'public broadcasting' – what Eric Michaels called 'the Aboriginal invention of television'. The ABC and SBS have developed Aboriginal employment strategies. A market in Aboriginal consultants has emerged. Aboriginal training is increasingly mandated as part of processes of filming Aboriginal and Islanders stories. Producer Rachel Perkins has spoken of the need for Aboriginal and Islanders to take over educating whites about Aboriginal and Islander culture. In their turn, governmental knowledges and sites are increasingly becoming Aboriginalized, with the advent of policies and institutions of Aboriginal and Islander self-determination like the Aboriginal and Torres Strait Islander Commission. Marcia Langton identifies the need for decolonizing public institutions, the film industry and the broader processes of public storytelling.

Aboriginal and Torres Strait Islanders are increasingly involved in film and television production and decisions on the use to which the filmic past which used them for its own purposes can be applied to Aboriginal purposes. The results can be unpredictable, as Teshome Gabriel and the Australian Film Commission found out in 1988:

> we hosted an Australian film series sponsored by the Australian Film Commission. I happened to have been one of the advisors and was shown the list of films and categories under which they were to be screened. One of the categories was 'aboriginal films', coming under the title of 'Savage Cinema'. I was shocked and surprised at this kind of open bigotry. We subsequently called the Australian Film Commission about the offensive nature of this title. They responded that they too had been astonished, but that the word 'savage' was used at the request of the Aborigines themselves. Little did anyone know that the (ab)Origines were screening the word 'savage' and reclaiming historical ruin, as a kind of privilege – as an emblem.
>
> (Teshome Gabriel 1993: 213)

And what turned out to be predictable (read 'normative') was 'our' non-Aboriginal response, our sense of what was a possible and available position for Aboriginal film-makers and curators. The excitement Gabriel finds in this reclaiming is surely one of pleasures to be had from Tracey Moffatt's work, in for example *Nice Coloured Girls* and *beDevil*.

David Bradbury's *State of Shock* culminates in a second climax late in the film. It is the most disturbing part of this documentary. The moment is a straightfoward observational recording of a drunk Peters, a failed marriage behind him, swaying to his feet after being bucked off in a rodeo. The camera lingers excruciatingly long on him. The image resonates culturally. Yes, he's a public spectacle. He's the drunk Aboriginal that the street derides. The image carries outside the film: a significant image which encapsulates the Aboriginal person as victim, as social problem. But the film also reaches out and 'wins back' this image. Peters is the human being we have come to know well and like during the film. The image of him out of control encapsulates his and his family's tragedy. By now, we look at him from his mother's point of view – a woman of extraordinary strength and humility who does not walk away from the situation no matter how critical she is of it and her own problems (her eyes are hidden behind sunglasses owing to the consequences of a stroke). Remembering this, I note that alcoholism and other drug addictions are not unusual among one's own relatives and friends. *State of Shock* helped me understand something more about these. Peter's mother made me reflect on my own limited capacity for compassion.

Some felt Bradbury's first Australian film should have been another big-picture issue, like his Vietnam war story, *Frontline*, his Nicaraguan story *Nicaragua no Pasaran* (1984) or his Chilean story *Chile: hasta Cuando?* (1985). Instead he focused on the Aboriginal social problem of male domestic violence and drunkenness, crafting these as having to do with dispossession and systematic mistreatment. Alcoholism became a political and personal issue. For some Aboriginal people Bradbury's showing of Peters in a drunken state was unethical. He breached all the rules and confirmed the worst stereotypes of Aboriginal people.

Wayne Barker, the director of *Milli Milli* (1993), felt impelled to tackle Bradbury, to 'not let him get away with it'. For her part Langton defended the film for its sympathetic consideration of drunkenness.

The national/international cleavage

National and international cleavages are important because they help establish a sense of collective identity by showing how we are different from 'them', and they clear space for identities other than 'ourselves'. As Schlesinger (1994: 27) observes:

> How we define the other and how the other simultaneously defines us are part of the unavoidable game of identity politics. We are defined, in part at least, by being different from how they are.

He argues that this process is part of *all* identity politics whether it is staged at an international, national or subnational level.

The national/international relation has been posed mostly as Australia versus the culturally proximate, stronger and larger UK, the USA and, to a lesser extent, continental European formations. But within the Pacific, this international relation is not based on Australian cultural, economic or military weakness or its post-colonial status. There Australia cannot be the victim, but is the culturally and economically strong power – particularly with New Zealand, Nui Guinea and the Pacific Island states. Australian cinema's interest in the Pacific is inescapably due to colonial expansion, particularly in Nui Guinea. The Pacific states are part of the larger Australian sphere of political, economic and cultural influence. Excluding New Zealand, its Pacific interests a *continuation* of Australia's own internal colonization of its Aboriginal and Torres Strait Islander populations. Many of Australia's best film-makers made Nui Guinea and Pacific films: Maslyn Williams, Lee Robinson, Robin Anderson, Bob Connolly, Dennis O'Rourke and Charles Chauvel. Their films are also an *extension* of the Australian film-making which deals with and involves Aboriginal and Torres Strait Islanders. It was a small step for Lee Robinson to move from the central Australian landscapes of his *Namitjira the Painter* (1946) and *The Phantom Stockman* to the Nui Guinea landscapes of *Walk into Paradise*.

Such film-makers are naturally less concerned with exotic indigenes than with societies in transition interacting with the wider world. They examine specific political agendas and fraught relations with modern lifeways, bureaucratic structures and policing methods. The deep ambivalences of O'Rourke's *Cannibal Tours* and *The Good Woman of Bangkok* are testimony to this. His work revolves around an uncomfortable degree of implication – on and off-screen – by the film-maker. He is the voyeuristic tourist consuming the 'Other' in his Nui Guinea film, *Cannibal Tours*; he is also the 'Other' looking back at us. His uncomfortable double vision is viewed as culturally insulting to the Other – how can he be both 'us' and 'them'? And what is he doing imagining himself as the Other (a Bangkok prostitute in *The Good Woman of Bangkok*, while using her like all the other drunken Western men?), or culturally sensitive (by being prepared to recognize the intersubjectivity involved and his own implication – daring to represent and be both white Western sex tourist and Thai prostitute?)

These Pacific and increasingly Asian ambivalences are structural to Australian film-making. Australians cannot easily talk about cultural distance without allowing that Asia-Pacific peoples are already *in their midst* and are an integral, longstanding if minor part of the Australian mix. 'They' are not other, they are 'ourselves'. A descendant of Australia's Pacific slave trade in the sugar industry in the nineteenth century, Mel Meninga, retired in 1994 as the well-loved and respected captain of the Australian rugby league team. Additionally, the peoples of the Pacific and Asia make up an increasingly significant minority population in Australia, whether they be the New Zealand Maoris of Port Headland and Bondi, the Fijian population of Sydney or the Singaporean population in Leeming, Perth. Pauline Chan is now an established film-maker with her first feature, *Traps* (other film-makers include Teck Tan and Laleen Jayamanne).

Joe Leahy's Neighbours (Connolly and Anderson 1988), as its title suggests, is about the neighbours of plantation owner and mixed race Joe Leahy (Nui Guinea mother, Australian father). Because it tries to explore the position of the indigenous man confronting and attempting to negotiate the first world and its international commodity trade, we feel deeply ambivalent about Joe Leahy. For some viewers he represents commodity capitalism 'ripping off the locals'.

By their next film, *Black Harvest* (1992), Joe Leahy unexpectedly becomes centred. We start to feel sorry for him. World coffee prices destroy his livelihood. Tribal conflict leaves the coffee unpicked. He becomes a pariah and he travels to Brisbane seeking immigration to Australia. The film-makers finally recognize their identity with Joe Leahy. Like him, they are outsiders. Unexpectedly the film forces its audience to recognize Joe Leahy not simply as a native Nui Guinea entrepreneur but as an Australian, socially, culturally and yes biologically. The film-makers show him inhabiting Australian culture, living in an Australian-style house. He sends his children to Australian boarding schools. When he is shown with his family in Brisbane seeking citizenship, *he manifestly belongs there*. But if Australia owes a duty of care to Joe Leahy it also owes one to his neighbours. The trilogy traces a movement back to the original Australian carpet-bagging involvement in the Nui Guinea highlands that produced the Australian-Nui Guinean Joe Leahy.

Within the (South-East and East-) Asian context, Australian cinema's interest is also part of a *fascination* with this more culturally distant but geographically proximate region, in titles as diverse as *The Man from Hong Kong*, *The Year of Living Dangerously* and *Bali Tryptich*. It is part of the larger European and Western regard for the predominantly Third World and the newly developing Asian countries. Australian film-makers are representatives of the stronger European-defined and -derived West, surveying a weaker Third World, Asia. A specialty of Australian film-making and academia alike is its Asian knowledges.

Australian directors produce and make films about Asia and the Pacific for international Western consumption. They provide representations of Asia in the dominant language of English and for first world consumption. *The Year of Living Dangerously* is one of the few international representations on film of the events leading up to Suharto's military takeover in Indonesia.

Australia's 'Asian interest' occupies a different ideological and conceptual space than its Pacific involvements, by virtue of these different histories. Australia is implicated in Asia not through colonial expansion but exclusionary settlement policies: it is a country founded in part on racial exclusion – on 'white Australia's' desire to remain British and European. It is also implicated by virtue of its participation in the decolonizing process. Its Vietnam adventure saw it fight on the losing side in what was, after all, also a civil war (something Vietnamese Australians often remind left liberals, who want to only see Australia's involvement in the Vietnam War as a neo-colonialist adventure imposed on the Vietnamese rather than part of the continuing struggles between the north and the south). It assisted the British in securing and guaranteeing the territorial integrity of the modern Malaysian state in the 1950s and 1960s. Such involvements parallel its contemporary role in attempting to broker the peace in Cambodia.

With Australia's Asia-Pacific identity becoming an issue, as trading and immigration dynamics configure Australia as increasingly 'part of Asia' and the Pacific, Australian storytelling – like its political and foreign affairs history – is coming under sustained scrutiny. In this context, the problem has become one of *looking*. Sylvie Shaw suggests Australian/Asian films such as *Blood Oath*, *Far East* and the mini-series *Bangkok Hilton* 'are looking more at our national psyche and say more about Australians than they do about Asia' (quoted in Berry 1994: 33). She thinks this is inappropriate: these texts should look more at Asia and Asians. Evidence for this failure of looking is found in the proliferation of insulting stereotypes. Sylvie Shaw suggests that Asians are typically 'the thug, the enemy, the prostitute, the victim, the drug baron and the drug runner'. For her part, Suvendrini Perera (1993: 17) writes that the *Year of Living Dangerously*, *Turtle Beach* (Wallace 1992) and the Australian drama series *Embassy* produce South-East Asia as 'a surrogate Middle East of Islam, despotism, violence, oil and sex, a storehouse where young boys as well as women circulate as endlessly accessible objects of desire and of destruction'.

For Shaw and Chris Berry, 'hetero-identification' seems to be the problem. Berry argues that Australian representations of Others should not 'function as metaphors for . . . [a] sense of collective identity' (Berry 1994: 33). It becomes a problem that the Other is not used for him or herself but to establish 'us' ('Westerners', Australians). The film-making featuring an Australian abroad – often an innocent, ignorant Australian – who gains knowledge and experience over the course of a film is, as Berry observes, a close relation to an ethnographic film-making describing a people and a place unfamiliar to the viewer. For Berry, Connolly and Anderson's documentary trilogy absents the local, turning Australians into observers rather than participants, telling stories about others without implicating themselves – 'Australians are not the same as "them"' (Berry 1994: 41, see also 42–6).

But Shaw and Berry overstate their case. 'Hetero-identification' as such is not the issue but, as Berry elsewhere recognizes, the kinds of 'hetero-identification'. Hetero-identifications are unexceptionally a part of all identity politics. The problem is not the path leading from innocence to knowledge, or various foreign nationals helping the Australian in his or her journey, the issue is the extent to which these stories include those peoples as part of their Australian and international audience.[8]

Like Langton's insistence on Aboriginal representation, Berry wants room for intersubjective negotiation. He insists on the unequal cultural exchanges involved, and the different speaking positions appropriate to them. It is not a problem, for example, that villains in Hong Kong cinema are Europeans (usually Americans) or African-Americans. It is defensible as an example of the colonized fighting back against the colonizer. The generic and action-base of the Hong Kong cinema also makes it inoffensive, calling as it does on a long tradition of Hollywood cinema in which screen monsters, villains and psychopaths are predominantly white and, to a lesser extent, black. Such casual 'racism' in the Hong Kong cinema does not get in the way of Western audiences appreciating Kung Fu movies, nor do they typically occasion diplomatic incidents. Part of Hollywood's very popularity turns on its capacity to show American evil through hyperbolic representations of its own social, cultural and political dysfunctionality. And this is a temptation to any national cinema to itself produce *American* villains as Phil Noyce did in *Dead Calm*, where Billy Zane played the monstrous (American) villain that the Nicole Kidman character needed to seduce and kill in order to rescue her husband.

Australian cinema and television's one-off basis and its often close connection to the historical record means it is often less fantasy-based than the Hong Kong or Hollywood cinemas. Even when it is at its most generic, as in *The Year of Living Dangerously*, Australian film-making is prone to public criticism within and outside Australia. Here the sensitivity of Malaysian, Singaporean and Indonesian governments meets the sensitivities of an Australian-based multiculturalism critical of representations of Australia's internal cultural diversity and its external relations. Both result in the most problematic area of Australian cinema's outreaching becoming its Asian-based storytelling and documentary depiction (Australia's Asian imaging is no worse than its Fijian, Nui Guinean and Pacific Islander imaging; it is just that this criticism carries more clout).

Perhaps the one area where 'hetero-identification' is unequivocally a *dialogue* is the Australian–Japanese relation. Thinking about Japan in Australian cinema takes us out of the simplistic 'Orientalist' frame. Japan is the world's second largest economy, it is Australia's largest trading partner. It was the imperial, fascist power whose aircraft levelled Darwin in the Second World War. It has a long and continuing history of racial exceptionalism. Its treatment of its Korean and now Philipino and Vietnamese minorities is as ugly as the treatment of some minorities in Australia. Its atrocities and genocide in the Pacific in the Second

World War parallel Australia's genocide of its Aborigines. The violence in the East- and South-East Asian theatres of the Second World War was massively and acutely a Japanese violence. Japan is patently not a 'victim'. It is a first world power. It can only project itself as 'a Third World country' in cultural terms if its terms of reference are the USA (Yoshimoto 1991: 256).

Between Australia and Japan is a set of reciprocations turning inevitably on the Second World War and the post-war peace. Nagisa Oshima's *Merry Christmas, Mr Lawrence* (1982) is a close relation to *Blood Oath* and the Kennedy-Miller produced mini-series, *Cowra Breakout* (Noyce and Noonan 1985). All encourage their audience to adopt the Asian and European Australian perspective simultaneously. In *Cowra Breakout*, this is achieved through its story of initial personal and national enmity and later personal friendship between an Australian soldier, Stan and a Japanese soldier, Gunji. Their enmity develops over the bloody Kokoda campaign, while their friendship in the prisoner-of-war camp develops at Cowra in New South Wales. Paralleling their friendship is the action of the officers in charge, who precipitate the events leading up to the breakout (both are shown to be cowards). The would-be Samurai and Stan's commanding officer become the representatives of the older order – just as Stan and Gunji are shown as the moral leaders, pointing to the understanding and commitment to work together marking the post-war period.

Cowra Breakout projects a space of Japanese–Australian dialogue and mutual understanding out of the ashes of an horrific war that is one utopian Australian projection of the special relationship between Australia and Japan. But there is, of course, limited scope for reciprocicity. Japan is becoming more important for Australia's symbolic economy; more important than Australia ever will be for the Japanese symbolic economy.[9]

CONCLUSION

Social problematization can usefully be regarded as part of the cultural materials of the cinema alongside technology, genre, formats, and audience preferences that all film-makers need to work with. The social and political problematizations have to be translated into film. This poses particular problems. One of the most successful producers of 'multicultural' film-making, Franco di Chiera, usefully distinguishes between political concepts and the requirements of attracting an audience:

> Look, 'multiculturalism' is fine, but it really is a political concept. It has some relevance to the everyday reality of Australia, but in the end when you're making television there's no point even discussing that, unless you make something that is going to attract an audience.
>
> You can be tokenistic as much as you like, but it's not going to be of interest to an audience. . . . Change only happens slowly. You can really get people's backs up otherwise.
>
> (Quoted in Schembri 1994)

I take di Chiera to be suggesting that social problematization has clear limits. It is not simply expressed in film; it is transformed on and by film including the cultural materials audiences bring to it. The sociologizing projects for Australian cinema run against the naturalizing aspects of the cinema: the available technical, economic, performative and generic repertoires of the cinema and its (international and nationally) politically determined market forms and business practices. These do not only function as services and instruments to be used to further the ends of the people-among-themselves; but they serve as ends in themselves, whether as entertainment or as cultural spaces to inhabit and through which to forge identities.

Outside the smaller, esoteric networks of circulation which permit relatively 'pure' expressions of social problematization in the political documentary, mainstream film-making requires that social problematization be made more impure, problematic, entertaining and riveting. To be successful a popular film's work of social problematization – its translation, mediation and hierarchization – needs to seduce, convince, enlist, divert and entertain its audience. In its turn, entertainment makes problematizations its own, enlisting the social purposes of problematization to its own diversionary purposes. When Tom Cowan made *Journey Among Women* he and his feminist collaborators produced a low budget feature that provided a statement about women and the colonial process, the colonization of women by men from the beginning of European settlement/invasion. One of the women involved wrote a novel based on the film published by Penguin. These were serious purposes, serious social problematizations. The film took the archetypes developed out of the Sydney feminist avant-garde filmmaking and literalized feminist-critical metaphors. But the film found another audience which made it, in return on investment terms, one of the most profitable of 1970s revival films. It found a niche in the then drive-in market. Its circulation remade it into the quintessential exploitation pic – naked women in the bush, a touch of the lesbian, men being 'punished' by women – that would have done Roger Corman proud. To be successful and sustain careers film-makers one must appreciate such ambiguities of circulation.

The cinema is built upon problematizations of various kinds. Our disputes as critics and concerned film-makers are often over kinds of problematizations, they turn on heirarchies of problematization. The film culture, society and the 'chattering classes' (of which I am a member) establish canonical problematizations that are ultimately matters of value. Governments do it, critics do it, film-makers do it, journalists do it. The ideological realism which presents us with, 'this is the way it is' or 'this is how it really is' is a facet of all film-making. Our social problematizations are associated with particular film-making strategies and formal techniques. The meaning, use and ideological value of a particular repertoire of film-making techniques turns on their positioning within a broader rhetorical, political and aesthetic field. Alternative independent cinema links progressive problematization with anti-realist and constructivist repertoires, such that the progressive independent film 'constructs' and self-consciously makes its case, while the mainstream film is seen to treat the social as self-evidently the way it is/ was. Some of these linkages between particular social problematizations and film-making techniques have been relatively durable – think here of the Brechtian legacy evident for at least three decades of political film-makers and most powerfully evident in John Hughes' Benjamin 'film essay' *One Way Street*, or the transnational stabilization of technique and social meaning in feminist cinema that connects Helen Grace's *Serious Undertakings* to Laura Mulvey and Peter Wollen's *Riddles of the Sphynx* (1977).

In 1988, Adrian Martin provocatively suggested that a cinema of good intentions which prides itself on its progressivist record is essentially a conservative cinema. At issue here is not whether there was too much social problematization in Australian cinema – as social problematization is an essential and indeed normative characteristic of the popular and political cinema, but the strong linkages between a cinema that self-consciously foregrounds its work of social problematization and a narrow band of film-making repertoires. His complaint was that film-makers took those film-making options closest to prevailing socio-cultural problematizations – social problem film-making, documentary, naturalist drama, television soap – and did not exploit more inventive *audiovisual* uses of the materials.

To an extent he is right. Critics and audiences foreground social problem-atization and use it as a central resource with which to inspect the cinema – whether for the 'Australian identity' or the representation of women – such that the social problematization becomes the story. This connects with the close relation to government funding and dovetails with Australian cinema's non-fiction traditions in literature and film.

My admiration for Esben Storm's feature *Deadly* is that it dared to use social problematization differently. It played with the liberal social problematization of structural racism in a country town, as a pretext to fool the audience and retrain them to see the 'real' crime behind the casual statistic: the police officer's crime of passion. He murders his Aboriginal prisoner for the prisoner's affair and sub-sequent child by his wife. Aboriginal–white relations are redrawn mythically as family matters. They are not 'out there' – but where they belong in the (Australian) family. It is an unreadable thriller because this textual politics is transgressive. It remakes the Aboriginal as (social) victim into a story of Aboriginal agency and ordinary crime. *Deadly*'s take is that the reality of Aboriginal/white sexual relations, elicit desire, love, passion is just as structural to the history of country towns and families as police and rednecks who need race awareness training supplied from the city. To embed social problematization in the thriller you have to be prepared to take such risks; the problematization has to be made legible through twisting and reordering it. *Deadly* could have been a better film and sometimes it was hard to follow. But its difficulties also stemmed from its confounding of audience and critical expectations for which the 'social problem' mode is the legitimate form for Aboriginal representation. James Ricketson's *Blackfellas* – made from the Archie Weller novel, *Day of the Dog* – presented no such problems. There Aboriginal youth are a social problem; white policing is a social problem. But like Stephen Muecke (1994) I prefer *Deadly*'s oedipal cultural politics.

Australian cinema is a series of cinema projects persisting and disappearing over time in relation to changing socio-cultural problematizations by critics, governments, activists and the changing raw materials of peoples and their lifeways in Australia. Stories of the Australian people and their diverse cultures provide a national cinema with templates, projects, discourses, and a critical distance on what is produced, as well as providing ways of seeing and creatively disposing pre-existing social materials into fictional and documentary form.

Chapter 12

Problematizing gender

INTRODUCTION

The gender cleavage is one of the most important structuring differences in front of and behind the camera in the cinema. Women have always been shown in Australian cinema, yet they still do not participate to the same extent as men do in creative, technical and administrative positions. The opportunities for, and wages of, women actors and performers are nowhere near as great as for men. And a distribution of roles limits what parts women can play in Australian film-making. Surveys show lower participation rates of women than men, their concentration in particular sectors of the film industry and the bias towards male leads and male-centred story-lines on-screen (see Cox and Laura 1992). The Media, Entertainment and Arts Alliance (MEAA) survey of films released from January 1993 to November 1994 listed six of thirty with female leads, and a further four with female co-leads – one third with women in central roles. And of these films, five were directed by women (Prisk 1994: 7). This roughly confirms that little has changed since 1991 and 1992.[1]

This picture contradicts Australian cinema's international reputation as a 'women-friendly' film industry which encourages the work of women. There are its high profile women directors (Campion, Armstrong, Turner, Moorhouse, Tass) – one of whom, Jane Campion, is Australasia's most high-profile and lionized auteur director. There are its important producers (Linda House, Pat Lovell, Patricia Edgar, Glenys Rowe, Margaret Fink, Joan Long) and actors (Judy Davis, Wendy Hughes, Nicole Kidman, Jacqueline McKenzie, Helen Morse, Sigrid Thornton). There is an impressive stream of feminist film-making with titles as diverse as *On Guard* (S. Gibson and Lambert 1983), *Serious Undertakings* and *For Love or Money*. There are the women who have been regularly employed at the highest levels of the film industry. At the time of writing, the chief executive of the Australian Film Commission (Cathy Robinson), the head of SBS-TV (Sawsan Madina), the director of Film Victoria (Jennifer Hooks), the head of the Australian Film Institute (Ruth Jones), and the head of ABC-drama (Penny Chapman) are all women.

Both representations of Australian cinema are true enough. The Australian film milieu is more progressive on the gender issue than are many other cinemas. Women directors are more prominent in the Australian cinema and the proportion of woman-centred stories appear – on my cursory inspection of cinema releases – to be much higher than in Hollywood. Equally, the Australian situation is not good. There is, on the basis of the evidence presented, a long way to go before there is an equality of outcome on and off-screen.

These two publicity images for Australian cinema are inextricably linked. The problematization of inequality in front of and behind the camera from the early 1970s, continues to work towards the second possibility of a more equal film milieu. Indeed the first underwrote the programmes, the development of women's networks, and forms of moral persuasion which helped give rise to the second. Surveys which provide evidence of a lack of equality of opportunity and on-screen outcome for women in a male-dominated industry produce information which is recognizable to and therefore potentially actionable by governments. These legitimate lobbyist arguments for affirmative action and equal outcomes. Such information collecting also fuels criticism and a sense of frustration with the film industry's treatment of women. For joint Federal Secretary of the Alliance, Ann Britton, the 1994 survey reveals a belief within the industry that 'women's stories are not as interesting to the audience' (Prisk 1994: 7). It also enables principled demands which go further than current film policy – as in calls for significant levels of childcare provision on film sets, and calls for a quota system in development and production funding which would equitably distribute funding between women and men (Prisk 1994: 7).

The broader public acceptance of the principle of gender equality organizes the collection of evidence of disadvantage and non-discrimination alike. It drives criticism from inside and outside the industry to meet the 'target' of equality; and it drives the celebration of women 'making waves' in publicity stories, curated festivals and the like.

In this chapter, I am concerned with the ways gender has been problematized on governmental, critical and industrial horizons in the broader film milieu. This problematizing of gender in social and cultural criticism and elsewhere impacts at the level of representation, politics, work practices and social organization.

FEMINISM AND THE PROBLEMATIZING OF GENDER

The major social and cultural project problematizing gender – and most particularly women's role in it – has been feminism. So important has feminism been in itself and in providing a model for alternative representational projects to emerge that it needs to be addressed in some detail. Feminism's problematizations of gender have not only been integral to organizing the representational and propositional contents of film-making, criticism and policy making, but have also supplied projects and targets for Australian cinema against which its achievements can be measured, assessed and found wanting. Gender problematization is a vehicle for industry and political change. It provides cinema with a socially ameliorative dimension.

Problematizing gender has centrally involved the domain of 'government' in both its particular sense of state apparatuses and policy and in its general sense of political parties, interest groups and other non-governmental organizations providing instruments for living and intervention into social life. Governments generate the need for and legitimate their intervention into the 'market', the film industry, and customary relations within them. Intervention can be direct in some institutions. The AFTRS, the ABC, SBS-TV, the AFC and the FFC can be held directly accountable to government on matters of gender equality, by virtue of direct government funding and reporting structures. In the private sector intervention is necessarily more indirect. Independent film and television production companies, the commercial television stations, exhibitors and distributors, are the targets of publicity campaigns – educational, moral persuasion and naming campaigns. The problematization of gender routinely encounters limits. These are not only limits of prejudice and misogyny but are the limits any social problematization encounters. Gender is only one of a number of problematizations competing for governmental attention and which is embedded in its routines. Its programmes run up against and intersect with, these other problematizations. All of our social problematizations are limited by the form and organization of audience entertainment choices and the economic structures of the cinema industry (feature films need to produce a return on investment; part of investor's calculations of viability is the track record of the film-maker.

Problematization and intervention unite knowledge and the exercise of power to 'bring new levels or departments of social existence into being' (Hunter 1994: 47). Gender problematization has created spaces of film-making activity which would not otherwise be as viable, complete and self-sustaining through commercial networks. Government funding was critical to feminist film-making in the 1970s – in 1979 Susan Alexander reported that '[w]omen seem to be more prepared to deal with government funding organizations than to enter the world of private finance' (quoted in Hawker 1987: 145). The important role the Federal Government plays in film-making involving women sustains a close relation to social problematization.[2]

The 'women and cinema' issue has brought into being two related 'new departments' of film: (1) the ideal of and limited accomplishment of a woman-friendly mainstream cinema and television industry producing titles like *Celia* and *The Piano*; and (2) a separate independent film-making space where women could develop capacities and explore ideas away from the immediate dictates of industry, producing the essay film *My Life without Steve* and the documentary experimental film *Ladies Rooms* (Gibson, Fiske, Lambert, MacKay 1977). These two ends of mainstreaming and separate development are integral to most forms of contemporary identity politics in liberal democratic societies. The alternative cultural space of feminist film-making has its own identity, limited budgets and exhibition, distribution and production circuits and is sustained by (limited) government funding and networks of varying degrees of formality based on a non-commercial calculus – political, social, aesthetic and communitarian. It provides women with experience and a track record on low budgets which helps them secure documentary contracts and the confidence of the mainstream funding institutions. In its turn the possibility of future mainstreaming provides a governmental *raison d'être* for underwriting marginal forms of film activity potentially inimical to various functions of the state.

Social problematization-driven film-making also provides materials, techniques and experience to be later utilized in the mainstream industry. It permits a film-making to evolve beside the market and develops strategies, expertise, policy and contents – for later inclusion in the mainstream market–industry nexus. A mutuality exists between gender problematization-derived film-making and the film milieu's need for new concepts, talent and forms of product development in front of and behind the camera. To some extent, feminist film-making is an extension of the logic that underwrites both ABC-TV and SBS-TV – providing a film-making and film training milieu partly justified by the social problematizations and community service obligations foundational to both services, but providing and developing programme concepts for later exploitation in the mainstream industry.

The capacity to win 'government' support for both projects of mainstreaming and separate development – whether through direct subsidy or through other means – lies in the acceptance of interest group identity politics as a legitimate and principled means of personal and political self-actualization. It also relies on governmental recognition of established disadvantage and victimization – including the failure of the market to meet aspirations, demands and grievances of women made legitimate by the action of problematization. When Sue Maslin argues that there is something dysfunctional about Australian cinema when its 'feature films continue to be overwhelmingly about men's stories' and these films don't 'reflect the society in which we live nor the cinematic fantasies of the majority of audiences' (Prisk 1994: 7), she is situating her critique firmly within accepted governmental logics for optimal utilization of societal resources.

FEMINISM AND CINEMA

Feminist problematization of cinema operates along four fronts. First, it brings into being a women's cinema: a cinema operating in and creating its own alternative cultural space, such as that attempted by the Sydney Women's Film Group from 1971, Reel Women in Melbourne from the mid-1970s to early 1980s, and Cinematrix in Perth in the 1980s and beyond. This is the 'urge to create their own cinema' (Blonski and Freiberg 1989: 192) found in titles like Jeni Thornley's autobiographical *Maidens* with its 'improvised, loosely poetic style' (Thornley 1987: 222). For Blonski and Freiberg (1989: 211) this film is 'a didactic history of the Australian family; the tracing of a personal journey from darkness to light . . . and the celebration of man-less sisterhood'.

Second, it argues for a feminist contribution to the different pathways of the cinema – whether in video, avant-garde (C. Cantrill's *In this Life's Body* 1984), the slice of life documentary (Armstrong's *Bingo, Bridesmaids and Braces*), political film-making (*Red Matildas*) or the mainstream feature film and television production industry (Campion's *Sweetie* and Hambly's *Fran*).

Third, it orchestrates a feminist intervention into the practices and routines of the film industry and with it film policy – in for example Women in Film and Television (WIFT) initiatives. This intervention is made of a family of projects aimed at the many different film institutions and agencies. It includes film training initiatives. Lobbying for, securing and maintaining ear-marked programmes like the AFC's Women's Film Fund in the 1970s and the Women's Program of the 1990s.

And lastly it develops both a feminist approach to the depiction of social reality (the 'strong urge to interrogate the language and institutions of the whole cinematic apparatus' (Blonski and Freiberg 1989: 192) in *Serious Undertakings* and *We Aim to Please* (Nash and Laurie 1977) and a feminist intervention into the presentation of the national past, its myths and symbols in the women in work documentary *For Love Alone* and *Bread and Dripping* (Wimmins Film Collective 1981) which 'reinterpeted aspects of Australian history from a feminist perspective' (McMurchy 1993: 197).

A feminist cinema means, at various times, all these (see Stern 1985; Blonski, Creed and Freiberg 1987 and Blonski and Freiberg 1989). As with all social and aesthetic movements and principled intellectual standpoints which attain some political and bureaucratic power, feminism is variously oppositional, mainstreaming, and incorporated at the heart of social meanings in Australian cinema. The umbrella organization (WIFT) was rejuvenated in the early 1990s in a concerted attempt to ensure these different components worked for, rather than against each other. WIFT marshalled these components together through a commitment 'not to create regulation and censorship' but to educate people about and promote the 'discrepancy in the gender treatments' (Prisk 1994: 7). Sue Maslin reported in 1993 (63) that it attracted 'most of its membership from women who look to its networking and employment opportunities rather than its political lobbying potential'.

The WIFT of the 1990s is a second generation feminist and cinema body. The first generation film activists of the 1970s and early 1980s were more concerned to create a separate space for a feminist cinema. Such a space was created under twin pressures: pressures from outside in terms of gender discrimination and lack of opportunities, and from within in terms of the construction of new spaces to one side and in opposition to the prevailing mainstream cinema.

From the mid-1970s, this activism has brought about a viable feminist minor stream of independent film-making, short fiction film (Campion's *A Girl's Own Story*), political documentary (*Film for Discussion*, Sydney Women's Film Group 1974), and experimental documentary work (as in Goldman and FitzSimons's *Snakes and Ladders*). This work was usually a combination of self-supported and government supported. Although starting as a minor stream of the avant-garde, counter-cultural and co-op movements, feminist cinema became increasingly central and provided their major, high profile successes. Like these broader aesthetic and political movements, it combined a critique of the mainstream by providing alternative and sometimes separatist spaces exploring women's lives. The resulting film-making had the limits and advantages of such film work: a largely intra-mural, consciousness-raising character, controlled circuits of film meaning and a shared feminist aesthetic controlling film meaning and film style alike so as not to produce misunderstanding. Barbara Alysen (1985: 313) described it as 'a feminist film genre' developing 'its own style' and allowing for experimentation within defined limits.

Chris Westwood, feminist activist and founder of the Belvoir Theatre, gestured to the strength and vitality of this minor stream when she confidently claimed in 1990 that:

> There's the mainstream feature film industry which doesn't even notice women in its ideas, in its intentions or what it's trying to do. And then there's the huge group of women film-makers doing interesting women's films, and they've been doing it since the early 1970s.
>
> (Watson 1990b: 226)

Annette Blonski, Barbara Creed and Freda Freiberg's edited book *Don't Shoot Darling!* (1987) focused mostly on this independent women's cinema. The book was designed as a statement in its own right – establishing the integrity, excellence and independent existence of this minor stream of film-making. It celebrated these filmworkers' dedication, commitment and use of their own funds to create an alternative cinema. Blonski summarized the common outlook of this 1970s and 1980s film-making:

> Independent cinema may have been diverse in form, but its practitioners had in common a position of difference and marginality, working outside the mainstream and in opposition to it.
>
> (Blonski 1987: 41)

By contrast, the 1990s has seen the mainstreaming of many of these women such that Maslin reported in 1993 (63) that 'contemporary women's film-making is no longer in opposition to, but an integral part of, the mainstream industry'. Arguably this mainstreaming would not have been possible without the separate and separatist film, theatre and other spaces of the 1970s and 1980s to provide a base from which to work. Maslin (1993: 63) does not see the result as totally beneficial. She argues that this mainstreaming has come at a cost to 'innovative and confronting feminist film-making' as 'documentaries are largely produced for a general television audience or corporate and government clients' and films are 'no longer a means of articulating feminism'.

Part of the process of mainstreaming is revealing a hidden history of women's contribution to Australian film, as in Andrée Wright and Stewart Young's compilation film on women in early Australian film, *Don't Call me Girlie* (1985),[3] in Alysen's 1984 (1985) essay 'Australian Women in Film'. Paulette McDonagh has become particularly important as a successful female writer-director of the silent cinema with *Those who Love* (1926), *The Far Paradise* (1928) and *The Cheaters* (1930); while the role of the women in the two significant film partnerships of the first sixty years of Australian cinema – that between Lottie Lyell and Raymond Longford and between Elsa and Charles Chauvel – is emphasized by both Wright and Alysen. The process of mainstreaming also involves valuing what might be called the local 'women centred cinema' in the 1970s classics – *My Brilliant Career*, *Caddie* and *Picnic at Hanging Rock*, and the 1980s and 1990s films – *Sweetie*, *Monkey Grip*, *The Last Days of Chez Nous* and *The Piano*.

The third trajectory of a feminist intervention into the film industry and policy development is integrally tied to inserting feminist understandings and gender problematizations into the ways the film industry 'knows and debates itself'. To this project, information collection is vital – and is driven by the kinds of questions asked. One of Cathy Robinson's achievements as head of the Australian Film Commission in the 1990s has been to make feminist agendas more central to industry policy, information gathering and public debate. The most important of these information gathering exercises were those provided by the report by Eva Cox and Sharon Laura entitled *'What Do I Wear for a Hurricane'* (1992) which reported on women in the Australian film, television, video and radio industries. Other reports corroborated these findings. The Australia Council's survey on performers' income showed male performers in 1992/93 earned a mean income of $14,000 while females an income of $8,300 (Prisk 1994: 7). These surveys serve a feminist agenda to interpret gender differences in employment and on-screen presence, as politically significant gender discrimination needing rectification.

In the fourth arena of feminist activity feminists intervene into the means of representation. Feminist critics and film-makers alike revealed and sought remedies for what they saw as the generally male bias in Western storytelling, the state of women to be 'looked at' – as objects of the gaze – and the narrative and documentary disposition and presentation of the sexes which saw the male having the authoritative voice. Margot Nash and Robin Laurie's *We Aim to Please* aims to disrupt such strategies. As Blonski and Freiberg (1989: 207–8) describe its strategies:

> It disturbs the complacency of the audience by throwing tomatoes at us, inscribing the titles on the bare breasts and buttocks of the film-makers, hissing and snickering conspiratorially, making jokes out of archetypal feminine symbols (the moon, the rose, the night), confronting us with naked as opposed to nude women's bodies in uncomfortable close-ups, addressing the audience aggressively.

Feminist critics and film-makers also seek the more local entailments of sexism in representations of nation, lifeways and the 'typical' Australian. Sophie Watson and Rosemary Pringle (1990: 232) have stated the feminist criticism of the Australian myth as follows:

> Australia has a long tradition of male 'mateship', and bases its national identity on the doings of these mates, the 'diggers' at Gallipoli. Women are largely excluded from the national myths that legitimate the Australian state. Australian egalitarianism is essentially of a masculine variety.

Feminist criticism of Peter Weir's *Gallipoli* was conducted in these terms. Annette Blonski described it as

> the purest expression of a nostalgia for an Australian identity that resides in some Elysian past of masculine beauty, anglo-celtic purity and bonding through war or the trials of the bush. Women, of course, are absent, thrown into the scrapheap of the alien other, along with crooked Turks and other untrustworthy foreigners. The Australian cinema had arrived.
>
> (Blonski 1987: 50)[4]

Sometimes the general critique of vision and film form and the particularist criticism of the nation's myths and symbols combine, as in Helen Grace's celebrated independent feminist film, *Serious Undertakings*. For Annette Blonski and Freda Freiberg *Serious Undertakings* 'rigorously questions our cultural myths and creative conventions' about Australian cinema, art and literature (1989: 197).

COPING WITH LIMITED SUCCESS

With the relative success of a generation of women through state institutions, state policy of access and equity, and success in Arts bureaucracies, women are overcoming being treated as the 'objects and participants of policy decisions rather than full participants in them' (Watson and Pringle 1990: 234). They are no longer excluded or marginalized to the extent they once were.

The rhetoric of 'outsiders trying to get in' is not applicable to women like Robinson, Hooks, Chapman, Armstrong and Garner who are insiders, working from powerful positions within the centres of power and prestige in Australian film-making and cultural policy development. These women are professionals in the film industry. They are not at the gates wanting to get in, they are inside, they belong there and create their own spaces. Here is novelist Helen Garner talking about her experience of film-making:

> My brief experience of film writing has been an intense pleasure, because of the calibre of the people who introduced me to it: Jan Chapman, who produced both films, and the directors, Jane Campion (*Two Friends*) and Gillian Armstrong (*The Last Days of Chez Nous*). Long script sessions with those three classy, generous and challenging professionals taught me to drop my defenses more.
>
> (Garner 1992: ix)

Garner does not make the fact these are women her topic, instead she emphasizes their professionalism. She allows the reader to recognize that all are women, she then underscores this as a positive attribute with the adjective 'classy' (a term that is not gender specific but usually applied to women in Australia) before she situates their professionalism.

The successful producers and directors already mentioned need an account of their success. Women's relation with the industry changes from time to time to one which recognizes how the Australian film-making milieu provides greater opportunities than those available to women in Europe and the Americas.

The Australian-based New Zealand film-maker, Marie Maclean, was asked in *Projections: A Forum for Film Makers*, why New Zealand and Australia produce so many women directors. She answered:

> I think it has something to do with it being a young, small industry that's more flexible and perhaps less initimidating than the American or European equivalent, with all its tradition and hierarchies. Because it's a young culture, you have to invent your own stories, and you gain a lot of confidence from doing that. There's very good support for women film-makers. I've never felt any barriers there in terms of having my films funded.
>
> (Fuller 1993: 89)

Similar accounts are given by women in bureaucracy. Sophie Watson and Rosemary Pringle, two prominent academic feminists, convert the 'young' country argument into a sign of 'immature' patriarchy. Interestingly, both are feminist appropriations of the 'developmentalist' metaphors long dominating the two Australasian polities. For Watson and Pringle:

> compared with the aura of long established patriarchal regimes, Australian 'fraternity' also has a certain adolescent quality which makes it vulnerable and malleable. The class structure probably is more open than its old-world equivalents, the high positions in the bureaucracy have been more accessible to the working class. Though this has mostly favoured men, the greater permeability of state structures has allowed for women's participation and, in recent years, made possible the rise of 'femocrats'.
>
> (Watson and Pringle 1990: 232)

Femocrats in this account have been able to intervene in Australia not only because of relative openness and accessibility, but also because of the state's adolescent immaturity and unachieved patriarchy. If this paedocratizes the Australian state and politics, positioning 'woman' as an agent for maturity of the errant child – the Australian state/society – it none the less marks a change of feminist strategies to do with the state and the mainstream industry.[5] The state is no longer treated as a male unity. Nor is it an evident political priority to either bring it down or disclose 'its weakest links and hence coming close to revolution' (Watson and Pringle 1990: 242). The focus has shifted to feminists conducting, after Foucault, 'a strategic analysis appropriate to political struggle, to struggles in the field of political power' (242). While this account of success is always and necessarily tempered by the stress on the distance still to go, it recognizes non-sexist attitudes and dispositions in the industry.

The exclusion argument is still forcefully made as structural and representational imbalances do remain. Underrepresentation behind and in front of the cameras still legitimates the need for separate 'women's film-making spaces' and the emergence of reverse discrimination in 'jobs for the girls networks'. Take Julie James Bailey's reported speech at a conference where she claimed that

> Australia's mainstream media was monopolized by males and therefore, 'by nature' was 'antagonistic to women, education and change'. She said a growing list of 'outrageous misogynist practices' had developed with 23% of women outlining general sexism as the reason for lack of progress in the industry. This resulted in men being the key decision-makers which meant hierarchical methods of working had been developed, she said. 'It is the men who determine what we see, read and hear'.
>
> (Towers 1994, Bailey 1994)

James Bailey claims for the film industry what an earlier generation of feminist researchers on the role of government was apt to conclude: that 'government [was] conducted as if men's interests are the only ones that exist' (Pringle and Watson 1990: 234). Such claims will continue to be made so long as the gap between male and female professional and representational statuses remains.

An important recent change is the emergence of a second generation feminist policy agenda for the mainstream industry, which moves from equal opportunity to equality of outcome. Equality of outcome is based on a different principle than equal opportunity. Equal opportunity removed impediments to women's participation in the workforce, film-making, film training institutions and the like as they were currently defined. It involved the women's right to participate on the same terms. American feminist Drucilla Cornell (1993: 143) characterizes such initiatives as a policy 'to enter a male world from which we have previously been shut out'. Equality of outcome has more expansive horizons. It wants to make up the gap that still exists *after* equal opportunity programmes. In the film industry, equal outcome involves accelerating participation rates of women in the industry and making on-screen indicators more equal. It wants the film industry's percentage of female workers to match that of women in the workforce generally. Cox and Laura (1992: 9) found that in 1992 39 per cent of the film industry's labourforce were women compared to the national labourforce figure of 42 per cent. Its ultimate goal is nothing less than the same number of women directors, producers, scriptwriters and roles for women as for men in the film industry (this is the film industry equivalent of the pressure on both major political parties to embrace policies geared to getting more women into Federal parliament).

Equality of outcome is also an expansive policy, in that it involves not simply recognizing 'equal rights' but 'equivalent rights'. Cornell (1993: 142) sees equivalent rights as demanding 'the restructuring of, not just accommodation to, the current world of work'. Such equivalent rights are not about helping women become more like men, they are self-consciously about women transforming political, symbolic and workplace cultures and male behaviours to 'enable women to value the choices we make about our lives and work without shame of our 'sex', even if such choices do not fit into the preestablished social world' (Cornell 1993: 143). In film-making such choices are also matters of representation and story.

EQUALITY OF OUTCOME AND DALLAS DOLL

The gap between equal opportunity and equal outcome can be seen as the difference between the 1976 *Caddie* directed by a man, Donald Crombie, but funded in part from federal monies made available for International Women's Year in 1975, and Ann Turner's 1993 telemovie *Dallas Doll*. Based on the memoirs of a Sydney bar-maid, *Caddie* is explicitly about making do in a class-based and gender-biased man's world of the public bar – where all women save the barmaid were excluded. The eponymous Caddie is a victim of domestic violence. She has to work in the problematic world of the bar (something respectable women would not do) because there is no other way to support her family. She brings up her family on the woman's lower wage. She and her co-workers suffer discrimination – including risk to health through backyard abortions. The film's logic sets Caddie up simultaneously as (female) battler and victim of social circumstances. Her romantic interests are two men; the 'flash' Jack Thompson character who nicknames her 'Caddie' and the Greek Australian Takis Emmanuel character, who has to break off the relationship due to family obligations that make it necessary for him to return to Greece.

Dallas Doll, by contrast, is self-consciously affirmative. It insists on unconventional choices. Women are agents not just victims of circumstances beyond their control. As in influential contemporary feminist thought (Monique Wittig, Luce Irigaray), the lesbian provides a utopian space in which women can define themselves and their sexuality for themselves rather than in relation to men. As Cornell glosses it:

> Lesbianism can provide us with a politically significant vision of a different engagement with a woman's own body and with a lover in which a woman's 'sex' is not repudiated.

(135–6)

Dallas Doll is unusual for an Australian film; as Barbara Creed put it in 1993 (11) '[l]esbians do not exist in mainstream Australian film'.

The lesbian romance in *Dallas Doll* becomes the agency of self-actualization both negatively with Dallas (Sarah Bernhart) who manipulates everyone including her lover Rosalind (Victoria Longley) to gain her own ends; and positively via Rosalind herself who finds her voice, personal fulfillment, sexuality and her dream as a farmer via the relationship with Dallas Doll. Through her lesbian affair she becomes herself rather than just an adjunct to the nuclear family.

This film's fantasy structure is to project an unconventional (even monstrous) trickster figure as a woman: a kind of female Frankfurter of *The Rocky Horror Picture Show*. And this too can be seen as opening a new representational terrain for women. Dallas is an ambiguous, malevolent figure who manipulates people. She enables the mother to fulfil her destiny as a farmer and a lesbian (hinted at earlier when her aunt points out an Indian painting of two women making love). She also becomes her own person and agent when she takes a rifle out and shoots at Dallas (precipitating a revenge structure, which sees the dog earlier injured by Dallas herding the cattle to crush her in a bizarre twist).

Although heterosexual desire and coupling is depicted, it is explicitly marginalized and made unnatural – just as a strand of contemporary feminism makes heterosexuality not 'natural' just 'common'.[6] The heterosexual relationship, between Dallas and the father, is never visualized but we do see, though, the father's progressive deterioration over the course of the film, with whip marks on his back and an inability to respond erotically to his wife.[7] The son who loses his virginity to Dallas Doll does so in a copulation scene designed not to eroticize but to render heterosex bestial and unnatural. The convention of chirping birds to 'love making' in the fields are turned on their head as the birds become voyeurs interrupting and objecting to an unnatural and scarcely erotic coupling. The later coupling between Dallas and the son is represented sonically through a banging of the filing cabinet. At this point the sex act is simply played out as a matter of power between two arch manipulators. It literalizes the separatist feminist metaphor of sex between men and women as a matter of power, with penetration disempowering women. Dallas's heterosexual coupling with the son undoes her and makes her a victim as the son reveals Dallas to his mother, Dallas's lover. In this scene, Dallas is, for the first time in the film, set up and destroyed by what she has created.

The erotic charge and central romance structure is between the two women. They play the game strip naked three times. The first time they are caught by the pre-pubescent daughter. The second time they make love. The third time they play the game on the golf links – the site of Dallas Doll's business venture, that she is using the family for – it is done as an expression of Rosalind's displeasure with Dallas for her manipulation of people. In these scenes the women look at each other erotically. Their eroticism is staged in their relationship, not in each woman's relationship to men.

Men are portrayed as women are often said to be in Australian cinema: as ciphers, cardboard characters, and as helpers. They are often cruelly treated and seem to deserve this treatment by virtue of their sex. The Mayor who is forced by Dallas to publicly display his mishapen sex organ is made the laughing stock of the community. This cruel scene is followed by broad farce, as the ex-mayor thanks Dallas for allowing his abnormality to become public: she has 'liberated him' too. The mayor gets in the way of Dallas's ambition so he must be removed.

He represents the patriarchal family – a smug satisfied and effeminate man whose humiliation is deserved by being diegetically represented as the father of too many children.

As in exploitation films, these men simply exist as counters to be moved, humiliated, assailed, assaulted and mercilessly abused. It even extends to children, as the young, apparently sensitive male adolescent – so often the focus of the teen pic – becomes a monster. The family is seen as something needing to be blown apart. Its exploitationist aesthetics make it a close relation of the knowing redisposition of societal archetypes in Philip Brophy's *Body Melt*, which like *Dallas Doll* cannot develop its characters much beyond caricature. It also literalizes the feminist imaginary where such an institution is to be treated with contempt and assumed to be naturally suppressive of female desire.

The most disturbing moments revolve around the transformation/possession of the son who unexpectedly provokes some sympathy. He moves from a boy afraid of his girlfriend's sexual advances, to losing his virginity to Dallas, to running away. Even Rosalind does not sustain her grief at his running away: her loss is turned into sexual passion for Dallas. Dallas Doll's legacy is to remake the son who we initially experience as a quite likeable person like her. Later he returns as a manipulating monster and the principal agent of Dallas' destruction. But unlike Dallas he is not as competent or stylish a manipulator. His attempted manipulation of his mother backfires. In revealing Dallas he reveals the sleazy person he has become. Rosalind says somewhat unconvincingly she will be 'there for him' but she will not consent to be part of his plans.

Now that Dallas is comfortably dead, Turner remakes the film as affirming the mother's right to choose to be what she always wanted to be – a farmer – and to reconcile her duty of care to her children and her ambition through pursuing that ambition. This is legitimated by her children – particularly her daughter – being seen to have preordained destinies which enable them to get on with things in spite of their parents. Throughout, the daughter retains her vision, does not come under Dallas's spell because she is both pre-pubescent and has an autonomous vision.

Dallas Doll enacts much of what feminist public discourse wants from a film. Unlike Campion's *The Piano*, where the woman's movement is between two men – one of whom becomes the agency by which she develops as a person and learns to speak (just as she transforms him in her turn), in *Dallas Doll* women simply do not need men for anything. Women can realize themselves without men. For this reason *The Piano* could be seen as ambiguous and regressive by some feminists, the feminist ideal of independence required either her death or her having nothing to do with men at the end. *The Piano* suggests implication and 'hetero-identification', whereas *Dallas Doll* is about the auto-identification of self-creating women. *Dallas Doll* has none of the ambiguities of *The Piano* in which the female and male are complicit and implicated. Instead it uses lesbianism as its utopian moment, allowing for female eroticism in relation to women, just as it compromises and denaturalizes it with men.

Each represents options for mainstreaming feminist perspectives in film-making. Campion recolonizes the film-making and film performance archive showing and affirming the central role of women in it. This even extends to the set, where on one day of the shoot there is a 'dress day' where all the crew are expected to wear a dress; apparently it helps Campion to work better with the men when she sees them in a dress.

The film of a woman's passion for her music and her love in *The Piano* is retold to refuse 'woman as victim' and the doomed scenario of its nineteenth-century forbears (just as the film plays with this, affirming life and her love) and objectifies and eroticizes the man as we look with her at him.

Jane Campion, Gillian Armstrong and Jackie McKimmie are the prominent practitioners of work in this domain. Such recolonizing leads to small changes of emphasis in other areas. Australian cinema's 'female friendly' teen-pics – Elfick's *Love in Limbo* and Dean Murphy's *Lex and Rory* (1993) – are something more than male coming-of-age films. The mother in *Love in Limbo* is unexpectedly centred and is neither humiliated nor made the victim of the 'ladies man' who pursues her. She accepts his companionship and sex on her terms. Her journey of sexual (re)awakening – she is a widow – parallels that of her son. There is a difference though: she has good sex, while her son's attempt to lose his virginity in a Kalgoorlie brothel develops into high farce as he is caught up in a 'union dispute' between the prostitutes and management over whether they should work or not. For its part, *Lex and Rory* insists that the Dai figure has on-screen autonomy – turning her into something more than the teen pic's male love interest – as the film centres her story and Lex becomes the means for her to establish her own identity, desires and future outside of her father's ambition that she should run a used-car yard with him.

By contrast, Turner in *Dallas Doll* and Anna Kokkinos in the acclaimed *Only the Brave*, attempt to create another separate and new space. Female protagonists are centred and foregrounded; they drive the story. Marginal identities and sexualities are explored. The goal is not simply a woman centred storytelling but a means of exploring new ways of rendering women characters in narration. Female characters can be 'married' as in *Muriel's Wedding* (this is, after all, what the two women who leave together can look forward to in the companionship and ordinariness of a life together – the traditional marriage).

FEMINIST PRECEDENT AS A MODAL LOGIC

The multifaceted character of the feminist agenda in Australian polity and film culture provided a model for other social problematizing to follow. Because it was both first at getting ear-marked funding, policy recognition and visibility, other 'minority' projects followed the modal logic provided by feminism. It provided a multifaceted trajectory and a sustainable model that governments could support. Here social problematization revealed the disadvantage, exclusion and marginalization of the female in the male/female cultural cleavage. It organized instruments and knowledges through which this disadvantage could be publicly established: statistically and qualitatively. It discriminated between domains of film-making and sorted those genres of film-making which were female friendly from those which were not – this also meant judging which genres of film-making were appropriate. Possibly one of the reasons *Lex and Rory* was not recognized as having a female co-lead in the Media, Arts and Entertainment Alliance Report was that its title suggested a male coming of age film.

There are three other domains in which similar trajectories of purpose and problematization are in evidence. These are: firstly, a multicultural cinema; secondly, an Aboriginal and Islander cinema; and thirdly, gay and lesbian film-making. In each the same logic can be discerned of establishing separate public spheres, special consideration, and governmental acceptance of the evidence of discrimination as the basis for action to facilitate future contributions to storytelling in its diverse forms. Without the centrality of social problematization none of these could be as effectively sustained or developed outside the market in order to build up resources and expertise to later enter the market.

Each appropriated the metaphor of colonization to map their respective grievances and legitimate their case for special consideration. The founding metaphor of the 1970s for the experience of women in Australia was Anne Summer's book *Damned Whores and God's Police: the Colonization of Women*. It metaphorized the social history of women in Australia through 'the analogy of colonial invasion, exploitation and dispossession' which was used to 'metaphorically, theoretically and rhetorically describe the experience of white women' (Curthoys and Muecke 1993: 191). In the 1980s and 1990s, the metaphor of colonization was attached to the experience of ethnic groups negotiating the broader Anglomorph culture: the treatment of ethnicity on television and the cinema is through colonizing the group concerned or, alternatively rendering ethnicity in the related fashion as a 'zoological feature' (Hage 1993: 153–67). Since the Mabo Decision, Aboriginal and Islander experience has become understood and publicly projected as a colonial experience. By the time it reaches the indigenous peoples, colonialism is no longer a metaphor. It describes what it was developed to describe – an experience of actual colonization.

Perhaps it is natural, given Australia's colonial past that colonial metaphors should be deployed to place firstly the settler culture, then women, then NES migrants and finally Aborigines, as victims of colonialism. But such a trajectory is not the usual one of a metaphorization getting further from actuality through usage. Rather the trajectory is resolutely towards the actuality of Aboriginal dispossession and giving the name colonialism to the victims of processes of colonialism and dispossession in the invasion and settlement of Australia.

The very success of feminist problematizations necessitates some acknowledgement that women may also be victimizers, colonizers and excluders of others. Ann Curthoys and Stephen Muecke (1993: 191) suggest the metaphor of colonization is no longer appropriate for white women, as it 'blurs and undermines the possibility of recognizing that white women were themselves *colonizers*'. Aboriginals become feminism's 'troubling other'. Using colonialism metaphorically can obscure the victims of Australian colonialism proper: Aboriginal women, men and children. Aboriginal woman activist, Bobbi Sykes actively resents the universalization of feminist problematizations. She sees them taking the place of other, much needed indigenous settler and racial problematizations:

> In Australia, the term 'equal rights' has been hijacked by the women's movement, and where 'equal opportunity' and 'equal rights' refer to equitable participation of Blacks in the USA, they refer only to the rights of women in this country.
>
> (Sykes 1989: 215)

Feminist problematizations have become mainstream. Like the patriarchal culture it began by attacking, settler culture women are now being required to recognize and acknowledge their implication and complicity. Sykes writes that it is time to 'recognize and explain ... the racially based privileges ... [and] the active racism of white women' (215). The very posing of this question indicates the achievements of the last twenty years.

Chapter 13

Problematizing nationhood

INTRODUCTION

In previous chapters I emphasized aspects of the 'people-among-themselves' as a series of cultural and gender cleavages internal to the society. In this chapter, I turn my attention to those aspects which produce a sense of Australia as a national society among national societies and Australians as a national people. Given the ascendance of nations as bureaucratic, political, market and social forms of organization and popular identity in the twentieth century, nationally defined societies are the unexceptionable norm.

Nationhood permeates many domains. Citizens are national subjects. Political parties promise new national directions. Feminist groups call for national redefinitions incorporating women into the national symbols and myths. National cinema activists call on the logic of national societyhood to legitimate ongoing public support. Governments develop multiculturalism as a national policy specifying who the Australian people are and the direction towards which these people and institutions of state should head. Ordinary people routinely define themselves 'in relation to other national peoples'. Film-makers exploit national materials and cultural archives. Audiences and critics recognize themselves in films and project their society as a certain kind of national society with its own directions and logics.

Policy-makers, film-makers, critics and audiences alike routinely produce political, civic and descriptive projects with which to represent the national society to itself and to the larger world. They also mundanely use such projects to create and make sense of local film-making. Specifying who its people are and what they and their society might become, is a routine social, political and cultural activity of a variety of agents inside and outside the film milieu. The various identities of the national society provide critics, policy-makers and audiences with standards against which to evaluate, query and celebrate the representational contents of Australian film-making. They provide a repertoire for film-makers to exploit in the films themselves and an identity and a mission for the cinema – something for it to represent and be. Agents problematize nationhood – sometimes to debunk it, but mostly they reconstruct it in the light of what it might be and what 'we' as a people might become.

In this chapter, I will examine four such problematizations and their translation into film. These are Australia as a

1 European derived society;
2 diasporic society;
3 new world society; and
4 multicultural society.

Despite the substantial non-European migration to Australia since the 1970s, Australian culture and its peoples are demonstrably the product of a European-derived society. A large proportion of its population is born outside the country or has at least one parent born overseas, and the visible ethnic communities persisting across several generations provide a basis for recognizing Australian society as a diasporic society. Australia is also obviously a settler society, a 'new world society' like those of North and Latin America where the 'dominant ethnicity' is a cultural hybrid not a particular ancestral ethnic group. The adoption of policies of multiculturalism, the increasing non-European settler presence and the public acceptance of Aboriginal and Islander claims as first peoples with a right to self-determination, found multiculturalism as an open-ended and culturally diverse social project.

These socio-cultural identities and the different projects associated with them compete for ascendancy, complement and are simply adjacent to each other. Each of these designations of Australian society and its cinema has a different utility. No claim for Australia as a European society can ignore the growing non-European elements in its cultural mix. No amount of wishing, cajoling or coercing is going to suspend the British, Chinese or Greek diaspora's experience of itself as such. No claim of 'we are all immigrants' – the ethnic strategy to rhetorically diminish the legitimacy of the settler culture and to retrospectively claim everyone as a member of a diaspora – can ignore Australia's indigenous peoples, or the absurdity of calling a 'diaspora' a people of several ancestries who are now into their tenth generation in the country. No claim for Australia as a multicultural society can void the continuing and dominant Anglo-Celtic, European and English-speaking character of Australian society which will continue into the forseeable future (Jupp 1991: 120).[1]

It follows that those looking for a pure version of any one of these cultural projects for the people-among-themselves – a European cinema, a new world cinema, a multicultural cinema, a diasporic cinema – are going to be disappointed with Australian cinema. Those pushing Australian cinema as a New World Cinema run against the survival of various diasporic logics in public institutions, film-making and society. Those pushing a diasporic cinema and multicultural cinema run against a settler culture of two hundred years standing with its own integrity, lifeways and traditions which have long ceased being diasporic and can be only expected – like the diasporic populations – to attenuate their identities so far. If these projects did not run aground of each other, it would be a surprise. Each disclose an aspect of Australian society and an aspect of its cinema. The society is fashioned from and will continue to be fashioned by its Anglo-Australian elements, ethnically unmarked Australians, a European sense of itself, diasporic migrant communities and identities, and multicultural combinations. This variety of projects jostling for ascendancy ensures that Australian cinema produces a messy combination capable of different description and viewer uptake.

Some would add to this list: Australia as a post-colonial society. I have not done so, because the term lacks precision. It is used to refer to: all these four specifications or combinations of these; to a process of decolonization with respect to Britain and the USA (the settler *and* Aboriginal culture become the colonized); and to a process of decolonization with respect to Australia's indigenous peoples (settler Australians *are* the colonizers). Postcolonialism also associates Australia with the African and Asian states gaining their independence after the Second World War. This is misleading. Australians – with the exception of Aboriginals and Islanders – are settler peoples not colonized subjects. Australia's 'nationhood' in a bureaucratic, administrative, governmental, political and popular sovereignty sense is not 'new' but rather quite old in comparison with many African, Asian and indeed European states. Although the term has wide usage in literary and cultural studies, I have opted here for more precise descriptions of the processes that typically go under its label. I have also chosen to talk about nationhood rather than nationalism, as I want to get at the ways society as a national whole is problematized, and the kind of nation that is, and has been, projected through such problematization (nationalism is only a bit player in this larger and more significant process of nationing).[2]

1 A European derived society

Courtesy of colonial settlement and a restrictive, racially-based immigration policy in force until the late 1960s Australia is a country of white European ancestry. The 1986 census put Australians of European ancestry at 95 per cent of the population (Jupp 1991: 96). The average Australian is typically a product of several, mostly European ancestries. Even with the substantial non-European migration to Australia since the 1970s, two thirds of the 22 per cent of the total population born outside Australia were born in Europe (one third in the UK/ Ireland; another third in continental Europe). Of those born outside Europe a significant proportion come from largely European-derived societies. The second largest overseas-born group in the 1991 census was the New Zealand-born (1.7 per cent of the total population).[3] From this vantage point films which turn on cultural differences within the nation – like *Metal Skin* (Wright 1995), *They're a Weird Mob*, *The Heartbreak Kid*, *Nirvana Street Murder* and *Strictly Ballroom* –

stage these within Australia's European family. The varieties of European identity become part of the larger identity of 'us' (white) Australians.

Australia's political, legal, social and cultural institutions are all European-derived. Its post-1788 history has been largely defined by European settlers and events in Europe. When philosopher John Passmore (1992: 14) called it a 'European country' he meant that Australia was a nation in which '[t]he most important events in our history, the ones which have done the most to make us what we are, occurred in Europe, taken now to include the British Isles, even in a Europe itself profoundly influenced by Egypt and the Middle East.' Until recently its cultural and political institutions favoured the reproduction of this European-ness with, for example, the major European languages being mostly taught in schools until the late 1980s when Asian languages started to rival these.

Film and television imports, influential production models and policy frameworks, and audiovisual exports have all been shaped within this mould. Australian cinema has most profitably circulated within Europe and North America and the extended markets of the different European languages. Its most productive international partnerships have been with European and European-derived producers and distributors (the British, US, French, German and Canadian). Despite the growing presence of Asian cinemas, Australia's cinema market is a market for European-derived Hollywood cinema and the various European cinemas (British, French, Italian, etc.). If film-makers have looked to Hollywood for inspiration, they have also looked to Europe. Their careers have usually been built on continental European and American connections in the larger and smaller festivals and retrospectives. The importance of continental Europe is further underscored by the significance of Cannes success to Australian film. Success with European and American audiences are significant arbiters of the value of Australian film. Bruce Beresford, Peter Weir and Jane Campion all launched their Hollywood careers via Europe.

Yet Australian cinema as a *European cinema* and Australia as 'demonstrably a *European society*' (Ross Gibson 1992: x) is a recent formulation. Calling it that can sometimes still be a progressive move, because it is insisting on the continental European influences besides the defining English and Celtic influences. The first wave multiculturalism of the late 1970s to the mid-1980s forged a space for a *continental European* component to the Australian identity. The aging of the continental European migrant experience (many of whose numbers are not being replenished (Jupp 1991: 89)), the general adoption of Mediterranean cultural practices and styles, and the significant intermarriage of people of different European ancestry is ensuring the convergence of these continental and Anglo-Celtic components. These dynamics undergird Charles Price's prediction of a composite of Anglo-Celtic and Non-Anglo-Celtic heritages as the dominant ethnic ancestral division emerging over the 1990s. For the child who is the product of several ancestries, it makes little sense to privilege one or other of these various European identities – they are simply (European) Australian. Storytellings involving this new ethnic division are becoming more 'representative'. In *Strictly*

Ballroom there is an explicitly represented convergence and melding of the Latin-Australian and the older Australian.

The increasing Asian, Pacific and non-European derived immigration is further encouraging an ethnic division along an Asian/European line. Australia is like the US in this respect where, as Michael Banton (1994: 16) observes, '[t]he sense of a common interest based on European origins has been reinforced by the arrival of Third World immigrants'. Such a European identity Others the increasing non-European migration to Australia.[4] As film-maker Teck Tan observed to Chris Berry (Berry 1993: 44), the European ethnic is becoming the unexceptionable cultural norm

> It seems we've got to the point where we're comfortable with European characters, and our culture is so Eurocentric that we can do that and do it pretty well. But when it comes to Asian characters, sometimes they make a good job of it, but very often they botch it up.

Berry goes on to suggest that Australian cinema affirms its Anglo-Celtic and European character by ignoring the 'forms of cultural hybridity' before the film-maker's eyes. The 'Vietnamese bakeries [that] abut Halal butchers' are 'only slowly appearing in a movie industry still dominated by Anglo-Celtic last names' (Berry 1992: 48). There was, he added, an absence of the kind of 'heterogeneity' that one routinely finds in Taiwanese and Hong Kong cinema.

If Australia's Europeanness is a cultural fact, it is also a public embarrassment given its non-inclusive and discriminatory history. Its ancestry is a product of non-European exclusion in the 'white Australia' policy conducted from the creation of the Federation in 1901 and abandoned in stages from 1956 to 1973 (Jupp 1991: 85–6). *Romper Stomper*, for example, insists on Davey's German background, refusing to sentimentalize his ethnicity and so let off the hook any part of the European Australian ancestral identity in its story of neo-Nazi activity against Asian-Australians.

Where once politicians, documentary film-makers (see Hurley's *A Nation is Built* 1938) and social commentators regarded Australia's European identity as an asset and even used it to legitimate Australia's postwar mass migration programme, it has now become a problem (Grant 1983: 311). It is an inappropriate civic and cultural identity given its exclusion of Aboriginal and Islander, non-European peoples and its strategic and economic place in the Asia-Pacific area.

Defining Australia as a European country is part and parcel of realistically renegotiating Australia's anomolous geographic and ethnic position in the Asia-Pacific region and accommodating its growing non-European populations. Passmore and Gibson envisage Australia 'meshing' with and evolving a productive relationship with its near neighbours not despite its differences but because of them. To recognize Australia as a European society is to recognize its provincial qualities and limitations (Gibson 1992: x). One facet of this new reality for Australia's European society is that 'the West' is no longer simply European or European-derived. Modernity, John Orr (1993: 6) observes has 'become global' and the 'scope of the modern film has been far broader' since 1970 than its older European-American axis.[5]

Helen Grace (1995: 133) discusses Pauline Chan's *Traps* as a film peculiarly about a contemporary 'crisis' of Australia's 'Anglo-Saxonness, or more generally, Europeanness'. The film revolves around a couple – a London-based Australian journalist, Michael (Robert Reynolds), and his photographer wife, Louise (Saskia Reeves) – who go to Indochina to write and photograph a publicity piece for a French colonial company. They stay with plantation head Daniel (Sami Frey), a friend of Michael's, and his daughter Viola (Jacqueline McKenzie). The French colonial period is coming to an end; Vietminh guerrilla activity is increasing. The relationship between the couple collapses – and their roles reverse – Louise becomes the dominant one as the film charts her own self-discovery in testing circumstances, Michael, for his part, is found wanting and even destroyed in the process. As Grace (137) observes, the story is, in part, the stuff of the classic situation of a European art film: 'angst, the painful journey of individual self-discovery, art versus journalism, the truth versus distortion, the repression of white women within bourgeois marriage – all the themes of the usual individualist psychodrama'.

But for Grace, what distinguishes the film is its tenuous link with Australia which, though 'barely spoken' is 'all the more significant because of the self-effacing sense of its presence' (137) – a sense of presence she reads in the awkwardness and hesitation in the performance of the Louise and Michael characters and in the way it works against 'the centrality and dominance of a European subjectivity' which 'self-destructs' as it pales into 'insignificance, coming to seem nothing more than sentimentality against the backdrop of, quite simply, more important things'. The couple are bit players in a colonial drama which is outside of their control and not substantially of their making but they are none the less happily complicit in and therefore a guilty party to. This process of decentring allows Grace to claim that the film marks out

> another kind of distance . . . between Europe and Asia and for a space between them to be opened up, in which the negotiation of a new relation becomes necessary but not in conventionally European terms. The neat structure of the classic opposition between the two terms, which is a feature of Orientalism ('east is east and west is west and never the twain shall meet') – is loosened and displaced.
>
> (137)

To underscore this point let me quote Chan because she has spoken of her own identification with the Louise character:

> There is actually a lot of myself in Louise, in the mirror effect as an Asian woman going to the West and feeling alienated and challenged by the culture and therefore having to find my own voice and my own identity.
>
> (Chan 1995: 68)

Here, it seems, is an Asian Australian woman negotiating her own negotiation of Australia's Europeanness through projecting that Europeanness in the problematic space of her own homeland Indochina in the 1950s![6]

Australia's Europeanness is a cultural fact and a mundane background in storytelling. Sometimes as in *Traps* it is usefully problematized in ideological and political recognitions. Mostly though, this Europeanness simply configures vernacular storytelling.

2 A diasporic society

If Australia as a European society predates 1970s and 1980s multiculturalism, so does Australia as a diasporic society. It has its roots in colonization and Australia as a British 'fragment' society under the British crown (Hartz 1964; Hodge and Mishra 1991). The idea of Australia as a diasporic nation is publicly embodied in the Union Jack in the Australian flag. It is also supported by the a continuing large-scale migration programme which, since 1970, has seen one fifth of the population born outside the country (at no time this century has the percentage of the Australian population born outside the country dipped below 10 per cent). Another way of looking at it is that 42 per cent of the total Australian population was either born overseas or had at least one parent born there (I. Castles 1992: 155) and 14 per cent of all households use a language other than English in the home. Given this, the experience of *expatriation* common to being a diaspora is particularly foregrounded in Australian social and cultural formations. Patterns of integration which involve changes to both the host and migrant cultures towards convergence do work themselves out over time. But the continuing high proportion of foreign-born and second generation Australians ensure that a diasporic sense of oneself and one's culture provides an important social and cultural cleavage.

These high proportions also ensure that the Australian host culture is in a comparatively weaker position of cultural and social dominance than in other social formations which migrants enter (in the older Canadian and US settler societies migrants make up only 16 per cent and 7 per cent of the population). This is further underwritten by an immigration programme which has historically favoured the skilled as much as the unskilled and so enabled many migrants to occupy significant positions of social and cultural power from the first generation. Such was the case for many skilled English, Scottish, German, Dutch and Hungarian migrants in the 1950s, and the skilled South Asian, Japanese, Singaporean and Hong Kong migrants of today. Consequently many prominent Australian film directors were born outside the country or are the second generation children of migrants. Because Australia is a peripheral rather than a metropolitan industrialized centre, this enables many 'European immigrants (to) feel superior to Anglo-Australians' (Bottomley 1992: 64). This sense of ethnic cultural superiority is narrativized in *Strictly Ballroom* as the ethnic gift of culture and style which rejuvenates Australian institutions.[7]

In this subsection, I will discuss three projects which have promoted Australia as a diasporic or part-diasporic society: Australia as a British diaspora; a collection of diasporas and a part-diasporic and part-non-diasporically defined host culture.[8] The British diaspora is the longest standing diasporic construction. It has its origins in the colonial (1788–1900) and dominion nation period (1901 to roughly 1950) – in which England was referred to as 'Home' by many Australian-born people and where those with British ancestry made up a large majority of the population. Routt's discussion of colonialism and family in the films of the 1920s and 1930s (1989) in which Australia could be 'the fairest child of the motherland' turn on a society, public ideologies and business conditions which unevenly and self-consciously projected the cinema and society as a continuation of British society. A nativist radical nationalism would have this as a colonial relationship and mentality persisting in an era of independence. But it is more than this – it is a diasporic logic.

Let me explain. William Safran (1991: 83–99) defines diasporas in terms of six characteristics – as Mishra (1995: 150) summarizes these:

(1) dispersal of people or their ancestors from a centre to two or more peripheries, (2) the retention of collective memory vision, or myth about the original homeland – its physical location, history, etc., (3) a feeling of non-acceptance, alienation or insulation in the host society, (4) a strong feeling that their ancestral homeland is their true, ideal home and the place to which they or their descendants would or should eventually return, (5) a responsibility for the maintenance of the homeland or its restoration, and (6) a self-conscious definition of one's ethnicity in terms of the existence of this homeland.

British migrants did disperse to different peripheries in North America, Australasia and Southern Africa. The Anglo-Australian retained the myth of the original homeland in England as 'home' and 'the old country'. Notions of exile and the British mother country are a consistent trope of cultural history with the convict system being seen as the first forced exile with no possibility of going back.[9] Feelings of responsibility for the maintenance of the British homeland underwrote the public support for Australian involvement in the two world wars. Despite a British oriented élite controlling the apparatuses of power and civil society, they projected their 'non-acceptance, alienation or insulation' in the new country as a consequence of the action of the supposedly inhospitable Australian landscape, which produced a sense of Australian oppressiveness acting on them. The then dominant Anglo-Australian ethnicity in the 1920s, 1930s and 1940s used its position self-consciously to project Australia as a 'British' society and Australia's British identity as a popular identity. In this dominion nation – and like dominion nations such as New Zealand – the figure of Miranda, the native born daughter, and not Caliban, the native Other, became the pivotal figure around which the imaginative drama of settlement was worked out (Routt 1989a: 36–42).

But there are important ways Australia's British diaspora is unlike many others. Most diasporas do not control the instruments of state they enter, most are not the dominant ethnicity, most are therefore not able to universalize their diasporic condition as a matter of state. Most are politically and culturally disempowered without significant cultural and political capital, and most are not explicitly and favourably connected to their homeland through close intergovernmental relations (first in the British Empire and later in the Commonwealth).[10]

Ken Hall and Charles Chauvel's cinema of the 1930s projected Australia's 'British' character. Such an identity 'united' both the English migrant and the (older) Australian,[11] just as it marginalized the minority settler ethnicities (in this period the Irish-, German-, Italian-descended) and Aboriginals and Islanders. Yet 'Britishness' conducted as an agency for Empire in which Australians were British agents of imperialism was, paradoxically, a more inclusive identity than Britishness is today. Now it simply refers to the geographical entity of Britain. England was then the international metropole and cultural core against which the provincial Australian society – and English language culture and society more generally – could be measured. A diasporic logic and link empowered oneself as part of the larger logic of Empire.

Hall and Chauvel's dominion nationalism attempted to make the British diaspora and the Australian mainstream congruent. Sometimes this entailed extravagant gestures of fealty to this ideal in, for example, Chauvel's *Heritage*. As Routt (1985: 57) describes the climax of this film:

> Frank Morrison has been confronted by his fellow graziers of the Northern Territory and pressed to go to Canberra to present the Territory's case for emergency aid. Yet when we see Frank in Parliament he is not speaking for the Territory. Instead he is eulogizing the entire Australian 'people' in a speech that climaxes with the exhortation that 'the bonds that bind us to the Empire should be bonds of steel!' All notion of Territorial separateness has vanished to be replaced by the complex 'race-Empire-nation', in which commonplace images of 'Australia' have been shifted to express 'England': the 'race', Empire, home, loyalty, tradition, greatness, destiny. National identity has been gathered up into Imperial identity and vice versa.

Generically, textually and content wise the Australian cinema of the 1920s and 1930s was obsessed by its British relation.

In Hall's *It isn't Done* the character's Australianness is revealed as a higher form of Britishness than that available in British high society. As Pike and Cooper (1980: 232) observe, this 'humble Australian farmer . . . unexpectedly inherits an old baronial estate' and goes to England to take it up. He finds himself, his family, their manners and their language out of place, unwanted and looked down upon by British '(high) society'. His ordinary 'Australianness' provides instance after instance of inappropriate behaviour (as the butler explains 'it isn't done'). But the film has the farmer reveal his true British nobility when he forges documents to show himself to the world as an imposter – this noble gesture enables his daughter's penniless English beau to inherit the estate and precipitates the family's return to Australia minus the daughter – but accompanied by the butler who by now knows the farmer's true blue-blood and therefore 'serves' nobility, even if that means in an Australia he initially professed to disdain.[12]

But, by the mid-1960s and 1970s, the very idea of Australia as British had definitively – if unevenly – changed. Jim Davidson (1979: 139–53) suggests that a process of de-dominionization of public recognitions and Australianist projects were under way. Britain still retained its place as a privileged point of comparison, but was now used to establish characteristics of a sovereign Australian society and people. They demonstrated just who Australians were by providing a culturally different foil, showing who they were not.

Some famous revival films of the 1970s and early 1980s embody these de-dominionizing strategies. In *The Adventures of Barry McKenzie*, *Gallipoli*, *Breaker Morant* an Australian identity and culture was defined against the British. In *Barry McKenzie* the British/Australian relationship had become banal – a point of differentiation represented by competing stereotypes. The very idea of Australia as British – and England as home – is set up as a conceit to reveal its sheer implausibility and as a lame plot excuse to put the fantastic and grotesque Barry McKenzie abroad as the half-wit 'Aussie innocent'. In *Gallipoli* the emerging mateship between the two men from opposite sides of the track and different ethnicities (Anglo-Australian and Irish-descended-Australian) shape an emerging composite Anglo-Celtic Australian identity which realizes itself more and more in the face of a callous and incompetent British high command. For its part, *Breaker Morant* disposes the figure of the Australian Legend (Hancock), dominion fealty (Whitton), the Englishman in Australia (Morant/Woodward) and the emergent independent Australian (the solicitor) into a composite *de-dominionizing* Australian identity. Their solidarity is achieved through their victimization, as the British Crown betrays its Australian-based fealty.

In the light of the post-war migration and changed external circumstance Australia as a British diaspora became a self-evidently problematic public identity.[13] By the mid-1960s in television drama, and by the mid-1980s in feature film-making and mini-series production, strategies of establishing oneself in relation to a British Other were replaced by Australianist strategies where the points of reference were as likely to be inwardly defined or externally defined in relation to America and Asia.

From the late 1980s, diasporic ideas about Australia and Australian identity and society started to return to the public culture and film-making, acquiring a progressive definition with the official mainstreaming of multiculturalism and the fashion of the period for foregrounding ethnic cleavages at the expense of other cultural cleavages. The large and diverse first and second generation of migrants created and sustained the reality of Australian society as, in part, a '*collection of diasporas*'. Official multiculturalism publicly legitimates various 'national' identities and (ethnic) identity politics within the Australian context. Australia is officially described now as a people of 'diverse heritages' and the principle of dual nationality and dual citizenship designed to secure greater continuity between ethnic homelands and the Australian host culture is a well accepted principle. Here the British diaspora was revised as simply one possible ethnic diaspora in the Australian context.

If Australia is a multiplicity of diasporas then what is the 'host' Australian culture, if not just another heritage, just another diaspora? The idea of Australia as a collection of diasporas remakes the '(white) Australian heritage' as just another heritage, this time an Anglo-Celtic or Anglo heritage with no special privilege, character or cultural primacy. The diasporic idea diminishes the claim of a pre-existing settler society to being the legitimate, distinctive public and private Australian cultural identity while at the same time upholding the claim of 'special status' to the new 'true' diasporas. The 'Anglo' heritage might have an Australian history, but its culture and lifeways are seen to be ethnically and ancestrally derived from its original diasporic condition.

This idea of Australia as several diasporas runs against a mainstream Australian society which recognizes itself as a distinctive culture in the family of nations and cultures. As such only a component of this mainstream will ever recognize itself as just another diaspora. Like other new world society identities, it also recognizes itself as a composite hybrid creation fashioned from several ancestries.

For those who see Australia as the sum of its diasporas, the fact that the mainstream does not see itself as a diaspora is seen to be both self-serving and in bad faith – it is 'colonialist'. For Elizabeth Gertsakis (1994: 48) it is 'a sentimental colonialist ethnicity of essentially Protestant Anglocentric lineages based on the cluster of inheritance of pioneer heritage (explorers, settlers and merchants) and now cultural entrepreneurs'.[14]

The paradox in the idea of Australia as a collection of diasporas is evident in *No Worries*. After spending much of the film sympathetically detailing the persistence across so many generations of farming of a distinctive Australian rural community with its own lifeways and traditions, the film rewrites Matilda and her family's culture as that of another immigrant culture by its move to the city. Matilda sits blankly in a classroom and hears, as an exemplary moral lesson, how everyone apart from the Aborigines and Islanders were once 'boat people'. The film works to show how different the city culture is from the rural culture while creating homologies between her Vietnamese refugee classmate and the dispossessed Matilda. As Matilda falters uneasily in the city, her rural culture must also be a diasporic culture (but of what? In the film's logic she has migrated to another country, the Australian city – but from where: the Australian countryside?) The older Australian becomes here a diaspora without a homeland – or rather a diaspora whose homeland is a disappearing Australia.

A third sense of diasporas turns on the actual and potential gap between the mainstream 'host' culture and diasporas within Australia. This relationship is also a repetition on a longstanding historical theme associated with migration. There was a notable cultural and linguistic gap between the currency lads and lasses of the nineteenth century and the British migrant, between the Aussies and the New Australians (continental Europeans) of the immediate post-war migration, and between the 'skips' (after *Skippy*) and the various 'imports' from around the world today. This gap also has a policy recognition in the late 1970s and 1980s versions of multiculturalism which were structured around the 'migrant in a host culture' relation. SBS-TV was initially called 'ethnic television'. And it continues to be the first generation migrant's channel (including first generation British migrants). Because multiculturalism in its first guise was founded on a diasporic logic it was therefore seen to be for migrants and not to involve the mainstream.

While the gap between the settler culture and the culture of the British Isles migrant is not as large as for other migrant groups, it is still a central cleavage in this diaspora/ host culture relation. Jupp notes a 1973 study which concluded that the majority of British migrants remain 'recognizably non-Australian throughout their lives' (Richardson quoted in Jupp 1991: 63). With close to 1.2 million of a population of 17 million born in the UK and Ireland (and mostly in the UK) and with many more times the number of British migrants than any other ethnic group, the British migrant figures largely in Australian storytelling. This results in a public sensitivity towards 'Pom bashing' and a usually sensitive portrayal of English migrants as when the de-dominionizing films – *Gallipoli* and *Breaker Morant* – invite the British diaspora to move closer toward the Australian position on national political, if not national cultural, grounds. It also fictionally naturalizes narrative trajectories from the British to the Australian and British parents interacting with their Australian children. The British time and efficiency expert in *Spotswood* played by Anthony Hopkins is humanized and won over by his encounters with Australian workers.

By contrast in 1980s mini-series productions – *Fields of Fire*, *The Dunera Boys*, *Palace of Dreams* (Lawrence *et al.* 1985) and *The Far Country* (G. Miller 1987) – the NESB migrant moves from the margins to the centre of the culture and the community, acquiring standing in the process. In these stories of reconciliation and accommodation the final result is the mainstream and the ethnic migrant alike being changed. Typically – though not always – reconciliation is staged through a romance plot in which there is a mutual heterosexual attraction between the peoples represented who synecdochically stand for their respective cultures. These storytellings are utopian projections of a larger socio-cultural reality of a gap and, at times, tension between the 'the skips' and the various 'imports'. These stories of integration and acceptance after initial difficulties, exclusion and marginalization took up where *They're a Weird Mob* left off.

But documentaries, cultural criticism and short fictional storytelling – like the social research of a generation of sociologists and anthropologists – is concerned to highlight and celebrate the persistence of these gaps. There, the gap is related to the racism, domination and oppression experienced by minority communities at the hands of the mainstream and the diaspora's own logics of cultural maintenance. This film-making accentuates irreconcilable and sustaining differences.

It rejects the utopian narrative of integration. Rose Capp (1993: 15) writes of Pellizari's short film *Rabbit on the Moon* as presenting

> the trials of an Italian-Australian upbringing in the exclusively Anglo-Australian Culture Club of Australia in the 1950s through the eyes of a child. For Guiseppina the potent magic of stories and songs from an imagined homeland are tainted by the racist slurs of schoolyard peers. The security of the family and home is threatened by Anglophiliac neighbours and the dawning comprehension of adult fallibility (when the adored pet rabbit is called up for family dinner duty).

Pellizari's work shifts the angle of incidence – making the 'us' of the films address the Italian-Australian and the 'them' the ordinary Australian, the 'foreigner'. We, the audience, are placed in the position of the Italian-Australian. Her work continues the prioritizing of the diaspora and its relations or non-relations with the wider Australian culture but it transforms the address. She produces cinema and television in Australia largely for Australian audiences, but provides a space which can be Australian-Italian and so count as such in the Italian context in a way *They're a Weird Mob* never could.

Somewhere in between these two storytellings is an emerging play for a popular storytelling represented in *The Heartbreak Kid* and *Gino*. Here the ethnic community is centred and is relatively self-contained. People from the wider culture are helpers. The central conceit of *Gino* is of a stand-up comic explaining his Italo-Australian family to the general (Australian) public, which includes his father and his prospective father-in-law. He explains Australian-Italian culture to the television and comic-club audience so his father and father-in-law might accept him for what the general audience know him to be – a standup comic. In this case, the romantic couple are entirely within the community. If the non-Italians simply exist on the margins of this story, so too does the Italian homeland which is reduced to a grainy 'memory' sequence sitting in an almost surreal relation to the rest of the narrative which makes the Australian Italians part of the Australian 'family'. This storytelling replicates the American television sit-com solution to identity politics: make the comedy wholly black or wholly white. If this creates separate spaces it also embeds the community and its contemporary Australian lifeways as one native to the country.

In *Reinventing Australia*, social researcher Hugh Mackay (1990: 164) observes tension between 'Australians' and 'ethnic minorities'. He sees this as a central characteristic of the national conversation about Australia, Australian identity and questions of heritage in a society comprised of a settler culture and a large cohort of first and second generation (migrant) Australians:

> Australians want migrants to become Australians first, and to let their ethnic origins recede before that commitment; migrants, for their part, want Aus-

tralians to accept not only that the emerging cultural identity *is* diverse and is all the richer for that, but also that migrants want to be part of the new emerging Australian identity.

(165)

These tensions are structural. They turn on the difference between diasporically defined identities and a non-diasporically defined settler culture. This is the Australian identity as a fragment of *somewhere else* versus the Australian identity as simply *itself*. This is the claim of ethnic origins versus an Australian status, which though formed out of a particular ethnic mix is none the less its own identity. Each wants to reconstruct the other. One wants the mainstream settler culture to accommodate the diasporic identity of migrant minorities, and to recognize its own one-time migrant status as a condition of reconstructing the meaning of the Australian to be consonant with the Australian as so many *diasporic* identities. The mainstream culture wants the diaspora to emphasize the Australian part of its two loyalties, to emphasize one part of its bi-cultural identity at the expense of the other. Because the older settler culture does not, by and large, see itself as having a diasporic identity but rather its own identity as 'simply Australian', the claim for the older settler culture to recognize itself as diasporic appears to it as a demand for it to acquire a colonial and neocolonial form.

3 New world society

The people who went to Australia are very much like the people who came to the US. We are peoples who are outcasts, exiles or bums, people with the excitement of going to a new place.

(Pauline Kael in Hamilton and Mathews 1986: 26–7)

Australian cinema is the cinema of a new world settler society just as is the cinema of the USA and Canada and, indeed, Latin America. Like the USA, Canada and Brazil, Australia has a large landmass, relatively large wilderness areas, low population densities outside the major urban centres and indigenous populations making up a small 'minority' within its polity. Writing about the 'youth revolt' of the late 1960s and early 1970s Bruce Grant observed that:

American films such as *Easy Rider* [1969] and *Zabriskie Point* [1969] had an immediate physical resonance in Australia, where the notion of freedom owes at least as much to surf beaches, long straight roads and the availability of the motorcar, as it does to the great European thinkers on liberty, or even the particular contribution in Australia of the libertarian disciples of the late Professor John Anderson.

(Grant 1983: 15)

If Britain and Europe are seen as Australia's past, the USA is often seen as 'an extreme version of an Australian future' (Bell and Bell 1993: 202).

The comparison with the USA and English Canada is apposite in that all are English-speaking 'settler cultures'. All created marginalized and disenfranchised small indigenous minorities which trouble the national identity of the majority and their sense of moral community (Strong and Van Winkle 1993: 9–26). As I wrote in another context:

> Each has traditions of dealing with many immigrant ethnicities. Each offers the promise of citizenship rather than guest worker status to immigrants. Each sees its culture as emergent and mixed producing a new society. None demands as stringently as do the more traditional 'nations' that change be constructed in accordance with 'primordial' national traditions. Each has a version of the 'bush' and the frontier which predisposes each to the 'western' and similar kinds of conceptions of the wilderness and the environment. Each shares common elements in political, legal and constitutional arrangements. . . . When added to the preeminent place of the USA in international audio-visual trade, these conditions help explain why the US – the major vision of 'America' – should have in Australia and Anglophone Canada its best television export markets.
>
> (O'Regan 1993: 19)

There are important structural, cultural and ideological similarities encouraging recognitions of Australia as a new world society akin to the USA. With the pre-eminent place of American cinema, American policy instruments and, increasingly, cultural criticism, 'new world' templates are encouraged for the understanding of Australian society. American programming provides rough maps of Australia, its values, and its institutions.

These societies are predicated upon an immigrant's preparedness to take on new identities, and an assumption that the existing native-born identities would attenuate themselves sufficiently to accommodate this new presence. These societies and their cultures are spoken of as 'developing', as just now being formed. But, at the same time, this openness promises a society which would not offend, would not be too different, and could be made into a *continuation* of the past settler culture, the culture from which one migrated, or to which it historically compares itself.

New world societies define themselves in their emergence, as a perpetual becoming, a coming into being in the here and now, continually differentiating, incorporating and moving on. For Jean-Luc Godard the charm of the American cinema is the fact that it is always in 'perpetuum, mobile, a core of irresistible energy colonizing the world through the feature movie because as a country America lacks a firm sense of self' (quoted in Orr 1993: 6). Without such a sense, there are many and multiple senses of self. As Routt (1994a: 220) observes: '[n]ot being sure of who you are is practically the dictionary definition of being Australian' and of 'being an American'. Such provisionality is foundational to thinking about the national culture of modern Australia (Lattas 1990: 54):

> The production of Australian nationalism is mediated through the production of an identity crisis. The continual questioning of who we really are is the essence of Australian nationalism. It produces the reflective space of distance, of removal, creating the alienation which we ascribe to ourselves as the secret truth constitutive of our identity.

The new world cinema places emphasis on the cultural diversity of the audience becoming in however a transitory way, a unity around a common story-space – a myth of convergence. So as Graeme Turner observes (1994: 131) '*The Heartbreak Kid* is not a tale of a unique, diasporic culture surviving within an ersatz host culture' *but* of a 'Greek community undeniably altered by its migration to Australia' – a community 'instantly recognizable as Australian'.

The 'new world cinema' is a cinema of the melting pot. It is populist in intent with its utopian ideological underpinnings. The worlds of the Spanish migrant and the older Australian are brought together in the finale of *Strictly Ballroom*. The romantic sexual union of the ethnically unmarked Australian man and the ethnically marked woman, parallels the solidarity between the Australian father and the woman's grandmother and father who, both socially marginal, lend their applause to the triangular relationship of the couple on the dance floor and become central in the reconstructed public world from which they have been hitherto excluded. The institution of ballroom dancing is infused with the flamenco steps remaking and rejuvenating itself so the son can fulfill his father's destiny. For Turner (1994: 129) 'Scott and Fran's performance has its roots both in Fran's Spanish family and in Scott's father's repressed history of attempting to challenge the dance competition's conventions himself.'

A predilection for such a utopian emergence, distinguishes Australia cinema as a new world settler society cinema. Like all such narratives – and the cinema more generally – this is a mythic narrative improbable in the real, and conforming to the aim of any entertainment cinema to present the imaginary as if it were the real.[15]

Like so many American films since the 1970s, what is 'Australian' about the context of *Death in Brunswick* is, in Turner's (1994: 132) words 'not its cultural purity but the mix of identity and accents – the play of ethnicity and class positions audible in the dialogue or legible in the clothing and physical appearances'. Ethnicity becomes subcultural lifestyle. Like its US counterpart of the 1970s to the present, 1990s Australian film-making is adding various ethnic identities to the subcultural identities it surveys and adding markers of different ancestries on screen. In Philip Brophy's schlock splatter feature *Body Melt* the Italian-Australian becomes simply one among a number of social types which include the middle-aged fitness fanatic, the thirty-something divorcee, the expectant mother, the steroid pumped-up body builders, the rural idiots, skippy and the mad doctor.

These caricatures are firmly in the service of the rich and 'unspeakably' gross spectacle provided by Brophy and his production designer, Maria Kozic. John Dingwall's *The Custodian* (1993) backgrounds ethnic and racial diversity, as the senior management of the newspaper breaking the police corruption story is represented by a first generation Chinese and a Continental European. Their Chineseness and NESB Europeanness does not enter the plot – it serves to provide colour and a big picture look. Of the central characters – the 'good guy', Anthony Paglia, looks Southern European.[16] A similar moment can be seen in Alexsi Vellis''s *Nirvana Street Murder* where Greekness becomes another subcultural identity. As Aleksi Vellis puts it:

> I set out in *Nirvana Street Murders* not to have two different types of characters. Everyone is nuts. None of the Greeks have [*sic*] bad back problems or language problems or cultural problems. They are dickheads like everybody else.
>
> (Quoted in Verhoeven 1993: 16)

Being a 'dickhead', by definition, is inclusive. He insists that 'characters' in drama should not be 'formulated to serve a [social] problem' but 'just be people in drama for entertainment'.

These films reflect the ways that in an immigrant society the protection of minorities tends toward the right of minorities to assimilate, integrate and contribute to the making of the broader culture. This is most explicit in *Strictly Ballroom*. Fran wants to be a ballroom dancer. She assimilates the established ballroom steps and adds something to them. As Philip Schlesinger notes (1994: 28), new world societies like the USA favour a social, cultural and political system where 'individual rather than group rights' are asserted. Fran stands up for herself. She asks to be Scott's partner. Her romantic interest is outside her ethnic community.

Such a film-making and that involving ethnically unmarked characters as in *The Man from Snowy River* and the *Mad Max* cycle maps out an Australian communication space where communicating with a multiethnic audience is a norm. Perhaps this explains the importance to American and indeed Australian cinema of myth – the sometimes maligned Australian mainstream cinema participates in the same 'democratic character' Adrian Martin and Geoffrey Nowell-Smith reserve for their description of American cinema – in that it is also a

> complex endeavour to unify what Nowell-Smith describes as 'an extremely diverse and largely immigrant public' around an image, a myth of 'America'. Thus a space is opened wherein cultural differences must necessarily be approached and negotiated, a rhetoric inevitably drawing in audiences of other nations.
>
> (Martin 1988b: 137–8)

The value and achievement of new world cinemas within their respective multi-ethnic contexts should not be underestimated. Douglas Gomery (1992: 171) observes that when Hollywood was creating and fashioning American identities as talkies came in during the late 1920s, the USA was 'a nation of first generation immigrants' such that '[t]wo of every three Americans consciously claimed membership in an ethnic community, either as foreign born or their descendants'. The new world Hollywood cinema was a commercial cinema. It did not set one ethnic group against the other – instead it fashioned the American as something else, neither one nor other of these identities. This *synthetic* identity was created by producers seeking to make money out of an ethnically diverse audience, by finding ways to combine them into a mass audience for a schedule of films and television programmes. Philip Schlesinger (1994: 34) points out that 'American film and television producers have for several generations addressed an ethnically diverse nation through a common language'. Here, as in society more generally, 'the consumer market', as Banton (1994: 5) notes, acts as 'a solvent of ethnic particularism'.

But, as the cinema of Douglas Sirk (*Written on the Wind* 1956), Paul Verhoeven (*Total Recall* 1990), James Cameron (*Terminator 2* 1991) and Billy Wilder (*Some Like it Hot* 1959) demonstrate, gaining the attention and solidarity of a culturally diverse audience need not involve centring ethnically marked identities. Like some of its American counterparts, *Crocodile Dundee* and *Gallipoli* worked with archetypal and abstracted figures. Their preference for the bushman/woman, the 'larrikin digger' are functional preferences for a diverse audience. Freda Freiberg (1994: 196), for example, notes that the larrikin city and bush figure in Australian cinema – a figure often associated with the Australian, and the Irish, and British immigrant – exhibited characteristics shared by the London 'cockney' Jews who were also transported or migrated in the same period. Her analysis is suggestive of the ways in which 'Australian stereotypes', so closely identified by multicultural critique with the Anglo-Celtic peoples, had resonances in the Jewish community and elsewhere, proffering spaces of identification if not direct inclusion.

An unmarked sense of 'unity' created out of the materials of diversity is clear in the 1960s and 1970s project in Australian cinema and television to create an 'Australian' voice and culture. This fashioned something new. Not only did it develop a stage and screen Australian accent different from what had been in place, but accents became more uniform from the mid-1960s compared to earlier productions (where as many as four or five different accents provided markers of class, ethnic, sectarian and gender differences in *They're a Weird Mob* and Hector and Dorothy Crawford's television series *Consider your Verdict* (1961)). The resulting Australian story space accentuated similarities within the culture and displayed its differences as those of competing values, generations, geography, class, gender and taste. This created – just as it reflected – a differently organized and non-British defined Australian identity, in which the Australian was consti-tuted largely through auto-identification. Ordinary television series from the 1960s articulated in the *vernacular* popular culture a non-diasporically defined

Australian identity. Similarly the quality films of the 1970s synecdochically registered the settler nation through the growth to maturity of its second generation in *My Brilliant Career, The Irishman* and *The Mango Tree.* The very idea of Australia as a derived society and a society of immigrants from elsewhere had gone into eclipse at the level of popular culture. Some of the relations of comparison were maintained with Britain and elsewhere but it was more likely that the American relation was foregrounded – most famously in *Crocodile Dundee.* Australia became, like America, another new world society. Australian popular culture – particularly in its most market-responsive audiovisual dramatic forms – created a myth of the Australian, deliberately focusing in front of the camera on the Australian as a character without any especial ethnic marking.

The popular products of this auto-identification – imposed as much by the commercial logic of differentiation in the symbolic goods market – are now seen by cultural critics to be homogenous, monocultural and exclusionary. For Graeme Turner (1994: 8) the cinema of the 1970s is an inward-directed cinema dedicated to a 'unitary nationalism' and restating Australian 'cultural purity'. But, like the Hollywood films of Billy Wilder, Douglas Sirk and Jean Renoir, some of the better known Australian titles were shaped by people of diverse ancestry. When they crafted *Mad Max, Careful he Might Hear You, Lonely Hearts, Bad Boy Bubby, Dot and the Kangaroo, Storm Boy* and *Coolangatta Gold* (Auzins 1984), Dr George Miller, Carl Schultz, Paul Cox, Rolf de Heer, Yoram Gross, Henri Safran and Igor Auzins were shaping an emergent Australian story space. Like Billy Wilder of the 1950s and 1960s (*The Apartment* (1960), *Some Like it Hot*) and Robert Zemeckis of today (*Forrest Gump* 1994), these were not simply people with 'ethnic last names'. They created a socially functional story space as it bypassed the communal idealism associated with ethnicity and sectarianism. It was also an audiovisual strategy meeting the objective market need for an Australian storytelling to define itself and supply its audience with a marketable entertainment identity (locally and internationally) and as something different from the United Kingdom and North American 'accents' on offer on the screen. This emergent culture and identity was not and is not monocultural, it was simply working from different principles of diversity – ones defined in a new world fashion.

Australian and American cinema has not sought so much to transcend ethnic particularism as to bypass it on the way to doing something else.[17] The strength of the new world societies and their cinemas has been to emphasize, create incentives, and expand the opportunities for relationships not governed by ethnic norms. One such opportunity has been provided by the important decision to emphasize a commercially-based and non-social policy driven screen culture. Such societies tend to offer members of a particular ethnic community more attractive benefits from incorporation 'in the wider society' than can ethnic organization and associations (Banton 1994: 15). Translated into the cinema, this results in the more attractive spectacle of *Muriel's Wedding* with its lurid, saturated colours, its energy and its excessive characterizations, or *Mad Max*'s powerful mix of action, spectacle and epic in dramatic landscapes in a mythical story frame. Do such films serve the Anglo-Celtic hegemony and a unitary and consensual version of the nation? It is certainly true that their Australia is that of Australian English and it has a European physiognomy. Like all cinemas, it was a cinema of the dominant ethnicity but this dominant ethnicity was in self-formation and was made by and of several ancestries. Like the American identity, this Australian identity was mythic.[18]

Additionally, many major cultural influences on this dominant culture, such as the huge American influence or the Western influence more generally in Australia are not based on immigration, colonial history, or ethnic ancestry. The dominant settler culture provides for an affiliation to, sense of kinship with and a relationship of solidarity with other English-speaking and Western cultures. Such affiliations do not need ancestral connections to be sustained, they make up a common Western vernacular.[19]

Priority given in state policy to equality, equity and access is mirrored in the narrative trajectories of film and television mini-series. They turn on the ultimate incorporation of the outsider and the outsider's culture into the broader Australian society, whether through the journey of the individual or family or the transformation of the broader community. This is Nino's journey into an acceptance and understanding of Australian culture in *They're a Weird Mob*. In *Gino* it is the resolution of pregnancy, marriage and career on the hybrid terms of the second generation Italian-Australian and not the traditional Italian values and cultural insularities of the first generation. Even when there is a failure of incorporation – as in the mini-series *Cowra Breakout* and *Always Afternoon*, where a massacre and a suicide result for the respective Japanese and German victims of Australian incomprehension and bastardry, this is resolved at the level of the viewer, as a moral imperative of reconciliation for the future.[20]

The achievement of a new world cinema is to downplay ethnicity and instead concentrate on other coordinates to describe the 'people-among-themselves'. This downplaying also has its base in social processes of ethnic intermixing at the most basic level of the family. The logic of Australian cinema as a new world cinema is strongly embedded. It has become even more dominant since the demise of its previous incarnations – Australian cinema as a kind of British cinema and with it the dominion and de-dominionizing relationships. What this cinema reminds us of is not only that the cinema is international, imaginary and emergent but that affiliations to its byways cross ethnic and social cleavages and in doing so create new demographic and cultural cleavages, *outside* the lottery of birth, ethnicity and familial structures. The capacity for popular cinema – road movies, musicals, schlock-splatter movies, cult movies – to expand these points of contact and multiply these points of differentiation in the context of palpable ethnic diversity is cause for modest celebration.

This popular culture of entertainment and consumerism, like the workplace, neighbourhood, schooling and intermarriage, is hybridized and incorporates diverse elements and ancestries into the dominant culture which so become powerful 'solvents' of ethnic cultural cleavages. It breaks down existing cleavages and reconstitutes them in terms of locality, urban/city, generational differences and composite ethnic divisions. The strength of Australian society and its culture historically has been its open cultural market-place which has given free rein to commercial and consumer culture, thereby accentuating non-traditionally defined spaces and points of contact.

Working within the domain of popular art, the 'new world identity' provides relatively unselfconscious public identities that can be readily consented to. It suffers the same opprobrium as do all such popular identities: it is consumer and fashion driven, it is ephemeral, it is utopian, it is not serious, it is hegemonic. By contrast, the multicultural society and multicultural cinema is a more critically acceptable identity. It is an official, critical intellectual and selfconscious creation. It can discount the authority, legitimacy and reach of the settler cultural and aesthetic traditions, which provide the basic grammar of Australian film and television production to imagine possibilities shaped by other less dominant interests. It sees itself as providing new vocabularies for film and television production and nationhood.

4 A multicultural society

Multiculturalism has several complementary guises. Cultural critics, film-makers, artists and people of difference own it as an alternative and oppositional Australian identity. It is a government policy designed to administer and 'control the dynamic process of the articulation of cultural difference, administering a consensus based on a norm that propagates cultural diversity' (Bhabha 1990: 208). Government agencies promote it as the basis for a new and general Australian identity which would make cultural difference 'constitutive of [national] identity' (Turner 1994: 124). And cultural critics celebrate it as postnational(ist) politics which would move beyond jingoism, the stultifying sameness of a monocultural nation, and allow for some Aboriginal and Islander accommodation.

What unites these versions is the idea of: affirming existing cultural diversity, bringing Australian cultural activity including film and television into alignment with this diversity, and projecting cultural diversity as an organizing social, aesthetic and national principle. Multiculturalism privileges social and cultural mixing, hybrid identities, hybrid cultural forms and cultural crossovers. It becomes simultaneously a critical ethic, a civic comportment, an aesthetic project propelling Australian cultural production forward, as well as a national project remaking Australia and the Australian into something more culturally open. It acknowledges the integrity of society's social margins, it promotes the action in and on Australian culture and society by its culturally diverse peoples – but most particularly the various NESB communities (diasporic and Aboriginal), and it sees these as positively reshaping Australian society and culture. In the multicultural vision Australia's cultural diversity – its multiethnic and multi-racial reality – is what is currently transforming Australian society and culture.

Multiculturalism proclaims the centrality – to society, nation, cultural production – of the disenfranchized and the recent immigrant. It is an international condition. Homi Bhabha (1994: 6) suggests that '[i]ncreasingly, "national" cultures are being produced from the perspective of disenfranchized minorities'. And '[t]he Western metropole must confront its postcolonial history, told by its influx of postwar migrants and refugees, as an indigenous or native narrative internal to its national identity'.[21]

The multicultural screen and arts critic claims cutting edge status for multicultural work, and simultaneously the space of the Australian. (For Carillo Gantner, one time Chair of the Performing Arts Board of the Australia Council 'work that is "cutting-edge" and uniquely Australian ... today that means multicultural' (quoted in Blonski 1994: 194).) The work of multicultural artists – i.e. cultural producers of a culturally diverse background – is a privileged site for the renegotiation of form and content:

> [R]ather than simply perpetrating old forms, one of the exciting new elements in the diasporic experience at the heart of multiculturalism is the idea that something quite new develops as a result of transplanting to a new context and interacting with other groups. It can generate a new hybridized cross-cultural art.
>
> (Gunew 1994: 6)

For a generation of critical intellectuals (Sneja Gunew, Audrey Yue, Elizabeth Gertzakis, Nikos Papastagiardis) and artists from a non-Anglo-Celtic background (Tan, Pellizari, Jayamenne) what is celebrated is the 'indeterminancy of identity' as a 'productive state' for the production of culture (Gunew 1994: 9). Thus Yue (1993: 21) writes in the context of discussing the work of Asian-Australian film-makers, Teck Tan and Lalleen Jayamenne that:

> Becoming Asian-Australian is a continually involving contemporaneity of not just crossing the territorial boundaries of one or the other, but of confronting them in their controversies. The challenge of this space is the realm in between outsider-in and insider-out, and beyond that which is predeterminately visible and familiar.

Such multiple identities and loyalties are even seen to be the coming global form as '[i]n political and economic term, cultural diversity is one of the central issues of our time' (Kalantzas and Cope 1994: 33).

Through the exercise of these logics, people of an NESB and Aboriginal and Islander background garner a public identity and a significance as cultural producers on several levels. They become the new emblematic national persona auguring 'a national identity which celebrates its hybridity rather than its purity'. They become those agents best equipped to dispose of the 'tired and irrelevant discourses of traditional Australian nationalism' (Turner 1994: 124). And they become the emergent groups: the marginalized social groups that challenge a morally and aesthetically spent mainstream.

Multiculturalism becomes a concept for everyone in its promise to 'dynamically open[ing] up the dominant culture' (Kalantzis and Cope 1993: 144). It is cosmopolitan. It embraces international 'contamination' in the place of insularity. It makes Australia a 'more interesting place'. For Curthoys and Muecke (1993: 180) this multiculturalism permits 'a postcolonial identity ... inherent in realizing the hybrid identities remaining to be developed out of the specific cultural materials at Australia's disposal'. It is distinguishable for its post-national characteristics:

> If the earlier nationalisms were predicated on unity (of race), exclusion (of Others), and by white exploitation of the land, then the post-national varieties can be predicated on difference (both internally and externally), inclusion (a multiculturalism not confined to the European) and a relegitimation of Aboriginal sovereignty over the land.
>
> (Curthoys and Muecke 1993: 179)

In this emerging version, Aborigines and Islanders have a central symbolic place, as do minority ethnic groups. A post-national multiculturalism promises a bringing together of the Aboriginal and the ethnic not to subsume one as part of the other but as part of a larger accommodation of the logic of first peoples and various forms of difference – ethnic and otherwise.

For this post-national project there is no more important figure than Aboriginal and Islander film-maker Tracey Moffatt. Moffatt's work is exemplary for a postnational multicultural criticism at several levels. It incorporates difference within the national space. Aboriginal and non-Aboriginal subjects negotiate the meaning and future of this space. A dialogue is set up between Aborigines and other culturally diverse peoples. In the process, the Australian society becomes unhinged and less fixed. This is precisely the promise for Jon Stratton and Ien Ang of Australian multiculturalism:

> Australian multiculturalism expressly incorporates ethnic difference within the space of the national, it provides a framework for a politics of negotiation over the very content of national culture, which is no longer imagined as something fixed and historically given but as something in the process of becoming. ...
> Thus, it is now possible to think about the distinctiveness of Australian national culture not in terms of an exclusive, pregiven racial/cultural particularity, but as an open-ended and provisional formation, as permanently unfinished business.[22]
>
> (1994b: 152)

As a photographer, visual artist and film-maker Moffatt's work is on the aesthetic cutting edge, crossing the conventional boundaries separating the different media and cultural forms. She provides evidence for Kalantzas and Cope's (1994:33) contention that 'diversity is where the cultural action is' and that 'the most exciting work is work that crosses cultural boundaries'. Moffatt demonstrates that the subjects best equipped for this project are 'NESB artists', now including Aboriginal and Islander artists, producing 'new hybridised cross-cultural art' (Gunew and Rizvi 1994b, xiii). Her work fits the satisfactions demanded by the cinephile and gallery-based appreciative audiences because, as Karen Jennings (1993: 73) notes, her work is often concerned 'with image and sound rather than expositary narrative' and realism. And it fits a feminist agenda too. For Patricia Mellencamp (1994: 128), Moffatt recovers 'history through fiction' and inscribes what has been 'missing in history and representation' – 'Aboriginal women'.

Moffatt's statements about herself foreground the 'indeterminacy of (her) identity'. She projects herself in a set of serial public identities which we read as her refusal to endorse a fixed identity, as a desire to disrupt conventional categories and confining stereotypes of Aboriginals and film-making. 'I want to be known as Tracey Moffatt interesting film-maker'; 'Tracey Moffatt, Aboriginal film-maker'; 'Yes I am Aboriginal, but I have the right to be *avant-garde* like any white artist',[23] or simply the beautiful Aboriginal woman unafraid to sensualize and eroticize herself as an actor in her feature, *beDevil*. Moffatt's public persona signals the possibility of (eventual) reconciliation; while being a palpable sign of an Aboriginal resistance to any such utopian rapprochement; her work is 'modern', *avant-garde* accessible and ponderable – she invites our interpretations, she goes out of her way to welcome them, while keeping open her options to later dispute the interpretations we produce. Rather than pre-empting our speculative interpretation, interrelatedness and the invitation to 'intersubjective dialogue' are foregrounded, so she can enlist us to project and assign meanings to her films and herself, just as she berates us for attempting to do so. We are still aware of being positioned as others appropriating black culture,[24] but this is on Aboriginal invitation, we are not those white film-makers and critics who activist and actor Gary Foley says are 'riding to success on the back of blacks' (quoted in S. Bell 1990: 35).

Moffatt is also important to the international standing of Australian cinema. This is not only a function of the standing of her work: its originality, its striking character, its use of theatrical design, its decidedly non-realist emphases – all *avant-garde* credentials; it is also her position as an indigenous film-maker of international standing. She is part of a new and emerging compartment of the international art cinema of which she is an innovator. And in this domain Australia is not a side player. Aboriginals and Islanders are one of the most known and foremost of indigenous peoples (T. Miller 1995: 7–17).

As an Aboriginal, a woman and simultaneously a victim and product of assimilationary logics she is doubly disadvantaged and disenfranchised. Her history is well-known. As a child she was taken from her Aboriginal mother and raised by – and I quote Moffatt here – 'an older white woman'. She embodies this shameful history of attempted cultural genocide as its victim, its storyteller, and its survivor (see Mellencamp 1994: 129). Moreover, as E. Ann Kaplan observes, her films are not simply in the business of 'locating and celebrating Aboriginal specificity' they are also about 'cultural inter-relatedness' (cited in Jennings 1993: 73). In all her major films – *Night Cries*, *Nice Coloured Girls* and *beDevil* – Moffatt insists on this interrelatedness while Aboriginalizing the viewing perspective.[25]

Moffatt does not forget or forgive the history of 'exclusion, exploitation and oppression' in order to become something else (perhaps more assimilated, well behaved, like the whites/Europeans/settlers); instead she confronts Aboriginal and Whites, to borrow Yue's expression, 'in their controversies'. In remembering and foregrounding Aboriginal white sexual and familial relations in *Nice Coloured Girls* and *Night Cries* she claims a positive heritage, an identity and Aboriginal women's agency snatched from this awful history.

Night Cries explicitly addresses her personal history. Karen Jennings (1993: 73) describes it as 'a film about a relationship between a middle aged Aboriginal woman . . . and an elderly white woman whom we assume to be her foster mother' (1993: 73). The focus of *Night Cries* is not on the moment of child stealing, or on growing up Aboriginal in a white family. It takes up the story later when identities are well established, interrelatedness is routine, embedded, ritualized *and* dysfunctional. As Marcia Langton (1993: 46) observes, these two women are 'independent beings, but perhaps they are not whole' (Langton plays the Aboriginal daughter).

The eventual death of the white mother can suggest that 'Aboriginal rebirth is conditional on the death of many prevailing white–black relationships' (S. Murray 1990: 22). But Moffatt invites a more personal reading by telling Murray that, as she developed the script, 'it became . . . more about me and my white foster mother' and that it was intentional that the little girl used in the flashback sequences 'looks a lot like me'. So, the film-maker not only imagines her mother's death, she is also admitting to matricidal feelings about her – and these feelings are crossed by an interracial history and politics of black exploitation, particularly as domestic servants in rural Australia.[26]

Throughout the film our attention is on the Langton character (she becomes simultaneously the film-maker's alter ego and the film-maker's screen surrogate as an older Moffatt). We see the mother through her eyes. We are made complicit in the middle-aged daughter's anger, frustration, bitterness and bad temper directed at her aged, decrepit, wheelchair-bound white mother. This anger can stand for wider Aboriginal anger towards the white society that usurped their land and marginalized them into servitude. So Scott Murray (1990: 20) can write 'the Old Mother's incontinence' suggests 'a white society clogged by its own cancers'.

In this logic, the mother's death frees the daughter of such self-destructive obligations to her white mother, yet there is nothing upbeat about her death – for how can a daughter gloat over her mother's death? Alongside the hatred of the white mother, stands the Aboriginal daughter's love and scarcely consolable grief. Aboriginal/white relations are firmly implicated within the family. Moffatt's films display the white mainstream if only to marginalize and displace it by Aboriginal presence and agency (she narrativizes white Australian impotence). Yet her films also speak of implication and mutual history. So Moffatt can cheekily claim that

> my film is universal, that it isn't particularly about black Australia and white Australia. It's about a child's being moulded and repressed – she's very sexually repressed. It could be the story of anyone stranded in the middle of the desert having to look after their ageing mother. American audiences understood it very well. They really liked it. It didn't matter that they didn't know the lead actress was Aboriginal.
>
> (Quoted in Scott Murray 1990: 79)

Her first feature *beDevil* also problematizes the settler mainstream and an Aboriginal history that will not go away. But even more than *Night Cries*, it endows this mainstream with what Carol Laseur (1993: 87) has called 'contradictory character traits'. By the third story of *beDevil*'s triptych structure, 'Love'n the Spin I'm In', the settler culture takes on a multicultural hue. But, as Laseur continues, this cultural difference 'whether it be Aboriginal, Greek, Torres Strait Islander, Chinese or Mexican, is not played upon in order to create a special or singular sense of meaning or identity'. Instead she sees spaces of 'intercultural dialogue'. Nowhere is this clearer than in the relation between Dimitri and his Islander tenant Emelda and her relatives in the 'Love'n' story.

Dimitri has a problem: he needs to evict Emelda and her extended family. Yet he cannot do it. Why? He also wants to remain on friendly terms with her. (Is this the settler culture's 'bad faith'? Wanting to remain friendly while doing over Aborigines and Islanders?) He promises his business associates something he cannot deliver. Laseur writes:

> Dimitri, Conos and Fong are negotiating prospects of a marina on the still occupied site, [when] Emelda's relatives turn up. All welcome Dimitri like a long lost family member. A reaction shot from Conos and Fong soon establishes the ironic and conflicting positionalities Dimitri occupies in his multifaceted relationships. In a desperate attempt to reconcile business connections with the sceptical observers, Dimitri stutters, 'It's all part of a traditional squatter's farewell ceremony'.
>
> (1993: 87)

In the process, the Islanders become the 'ghosts in the (capitalist) machine'. They refuse to go away, and what is more, Dimitri does not ultimately want them to although he does not admit to it. In this final story, the successfully buried Aboriginal and other history/presence cannot be replaced by the canal developments of the middle story. Islander resistance and occupation prevents it. The tenant/landlord relation is inverted and the would-be developer settles for drinking till late with his black neighbours.

Film-makers like Pauline Chan, Monica Pellizari and Clara Law (*Floating Life*) are also creating a *diasporic multicultural cinema* – but they suffer the same problems as the mainstream – they can only ever be another instance or a significant variant of a larger international whole. Chan and Law of the diasporic Chinese/Asian cinema of North America, Taiwan and Hong Kong. Pellizari of the Italian-American. The space once occupied by the European art film becomes occupied in the 1990s by the prospect of a multicultural cinema largely in English. The multicultural cinema that emerges in their work, and that of Moffatt, requires as did its earlier 'quality cinema' incarnations, government action to secure it.

In enacting and occupying the spaces of 'collective aspiration', the 'multicultural cinema' is a close relation to the 'new world cinema'. The major difference between them is the greater store that multicultural projects place upon acknowledging cultural difference, distinct cultural spaces within the country, and unmeltable racial and ethnic differences. Whether as a cinema of cultural openness and respect for diversity or the cinema of an emerging composite NESB ethnicity capable of taking on the dominant ethnicity – or even a new dominant and open-ended ethnicity – this 'multicultural cinema' distinguishes itself from the project of a new world settler society by its foregrounding of cultural diversity as matters of symbolic and political self-determination within the nation.

From a multicultural standpoint the new world cinema was interested in de-differentiating strategies. It emphasized commonalities rather than differences, consensus rather than plurality, a singular Australian identity rather than multiple identities. The new world cinema configures incursions, increments and alterations to existing forms and means of representation. A multicultural cinema imagines its task as one of accentuating differences. It projects the expression of differences as an ethical principle. It projects itself on the side of the emergent and the open-ended. It imagines another beginning in the cinema and another chance for Australia.

If, as we have seen, the new world project was also emergent, open-ended and composite, the multicultural project distinguishes itself by leaving more space for negotiation by minorities. For example, it more easily allows an integral place in the 'national community' for Aboriginal and Islander peoples. What is envisaged here are sovereign individual cultures and communities existing within the nation space and laying claim to that national space. By contrast, the new world identity incorporates producing a changing dominant ethnicity over my lifetime – from British to Anglo-Celt to European.

CONCLUSION

Australia's changing migration patterns and the need to publicly recognize the special status of its first peoples makes necessary post-national multiculturalism and diasporic projections alike. They provide a foil to the continuing and hegemonic Anglo-Celtic, European and English-speaking society routinely produced in the mainstream cinema and television. Multicultural and diasporic understandings also underwrite the frustration the critic, policy-maker and the NESB and Aboriginal film director feel, that in spite of a decade of multiculturalism, a national broadcaster dedicated to cultural diversity and, of late, a more responsive mainstream public broadcaster in the ABC they still face the uneven marginalization from the centres of Australian popular cinema. Andrew Jakubowicz (1994: 104) reports findings that the Australian mass audience is 'significantly racist' and this is evidenced by the fact 'substantial minorities' in Australia are unable to 'exert very little real effect on the [on screen] outcomes'. The mainstream still holds 'conventional monocultural views of nation and national identity' which stand in the way of the multicultural ideal.

For this position, changes in population demography and in the culture of the new world society never seem quick enough. They routinely encounter the screen culture's representational limits. The popular symbolic screen culture gives priority to the majority of the population who are Australian born and are of several ancestries. It still prioritizes at a public level those with no special allegiances other than to Australia. It will remain an English-language cinema participating in that cultural area's broader conversations. It does not privilege biculturalism and hybridity.[27] It continues to foreground an ethnically unmarked and non-diasporically defined Australian identity, alongside markers of cultural diversity, as in Hollywood film and television. Australian screen culture and society continues to be Eurocentric in its outlooks and norms. Neither a multicultural cinema nor SBS-TV will make significant incursions into Hollywood's and the popular Australian cinema and television's lion's share of the viewing of all audiences, including ethnic audiences.

The cultural specificities and socio-political projects dealt with here variously project and describe Australian lifeways, society and its ethnicities. Each encapsulates a dynamic of interpenetration and hybridization. Each has its own utility. Each requires a medium and a means of translation to find filmic form. These projects provide materials and orientations for critics, film-makers, policy makers and audiences alike. Some of these projects are antagonistic, some are complementary. Sometimes films can be interpreted within each of these terms. Jackie McKimmie's *Gino* is simultaneously a film about the Italian diaspora in Australia, emphasizing its self containment and its continuities with the old country. It is a multicultural film-making demonstrating cultural hybridization and mixing, as the various aspects of settler Australian lifeways are taken on, friendships and business partnerships are organized (Gino has a non-Italian manager, his girlfriend has an Anglo best friend), and as Italian-Australian culture is given its own integrity as part of Australian society. It is an example of the new world cinema, because the story is marked as a story for all, by the stand-up comedian marking out a space that is something more than the Italian, but a part of the Australian, thus becoming the property of everyone. And it depicts an obviously European society with difference clearly marked as persisting within European Australia.

My personal preference is for the less idealized and more composite of these formations – like the new world and multicultural identities – which do not turn so crucially on the lottery of birth and ancestry. But I still need to acknowledge the integrity of imported nationalities and their attendant identity politics, the reality of longstanding diasporas and, if we are to be symmetrical in criticism, the integrity of a dominant European ethnicity. I also need to acknowledge the limits of all such macro-level problematizations. These society-wide and nationhood differentiations do not provide the various cultural differentiations of gender, region, demography and class mapped out previously with a larger direction and coherence. Problematizations of nation do not structure all the other social problematizations. They are simply one more problematization to be coordinated, ranked and associated with other such problematizations in the film milieu.

Chapter 14

Critical dispositions

INTRODUCTION

In her discussion of French cinema, Susan Hayward (1993: 6–7) identifies a
number of 'modalities' that 're-present the cinema'. She distinguishes 'critical
discourses', 'historical' and 'state' discourses. Both the critical discourses (ranging 'from film criticism to film theory') and the historical discourses are in the
business of 'identifying the nature of the national cinema' and 'in privileging a
certain type of cinema'. In this final chapter, I want to examine these critical and
historical discourses and the institutional networks that support them.

EXPLICATORY AND SYMPTOMATIC FILM CRITICISM

In *Making Meaning* (1989: 43), David Bordwell argues that the most general
division in criticism is between explicatory and symptomatic criticism. Explicatory criticism 'rests upon the belief that the principal goal of critical activity
is to ascribe implicit meanings to films'. Here critics take 'referential or explicit
meaning as only the point of departure or inferences about implicit meanings'. By
contrast, symptomatic criticism is concerned with diagnosis, practising 'a "hermeneutics of suspicion", a scholarly debunking, a strategy that sees apparently
innocent interactions as masking unflattering impulses'. It involves asking Nietzs-
che's questions:

> When we are confronted with any manifestation which someone has permitted
> us to see, we may ask: what is it meant to conceal? what is it meant to draw our
> attention from? what prejudice does it seek to raise? and again, how far does the
> subtlety of the dissimulation go? and in what respect is the man mistaken?
>
> (Nietzsche, quoted in Bordwell 1989: 72)

In contemporary film criticism, Bordwell suggests, a particular kind of symptomatic interpretation has ruled: it is one that 'rewards the interpreter who seems to
analyse a publicly accessible "work" or "text"'. The critic shows 'how repressed
material has social sources and consequences'. Film secretes 'something significant about the culture which produces or consumes it' (73). Bordwell further
suggests that there is often a division of labour between these two critical

repertoires, as explicatory criticism is reserved for 'good objects' and sympto-matic criticism for 'bad objects'.

Such a critical division of labour entails different text and commentary rela-tions. The explicatory critic starts from a position of respect which assumes the semiotic richness and density of the work. The critic works inside out and pays close and sympathetic attention to film meanings. S/he enters a dialogue with the film. Film meaning is expansive. And this expansiveness owes itself to the labour of the film and of the film-maker. By contrast, the symptomatic critic is often at war with the text. As this is politics by other means, no quarter is given. Criticism evens the score by giving full weight to that which is suppressed, repressed, elided and excluded. The critic reveals the flaws of the film through an often un-sympathetic attention. Critics have skirmishes with the films they examine.

Film critics typically reconcile both these practices by pursuing one at a time. They are encouraged in this by a relatively stable division of labour and value which distributes explicatory and symptomatic criticism to different film-making domains. Film intellectuals treat the short film and the alternative film in an explicatory fashion, drawing out its implicit meanings. They treat the mainstream features and mini-series production symptomatically, drawing out their repressed meanings. (Explicatory criticism – when undertaken on mainstream cinema – tends to be reserved for reviews in the highly transient and ephemeral discussions in the film trade publications; sometimes cultural critics make such a claim for a mainstream film which is seen to be worthy despite being mainstream.) Independ-ent or 'eccentric' films readily impel implicit readings because they are seen to supply 'the missing' not the main 'beat'. A neat symmetry emerges: the virtual audiences of these independent film-makers is underwritten by the emergent cinema promised by film critics. On the other hand, symptomatic criticism is rarely undertaken on independent cinema. Rather, it is a cinema with a 'discern-ible "freedom" where ideas not budgets were the distinguishing factor' (*Adelaide Advertiser* 6 October 1994, 'Focusing on Frames'). There is often good reason here, in that some of this cinema is more *read about* than viewed. Sympathetic writing matters more to this cinema.

Furthermore, the best writing on Australian cinema is often explicitly debunk-ing and wary. Perhaps this is most classically embodied in Helen Grace and Jeni Thornley's ascerbic comment (1981: 4) about the then 'film export' drive:

> Films are fast becoming Australia's sheep. It's no longer wool for the world,
> it's films for the world. The new nationalistic fervour that surrounds Australia's
> latest export commodity is not much different from the nationalism that has
> surged through the white Australian history of two hundred years.
>
> (Grace and Thornley 1981: 4)

Australian writing on the cinema and television is often measured by the amount of indignation capable of being registered about a film or programme. Critical writing thrives on problematic and ambiguous objects like *Romper Stomper*, *Crocodile Dundee* or the television series *Embassy*: '[i]ndeed some of the most lively criticism in Australia has surrounded "popular" films' (AFC, 1991: 61). There are reasons for this. Critics are now trained in a 'hermeneutics of suspicion' more than in explicatory protocols. And symptomatic criticism thrives on problematic objects. Popular films also have the added advantage that readers can be expected to be familiar with them, so critics can work from a shared and ubiquitous object. As the AFC (1991: 61) submission to The Moving Pictures Inquiry put it: 'the homogenous "good" critical response is not necessarily the "best" result for the film, its film-makers or film culture in Australia'.[1] So:

> A warm and forgettably uncritical response to a film may be less satisfying than passionate disagreement amongst audiences and critics about its moral choices. Panning a bad film may provide the vehicle for an energetic discussion about the state of Australian or world cinema. Assessing critical response is certainly not about setting up a simple opposition to commercial success.

These fractures are evident in the work of Dermody and Jacka. The second volume of *The Screening of Australia* (1988a) is mostly made up of symptomatic film criticism. They locate the repressed masculinist meanings of Australian cinema. They find an 'inward national drama' at work. They see Australian cinema locked into a series of textual and economic 'double binds' of a 'second cinema'. They debunk the claims of this cinema by diminishing the value and possible meanings of films deriving from an 'adolescent' industry. They find Australian cinema as a whole – particularly after 1981 – as having a distressing blandness attributable to its deep strategic orientations:

> the result of the circumscribing effect of middle-brow good intentions above . . . and a culturally stupid 'commercialism' below . . . The distressing staleness of the pattern, maintained with little change for more than a decade, is also attributable to the entrenched notion that here is identifiable 'quality', and that it is the answer to the 'natural', ever-present threat of the carpetbagger mentality.
>
> (1988a: 49)

While this work is perhaps the best known symptomatic criticism, similar criticisms are sustained at a public, academic and industry level. Characteristically, films are taken as having one set of meanings and are made to mean something else and less. *The Dismissal* becomes an example of 'declared nationalism and male Australianness' (1988a: 32). Denouncing what is not there becomes a means of denouncing what *is* there: formally, thematically and stylistically.

But Dermody and Jacka's enterprise would not be so persuasive if symptomatic criticism was all they undertook. In parts of volume two of *The Screening of Australia*, and Dermody's (1988) 'The Company of Eccentrics' published soon afterwards, explicatory criticism is undertaken of films that apparently escape their historical and production industry constraints. This film-making is held to escape, the stifling prescription of middle-brow good intentions and commercialism, and is often against the grain of the 'male ensemble' film. These films are the 'some exceptions, some local effects' that 'have squeezed by' – which have come about despite prevailing conditions rather than because of them. The 'eccentrics' also enables Dermody and Jacka to keep alive the 'dream' of Australian cinema affording some pleasurable investment in at least part of its archive.

Dermody and Jacka's criticism is a local variant of internationally shared norms of film and cultural criticism for which debunking symptomatic criticism is the dominant repertoire, while explicatory criticism is a minor component held over for those filmic objects invested with progressive aesthetic, political or social outcomes. Most disturbingly, Bordwell (1989: 21–9) suggests the origins for these critical choices do not lie in the films but in the institution of film criticism and the moral imperatives that sustain it. These select some rather than other topics; label some film-making as progressive and worthy, and others not.

REMYTHOLOGIZING AND DEMYTHOLOGIZING FILM CRITICISM

Remythologizing criticism

There is also another way to characterize the divides in film criticism. This is to identify criticism which demythologizes and which remythologizes. Demythologizing or debunking the films is central to contemporary symptomatic criticism's explicit project of regulating film meaning. The more popular the cinema, the greater critics perceive the necessity to debunk as a socially useful act. But symptomatic film criticism, as Bordwell observes, emerged to facilitate film meaning.

For Parker Tyler's film criticism of the 1940s it resolved itself in what Bordwell describes as an '"irrational enlargement" of scenes from favourite films' (1989: 73, see also 76–8). Symptomatic criticism, like its explicatory counterpart, 'remythologizes' film meaning as the critic 'reflects on her or his idiosyncratic associations' (Bordwell 1989: 73). André Bazin – for Bordwell the high priest of explicatory criticism – and his followers also enlarge on film meaning. Their claim that their imputed meanings are 'in the text' only make clear their interventionist ends, in Adrian Martin's words (1988a: 92), to extract 'the contours of a possible cinema, unlike any other yet seen'. For Martin this is also the domain of Manny Farber's 'termite criticism':

> Termite criticism ... ignores the obvious hooks of a movie (such as linear narrative or formulaic ploys) and burrows deep in order to find the really juicy or interesting stuff – details, gestures, atmospheres. Just as Durgnat dissolves the film-text into a semantic mass, Farber and those he has influenced ... restructure movies into worlds or environments – texts you can inhabit and walk around – in order to grasp better the aesthetic and cultural sensibilities that they picture and figure.
>
> (1992: 128)

What is important about film criticism is 'the action of critical writing, what it can conjure, perform, circulate, transform' (Martin 1992: 131). Explicatory criticism can be as regulative and stipulative as symptomatic criticism. Indeed one of the reasons symptomatic criticism emerged was the limitations of explicatory criticism, the narrow canons it delivered and the prescription of topics and standpoints of analysis. Equally symptomatic criticism can be just as facilitatory and enlarging as can explicatory criticism. Symptomatic criticism need not be denunciatory; explicatory criticism need not be celebratory. That they have each become so is an historical circumstance of screen and cultural studies trajectories, and a cultural politics driven on the one hand by an identity politics concerned to find exclusion, excorporation, tokenism and victimization, and on the other by a technique of self-examination which interrogates rather than takes for granted the grounds of one's own pleasures.

Remythologizing critical writing is sometimes encouraged. In 1980, Scott Murray drew together a number of critics to create the coffee-table book, *New Australian Cinema*. It contained a number of essays that *remythologized* Australian cinema. The most important of these were by Meaghan Morris ('Personal Relationships and Sexuality') and Tom Ryan ('Historical Films') – both of which underwrote subsequent demythologizing criticism by Susan Dermody, Liz Jacka and Graeme Turner. Fourteen years later, *Cinema Papers* invited a number of film critics to write about those neglected 'films we love'. The result was one of the few formal attempts since 1980 to 'remythologize' Australian cinema, as critics were invited to make something more of a handful of 'forgotten films'. Most particularly it gave scope to idiosyncratic 'irrational enlargements' as is evidenced in Lorraine Mortimer (1994) on *The Clinic*, Adrian Martin (1994e) on *Going Down*, Raffaele Caputo on *Bello Onesto Emigrato*, or my own essay (O'Regan 1994b) on *King of the Coral Sea*.

Some of Australia's finest film critics – Meaghan Morris, Adrian Martin, William Routt, Susan Dermody, Ross Gibson and Stuart Cunningham – practice symptomatic and explicatory criticism at the same time. They do so to enlarge and not simply detract. Gibson demythologizes the use of landscape in Australian cinema in both his essay 'Formative Landscapes' (1988) and his film, *Camera Natura*. Yet he remythologizes it in his criticism (1992: 158–77) of *Mad Max III: Beyond Thunderdome* and his film of the Piliga Forest, *Wild*. Morris, Martin and Routt openly acknowledged their debt to 'enlargers': Morris to Parker Tylor, Martin to Manny Farber and Routt to *Cahiers du Cinéma* and *Positif* critics of the 1950s and 1960s. Morris once worked and Martin still works as a professional reviewer. Both have a keen and fundamental respect for the hybrid spaces of public commentary. For his part, Routt's singular take on Australian cinema is animated by his larger project of evolving an adequate critical response to popular film as a domain of cultural and aesthetic experience. His Australian film criticism sits congruently with his work on naïve art, gangster films, the exploitation film-making of Roger Corman, creature features, Hollywood musicals and popular music. Morris's celebrated essay on *Crocodile Dundee* (1988: 241–69) creates a *feminist supplement* to that film which draws the reader back into it. Morris acknowledges the film's 'entrepreneurial zest' while giving due weight to its 'political hostilities'. Cunningham's (1991) book on Chauvel, *Featuring Australia* and his work (1988, 1989b) on the Kennedy-Miller mini-series both find a vital and serious cultural dialectic in what first appears unlikely material – the kitsch of Chauvel's bizarre *Uncivilized* (1936) and the 'hyper-real' melodrama of the Kennedy-Miller *Dirtwater Dynasty* with its staggering coincidences and elemental forces reminiscent of the nineteenth-century stage. Criticism does not give us the last word here. It opens up and does not close down.

The habits of denunciation and remythologizing produce different interests in Australian cinema. Each holds the critic and the reader to the cinema in a different way. Remythologizing criticism is devious, seductive, subtly incorporating and gently persuading the reader. It takes the 'bad object' and finds, wishes and creates out of it, 'good' objects which stand alongside the film. It reappropriates in 'feral' ways (miming the very characteristics Ross Gibson finds in some Australian cinema). And like those remythologizing moments of Gibson's book, it says 'try thinking this way, with these tools about these objects'. It facilitates an interest in the cinema by making a play for the intrinsic interest of the texts for themselves as opportunities for critical play.

But remythologizing carries its own risks. In staying with the object – rather than taking an explicit distance from it – its attachment to the film can appear ultimately supportive of it. It risks excusing, through its loving regard, some racist and patriarchal storytelling. It can support the existing film culture's divisions of labour between film criticism and film-making at the expense of dreaming new beginnings of making something else possible. It can't let go of the past. Perhaps the problem with remythologizing criticism is that it risks being seen to go over to the side of the enemy – because it does not 'talk straight and strong'. But its ambiguity and elusiveness is also its strength as a persuasive rhetoric.

Demythologizing criticism

Demythologizing criticism is unambiguous. Critics find badness where we thought there was goodness. Debunking is motivated by a desire to break apart the object and to inspect ones desires, to be suspicious about the way the self is being made over in its dialogue with the text. As a coming into *awareness* out of a kind of enslavement, it is declamatory and hectoring. It establishes a clear separation between itself and the text. It works hard not to be *implicated*, it tries to sever its attachment to the existing cinema (thus demythologizing, repudiating, renouncing). The critic 'others' herself/himself from what is before him/her. The love object, the cinema, has – due to its own actions – become dubious. But love can be restored. Demythologizing becomes a means to project a future in which the bad things it identifies can be made good.

For that future criticism's *denigratory* play becomes the *intrinsic* interest; the pleasure and progressivism lies in the declamation not the films. Since denunciation requires passionate engagement, spending time developing scenarios of awfulness requires a commitment to criticism and a faith in new objects rising from the ashes of the one under scrutiny. To demythologize is to talk 'straight and strong'. It is an important repertoire for consciousness-raising and has as its close relation, identity politics. It is often intramural in that it often does not need to convince its readers about those things that it takes to be politically and aesthetically self-evident. And it has an overtly *political* character, undertaking criticism as a *political instrument*. Such criticism circulates as evidence, as part of a larger case, defining the bounds of a larger solidarity. Because it does not implicate the reader, because it expels as licit its own attachment to the cinema, an extra-cinematic compact is created between reader and critic – a cultural critical space – which enables contemplation of the cinema and television, its mundane choices, and what it delivers.

Demythologizing proves its practical, policy and political credentials by being *future-oriented* and not stuck in the past. It promises a cinema slate clean for an emerging generation of film-makers, critics and policy-makers who can readily walk *in the face of* their predecessors. It narrows the field of possible exemplars. It clears the way for new beginnings. It carries the injunction: 'try better next time'. We read demythologizing criticism in order to know *where else* to go. We read it to remake our understandings and interpretations of what is criticized.

We don't read such criticism to attach ourselves to the past (a tradition-forming practice). The past shows us what not to do, what not to be, where not to go. It cannot instruct us. Demythologizing critics dwell in the past to exorcize and have done with it. Today's principled critic for whom Australian cinema is variously an Anglo, racist, homophobic and/or misogynist cinema – and the McFarlane and Mayer of *New Australian Cinema* (1992) – all provide the reader with just such an experience of being done with the past. They demonstrate that the past and present film-making should not weigh too heavily on film-making and critical horizons. Their work enables us – critics, film-makers and reader/audiences – to move on. Such work supplies the heterogeneity, difference and excellence lacking in the existing cinema.

Demythologizing's problems are tied into its advantages. First, it not only risks 'rubbing out' the text but also criticism's very reason for being. Students I have taught sometimes respond to the wealth of demythologizing critical writing in Dermody and Jacka's important work by asking: 'Why bother reading about these films if they are no good?' or 'why are you making us watch these (politically incorrect) films?' or 'why are you presenting all these "boys stories"?' and, more rarely, 'why bother writing about the cinema if you are *only* going to criticize it?' Their problem is that they know only a handful of the films – demythologizing criticism does not encourage them to go back to these films because it makes them *uninteresting*. Symptomatic critical technologies exhaust and pigeonhole these films, unless they are the canonical Hollywood classics which are returned to again and again – and screened in courses enabling students to be both complicit with the film and resist it simultaneously. Whereas Dermody and Jacka wrote in a milieu where their work was simply one more critical voice; in a classroom situation and for a new generation these films are known through Dermody and Jacka's writing. Their books – not the films – have become the monuments, their writing the canonical repertoire. What was wonderfully provocative in the mid- to late 1980s can look uncharitable in the 1990s – very little of what Weir, Schepisi, Crombie, Kennedy-Miller and Armstrong did in the 1970s and 1980s is worthy of reconsideration. The films are simply nostalgia films, costume dramas, a sexist cinema, the AFC genre, a monocultural cinema. The downsides to the contemporary ascendance of demythologizing criticism are clear enough: positive achievement outside the narrow sphere of the peripheral cinema goes largely unremarked; cultural politics is not always the best way to address the cinema, as the aesthetic is too quickly collapsed into a rigid cultural politics; and ignorance of Australian film and cultural history becomes acceptable.

Yet Dermody and Jacka's denunciatory criticism did hold the reader, particularly when it was an account of contemporary cinema. It did so in two ways. First, it encouraged self-examination and dialogue by the reader/viewer, particularly if it was about an Australian film that one had seen and liked. Denunciation schools our likes, showing us how to make them into dislikes and providing the reader with new and complex ways to diagnose these texts. Second, extreme principled positions – like considering the landmark mini-series, *The Dismissal*, as just another sexist male ensemble film/mini-series – can be readily entertained and tossed around by the reader in ways that more considered and balanced judgements cannot.

In a similar fashion, Stuart Cunningham's controversial *Framing Culture* (1992) demythologized contemporary Australian cultural criticism. It became a 'must argue' book precisely because of what were seen as its extreme pro-policy and anti-cultural studies positions. People read such demythologizing criticism to find the author as being 'a bit hard' on this or that film or critical practice. Such readings serve as incomplete texts to be 'raided' by other readers and they can be readily compared with the reader's own recollections and makings. Denunciation is tailor-made for readers and writers prepared to work through and contest meanings.

As a film criticism, denunciation can be functional – particularly when it sounds out another view on a popular film or television programme attracting a generally positive press. In the domain of the popular film already on the way to success, critics have no chance of 'killing' the film. Instead they sound a note of caution. Their denunciation becomes part of the uptake. Such criticism becomes dysfunctional with more specialized product – then critics 'can make it more difficult to generate substantial audiences' (AFC 1991: 60). Given the more specialized character of much Australian feature film-making and documentary production, denunciatory criticism may be often dysfunctional.

Demythologizing and remythologizing have their place. Demythologizing also opens out onto a form of remythologizing – even if only as a 'negative' narrative image for Australian cinema and culture. It is associated with positive agendas that, in a sense, its negativity clears the way for, and for which it acts as an instrument. Dermody and Jacka's demythologizing criticism secures a place for, and legitimates the standing of the 'eccentric films' and a feminist film-making and critical perspective. Their work makes the local alternatives they espouse that much more startling, original and different. Debunking here clears space for and legitimates emergent cinemas.

THE CINEPHILE, THE CRITICAL INTELLECTUAL AND THE CULTURAL HISTORIAN

To these different critical practices – explicatory and symptomatic and remythologizing and demythologizing – another critical practice needs to be added: that of historical criticism. These different critical practices roughly match up with three competing personae for the critic: the cinephile, the critical intellectual and the cultural historian. While there is often considerable interconnection between these personae, each is attached to different parts of the critical landscape – different institutional spaces, performance styles and critical agendas.

Each of these three critical comportments involve different critical practices. Cinephile criticism is often an explicatory criticism, in that it is producing a supplement to the film in its usually contemporary circulation; critical intellectual institutions typically engage a symptomatic criticism which produces a debunking of film meaning and institutions; and historical institutions of historical criticism produce a record of an industry and film milieu. Cinephile institutions transform through remythologizing film meaning; critical institutions through demythologizing the meaning of films; and historical institutions through narrativizing the relation between past filmic trajectories.

Each comportment of the person here – the cinephile, the critical intellectual and the historian – is responsible to different publics: the cinephile to a public for whom the cinema is a goal in itself – an internally conceived cultural politics of the 'film world'; the critical intellectual to a public for whom the constituencies are more broadly conceived categories of social persons and movements – an externally conceived cultural politics; and the historian to a professional community and a variety of curatorial functions.

1 The cinephile

The cinephile film criticism of what can be loosely called the 'cinema' institutions in film magazines, reviews and journals – is concerned with film as its object, topic and end of discussion. Although it is a term usually reserved for a more specific attachment to the cinema, it is useful to think of these institutions as the 'cinephile institutions', given their significant attachment to and connection with the cinema/ industry.

Film is conceived in predominantly expressive terms within this broadly conceived film milieu. It is rendered as a performance text to be judged, appraised and considered in relation to critical, technical and aesthetic values developed for film criticism. This involves a cultural politics of direction/creation – disposing of cinematic materials, forms and genres, forging and identifying connections between films, constructing a cinematic legacy. Films are held aesthetically accountable. The concern is for the position of the film-maker as film-maker; taken for granted here is the relative autonomy of the film world. Perhaps Adrian Martin has stated this in its purest form when he ruminated on the importance to critics and film-makers alike of Bazin's question: 'What is cinema?'

> In a sense, every practising film-maker must ask himself or herself, 'What is cinema for me?' Every film-maker must, in the first place, be able to dream or imagine the cinema that he or she desires. I tend to believe that, for true film-makers (from F. W. Murnau to Jim McBride), this imagining is not primarily expressed in terms of, 'What do I want to say with film?', but, rather, 'What do I want to see and hear on film?'. That is, the ability to imagine certain configurations of image, sound, movement, form, fiction and mood matters more than convictions concerning which social issues, types of behavior and so on should be presented on screen. Perhaps for true film-makers the two stages happen simultaneously; for to imagine a form of cinema is naturally to project certain images and shapes of life in action.
>
> (1988a: 92)

Martin's cinephile worries about how much the 'cultural terrain has been paved over by good intentions'. There is, he thinks, too much of a demand for the cinema to deliver preferred outcomes without paying due regard to the necessity for translation through the materials available to the film-maker (Martin 1988a: 101). With such a fundamental respect for the cinema, the cinephile intellectual necessarily foregrounds remythologizing in the work of film-makers and critics alike; reserving demythologizing for 'lesser films' and 'filming'. S/he also sees cultural politics in performance issues of staging, *mise-en-scène*, action. The cinema is not seen through to its social meaning, it is looked at in opacity and density. As Martin puts it: what is important is not what it has to say, but what it presents for us to see and hear. In film reviewing, critical commentary and polemic, the cinephile intellectual has a centrality to the work of the cinematic institution. S/he does functional work which is not pure critique nor ficto-criticism but a critical manoevre that can, in conjuring, miming and performing, be like film-making.

2 The critical intellectual

The film criticism of the critical intellectual institutions are concerned with a film's social and ideological meaning. Since the mid-1970s, writing on the cinema in the dominant Anglophone currents of cultural criticism and cultural studies has become dominated by the assaying of a film or cinema's cultural politics. Such criticism is conducted in a wide number of places – from cultural journalism to critical commentary and is possibly the most widespread critical practice in

Australian cinema. Characteristically, films are pulled into those spaces. What is important about film is that it is a social act. Film becomes a social practice (significantly the title of Graeme Turner's introductory cinema book). Films are held socially accountable by diverse peoples and political standpoints. The preferred means to do so is ideological critique.

For the persona of the critical intellectual, social problematizations are never far away. Because of the centrality to criticism of social problematization, a naturalist ideology is close by, as Australian films are expected to express what is there, to be true to the real and the possible – the central dispute is over what constitutes the actual and a desirable outcome. (Correspondingly, and in reaction to this criticism, there is a minor countervailing critical tendency to view Australian films as excessively dominated by naturalism at the expense of mythic, imaginary, mediated, and cinephilic work.)

As cultural politics, criticism owes a direct responsibility to the industry to the extent that it has social effects within it. It is not animated by a relation with a broad film-making milieu, except for its 'progressive' elements. It is not principally concerned with aesthetic issues as ends in themselves. Aesthetic value is mixed up with political value in a cultural politics or political aesthetic. It is about questions of value being displaced for progressive politics.

This cultural criticism is sustained by the availability in the Australian context of the stances and standpoints developed from the cultural and social criticism of the critical intellectual. This capacity is relatively new. It is largely a consequence of the institutionalization in tertiary education – the universities and former colleges turned universities of screen studies and cultural studies. Academic posts have supported, on a part-time and full-time basis, many of the people who professionally perform film criticism in Australia (there is writing on the Australian cinema driven by far less grandiloquent ambitions and for which a 'staff function' is an important component in the film reviews, for example, of the major metropolitan dailies and general journals such as the *Bulletin*). And those with positions in the critical institution do not always behave as critical intellectuals.

Such criticism is conducted by what Robert Merton once called 'unattached' as opposed to 'bureaucratic' intellectuals (Merton 1968: 266). (For Merton, unattached intellectuals are those 'intellectuals who do not perform a staff function in helping to formulate and implement policies of a bureaucracy'. Academics are unattached intellectuals despite their connection with academic bureaucracy in that 'they typically are not expected to utilize their specialized knowledge for shaping the policies of the bureaucracy' (Merton 1968: 266).) In these circumstances, the bulk of the written critical discourse on Australian cinema, as opposed to the marketing, major dailies reviewing and promotional discourses of the cinema, is conducted by critical intellectuals for whom writing on the cinema is their expertise but not their professional staff-function.

Hunter suggests that critical intellectuals have a role to play. He sees their 'bureaucratic role' as 'their moral comportment'. He further suggests that their 'practice of critique is inapplicable to the system in which they are employed, except as a prestigious model for a desired way of life' (168). Here the film critical intellectual is playing the simultaneous role of moral conscience for a film-making milieu, bearer of an aesthetic sensibility apparently unavailable except to all but a few favoured film-makers, and articulate supporter of the more marginal zones of film activity (particularly those closest to his or her social, political and aesthetic agenda. This selection of critical vocabulary and development of critical ends is one ideally suited to a cultural politics, marrying as it does socio-political ends of difference and diversity with aesthetic ends favouring multiplicity, heterogeneity and an open-ended and multi-generic film practice.

Principled criticism favours demythologizing repertoires of discursivization and social problematization. There is an ongoing emphasis upon the arbitrariness, contingency, imaginary and constructed nature of a national cinema – national identity, national culture – alongside a generalized suspicion about the motives of popular film-makers, the formal and aesthetic choices they make, the politics they espouse especially where the mainstream cinema is concerned. The close association of the Australian cinema on the public record to notions of nation, national culture, national myths and symbols further encourages demythologizing criticism of, for example, Graeme Turner's recent book *Making it National* (1994), where popular images of national identity in film and the broader media culture are shown to serve specific interests. While demythologizing is critical of Australian cinema and lifeways it reinforces the terms of cinema as a socio-cultural dialogue with Australian national specificities.

Critical intellectuals maintain a professional separation from the film market. They are not just film critics. To protect their integrity within their own academic community they need to occupy an unattached space. They cannot afford to be seen as 'popular culture used-car salesmen'.[2] These, together with the prevailing and dominant rhetoric of cultural politics derived from the principally English language currents of film, television and cultural criticism, ensure that the cultural criticism of Australian film is often conducted a long way away from the film production – circulation – consumption contexts and the 'popular art' understandings developed in that context. Instead it circulates in professional academic and public journals of cultural criticism where Australian film is not so much related to other films, to trends in the international cinema and the like but to Australian culture, Australian lifeways, popular culture, minority identity politics and the topics of the day in the field. Australian cinema is drawn into a number of spaces and made to do its work in these spaces.

As critical intellectuals, film intellectuals are concerned to identify and celebrate (where it exists) the 'missing beat', and to adopt a 'hermeneutics of suspicion' towards mainstream cinema recommending needed directions, denouncing its current form, and finding supportable tendencies. The critical intellectual is naturally drawn to the peripheral cinemas and the institutions and film-makers that support them. There is a deal of interchange between the critical intellectual and this film-making milieu. Not surprisingly their work is based on a mix of explicatory (to support the 'eccentric', the 'independent', the 'oppositional' and the 'experimental' closer to the critical intellectual's standpoints) and symptomatic readings (to denigrate and ameliorate the mainstream and its dominant aesthetic and cultural norms).

Australian cinema also fits this cinema. It is probably a lot more 'worthy' (or 'politically correct') than the product of a number of national cinemas. Certainly, visiting *Cahiers du Cinéma*'s critic Serge Grunberg (1994: 29) thought so when he wrote:

> those who are empowered to allow creativity often generate ... an ambience that is above all politically correct, in which one is forbidden to overlook even the least minority.

Such worthiness is further sustained by the close connections between fact and fiction (the truth to the actual and the truth to the probable), the proximity of governmental funding and the importance to the national cinema of social problematization.

3 The film historian

Third, there are, as noted, the film histories with their careful protocols of archival scholarship and attention to film release, contemporary reviews and industrial conditions – film as archival record. In her discussion of French cinema, Susan Hayward (1993: 7) draws attention to the importance to a national cinema of discussions of a national past and the institutions and discourses which secure that discussion. This work of curating Australian cinema's past is not as exclusively driven by the critical repertoires of symptomatic and explicatory criticism, or demythologizing and remythologizing criticism. It is also driven by other documentation and evaluative practices: historical and archival practices of the National Film and Sound Archive with their different estimations of value, encyclopedism and passion for the industry as a network of people and enterprises (all qualities evident in the work of Graham Shirley, Brian Adams, Eric Reade, Ina Bertrand, Andrée Wright, Andrew Pike, Ross Cooper, John Tulloch and more recently Chris Long, Philip Dutchak and Deane Williams).[3] For those undertaking this practice, curating the past is a public good – and sometimes a bureaucratic and citizenship enterprise. It involves suspension of certain kinds of judgement about whether this or that film is worthy or has political sentiments with which they might agree. It tends to be a more open-ended enterprise than the stance that film and cultural critics take towards film objects.

Historical discourses are central to Australian culture. Popular and academic history is an important part of Australian non-fiction publishing and image making. Within this context cultural histories, although a relatively recent phenomenon, are becoming increasingly central. The strength, insitutional separateness and self-sustaining Australian publication infrastructures for history make cultural histories as much adjuncts to the general historical record as to the Australian film and television industries. Writing Australian film histories are one way of engaging with the Australian cinema in an extended fashion. The result: a space is created for greatly developed critical work loosely drawing on the public value – and the institutional support that follows from this – of Australian history.

HYBRID SPACES, IMPURE COLLOCATIONS

Typically the cinephile, the critical intellectual and the historian persist in the same person and in the same space just as the publics for each overlap. Film criticism is often a hybrid of each of these elements. William Routt is the cinephile exploring the archive with an eye for popular cinema and naïve style; he is also a professional historian concerned to establish and describe – even if it goes against the logic he is developing – a film production and reception milieu, and he is the critical intellectual providing a symptomatic reading of the Rudd cycle, colonialism and the inclusions and exclusions engendered. Morris's work is simultaneously explicatory, demythologizing and remythologizing. Susan Dermody is a cinephile and a critical intellectual. Even Adrian Martin can't resist the invitation to be a critical intellectual (see his chapter in *Phantasms* on 'political correctness', 1994b: 139–48). Australian cinema criticism is a movement involving all these comportments. Sometimes this means a division of labour on the page and within the same piece of writing, at other times it is a division of labour expressed in different writing and speaking contexts.

Some of the ways each of these dimensions to cinema criticism can occur in the one place can be seen in the diverse contemporary uptake of *The Birth of White Australia* (Walsh 1928). In 1994, it was screened in Italy at the Pordenone silent film festival. This was the first time that Australian and New Zealand film-making was showcased at this event. Pordenone is a curated event in which archival knowledges are brought to bear on the cinema. Paolo Cherchi Usai justified the programming of *Birth* on the grounds of it being a 'racist testament chosen to represent the culture of Australia at that period' (Shirley 1994: 43). Usai was combining here an historical, critical and aesthetic function simultaneously.

By contrast, the Australian film historian, Graham Shirley (1994: 43), found this film a 'surprising' choice, as it is not so straightforwardly representative. Pike and Cooper (1980: 191) note that 'no commercial screening in Sydney or other state capitals seems to have taken place'. The film-maker, Phil K. Walsh 'had no further association with feature production' and the investors 'lost heavily'. The film was also produced in unusual circumstances. Investment for the film came from the country town of Young which also seems to have been its principal audience. The film could be seen as working from 'booster' images of towns and cities: it tried to capitalize on the town's now dubious claim to be the birthplace of the White Australia policy in order to distinguish itself. The fact that it was possible for the film to be made provides evidence of Australian racism. It is representative of the culture in the period, in so far as any unsuccessful film made outside the usual trade investment, producer and distributor linkages can be.

Certainly its investors and film-maker saw possibilities in recasting the successful American original, *The Birth of a Nation* (Griffith 1915), into an Australian imitation in which the Chinese occupy the place of African-Americans. Its lack of success in even convincing exhibitors to screen it makes it difficult to see the film as significantly participating and shaping the public record. The film's failure to be judged suitable for commercial exploitation suggests the film project was inappropriate in some way. This may have been due to its lack of quality, it may also be due to its producing an 'unacceptable ideological face' to the white Australia policy. Either way, historical evidence suggests that the film's place on the Australian social imaginary was limited. Its failure to cross into anything more than marginal public recognition outside the town of Young might just as well provide evidence of a much less virulent form of racism in the public culture than the film itself displays. For Graham Shirley, as a cinephile intellectual, the film is also a bad film, poorly and unprofessionally constructed, lacking the quality of films like *The Breaking of the Drought* that were overlooked for this selection.

Within cultural studies the film has been revived to provide filmic evidence of the White Australia policy. For Siew Keng Chua (1993: 29) it is a founding text of an endemic and systemic Australian racism that runs in a line from 1928 to the 1980s cinema of *The Year of Living Dangerously* and *Echoes of Paradise*, and into the 1990s with *Turtle Beach*:

> This film has set the boundaries of the discourse against which subsequent Australian films with Asian, particularly Southeast Asian, settings and characters are delined. Viewing this film recently, even with the knowledge of today's official Australian discourse locating this country in the Asian region, I still felt the chill of confronting such an overtly racist text. The study of Australian films must deal with the analysis of this film just as the study of American films must engage with Griffith's *Birth of a Nation*. Whereas the latter contains aesthetic and technical innovations of interest to film scholars, the former is technically and aesthetically irredeemable. Nevertheless, the film is historically important in locating one (extreme) set of the hierarchy of orientalist discourses in Australian films.

Given that there is no direct historical evidence to connect *The Birth of White Australia* with the subsequent film-making of small 'l' liberals like Phil Noyce (in his 1980s incarnation), Stephen Wallace or Peter Weir, the connection Chua makes is a critical association produced by orientalist criticism and a devastating experience of viewing. The extremities of *The Birth of White Australia* 'rub off' on to the modern films. The cultural critic creates the continuities as symptomatic continuities.

By contrast, the remythologizing cinephile historian, Routt, qualifies this Australian racism. He notes that Australian racism of the 1920s and 1930s

> is articulated . . . as a relation of domination and subordination rather than one of simple hatred. The 'inferior beings' in such films as *A Girl of the Bush*, *The Jungle Woman* and *The Birth of White Australia* (only the Aboriginal people in

the latter case) are often possessed of definite virtues, even if those virtues do not make them the equal of whites.

(Routt 1989a: 40)

The Birth of White Australia mobilizes hatred against the Chinese on the gold fields while simultaneously mobilizing sympathies for its Aboriginal characters. A really popular film like Ken Hall's 1933 film, *The Squatter's Daughter* has as one sub-plot the heroine's (Joan) crippled brother, Jimmy, finding happiness with Zena, the daughter of an itinerant Afghani hawker. As Routt (1989a: 40) describes it:

> Jimmy's physical (and moral) handicap certainly can be read as 'justifying' his attraction to Zena, but in the ordinary course of fictional events, this compounded 'weakness' would lead inevitably to his death, not to a coupling which parallels the pairing of Joan and the rightful heir, Wayne Ridgeway. In this case, the narrative demand or a 'happy end' seems to have undermined racial/cultural prescriptions.

Such pragmatic qualifications can also be found in the exercise of the White Australia policy in this same period, where some Chinese migration to Australia continued despite the avowed public policy – because of the importance to parts of the Australian economy of that Chinese labour and expertise.

None of the several comportments of cinephile, critical intellectual and film historian need communicate. For the film historian *The Birth of White Australia* is not a significant film. It shows, if anything, what was unacceptable to the trade at this time. For the social historian it is an example of the use of racism as a community-binding event in a small country town. For the critical intellectual it becomes representative of Australia during and after the White Australia policy.

Australian film criticism often attempts a combination of these different comportments. It does so because it has to. In a small publishing market like Australia the combination of the repertoires of the cinephile, the critical intellectual and the historian in the one place is part of a necessary strategy to cover a number of bases. If the critical work is to be sustainable in the book market it has to be available to upper secondary, university students and a film-going public. It must find ways of translating critical intellectual stances into film-going, translating cinephilia into critical intellectual comportments, and making historical practices consonant with cinephile and critical intellectual practice.

The strength of each of these different critical appropriations of Australian cinema has ensured a powerful and multifaceted naturalization of Australian cinema as an object, target and point of interest across a wide social and cultural spectrum. These different critical strategies attach the local cinema to mainstream cultural and social conversation. They shape Australian cinema as having to do with all the important and contemporaneous social problematizations. They embed it within the larger history of the people and the nation. They establish an ideal against which present Australian cinema and actions within the cinematic institution can be measured. By showing how it fails the ideal, there is room for governmental problematization and for a redoubling of efforts. Through re-mythologizing, the cinema is made ever more meaningful and turned into an object to be returned to. The combination of these activities make Australian cinema socially and culturally central rather than simply another entertainment institution. These conditions ensured that 'critical response to Australian films in the 1980s . . . appeared in a huge range of places' (AFC 1991: 61). This huge range ensures a 'democracy' of involvement in and purchase on Australian cinema.

Careers of critics have been built around these hybrid spaces. Critics often do work on cultural and film history, produce cinephile essays and write principled criticism of Australian cinema (when the cinema as a whole is addressed they demythologize; when an individual film is discussed there is just as often a remythologizing practice at work). This book practices a mixed space working off all of these different critical comportments. For all the advantages of these 'hybrid' spaces, they come at a cost. In being not just a cinephile, the terrain a cinephile would cover is curtailed. In being not just a critical intellectual, limits are imposed on how far concepts and criticism can be taken. In being not just an historian, corners are cut, secondary materials are relied on and much historical work on Australian cinema that needs to be done remains untouched. Many of Australia's screen journals – *Metro, Continuum, Filmnews* (1970–1995), *Media International Australia* – are made of such hybrid, impure collocations. They provide Australian criticism with an impurity that is its strength and its weakness.

REPUDIATING, PROBLEMATIZING AND CLOSURE

In his considered response to Stuart Cunningham's *Framing Culture* (1992) – a book which made similar criticisms of the prevalence of the principled criticism of critical intellectuals as I do here – Tim Rowse (1993) defended critical intellectual standpoints by identifying three moves critical intellectuals make – repudiation, problematization and closure. Repudiating is a debunking repertoire in which demythologizing takes an 'all or nothing' form. Rowse acknowledges it, notes its excess at times, but has little to say about it save to note how Cunningham's criticisms make it stand for the whole. Instead he concentrates on what it is a part of: the larger activity of problematizing. Such problematizing is an activity central to the cultural critic's duty of care:

> It is most important that cultural critics convey the problematic nature of all representations, not least those in which senses of common concern as 'cit-izens' or 'the people' or 'Australians' are constructed.
>
> (Rowse 1993: 104)

Problematizing can be repudiating, denunciatory, debunking and demythologiz-ing, it may equally be critical, contemplative, positive and remythologizing. It can be both a means to denounce the 'national popular' and a 'progressive articu-lation' of it (Rowse 1993: 104). Rowse defends problematizing as a necessary principle. I situate my problematizing here of film criticism's normative problem-atizations as part of this same duty of care.

Rowse argues that problematizing is one of the two 'moments' of 'an engaged cultural criticism' that are essential to its make-up. The other moment is 'closure'. This is when '"we" base "our" projects on certain defensible representations of the common or public interest, on certain representations of the "national" and on certain "nodal" rhetorics' (Rowse 1993: 104). Closure is essentially a matter of political judgement. These moments of problematizing and closure 'do not merely coexist, sealed off from each other' and the relations between them – as is evident from Rowse's disagreements with Cunningham – they are 'fraught'. Judgements as to when to problematize and when to close, orient research and criticism just as differing judgements over closure and problematizations orient Rowse's dispute with Cunningham. These too are political matters. As such, the principled criticism of the critical intellectual is a pragmatic criticism. It practices politics with criticism as its vehicle. Those that take such criticism at its word – that is precisely as principled – are bound to overlook its strategic preparation. As the product of an adversarial political culture, principled criticism is necessarily and unashamedly partisan and propagandistic.

We can surely agree with Rowse that 'the imaging of the nation is more powerfully practiced by some than others' (Rowse 1993: 104). Aborigines, women and NESB Australians are not as powerful or central to this imaging practice. But history, the imaging of nation, policy and prevailing social problem-atizations are also about 'approved classes of human being' and not just 'dominant groups' (L. Murray 1984: 159). For Les Murray, this means that the unfashionable group he identifies with – country people – miss out:

> History is not just the propaganda of dominant groups, but also the public record of approved classes of human beings, and there is a way in which country people in Australia are apt to miss out on their due by being neither acceptably Upper nor recognisably proletarian, and their wary reticences compound this still further.

Since the advent of SBS-TV, the Mabo decision, the mainstreaming of multi-culturalism and equal opportunity and sex discriminations structures – NESB Australians, Aborigines and women have become part of these 'approved classes'. (This same period has seen a winding back of the ABC-TV's commitment to regional Australia, a federal political agenda dominated by a party for whom country votes are not as critical as ethnic votes in their marginal electorates, and a criticism for which the Australian is to be known as the urban Australian.) Our critical technologies favour recognition of some kinds of disadvantage not others. They problematize in certain directions.

But problematization and closure are closer than Rowse suggests. Different kinds of closure are central to problematizing. Choosing what to problematize entails excluding as much as including. Problematizing constrains so as to enable. The contemporary emphasis upon ethnicity and gender turns them into determining categories. They function as determinations in the last instance, like the economy and social class for an older Marxism. This is their closure. Rowse's political judgement involved in closure is another constraint placed upon an existing closure. Because problematizing always excludes as a means to include, closes as a means to open, it needs to be careful with repudiation. As Nicholas Thomas (1993: 132) has put it '[i]f one privileges an insight, one must correspondingly privilege a blindness' such that our ways of describing 'necessarily' produce 'lacunae as well as presences'.

Demythologizing criticism justifies itself as a response to a society – its symbolic culture, its cultural strategies, its celebrations. It challenges the complacency that comes to us through the advertising, mass marketing, commercial television, the political record and the degeneracies of a complacent, 'sheltered', 'racist', unoriginal society. It wants to insist upon the problematic nature of national representations and feels this insistence too is under challenge from a virulent nationalism:

> Nationalism at present is the cultural strategy which most effectively disenfranchizes the indecorous and dissatisfied communities inhabiting the island. In the context of 'celebrations' such as the Bicentenary or the sundry sporting ceremonies that roll around annually, factional agitation and criticism are deemed meanminded and self-pitying. There is something especially invidious about this cajoling, condescending method of authorizing middle-Australia as natural, fun-loving, confident . . . and unified.
>
> (Gibson 1992: 194)

Yet inside cultural criticism the 'indecorous' and the 'dissatisfied' are far from disenfranchized. Here such voices are the unexceptionable norm and debunking a dominant cultural and ethical style. For this reason it is necessary to ask the question of its question.

A particular film criticism and film culture results from the prevalence of principled criticism in the spaces of cultural criticism and the routine self-positioning of the critic as speaking his mind and challenging the view of Australian cinema as something good. Film meaning and film criticism is structured through social problematization. Critics call upon a longstanding tradition of cultural criticism which lambasts notions of tradition and delegitimizes the mainstream culture and its social lifeways, cultural choices and existing aesthetic productions. Such a criticism is, perhaps, culturally appropriate to a film industry which is largely of a 'one-off' character (and therefore of perpetual new beginnings), which makes several contributions to the diverse pathways of the cinema, and which characteristically operates stylistically as 'human drama' even when making generic films.

The demythologizing rhetorics also dovetail with longstanding cultural and social orthodoxies, in which Australian culture is an emergent culture for which new beginnings and Australian culture as unfinished business are *de rigueur*. Such orthodoxies permit the critical intellectual to readily wipe the production slate clean. A daggy, rather than glorious past is a natural consequence of demythologizing repertoires (remythologizing criticism compromizes the image of a clean slate, constructing an Australian cinema with reference to a present and meaningful screen past – its very resistance to these prevailing orthodoxies is one of its most attractive aspects).

Repudiation attracts notice through overstating its case. A repudiating critical multiculturalism sometimes constructs the past and present mainstream as simply an homogenous, monocultural, homophobic and racist cinema predicated on the exclusion of NES peoples, Asians, gays and lesbians. Critical interest in film history, contemporary film-making and popular culture is in finding exploitation, exclusions, absences in front of and behind the camera – in short what not to do. It forgets that, for example, the problem of meeting and dealing with cultural and ethnic diversity is not a new one for Australian cinema. Contemporary multicultural films still redispose the values, strategies and archetypes of *They're a Weird Mob*. The cultural diversity of the ABC's *Chequerboard* series of the late 1960s and early 1970s matches that of today's offerings. Indeed it routinely adopted and presented lifeways within a more 'pluralist' frame than that of today's 'cultural diversity' which sees diversity in the more settled terms of gender, sexual orientation, ethnicity, and race. The contemporary move towards mainstreaming gay lifestyles was built on the gays of the most popular Australian television soap ever – *Number 96* (1972). Its disreputable offspring – *Prisoner: Cell Block H* (1979), mainstreamed lesbianism and is the closest thing Australian audiovisual culture has to the progressive politics of American exploitation cinema. A quick inspection of the producers of Australian culture demonstrates that it has never been exclusivist. As noted earlier people of a NESB background produced many classics of Australian cinema from *Mad Max* to *Careful he Might Hear You*; from *Lonely Hearts* to *Malcolm*; from *Bad Boy Bubby* to *Storm Boy* and *Dot and the Kangaroo*. When critical multiculturalism is a problematizing gesture able to generate new meanings, possibilities and tentative closures, I *endorse* it.

Closure of various kinds is part of every critical exercise. I have closed here around the notion of Australian cinema, in my insistence upon it as natural, social and imaginary. Some would dispute this closure as it starts from 'Australian cinema'. Its problematizations are designed to expand this category. Some will see this as a defence of something already superceded. I have not started from feminism, Aboriginal and Islander positions or multicultural positions, but from the position of a film-making and film reception milieu in which these positions have a place, but not a determining place. My allegiance, my sense of responsibility is towards Australian cinema as a critical, film-making and cultural milieu within a broad social context.

CONCLUSION

The problems identified in Australian film criticism – the extremes of demythologizing and symptomatic criticism and the centrality of the critical intellectual

– underwrite a desire for Australian film-making to be 'good' (aesthetically, culturally and politically). We do not want to know 'about the dull films', instead we want to 'make "Australia" and "good" the same thing' (Routt 1994a: 219). But the need for this vision runs aground against an Australian cinema which can only ever be in a real sense, dull. As with every other national cinema, Australian cinema is a mundane, hybrid cinema that will always lack the purity demanded by social, aesthetic and political problematization. So, to sustain this ambition criticism must see *itself* as providing what the cinema lacks. And because it usurps the place of the films – it needs to blame the films for criticism having to take this action.

The problem with wanting Australian cinema to be all 'good' is that it lends itself to critical presumption. With criticism occupying its own centre stage, its desire for the cinema to be good boils down to normative prescriptions: wanting only (their) socially approved kinds of people to make films, wanting films to follow only socially approved topics and film-making traditions. Criticism can too readily become prescriptive of the time periods that Australian cinema should engage with, and those parts of the cultural archive that are to be foregrounded. The reader and critic alike run the danger of being too readily superior to the lifeways of other Australians, to the film-makers who fashion this product, to the writers who might explicate and celebrate it.

If all criticism is prescriptive, my complaint here is over critical style. I favour a criticism which makes films come alive and not just belittles them, which recognizes critics' *implication* and not their separation from what is before them, which encourages critical humility and interrogates its own expansive and imperializing horizons. I want to accord to film-makers the necessary agency and intelligence to make strategic decisions, to behave ethically, to take criticism into account and to be commercial.

Australian cinema will be always something more and something less than the representations critics make of it. film-making is necessarily a mundane, ambiguous, multivalent, rhetorically strong assemblage within which the same resources permit and even encourage widely divergent uptakes by audiences, critics and film-makers. film-makers pursue aesthetic concerns and social problematizations, not those currently in fashion in cultural criticism and government policy but of interest to diverse audiences. The 1994 mini-series from Kylie Tennant's left-wing novel of the 1930s, *The Battlers* did well in television ratings but attracted little favourable critical comment. Mainstream critics described it as a throwback to an earlier period in that it was set in the past, a nostalgia film, and 'old-fashioned' in its monoculturalism. Critics could have noticed – but did not – the film's work to connect the Great Depression of the 1930s to the worst recession since then of the early 1990s. They could have noted its emphases on homelessness, structural unemployment, exploitative labour contracts, fractured families, the issue of the biological/non-biological mother, and the proximity of jail to a marginalized, shiftless and itinerant population. Such emphases connected the present and recent past to *The Battlers*.

My own position on Australian cinema is that critics should not expect or hold out for an ideal of complete development of the national culture, Australian identity or Australian film-making. film-making is something less than criticism. It can rarely function in anywhere near the didactic way criticism can. But film-making is something more than criticism, owing to its polysemy and its encouragement of diverse uptake. An awareness of this difference is crucial to the conduct of an informed film and television criticism.

Our problematizations are then always 'a bit narrow'. They are always partial and 'unable to take up an object in its entirety' (Malpas and Wickham 1995: 14). I believe the best approach is to adopt pluralist ethics which allows for a diversity of equally valid ends. Pluralism is appropriate to a situation in which problematizing is constitutionally incomplete, partial and therefore prone to failure. Because failure is foundational to any governmental programme, it is not ultimately remediable (Malpas and Wickham 1995: 8).[4] Solutions to one problem give rise to unforeseen problems in other areas and so on. Pluralism also allows for a style which recognizes equally valid ends and the difficultly of our painful choices. It is one which not only entails a modesty, by recognizing constitutional partiality and incompleteness, but it also recognizes incommensurabilities; incommensurabilities which, since they provide our very grammar for a national cinema and enable it to be a commodious object, we cannot wish away.

Am I recommending a relativism of values holding among questions of gender, national cinema, of enduring social differentiations, of criticism, nation and society? I don't think so. This study is pluralist, not relativist. For Isaiah Berlin (1991: 87) pluralism 'merely denies that there is one, and only one, true morality or aesthetics or theology, and allows equally objective alternative values or systems of value'. As he (65) has defined cultural pluralism, it is:

a panorama of a variety of cultures, the pursuit of different, and sometimes incompatible, ways of life, ideals, standards of value. This, in its turn, entails that the perennial idea of the perfect society, in which truth, justice, freedom, happiness, virtue coalesce in their most perfect forms, is not merely Utopian (which few deny), but intrinsically incoherent; for if some of these values prove to be incompatible, they cannot – conceptually cannot – coalesce.

Pluralism refuses to concede that 'to all genuine questions there can only be one correct answer, all the other answers being incorrect' (24), instead it says 'to all genuine questions there are a number of correct answers.' It insists that 'no one method exists for the discovery of these answers' (24) – there are a number of methods. It recognizes that it is impossible for 'all the correct answers to be compatible' because '[c]orrect answers are [often] incommensurable'. They do not entail one another in a 'single, systematic, interconnected whole' (25). This study of Australian cinema has been animated by these concerns.

Notes

1 INTRODUCING AUSTRALIAN NATIONAL CINEMA

1 George Miller is a medical doctor, but that is not why I use the title for him. Rather I use it to distinguish between him and the other George Miller. Dr Miller is the director of the *Mad Max* cycle and the Miller of Kennedy-Miller, George Miller is the director of *The Man from Snowy River* (1982).

2 THEORIZING AUSTRALIAN CINEMA

1 E. G. Whitlam, quoted in *Australian Film and Television School Newsletter*, 8 (1975).
2 For an important discussion of the way our modern entities, of which cinema is part, define our bond by their circulation, see Latour 1993: 89.
3 Sacks explains private calendars as follows 'what private calendars do is to provide for the locating of not only events within that relationship, but events of the world in general, by reference to that relationship'.
4 It is possible to see film-makers as 'selling out' and as using the political film/social concern route as their entree to the mainstream industry. But it is equally possible to see this as a consequence of state funding where the closer the proximity to the state dictates a certain level of problematization which focuses on the domains of state activity; once in the commercial industry, different kinds of public domains and publics are being addressed. Film-makers move from the virtual public of the small film, to the entertainment choices and ratings-driven publics of the mainstream industry. This entails negotiating spheres of social life which are not state-driven and relying less on social problematizations to drive the narrative.
5 *The Pictures that Moved* (1968) was directed by Alan Anderson and written by Joan Long.
6 Perhaps the most seminal texts in which this agitational discourse appeared were: Sylvia Lawson, 'Not for the Likes of Us' (1965) and 'Australian Film' (1969); Michael Thornhill, 'The Australian Film' (1967); and the compilation documentaries involving Joan Long – *The Pictures that Moved* (1968), directed by Alan Anderson; and *The Passionate Industry* (1972 script and direction Joan Long). Both films were made for the Commonwealth Film Unit and were widely circulated.
7 A useful reference for this discourse is John Douglas Pringle's *Australian Accent* (1958, 1978: 113–37).
8 *The Vincent Report*, as it was commonly called, had a more official designation, as the Report from the Select Committee on the Encouragement of Australian Productions for TV (Canberra: Commonwealth Government Printer, October 1963).

9 The report reiterated much of *The Vincent Report*'s assertions – though with brevity.

10 There are those like myself who describe Australian cinema by applying a theoretical construct of national cinemas, thereby routinely conceptualizing, analysing and framing 'national cinemas' in particular ways both for our readers and disciplinary purposes.

11 As Gilles Deleuze would have it, Foucault sees problematization as bound up in truth, as 'truth offers itself to knowledge only through a series of "problematizations"' (Deleuze 1988: 64).

3 A NATIONAL CINEMA

1 The only exception I can think of is the 1979 Peat Marwick, Mitchell Services report on the Australian Film Commission, which imagined unlimited horizons for Australian cinema, enacting the dream so chimerically available to the non-Hollywood English-language producers, in gaining equivalent American success. See PMM, 1979: 18–20.

2 Bill Routt, personal correspondence, August 1994.

3 The earlier film – a British location film – was directed by Ralph Smart and released in 1947.

4 The 'clever New Zealander' quotation is taken from the trade press of the time (see Berryman, 1990: 26).

4 A MEDIUM-SIZED ENGLISH-LANGUAGE CINEMA

1 Sometimes the situation can be reversed, as when a number of local blockbusters come on to the market. For example in 1988 the Australian figure was 153,000 per Australian film and 120,000 for all films (*Screen Digest*, April 1992: 86).

2 Because of Australia's size and the limited economies of scale available to producers, the lower economic thresholds created by pay-TV and video will not be able to produce, in a multifaceted commercial form, the phenomenon familiar from the USA with developments in the Hispanic and Middle Eastern language markets.

3 The informal community circulation of videos, semi-commercial distribution of ethnic videos remains largely outside the purview of the censor, being imported directly and circulated in that grey area between commerce and community so characteristic of ethnic communities in Australia. (Some of the consequences of this are noticeable in the 1986 censorship registrations which saw the proportion of English-language features *increase*: the US figure was 9 per cent higher at 39 per cent, the UK figure approached 10 per cent and the Australian at 5 per cent and these three English language producers made up 54 per cent of registered films. The repertory cinema and video and legal ethnic cinema and video trade is shown in the figures for France (5 per cent), West Germany (3 per cent), Italy (1 per cent), Hong Kong (15 per cent), Taiwan (3 per cent), the USSR (2 per cent), Japan (6 per cent) and other (9 per cent).)

4 In 1980 Bob Ellicott, as the Federal Minister responsible for film policy, made this quite explicit when he said in parliamentary debate that: 'I believe that the Australian film industry has to find those themes which on the one hand, identify our own Australian character, but at the same time have an appeal to all English speaking human beings' (*Commonwealth Parliamentary Debates*, House of Representatives, 118 13/5/1980, 2665).

5 Recognition of this is behind the continental European strategy to shoot films in English. But continental European films in English suffer the same constraints as other non-Hollywood English producers. That is, they are in permanently unequal competition with Hollywood such that occasional success is more likely.

6 These are mid-1992 population estimates. The Australasian breakdown was: Australia 17.5 million and New Zealand 3.4 million. See United Nations. 1994. *Population and Vital Statistics Report*. Statistical Papers, Series A, XLVI: 2, 1 April, 14.

7 There are exceptions. For example Australia's slow uptake of cable television and its comparatively late introduction of colour television.

8 These French and Italian figures for Hollywood are among the highest they have been. In 1980, for example the US share of the French market was 35.2 per cent and the Italian 33.7 per cent (source *Screen Digest*, April 1992: 84).

9 It is doubtful they would have had as much of an impact anyway. A less organized exhibition market would have led to more organization from the distributors, as the major exhibitors functioned to provide a de facto distribution structure for distributors.

10 The French cinema had twenty-one German releases in 1993 (Kindred 1995: 177), compared to Australian cinema's four releases in that market (*Frauds* (Elliott 1993), *The Piano*, *Death in Brunswick* and *Romper Stomper*) (Reid 1994: 111).

11 David Thomson (1980: 568) in his *A Bibliographical Dictionary of the Cinema* connects *To the Distant Shore* with *Under Capricorn*. He also judges this film Sirk's best German film.

12 But is this 'Anglo' culture of Australia and English-speaking Canada manifesting itself?

13 Despite its proximity to Australia, the Singaporean community in Australia, and the important and ongoing trading links between Singapore and Australia, Singaporean television rarely runs an Australian film or television series.

5 FORMATIONS OF VALUE

1 These are observations drawn from interviews with video shop proprietors undertaken by my 1995 Australian cinema class.

2 Herrnstein Smith (1988) and Frow (1985) calls these 'economies of value'.

3 Co-productions are mechanisms of a formalized kind, which provide a mechanism to trigger finances accessible only to local film-makers in their respective co-production countries. Australia has co-production treaties or memoranda of understanding agreements with France, the UK, Canada, New Zealand and Italy.

4 As I have indicated elsewhere (O'Regan 1994a) an ideal model of conversation is proposed here which does not mesh with the pragmatics of conversation, nor indeed the philosophy of communication as conversation, derived from John Dewey. If we started from more appropriate models of conversation and construe these as the 'natural' condition we could note the constitutionally unequal character of conversation, its capacity at best for approximation and so on.

5 Williamson's script writing credits include *Gallipoli*, *Don's Party* and *The Year of Living Dangerously*.

6 This sense of legitimate self-protecting resistance extends to other nations. Australians feel justified in railing against the dead hand of British imperialism in Australian culture and cinema.

7 See *Script. Screen and Stage*, January 1971, for a number of viewpoints on this idea of two separate, opposed industries.

8 The Australian Film Council claimed among its members: cinema-goers, directors, producers, writers, actors, camera men, studio executives, union and guilds. See *Australian Film Council Newsletter*, August 1969: 5.

9 The Tariff Board's brief was to report to the government on what measures should be undertaken to encourage film and TV production. It also had to investigate whether it was necessary to introduce measures to ensure Australian film and television texts got

a reasonable share of the market in exhibition and distribution. See *Financial Review*, 28 March 1972.

10 This combination proved effective for Hollywood cinema, in that it reached into and enlisted the support of local commercial élites to actively work for the imported product at the expense of local product.

11 Of course, there are exceptions. Elsaesser (1989) maps the importance of the conditions of production to New German Cinema. His exemplary analysis instructs mine. One source of Elsaesser's achievement is to read this exceptional cinema mundanely as if he were discussing British cinema. Susan Hayward (1993) does likewise with French cinema.

12 It is worth noting in passing here that Paul Willemen's support for *Serious Undertakings* (1983) enabled Helen Grace to obtain the funds necessary to complete her project. Willemen has over a number of years taken a consistent interest in Australian cinema – particularly Australian independent cinema (he was instrumental in *Framework*'s two 'Australian issues' in the 1980s) and his work on national specificity draws on Australian debates (1994: 206–7).

13 What is brought into question is the finality of ends for a national cinema – its debt to a rigid *cultural utility* which does not admit as a good nonproductive expenditure.

14 Correspondence with author August 1994.

15 Support for this comes from David Cronenberg who says '[y]ou cannot worry about what the structure of your own particular segment of society considers bad behaviour, good behaviour; good exploration, bad exploration'; and that 'at the time you're being an artist, you're not a citizen . . . you don't have the social responsibility of a citizen' (Rodley 1993: 158).

16 The French would see this as yet another example of Anglo-Saxon pragmatism. British and Australian policy-makers would claim it was the only policy option available to a country operating in the English language. Sometimes it is claimed it is due to the standing of film art in markets where Hollywood gets its best audiences on a per capita basis – film policy projects 'quality' rather than the more élitist position of film art.

6 MAKING MEANING

1 This is drawn from Nicole Mitchell's 'Essay on *Romper Stomper*' for my 1994, Australian Cinema class at Murdoch University.

7 DIVERSITY

1 Although a Hollywood location film, *The Sundowners* is included here as it contributes to the Australian Western vernacular embodied in Cleary's novel.

2 For an overview of John Hughes's films see Peter Hughes (1993).

3 Working through Pike and Cooper's book on Australian cinema up until 1977 only one other film made before this seems to qualify: Dusan Marek's 1971 experimental feature *And the Word was Made Flesh*.

4 Gillian Bottomley (1994: 146) argues that this case cast a slur on Greek-speakers, was the longest and most expensive legal proceedings in the history of British law and involved shady practices by public authorities.

5 See Adrian Martin's criticism of my work on 1960s film culture for being 'superficial and contradictory' in his 'No Flowers for the Cinephile' (1988b: 124).

6 See *Continuum*'s 500 pp. 'Electronic Arts in Australia' issue edited by Nicholas Zurbrugg 1994; Martin 1989, 1994c, 1994d.

8 UNITY

1 As I put it in 1987 'the absence of an economically secure film production industry has meant that theatrical codes, ideas, norms and personnel constitute an important resource for film production' (117). See also Dean Williams (1994/1995: 36–9).

2 Their closeness to this public record is one reason why it is so masculinist and will remain so while the public record and public culture are male-dominated domains. In Chapter 10, I identify this non-fiction relation as one of Australian cinema's distinctive features.

3 Australians also have their own experience of state, politics and government. Australia is, for instance, often thought of as an 'over governed' country with citizens entertaining higher expectations of the state and its role than in comparable countries.

4 By contrast, Morris (1989: 117) acknowledges an Australian television drama – most evidently the soaps – where the reverse is often the norm.

5 Blakemore has spoken of the cultural appropriateness of such adaptations from the Russian playwright, given the provincial/metropolitan/nativist standing of the European in Russian 'society'.

6 So much so, that when I watched this series on Australian television I kept being distracted by the American accents, so habituated had I become to this style of realization as an ordinary marker of an Australian programme.

9 NEGOTIATING CULTURAL TRANSFERS

1 Hollywood predominantly interacts with 'foreign' cinemas and television in this way.

2 Significantly, David Stratton (1980) entitles his study of 1970s Australian cinema *The Last New Wave*.

10 A DISTINCT PLACE IN THE CINEMA

1 My favourite example here is drawn from an episode of the much maligned *Embassy* television series. The Australian Ambassador to Ragaan betrays her country over the issue of Australian arms sales to get the best 'friendship between peoples' and regional outcome. The 'strong man' leader of Ragaan comments on this strange behaviour from an Australian diplomat. He also means it as a compliment.

2 *Blood Oath* also develops an Australian-Japanese psycho-drama, where it adopts a current of progressive thinking in Australia about the need to establish 'people connections' with minority and marginal groups in Asia. This film was made when Australia's 'great and powerful friends' were America and Japan, neither of which needed Australia as much as in the past.

3 In 1994, television comedian, Elle McFeast remade the sex investigation film with her ABC-TV special, targeting men's sexuality as an object of the female narrator's curiosity.

4 Yet the documentary mode only binds some Australian audiences into a film or television programme, the argument for a film industry was partly made so as to create opportunities for that binding in feature and television drama formats.

5 For a discussion of this film, its controversy and its textual politics see O'Regan 1985b, Sykes 1979: 113.

6 So too the reality of a drastically new diet (flour and sugar), new drugs (alcohol, tobacco and in the nineteenth century, opium), new forms and technologies of living, and new diseases (measles, chickenpox, influenza, VD and now AIDS) – when coupled with

dispossession, decimated and continue to decimate Aboriginal populations more than direct racist violence ever did. But colonialism as an Aboriginal health issue is not as filmic and telegenic as is violence and overt discrimination meted out by a bunch of ugly white Australian men.

7 Part of *Blood Oath*'s problem at the domestic box-office was that its Japanese release came after its Australian one. It would have had a more successful release if the Japanese release had come first and therefore foregrounded the film's Japanese/Australian dialogue. As it was, the two were not integrated and the film could be mistakenly read in Australia as Japan-bashing.

8 On this film see Caputo 1994.

9 Powell says more about his later Australian film, the remake of Norman Lindsay's novel *The Age of Consent*, and that is a sexist comment about how lovely Helen Mirren looked without any clothes!

10 Such scenes have their 'real' effects. Not long after travelling around South-East Asia wondering whether I was Australian or not (itself the product of these practices of Australian alterity), I saw *Caddie*'s sentimental rendition of *They're a Weird Mob*'s ethnic party. There, its solid image of Greek familial and communal solidarities, dancing and a desegregated sexual division of labour was counterposed to the drunken and 'segregationist norm' of the six-o'clock swill culture that Caddie pulled beers for. Not long after, I talked to an Australian woman of Greek and English extraction about her trip back to her mother's homeland, Greece. With *Caddie* in mind I said something like: 'it must have been a relief to be in a less sexist society'. She looked back at me with some bemusement and said that at least in Australia men have the good grace not to pinch your behind!

11 The resemblances do not end there: like the Bloke and Doreen's milieu, Nino and Kay's is the city. The Bloke hawks fruit and vegetables, Nino works on building sites. Each is upwardly mobile: the Bloke through hard work and becoming an orchard-owner through the gift of his wife's uncle, Nino through hardwork and his association with Kay and, one presumes eventually her father, and his canny sense of real estate by buying a plot of land overlooking the sea.

11 PROBLEMATIZING THE SOCIAL

1 Nowhere have country sensibilities most evidently failed to resonate in the urban setting than in the maintenance through the past two hundred years of this 'myth of the alien bush'. It is sustained not just by metropolitan sensibilities universalizing their own non-relation to the countryside but also by migration to Australia – for these migrants these trees, these shrubs, these landscapes are 'alien'. Growing up in the country I was astonished by the very idea of deciduous trees: trees that were for half of the year *not trees*.

2 This is in marked contrast to his earlier example of representations work, *Camera Natura* which takes little account of such sensibilities or the possibility that these might be animating some of the films dealt with in it.

3 I owe this formulation to William Routt. Personal correspondence with the author. October 1994.

4 Schepisi's film was set in a seminary for boys. The film emphasized the boy's boarding school aspect incorporating the teachers as the sexually repressed and sometimes deviant persons, as in the teachers of the girls' boarding school films of its time *Picnic at Hanging Rock* and *The Getting of Wisdom*. The Catholic references were downplayed to the extent that any viewer was encouraged to see the general in the particular.

5 Routt has pointed out to me the proximity of the evangelical Christian tradition in the

USA to exploitation film-making: combining high-minded moral messages with exploitationist prurience. There is no Australian equivalent.

6 It is probably worth noting that my father is of Irish descent, my mother of mixed English, Scottish and Norwegian descent via New Zealand and that 'mixed marriages' in this period were more often between Catholic women and Protestant men.

7 This benign image does violence to some contemporary realities for Aboriginal and Islander fringe dwellers, urbanites and people with no family structure. The 'positive' image erases some of the consequences of dispossession and colonization, which has been to make identity and belongingness less than a secure thing for many Aboriginal and Islanders.

8 The attempt to outreach not only in representation but also in audience is evident in ABC's ATVI satellite TV service which after fifteen months of operation in June 1994 was claiming an Asian regional audience of some 24 million, matching to some extent the ABC Radio Australia reach. The feedback was producing odd demands: viewers who wanted more on Australian domestic politics (because of their Australian invest-ments and children at University there) or alternatively the demand for 'Australian' colour stories – more on Australia's sheep dog trials.

9 Siew Keng Chua (1992, 1993) and Sylvie Shaw (1992) berate Australian film-makers for failing to make distinctions between the different Asian countries. A failure they compound by not theorizing the differences in Australia's relation with Indonesia and with Japan on film.

12 PROBLEMATIZING GENDER

1 This survey strangely does not list Fiona MacGregor's co-leading role in *Lex and Rory* or Charlotte Rampling's in *Hammers over the Anvil* (Turner 1993). If billing is a measure then these two films would be included, as too would *Map of the Human Heart*. A more reliable indication might be sheer screen time. On this score, Fiona MacGregor is evidently the co-lead of *Lex and Rory* and is listed as such in the credits. It is her story as much as Lex's. For its part, *Hammers over the Anvil* is a story in the mould of *The Go-Between* (Losey 1970) which makes it – and does not make it – a 'male rites of passage story'. If *Lex and Rory* and *Hammers over the Anvil* were included, then the figure would be the more respectable 40 per cent lead or co-lead.

2 Sometimes this ameliorative dimension is achieved through special programmes within governmental film agencies like the Women's Film Fund of the 1980s.

3 Wright and Young unnecessarily marred their case by leaving unchallenged the claim that Lyell, not Longford was the true creator of the classic films which Longford, Lyell and Higgins collaborated on. This is an opinion no other film historian shares and one which Ken Hall advised Wright against including!

4 Blonski makes an error here: the Egyptians not the Turks are the untrustworthy ones (of course, this does not make it any better just a little more complicated, as the film subscribes to the ANZAC legend of the 'noble enemy, the Turk' – the vile enemy of this legend is the German). The film was a success in Turkey and had a successful revival in 1994 in Istanbul as part of a festival of Australian films. Proceeds from its screenings to packed audiences went to a reafforestation project on the Gallipoli peninsular, which had been destroyed by bushfire (see Simpson 1995).

5 There is an alternative representation of the Australian state: its openness would be the historical consequence of a mature, democratic polity which has taken figures of (in)equality seriously over a long period. Such an account foregrounds Australia's extension of suffrage to women, the involvement and successes of the Chartist, temperance and feminist movement, and the various social programmes of a pro-gressive welfare state over the century.

6 Lesbianism is significant in the feminist project of auto-identification because hetero-identifications – involved, for example, in heterosexual identity – are seen to have disempowered women, their identity and their sex.

7 Interestingly Barbara Creed described Turner's earlier film, *Flesh on Glass* (a story of doomed lesbian love, 1981) as 'a powerful critique of heterosexuality and of masculinity, which is associated with the repressive sadistic powers of the law' (Creed 1993: 11).

13 PROBLEMATIZING NATIONHOOD

1 Jupp's (1991: 120) predictions of Australian demography by 2010 are that 'about 7 per cent of Australians will be of South-East or East Asian descent. Chinese, Arabic and Vietnamese will rival Italian and Greek as the most widely used languages after English. Perhaps 2 per cent of the population will be Muslim. Australia will be even more multicultural than it is today. ... Australia will by then still be much less multiracial than the United States or New Zealand. ... English will still be the language of three-quarters of Australians and two-thirds will still be able to trace their ancestry back to Britain and Ireland.'

2 Berlin (1991: 176–7) considers that 'nationalism is not consciousness of the reality of national character, nor pride in it'. Rather it is is a belief 'in the unique mission of a nation, as being intrinsically superior to the goals or attributes of whatever is outside it'. In short we should make distinctions among forms of national consciousness only one of which is nationalism.

3 Of these New Zealand born, a visible minority were New Zealanders of Maori ancestry. The 1.7 per cent figure is taken from Ian Castles (1992: 155) and is based on the 1991 census.

4 Australia's post 1976/77 migration history saw Asian migration become over one third of the overall migration in some years (Jupp 1991: 87).

5 Given such shared international cultural forms Western intellectuals need to take Chua Beng-Huat's advice (1990, cited in Frost 1994b: 23) and 'cease to lay proprietary claims to several concepts and societal developments that have Western origin but now have gained global proportions'. His candidates are 'capitalism, Modernity, and its political entailment, democracy'.

6 Michael can be interpreted as the blustering misogynist Australian male ready to prostitute his integrity for the sake of the company (Empire); Louise the more sensitive British/Australian woman prepared to experience the Other more humbly and directly. His diffidence is a preparedness to abase himself; hers a capacity to change.

7 It can also be curiously internalized. I sometimes hear my friends of English ancestry say they come from a 'boring background'.

8 None of these diasporic recognitions include Aboriginal and Islanders unless, of course, we understand the reassemblage of contemporary Aboriginality as the formation of a diaspora-like identity through processes of dispossession and exile.

9 The only two groups forcibly removed to Australia are Anglo-Celts and South Sea Islanders.

10 Not surprisingly radical (fascist and communist) politics, progressive politics and that of minority ethnic groups advocated, in the first seventy years of this century, those nationalist and Australianist positions intent on removing the diasporic element in Australia's public sense of itself.

11 These terms are derived from Banton (1982) 'The Two Ethnicities'.

12 There is significant continuity between Australian films of the 1930s and today's diasporic multicultural film-making, in the same anxious concern about the diaspora's relationships with the absent homeland and in the attempt to declare oneself 'the fairest

child' – as when Fremantle Italians of Franco di Chiera's *The Joys of the Women* preserve Italian traditions and songs no longer kept alive in Italy, thus becoming 'more Italian than the Italians'.

13 As Kalantzis and Cope observe, when 'an ethnically singular Britain and an ethnically singular Australia are aligned as a civic and cultural continuum ... other immigrants become seditious outsiders' (1993: 134).

14 Gertsakis was writing in an Australia Council sponsored publication *Culture, Difference and the Arts* (Gunew and Rizvi 1994a). This otherwise useful book is marred by denigrations of this kind (see also Winikoff 1994).

15 What is not improbable is the social norm of sexual union outside of ancestral groups as evidenced in marriage and ancestral statistics. What is improbable is the hyperreal social institutions and characters represented.

16 The film is one which meets the demand made by the MEAA for ethnic actors to play roles marked as the 'normal Australian'.

17 Banton (1994: 5) argues that 'change in ethnic relations often comes about not because people change the value they place upon associations with co-ethnics, but because they change their ideas about which relationships can be governed by ethnic norms'.

18 The very expression Anglo-Celtic to describe the dominant culture and peoples of Australia indicates the success of the new world cultural and audiovisual ideal in creating something new and durable out of the antagonistic cultural and human materials at its disposal. Remember the term Anglo-Celt is 'an extraordinary cultural hybrid' (Kalantzas 1990: 48) which 'aggregates groups amongst whom no love has been lost, and who don't even share common religious or ancestral languages' (Kalantzis and Bill Cope 1993: 134).

19 Sean Glynn (1992: 239) notes Australian cities do have 'remarkable similarities – in popular culture, technology, social structure and way of life' not only with each other but with 'British, American and other cities of the Western world'.

20 Banton (1994: 14) writes of the process of trading off 'preferences for association with co-ethnics against other values'. New world societies and cinemas strive, however unsuccessfully, to offer other such values.

21 Australia is not a Western metropole but a displaced European society; and like Brazil its settler culture which the 'disenfranchized' enter is already 'creole' and 'syncretic'.

22 Multicultural rhetoric needs to fashion itself as a break with the past. My argument here has been that the content of the national culture in Australia has always been in 'the process of becoming', that it was never 'fixed and historically given', and that it was always 'permanently unfinished business'. The real issue is the extent and degree of 'becoming' contemplated. Stratton and Ang are talking of degrees here.

23 The first two quotes I heard in two ABC Radio National interviews. The last quote is from Scott Murray (1990: 21).

24 A measure of this invitation to co-produce the film's meaning is Laleen Jayamenne's 1992) explicitly 'Sri Lankan reading' of *Night Cries.*

25 So Scott Murray (1990: 19) can write of *Night Cries* that 'the principal needs are those of the Australian Aborigines, whose time since the white settlement began has been, among many other things, a battle to retain cultural and spiritual independence in the face of powerful white repositioning.'

26 When I first watched this film I was confused about just who the Langton character was – Aboriginal servant, lover or daughter.

27 Multicultural critics claim biculturalism and hybridity as the special status, Australianness and intrinsic advantage of culturally diverse film-makers producing cutting edge hybrid work. The boosterism of such publicity invests ancestral identity and being born somewhere else with especial advantages over other ancestral identities and ordinary

Australians. In the process, such critics conflate innovative hybrid cinema forms with the lottery of birth; hybrid peoples necessarily give rise to innovative hybrid art. Such claims of privileged status are part of the publicity cycle of any interest group and stem from the many disadvantages some NESB migrants face in negotiating Australian cultural institutions. This association of hybrid people and hybrid art is, of course, overly prescriptive and legislative – hybrid art forms are, of course, not the prerogative of recently arrived migrants or their second generation offspring.

14 CRITICAL DISPOSITIONS

1 By contrast, explicatory criticism is almost a 'kiss of death' for a film as a critical gathering point.
2 The most damning indictment Eric Michaels and Nick Zurbrugg could muster to describe a Brisbane paper by a prominent Australian cultural critic, Michaels (1990: 112).
3 See Shirley and Adams (1983), Reade (1979), Bertrand (1989), Wright (1986), Pike and Cooper (1980), Tulloch (1981, 1982), Long (1994a – part of a continuing series charting 'Australia's First Films'), and Williams (1995). Dutchak has presented his work on Longford, Lyell and Higgins at the 1993 History and Film Conference in Melbourne.
4 As Malpas and Wickham (1995: 8) put it 'the practice of governance is characterized, not by finality and success, but by incompleteness and failure'.

List of films cited

FEATURE FILMS, DOCUMENTARIES, SHORT FILMS, TV MINI-SERIES AND SERIES

ABC of Love and Sex Australian Style, The, documentary dir. John Lamond 1978
Acropolis Now, TV series prod. Crawford Productions 1989
Act of Betrayal, The, mini-series dir. Lawrence Clark 1988
Adventures of Barry McKenzie, The, dir. Bruce Beresford 1972
Adventures of Priscilla: Queen of the Desert, The, dir. Stephan Elliott 1994
Age of Consent, The, dir. Michael Powell 1969
Alice to Nowhere, mini-series dir. John Power 1986
All that is Solid, documentary dir. John Hughes 1988
All the Rivers Run, mini-series dir. George Miller, John Power and Pino Amenta
Alvin Purple, dir. Tim Burstall 1973
Always Afternoon, mini-series dir. David Stevens 1988
American in Paris, An, dir. Vincente Minnelli 1951
And the World was Made Flesh, dir. Dusan Markek 1971
Angel at my Table, An, dir. Jane Campion 1990, New Zealand
Animal House, dir. John Landis 1978
Ann of Green Gables, mini-series dir. Kevin Sullivan 1985
Annie's Coming Out, dir. Gil Brealey 1984
ANZACS, mini-series dir. John Dixon, George Miller and Pino Amenta 1985
Apartment, The, dir. Billy Wilder 1960
Around the World in 80 Ways, dir. Stephen MacLean 1988
As Times Goes By, dir. Barry Peak 1988
Aussie Rules, documentary dir. Barbara Chobocky 1993
Australia Live, documentary dir. Peter Faiman 1988
Australian Dream, dir. Jackie McKimmie 1987
Avalon, dir. Barry Levinson 1990
Aya, dir. Solrun Hoaas 1991
Babe, dir. Chris Noonan 1995
Back of Beyond, The, documentary dir. John Heyer 1954
Backroads, dir. Phillip Noyce 1977
Bad Boy Bubby, dir. Rolf de Heer 1994
Bali Hash, documentary dir. John Darling 1989
Bali Triptych, documentary dir. John Darling 1987
Bananas in Pyjamas, TV series prod. ABC 1991
Bangkok Hilton, mini-series dir. Ken Cameron 1989

Banjo Patterson's The Man from Snowy River, mini-series dir. Tim Burstall, Denny Lawrence, Dan Burstall 1994
Barbarosa, dir. Fred Schepisi 1982
Barton Fink, dir. Joel Coen 1991
Battlers, The, mini-series dir. George Ogilvie 1994
Battleship Potemkin, dir. Sergei Eisenstein 1925
Baywatch, TV series prod. All American Television Inc. 1989–
beDevil, dir. Tracey Moffat 1993
Bellbird, TV serial prod. ABC 1967–77
Bello Onesto Emigrato Australia Sposerebbe Compaesana Illibata, aka *Girl in Australia*, dir. Luigi Zampa 1971
Below the Wind, documentary dir. John Darling 1994
Betrayer, The, dir. Beaumont Smith 1921
Between Wars, dir. Michael Thornhill 1974
Big Country, The, documentary TV series ABC 1968–88
Big Sleep, The, dir. Howard Hawks 1946
Bigger than Texas: The Ghosts that Never Die, documentary dir. David Noakes 1992
Bingo, Bridesmaids and Braces, documentary dir. Gillian Armstrong 1988
Birds, The, dir. Alfred Hitchcock 1963
Birth of Nation, The, dir. D. W. Griffiths 1915
Birth of White Australia, The, dir. Phil K. Walsh 1928
Bitter Springs, dir. Ralph Smart 1950
Black Harvest, documentary dir. Bob Connolly and Robin Anderson 1992
Black Robe, The, dir. Bruce Beresford 1992
Blackfellas, dir. James Ricketson 1993
Blinky Bill, TV series dir. Yoram Gross 1994
Blood Oath, dir. Stephen Wallace 1990
BMX Bandits, dir. Brian Trenchard-Smith 1983
Body Melt, dir. Phillip Brophy 1994
Bodyline, mini-series dir. Carl Schultz, George Ogilvie, Lex Mamnos and Denny Lawrence 1984
Bolero, dir. Albie Thoms 1967
Bread and Dripping, dir. Wimmins Film Collective 1981
Break of Day, dir. Ken Hannam 1976
Breaker Morant, dir. Bruce Beresford 1980
Breaking of the Drought, The, dir. Franklyn Barrett 1920
Breathing Under Water, dir. Susan Dermody 1992
Brides of Christ, mini-series dir. Ken Cameron 1991
Broken Melody, dir. Ken G. Hall 1938
Buddies, dir. Arch Nicholson 1983
Burke and Wills, dir. Graeme Clifford 1985
Bush Christmas, dir. Ralph Smart 1947
Bush Christmas, dir. Henri Safran 1983
Caddie, dir. Donald Crombie 1976
Camera Natura, documentary dir. Ross Gibson 1984
Cane Toads, documentary dir. Mark Lewis 1987
Cannibal Tours, documentary dir. Dennis O'Rourke 1988
Captain Thunderbolt, dir. Cecil Holmes 1953
Careful He Might Hear You, dir. Carl Schultz 1983
Cars that Ate Paris, The, dir. Peter Weir 1974
Celia, dir. Anne Turner 1989
Celso and Cora: A Manila Story, documentary dir. Gary Kildea 1983

Change of Face, A, documentary dir. Franco de Chiera 1988
Chant of Jimmie Blacksmith, The, dir. Fred Schepisi 1978
Chariots of Fire, dir. Hugh Hudson 1981
Cheaters, The, dir. Paulette McDonagh 1930
Chequerboard, documentary series prod. ABC 1969–75
Children of the Dragon, mini-series dir. Peter Smith 1992
Chile: hasta Cuando?, documentary dir. David Bradbury 1985
Clay, dir. Giorgio Mangiamele 1965
Clear and Present Danger, dir. Phillip Noyce 1994
Clinic, The, dir. David Stevens 1983
Club, The, dir. Bruce Beresford 1976
Coca-Cola Kid, The, dir. Dusan Makavejev 1985
Coniston Muster: Scenes from a Stockman's Life, documentary dir. Roger Sandall 1972
Consider Your Verdict, TV series prod. Crawford Productions 1961
Coolangatta Gold, dir. Igor Auzins 1984
Countdown, TV series prod. ABC 1978–87
Country Life, dir. Michael Blakemore 1994
Country Practice, A, TV serial prod. JNP Films Pty Ltd. 1981
Cowra Breakout, mini-series dir. Phillip Noyce and Chris Noonan 1985
Crocodile Dundee, dir. Peter Faiman 1986
Crocodile Dundee II, dir. John Corrall 1988
Crossing Delancey, dir. Joan Silver 1988
Crystal Voyager, documentary dir. Albert Falzon 1973
Custodian, The, dir. John Dingwall 1993
Dad and Dave Come to Town, dir. Ken G. Hall 1938
Dad Rudd, M.P., dir. Ken G. Hall 1940
Dallas, TV series prod. Lorimar 1978–91
Dallas Doll, dir. Ann Turner 1993
Damnation of Harvey McHugh, The, mini-series dir. Richard Sarell, Peter Dodds, Nandy Smith and Brendan Maher 1994
Dances with Wolves, dir. Kevin Costner 1991
Dangerous Game, dir. Stephen Hopkins (prod. 1988) released 1991
Dawn!, dir. Ken Hannam 1979
Dead Calm, dir. Phil Noyce 1989
Deadly, dir. Esben Storm 1992
Death in Brunswick, dir. John Ruane 1991
Death of a Soldier, dir. Phillipe Mora 1986
Delinquents, The, dir. Chris Thomson 1989
Devil in the Flesh, aka *Beyond Innocence*, dir. Scott Murray 1989
Devil's Playground, The, dir. Fred Schepisi 1976
Dingo, dir. Rolf de Heer 1992
Dirtwater Dynasty, mini-series dir. Michael Jenkins and John Power 1988
Dismissal, The, dir. Dr George Miller, Phil Noyce, Carl Schultz, George Ogilvie, John Power 1983
Division 4, TV series Crawford Productions 1969–75
Dogs in Space, dir. Richard Lowenstein 1987
Don's Party, dir. Bruce Beresford 1976
Don't Call me Girlie, documentary dir. Andrée Wright and Stewart Young 1985
Dot and the Kangaroo, dir. Yoram Gross 1977
Driving Miss Daisy, dir. Bruce Beresford 1989
Duel in the Sun, dir. King Vidor 1946
Dunera Boys, The, mini-series dir. Ben Lewin 1985

Dynasty, TV series prod. Aaron Spelling Productions 1981–9
Easy Rider, dir. Dennis Hopper 1969
Eat Carpet, TV series SBS-TV 1988
Echoes of Paradise, dir. Phillip Noyce 1988
Edge of Darkness, BBC mini-series dir. Martin Campbell 1985
El Angelito, dir. Guillermo Sepulveda 1993
El Cid, dir. Anthony Mann 1961
Eliza Fraser, dir. Tim Burstall 1976
Embassy, TV serial prod. ABC and Grundy 1990–2
Emerald City, aka *David Williamson's Emerald City*, dir. Michael Jenkins 1989
Escape from Absolon, dir. Martin Campbell 1994
E.T., dir. Steven Spielberg 1982
Eureka Stockade, dir. Harry Watt 1949
Eureka Stockade, mini-series dir. Rod Hardy 1984
Every Night ... Every Night, dir. Alkinos Tsilimidos 1994
Evil Angels, aka *A Cry in the Dark*, dir. Fred Schepisi 1988
Exile, dir. Paul Cox 1993
Exile and the Kingdom, documentary dir. Frank Rijavek 1994
F/X, dir. Robert Mandel 1985
F/X 2: The Deadly Art of Illusion, dir. Richard Franklin 1991
Far Country, The, mini-series dir. George Miller 1987
Far East, dir. John Duigan 1982
Far Paradise, The, dir. Paulette McDonagh 1928
Fast Talking, dir. Ken Cameron 1984
Fearless, dir. Peter Weir 1994
Fields of Fire, mini-series dir. David Elfick and Rob Marchand 1987, 1988, 1989
Fighting Back, dir. Michael Caulfield 1983
Film for Discussion, documentary dir. Sydney Women's Film Group 1974
First Contact, documentary dir. Robyn Anderson and Bob Connelly 1982
Flesh on Glass, dir. Ann Turner 1981
Flirting, dir. John Duigan 1991
Floating Life, dir. Clara Law 1996
Fly, The, dir. David Cronenberg 1986
Flying Doctors, The TV series prod. Crawford Productions 1985– 9
For Love or Money, documentary dir. Megan McMurchy, Margot Nash, Margot Oliver, Jeni Thornley 1983
For the Term of his Natural Life, dir. Norman Dawn 1927
Forrest Gump, dir. Robert Zemeckis 1994
Fortress, dir. Steve Gordon 1993
Fortunate Life, A, mini-series dir. Marcus Cole, Henri Safran 1986
Forty Thousand Horsemen, dir. Charles Chauvel 1940
Four Weddings and a Funeral, dir. Mike Newell 1994
14's Good, 18's Better, documentary dir. Gillian Armstrong 1981
Fran, dir. Glenda Hambly 1985
Frauds, dir. Stephen Elliott 1993
Free Willy, dir. Simon Wincer 1993
Fringe Dwellers, dir. Bruce Beresford 1986
From the Tropics to the Snow, documentary dir. Richard Mason and Jack Lee 1964
Frontline, documentary dir. David Bradbury 1980
Gallipoli, dir. Peter Weir 1981
Genocide, documentary dir. Richard Oxenburgh 1990
Getting of Wisdom, The, dir. Bruce Beresford 1977

Ghosts . . . of the Civil Dead, dir. John Hillcoat 1989
Gino, dir. Jackie McKimmie 1994
Girl of the Bush, A dir. Franklyn Barrett 1921
Girl's Own Story, A, dir. Jane Campion 1983
Go-Between, The dir. Joseph Losey 1970
God Knows Why But it Works, documentary dir. Phillip Noyce 1975
Godfather, The, dir. Francis Ford Coppola 1972
Going Down, dir. Haydn Keenan 1983
Good Woman of Bangkok, The, documentary-fiction dir. Denis O'Rourke 1992
Goodbye Paradise, dir. Carl Schultz 1983
G.P., TV series prod. Roadshow, Coote and Carroll and ABC-TV 1989–
Green Card, dir. Peter Weir 1991
Grendel Grendel Grendel, dir. Alex Stitt 1981
Gross Misconduct, dir. George Miller 1993
Ground Zero, dir. Michael Pattinson 1987
GTK, TV series prod. ABC 1969–75
Halloween, dir. Dwight Little 1978
Hammers over the Anvil, dir. Ann Turner 1993
Harlequin, dir. Simon Wincer 1980
Heartbreak High, TV series Gannon Television 1994–
Heartbreak Kid, The, dir. Michael Jenkins 1993
Heartland, mini-series ABC dir. 1994
Heatwave, dir. Phillip Noyce 1982
Heavenly Creatures, dir. Peter Jackson 1995
Heimat, mini-series dir. Edgar Reitz 1984
Heritage, dir. Charles Chauvel 1935
Hester Street, dir. Joan Silver 1974
High Rolling, dir. Igor Auzins 1977
Hightide, dir. Gillian Armstrong 1987
Home and Away, TV serial prod. ATN Channel 7 1988–
Homicide, TV series prod. Crawford Productions 1964–75
Hostage, dir. Frank Shields 1983
Hotel Sorrento, dir. Richard Franklin 1995
House Opening, The, dir. Judith MacDougall 1980
How the West was Lost, dir. David Noakes 1987
Howling III: The Marsupials, dir. Phillipe Mora 1987
I Love Lucy, TV series prod. Desilu 1951–7
Ileksen, dir. Dennis O'Rourke 1978
Illustrated Auschwitz, The, documentary dir. Jackie Farkas 1992
In the Wake of the Bounty, documentary dir. Charles Chauvel 1933
In this Life's Body, dir. Corinne Cantrill 1984
Incident at Raven's Gate, dir. Rolf de Heer 1989
Indecent Obsession, dir. Lex Marinos 1985
Indecent Proposal, dir. Andrew Bergman 1993
Indonesia Calling, documentary dir. Joris Ivens 1946
Irishman, The, dir. Donald Crombie 1978
Island of Lies, documentary dir. Gillian Coote 1990
It isn't Done, dir. Ken G. Hall 1937
Jedda, dir. Charles Chauvel 1955
Jenny Kissed Me, dir. Brian Trenchard-Smith 1986
Jilted, dir. Bill Bennett 1987.
Joe Leahy's Neighbours, documentary dir. Bob Connolly and Robin Anderson 1988

Joh's Jury, dir. Ken Cameron 1993
Journey among Women, dir. Tom Cowan 1977
Joys of the Women, The, documentary dir. Franco di Chiera 1993
Jungle Woman, dir. Frank Hurley 1926
Just Desserts, dir. Monica Pellizari 1993
Killing of Angel Street, The, dir. Donald Crombie 1981
King of the Coral Sea, dir. Lee Robinson 1954
Kings of the Road, dir. Wim Wenders 1975
Kostas, dir. Paul Cox 1979
Ladies Rooms, documentary dir. Sarah Gibson, Pat Fiske, Susan Lambert, Jan MacKay
     1977
Landslides, documentary dir. Gibson and Lambert 1986
Last Days of Chez Nous, The, dir. Gillian Armstrong 1992
Last of the Knucklemen, The, dir. Tim Burstall 1979
Last Outlaw, The, mini-series dir. Kevin Dobson and George Miller 1980
Last Tasmanian, The, dir. Tom Haydon 1978
Last Wave, The, dir. Peter Weir 1977
Law of the Land, TV serial prod. Roadshow, Coote and Carroll 1993
Learning the Ropes, documentary dir. Barbara Chobocky 1993
Leaving of Liverpool, The, mini-series dir. Michael Jenkins 1992
Lempad of Bali, documentary dir. John Darling 1980
Les Diaboliques, dir. Henri-Georges Clouzot 1954
Les Enfants du Paradis, dir. Marcel Carne 1943
Lethal Weapon, dir. Richard Donner 1987, 1989, 1992
Lex and Rory, dir. Dean Murphy 1993
Life and Times of Rosie the Riveter, The, documentary dir. Connie Field 1980
Lion King, The, dir. Roger Allers and Rob Mincoff 1994
Little Women, dir. Gillian Armstrong 1994
Lonely Hearts, dir. Paul Cox 1982
Lonesome Dove, dir. Simon Wincer 1989
Longtime Companion, dir. Norman Rene 1990
Lorenzo's Oil, dir. George Miller 1992
Lost Honour of Katharina Blum, The, dir. Margarethe von Trotta 1975
Lousy Little Sixpence, documentary dir. Alec Morgan 1983
Love in Limbo, dir. David Elfick 1993
Love Letters from Teralba Road, dir. Stephen Wallace 1977
Lover Boy, dir. Geoffrey Wright 1988
Mad Dog Morgan, dir. Phillippe Mora's 1976
Mad Max, dir. Dr George Miller 1979
Mad Max II, aka *The Road Warrior*, dir. Dr George Miller 1981
Mad Max III: Beyond Thunderdome, dir. Dr George Miller and George Ogilvie 1985
Magistrate, The, mini-series dir. Kathy Mueller 1989
Maidens, dir. Jeni Thornley 1978
Making Love, dir. Arthur Hiller 1982
Malcolm, dir. Nadia Tass 1986
Man from Hong Kong, The, dir. Brian Trenchard-Smith 1975
Man from Snowy River, The, dir. George Miller 1982
Man of Flowers, dir. Paul Cox 1983
Manganinnie, dir. John Honey 1980
Mango Tree, The, dir. Kevin Dobson 1977
Manon des Sources, dir. Claude Berri 1987
Maori Maid's Love, A, dir. Raymond Longford 1916

Map of the Human Heart, dir. Vincent Ward 1993
Marco Polo Junior and the Red Dragon, dir. Eric Porter 1972
Maria, documentary dir. Barbara Chobocky 1991
Matlock Police, TV-series prod. Crawford Productions 1971–5
Merry Christmas, Mr Lawrence, dir. Nagisa Oshima 1982
Metal Skin, dir. Geoffrey Wright 1995
Midnight Express, dir. Alan Parker 1978
Mike and Stefani, documentary dir. Ron Maslyn Williams 1952
Milli Milli, documentary dir. Wayne Barker 1993
Mission Impossible, TV series dir. Cliff Bole and Kim Manners 1989
Models Inc., TV series prod. Spelleng Television Inc. 1994
Modern Times, documentary dir. Graeme Chase 1992
Monkey Grip, dir. Ken Cameron 1982
Morning of the Earth, documentary dir. Albert Falzon 1972
Mother and Son, TV series prod. ABC 1985–
Mourning for Mangatopi: A Tiwi Bereavement Ceremony, documentary dir. Curtis Levy
    1975
Mouth to Mouth, dir. John Duigan 1978
Moving Out, dir. Michael Pattinson 1983
Muriel's Wedding, dir. Paul J. Hogan 1994
My Beautiful Laundrette, dir. Stephen Frears 1985
My Brilliant Career, dir. Gillian Armstrong 1979
My First Wife, dir. Paul Cox 1984
My Life without Steve, dir. Gillian Leahy 1986
My Survival as an Aborigine, documentary dir. Essie Coffey 1979
Mystical Rose, dir. Michael Lee 1976
Naked Bunyip, The, dir. John B. Murray 1970
Naked Lunch, The, dir. David Cronenberg 1991
Namitjira the Painter, documentary dir. Lee Robinson 1946
Nation is Built, A, documentary dir. Frank Hurley 1938
Navigator: A Medieval Odyssey, The, dir. Vincent Ward 1988
Nazi Supergrass, documentary dir. David Bradbury 1993
Ned Kelly, dir. Tony Richardson 1970
Neighbours, TV serial prod. Grundy Television 1985–
Newsfront, dir. Phillip Noyce 1979
Nicaragua no Pasaran, documentary dir. David Bradbury 1984
Nice Coloured Girls, dir. Tracey Moffatt 1987
Night Belongs to the Novelist, The, dir. Christina Wilcox 1987
Night Cries – A Rural Tragedy, dir. Tracey Moffatt 1989
Night the Prowler, The, dir. Jim Sharman 1979
Nightmare on Elm Street 5, A, dir. Stephen Hopkins 1989
Nirvana Street Murder, dir. Aleksi Vellis 1991
No Worries, dir. David Elfick 1993
Norman Loves Rose, dir. Henri Safran 1982
Nostradamus Kid, The, dir. Bob Ellis 1993
Number 96, TV serial prod. Cash-Harmon Productions 1972– 9
Odd Angry Shot, The, dir. Tom Jeffery 1979
On Guard, dir. Sarah Gibson and Susan Lambert 1983
On our Selection, dir. Raymond Longford 1920
On our Selection, dir. Ken G. Hall 1932
On our Selection, dir. George Whaley 1995
On the Beach, dir. Stanley Kramer 1959

Once Upon a Time in the West, dir. Sergio Leone 1968
Once were Warriors, dir. Lee Tamahori 1994
One Australia? The Future Starts Here, documentary dir. Christine Sammers 1991
One Way Street, documentary dir. John Hughes 1993
Only the Brave, dir. Ana Kokkinos 1994
Overlanders, The, dir. Harry Watt 1946
Palace of Dreams, mini-series dir. Denny Lawrence, Geoffrey Nottage, Graham Thorburn, David Goldie and Richard Pellizzeri 1985
Palm Beach, dir. Albie Thoms 1979
Paradise Beach, TV serial prod. Village Roadshow and New World International 1993–94
Patrick, dir. Richard Franklin 1978
Patriot Games, dir. Phillip Noyce 1992
Peel, dir. Jane Campion 1982
Peeping Tom, dir. Michael Powell 1959
Peter Kenna's Umbrella Woman, dir. Ken Cameron 1987
Petersen, dir. Tim Burstall 1974
Phantom Stockman, The, dir. Lee Robinson 1953
Phar Lap, dir. Simon Wincer 1983
Piano, The, dir. Jane Campion 1993
Picnic at Hanging Rock, dir. Peter Weir 1975
Pictures that Moved, The, documentary dir. Alan Anderson 1968
Police Rescue, TV series prod. Southern Star Xanadu, the ABC and the BBC 1992–
Predator 2, dir. Stephen Hopkins 1990
Prisoner: Cell Block H, TV serial prod. Grundy Organisation 1979–86
Prisoner of St Petersburg, dir. Ian Pringle 1990
Proof, dir. Jocelyn Moorhouse 1 1985
Psycho II, dir. Richard Franklin 1983
Puberty Blues, dir. Bruce Beresford 1981
Pure 5, dir. Bert Deling 1976
Queensland, dir. John Ruane 1976
Quigley Down Under, dir. Simon Wincer 1992
Rabbit on the Moon, dir. Monica Pellizari 1987
Race for the Yankee Zephyr, dir. David Hemmings 1981
Rage, TV series prod. ABC-TV 1985–
Razorback, dir. Russell Mulcahy 1984
Rebecca, dir. Alfred Hitchcock 1940
Rebel, dir. Michael Jenkins 1985
Reckless Kelly, dir. Yahoo Serious 1993
Red Matildas, documentary dir. Sharon Connolly and Trevor Graham 1985
Red Shoes, The, dir. Michael Powell and Emeric Pressburger 1948
Removalists, The, dir. Tom Jeffrey 1975
Return Home, dir. Ray Argall 1990
Return to Eden, mini-series dir. Karen Arthur, Rod Hardy, Arch Nicholson and Kevin Dobson (series 1) 1983 (series 2) 1986
Riddles of the Sphynx, dir. Laura Mulvey and Peter Wollen 1977
Roadgames, dir. Richard Franklin 1981
Robbery under Arms, dir. Jack Lee 1957
Rocky Horror Picture Show, The, dir. Jim Sharman 1975
Rolling Home, documentary dir. Paul Witzig 1974
Roly Poly Man, dir. Kym Goldsworthy 1994
Romper Stomper, dir. Geoffrey Wright 1992

Rudd's New Selection!, dir. Raymond Longford 1921
Rush, mini-series dir. Frank Arnold, Eric Taylor and Michael Jenkins (series 1) 1974 (series 2) 1976
Russia House, The, dir. Fred Schepisi 1990
Sammy and Rosie Get Laid, dir. Stephen Frears 1987
Say a Little Prayer, dir. Richard Lowenstein 1993
Scales of Justice, mini-series dir. Michael Jenkins 1983
Schindler's List, dir. Steven Spielberg 1992
Sentimental Bloke, The, dir. Raymond Longford 1919
Serious Undertakings, dir. Helen Grace 1983
Shadow of Lightning Ridge, The, dir. Wilfred Lucas 1920
Shame, dir. Steve Jodrell 1988
Shirley Thompson versus the Aliens, dir. Jim Sharman 1972
Siege of Pinchgut, The, dir. Harry Watt 1959
Silence of Dean Maitland, The, dir. Ken G. Hall 1934
Silver City, dir. Sophia Turkiewicz 1984
Singin' in the Rain, dir. Gene Kelly and Stanley Donen 1952
Sirens, dir. John Duigan 1994
Six Degrees of Separation, dir. Fred Schepisi 1993
Six Pack, mini-series dir. Kay Pavlou, Di Drew, Sue Brooks, Rodney Fisher, Megan Simpson and Karin Altmann 1991
Skippy, TV series prod. Fauna Productions/Norfolk International Productions 1968–70
Sliver, dir. Phillip Noyce 1993
Smokes and Lollies, documentary dir. Gillian Armstrong 1976
Snakes and Ladders, documentary dir. Mitzi Goldman and Trish FitzSimons 1987
Sniper, dir. Luis Llosa 1992
Soldiers of the Cross, dir. Joseph Perry and Herbert Booth 1900
Some Like it Hot, dir. Billy Wilder 1959
Sons of Matthew, The, dir. Charles Chauvel 1949
Speed, dir. Jan de Bont 1994
Spider and Rose, dir. Bill Bennett 1994
Spotswood, dir. Mark Joffe 1992
Square Bashing, dir. Stephen Harrop 1982
Squatter's Daughter, The, dir. Ken G. Hall 1933
Star Struck, dir. Gillian Armstrong 1982
Star Wars, dir. George Lucas 1977
State of Shock, documentary dir. David Bradbury 1989
Stir!, dir. Stephen Wallace, 1980
Stone, dir. Sandy Harbutt 1974
Stork, dir. Tim Burstall 1971
Storm Boy, dir. Henri Safran 1976
Story of the Kelly Gang, The, dir. Charles Tait 1906
Stowaway, The, dir. Lee Robinson and Ralph Habib 1958
Street Fighter, dir. Stephen E. de Souza 1995
Street Hero, dir. Michael Pattinson 1984
Strictly Ballroom, dir. Baz Luhrmann 1992
Strikebound, dir. Richard Lowenstein 1984
Struck by Lightning, dir. Jerzy Domaradzki 1990
Sum of Us, The, dir. Geoff Burton and Kevin Dowling 1994
Sunday Too Far Away, dir. Ken Hannam 1975
Sundowners, The, dir. Fred Zinnemann 1960
Surf Movies, documentary dir. Albie Thoms 1981

Sweetie, dir. Jane Campion 1989
Sylvania Waters, TV documentary series dir. Brian Hill and Kate Woods 1992
Takeover, documentary dir. David MacDougall and Judith MacDougall 1980
Tale of Ruby Rose, The, dir. Robert Scholes 1988
Talk, dir. Susan Lambert 1994
Tell England, dir. Anthony Asquith and Gerald Barkas 1931
Tender Mercies, dir. Bruce Beresford 1982
Terminator 2, dir. James Cameron 1991
Terra Nullius, dir. Anne Pratten 1993
They're a Weird Mob, dir. Michael Powell 1966
Those who Love, dir. Paulette McDonagh 1926
Thread of Voice, dir. Arf Arf 1994
Three in One, dir. Cecil Holmes 1957
Three to Go, dir. Peter Weir, Brian Hannant, Oliver Howes 1971
To the Distant Shore, aka *Zu Neuen Ufern*, dir. Hans Detlief Sierck aka Douglas Sirk
    1937
Topaz, dir. Alfred Hitchcock 1968
Total Recall, dir. Paul Verhoeven 1990
Town Like Alice, A, dir. Jack Lee 1956
Town Like Alice, A, mini-series dir. David Stevens 1981
Traps, documentary dir. John Hughes 1986
Traps, dir. Pauline Chan 1994
Tripe, dir. Greg Woodland 1985
Turkey Shoot, dir. Brian Trenchard-Smith 1982
Turtle Beach, dir. Stephen Wallace 1992
Two Friends, dir. Jane Campion 1985
Two Laws, documentary dir. Alessandro Cavadini and Carolyn Strachan, 1981
Two Thousand Weeks, dir. Tim Burstall 1969
Umbrella Woman, The, dir. Ken Cameron 1987
Uncivilized, dir. Charles Chauvel 1936
Under Capricorn, dir. Alfred Hitchcock 1949
Under the Skin, TV mini-series Film Australia 1994
Union Maids, documentary dir. J. Reichert and J. Klein 1976
Until the End of the World, dir. Wim Wenders 1992
Vacant Possession, dir. Margot Nash 1995
Velo Nero, dir Monica Pellizari 1987
Vietnam, mini-series dir. John Diugan and Chris Nooran (1987)
Waiting, dir. Jackie McKimmie 1991
Waiting for Harry, documentary dir. Kim McKenzie 1980
Wake in Fright, dir. Ted Kotcheff 1971
Walk into Paradise, dir. Lee Robinson and Giorgio Pagliero 1956
Walkabout, dir. Nicolas Roeg 1971
Waterfall, dir. Arthur and Corrinne Cantrill 1984
Waterfront, mini-series dir. Chris Thomson 1984
Waterworld, dir. Kevin Reynolds 1995
We Aim to Please, dir. Margot Nash and Robin Laurie 1977
We of the Never Never, dir. Igor Auzins 1982
Weekend of Shadows, dir. Tom Jeffrey 1978
When Mrs Hegarty Comes to Japan, documentary dir. Noriko Sekiguchi 1992
Where the Green Ants Dream, dir. Werner Herzog 1984
Whiplash, mini-series dir. John Lucas and Peter Maxwell 1961
Wild, documentary dir. Ross Gibson 1993

Witch Hunt, documentary dir. Barbara Chobocky 1986
Witches of Eastwick, The, dir. George Miller 1987
Wizard of Oz, The, dir. Victor Fleming 1939
Woman Suffers ... While the Man Goes Free, The, dir. Raymond Longford 1918
Woman's Tale, A, dir. Paul Cox 1991
Women of the Sun, mini-series dir. James Ricketson, David Stevens, Stephen Wallace and
    Geoffrey Nottage 1982
Written on the Wind, dir. Douglas Sirk 1956
Wrong Side of the Road, dir. Ned Lander 1981
Wrong World, dir. Ian Pringle 1986
Year My Voice Broke, The, dir. John Duigan, 1987
Year of Living Dangerously, The, dir. Peter Weir 1982
Young Einstein, dir. Yahoo Serious 1988
Young Soul Rebels, dir. Isaac Julien 1991
Yumi Yet, documentary dir. Dennis O'Rourke 1976
Zabriskie Point, dir. Michelangelo Antonioni 1969

Bibliography

Abbey, Ruth and Jo Crawford (1987) 'Crocodile Dundee or Davey Crockett?', *Meanjin* 2: 145–53.

Adams, Phillip (1971) 'Adam's Rib', *The Age*, 4 December 1971, Review 11.

—— (1982) 'The Importance of Remaining Australian', *The Bulletin* 12 January: 32–3.

—— (1995) 'Introduction'. In James Sabine (ed.) *A Century of Australian Cinema*, Port Melbourne: Reed Books, 1995, vii–xi.

Alomes, Stephen (1988) *A Nation at Last?: The Changing Character of Australian Nationalism 1880–1988*, North Ryde, Sydney: Angus and Robertson.

Alysen, Barbara (1985) 'Australian Women in Film'. In A. Moran and T. O'Regan (eds.) *An Australian Film Reader*, 302–13.

Anderson, Benedict (1983, 1991) *Imagined Communities*, London: Verso.

Armes, Roy (1987) *Third World film-making and the West*, Berkeley: University of California Press.

Australian Broadcasting Tribunal (1991) *Broadcasting in Australia*, Sydney: Australian Broadcasting Tribunal.

Australian Film Commission (1986) *Film Assistance: Future Options*, Sydney: Allen & Unwin.

Australian Film Commission (1991) *Analysis of the Performance of Australian Films since 1980*, A Paper for the House of Representatives Standing Committee on Environment, Recreation and the Arts Inquiry into the Performance of Australian Film – 'The Moving Pictures Enquiry', Sydney: AFC. October.

Australian Film Television and Radio School Annual Report 1992/93, Sydney: Australian Film Television and Radio School.

Bailey, Julie James (1994) 'Labels Proposed to Identify Gender', *Encore* 31 October–13 November, 12:17, 18.

Balázs, Béla (1970) *The Theory of the Film: Character and Growth of a New Art*, trans. Edith Bone, New York: Dover Publications.

Banton, Michael (1982) 'The Two Ethnicities', *Journal of Intercultural Studies* 3: 1, 25–35.

—— (1994) 'Modelling Ethnic and National Relations', *Ethnic and Racial Studies* 17: 1, 1–19.

Barry, Ramona (1994) 'Learning to Walk, All over Again', *Overland* 135: 8–10.

Baxter, John (1970) *Australian Cinema*, Sydney: Pacific Books.

—— (1986) *Filmstruck: Australia at the Movies*, Sydney: Australian Broadcasting Corporation.

Bazin, André (1971) *What is Cinema*, vol. 2, Berkeley: University of California Press.

Bean, Jeremy and David Court (1994) 'Production'. In R. Curtis and S. Spriggs (eds) *Get the Picture*, 30–67.

Bell, Philip and Roger Bell (1993) *Implicated: the United States in Australia*, Melbourne: Oxford University Press.

Bell, Sharon (1990) 'Filming Radio Redfern: "Riding to Success on the Backs of Blacks"?', *Media Information Australia* 56: 35–7.

Bennett, Colin (1978) 'Cloud Hangs over our Silver Screen', *The Age*, 20 May, Review 11.

Berlin, Isaiah (1991) *The Crooked Timber of Humanity: Chapters in the History of Ideas*, New York: Knopf.

Berry, Chris (1992) 'Heterogeneity as Identity', *Metro* 91 (Spring): 48–51.

—— (1993) 'Australia in Asia/Asia in Australia: An Interview with Teck Tan', *Metro* 94 (Winter): 42–4.

—— (1994) *A Bit on the Side: East–West Topographies of Desire*, Sydney: EMPress.

—— (1995) 'Pauline Chan: Interview', *Cinemaya* vols 25–6: 65–7.

Berryman, Ken (1990) 'A Girl of the Bush'. In K. Berryman (ed.) *Focus on Reel Australia*, Hendon SA: Australian Council of Government Film Libraries in association with the National Film and Sound Archive.

Bertrand, Ina (ed.) (1989) *Cinema in Australia: A Documentary History*, Kensington: University of New South Wales Press.

Bertrand, Ina and Diane Collins (1981) *Government and Film in Australia*, Sydney: Currency Press.

Bertrand, Ina and William Routt (1989) 'The Big Bad Combine: Some Aspects of National Aspirations and International Constraints in the Australian Cinema, 1896–1929'. In A. Moran and T. O'Regan (eds.) *The Australian Screen*, 23–7.

Bhabha, Homi (1990) 'The Third Space: Interview with Homi Bhabha'. In Jonathan Rutherford (ed.) *Identity: Community, Culture, Difference*, London: Lawrence & Wishart, 207–21.

—— (1994) *The Location of Culture*, London and New York: Routledge.

Blonski, Annette (1987) 'At the Government's Pleasure: Independent Cinema'. In A. Blonski, B. Creed and F. Freiberg (eds) *Don't Shoot Darling*, 40–60.

—— (1994) 'Persistent Encounters: The Australia Council and Multiculturalism'. In S. Gunew and F. Rizvi (eds) *Culture, Difference and the Arts*, 192–206.

Blonski, Annette and Freda Freiberg (1989) 'Double Trouble: Women's Films'. In A. Moran and T. O'Regan (eds) *Australian Screen*, 191–215.

Blonski, Annette, Barbara Creed and Freda Freiberg (eds) (1987) *Don't Shoot Darling!: Women's Independent film-making in Australia*, Richmond, Melbourne: Greenhouse Publications.

Blum, Richard A. (1984) *American Film Acting: The Stanislavski Heritage*, Ann Arbor, Michigan: UMI Research Press.

Bordwell, David (1985) *Narration and the Fiction Film*, London: Methuen.

—— (1989) *Making Meaning: Inference and Rhetoric in the Interpretation of Cinema*, Cambridge, Mass: Harvard University Press.

Bordwell, David and Kristin Thompson (1986) *Film Art: An Introduction*, 2nd edn, New York: Alfred Knopf.

Bottomley, Gillian (1992) *From Another Place*, Oakleigh, Victoria: Cambridge University Press.

—— (1994) 'Post-Multiculturalism? The Theory and Practice of Heterogeneity', *Culture and Policy* 6: 139–52.

Broderick, Peter (1988) 'Introduction'. In Scott Murray (ed.) *Back of Beyond: Discovering Australian Film and Television*, Sydney: AFC, vi–vii.

Bromby, Robin (1979) 'Test for Australia', *Sight & Sound* 48: 2 (Spring): 85–7.

Burch, Noel (1979) *To the Distant Observer: Form and Meaning in Japanese Cinema*, London: Scolar Press.

Burstall, Tim (1977) 'The Triumph and Disaster for Australian Films', *Bulletin* 24 September: 50, 53.

Butler, Alison (1992) 'New Film Histories and the Politics of Location', *Screen* 33: 4 (Winter): 413–26.

Cafarella, Jane (1994) 'Filipino Women blast *Priscilla* for Portrayal of Worst Stereotype', *The Age*, 7 October. In *Cinedossier* Issue 656, 11 October 1994, 20.

Cameron-Wilson, James and F. Maurice Speed (1993) *Film Review 1993–4 Including Video Releases*, London: Virgin Books.

Capp, Rose (1993) 'Monica Pellizari's Short Black Look at the Australian-Italian Experience', *Artlink* 13: 1 (March–May): 15–16.

Caputo, Raffaele (1993) *'Mouth to Mouth'*. In Scott Murray (ed.) *Australian Film 1978–1992*, 19.

—— (1994) *'Bello Onesto Emigrato Australia Sposerebbe Compaesana Illibata'*, *Cinema Papers* 101 (October): 19, 79.

Carroll, John (1982) 'National Identity'. In J. Carroll (ed.) *Intruders in the Bush*, Melbourne: Oxford University Press, 209–25.

Castaldi, Peter (1994) 'Movie of the Week', *The Sunday Herald Sun*, TV Extra, 23 October. In *Cinedossier* Issue 656, 25 October 1994, 52.

Castles, Ian (1992) *Year Book. Australia 1992*, no. 75 Australian Bureau of Statistics: Canberra.

Caughie, John (1990) 'Playing at being American: Games and Tactics'. In Patricia Mellancamp (ed.) *Logics of Television*, Indiana: Indiana University Press, 44–58.

Chan, Pauline (1995) 'Director's Comment', *Cinemaya* 25–6, 68.

Chua, Beng-Huat (1990) 'Confucianization in Modernizing Singapore'. Beyond the Culture? The Social Sciences and the Problem of Cross Cultural Comparison Conference. Loccum, West Germany, 22–5 August. Cited in Frost (1994a).

Chua, Siew Keng (1992) 'A Half-Opened Door: Australian Perspectives on Asia', *Cinemaya*, Autumn/Winter: 17–18.

—— (1993) 'Reel Neighbourly: the Construction of Southeast Asian Subjectivities', *Media Information Australia* 70 (November): 28–33.

Ciment, Michel (1995) 'France'. In P. Cowie (ed.) *Variety International Film Guide 1995*, 164–73.

Clayton, Peter (1994) 'Short Route Discovery', *The Australian Financial Review*, 17 June, Weekend 15.

Collins, Diane (1987) *Hollywood Down Under –Australians at the Movies: 1886 to the Present Day*, North Ryde, Sydney: Angus & Robertson.

Collins, Richard (1990) *Television: Policy and Culture*, London and Cambridge, Mass: Unwin Hyman.

Conomos, John (1993) *'Nirvana Street Murder'*. In Scott Murray (ed.) *Australian Film 1978–1992*, 321.

Coombs, H. C. (1981) *A Trial Balance*, Melbourne: Macmillan.

Cornell, Drucilla (1993) *Transformations: Recollective Imagination and Sexual Difference*, New York and London: Routledge.

Corrigan, Timothy (1983) *New German Film: the Displaced Image*, Austin: University of Texas Press.

Cowie, Peter (ed.) (1995) *Variety International Film Guide 1995*, London: Hamlyn; Hollywood: Samuel French Trade.

Cox, Eva and Sharon Laura (1992) *'What do I wear for a Hurricane?' Women in Australian Film, Television, Video and Radio Industries*, Australian Film Commission and the National Working Party on the Portrayal of Women in the Media, November.

Crawford, Anne-Marie and Adrian Martin (1989) 'Review of *Sweetie*', *Cinema Papers* 73 (May): 56–7.

Creed, Barbara (1992) 'Mothers and Lovers: Oedipal Transgressions in Recent Australian Cinema', *Metro* 91: 14–22.

—— (1993) 'Lesbian Independent Cinema and Queer Theory', *Artlink* 12: 3, 11–12.

Crofts, Stephen (1980). '*Breaker Morant*: Rethought', *Cinema Papers*, vol. 7 issue 30: 420.

—— (1992) 'Cross-Cultural Reception: Variant Readings of *Crocodile Dundee*', *Continuum* 5: 2, 213–27.

—— (1993) *Identification, Gender and Genre in Film: The Case of Shame* with *Shame: The Screenplay* by Beverly Blankenship and Michael Brindley, Melbourne: Australian Film Institute, The Moving Image, no. 2.

Cunningham, Stuart (1978) 'Australian Film', *Australian Journal of Screen Theory* 5 and 6: 36–47.

—— (1985) 'Hollywood Genres, Australian Movies'. In A. Moran and T. O'Regan (eds) *An Australian Film Reader*, 235–41.

—— (1987a) 'The Chauvel School of Scenario Writing'. In T. O'Regan and B. Shoesmith (eds) *History on/and/in Film*, Perth: History and Film Association of Australia (WA), 81–9.

—— (1987b) 'Nascent Innovation: Notes on Some Features from the 1950s', *Continuum* 1: 1, 93–9.

—— (1988) 'Kennedy-Miller: "House Style" in Australian Television'. In S. Dermody and E. Jacka (eds) *The Imaginary Industry*, 178–99.

—— (1988/89) 'To Go Back of Beyond', *Continuum* 2: 1, 159–64.

—— (1989a) 'The Decades of Survival: Australian Film 1930–1970'. In A. Moran and T. O'Regan (eds) *Australian Screen*, 53–74.

—— (1989b) 'Textual innovation in the Australian historical mini-series'. In J. Tulluch and G. Turner (eds) *Australian Television: Programs, Pleasures and Politics*, Sydney: Allen & Unwin, 39–51.

—— (1991) *Featuring Australia: The Cinema of Charles Chauvel*, Sydney: Allen & Unwin.

—— (1992) *Framing Culture: Criticism and Policy in Australia*, Sydney: Allen & Unwin.

Cunningham, Stuart and Graeme Turner (eds) (1993) *The Media in Australia: Industries, Texts, Audiences*, Sydney: Allen & Unwin.

Curthoys, Ann and Stephen Muecke (1993) 'Australia, For Example'. In W. Hudson and D. Carter (eds) *The Republicanism Debate*, 177–200.

Curtis, Rosemary and Shelley Spriggs (eds) (1992) *Get the Picture: Essential Data on Australian Film, Television and Video*, 2nd edn, Sydney: Australian Film Commission.

—— (eds) (1994) *Get the Picture: Essential Data on Australian Film, Television and Video*, 3rd edn, Sydney: Australian Film Commission.

Davidson, Jim (1979) 'The De-dominionisation of Australia', *Meanjin* 38: 2 (July), 139–53.

Di Chiera, Frank (1979) *Foreign Language Film Exhibition and Distribution in Australia*, Sydney: Research and Survey Unit Monograph no. 13, Australian Film Television and Radio School.

Deleuze, Gilles (1988) *Foucault*, trans. and ed. Sean Hand, forward by Paul Bove, Minneapolis: University of Minnesota Press.

Dermody, Susan (1981) 'Rugged Individualists or Neocolonial Boys? The Early Sound Period in Australian Film, 1931/2', *Media Papers* no. 12, Sydney: New South Wales Institute of Technology.

—— (1988) 'The Company of Eccentrics'. In S. Dermody and E. Jacka *The Imaginary Industry*, 132–54.

Dermody, Susan and Elizabeth Jacka (1987a) 'An Australian Film Reader in Question', Continuum 1: 1, 140–55.
—— (1987b) The Screening of Australia, vol. 1: Anatomy of a Film Industry, Sydney: Currency Press.
—— (1988a) The Screening of Australia, vol. 2: Anatomy of a National Cinema, Sydney: Currency Press.
—— (eds) (1988b) The Imaginary Industry: Australian Film in the late '80s, Sydney: Australian Film Television and Radio School.
Devine, Frank (1994) 'Local Films find a Caste of their Own', The Australian 10 October. In Cinedossier Issue 654, 11 October 1994, 26.
Diawara, Manthia (1992) African Cinema: Politics and Culture, Bloomington: Indiana University Press.
Dissanayake, Wimal (ed.) (1988) Cinema and Cultural Identity: Reflections on Films from Japan, India and China, Lanham, MD: University Press of America.
Docker, John (1991) 'Popular culture versus the state: an argument against Australian content regulations for television', Media Information Australia 59: 7–26.
Ellis, Bob (1994) 'Rough Cut', Encore 12: 13, 20.
Elsaesser, Thomas (1989) New German Cinema: a History, London: BFI and Macmillan.
—— (1994) 'Putting on a Show: The European Art Movie', Sight and Sound 4 (April): 22–7.
Enker, Debi (1994) 'Australia and Australians'. In Scott Murray (ed.) Australian Cinema, 211–225.
Epstein, Jan (1992) 'Australian Films at Cannes', Cinema Papers no. 89 (August): 22–5.
—— (1993) 'As Time Goes By'. In Scott Murray (ed.) Australian Film 1978–1992, 241.
—— (1994) 'Stephan Elliott: The Adventures of Priscilla, Queen of the Desert, Interview', Cinema Papers 101: 4–10, 86.
Foucault, Michel (1981) 'Questions of Method: an Interview with Michel Foucault', trans. Colin Gordon, Ideology and Consciousness 8 (Spring): 3–14.
Franklin, Richard (1980) 'Letters: Uri Windt', Cinema Papers 30: 411.
Freiberg, Freda (1994) 'Lost in Oz?: Jews in the Australian Cinema', Continuum 8: 2, 196–205.
Friedman, Eva (1992) 'Geoffrey Wright's Romper Stomper – a location Report', Cinema Papers 86 (January): 6–11.
Frost, Stephen (1994a) 'Broinowski versus Passmore: A dialogue of our Times', Continuum 8: 2, 20–48.
—— (1994b) 'Embassy and the New Orthodoxy in Australian–Southeast Asian Relations', Southeast Asian Journal of Social Science 22: 189–208.
Frow, John (1995) Cultural Studies and Cultural Value, Oxford: Clarendon Press.
Fuller, Graham (1993) 'Searching for the Serpent: An Interview with Alison Maclean'. In John Boorman and Walter Donohue (eds) Projections 2: A forum for Film-makers, London and Boston: Faber & Faber, 81–8.
Gabriel, Teshome H. (1993) 'Ruin and the Other: Towards a Language of Memory'. In Hamid Naficy and Teshome H. Gabriel (eds) Otherness and the Meida: The Ethnography of the Imagined and the Imaged, Langhorne, Penn: Harwood Academic Publishers, 211–19.
Gardner, Geoff (1993a) 'Palm Beach'. In Scott Murray (ed.) Australian Film 1978–1992, 65.
—— (1993b) 'Moving Out'. In Scott Murray (ed.) Australian Film 1978–1992, 134.
Garner, Helen (1992) 'Introduction', The Last Days of Chez Nous and Two Friends, Ringwood, Vic: McPhee Gribble, vii–xiii.
Gertsakis, Elizabeth (1994) 'An Inconstant Politics: Thinking about the Traditional and the

Contemporary'. In S. Gunew and F. Rizvi (eds) *Culture, Difference and the Arts*, 35–53.

Gibson, Ross (1988) 'Formative Landscapes'. In Scott Murray (ed.) *Back of Beyond*, 20–32.

—— (1992) *South of the West*, Bloomington and Indianapolis: Indiana University Press.

Gillespie, Pat (1993) '*Strictly Ballroom*', *Cinema Papers* 91 (January): 52.

Given, Jock (1994) 'Review: 1992–93'. In R. Curtis and S. Spriggs (eds.) *Get the Picture* 3rd edn, 12–28.

Glynn, Sean (1992) 'Urbanization in Australian History'. In Gillian Whitlock and David Carter (eds) *Images of Australia*, St Lucia: University of Queensland Press, 229–39.

Gomery, Douglas (1992) *Shared Pleasures: A History of Movie Presentation in the United States*, Madison: University of Wisconsin Press.

Grace, Helen (1995) 'Everywhere Toilet: Defilement: the Views in Wide Shot', *Communal Plural 4* (University of Western Sydney, Nepean, Research Centre in Intercommunal Studies), 131–43.

Grace, Helen and Jeni Thornley (1981) '28th Sydney Film Festival Program', *Filmnews* 11: 7, 4.

Grant, Bruce (1983) *The Australian Dilemma: A New Kind of Western Society*, Ruschcutters Bay, Sydney: Macdonald Futura.

Grunberg, Serge (1994) 'Australia, From the Desert to Hollywood', *Metro* 100: 27–31.

Guback, Thomas (1969) *The International Film Industry*, Bloomington: Indiana University Press.

Gul, Anna (1993) '*Dangerous Game*'. In Scott Murray (ed.) *Australian Film 1978–1992*, 311.

Gunew, Sneja (1994) 'Arts for a Multicultural Australia: Redefining the Culture'. In S. Gunew and F. Rizvi (eds) *Culture, Difference and the Arts*, 1–12.

Gunew, Sneja and Fazal Rizvi (eds) (1994a) *Culture, Difference and the Arts*, St Leonards: Allen & Unwin.

—— (1994b) 'Introduction'. In S. Gunew and F. Rizvi (eds) *Culture, Difference and the Arts*, xi–xci.

Hage, Ghassan (1993) 'Republicanism, Multiculturalism, Zoology', *Communal/Plural* 2 (University of Western Sydney, Nepean, Research Centre in Intercommunal Studies), 153–67.

—— (1995) 'The Limits of "Anti-Racist Sociology"', *UTS Review* 1: 1, 59–82.

Hall, Ken G. (1980) *Australian Film: The Inside Story*, Sydney: Summit Books.

Hamilton, Peter and Sue Mathews (1986) *American Dreams: Australian Movies*, Sydney: Currency Press.

Hancock, W. K. (1930, 1961) *Australia*, Brisbane: Jacaranda Press.

Harari, Fiona (1995) 'The Risk Takers', *The Australian Magazine*, *Weekend Australian* 18–9 November: 20–3.

Harris, Max (1964) 'Document of Our Time', *Overland* 29: 25–6.

—— (1979) 'Sense and Sensibility in the Film World', *Weekend Australian* 21–2 April, Supplement, 4.

—— (1980) 'What's Yank for Stupid?' *Weekend Australian* 3–4 May, Magazine, 4.

Harris, Mike (1990) 'Aunty Strikes Again', *The Bulletin* 11 September: 158.

Hartley, John (1992) 'Television and the power of dirt', *Tele-ology*, London: Routledge.

Hartz, Louis (1964) *The Founding of New Societies*, New York: Harcourt, Brace & World.

Hawker, Philippa (1987) 'Women in Training or "I would like to work for Kennedy Miller when they stop making boy's films"'. In A. Blonski, B. Creed and F. Freiberg (eds) *Don't Shoot Darling!*, 135–552.

Hawley, Janet (1994) 'Cringe no More', *The Age-Good Weekend*, 8 October.

Hay, James (1987) *Popular Film Culture in Fascist Italy*, Bloomington and Indianapolis: Indiana University Press.

Hayward, Susan (1993) *French National Cinema*, London and New York: Routledge.

Higson, Andrew (1989) 'The Concept of National Cinema', *Screen* 30: 4, 36–46.

Hinde, John (1981) *Other People's Pictures*, Sydney: Australian Broadcasting Corporation.

Hodge, Bob and Vijay Mishra (1991) *The Dark Side of the Dream*, Sydney: Allen & Unwin.

Hooks, Barbara (1990) 'Hurrah for *Embassy*: a Foreign Affair to Remember', *The Age* 12 September, 14.

Horton, Robert (1993) 'Dancing the Light Down Under', *Film Comment* 29: 1 (January/February), 6–7.

House of Representatives Standing Committee on Environment, Recreation and the Arts (1992) *Report of the Moving Pictures Inquiry*, Canberra: Australian Government Publishing Service, June.

Hudson, Wayne and David Carter (eds) (1993) *The Republicanism Debate*, Sydney: University of New South Wales Press.

Hughes, Peter (1993) 'A way of Being Engaged with the World: The Films of John Hughes', *Metro* 93: 46–55.

Hunter, Ian (1976, 1985) 'Corsetway to Heaven: Looking Back to Hanging Rock'. In A. Moran and T. O'Regan (eds) *An Australian Film Reader*, 190–4.

—— (1994) *Re-thinking the School*, St Leonards, Sydney: Allen & Unwin.

Interim Board of the Australian Film Commission (1975) 'Report of the Interim Board of the AFC', February.

Interim Report of the [Film] Committee, Australian Council for the Arts (May 1969, 1985), reprinted in A. Moran and T. O'Regan (eds) *An Australian Film Reader*, 171–4.

Jacka, Elizabeth (1988a) 'Australian Cinema: an Anachronism in the '80s?'. In S. Dermody and E. Jacka (eds) *The Imaginary Industry*, 117–130.

—— (1988b) 'Films'. In S. Dermody and E. Jacka (eds) *The Imaginary Industry*, 65–130.

—— (1991) *The ABC of Drama: 1975–1990*, Sydney: Australian Film Television and Radio School.

—— (1992) 'Globalization and Australian Film and Television'. In A. Moran (ed.) *Stay Tuned: an Australian Broadcast Reader*, Sydney: Allen & Unwin, 185–91.

—— (1993) 'Film'. In Stuart Cunningham and Graeme Turner (eds) *The Media in Australia: Industries, Texts, Audiences*, Sydney: Allen & Unwin, 72–85.

Jacka, Elizabeth and Stuart Cunningham (1993) 'Australian Television: An International Player', *Media Information Australia* 70 (November): 17–27.

Jahiel, Edwin (1995) 'Tribute: International Film Festival of La Rochelle'. In P. Cowie (ed.) *Variety International Film Guide 1995*, 377–86.

Jakubowicz, Andrew (1994) 'Australian (Dis)Contents: Film, Mass Media and Multi-culturalism'. In S. Gunew and F. Rizvi (eds) *Culture, Difference and the Arts*, 86–107.

Jayamenne, Laleen (1992) 'Love Me Tender, Love Me True, Never Let Me Go ... A Sri Lankan Reading of Tracey Moffat's *Night Cries*', *Framework* 38/39: 87–94.

Jennings, Karen (1993) *Sites of Difference: Cinematic Representations of Aboriginality and Gender*, Melbourne: Australian Film Institute.

Johnson, Colin (Mudrooroo) (1987) 'Chauvel and the Centering of the Aboriginal Male in Australian Film', *Continuum* 1: 1, 47–56.

Jones, Deborah (1992) 'Waltzing out of the Outback into the Ballroom'. In Baz Luhrmann and Craig Pearce (eds) *Strictly Ballroom. From a Screenplay by Baz Lurhmann and Andrew Bovell*, Sydney: Currency Press, xiii–xiv.

Jupp, James (1991) *Immigration*, Sydney: Sydney University Press and Oxford University Press.

Kael, Pauline (1980, 1985) 'A Dreamlike Requiem for a Nation's Lost Honour'. First published *New Yorker* 15 September 1980; republished in A. Moran and T. O'Regan (eds) *An Australian Film Reader*, 204–10.

—— (1986) *Taking it All in: Film Writings 1980–1983*, London: Arena.

Kaes, Anton (1989) *From Hitler to Heimat: The Return of History as Film*, Cambridge, Mass.: Harvard University Press.

Kalantzis, Mary (1990) 'Ethnicity meets Gender meets Class in Australia'. In S. Watson (ed.) *Playing the State*, 39–59.

Kalantzis, Mary and Bill Cope (1993) 'Republicanism and Cultural Diversity'. In W. Hudson and D. Carter (eds) *The Republicanism Debate*, 118–44.

—— (1994) 'Vocabularies of Excellence: Reworking Multicultural Arts Policy'. In S. Gunew and F. Rizvi (eds) *Culture, Difference and the Arts*, 13–34.

Kapferer, Bruce (1988) *Legends of People, Myths of State*, Washington: Smithsonian Institution Press.

Kaufman, Tina and Peter Page (1979) '*Mad Max* (Interview with George Miller)', *Filmnews* 9: 7, 9.

Kennedy, Harlan (1989) 'The New Wizards of Oz', *Film Comment* 25: 5 (September–October), 73–7.

—— (1994) 'Cannes '94: My GATT is Quick', *Film Comment* 30: 4 (July–August), 5–6, 11.

Kindred, Jack (1995) 'Germany'. In P. Cowie (ed.) *Variety International Film Guide 1995*, 175–80.

King, Stephen (1981) *Stephen King's Danse Macabre*, New York: Berkley Books.

Koval, Ramona (1992) *One to One*, Sydney: Australian Broadcasting Corporation.

Kuhn, Thomas (1970) *The Structure of Scientific Revolutions*, Chicago: University of Chicago Press.

Langton, Marcia (1993) *'Well, I heard it on the radio and I saw it on the television . . . '* An Essay for the Australian Film Commission on the politics and aesthetics of film-making by and about Aboriginal people and things, Sydney: AFC.

Laseur, Carol (1992) 'Australian Exploitation: The Politics of Bad Taste', *Continuum* 5: 2, 366–77.

—— (1993) '*beDevil*: Colonial Images, Aboriginal Memories', *Span* 37 (December): 76–88.

Latour, Bruno (1987) *Science in Action*, Cambridge Mass.: Harvard University Press.

—— (1993) *We Have Never Been Modern*, trans. C. Porter, Cambridge, Mass.: Harvard University Press.

Lattas, Andrew (1990) 'Aborigines and contemporary Australian nationalism: primordiality and the cultural politics of otherness'. In Julie Marcus (ed.) *Writing Australian Culture, Social Analysis* 27: 50–69.

Lawson, Sylvia (1965, 1985a) 'Not for the Likes of Us'. Reprinted in A. Moran and T. O'Regan (eds) *An Australian Film Reader*, 150–7.

—— (1969, 1985b) 'Australian Film, 1969'. Reprinted in A. Moran and T. O'Regan (eds) *An Australian Film Reader*, 175–83.

—— (1982) 'Towards Decolonization: Film History in Australia'. In S. Dermody, J. Docker and D. Modjeska (eds) *Nellie Melba, Ginger Meggs and Friends: Essays in Australian Cultural History*, Malmsbury: Kibble, 19–32.

—— (1985c) '*Serious Undertakings*'. In A. Moran and T. O'Regan (eds) *An Australian Film Reader*, 327–32.

Leahy, Gillian and Noel King (1994) '"I'd thought for a long time that I'd make an experimental film about love": An Interview with Gillian Leahy about *My Life Without Steve*', *Continuum* 7: 2, 238–53.

Leigh, Michael (1988) 'Curiouser and curioser'. In Scott Murray (ed.) *Back of Beyond: Discovering Australian Film and Television*, 78–89.

Lewis, Glen (1987) *Australian Movies and the American Dream*, New York: Praeger.

Lohrey, Amanda (1981) '*Gallipoli*: male innocence as a marketable commodity', *Island Magazine* 9/10 (March): 29–34.

Loizos, Peter (1993) *Innovation in Ethnographic Film*, Chicago: University of Chicago Press.

Lombard, George (1993) 'The Australian Example', *Refugees* 93: 18–19.

Long, Chris (1994) 'Australia's First Films: Federation Film', *Cinema Papers* 101 (October): 56–61, 82–3.

Lotman, Yuri M. (1990) *Universe of the mind: a semiotic theory of culture*, trans. Ann Shukman, Bloomington and Indianapolis: Indiana University Press.

Lucas, Rose (1993) '*The Man from Snowy River*'. In Scott Murray (ed.) *Australian Film 1978–1992*, 103.

Lunden, Rolf and Erik Asard (eds.) (1992) *Networks of Americanization: Aspects of the American Influence in Sweden*, Acta Universitatis Upsaliensis, Uppsala: Studia Anglistica Upsaliensia 79.

McClelland, James (1987) 'Time to Confess – Paul Hogan is simply the Greatest', *Sydney Morning Herald* 10 December, 15.

MacDonald, Amanda (1995) 'French Film–Crit Takes a Holiday', *Metro* 103: 57–65.

McDonald, Peter (1993) 'Households and Family Trends in Australia'. In Ian Castles (ed.) *Year Book Australia 1994*, no. 77, Canberra: Australian Bureaux of Statistics, 149–65.

McFarlane, Brian (1980) 'Horror and Suspense'. In Scott Murray (ed.) *The New Australian Cinema*, 61–77.

—— (1987) *Australian Cinema 1970–1985*, Richmond, Melbourne: William Heinemann Australia.

McFarlane, Brian and Geoff Mayer (1992) *New Australian Cinema: Sources and Parallels in American and British Films*, Cambridge and Oakleigh, Vic.: Cambridge University Press.

McGuinness, P. P. (1975, 1985) 'Peter Weir's Hauntingly Beautiful Film Makes the Film World Stand Up'. Reprinted in A. Moran and T. O'Regan (eds) *An Australian Film Reader*, 188–9.

McIntosh, Trudi (1994) 'Time short for local multimedia industry', *Australian* 30 August. In *Cinedossier* Issue 648, 30 August 1994, 6–7.

MacKay, Hugh (1993) *Reinventing Australia: The Mind and Mood of Australia in 1990*, Pymble, Sydney: Angus & Robertson.

McMurchy, Megan (1993) 'The Documentary'. In Scott Murray (ed.) *Australian Cinema*, 179–98.

Malone, Peter (1987) *In Black and White and Colour*, Jabiru, NT and Leura, NSW: Nelen Yubu Missiological Unit Series no. 4.

—— (1994) '*The Roly Poly Man*', *Cinema Papers* 101: 69.

Malpas, Jeff and Gary Wickham (1995) 'Governance and Failure: On the Limits of Sociology', unpublished paper, Murdoch University.

Marshall, P., David and Rea Turner (1992) 'At Last a Co-Production that We can all Enjoy: The Australian Canadian Co-Productions of *Black Robe* and *Golden Fiddles*', *Media Information Australia* 66 (November): 93–8.

Martin, Adrian (1980) 'Fantasy'. In Scott Murray (ed.) *New Australian Cinema*, 97–111.

—— (1988a) 'Nurturing the Next Wave: What is Cinema?'. In P. Broderick (ed.) *Back of Beyond*, 90–101.

Martin, Adrian (1988b) 'No Flowers for the Cinephile: The Fates of Cultural Populism 1960–1988'. In Paul Foss (ed.) *Island in the Stream*, Leichardt, Sydney: Pluto Press, 117–38.

—— (1992) '*Mise en Scène* is Dead: the Expressive, the Technical and the Stylish', *Continuum* 5: 2, 89–140.

—— (1993) *Peter Kenna's The Umbrella Woman*. In Scott Murray (ed.) *Australian Film, 1978–1992*, 225.

—— (1994a) 'Ghosts . . . of a national cinema', *Cinema Papers* April 97–8: 14–15.

—— (1994b) *Phantasms*, Ringwood: Penguin.

—— (1994c) 'The Short Film'. In Scott Murray (ed.) *Australian Cinema*, 201–10.

—— (1994d) 'Hold Back the Dawn: Notes on the Position of Experimental Film in Australia 1993', *Continuum* 8: 1 292–301.

—— (1994e) '*Going Down*', *Cinema Papers* 100 (August): 16–17.

Maslin, Sue (1993) 'The End of Independence? Women's Film and Video in the 90s', *Artlink* 13: 1, 63–4.

'Meaning of Compliance, The' (1981) *Filmnews* 11: 8, 7.

Medhurst, Andy (1995) 'Inside the British Wardrobe', *Sight and Sound* March: 16–17.

Mellencamp, Patricia (1994) 'Haunted History: Tracey Moffatt and Julie Dash', *Discourse* 16: 2 (1993–4), 127–63.

Merton, Robert K. (1968) *Social Theory and Social Structure*, New York: Free Press.

Metz, Christian (1974) *Language and Cinema*, trans. Donna Umiker-Sebeok, The Hague: Mouton.

Michaels, Eric (1990) *Unbecoming: an AIDS Diary*, Sydney: EMPress.

Miller, Toby (1993) *The Well-Tempered Self: Citizenship, Culture and the Postmodern Subject*, Baltimore and London: The Johns Hopkins University Press.

—— (1994a) 'Introducing *Screening Cultural Studies*', *Continuum* 7: 2, 11–44.

—— (1994b) 'How do you Turn Indooroopilly into Africa? Mission: Impossible, Second World Television, and The New International Division of Cultural Labour', unpublished paper, Division of Cinema States, New York University.

—— (1995) 'Exporting Truth about Aboriginal Australia: "Portions of Our Past Become Present Again, Where Only the Melancholy Light of Origin Shines"', *Media Information Australia* 76: May, 7–17.

Mishra, Vijay (1995) 'New Lamps for Old: Diasporas Migrancy Borders', *Studies in Humanities and Social Sciences* II: 1, 147–64.

Mitchell, Tony (1993) 'Through Anglo Lenses: Italians in Australian Television Drama', *Australasian Drama Studies* 22 (April): 20–32.

Molloy, Simon and Barry Burgan (1993) *The Economics of Film and Television in Australia*, Sydney: Australian Film Commission.

Moran, Albert (1991) *Projecting Australia: Government Film Since 1945*, Sydney: Currency Press.

—— (1993) *Moran's Guide to Australian TV Series*, Sydney: Australian Film Television and Radio School.

—— (ed.) (1994) *Film Policy: An Australian Reader*, Brisbane: Institute for Cultural Policy Studies (Griffith University).

Moran, Albert and Tom O'Regan (eds) (1985) *An Australian Film Reader*, Sydney: Currency Press.

—— (eds) (1989) *The Australian Screen*, Ringwood, Vic.: Penguin.

Morin, Edgar (1961) *The Stars*, trans. Richard Howard, London: Evergreen.

Morris, Meaghan (1980) 'Personal Relationships and Sexuality'. In Scott Murray (ed.) *The New Australian Cinema*, 133–51.

—— (1988) 'Tooth and Claw: tales of Survival and *Crocodile Dundee*'. In *Pirate's Fiancée: Feminism, Reading and Postmodernism*, London: Verso, 241–69.

—— (1989) 'Fate and the Family Sedan', *East-West Film Journal* 4: 1, 113–34.

Morris, Meaghan (1993) 'The Very Idea of a Popular Debate (Or, Not Lunching with Thomas Kenneally'), *Communal/Plural* 2: 153–67.

Mortimer, Lorraine (1994) '*The Clinic*', *Cinema Papers* 101 (October): 16, 18.

Mudrooroo (Colin Johnson) (1987) 'Chauvel and the Centering of the Aboriginal Male in Australian Film', *Continuum* 1: 1, 47–56.

Muecke, Stephen (1992) *Textual Spaces: Aboriginality and Cultural Studies*, Sydney: University of New South Wales Press.

—— (1994) 'Narrative and Intervention in Aboriginal film-making Policy', *Continuum* 8: 2, 248–57.

Murnane, Gerald (1984) *The Plains*, Ringwood, Vic.: Penguin.

Murray, Les A. (1984) *Persistence in Folly*, Sydney and London: Sirius Books.

Murray, Scott (ed.) (1980) *The New Australian Cinema*, Melbourne: Nelson/Cinema Papers.

—— (ed.) (1988a) *Back of Beyond: Discovering Australian Film and Television*, Sydney: Australian Film Commission.

—— (1988b) 'George Miller: Interview'. In Scott Murray (ed.) *Back of Beyond*, 34–43.

—— (1990) 'Tracey Moffatt, *Night Cries – A Rural Tragedy*. Report by Scott Murray', *Cinema Papers* 79 (May): 18–22.

—— (ed.) (1993a) *Australian Film 1978–1992: A Survey of Theatrical Features*, Melbourne: Oxford University Press in association with the Australian Film Commission and Cinema Papers.

—— (1993b) '*The Navigator: A Medieval Odyssey*'. In Scott Murray (ed.) *Australian Film 1978–1992*, 254.

—— (1993c) '*The ABC of Love and Sex Australian Style*'. In Scott Murray (ed.) *Australian Film 1978–1992*, 14.

—— (ed.) (1994a) *Australian Cinema*, St Leonards, Sydney: Allen & Unwin in association with the Australian Film Commission.

—— (1994b) 'Australian Cinema in the 1970s and 1980s'. In Scott Murray (ed.) *Australian Cinema*, 71–146.

—— (1995) 'Returning Home: Richard Franklin Interviewed by Scott Murray', *Cinema Papers* 104: 24–7, 57.

Murray, Sue (1992) 'Distribution and Marketing'. In R. Curtis and S. Spriggs (eds) *Get the Picture*, 2nd edn, 62–70.

Neale, Steve (1981) 'Art Cinema as Institution', *Screen* 22: 1, 11–40.

Nichols, Bill (1994) 'Global Image Consumption in the Age of Late Capitalism', *East–West Film Journal* 8:1, 68–85.

Nowell-Smith, Geoffrey (1985) 'But do we need it?'. In Martin Auty and Nick Roddick (eds) *British Cinema Now*, London: British Film Institute.

Office of Film and Literature Classification and Film and Literature Board of Review (1993) *Report on Activities 1992–93*, Canberra: Australian Government Publishing Service.

O'Grady, John (writing under the pseudonym of Nino Culotta) (1974) *They're a Weird Mob: A Novel by Nino Culotta*, reprint, Sydney: Ure Smith, orig. pub. 1957.

O'Regan, Tom (1984a) 'Australian Film Making: Its Public Circulation', *Framework* 22/23: 31–6.

—— (1984b) 'Writing an Australian Film History – Some Methodological Notes', Sydney: Local Consumption Publications, Occasional Paper. no. 5.

—— (1985a) '*The Man From Snowy River* and Australian Popular Culture'. In A. Moran and T. O'Regan (eds) *An Australian Film Reader*, 242–51.

—— (1985b) 'Documentary in Controversy: *The Last Tasmanian*'. In A. Moran and T. O'Regan (eds) *An Australian Film Reader*, 127–36.

O'Regan, Tom (1986) 'Aspects of the Australian Film and Television Interface', *Australian Journal of Screen Theory* 17/18: 5–33.

—— (1987) 'The Historical Relations between Theatre and Film: *The Summer of the Seventeenth Doll*', *Continuum* 1: 1, 116–20.

—— (1988) '"Fair Dinkum Fillums": the *Crocodile Dundee* Phenomenon'. In S. Dermody and E. Jacka (eds) *The Imaginary Industry*, Sydney: Australian Film Television and Radio School, 155–75.

—— (1989a) 'Cinema Oz: the Ocker Films'. In A. Moran and T. O'Regan (eds) *Australian Screen* 75–98.

—— (1989b) 'The Enchantment with the Cinema: Film in the 1980s'. In A. Moran and T. O'Regan (eds) *Australian Screen* 118–145.

—— (1993) *Australian Television Culture*, Sydney: Allen & Unwin.

—— (1994a) 'Two or Three Things I Know about Meaning', *Continuum* 7: 2, 327–74.

—— (1994b) '*King of the Coral Sea*', *Cinema Papers* 101 (October): 14–16.

Orr, John (1993) *Cinema and Modernity*, Cambridge and Oxford: Polity Press.

Parker, Andrew (1993) 'Grafting David Cronenberg: Monstrosity, AIDS Media, National/Sexual Difference'. In Marjorie Garber, Jann Matlock & Rebecca L. Walkowitz (eds.) *Media Spectacles*, New York: Routledge, 209–31.

Partridge, Dinah (1988) '*Shame*, and the Representation of Women', *Filmviews* 33: 137, 37–8.

Passmore, John (1992) 'Europe in the Pacific'. A public lecture delivered under the auspices of the Australian National University, 10 June, mimeo.

Peary, Danny (1989) '*The Road Warrior*'. In Peary's *Cult Movies 3*, London: Sidgewick & Jackson, 206–11.

Peat, Marwick, Mitchell Services (1979) *Towards a More Effective Commission: the AFC in the 1980s*, Sydney: Peat, Marwick, Mitchell Services.

Pellizari, Monica (1991) 'A Matter of Representation', *Artlink* 11: 1 and 2, 80–1.

Pendakur, Manjunath (1990) *Canadian Dreams and American Control: the Political Economy of the Canadian Film Industry*, Detroit: Wayne State University Press.

Penny, Simon (1994) 'Working in Electronic Media', *Continuum* 8:1 (*Electronic Arts in Australia* (ed.) N. Zurbrugg), 328–37.

Perera, Suvendrini (1993) 'Representation wars: Malaysia, *Embassy*, and Australia's Corps Diplomatique', *Australian Cultural Studies: A Reader*, In M. Morris and J. Frow (eds.) Sydney: Allen & Unwin, 15–29.

Pike, Andrew and Ross Cooper (1980), *Australian Film 1900–1977: A Guide to Feature Film Production*, Melbourne: Oxford University Press.

Pines, Jim and Paul Willemen (eds) (1989) *Questions of Third Cinema*, London: British Film Institute.

Political and Economic Planning (1952) *The British Film Industry*, London: Political and Economic Planning.

Powell, Dilys (1989) *The Golden Screen: Fifty Years of Films*, ed. George Perry, London: Pavilion Books (in assoc. with Michael Joseph).

Price, Charles A. (1989) 'Ethnic groups in Australia'. In J. Jupp (ed.) *The Challenge of Diversity*, Canberra: AGPS, 6–19.

Pringle, John Douglas (1978) *Australian Accent* (1958), rpt, Adelaide: Rigby.

Prisk, Tracey (1994) 'Women still find the going tough', *Encore*, 28 November–11 December, 12: 19.

Quinn, Karl (1993a) '*Romper Stomper*', *Metro* 92 (Summer): 4–7.

—— (1993b) '*Proof*'. In Scott Murray (ed.) *Australian Film 1978–1992*, 322.

—— (1994/5) 'Drags, Dags and the Suburban Surreal', *Metro* 100 (Summer): 23–6.

Rajadhyaksha, Ashish (1986) 'Neo-traditionalism: Film as Popular Art in India', *Framework* 32/33: 20–67.

Reade, Eric (1979) *History and Heartburn: the Saga of Australian Film, 1896–1978*, Sydney: Harper & Row.

Reid, Mary Anne (1993) *Long Shots to Favourites: Australian Cinema Sucesses in the 90s*, Sydney: Australian Film Commission.

—— (1994) 'Distribution'. In R. Curtis and S. Spriggs (eds) *Get the Picture*, 3rd edn, 67–129.

Richie, Donald (1991) *A Lateral View*, Tokyo: The Japan Times, Ltd.

Ricketson, James (1979) 'Poor Movies, Rich Movies'. *Filmnews* 9: 1, May. In A. Moran and T. O'Regan (eds) *Australian Film Reader*, 223–7.

Robinson, Cathy and Jock Given (1994) 'Films, Policies, Audiences and Australia'. In A. Moran (ed.) *Film Policy: An Australian Reader*, Nathan: Institute for Cultural Policy Studies, Griffith University, 17–26.

Robinson, David (1994) *Chronicle of the Cinema 1895–1995 – no. 5 1980–1994*, London: British Film Institute.

Rockett, Kevin, Luke Gibbons and John Hill (1988) *Cinema and Ireland*, London: Routledge.

Roddick, Nick (1995) '*Four Weddings* and a Final Reckoning', *Sight and Sound*, January, 12–15.

Rodley, Chris (ed.) (1993) *Cronenberg on Cronenberg*, London and Boston: Faber & Faber.

Rohdie, Sam (1982a) 'Review', *Cinema Papers* 39 (August): 375–77.

—— (1982b) '*Gallipoli* as World Cinema Fodder', *Arena* 60: 36–55.

—— (1983, 1985) 'The Australian State, A National Cinema'. In A. Moran and T. O'Regan (eds) *An Australian Film Reader*, 264–73.

Rose, Deborah Bird (1990) 'A Distant Constellation', *Continuum* 3: 2, 163–70.

Rose, Nikolas and Peter Miller (1992) 'Political Power beyond the State: Problematics of Government', *British Journal of Sociology* 43: 2, 173–205.

Routt, William (1985) 'On the Expression of Colonialism in Early Australian Films – Charles Chauvel and Naive Cinema'. In A. Moran and T. O'Regan (eds) *An Australian Film Reader*, 55–71.

—— (1989a) 'The Fairest Child of the Motherland: Colonialism and Family in Films of the 1920s and 1930s'. In A. Moran and T. O'Regan (eds) *Australian Screen* 28–52.

—— (1989b) 'Todorov amongst the Gangsters', *Art & Text* 34 (Spring): 109–26.

—— (1994a) 'Are You a Fish? Are You a Snake?: An Obvious Lecture and Some Notes on *The Last Wave*', *Continuum* 8: 2, 215–31.

—— (1994b) 'Some Early British Films Considered in the Light of Early Australian Production', *Metro* 99 (Summer): 65–9.

Routt, William and Richard Thompson (1987) '"Keep Young and Beautiful" – Surplus and Subversion in *Roman Scandals*'. In T. O'Regan & B. Shoesmith (eds) *History on/and/in Film*, Perth: History and Film Association, 31–44.

Rowe, David (1994) 'The Federal Republic of *Sylvania Waters*', *Metro* 98: 14–23.

Rowse, Tim (1985) *Arguing the Arts*, Ringwood: Penguin.

—— (1993) 'Searching for Cultural Connections', *Media Information Australia* 68 (May): 100–5.

Rowse, Tim and Albert Moran (1984) '"Peculiarly Australian" – the Political Construction of Cultural Identity'. In S. Encel and L. Bryson (eds.) *Australian Society: Introductory Essays*, 4th edn, Melbourne: Longman Cheshire, 229–77.

Ruthrof, Horst (1980) *The Reader's Construction of Narrative*, London: Routledge Kegan Paul.

Ryan, Tom (1980) 'Historical Films'. In Scott Murray (ed.) *The New Australian Cinema*, 113–31.

Sacks, Harvey (1992) 'Suicide as a device for discovering if anybody cares'. In Gail Jefferson (ed.) *Lectures on Conversation*, vol. 1, Oxford: Basil Blackwell, 30–9.

Safford, Tony (1995) 'Two or Three Things I Know about Australian Cinema', *Media International Australia* 76 (May): 27–9.

Safran, William (1991) 'Diasporas in Modern Societies: Myths of Homeland and Return', *Diaspora* 1: 1, 83–99.

Sammers, Christine (1993) 'You're Exotic – I'm Exotic'. In *The Big Picture: Documentary Film-making in Australia*, Clayton, Vic.: National Centre for Australian Studies, Monash University, 163–7.

Saunders, Wal (1994) 'The Owning of Images and the Right to Represent', *Filmnews* May: 6–7.

Schembri, Jim (1994) 'SBS breaks the TV stereotype barrier', *The Age Green Guide* 10 February. In *Cinedossier* Issue 620, 15 February 1994, 25.

Schiller, Herbert I. (1993) 'Transnational Media: Creating Consumers Worldwide', *Journal of International Affairs* 47: 3, 47–58.

Schlesinger, Philip R. (1993) 'Wishful Thinking: Cultural Politics, Media and Collective Identities in Europe', *Journal of Communication* 43: 2, 6–17.

—— (1994) 'Europe's Contradictory Communicative Space', *Daedalus* 123: 2, 25–52.

Schou, Søren (1992) 'Postwar Americanisation and the revitalisation of European culture'. In K. Schrøder and M. Skovmand (eds) *Media Cultures*, 142–60.

Schrøder, Kim Christian and Michael Skovmand (eds) (1992a) *Media Cultures: Reappraising Transnational Media*, London: Routledge.

—— (1992b) 'Introduction'. In K. Schrøder and M. Skovmand (eds) *Media Cultures*, London: Routledge, 1–16.

Schudson, Michael (1994) 'Culture and the Integration of National Societies'. In Diana Crane (ed.) *The Sociology of Culture*, Oxford and Cambridge, Mass.: Blackwell, 21–43.

Shaw, Sylvie (1992) 'The Asian screen test', *Cinema Papers* 87: 34–40.

Shirley, Graham (1994) 'Le Gionate del Cinema Muto: 12th Pordenone Silent Film Festival 9–16 October 1993', *Cinema Papers* 97/98 (April): 42–6.

Shirley, Graham and Brian Adams (1983) *Australian Cinema: The First Eighty Years*, Sydney: Angus & Robertson and Currency Press.

Simpson, Catherine (1995) 'Anything is Possible in Istanbul', unpublished paper, School of Humanities, Murdoch University. Available for inspection at the Oz Film Web Site at Murdoch University.

Sjögren, Olle (1992) 'The Swedish Star-Spangled Banner: An Essay on Blended Images in Film'. In R. Lunden and E. Asard (eds) *Networks of Americanization*, Abstract by Richard Holm, 156–60.

Smith, Anthony D. (1986) *The Ethnic Origins of Nations*, Oxford: Basil Blackwell.

—— (1991) *National Identity*, London: Penguin.

Smith, Barbara Herrnstein (1988) *Contingencies of Value: Alternative Perspectives for Critical Theory*, Cambridge, Mass.: Harvard University Press.

Spectrum Research (1978) 'The Spectrum Report on Australian Film Audiences', *Cinema Papers* 15: 236–7.

Stam, Robert (1993) 'Review Essay: Eurocentrism, Afrocentrism, Polycentrism: Theories of Third Cinema'. In Hamid Naficy and Teshome H. Gabriel (eds) *Otherness and the Media: The Ethnography of the Imagined and the Imaged*, Langhorne, Penn.: Harwood Academic Publishers, 233–54.

Stern, Lesley (1985) 'Independent Feminist film-making in Australia'. In A. Moran and T. O'Regan (eds) *An Australian Film Reader*, 314–26.

Stratton, David (1980) *The Last New Wave: The Australian Film Revival*, Sydney: Angus & Robertson.

Stratton, David (1990) *The Avocado Plantation: Boom and Bust in the Australian Film Industry*, Sydney: Pan Macmillan.

—— (1995) 'Australia'. In P. Cowie (ed.) *Variety International Film Guide 1995*, 94–102.

Stratton, Jon and Ien Ang (1994a) '*Sylvania Waters* and the Spectacular Exploding Family', *Screen* 34: 1 (Spring): 1–21.

—— (1994b) 'Multicultural Imagined Communities: Cultural Difference and National Identity in Australia and the USA', *Continuum* 8: 2, 124–58.

Strong, Pauline Turner and Barrik Van Winkle (1993) 'Tribe and Nation: American Indians and American Nationalism', *Social Analysis* 33 (September): 9–26.

Sturgess, Gary (1982) 'The Emerging New Nationalism', *Bulletin*, 2 February, 58–70.

Summers, Anne (1975) *Damned Whores and God's Police: the Colonization of Women in Australia*, London: Allen Lane.

Sykes, Roberta (1979) '*The Last Tasmanian*, A Re-make: This Time with a Camera', *Filmnews* January 13.

—— (1989) *Black Majority*, Hawthorn, Melb.: Hudson Publishing.

Tariff Board (1973) *Tarifff Board Report: Motion Picture Films and Television Programs*, Canberra: Australian Government Publishing Service.

Taylor, Ronnie (1992) 'Baz Luhrmann's *Strictly Ballroom*', *Cinema Papers* 88 (May–June): 6–10.

Teo, Stephen (1995) '*Traps*: A Review', *Cinemaya* 25–6 (1994–5): 63–4.

Thomas, Nicholas (1993) 'Related Things', *Social Analysis*, 34 December, 132–42.

Thompson, Kristin (1985) *Exporting Entertainment: America in the World Film Market 1907–1934*, London: British Film Institute.

—— (1987) 'The End of the "Film Europe" Movement'. In T. O'Regan and B. Shoesmith (eds) *History on/and/in Film*, Perth: History and Film Association of Australia (WA), 45–56.

Thompson, Peter (1994) 'Mind Your Show Business', *Herald Sun* (Melbourne), 24 October. In *Cinedossier*, Issue 656, 25 October 1994, 18.

Thoms, Albie (1978) *Polemics for a New Cinema: Writings to Stimulate New Approaches to Film*, Sydney: Wild and Woolley.

Thomson, David (1980) *A Bibliographical Dictionary of the Cinema*, London: Secker & Warburg.

Thornhill, Michael (1967) 'The Australian Film', *Current Affairs Bulletin* 41: 2.

Thornley, Jeni (1987) 'Personal Statement'. In A. Blonski, B. Creed and F. Freiberg (eds) *Don't Shoot Darling! Women's Independent film-making in Australia*, 221–3.

Towers, Katherine (1994) 'Call for Movies to be Gender Rated', *The Australian*, 11 October. In *Cinedossier* Issue 654, 11 October 1994, 36.

Tulloch, John (1981) *Legends on the Screen*, Sydney: Currency Press.

—— (1982) *Australian Cinema*, Sydney: Allen & Unwin.

Turner, Graeme (1986, 1993c) *National Fictions: Literature, film and the construction of Australian narrative*, Sydney: Allen & Unwin.

—— (1988) 'Mixing Fact and Fiction'. In Scott Murray (ed.) *Back of Beyond*, 68–75.

—— (1989) 'Art Directing History: the Period Film'. In T. O'Regan and A. Moran (eds) *Australian Screen*, 99–117.

—— (ed.) (1993a) *Nation, Culture, Text: Australian Cultural and Media Studies*, London: Routledge.

—— (1993b) 'Cultural Policy and National Culture'. In G. Turner (ed.) *Nation, Culture, Text*, 67–71.

—— (1994) *Making it National: Nationalism and Australian Popular Culture*, Sydney: Allen & Unwin.

Verhoeven, Deb (1993) 'Aleksi Vellis', *Artlink* 13: 1 (March–May), 16.

Vincent Report (1964) 'The Vincent Report', *Overland* 29 (April): 27–38. Its official title was: *Report from The Select Committee on the Encouragement of Australian Production for Television*, October 1963.

Walsh, Maureen (ed.) (1976) *Entertainment is Big Business Let's Invest in It*, Double Bay, Sydney: Producers and Directors Guild of Australia.

Ward, Russell (1958, 1980) *The Australian Legend*, Melbourne: Oxford University Press.

Wark, McKenzie (1992) 'Speaking Trajectories: Meaghan Morris, Antipodean Theory and Australian Cultural Studies', *Cultural Studies* 6: 3, 433–48.

Watson, Sophie (ed.) (1990a) *Playing the State: Australian Feminist Interventions*, Sydney: Allen & Unwin.

—— (1990b) 'Feminist Cultural Production: The Tampax Mafia, an Interview with Chris Westwood of the Belvoir Street Theatre'. In S. Watson (ed.) *Playing the State*, 219–28.

Watson, Sophie and Rosemary Pringle (1990) 'Fathers, Brothers, Mates: The Fraternal State in Australia'. In S. Watson (ed.) *Playing the State*, 229–43.

Weir, Tom (Tom Fitzgerald) (1958, 1985) 'No Daydreams of Our Own'. In A. Moran and T. O'Regan (eds.) *An Australian Film Reader*, 144–9.

White, David (1984) *Australian Movies to the World*, Sydney: Fontana and Cinema Papers.

Wignall, Louise (1994) 'The Extraordinary in the Ordinary: P. J. Hogan talks about *Muriel's Wedding*', *Metro* no. 99: 31–4.

Wildman, Steven and Stephen Siwek (1988) *International Trade in Films and Television Programs*, Cambridge, Mass.: Ballinger Publishing.

Willemen, Paul (1994) *Looks and Frictions: Essays in Cultural Studies and Film Theory*, London and Bloomington: BFI and Indiana University Press.

Willemen, Paul and Jim Pines (eds) (1989) *Third Cinema*, London: British Film Institute.

Williams, Alan (1992) *Republic of Images: A History of French film-making*, Cambridge, Mass.: Harvard University Press.

Williams, Dean (1994/1995) 'All that is Left: The Early Life and Work of Cecil Holmes', *Metro* 100: 36–9.

—— (1995) 'The Commonwealth Film Unit: Predecessors and Precursors', *Metro* 104: 52–7.

Williams, Sue (1994) 'Action Films Find a Sensitive Soul', *Weekend Australian* 27 August, Weekend Review 'Arts Section', 13.

Williamson, J. W. (1995) *Hillbillyland: What the Movies did to the Mountains and What the Mountains did to the Movies*, Chapel Hill: University of North Carolina Press.

Winikoff, Tamara (1994) 'Big Banana and Little Italy: Multicultural Planning and Urban Design in Australia'. In S. Gunew and F. Rizvi (eds) *Culture, Difference and the Arts*, 130–46.

Wright, Andrée (1986) *Brilliant Careers: Women in Australian Cinema*, Sydney: Pan Books.

'Writer's Offensive' (1980) *Filmnews* 10: 6, 1.

Yoshimoto, Mitsuhiro (1991) 'The Difficulty of Being Radical: The Discipline of Film Studies and the Postcolonial World Order', *Boundary 2* 18: 3, 242–57.

Yue, Audrey (1993) '"I am Like You, I am Different": Beyond Ethnicity, Becoming Asian Australian', *Artlink* 13: 1 (March–May), 19–21.

Zetlin, Monica (1994) 'Review: *Country Life*', *Cinema Papers* 101: 64.

Zurbrugg, Nicholas (ed.) (1994) *Electronic Arts in Australia, Continuum* 8: 1.

Subject index

Aboriginal and Torres Strait Islander: and feminism 302–3; representations 57–9, 93, 104, 174, 191–3, 209–10, 241–2, 286–7, 326–9; settler relations 191, 275–80; women 327–9

Australian Film Commission 15, 18, 47, 74–75, 86, 113, 117, 177, 186, 203, 278–9, 288, 290, 292, 294, 335, 340, 349

Australian cinema as a national cinema: as a festival cinema 61–5, 79, 96, 111–5; Hollywood and national cinemas 45–50, 115–21, 131–44; hybridity of national cinemas 71–6, 121–8; local and international characteristics 50–61; nation-state, relation to 65–71; *see also* characteristics of Australian cinema

Australian representations of other places: American 103, 110, 283–4; Asian 98, 184, 280–4, 309–10; British 95, 96, 97, 311–3; Outward orientation 178–81; Pacific 184–5, 280–1

characteristics of Australian cinema: antipodal cinema 106–10; blending fact and fiction (faction) 238–43; blending of melodrama and art film 237–8; cultural stereotypes 92–5; diversity 167–88; genre 194–6; medium sized and English language 77–106; narrative and thematic preoccupations 195–201; national specificities 189–94; naturalism 202–8; negotiating political weakness 235–6; othering the Australian 250–6; positive unoriginality 226–8; setting and landscape 208–11; stylistic preoccupations 201–8; ugliness and

ordinariness 243–50; unity 189–212; speech 193, 253

cinema conceptualized as: apparatus 5, 10–7; domain of social action 1–4, 38–41; object of knowledge 27–34; problem of knowledge 8–9, 34–8; social bond 17–27

circulation of meanings: complementary uptakes 148–9; dissenting readings 149–56; public repertoires 145–8, 160–3; selective uptake 156–60

critical value 111–44; functional character of regimes of value 141–4; Hollywood and national cinemas 115–21, 131–41; ranking national cinemas 121–7; rankings within a national cinema 127–131

criticism 181–5, 333–54; cinephile 341–2; critical closure 349–52; cultural criticism 342–5; demythologizing 338–41; diverse film criticism 181–5, 346–9; explicatory 333–6; film historian 345–6; remythologizing 336–38; symptomatic 333–6

cultural transfers 213–31; antipodality 106–10; cultural cringe 216–7; cultural imperialism 116–9; Lotman's model 214–22; Morris' model 226–8; stages in Australian cinema 222–25

diasporas within Australia: British 311–5; Chinese 79–81, 346–8; Greek 80–1, 193, 319–20; Italian 79–81, 97, 254–5; South-East Asian 141, 149–50, 309–10; Spanish 319

Name index

DIRECTORS CITED (SELECTED PRODUCERS AND SCRIPTWRITERS CITED)

Feature films, documentaries, short films, TV-mini-series and series cited